Life in America

To Sabrina and Yaa

LIFE IN AMERICA

Identity and Everyday Experience

Edited by

Lee D. Baker

350 Main Street, Malden, MA 02148-5018, USA
108 Cowley Road, Oxford OX4 1JF, UK
550 Swanston Street, Carlton, Victoria 3053, Australia
Kurfürstendamm 57, 10707 Berlin, Germany

First published 2004 by Blackwell Publishing Ltd

Library of Congress Cataloging-in-Publication Data

Life in America : identity and everyday experience / edited by Lee D. Baker.
p. cm.
Includes bibliographical references and index.
ISBN 1-4051-0563-1 (alk. paper) — ISBN 1-4051-0564-X (pbk. : alk. paper)
1. United States—Social conditions—1980–2. National characteristics, American. 3. Identity (Psychology)—United States. 4. Social classes—United States. 5. United States—Race relations. 6. United States—Social life and customs. I. Baker, Lee D., 1966–

HN59.2L53 2003
306′.0973—dc21 2003044371

A catalogue record for this title is available from the British Library.

Set in 9.5/11.5pt Ehrhardt
by Kolam Information Services Pvt. Ltd. Pondicherry, India.

Printed and bound in the United Kingdom
by TJ International Ltd, Padstow, Cornwall

For further information on
Blackwell Publishing, visit our website:
http://www.blackwellpublishing.com

Contents

Acknowledgments

I cannot begin to thank all of the people who encouraged and supported me as I undertook this daunting project, but I do want to recognize a number of people who offered specific help, feedback, inspiration, and guidance. First and foremost, I want to thank my wife Sabrina L. Thomas who always knows (much to my chagrin) exactly when to support my scholarly efforts and when to encourage me to focus on the family.

I suppose I should also thank the Virginia State trooper who pulled me over on Interstate 95, just outside of Petersburg. I have been pulled over many times, but this time the trooper saw someone else. Instead of seeing a "young black man," he saw my receding hairline, my wife in the front seat, our toddler crying in the backseat, and in the rear of our well-worn sport utility vehicle, the family dog barking up a storm. As I saw the trooper come back to the car after checking my driver's license, he explained that the taillight was indeed out, but we were free to go and "to have a safe trip back to North Carolina." My wife said, with more than a hint of sarcasm, "you're just getting old sweetheart." We both knew that it was more than that: our family is often identified as the typical middle-class heteronormative family, which packs a rather powerful punch of privilege. Although we are far from typical, this motivated me to begin exploring and teaching about the tension between the way people identify themselves and get identified by others in the context of everyday experiences, and how often unstable identity formations change in different contexts and throughout the lifespan.

The students and faculty at Duke University have been instrumental in breathing life into this project. Over the last two years, I have taught a course entitled "Identity and Everyday Life in America" and my many discussions with these students have helped me shape this volume. The year I spent as one of the conveners of the Franklin Seminars at the John Hope Franklin Humanities Institute at Duke University was very rewarding and the participants of the seminar convinced me to push the limits of interdisciplinarity. Special thanks to all of the seminar participants, especially Cynthia Herrup (my co-convener), Trina Jones, Ada Noris, Amy Ongiri, Richard Powell, Priscilla Wald, and Maurice Wallace. The departments of cultural anthropology and African and African American studies have also been very supportive. John L. Jackson, Jr. and Deborah A. Thomas both read and commented on the introduction, and Kathy Ewing shared with me key resources, sources, and important theoretical distinctions. Anne Allison and Charles Piot gave me the confidence "to just go for it" when I was really doubting some of the essentialist implications that this volume was sure to raise. Other scholars who provided important feedback and encouragement included Kevin Yelvington, Thomas C. Patterson, Richard Handler, Connie Blackmore, William A. Little, and several anonymous reviewers – thanks.

The initial encouragement and consistent commitment of Jane Huber at Blackwell Publishing was integral to the culmination of this project. In Blackwell's Oxford offices, I would like to thank Janet Moth for her editorial magic. This volume could not have been completed without the steadfast work and research of Bianca Robinson who provided a role that exceeded her title of "research assistant."

I would like to thank all the authors, but offer my special thanks to Anne Allison, Judith Goode, John L. Jackson, Jr., Maureen Mahon, Aihwa Ong, Jeff Maskovsky, and Mary Pattillo-McCoy.

Sabrina L. Thomas, my lovely wife, however, is the single most important person I need to thank. She teaches and conducts research on human development and family relations at North Carolina Central University and our many conversations and discussions form the scaffolding of this volume. It has been her expertise, insight, and our conversations about the human lifespan, identity, and the family that have shaped my research, writing, and teaching about issues surrounding identity and American culture.

Our 3-year-old daughter, Yaa Asantewa Baker, remains our greatest inspiration.

In many respects, this is the first time I have ventured away from the history of anthropology, which is produced by a fairly small and intimate group of scholars, and into the much more fractious and politically fraught field of identity and American culture. Organizing this volume was not without risk—several close friends cautioned me but many, many others were positive and applauded my efforts to use ethnographic research to explore identity and American culture. I am still frustrated that I could not find a way to better incorporate the experiences of American Indians. Whatever the outcome, I stand by my work and hope that it will lay bare some of the rifts between ethnic studies and cultural anthropology in an effort to begin to bridge those rifts and encourage more cross-disciplinary discussions about identity in the United States.

The editor and publishers wish to thank the following for permission to use copyright material:

1 Anne Allison, "Cyborg Violence: Bursting Bodies and Borders with Queer Machines," *Cultural Anthropology*, 2000, 16 (2): 237–266. Reproduced by permission of the American Anthropological Association. Not for sale or further reproduction.

2 Marcelo M. Suárez-Orozco, "Everything you ever wanted to know about assimilation but were afraid to ask," *Daedalus*, 2000, 129 (4): 1–30. Published by the Russell Sage Foundation.

3 Judith Goode, "Dousing the Fire or Fanning the Flames: The Role of Human Relations Practitioners in Intergroup Conflicts," *Transforming Anthropology* 2004, 12. Reproduced by permission of the American Anthropological Association. Not for sale or further reproduction.

4 Kelly H. Chong, "What it means to be Christian: The role of religion in the construction of ethnic identity and boundary among second-generation Korean Americans,"

Sociology of Religion, 1998, 59 (3): 259–287. © Association for the Sociology of Religion, Inc. All rights reserved. Reprinted by permission of the publisher and author.

5 Karen Pyke, "'The Normal American Family' as an Interpretive Structure of Family Life among Grown Children of Korean and Vietnamese Immigrants," *Journal of Marriage and the Family*, 2000, 62 (1): 240–256. © 2000 by the National Council on Family Relations, 3989 Central Ave. NE, Suite 550, Minneapolis, MN 55421. Reprinted by permission.

6 Kyeyoung Park, "'I Really Do Feel I'm 1.5!': The Construction of Self and Community by Young Korean Americans," *Amerasia Journal*, 1999, 25 (1): 139–163. Published by Asian American Studies Center Press. Reprinted by permission of the publisher.

7 Susan J. Ferguson, "Challenging Traditional Marriage: Never Married Chinese American and Japanese American Women," *Gender & Society*, 2000, 14 (1): 136–160. © 2000 Sage Publications. Reprinted by permission of Sage Publications.

8 Aihwa Ong, "Cultural Citizenship as Subject-Making," *Current Anthropology*, 1996, 37 (5): 737–753. © 1996 University of Chicago Press.

9 Stacey J. Lee, "More than 'Model Minorities' or 'Delinquents': A Look at Hmong American High School Students," *Harvard Educational Review*, (Fall 2001), 71 (3): 505–529. 2001 by the President and Fellows of Harvard College. All rights reserved. Reprinted with permission.

10 Yen Le Espiritu, "'We don't sleep around like white girls do': Family, Culture, and Gender in Filipina American Lives," *Signs*, 2001, 26 (2): 415–441. © 2001 University of Chicago Press. Reprinted by permission of the publisher and author.

11 Nazli Kibria, "College and the Notions of 'Asian American': Second-Generation Chinese and Korean Americans Negotiate Race and Identity," *Amerasia Journal*, 1999, 25 (1): 29–51. Published by Asian American Studies Center Press. Reprinted by permission of the publisher.

12 Jeff Maskovsky, "Sexual Minorities and the New Urban Poverty," in *Cultural Diversity in the United States: A Critical Reader*, Ida Susser and Thomas Patterson, eds, pp. 322–342. Published by Blackwell Publishing.

13 Kathryn Herr, "Institutional Violence in the Everyday Practices of School: The Narrative of a Young Lesbian," *Journal for a Just and Caring Education*, 1999, 5 (3): 242–256. ©1999 by Sage Publications. Reprinted by permission of Sage Publications Inc.

14 Alyssa Cymene Howe, "Queer Pilgrimage: The San Francisco Homeland and Identity Tourism," *Cultural Anthropology*, 2001, 16 (1): 35–62. Reproduced by permission of the American Anthropological Association and the author. Not for sale or further reproduction.

15 John L. Jackson, "Birthdays, Basketball, and Breaking Bread: Negotiating with Class in Contemporary Black America," *Harlemworld: Doing Race and Class in Contemporary Black America*, 2001, pp. 88–122. © 2001 University of Chicago Press. Reprinted by permission of the publisher and author.

16 Mary Pattillo-McCoy, "Nike's Reign," *Black Picket Fences: Privilege and Peril Among the Black Middle Class*, 2000, pp. 46–67. Published by University of Chicago Press. © 2000 University of Chicago Press. Reprinted by permission of the publisher and author.

17 Maureen Mahon, "Black Like This: Race, Generation, and Rock in the Post-Civil Rights Era," *American Ethnologist*, 2000, 27 (2): 283–312. Reproduced by permission of the American Anthropological Association and the author. Not for sale or further reproduction.

18 Julia Hall, "It Hurts To Be a Girl: Growing Up Poor, White, and Female," *Gender & Society*, 2000, 14 (5): 630–644. © 2000 Sage Publications. Reprinted by permission of Sage Publications.

19 Pamela Perry, "White Means Never Having To Say You're Ethnic," *Journal of Contemporary Ethnography*, 2001, 30 (1): 56–92. © 2001 Sage Publications. Reprinted by permission of Sage Publications.

20 Kyle W. Kusz, "'I Want To Be the Minority': The Politics of Youthful White Masculinities in Sport and Popular Culture in 1990s America," *Journal of Sport and Social Issues*, 2001, 25 (4): 390–417. © 2001 Sage Publications. Reprinted by permission of Sage Publications.

21 Suzanne Oboler, "The Politics of Labeling: Latino/a Cultural Identities of Self and Others," *Latin American Perspectives*, 75 19 (4): 18–36. © 1992 by Sage Publications. Reprinted by permission of Sage Publications Ltd.

22 Brenda Bright, "'Heart Like a Car': Hispano/Chicano Culture in Northern New Mexico," *American Ethnologist*, 1998, 25 (4): 583–610. Reproduced by permission of the American Anthropological Association and the author. Not for sale or further reproduction.

23 Angela Valenzuela, "'Checkin' Up on My Guy': Chicanas, Social Capital, and the Culture of Romance," *Frontiers*, 1999, 20 (1): 60–80. © 1999 Frontiers Editorial Collection. Reprinted by permission of the University of Nebraska Press.

"Ending Poem" in *Getting Home Alive* By Aurora Levins-Morales and Rosario Morales. © 1986 by Firebrand Books, Ithaca, New York.

"I Left My Heart in San Francisco," music by George C. Cory Jr., lyrics by Douglas Cross, sung by Tony Bennett. © 1954 by General Music Publishing Co., Inc.

"Mean Risk Behavior by Ethnic Group and Immigrant Status," *From Generation to Generation: The Health and Well-Being of Children in Immigrant Families*, edited by Donald Hernandez and Evan Charney. Copyright © 1998 by the National Academies of Sciences; courtesy of the National Academy Press, Washington, DC.

Lowrider Magazine cover featuring the Santuario de Chimayó. © 1990 Lowrider Publishing Group.

Every effort has been made to trace copyright holders and to obtain their permission for the use of copyright material. The authors and publishers will gladly receive any information enabling them to rectify any error or omission in subsequent editions.

Introduction: Identity and Everyday Life in America

Lee D. Baker

What is American culture? This question is impossible to answer. However, social scientists, artists, novelists, and politicians have been trying to unlock the mysteries of what makes people in the United States "American" since the founding of the republic. One of the many difficulties is that culture itself is not a "thing," and American cultural patterns and practices are continuously in flux, changing in step with shifts in technology, migration patterns, class relations, economic cycles, and global relations. There are nonetheless certain beliefs, practices, and experiences that are shared by most Americans.[1] And although specific cultural patterns and practices themselves change over time, it is important to understand that individuals and specific groups of Americans experience those patterns and articulate these practices in very different ways. An effective way to explore American culture is to identify those institutions, practices, and activities that are shared by many people every day in the United States while investigating how individuals and groups experience them in different or similar ways.

Something as simple as going to the mall is a good example. Going to the mall is a shared experience for many Americans. Along with the ideology of the American Dream, it is the belief in inalienable rights, the sanctity of liberty, run-away individualism, and consumerism that makes us distinctly American. From Honolulu, Hawaii to Hanover, New Hampshire, malls across the United States are increasingly homogeneous and offer a shared experience. The ubiquitous Gap, Mrs. Field's Cookies, Victoria's Secret, and Footlocker make these climate-controlled public spaces American institutions. Although many Americans visit the mall, their individual experiences may be in stark contrast to one another.

Affluent teens that meet at the mall to flirt and pick up the latest gear from Abercrombie and Fitch experience the mall differently than retired Jewish women who meet to walk, gossip, and pick up something for the grandchildren. Black teenage boys are surveyed by security cameras and shrouded by suspicion that is often masked by a polite "may I help you?" Yet, the Mexican-American woman in a janitorial uniform cleaning off tables at the food court or sweeping up candy-bar wrappers from carefully buffed floors is rendered invisible, not even noticed by the impatient mother trying to calm the temper tantrum of her 2-year-old or the department store diva misting each passer-by with designer perfume. There are countless examples of activities, spaces, and institutions in the United States that are shared but experienced differently: watching TV, going to high school, falling in love, going to church, working to achieve the American Dream, raising children, sharing leisure time, going to funerals; the list goes on.

Why are Americans so similar, yet experience things so differently? The short and simple answer is that the U.S. is a nation of immigrants, colonized subjects, enslaved Africans, and displaced American Indians and Mexicans, and each specific group has a very different history and cultural heritage. This simple answer neither explains the way individuals negotiate and navigate their ethnic heritage, nor speaks to the uniquely American way gender, sexuality, race, and class articulate to shape and reshape the lives of individuals. It also does not address the muddy middle: the vast sum of people who do not "fit" neatly within the traditional categories of man, woman, black, white, gay, straight; moreover, it does not even begin to question the veracity of the categories themselves. Finally, that simple answer cannot explain the dynamics and dualities embedded in such comfortable categories as "Latino" or "Asian," which are often viewed through a lens of ethnicity, but are in fact groups of disparate peoples that have been racialized as a homogeneous group. After all, what does a middle-class Japanese American woman working as a physician-assistant and raising her kids in the suburbs of Charlotte, North Carolina have in common with a poor Filipina American working as a domestic and raising her children in San Diego, California? They do not share the same traditional language, history, or religion; however, they are both mothers and both women, and one can safely assume that they both experience the imposition of similar stereotypes – so-called "Asian women" are exotic and erotic or hard-working and subservient.

A longer and more complex answer to "why Americans are so similar, yet experience things so differently" lies in exploring how identity is formed, deployed, negotiated, and manipulated in people's everyday lives. By focusing on the politics and pain, celebration and solemnity that emerge from the tug-of-war between the way an individual chooses to identify him or herself (what I will call identity) and the way others identify that individual (what I will call identification), the answers to why Americans experience things so differently begin to trickle out.[2] Surveying how Americans identify themselves and others illuminates the way culture, power, and history structure society in ways that shape and impact the everyday lives of all Americans, which helps to answer that impossible question "What is American culture?" The cultural patterns and processes involved in the practices of identity in the United States create a shared experience shaped by popular culture, history, law, migration patterns, etc. and structured by race, class, and gender. Practices of identity and identification, therefore, can be that proverbial lens through which to view American culture.

What exactly is "surveyed" when exploring American identity? Like the ideas of culture, tradition, nation, and race, this term is used every day as shorthand to express often complicated relationships, historical processes, or particular practices. Moreover, these words are quite literally "loaded" terms that politicians, advertising executives, and journalists deftly employ to cultivate a particular effect with great impact. It is the social scientist's job to unpack or unload these terms by tackling their epistemological presuppositions.

Social scientists have indeed explored the epistemological issues linking such terms as nation, community, and tradition to reified, bounded, ahistorical, and static understandings of cultural practices and social groups, yet these same critics often resort comfortably to the notion of identity to replace such terms as race, ethnicity, or sexuality. Richard Handler explains how "reification is an epistemological problem not easily vanquished, for it pervades the rhetorical and conceptual apparatus of our scientific world view. Thus we may succeed in discarding one set of reifying concepts from our scholarly tool kit, only to find ourselves employing others in their stead" (Handler 1994:27). Reification (the process of making something abstract seem real or concrete) not only dominates the apparatus of science, but also dominates countless domains of everyday life that range from exchanging a piece of paper (money) for a Coke to having "fun" at the amusement park, dropping 165 feet at 80 miles an hour, for example, on the "Hypersonic XLC" at Paramount's Kings Dominion.

That identity reifies notions of homogeneity, hierarchy, and essentialism should not be surprising; that social scientists analyze identity in ways that reify homogeneity, hierarchy, and essentialism is also not surprising but is particularly troublesome. Is there a way to write about identity without reifying it? One suggestive approach is to view identity as a category of practice, opposed to a category of analysis.[3]

Analytical leverage is actually increased by viewing identity as a rather sloppy category of practice, opposed to the cleaner category of analysis because the use of practical (or bottom-up) categories can easily incorporate the fluidity involved in the way social and power relations shape identity and vice versa. By surveying identity as an everyday category of practice, one can dynamically map the way people maintain, contest, and negotiate the boundaries and borders of race, class, gender, and sexuality. My aim is not to just report "native" categories of practice, rather offer some analysis, or provide a way of abstracting from raw experience. Evoking the language of cartography, a discipline delirious with reification, may not be appropriate. Conceptually, however, the idea of mapping the topography of a landscape or surveying the trends and relationships within an ecosystem is different than using set theories and arbitrary categories to classify, organize, and describe a landscape or flora and fauna. Although it ultimately may be impossible to analyze identity without reifying abstract ideas, surveying how Americans practice identity is a slightly different project than attempting to theorize and analyze identity as a conceptual apparatus.

The practice and performance of identity takes on a variety of different forms and functions, but critical to any practice is the reference to that practice. An important aspect of this survey will be identifying how Americans consistently use "identity" to reference three aspects of social life that shuttle constantly between questions of "who and what" am I, are you, are we, are they. The first reference concerns individual identity or personality, the second refers to collectives or groups of human beings that are imagined to have some commonality or common cause with which individuals can identify, for example "I really identify with Chicanas." Critical to this reference is the ability for people within the group to distinguish themselves from other imagined communities. Finally, many people use the notion of identity to explain the relationship between the two other references and therefore assume that people assimilate elements of so-called collective identities into their unique personal identities (Handler 1994:28). This third reference is the most salient as people identify others, because too often people actually believe that one can correctly identify someone's individual identity as a result of their outward appearance.

The tension between the ways people self-identify (identity) and get identified (identification) by other people and institutions is critical to understanding practices of identity in America. It is never a simple "choice" in terms of one's own identity because individuals are always situated within a matrix of laws, rules, institutions, and expectations. Yet, people have choices and take actions. What people do, individually and collectively, can reconfigure power relationships, alter cultural practices, and change the sweep of history.

Although this argument appears to be a simple "negative feedback loop," it constitutes more of a dialectic and is driven by the theory that people are agents who effect change and impact lives – their own, their family's and community's, and indeed the nation's – but that impact or an individual's agency is limited or enhanced or determined by their circumstances.[4] In other words, by surveying the circumstances with which people make, reject, and navigate identities in everyday life, one can better understand the social and historical forces – macro-level dynamics – that shape those very circumstances. By doing so, a picture, albeit incomplete, of what American culture looks like begins to emerge.

"What is American culture?" and "Why do Americans act the way they do?" are important questions. The essays selected for this collection, however, describe how identity is practiced, not how or why it is established. The essays focus specifically on how identity and identification commingle as multivalent cultural patterns and processes that people must contend with as they make sense of everyday life in America. And it is this "how question" that organizes the essays. By surveying how people practice, perform, and negotiate the admittedly vague notion of identity within a series of spheres in everyday life – school, family, romance, church, and shopping – one can better understand how issues surrounding identity shape people's lives and conversely how issues of everyday life shape aspects of people's identity. Viewing identity as practiced through lived experience allows us to explore a number of key questions that plumb American cultural practices to demonstrate how specific groups of Americans articulate shared experiences in different ways. In other words, this book attempts to explore three seemingly contradictory aspects of identity and American culture: it explores those aspects of American culture that constitute a shared experience across categories of identities, yet also demonstrates how specific groups of Americans articulate unique cultural practices as a part of their experience within social and cultural groups; at the same time it incorporates the fact that each individual stitches together an identity that is idiosyncratic and shifts on the fly.

The types of questions these essays seek to answer can be quite ordinary. They include: How do folks come to define themselves while defining others? How do people find a place to live and people with which to live, or how do people come to find a place to work and worship? But these same types of questions can also wax philosophical, including looking at how people envision a future and mobilize towards that realization. The types of questions surrounding how people practice identity are endless, and range from managing basic bodily functions to satisfying the ephemeral desires of holy spirits. The use of ethnographic methods and anthropological theory which seek to describe and interpret how people's actions and voices are deployed in order to navigate the turbulent seas of American identity is one way to begin to explain why people do what they do. Nonetheless, it is important to remember that this approach toward explaining why people behave as they do is generated by the people themselves and is quite different from the reasons "why" proffered by putative experts.

There is of course no way to explain exactly "why" a small organization of individuals would hijack domestic airlines to blow up the towers of the World Trade Center, or exactly why otherwise mild-mannered kids would gun down fellow students at suburban high schools. Yet, it is critically important to understand that there are reasons that motivate hate, violence, and dehumanization, and many of those reasons are fueled by a lack of understanding and empathy, or a fear of diversity. When people begin to transcend their fears and move to a greater understanding of the differences that make the United States so unique, strong, and complex, we will all live in a safer, more humane world.

Identity and Identification

On the evening of October 6, 1998 two bicyclists on the outskirts of Laramie, Wyoming, saw what they thought was a scarecrow off in the distance. The crumpled form lashed to one of the many barbed-wire fences that crisscross the windswept plains of Wyoming was not what they had expected: it was Matthew Shepard – beaten, burned, and tortured. Shepard had been tied to the fence for 18 hours before he was transported to the local hospital. Tears of pain and suffering left streaks down the mud and blood that covered his face. After several days, Shepard slipped into a coma and eventually died of severe head injuries.

Matthew Shepard was born in Casper, the heart of Wyoming's oil belt. The son of an affluent oil safety inspector, he traveled extensively and attended boarding schools in Switzerland. Shepard returned to the United States to attend college at his father's alma mater. At the time of his death, Matthew Shepard was a 21-year-old college student at the University of Wyoming who was passionate about politics and foreign affairs, and fluent in German and Arabic. He was also gay.

Like all Americans, Shepard had many facets to his identity. During that ill-fated evening, however, two town toughs identified only one – his sexuality. This sparked the rage that precipitated a chain of events leading to Shepard's homicide. Luring Shepard from a local tavern into their pickup, the two young assailants grappled with a mix of furor and fear that fueled their compulsion to torture and humiliate this young man, who stood only 5 feet 2 inches tall (Brooke 1998; Kenworthy 1998).

The Shepard incident in Wyoming came on the heels of another grizzly murder meted out with similar vengeance. On June 7, 1998, two ex-convicts brutally murdered 49-year-old James Byrd, Jr. in Texas. Fueled by the same mix of fear and furor that engulfed Shepard's assailants, these men kidnaped Byrd and beat him unconscious. After spray-painting his face black, they dropped his pants and tied his ankles to the back of their pick-up truck. The two men dragged James Byrd behind the truck for two and a half miles, leaving skin, blood, arms, genitalia, and his head strewn along the highway. What remained of his tattered corpse, the two perpetrators dumped in front of a black cemetery. James Byrd was a grandfather and the father of three children. He was also black. The two ex-convicts who had affiliations with a racist gang, however, only identified one aspect of Byrd's identity – his race (Texas NAACP 1999). Both the Byrd and Shepard incidents are examples of the ritual violence of lynching, which was fairly common during the late 19th and early 20th centuries, yet remains a sporadic but lethal occurrence today. This sort of terror and violence is easily condemned and often dismissed as the work of only a handful of unstable individuals, yet in many cases these dramatic hate crimes are quite literally the tip of the iceberg, while many less newsworthy assaults, attacks, and nonviolent incidents of oppression occur on a daily basis and are motivated by the same hate, misunderstanding, and fear of diversity. The violence and terror triggered by trained police officers who misidentify a person is more complicated, yet demonstrates how racialized violence has become institutionalized within structures of power in the United States.

On February 4, 1999, Amadou Diallo, an unarmed, Guinea-born street vendor, was gunned down in the Bronx, New York by a hail of 41 bullets fired by members of the New York City Police Department's Special Crime Unit. Using the same cultural processes of "identification" employed by many Americans, the officers believed that Amadou Diallo was the serial rapist they had been looking to apprehend. What these members of New York's finest did not see was a hard-working ethnic immigrant seeking his American Dream; they operated from a racialized worldview that often eclipses the Constitution and somehow justifies a frenzied racial violence that has filled the bloodstained pages of United States history.

The tension between identity and identification does not always trigger lethal consequences, but when people cannot or do not successfully negotiate the complicated issues surrounding one's identity or that of others, it can be and often is deadly. For example, the rash of high-school shootings instigated by white male students who did not "fit in" and resented the various cliques of athletes and achievers, or the epidemic of young women plagued by eating disorders who feel compelled to achieve the supposed ideal body-type of waif supermodels and actresses like Calista Flockhart.

On the other end of the spectrum, the tension between identity and identification is much more benign and mundane. It can be as simple as choosing the character "you want to be" when loading the Tekken II video game, or how often you mow the lawn. Quite literally from womb to tomb and head to toe, issues surrounding identity shape the lives of virtually all Americans and are an integral part of American culture. When someone slips on a pair of Nike Shox R4s or a pair of Cole Haan Trudys, it tells you something about their identity. When someone half-heartedly swoops hair from one side of their head to another to cover a bald spot, or meticulously grooms their dreadlocks, it tells you something about their identity. The church people attend, the gods to whom they pray, the individuals they call family, and the partners with whom they make love: all tell you something about their identity. In each of these cases, individuals have many choices how to represent such aspects of identity. There is a lot less choice, but perhaps more creativity, involved in the way people represent race and gender. When it comes to class and sexuality, integral aspects of any identity, the interpretation of that tension between identity and identification becomes even more complicated.

People stitch together complicated and often shifting identities every day. They can shift quickly, as in code-switching teenagers who switch from Ebonics to Standard American English in a matter of seconds, or church-going Koreans who emphasize their Christian identity on Sunday, but their Asian heritage at school or the office Monday morning. The shift from adolescent to senior citizen takes a lifetime. Most Americans understand how identity shifts and swings as moods and contexts change. Intuitively, most people realize that while at work one might be a computer programmer, while at home that same person is suddenly "Mommy" – magically transferred from barcodes to Barney in a single commute. The fluidity with which Americans understand their own lives in terms of shifting identities, however, is rarely employed when people identify others.

Actually, shifting may not be the best verb or metaphor to explain these subtle transformations that often involve surfing within and between dimensions of personal identity and collective or cultural identity. Americans love choices, and go to great lengths to insure that they have them. Much like surfing the Internet or channels on Direct TV, people surf the repertoires of identity available to them. Some Americans do indeed have more choices than others.

Although one's class position is the leading indicator of choices available, the processes of identification (ascriptive identity or the imposition of an ascribed status) actually curtail the performance of particular forms of identity and structure the expected repertoires people *should* and often do perform, practice, or inhabit. Stories often act as the medium of such repertoires. People tell stories about themselves and others, and usually locate themselves within variations of the available repertoire of stories. Charles Tilley, who views identity as a concept that is "blurred but indispensable," best articulates this idea about the repertoire of possible narratives. He defines identity as "an actor's experience of a category, tie, role, network, group, or organization, coupled with a public representation of that experience; the public representation often takes the form of a shared story, a narrative" (Tilly 1996:7).

Although it is analytically useful to view identity in terms of performance, acting, or storytelling, it is important to understand that it is not pretend or imaginary play; these roles, repertoires, and performances are adopted and integrated into an individual's self-concept throughout one's lifespan, and it begins early. The essays in this book focus on the cultural processes at work as people negotiate a self-identity within an American society that routinely misidentifies people based on a set of cultural categories that are often viewed as biological.

The essays in this book will not explicitly address the psychology involved in identity formation, but they will address identity formation and the formation of an individual's self-concept as an integral part of the cultural processes at work as people craft an identity for themselves as well as identify others. It is important to note, however, that the formation of an individual's self-concept in the United States is tethered to the callous ascription of labels, stereotypes, and expectations imposed upon people who putatively fall within particular categories. Erik Erikson long ago argued that the most important developmental task of adolescence was to forge a coherent sense of identity. For optimal development, Erikson argued, an individual needed a good fit between the individual's sense of self and the varied social milieus he or she must traverse. In other words, the social world should complement the sense of self-being forged by the adolescent. A flexible and adaptive identity, Erikson continued, could not develop if there was a heavy concentration of hostility, role confusion, or cultural dissonance and strife involved in forming the concept of self (Erikson 1963).

Many social scientists have updated Erikson's work so it can be used to address and understand how "identities are crafted and recrafted as youth make their way in varied social settings" (Suárez-Orozco and Suárez-Orozco 2001:92). As Carola and Marcelo Suárez-Orozco note, "immigrant children today may have their breakfast conversation in Farsi, listen to African American rap with their peers on the way to school, and learn about the New Deal from their social studies teacher in mainstream English" (Suárez-Orozco and Suárez-Orozco 2001:92).

It is not exactly accurate to say that people somehow negotiate identity and identification as if they are two separate cultural processes. As people develop psychologically and emotionally, the sense of self is shaped in large part by reflections mirrored back by significant others. In addition to one's reflection, the concept of self is created in a process of recognizing and defining oneself in relation to others (Van Ausdale and Feagin 2001:91).

Self-identity is quite often influenced by the identification of others. According to psychoanalyst D. W. Winnicott, when the reflected image is generally positive, the child or adult is more likely to feel worthwhile and competent, but when the reflection is generally negative, the child or adult is more likely to have difficulty maintaining an unblemished sense of self (Suárez-Orozco and Suárez-Orozco 2001:98; Winnicott 1971). Difficult is not impossible, and gender, cultural, class or sexual identity need not be, and is not often a deep, basic or abiding aspect of one's self-concept.

This is, however, where Americans' love affair with choice comes into play. As a way to deflect, hedge, or challenge the imposition of conflict, negative perceptions, etc., people will surf through their available repertoires and select context-specific identity narratives to inhabit or perform. For example, a young black man might use his "white voice" to bank by phone, or his Internet browser to shop online to mitigate stress in retail spaces. This same guy might use his "defiant look" to cast at the driver of a car that stops suddenly as he crosses the street against the light, thus challenging or re-appropriating negative perceptions.

The converse is also typical. People deploy context-specific identity narratives to foster commonality and connectedness or enhance and cultivate positive perceptions of self. At the 2000 Lumbee Powwow, in Pembroke, North Carolina, for example, one of the champion drummers featured in the traditional drumming contest was a student in the School of Engineering and Applied Science at Princeton University. At the Powwow, this Ivy League undergraduate donned his feathers and finest regalia. An official announcement over the loudspeaker, only echoing the many warm sentiments the young man had received, congratulated him for "not forgetting where he came from" – at once describing and inscribing his ability to connect and be embraced by this particular community and in this context.

Although I did not get a chance to chat with this young man, it is reasonable to assume that he dons different attire and quite literally performs a different routine within the engineering labs at Princeton, and probably employs still another routine, spins a different identity narrative, and dons an altogether different attire as he dines at the selective dining clubs along Prospect Avenue, where many a storied Princeton alum first learned the exotic rituals of wining and dining, networking and deal-making.

The processes of surfing, adorning, combining, layering, and selecting the identity a person wants to present, or the story a person wants to tell, actually refracts and collides with the deeper and more psychological concept of self in a variety of complex and unstable ways. Yet, these fragmented and morphing identities, which often stabilize or become more routine in middle adulthood, are pieced together with, or in response to, the constitutive elements of race, class, gender, and sexuality that are surprisingly stable, and often viewed as static, natural, and rooted in biology. It is these stock and seemingly immutable categories and symbols that are used to identify others in a quick and simplistic manner.

The Nature of Categories

In the United States, race, gender, and age grade (e.g., teenager, middle-aged, senior citizen) are the social categories most routinely used to identify people, yet they rarely top the list of the most important aspects of people's individual identity. Although class, sexuality, and ethnicity are tightly interwoven within these markers of identity, there are a variety of reasons that those categories do not lend themselves to the quick and routine process of identification or stand-alone markers of identity. One reason, perhaps, is that race, gender and age grade are the first social categories by which toddlers learn to classify and differentiate people (Van Ausdale and Feagin 2001:126). As well, the perception is that class, sexuality, and ethnicity are muddier and more malleable categories that people can more easily manipulate – they can stay in the closet, pretend they're rich, or downplay their Swedish heritage.

Categories of race, gender, and age in the United States are social and cultural constructs, although they are very real and embody tangible value; they are based in history, stereotypes, and inequitable power relationships. In terms of race and gender, they are not based in biology, science, or any detectable substance. Part of the cultural belief system that reinforces gender and racial differences is the idea that race and gender are natural categories. The idea that nature shapes these categories has particular staying power in the United States. This is because sex and cultural groups that reproduce some insignificant genetic traits to a certain extent line up with the roles, expectations, and identities that have emerged historically through social and cultural processes to form the categories of gender and race. This is not to say that women and men are the same or that there is no physical difference between Shaquille O'Neal and George W. Bush. There are no race-based traits, however, that enable Shaq to excel in basketball or George W. in politics. Similarly, there is nothing on the Y-chromosome that enables men to run virtually all Fortune 500 companies.

Across the world and throughout history there is tremendous diversity in the way societies have assigned men and women different tasks, roles, and activities, expectations and stereotypes, and positions within a social hierarchy. Simply put, there is not a set of things that males and females do to make them men and women, nor is there a set of things women and men do that make them specifically female and male (Ortner 1996:59–115). Over time in the United States, a set of tasks women and men are supposed to do has emerged, but even these are in continuous flux. The progressive gender roles depicted by Mary Tyler Moore, for example, on her popular 1970s television show are quite different from the equally progressive roles depicted by Sarah Jessica Parker on her popular 2000s show *Sex and the City*.

Although somewhat different, racial categories in the United States have been forged by a unique history and particular patterns of enslavement, migration, displacement, class relations, and genocide. These categories have also been shaped by the inherent contradiction within American democracy that entails a belief in equality and justice, but a reality of racial injustice and inequality. Like gender, the cultural terms and conditions of racial categories change over time.

During the last 50 years in the United States, class status and assimilation have broadened the types of roles, stereotypes, and expectations assigned to specific racial categories. For example, being identified as a Negro in Raleigh, North Carolina in 1950 is very different than being identified as an African American in "the Triangle" in 2002. Moreover, the very notion of a poor working-class immigrant is very different today than it was even 50 years ago. Phones, e-mail, and relatively inexpensive air transportation enable non-white immigrants to remain integrated into the lives and livelihood of people "back home," thus enabling many immigrants to side-step the path to assimilation, which for poor non-white immigrants remains a steep and rutted path.

Gender cuts across racial, ethnic, and class lines, but throughout United States history, race, class, and gender have been so tightly bound to one another that one cannot be analyzed without the other (Andersen and Collins 2001; Collins 2000; Lancaster and di Leonardo 1997; Pollard and Hyatt 1999; Williams 1991).

Categories of age or age grades are also social constructs that cut across race, class, and gender. Although significant hormonal and biological changes occur throughout the life-span, the terms and conditions of such social categories as child, adolescent, adult, or senior citizen vary across time and space. These categories are believed to be set and natural. They, too, are changing as juveniles are tried in court as "adults," and the aging baby-boomer cohort barrels toward retirement, destined to live longer, healthier, more active lives in their golden years.

Within many societies, children are forced to grow up fast, usually to work or have children. In the United States, the settings of the social clock, or the culturally set timetable that establishes when it is appropriate to engage in various activities like getting married, having children or retiring has been moving up over the last century. Like race and gender, an individual's socioeconomic status and class position shape both identity and identification. Class often sets the social clock for age-grades, moving the clock forward as affluence increases. It's common for poor people in the United States to have children at 20, and to be considered old at 65, while more affluent Americans might have children at 38 or 40 and be considered old at 80.

Like age and gender, categories of class and socioeconomic status are social constructs that cut through and across racial groups. Additionally, like race and gender, many Americans presume that class difference is based on natural and often moral distinctions. The images, ideas, and stereotypes that are evoked when one person identifies another as a member of the under class, working class, middle class, or upper class are often quite distinct. Although divisions of labor are material, not constructs or reified abstractions, there is a social stratification assigned to particular jobs that has nothing to do with the amount of money one earns. Americans will often identify a Mexican poultry worker as less valuable than an African-American nursing aid, or a white waitress at Waffle House, even though the wages may be similar. Bus operators for the Metropolitan Transit Authority in Los Angeles get paid on average more than schoolteachers for the Los Angeles Unified School System, but Americans tend to view the class status of a teacher as higher than that of a bus driver (Bass 2001; Treviõ 2000).

The idea that if one "works hard and plays by the rules" one can be successful in America is a principal ideology that binds the majority of Americans (rich and poor) together – it is indeed the American Dream (Hochschild 1995). In many respects, this ideology masks the distribution and maintenance of wealth in America and shifts the structure of wages, patterns of home ownership and policies that shape the economy away from social and structural dynamics and onto the individual, often coming to rest on the idea of "individual initiative" and work ethic. There are countless Americans who work hard every day and play by the rules, yet don't find success in their work lives. For many women and men of color, it is people in the middle classes who find hitting that glass ceiling the most frustrating. Others find it impossible to break out of the lose-lose cycle of poverty, while still others view themselves as unsuccessful because they lost high-paying industrial jobs only to find low-paying, service-sector jobs.

Using social categories to identify people is such an embedded cultural practice that people rarely stop to consider how or why they do it – it is simply part of American culture. People do stop, however, when individuals do not or will not fit neatly within those comfortable social categories that have taken on very biological overtones. Many Americans will experience a puzzling moment when passing, on the street, in the subway or at the mall, a person whose race or gender is ambiguous.

For racially ambiguous individuals, the indefiniteness often elicits uninvited questions by strangers who, for some reason, must know, or want to test their skill at ethnological categorization. It is not uncommon for people to randomly ask me, "Are you Puerto Rican, mixed, or what?" A subtler, but equally intrusive query is, "Where did you get those eyes?" My stock answer is Wal-Mart, but if I say "My mother," people immediately, ask me "Is she white?" Similarly, in my many interviews of people with indefinite racial or gender assignment, respondents often explain that strangers are often "unsettled" by racial or gender ambiguity. The converse is that the vast majority of people don't elicit such cognitive dissonance.

In terms of race, this reaction is quite profound. There is a vast amount of human diversity that simply belies any rational or scientific categorization, but Americans efficiently parse such complicated mosaics of traits, proteins, and alleles into putative natural categories. Over the last three centuries, Americans have participated in complicated historical and cultural processes that have crystallized a collective and deeply held belief that racial categories are part of the natural world and are based on rational presuppositions (Baker 1998; Degler 1991; Gossett 1968; Smedley 1993).

For individuals belonging to the many African American communities, the so-called natural category of race, as practiced as a tool of identification, encompasses a dizzying array of physical types – short, tall, fat, skinny, dark, light, straight hair, curly hair, long hair, no hair, wide noses, narrow noses, fat lips, skinny lips, big feet, small feet, lactose tolerant, lactose intolerant, blue eyes, brown eyes, A+ blood type, O– blood type, etc. Although racial assignment seems immutable in the United States, many African Americans who would be racially identified as black in Los Angeles would not be considered black in Johannesburg, South Africa, Kingston, Jamaica, Accra, Ghana, or Rio de Janeiro, Brazil.

Analyzing and describing identity in the United States is difficult because it is an analysis of the self and society, culture and personality, gender and sexuality. At the same time, one must study racism, sexism, heterosexism, and class privilege. There are many moving, morphing, and entangled features to isolate and explain. Moreover, there is a wide range of meanings people attribute to the word "identity," and a growing number of scholars who believe the term is too worn and ambiguous for use in social analysis (Brubaker and Cooper 2000:2).

It is also difficult to make generalizations about the very idiosyncratic attributes that any one person stitches together to form an identity as an individual and as a member of various communities. Any visitor to the various Star Trek convocations can attest to the idiosyncratic nature of identity, which often flies in the face of generalization. The difficulty in studying identity is further compounded by the fact that different disciplines approach the study of identity from very different perspectives, methods, and research strategies, invariably privileging different aspects of that amorphous term.

Practicing identity in everyday life is much simpler than analyzing it. In the same way one need not be a soil scientist to plant a garden, a software engineer to check e-mail, or an economist to trade stocks, the vast majority of people in America negotiate and navigate between and within the complexities of identity and identification with skill, grace, and creativity on a daily basis. Moreover, people who migrate to the United States learn the rules of the road very quickly when it comes to the complex social forces involving race, class, and gender formation. The ease and comfort people express when it comes to racial hierarchies, gender expectations, and stereotypes of homosexuals is part of the reason that the pillars of democracy have never stood for all Americans. The folklore, commonsense, and steadfast belief in natural or essential distinctions between people are embedded and routinized within an American culture that reproduces inequality and maintains racial, gender, and class hierarchies. Moreover, these unquestioned categories fuel a wide range of misconceptions, including the laziness of poor people, the sexual proclivities of black people, and the idea that homosexuality is a disease.

The essays selected in this volume survey the everyday practices of identity – self-identification, the identification of others, and the way people do or do not affiliate, belong, and experience commonality, connectedness, and cohesion within a racial or ethnic group. There are two conceptual perspectives about the practice of identity, which the essays selected in this volume highlight. Although none of the articles explicitly articulates these concepts, one can use these concepts to better understand how forms of identity are practiced in the U.S.

The first concept involves an understanding that identity should be viewed as a category of practice, not a category of analysis, and it is a practice that often belies rational or scientific analysis. The second is that one's self-identity is unstable, is complicated, and an ongoing process, and the third concept relates to what W. E. B. Du Bois often referred to as "life behind the veil," or an understanding that people live within and between different cultural worlds that are salient, registered, and manipulated with purpose and agency.

The Politics of Organization

In the United States, the reality of everyday life is shaped by interlocking systems of racism, sexism, class difference, and heterosexism that structure the distribution of profit, power, and privilege. It is a cultural system, not unlike a kinship system or exchange system that many an anthropologist has tried to decipher to find the key to understanding a particular culture. Analytically, it is important to distinguish between sexism and class difference or between racism and heterosexism. However, in everyday life, these elements operate within a system of oppression and opportunity that collude and contradict each other in a myriad of sometimes predictable and oftentimes unpredictable ways. A variety of scholars have successfully and comprehensively untangled the thorny thicket of race, class, and gender that has forever bedeviled America's democratic ideals, but this collection of essays focuses on how people negotiate the tensions between identity and identification, and thus navigate the perils and perks of everyday life in America. These processes of negotiation and navigation are cultural practices, oftentimes developed in response to the pernicious and contradictory intersection of inequitable race, class, and gender relations.

In the United States, virtually all individuals have an ethnic background, an age and class status, a religious and sexual orientation, a gender, hobbies, family members, goals and aspirations, etc. that go into the way one's particular identity is formed. At the same time, this same person (even if he or she is a tourist from a different country) must operate in a society that ranks, judges, and assigns value to differences.

There are a number of ways one could organize a collection of essays that surveys the way identity is practiced in the United States in an effort to describe aspects of American culture. Each method has advantages and disadvantages. One could focus on children, and look at the way patterns of child development differ across region, class, gender, race, etc. One could also focus on women across ethnic groups; on class relations; on race, class, and gender, etc. One could, and should, incorporate a historical perspective into any discussion of racial or gender categories in the United States. Each editor's particular angle of focus inevitably privileges some areas while ignoring others.

I chose to focus on the way social and cultural groups of Americans – Chinese Americans, African Americans, Korean Americans, etc. – experience institutions, develop desires, and articulate practices. The articles tend to focus on school and education, shopping and consumption, church and spirituality, family and kinship, and love and romance. This is a particularly dangerous way to organize a book because I leave out many groups, which should not be seen as a slight or as indicating that I view groups not addressed as unimportant. Moreover, this type of organization lends itself to re-articulating the notion of homogeneity in the face of diversity within groups. One of the reasons I chose to organize this reader along these lines is because a lot of important work has been written on the way articulating difference, otherness, and marginality has shaped society. However, people do not use differences to organize themselves into communities, political entities, or electronic discussion groups; they use similarities and solidarities – real or imagined. These similarities, of course, are not limited to race, ethnicity, etc., and "issues" or religion, or even a proposed cellphone tower, can be as salient as race, ethnicity or gender to cement common cause, which often cultivates coalitions that bring otherwise disparate groups together (Sanjek 1998). Although focusing on the oppression and opportunity that is articulated by the interlocking system of racism, sexism, and class hierarchies is critical to understanding identity in the United States, focusing specifically on race and class can overshadow the creative and specific ways people collectively negotiate these constraints and opportunities within social groups. This book includes eight sections with two or three authors contributing to each section.

Conditions of Identity, Violence, and Technologies

In this opening section, Anne Allison, Marcelo M. Suárez-Orozco, and Judith Goode each highlight and probe some of the conditions within which identity is practiced in the United States today. Cities, immigration, and the adolescent experience have undergone tremendous changes in the last 20 years. With technological shifts, the rise of multiculturalism, and a general shift in the economy from industry and manufacturing to information, service, and finance, American culture and the way people practice identity have become exceedingly complex and fragmented, unpredictable and unstable.

Anne Allison explores identity and media violence in a postmodern world. Steering away from the easy condemnation of media violence, she focuses instead on the popularity of cyborgs in children's imaginary play. Cyborgs, as she points out, are part human, part machine, part killer and part hero. And like many kids today, cyborgs are tethered to technology and lead fragmented lives. She uses the rash of high-school shootings as a gritty backdrop to challenge the way pundits and presidents link the violence perpetrated by teenagers who gun down classmates to the violence that saturates many of the mediums of children's imaginary play, including video games, action figures, movies, and comics. Exploring such characters as Sailor Moon, Mighty Morphin Power Rangers, and RoboCop, she explains that the popularity of these fragmented superheroes "stands for the type of hyper-technologicalized world we now live in; for the embeddedness of this technology in our everyday lifestyles, identities and skins; and for the fluctuations and the dispersals of a postmodern existence, both because of and apart from technology" (p. 36).

Marcelo M. Suárez-Orozco outlines the dramatic changes in the types of immigration to the United States in recent years. Questioning basic assumptions about assimilation and accommodation, Suárez-Orozco demonstrates that technology, globalization, and social segregation contribute to reasons why immigrants today do not have to make a clean break with their country of origin. Thanks in large part to new technologies, "immigrants today are more likely to be at once 'here' *and* 'there,' articulating dual consciousness and dual identities and, in the process, bridging increasingly unbounded national spaces" (p. 51).

Judith Goode addresses the instability and contingency of ethnic or racial identity and demonstrates how multi-racial communities can be forged within neighborhoods. She eloquently identifies the way well-meaning human relations workers employ rather static and uninformed ideas about racial and ethnic identity. Goode's work demonstrates, better than most, that life in America is full of ironic, contingent, and complex articulations of identity, where individuals must negotiate the pull of class, neighborhood, and local histories in addition to the push of racial and ethnic solidarity as an effective bulwark against structural racism.

Although all three authors address strikingly different issues, each highlights the importance of setting aside concepts and ideas that were employed to make sense of the way Americans practiced identity, even ten years ago. The way identity is practiced today is very fluid, contingent, and unstable.

Church, Family and the Dynamics of Post-Civil Rights Migration

In this section, Kelly Chong, Karen Pyke, and Kyeyoung Park explore and document several important factors that contribute to the performances and practices of identity within Korean American communities. A unique history and specific patterns of migration to the United States has contributed to the formation of Korean American communities that often center around family, church, money, and education.

According to Census 2000, the U.S. government numbers those who consider themselves Korean at just over 1.2 million people, which includes those who consider themselves Korean in combination with another ethnic group. Although fraught with essentialist assumptions and awkward language, the census can help determine the relative size of specific Asian communities. For example, people who specified Korean on the census numbered about the same as people who considered themselves Japanese and Vietnamese, but about half the number of people who identified themselves as Chinese or Filipino. People who identified themselves as Korean American make up roughly 10 percent of the overall Asian population that Census 2000 enumerated at 11.9 million out of 281.4 million or 4 percent of the overall population in the United States.

Often people who identify themselves as Korean American embrace beliefs about filial piety, parental authority, and individual sacrifice. Values like these often do not square with the rugged individualism, sense of an individuated self, and notions of freedom that many Americans hold to be normal or self-evident. The authors of this section document how people negotiate these often conflicting values as the second generation of the largest wave of Korean immigrants reaches middle adulthood.

Consumption, Class, and Traditions of Negotiation and Investment

In this section, Susan J. Ferguson and Aihwa Ong document and explore various aspects of identity and identification as it relates to people who consider themselves Chinese American. Although Ferguson and Ong offer comparative analyses, each author focuses on this extremely complex and diverse group. Steeped in a long and complex history in the United States, Chinese Americans are the largest and most socially, linguistically, and economically diverse group of Asian Americans.

Census 2000 reports that 2.7 million people identified themselves as Chinese alone "or in combination with one or more races or Asian groups." Chinese Americans are very diverse – ranging from the "uptown" Chinese who assimilate unnoticed in many of America's suburbs, to the so-called "downtown" Chinese who maintain networks, language, and business practices in the Chinatowns that form enduring neighborhoods within many urban landscapes. In a variety of ways, the experiences of those who claim Chinese American identity exemplify the impossibility of generalizing about a particular ethnic group, and yet Chinese Americans all share a history of many years of racial oppression in the United States (Louie 2001:445). While that racial construct has changed over time, Aihwa Ong demonstrates that, despite one's economic gains, racial differences continue to dog democracy.

The Politics and Perils of Assimilation

Stacey J. Lee and Yen Le Espiritu follow up on the themes articulated by Marcelo M. Suárez-Orozco, who questioned the import of immigrants assimilating so-called American culture and values. Immigrants have long believed that assimilating American values and behaviors was the key that opened the door to the American dream. Many immigrant parents today, who may not fully understand hip-hop culture or perceive rather loose sexual relations among American youth, are asking their children to reject so-called American culture while embracing their more conservative "traditional culture."

Stacey J. Lee documents how the push and pull of popular culture and American values force youth to produce creative ways to be Hmong in America. Yen Le Espiritu demonstrates how gender is key to immigrant identity by describing how Filipina women use the sexual stereotypes of white women to assert a sense of their own cultural superiority. Both authors challenge the long-held belief that the goal of immigrants to the United States, whether first-, 1.5-, or second-generation, is the assimilation of so-called American culture. They illustrate how – in an era where identity and values of immigrants are maintained by constant flows of information, people, and money between their country of origin and the United States – the rejection of some American values, while maintaining language, behaviors, and other values, or not making that clean break, is now as American as hamburgers.

Nazli Kibria, in many respects, shows the opposite head of the same coin. Kibria demonstrates how some college students reject the politics and performances involved in the category "Asian American," finding it cliquish and constricting. Although the students Kibria interviewed rejected the construct of such a politically inspired category, there is an implicit desire for these students to assimilate the ideals and behavior of so-called "American" or "normal" culture, which really means white cultural practices. To accomplish this they must challenge the terms and conditions of the Asian American category, exemplifying that frequent disconnection between identity and identification. Following Aihwa Ong's article, it is important to note that the students who could choose to reject or distance themselves from the community with which they are identified as members are racialized differently than their Hmong or Filipino peers.

More than Consumption: Experiencing Gender, Class, and Race

Sexuality is an important facet of everyone's identity. Like many whites who view their cultural practices as normal or not unique, many heterosexuals do not realize how integral sexuality is as a component of one's identity. Like other facets of identity, including language, culture, and race, when dominant institutions and discourses identify one as "different" or it attracts discrimination, that particular facet often becomes the site where individuals forge the most salient aspects of their identity. They do this by participating in communities, forming political commitments, and patterning and performing particular behavioral practices. Jeff Maskovsky, Kathryn Herr, and Alyssa Cymene Howe explore very different aspects of queer identity, but each demonstrates how particular facets of identity are never exempted from the interlocking forms of oppression in the United States where race, class, and gender circumscribe the choices and repertoires available to each individual as they experience life in America.

Policing Blackness, Authenticity and the Soul Patrol

According to Census 2000, 12.9 percent of the U.S. population is black or African American. Two million people, however, identified themselves as black in combination with another race. What does it mean to be black in America today? Is it determined by identity or identification? Each of the authors in this section demonstrates that within black communities it is more important how one acts than how one is identified.

John L. Jackson, Jr., Mary Pattillo-McCoy, and Maureen Mahon each explore how black people negotiate the politics and performances involved in defining and negotiating the meaning of blackness. In each case, class confounded and delimited the way each of the people they observed and interviewed organized their lives and structured their behavior, from the types of birthday parties they threw, to the shoes they bought, to the music they played. Each of these seemingly innocuous class-inflected behaviors was staged to perform or redefine a putative authentic blackness. Implicitly, each author outlines the boundaries of blackness where seemingly poor blacks have more of a claim to this blackness than middle- and upper-class blacks. However, as Mary Pattillo-McCoy's ethnography of Groveland (a pseudonym for a suburb of Chicago) points out, many less affluent blacks symbolically try to make up economic gaps by buying things and looking "good" or more "middle-class," while marketing executives exploit and manipulate this desire.

Privilege, Power, and Anxiety of the Norm

With just over 75 percent of the U.S. population recording themselves as white in Census 2000, it is no wonder that many people equate American culture with whiteness. More specifically, as Pamela Perry argues in "White Means Never Having to Say You're Ethnic," many whites don't view their behavior and identities as cultural but rather "cultureless." Even in states like New York, California, and Texas, where whites are minorities in the urban landscape, the norm is always pegged by the activities and identities of whites. Perry demonstrates how this notion of cultureless identity acts as a tool that articulates racial superiority.

Julia Hall, in "It Hurts to be a Girl: Growing Up Poor, White and Female," depicts how the toll of white-on-white violence meted out upon the bodies of young girls shapes their identities in enduring ways. Moreover, Hall documents how institutions are complicit in furthering a pernicious form of sexism that may be the norm but hard to call normal. Finally, Kyle W. Kusz, in "'I Want to be the Minority': The Politics of Youthful White Masculinities in Sport and Popular Culture in 1990s America," shows the anxiety many whites feel. Like Anne Allison, Kusz explores the rash of high-school shootings, but as a way to explore the "white man as victim" trope, a popular theme in print and radio media. He also uses sports and popular culture as a way to examine the way certain white men construct their identity as victims.

Language, History, and Specificity

The final section explores the aspects of identity and everyday life that Mexican Americans tend to experience. According to the cumbersome categories of Census 2000, 12.5 percent of the U.S. population considered themselves Hispanic or Latino (of any race). Almost 60 percent of this Latino population identified themselves as Mexican, making this category 7.3 percent of the entire U.S. population. Like the pan-ethnic category "Asian American," the term "Latino" encompasses very diverse peoples. In her classic essay, "The Politics of Labeling: Latino/a Cultural Identities of Self and Others," Suzanne Oboler explores the specific identity politics involved within and between the various labels used to describe Spanish-speaking people in the United States. Brenda Bright and Angela Valenzuela describe in detail the articulation of identity within the everyday life of particular Mexican American or Chicana/o communities. In all three essays, the authors forefront the fact that class, gender, and age all shape the way Mexican Americans identify and get identified.

Essentially it is Essentialism, but ...

> Critics, both inside and outside of anthropology, have called "culture" into question as "essentializing" – the conceptual mirror image, as it were, of traditional racialist assumption; paradoxically, it has at the same time become the badge of identity of a multicultural multitude of minority groups – who may in fact deny the possibility that outsiders (anthropologists included) are capable of understanding or representing their cultural essence. (Stocking 2001:324)

Exploring the idea of the sameness, togetherness, and community of any group takes the reader down the slippery slope of essentialism. As Diane Fuss explains, essentialism "is most commonly understood as a belief in the real, true essence of things, the invariable and fixed properties which define the 'whatness' of a given entity" (Fuss 1989:xi–xii). This belief in essentialism as it relates to groups of people has filled America's collective memory with many stereotypes that have become a part of everyday life, and punctuated its legal record with statutes that enforce rights and responsibilities based on race, gender, and sexuality. It was the belief in essentialism that allowed Americans to abrogate the 5th and 14th Amendments to the U.S. Constitution, as agents of the federal government snatched American families from their homes to relocate them to the internment camps scattered throughout the western states during World War II. Like many ideologies, essentialism has teeth that inflict pain and anguish.

Essentialism is the ideological glue that enables people to engage in colonialism, racism, sexism, etc. It allows people to believe there is some sort of tangible difference between "us" and "them." In its most dramatic form, the belief in the essential qualities of all X, Y, and Z people allows men and women in combat to kill a dehumanized enemy. Less dramatic forms of essentialism include people believing that women are more nurturing or possess some sort of "mothering" instinct and that gay guys really can decorate better than straight ones. There are, however, some empowering aspects of essentialism. Like many other aspects of American culture, essentialism is often ironic and cuts both ways, which contributes to its tenacity. The way many Americans believe in the metaphysical essences and natural qualities of particular types of people can actually serve to unite people through social and political solidarity. Whether it is the black power movement of the late 1960s, or a political action committee formed by a group of Chinese Americans in the year 2003, the processes of unification are at once a process of dividing and policing who is accepted and who is not accepted. The idea of a unified whole is fiction, but it is a foundational fiction that, at once, veils and affirms social groups that experience some sense of connectedness or cohesion, unity or solidarity.

Black student solidarity on predominately white college campuses is one of the many examples of how essentialism can cut both ways. Despite claims of self-segregation, many black students are regularly alienated within institutions of higher education. Associating with peers of similar racial backgrounds enables many black students to inhabit particular spaces that are filled with social camaraderie and cultural familiarity. But what is the tangible common denominator that unites an international student from Jamaica, a rich kid from the D.C. suburbs, a poor kid from Bremerton, Washington and a student-athlete from Pasadena, California? Although one could make the argument that it is history and culture, the more salient factors include the way students of African descent are identified as "black," with all of its historical and social baggage. In most cases, the black student boundary is drawn on the identification side of the equation, but many believe there are indeed some commonalities uniting black people: They share a creative and soulful spirit, customs, aesthetics, and history, or simply a sense of pride in who they are as black people. Like so many groups, social organizations, or cliques, one not only needs to be black, one must also act "black" to participate fully in the solidarity, safety, and camaraderie of the social/political group. The policing of boundaries that determine who is in and who is out of the group often turn on behavior, ideas of authenticity, and cultural competence. Affectionately known as the "soul patrol," the people who maintain the boundaries of blackness, within what are basically cliques on predominately white college campuses, often alienate those who do not or will not conform. At historically black colleges and universities, a whole different set of social politics is at play, and those boundaries are often drawn and performed along class lines. Even though blackness is performed very differently within these different contexts, all black students are keenly aware that they are identified as being black in America, and each student embraces or rejects this identification in various ways.

The boundaries and performances enacted by black students on college campuses are practices of identity shored up by essentialist beliefs that turn on the "whatness" of these black students. The binding of patterned behavior and essentialist beliefs is quite routine in the United States and occurs within and between nearly every social and political group. It is the same sort of essentialism that quickly reversed the Asian-as-model-minority back to the Asian-as-double-dealing-and-disloyal in the wake of the Win Ho Lee case and former President Bill Clinton's campaign finance scandal. Essentialism is a powerful and explosive ingredient when calling for political action and remains the basis of much nationalist rhetoric.

Americans in general practice identity in essentialist ways. This is the main reason I chose to organize this book by employing categories that are inherently vacuous, ephemeral, and based more in folklore and perception than tangible facts. This approach is not without risk. For example, by highlighting the experiences of Korean Americans, I risk reproducing a discourse, however critical, that there is something authentic, real, or essential that makes someone with a Korean background in the United States really a Korean American.

I do this in an attempt to deconstruct stereotypes, critique essentialist beliefs, and complicate accepted assumptions about American cultural groups. However, I am not necessarily committed to this approach, and invite the reader to study all the articles about consumption and shopping together and then read the ones on church and religion together, etc. This would offer an interesting understanding of identity across various social groups. The way it is currently organized, however, is ethnographically sound.

Anthropology has always privileged the views of the people it studies. To study shamanism, magic, or ancestor worship, anthropologists cannot immediately discount these practices and must incorporate an insider's perspective as part of their analysis. From my perspective, as a social scientist, to say that there is some sort of essence that Chinese or black or Koreans in the United States share in common is like saying that magic is a real force of nature. As an ethnographer of American culture, however, I have to set aside my beliefs and follow the way people actually organize themselves into communities, even though this often reproduces ideas about essentialism. It is because people do organize and identify themselves in such a fashion that I chose to organize this book in a way that mirrors how many Americans organize their lives.

NOTES

1 Throughout this introduction, I use the term "American" as the general public uses it, referring to people who reside in the United States. Technically this is not correct because the term American includes everyone from the top of North America to the bottom of South America.

2 Actually, these distinctions I am making are glossed from the more technical distinctions made by Rogers Brubaker and Fredrick Cooper, who label this as a "distinction between self-identification and the identification and categorization of oneself by others." Drawing from anthropologist Richard Jenkins (1994), these authors explain that "Self-identification takes place in dialectical interplay with external identification . . . External identification is itself a varied process. In the ordinary ebb and flow of social life, people identify and categorize others, just as they identify and categorize themselves. But there is another key type of external identification that has no counterpart in the domain of self-identification: the formalized, codified, objectified systems of categorization developed by powerful, authoritative institutions." When the authors note "no counterpart" they do not imply "no part" in those processes.

3 Brubaker and Cooper (2000) offer a nice explanation of "categories of practice" as they relate to identity. Explicitly "following [Pierre] Bourdieu," the authors explain that these categories are "something akin to what others have called 'native' or 'folk' or 'lay' categories." These are categories of everyday social experience, developed and deployed by ordinary social actors, as distinguished from the experience-distant categories used by social analysts (Brubaker and Cooper 2000: 4). Mara Loveman (1997) also deftly argues that using categories of practice mitigates the processes of reification and enables social analysts to focus their attention "on processes of boundary construction, maintenance, and decline" (Loveman 1997: 891).

4 The word circumstance is used often, but I use it here deliberately as a way to capture the tension between an individual's choices, acts, and actions and the social, economic, and racial realities that circumscribe, in some respects structure, the everyday life of each individual – what some critical theorists describe as someone's "positionality." In addition, the word is flexible enough to describe the instances when people actually do "change their circumstances."

REFERENCES

Andersen, Margaret L. and Patricia H. Collins. 2001. *Race, Class, and Gender: An Anthology*. 4th edn. Belmont, CA: Wadsworth.

Baker, Lee D. 1998. *From Savage to Negro: Anthropology and the Construction of Race, 1896–1954*. Berkeley: University of California Press.

Bass, Janet. 2001. Teacher Salaries Fail to Keep up with Inflation: AFT Releases Annual State-by-State Teacher Salary Survey [web page]. Accessed July 19, 2001. Available at http://www.aft.org/press/2001/download/1-1.pdf.

Brooke, James. 1998. Gay Man Beaten and Left for Dead; 2 Are Charged. *The New York Times* (New York), October, 10: Section A, p. 9.

Brubaker, Rogers and Frederick Cooper. 2000. Beyond Identity. *Theory and Society* 29:1–47.

Collins, Patricia H. 2000. *Back Feminist Thought: Knowledge, Consciousness, and the Politics of Empowerment*. New York: Routledge.

Degler, Carl N. 1991. *In Search of Human Nature: The Decline and Revival of Darwinism in American Social Thought*. New York: Oxford University Press.

Erikson, Erik. 1963. *Childhood and Society*. New York: W. W. Norton.

Fuss, Diana. 1989. *Essentially Speaking: Feminism, Nature and Difference*. New York: Routledge.

Gossett, Thomas F. 1968. *Race: The History of an Idea in America*. New York: Schocken Books.

Handler, Richard. 1994. Is "Identity" a Useful Cross-Cultural Concept? In *Commemorations: The Politics of National Identity*, John R. Gillis, ed., Pp. 27–40. Princeton, NJ: Princeton University Press.

Hochschild, Jennifer L. 1995. *Facing Up to the American Dream: Race, Class, and the Soul of the Nation*. Princeton, NJ: Princeton University Press.

Jenkins, Richard. 1994. Rethinking Ethnicity: Identity, Categorization, and Power. *Ethnic and Racial Studies* 17(2):197–223.

Kenworthy, Tom. 1998. Gay Man Near Death After Beating, Burning; Three Held in Wyoming Attack Near Campus; Hate Crime Suspected. *The Washington Post* (Washington, DC), October 10: Section A, p. 1.

Lancaster, Roger N. and Micaela di Leonardo. 1997. *The Gender/Sexuality Reader: Culture, History, Political Economy*. New York: Routledge.

Louie, Vivian. 2001. Parents' Aspirations and Investment: The Role of Social Class in the Educational Experiences of 1.5 and Second-Generation Chinese Americans. *Harvard Educational Review* 71 (3):438–474.

Loveman, Mara. 1999. Is "Race" Essential? *American Sociological Review* 64(6):891–899.

Ortner, Sherry. 1996. *Making Gender: The Politics and Erotics of Culture*. Boston: Beacon Press.

Pollard, Tessa M. and Susan B. Hyatt. 1999. *Sex, Gender, and Health*. New York: Cambridge University Press.

Sanjek, Roger. 1998. *The Future of Us All: Race and Neighborhood Politics in New York City*. Ithaca, NY: Cornell University Press.

Smedley, Audrey. 1993. *Race in North America: Origin and Evolution of a Worldview*. Boulder: Westview.

Stocking, George W. Jr. 2001. *Delimiting Anthropology: Occasional Essays and Reflections*. Madison: University of Wisconsin Press.

Suárez-Orozco, Carola and Marcelo M. Suárez-Orozco. 2001. *Children of Immigration*. Cambridge, MA: Harvard University Press.

Texas NAACP. 1999. James Byrd, Jr. [web page]. Accessed July 27, 2001. Available at http://www.texasnaacp.org/jasper.htm

Tilly, Charles. 1996. Citizenship, Identity and Social History. In *Citizenship, Identity and Social History*, Charles Tilly, ed. Pp. 1–7. Cambridge: Cambridge University Press.

Treviõ, Joseph. 2000. Tensions on Board: Many Latino Bus Riders at Odds with Drivers and MTA Strike [web page]. Accessed July 19, 2001. Available at http://www.laweekly.com/ink/00/46/news-trevino.shtml.

Van Ausdale, Debra and Joe R. Feagin. 2001. *The First R: How Children Learn Race and Racism*. New York: Rowman & Littlefield.

Williams, Patricia J. 1991. *The Alchemy of Race and Rights*. Cambridge, MA: Harvard University Press.

Winnicott, D. W. 1971. *Playing and Reality*. Harmondsworth, England: Penguin.

Part I

Conditions of Identity, Violence, and Technologies

1

Cyborg Violence: Bursting Borders and Bodies with Queer Machines

Anne Allison

A new killer drug has hit the streets of Detroit and the cyborg RoboCop is hunting down its creator. Entering the warehouse where his computer tells him "nuke" is being made, RoboCop sees the drug-lord and tells him, "Dead or alive, you're coming with me." Cain laughs as his underlings emerge from the shadows. Carrying guns, they move in and shoot; a boy blasts off RoboCop's hands and a woman lacerates his stomach with laser fire. Forced to his knees, RoboCop vows, "I will kill you" to Cain.

The thugs now encircle him and one, maneuvering a huge magnet, picks up the cyborg's metal body then drops it onto a bed of warehouse scraps. Before RoboCop can move, he is pinned down at his hands and feet with metal stakes. Standing over him, Cain holds up a vial of Nuke and plunges it rapturously into his neck. Armed with tools, the minions approach RoboCop and start dismembering him. They hack, saw, and drill his body; a fade-out follows the severing of his left leg.

The fragments of RoboCop are delivered to the precinct police station. What remains of him forms a pile that a technician moves to her lab to start rebuilding. But her bosses – executives at Omni Consumer Products (OCP) who own the police force as well as the cyber-cop – have not yet decided whether RoboCop is worth the cost of reconstruction. Saying he's "just a machine," they halt his repair. But the police who have gathered around the cyber-cop see this differently: "It's like you're killing him."

Two scenes later, RoboCop has yet to be reassembled. His body is strung up in the lab; the torso with attached head is hung eerily on a line. The police chief pleads for OCP to save him because he's "one of ours" and needed back on the job. A corporate executive responds to this that they may just sell him as scrap. When OCP does decide to fix him, they pay particular attention to weeding out any human remains in the cyborg. Yet, when asked who he is at the end, RoboCop answers "Murphy" – the person he was before and whose remnants were used to build the cybercop. Told this is an illusion, he is rewired to identify himself as "RoboCop."

Shortly afterward, RoboCop walks out the door. When he is greeted by his fellow cops, they call him "Murphy."

Scenes from *RoboCop 2*, Directed by Irvin Kershner

The Media and Kids: Violent Connections?

When I was first writing this paper in June 1998, the U.S. news media was awash in what was then reported to be the latest episode of "teenage rage." Predating the much more spectacularly horrific events at Columbine a few months later, this was a shooting by a 15-year-old boy on the premises of his school in Springfield, Oregon. In this case, a boy who had been expelled the day before for harboring a gun, opened fire at his school and, shooting randomly, killed two children and wounded 22 others. As in my local paper (the *News and Observer* in Raleigh, North Carolina), the press represented this as part of a national "rash": shootings that took place at schools, in "unlikely" settings (backwater towns and, with Columbine, in the upscale suburb of Littleton, Colorado), with brutal results (26 dead excluding parents shot elsewhere and scores wounded), and at the hands of white, teenage boys. Stunned by the savagery of these acts, people across the country were also stricken by their eruption in the "bedrock" of America and by homegrown boys driven to murder over alleged slights and rebuffs. Although commentary struggled with explanations (getting little further, though, than "boys caught up in teenage rage" [Cannon 1998:19A]), more profound was the incessant questioning "WHY?" as posed by the *News and Observer* in its headline following Springfield (Cannon 1998:19A).

Making the same query two days earlier on National Public Radio (NPR), a reporter suggested the answer lay in today's culture of violence. On this view, recourse to violence, particularly with guns, has become insinuated into everyday life in the United States like a national habit. Citing the example of two Hollywood movies, *Die Hard* (1988) and *RoboCop 2* (1990), with their litanies of shootings (61 in the case of *RoboCop 2*), the report noted the normalization of such violence and how its presence in mass culture matches its spread in real life. Gun usage has now become commonplace; a gun-laden movie like *RoboCop 2* has been watched by millions of kids;[1] and the recent school shootings have occurred in "middle" America rather than the inner cities (where the everydayness of violence goes unnoted). As picked up in this story, it is the mainstreaming of violence that seems disturbingly new to so many people in the United States today. And, with this perception, comes criticism of mainstream media, a staple of everyday life here and well-known for its diet of violence.

But how are these two forms of common violence actually related? Research on what is called "violent entertainment" or "media violence" was proliferating already when stimulated by the recent shootings. To date, the bulk of this has been conducted by people who assume a clear-cut definition of media violence, use quantitative methods in studying the effects it has on various audiences, and conclude that violent media are harmful for viewers, particularly children. In this research (conducted predominantly by scholars and officials in the fields of public policy, violence prevention, law, medicine, education, psychology, communication, and media studies),[2] media violence refers, as it does in Sissela Bok's and James Hamilton's recent studies, to any media coverage or representation of bodily damage, destruction, or death including graphic reportage of murder in the news, video games that feature killers and killing, and the constancy of attack scenes and shoot-outs in movies and television including children's cartoons (Bok 1998; Hamilton 1998). Focusing on the effect(s) violent media have on various audiences, research such as Bok's has pointed to primarily four: increased fear or anxiety about one's world, an appetite for more violence (in whatever form), desensitization to violence, and aggression. Where it has been most conclusive is in showing how children, particularly under the age of 6 and particularly for the medium of television, repeatedly demonstrate higher levels of aggression after viewing scenes of injury and destruction (Hamilton 1998). The most common explanation for this is that young children, incapable of distinguishing the fantasy of mass media from reality, mimic the former in socially inappropriate ways in their behavior (Bok 1998).

But the mimicry of violent images and scripts goes far beyond the age of young childhood, many suggest, and is at root in the new genus of casual brutality erupting in the (school)yards of middle America. In his remarks following the Springfield shooting, for example, President Clinton declared that youth today in the United States have become desensitized to violence by the degree it inhabits their world(s) of (video) games, television, and movies. This view was even more strongly endorsed at the conference Clinton held on violence after Columbine – and in the report on "Marketing Violent Entertainment to Children" by the Federal Trade Commission (FTC) that ensued[3] – where Hollywood's role in inciting youth to violence is treated as a foregone conclusion (unjustified, as a number of studies have shown, by the "evidence").[4] The premise here is that media violence, even when not literally mimicked, engenders a mindset that sees violence as not only acceptable but "cool." As Sissela Bok (1998) has argued for children's shows like *The Mighty Morphin Power Rangers*, fighting that leads to obliteration of one's opponent is normalized, glamorized, and made fun. Kids laugh when enemies are blasted and come to associate aggression with excitement, pleasure, and ego-boosts – a dangerous message, Bok concludes, for how children view both the world and themselves.

It is this conceptualization of violent entertainment and the impact it has on youth I wish to challenge in my paper by considering a specific genre – violent cyborgs popularized since the 1980s by such blockbuster hits as *RoboCop* and

Terminator. By almost any definition, these movies are violent. But it is the meaning and organization of this violence I wish to pay attention to here as few in the category of killer cyborg – cyborgs are hybrids of living matter melded with cybernetic devices; and killer cyborgs, often indistinguishable from cyborgs, are cyborgs programmed to fight, kill, or attack – are as neatly and unambiguously drawn as critics like Bok would suggest. Although their bodies both are and bear lethal weapons, the cyborg's identity is complicated beyond that of mere aggressor. Created themselves out of body-parts from dead (often killed) human beings, these cyborgs undergo constant attack and continual reconstruction. Who or what the cyborg is, in fact, is a concern that both troubles and constitutes the plot, and establishing one's identity is a desire that drives as much as eludes the cyborg subject. Destruction then, though a dominant trope in cyborg stories, is intrinsically linked to another theme – identity construction – as cyborgs not only produce violence but are produced themselves out of violent acts. Thus while images of cutting, exploding, and splattering (re)cycle in this genre, "life" is both destroyed and reemployed as a result.

In considering a movie like *RoboCop 2*, I propose that we look at violence as a force that not only "inflicts injury" (as the *Oxford English Dictionary* defines violence) but also produces identity in a realm of media entertainment where destruction is particularly enmeshed in the making of a new subject, the cyborg. Such an emphasis on what is productive rather than merely destructive in mass culture differs considerably from the standard conceptualization of violence within scholarly and public discourse on media violence. For example, in his recent book, *Channeling Violence: The Economic Market for Violent Television Programming* (1998), James Hamilton defined violence as the number of incidents of the exercise of physical force so as to inflict injury or damage to persons or property. By this definition, violence is something that is quantifiable, visible, and willful. The assumption is that we know violence when we see it, and its meaning is limited to one thing – it destroys. Further, what is said about violence within media is also said about the impact it has on viewing audiences: violence attacks viewers by breaking down their sensitivity and resistance to aggression. Hence we get the NPR description of *RoboCop 2* as a movie with 61 shootings and the explosive statistics, much circulated in the 1990s, that the average child in the United States will have viewed 8,000 murders and more than 100,000 acts of violence by the time they leave elementary school (Bok 1998:59). Reduced to such numbers, there seems little else to say except that media violence holds a meaning for kids that is only deleterious.

This position is not unlike that of the anti-pornography contingency of 1980s feminism spearheaded by Dworkin and MacKinnon that treated pornography only in terms of the violence it renders on women and failed to consider why and how it produces other effects, such as meaning and pleasure for regular consumers. As critics (including Williams 1989; Kipnis 1992; Bright 1995; F.A.C.T. Book Committee 1992; Ross 1989; and Allison 2000) argued, any behavior with mass or popular appeal is drawing in people for reasons that must be understood rather than merely condemned. So too, I argue, about media violence where research to date has been narrowly confined to interrogating effects using an apriori definition (quantifiable, injurious acts) that limits the answers we get. Such an approach cannot account for the vast appeal of violent media across what is a broad spectrum of children today in the United States. Nor does this approach adequately examine the terrain and landscape of the violent worlds so intensely imagined in movies like *RoboCop 2* whose fantasies of disconnected and reconnected body-parts are speaking somehow to children and of something(s) in the lives they are leading today. My aim in this paper is to start making these connections – between the worlds that kids live in and their imaginary worlds of violent play populated with the continually disintegrating and reintegrated body-parts of humans, machines, killers, and heroes. What I will propose is that fragmentation centers the violence in one genre of media entertainment – cyborgs – and that this trope both reflects a ("real") world of flux, migration, and deterritorialization, and produces ("imaginary") new subjects whose queerness bears the seeds of a constructive potential for U.S. children today.[5]

Postmodernism

Today's world of global capitalism and proliferating technologies is often described in terms of flows. Flows – of people, goods, money, ideas, images – move between borders – of nations, economies, cultures – making this an age of deterritorialization as much as reterritorialization. Production has shifted from the Fordist model (Harvey 1989) of a rationalized labor force: of core workers who stay in one place and earn enough wages to consume what they produce – the mass-produced goods that embed both the desires and discipline of a modern lifestyle. Today, production is based on "flexible accumulation" where, geared to quick turn-over and a constantly changing market, companies have downsized their core workers, diversified their holdings and product lines, and rely more on subcontractors, peripheral workers and outsourcing. Increasingly there is a gap between those who produce and consume brand name goods – Nike or Adidas shoes, for instance – and continually, in the United States at least, the gap is rising between the so-called haves and have-nots accompanied by a shrinkage of the middle class in-between.

The condition of postmodernity in which we live is one of shifts and dispersals, instability and movement, speed and ephemerality. Ever more our world is being remade and redrawn through various technologies – image and information production, medical and genetic advances, military and starwar networks. Our connections are quicker (whether by travel, phone, email, or CNN) to places and peoples further away; disconnections are quick too – ruptures of families, communities, workplaces, schools. David Harvey (1989) speaks of time-space compression and the increased attention placed on the immediate and instantaneous in postmodern lifestyle. Consumption is more important than ever in advanced capitalist economies and images not only sell commodities but are commodities themselves, operating in an economy that reifies the surfaces and impressions of things. Major consumer values are instantaneity – fast food and speedy services – and disposability – goods that can be easily and quickly thrown out. Reproductions or simulacra are valued over originals and the cultural logic of postmodernity, as theorized by Frederic Jameson (1984), is marked by an aesthetic of the pastiche – the jumbling of mixed genres and past and present time periods – and schizophrenia – the experience of life as disjointed, incoherent, and lacking linear continuity.

It is against this backdrop that I want to read children's play and, in particular, a form of play in which the media in the United States has taken such a keen interest: violent entertainment. Within this category characterized by a prominence of attacks, shootings, ruptured body-parts, and hyper-weapons is a sub-set in which the explosiveness of violence is coupled with another, far less studied dimension, the making and remaking of a new kind of subject – the cyborg. Following Donna Haraway (1991), I take cyborg to be a fusion of artificial machinery and living (animal, human, or alien) organism that confuses prior identity borders. This confusion is marked by both a dislocation and reaggregation of bodies and body parts (of and between nature, nation, race, community, gender, commodity, and/or culture) – what I trace here through violence and queerness. The figure of the cyborg has become exceedingly popular in (and circulates between) two sites I pay attention to – mass-produced play in Japan and the United States since the 1980s that spreads across the multimedia of comic books (*manga* in Japan), cartoons (*anime*), film, live action television, video (and gameboy) games, and merchandise such as action figures.[6] Replicants, terminators, RoboCops, and power rangers are the figures of this play world. And all are identified as not only cyborgs but also fighting machines: beings whose bodies – amalgamations of weaponry, machinery, and powers – are programmed to fight, eradicate, disintegrate, splatter, shoot, mutilate, or kill. The stories, what there are of them, are orchestrated around the theme and staging of excessive destruction. In the *RoboCop* movies, for instance, scenes of slaughter or mutilation occur ritualistically about every ten minutes and, in *The Mighty Morphin Power Rangers*, based on a live action television series that has run continuously in Japan since 1973 and in the United States since 1993, the team of clean-scrubbed teenagers who morph into power-suited warrior rangers, battle and defeat at least one grotesque-looking beast every show.

What is the pleasure engaged by fans with such programming and how is violence conceptualized? My own son, recently turned 15, was a consumer and player of the violent cyborg genre for years. He delighted in the gore of both the *RoboCop* and *Terminator* series, loved all the masked warrior cyborgs when he lived in Japan as a young child, and played continually (until 12 or 13) with his cyborg action figures that he mobilized into intense battles peppered with an arsenal of blaster guns and fantasy super-weapons that ended in downed figures, severed limbs, and scattered body-parts. Adam is an uncommonly sweet, gentle, feminist boy, yet he was drawn to a fantasy play of macho warriors with heightened powers and killer instincts. When asked what he liked in this play-world, his answer was simply "it's cool." When pushed to elaborate, however, Adam described not only the thrill and excitement of multiple explosions, fast action, and powerful heroes, but also more studied and aesthetic pleasures taken in knowing, discriminating, and appreciating the details of this universe – the plots and particularly the makeup of characters' bodies that fuse with weapons, powers, and vehicles.

In research I have done on children's mass culture in both Japan and the United States, I am struck by a similar pattern: fascination with both the break-down and make-up of key characters. This is true in the case of *Sailor Moon*, for example, a highly popular, long-running (1992–97) *manga* (comic book) and television *anime* (cartoon) in Japan that, exported to several other countries including the United States, features a group of teenage girls who transform into the superheroines, the Sailor Scouts led by Sailor Moon, to fight the evil Negaverse. As to the appeal of *Sailor Moon*, fans are most likely to cite the composition and array of characters – five different girls who shift from their own version of normalcy (one is smart, another lives at a temple, the lead character is a sleepyhead who loves to eat and play rather than study) to superheroism (each with distinctive powers, costumes, and names).[7] And yet, when observing children actually watching episodes of *Sailor Moon* in the United States, I noticed how attentive they were to the action scenes – the moments of battle when, threatened by destruction, the girls upgrade their powers and shape-shift to zap, blast, cream, or otherwise eviscerate their foes. In asking later whether any of the kids had found these battles to be "violent," one 12-year-old shouted "yes," adding that this was his favorite part of *Sailor Moon*. Becoming highly animated, he went over this and other attack scenes from the show in which bodies break apart, disintegrate in mid-air, and mutate their form (an arm changes into a blade or what looks human transmutes into a monster, for example).

Of the other 12 children in this particular group, only one agreed with the characterization of *Sailor Moon* as violent, adding that she liked violence in entertainment (as in slasher films like the *Halloween* series, which started in 1978). The others, as is the far more typical reaction, thought "soft" and "cute" better described *Sailor Moon* given its gentle story and subdued graphics. Yet, for all these viewers (and fans in general), the appeal of the story is in the shifts and multipartedness of the characters: girls who transform and are, at either end, a complex of attributes. As a girl, Serena (the main character whose name is Usagi in the Japanese version) has a mixture of traits and, as the superhero, Sailor Moon, a constellation of powers – weapons (tiara and moon prism wand), strengths (the ability to shift form, impersonate others, execute multiple attacks), and a make-over appearance (that, with new cleavage, jewels, and a uniform that is now mini-skirted, turns her sexy and beautiful). All of the latter, it is important to note, are only revealed in the course of battle. This means that transformation, the keyword in *Sailor Moon*, is always and inextricably linked to destruction;[8] the girls transform only with the arrival of (and to counter-attack) the destructive Negaverse, and, as superheroes, they use their powers to destroy. As the full name of the show (*Bishōjo Shenshi Se-ra Mun*-[Pretty Soldier, Sailor Moon]) suggests, the construction of superheroism here is coupled to, and dependent on, the persona of warrior-destroyer. So even in this mild, sweet version of a cyborg killer, violence defined as acts intended to damage or destroy others is fundamental to the identity and appeal of the main character(s).[9] As I pushed this point with the children in my study, most admitted that they found the action scenes interesting not only for the transformations that reconfigure the heroes but also for the disaggregation that unravels the enemies – a slow dissolution, as one gave the example, of a monster who crumbled first with her hands, then arms, next the head, and finally the rest of the body. "Cool" was the reaction.

What the above responses by fans of violent cyborgs and transforming superheroes point to is a fascination in what could be called the dissection of transhuman characters whether the focus is on the make-up or break-down of a subject – a distinction that becomes, itself, indistinguishable. Hence, an interest in the composition of how cyborg bodies are built on and from multiple parts (chest-plates, armor, power belts, tiaras) bleeds into an interest in the decomposition (splattering, smashing, chopping, firing) bodies undergo as a consequence of violent fighting. Thus, though coming at it from opposite ends as it were, both the constructive and destructive components of cyborg violence are part and parcel of the same geometry: power as it fuses and defuses in bodies with shifting and exploding borders of identity. That is also to say, violence is not only the end to things, but also the beginning. In the case of cyborg myths, killing terminates the life of one kind of being (human) but also initiates the life of another (cyborg).

David Harvey (1989:311) has written critically of the "creative destruction" fostered by the cyberpunk movie *Blade Runner* (1982), arguing, in accord with the common criticisms of media violence, that its violence is excessive and encourages an aggressive stance of dealing with adversity by zapping and whacking one's opponent. With this perspective, violence is seen only in terms of its destructiveness: as acts that injure, damage, or ruin people and things and get glorified in the mass media by hyped-up special effects, inattention to the consequences of violence, and the heroization of violent characters (Bok 1998). Yet, as fans of cyborg action have suggested to me, "destruction" is a far more complicated operation and has implications for the construction of new kinds of subjects as well: subjects who, made in the nexus of violence, emerge with their lines of "humanness" and "selfhood" redrawn.[10] Unanchored from the semblance of monolithic roots, these new subjects exceed the parameters of a singular identity and, in this sense, are queer. In the case of *Sailor Moon*, for example, the supergirls have bodies/identities that (con)fuse prettiness with warriorship and have desires that roam towards each other as well as toward boys.[11]

Accordingly, my position is that it is important to consider what might be productive as well as counter-productive for children today in the "creative destructiveness" of cyborg fantasy. In this I am guided by what Donna Haraway (1991) sees as the progressive potential of cyborgs: artifice that can help overcome the power inequities bred by worldviews that treat bodies as naturalistic, where nature of one kind is taken to be inherently superior – self versus other, white versus black, male versus female. Today's cyborg heroes have bodies that complicate, rather than reduce to, nature and are possessed with powers that are far more contingent and diffuse than those of earlier cultural heroes – the Superman of the 1950s television show, for example, where his powers were centered in and secured by a holistic, natural (male) body.[12] If that was the Fordist model of fantasy phallicism, today's cyborgs are the flexible, postmodern model despite, or precisely because of, the fact they continually explode.

Unlike those who commonly argue that heroes of violent entertainment, including cyborg violence, are drawn according to a modernist model of stable coherency and "invincible" machoism (Springer 1993; Balsamo 1996; Bok 1998), I stress the ruptures, slippages, and excesses to which cyborg heroes are not only subjected (through the constant attacks, incisions, intrusions, and penetrations to their bodies) but also assume subjectivity itself.[13] To do so, I use the example of a movie series, the *RoboCop* trilogy (*RoboCop* [1987], *RoboCop 2* [1990], *RoboCop 3* [1993]), in which the volatility of the world portrayed and the cyborg it produces are particularly clear if also excessive. My attempt here is to scrutinize the dimensions of both the violence and subjectivity in this specific text before speaking more generally of the genre of cyborg violence and its situatedness within the world of media entertainment and the socio-economic conditions of late capitalism.

Robo-Violence

The movie *RoboCop*, the first in a series of three, starts off with a scene of violence.[14] Set in the crime-ridden city of Detroit where a newscast announces that three police officers have just been killed, executives at OCP discuss plans to build what is to be a corporately run new city. Hoping to arm this city with fail-safe police who can maintain order over the rising, alienated underclass, OCP designs a robotic cop, Ed 209, whose test-run dramatically fails, brutally killing an executive. It is the next design, this time for a cybernetic cop, that constitutes the story of RoboCop. These plans require a model policeman who must die in order to be rebuilt as a lethally superior model cop. Targeted as the victim, Alex Murphy is sent into an ambush with his partner, Anne Lewis, and savagely blown apart by a group of thugs who taunt and tease him by first shooting off his hand. The scene is graphic and gruesome, and Murphy is finally killed by a shot to his head.

The violence of this act is not only intense and drawn out, but takes place at the beginning of the story to unfold; indeed, the protagonist's murder is the very condition of and for his rebirth as cyborg cop. The need to kill Murphy is driven home in the process of rebuilding that follows. When, at one point the doctors working on him discover that they can save one arm, the OCP executive in charge tells them to "kill it, shut him down, we want total prosthesis" and, leaning over Murphy's still human-looking body, barks "you're going to be one mean motherfucker." By the next scene, Murphy has become a machine: a fact we experience through RoboCop's perspective, looking up from where he's lying on the table having his monitor adjusted, and seeing, as does he, through the scanner of his computer. RoboCop's position here and ours, if we identify with it, is one of vulnerability and unease: a state that continues when RoboCop is soon programmed, as a machine, to obey the directives dictated him by OCP. He repeats back his orders: serve the public trust, protect the innocent, uphold the law.

Immediately, however, his weakness shifts to strength as the completed RoboCop walks powerfully now down the hall of the police precinct in his bulky armature. His appearance and performance in the police shooting gallery impress all the human cops; the citizens of Detroit are similarly awed with his superlative feats. As we see (all in a few seconds of movie-time): RoboCop stops a hold-up, saves the mayor being held hostage, and rescues a rape victim. In all these acts, RoboCop performs with both the accuracy and dispassion of a machine; the hostage-taker is thrown out of a window and the rapist is shot (significantly) in the crotch. Although RoboCop's phallic powers are recognized by all, the question of his identity is far more troubling. As posed by a newscaster, "Who is he? What is he? Where does he come from?" In her own answer, "He is OCP's new warrior," RoboCop is identified as both a cyberpower and corporate property. What we learn from this statement is that, whatever and whomever RoboCop is, he is controlled by someone else: the classic state of alienation. This state and the unease and resistance it provokes are not only the threads of the narrative but also the sites compelling the many spectacles of violence that explode rhythmically throughout the film.

It is the struggle to gain control over his life and the remnants of his human identity that launches RoboCop into the line of fire time and time again. In the Frankenstein trope formulaic in many cyborg stories,[15] the machine created by humans develops a mind of his own thereby turning on its creator. So too with RoboCop who rebels against OCP by developing an identity and power that elude their control. This starts with his gun, made originally by OCP engineers as a high-tech machine, that is "remade" by RoboCop who gives it his signature gun-hold.

It is this gesture (a twirl before returning the gun to its holster) that Lewis recognizes as that of her old (and now dead) partner, Murphy. Sharing this insight with RoboCop triggers his own recollection of a past that he now recalls, but only sketchily, through two memories, both involving guns, that keep recycling (in Murphy's head and on the screen). The first is of Murphy's murder that is a replay of the onslaught of guns and shots that killed him. This, needless to say, is a terrifying image – of savage penetration and obliteration of the self. The second memory also calls up great loss: recollections of his wife and child who Murphy remembers from the time his son, watching his cowboy idol twirl his gun on television, asked, "Hey, Dad, can you do that?"

As a father, Murphy appropriated this gesture to impress his kid. For RoboCop, the mimicry stands for even more: a performance of manhood that is his only link to human memory, relationality, and will. This is a postmodern move, if there ever was one: a television image copied by the father to phallicize himself in the eyes of his son and by the cyborg to humanize himself in his own eyes and those of the viewer. Of course, RoboCop's gun stands for much more than the traces of his human self. It is also the tool that stands metaphorically for, and metonymically in for, his cyborg system. Unlike any other's, RoboCop's gun is not only more potent and deadly accurate, it is also housed inside his cyborg leg – literally a part of the body of cyber-cop.

Twirling then firing his gun, RoboCop has both the powers of a cyborg and, as the narrative develops, the sensitivity of a human. It is the latter – in quest of truth, justice, and vengeance – that compels him to discover the identity of Murphy's killers and the complicity of OCP vice-president, Dick Jones, in the murder. This discovery re-exposes RoboCop to danger as Dick Jones decides to eliminate him, programming Ed 209, to do the kill. Being a better model, though, RoboCop survives, disabling the robot. In the most grueling scene in the film, he is attacked by masses of armed police who have been ordered, by their chief through OCP, to take him down. As they encircle a parking lot all firing guns, the scene resembles the earlier one when Murphy was repeatedly shot. This scene too gets drawn out and RoboCop incurs incredible damage until he is whisked off to safety by Lewis.

In a scenario distinctive to the cyborg genre, RoboCop repairs his own wounds, using tools brought to him by Lewis to open up his compartments and retool his insides. In the end, RoboCop removes his helmet, thereby exposing his hybridized head – half human, half machine – in which state he finally refers to himself as Murphy. After another blow-out encounter in the warehouse where Murphy was originally shot, the finale has RoboCop confronting OCP officials with proof of Dick Jones' crimes. The president fires Jones, thereby allowing RoboCop to kill him (which his directive against killing any senior OCP official would otherwise have blocked). Turning to RoboCop, the president says "Nice shooting. What's your name, son?" RoboCop answers "Murphy," ending the movie.

The Sensuality of Violence

One of the most obvious and memorable aspects of *RoboCop* and other members of the fantasy cyborg genre (whether film, anime, cartoon, or comic) is its kinetic energy, fast-paced action, and intense explosions of fire, shooting, killing, and carnage. Some describe this, of course, in terms of violence: a violence that is over-the-top, gratuitous, or excessive – an excess, it is said, beyond what the narrative needs or is all about. Yet it is precisely this surplus of violation that repeatedly cuts apart and into body lines as we know or have known them that defines the genre, lending it the flashes of intensity that pulsate jaggedly rather than conjoin smoothly in narrative linearity. This is the earmark of a postmodern aesthetic: one, as Jameson (1984) has described it, that displaces a sense of history with an overload of sensations that play off and with various surfaces. The fact that machines constitute one of the main surfaces in this genre, assuming exciting if troubling new interactions with and for humans, categorizes cyborg fantasy also as science fiction: stories that imagine a time and space other than the here and now, usually with primacy given the theme of technology. In the science fiction imaginary, a world of increased or different machinery is envisioned with images that, while futuristic, also serve to re-imagine the present. Again, according to Jameson, science fiction works to "defamiliarize and restructure our experience of our own present" and does "so in specific ways distinct from all other forms of defamiliarization" (1982:150).

Cyborgs, in the forms populating mass culture today – RoboCops, terminators, androids, morphin rangers – both are and are not imaginable. Or, better stated, while cyborgs like this are not yet real, the reality they represent of the interpenetration of machinery into the lives, homes, and bodies of people is certainly familiar to us all. Cyborg fantasies all bear worlds heavily inlaid with machines: both familiar – like phones, walkman, answering machines, and televisions – and unfamiliar – new kinds of vehicles, imaging screens, communicators, and weapons. Typically these stories are set in large cities such as Detroit,[16] Los Angeles, and Tokyo, often following a world war or apocalyptic event. Their time-frame is the future, but within two or three decades of the present, and an emphasis is placed on space, visualized in terms of a pastiche that jumbles high-tech with low-tech, and signs of material progress are abutted against those of social, moral, and environmental decay. *Akira* (1988) and *Blade Runner* are both classics in this sense with landscapes littered with garbage and crumbling buildings but also sophisticated machines; where everything is bleak and somber, almost entirely devoid of nature (which itself is indistinguishable from artifice); and whose inhabitants are affectless, alienated, angry, and often alone, strained and divided by limited resources that are controlled by corrupt authority figures – politicians, military commanders, and corporate executives.

When the tone is so dark, the impression rendered of a technologized cyber-world is dystopic and the warning given is that technology breeds violence and corruption, and its seepage into our lives and bodies must be watched, even resisted. Yet not all cyborg sci-fi is dystopic. And even when this is its overt message as in *RoboCop* – with its vile cyborg-makers and the cyborg's nostalgia for the humanness it has lost – cyber sci-fi still yields a pleasure and aesthetics in its technocraft. Constance Penley (1991) has described this as "technoir": where, while the narrative in *RoboCop* is critical of technology, the aura of its technologized images is celebratory undercutting the text's dystopia at the level of cinematic pleasure. Yet others writing about cyborg sci-fi pay little attention to the narrative altogether, concentrating instead on the sensory intensity and sensuality of the visual and sometimes aural presentation. Dan Rubey (1997), for example, in writing about *Star Wars* (1977), George Lucas's blockbuster trilogy, speaks of its "machine aesthetic": the spectacle made of sci-fi machines enhanced, indeed produced, by the cinematic technology of spectacular special effects. Rubey argues that this fetish of *Star Wars* machinery creates the sensation of mergence in viewers with the machines on the screen. The emotions this conjures up are ambivalent; the rush of mastery from feeling one's body and powers augmented yet also a sense of vulnerability, even obliteration, when imagining machines as controlling, dominating, or wiping out oneself.

In either case, of course, there is a play with the borders of human powers, existence, and mortality in fantasizing new machines. And, as anthropologists have known for a long time, borders always provoke a mixture of danger and pleasure, and border-crossing is steeped in rituals, tinged often with violence as in initiation rites. Carol Clover (1992), in her study of the violent genre of slasher films watched primarily by adolescent boys in the United States, has argued, similarly to Rubey, that viewers shift in their identification with the characters (or machines) on the screen. Viewers delight in both the predatory pursuit of victim by the slasher, and the fighting back of the "final girl" in defending herself from attack. There is also what Clover takes to be gender-shifting in that boy viewers identify with not only the male slasher but also the female heroine on the screen. Film theorist Steven Shaviro (1993) has pushed this point even further, proposing that viewers of horror, violent, and slasher films identify or invest with the victims of attack not only when they are victoriously overcoming their attackers (as with the "final girl") but also, and more importantly, when they are being pursued, dismembered, and slaughtered. For Shaviro, following the work of Bersani (1986), Bataille (1994), and Deleuze and Guattari (1983, 1987), cinematic pleasure is structured more in terms of masochism than mastery. Viewers less identify with lead characters than they are brought into contact with images through a process of contagion or mimesis; the dissolution of fixed identities and borders transfixes viewers by images that are horrific yet "strangely attractive" (Shaviro 1993:53). As he argues, "Anxiety over the disruption of identity is concomitant with, and perhaps necessary to, the very intensity of sensual gratification" (1993:56).

Such shifts, fluidity, and ambivalence are also at work in a cyber fantasy like *RoboCop*. The destructive action in the film continually explodes out of but also, and more interestingly, implodes into the key figure, RoboCop, with whom most viewers I have spoken to center their attention. Right from the start, Murphy/RoboCop is the object as much as the subject of brutal attack; as a human, he is savagely killed, and, as a cyborg, he is cruelly remade and perpetually hunted, shot, sawed, sliced, blasted, maimed, and retooled. Of course, RoboCop is hardly a passive victim and is aggressive himself in pursuing those who transgress the codes of civil obedience that he has been programmed to uphold. Accordingly, RoboCop uses his cybernetic powers and weapons to subdue, disengage, or otherwise eliminate criminals in acts that range from breaking limbs and throwing people out of windows to shooting, firing, exploding, and cracking bodies. Thus, while eruptions of force constantly pulsate throughout all three films in the *RoboCop* series, the flow is constantly shifting – emanating from as much as targeting both the "good" and "bad" characters in the films. Not only does this make the explosiveness in the film both morally and ontologically variable – it is connected to good as well as bad forces and to both destructive and constructive ends – it also portrays the hero as someone whose powers are far more fluctuating and fluid than stable and set: a character whose state of being constantly shifts between invincibility and destruction, potency and impotency, and immortality and death.

Phallic Powers/Gendered Self

Despite the volatility (and viability) of its powers, the violent cyborg is consistently described in metaphors of gravity, denseness, and stability – as a "fortress" with "rock solid masculinity," for example (Springer 1993). This stance is held by media scholar Claudia Springer who, writing of the *RoboCop* and *Terminator* films (*Terminator* [1984] and *Terminator 2: Judgment Day* [1991]), argues that cyborgs in mass culture are dominantly figured as not only violent, but also bulked up and macho.[17] The choice of Arnold Schwarzenegger as lead cyborg in the *Terminator* series seems prima facie evidence for this thesis: an actor whose "aggressively corporeal" body literally signifies power as physically large, visible, and phallic. To Springer, such a bodily image is retrograde on two scores. First, it misrepresents today's postindustrial, postmodern technology that, unlike the massive steam and hydraulic engines of an earlier era, runs on micro-electronic circuitry that is more passive and hidden from view. To impersonate the labyrinthine technological networks of our computer age with the beefed-up body of a Schwarzenegger is not only inaccurate but also reactionary, signaling an unease with the technologization of today's world.

The "externally visible musculature" of RoboCop is also masculinist, signaling a second way in which it is regressive, according to Springer (1993). The gendering of the cyborg here relies on tropes of conquest, aggression, and bulk – trademarks of the modernist male hero played by a John Wayne or Sylvester Stallone – which are old-time survivals, superimposed onto, rather than radicalized by, the newness of cyborg technology. This view, common amongst those writing about cyborgs in mass culture, is that, despite cyber-technology's promise to rewrite human flesh, identity still gets drawn using rigid, naturalist, and masculinist notions of body and gender.[18] Anne Balsamo (1996), Constance Penley (1991), and Fred Pfeil (1990), for example, all agree that, while certain borders get dissolved in cyborg fantasy, the border of gender remains "stuck," as Pfeil puts it, "in a masculinist frame" (Pfeil 1990:88). And in her study of a cognate to cyborgs, the *Teenage Mutant Ninja Turtles* on television, Marsha Kinder (1991) has similarly observed that, while the mutant turtles variously border-cross, the borders between female and male, and good and evil, stay unbendingly fixed.

But how static or stable *is* the identity of a RoboCop so commonly described as holistically "male"? Not very, was the response given by undergraduate students I taught in a semester-long course on cyborgs at Duke in spring 1998.[19] According to them, RoboCop is a far more ambiguous and muddied character than clear-cut along any plane – hero, public citizen, man. The strongest reaction evoked by watching *RoboCop* (shared for the other most graphically violent cyborg movie we viewed, *Akira*) was a sense of discomfiture, experienced as stimulating, both viscerally and intellectually, by about one-third of the students, but repulsive and distasteful by another third (almost as many males as females). None of the students (including the third who felt less strongly either way) said their viewing of *RoboCop* inspired feelings of unequivocal mastery or reassurance, and those who said they identified with the lead character did so in ways they described as complex and ambivalent (I will come back to this point later). As one student stated it, the film is "troubling."

As such reactions suggest, masculinity construed as "rock solid" – with its evocations, I will later suggest, of the very bedrock of middle America felt so transgressed upon in the recent school shootings – misidentifies RoboCop as (dis)embodied in these films.[20] Aggression is central to his character(ization), without a doubt, but RoboCop is as much a violent figure – the macho warrior bent on old-time revenge and killing one's foes – as reconfigured by violence into something else – a bullet-holed carcass, a remade machine, a pile of scrap. Violence, in other words, works here to not only portray the cyborg as a (traditional) aggressor, but also to dislodge, explode, and redraw the boundaries/boundedness of this very portrayal. Thus while the corporeality of a Schwarzenegger may well trigger a set of associations in viewers of macho masculinism, this grammar is disrupted when that body is also a machine that is owned, engineered, and continually fractured apart – conditions that make phallicism here far more fragile and unstable than sturdy and fixed. Indeed, RoboCop lacks the very body-part – a penis – central to the (Western) signification of not only maleness but (genital-based) meaning, subjectivity, and social order as well. In this sense, RoboCop exceeds rather than accedes to identity, and is less a gendered than transgendered (queer) subject.[21]

What makes RoboCop a "man," after all? If, as Springer asserts, it is the "fortress" of his body, this is a body built from "technological adornments" (1993:95) – an artifice of cyborg construction that, as Haraway (1991) has argued, breeds bodies and body parts no longer constrained or dictated by nature. This makes RoboCop's body mechanical rather than natural: a technological engineering that can be used on anybody (any body) no matter their (gendered, ethnic, corporeal) condition of birth. As RoboCop says to Lewis after she has been shot at the warehouse in the blow-out scene near the end of the (first) film: "They'll fix you. They fix everything." RoboCop himself is a mess after having had a pile of metal dropped on him, a stake driven through his chest, and his body riddled with bullets. But in his words about technological retooling – a process that can remake Lewis, the woman, as it once did Murphy, the man – there is more caution than celebration for, as we all know by this point in the story, a "cyborgian" make-over entails savagery and loss as much as it does mastery and gain.

Powers, what the cyborg's identity is critically founded on, transcend and displace human flesh. Not only is the "natural" body remade with artificial machinery, however, the cyborg subject also decomposes and segments into multiple parts, none of which holds or centers the "self." The visual representation given cyborg killers – RoboCop but also others such as Terminator, Spawn, Tetsuo (in *Akira* as well as Tetsuo in *Tetsuo, the Iron Man* [1988]), and the Power Rangers – is of multi-parted beings who keep shifting and transforming according to which parts are being activated or retracted. For most, these involve human-looking components (fleshy faces, human proportions, two arms, and two legs) that fuse with, disaggregate into, or transform to nonhumanoid materials, mainly machines but also demons, monsters, or any physical surface (as with the T-1000 and its liquid alloy in *Terminator 2*). Powers for such creatures are organized more as circuits than "fortresses" and include weapons or machines that are often melded into or with the body (such as in the Japanese warrior show *Kamen Raida* where the hero's powers crystallize on a belt that emerges from the boy's stomach when he transforms), making the border between "inside" and "outside" blurry and unstable. As complex and multiparted the machinery of the cyborg, so is its overall coherence that is in constant flux triggered mainly by violent attacks; RoboCop loses (and gets reconstructed) hands, legs, brainparts, circuits, and various operating functions all the time. In this, the cyborg's powers are far more diffused and decentered than those of popular heroes in the modernist mode – Superman, for example, whose phallicism was signified by a single costume change that drew attention to the wholeness and corporeality of his masculine physique. By contrast, the powers of RoboCop are multiple, detachable, and artificial, which makes them also more scattered, contingent, and transferable.

The issue of agency (as well as alienation) is also significantly raised in such a flexible model of detachable, contingent powers. Its assemblage of weapons, machines, body parts, and powers are rarely in the cyborg's control. Not only are there the risks of break-down, shut-down, or attack, but cyborgs typically serve an owner and lack the qualities depicted in the movie as "essentially" human – independence, agency, family, home, and emotion. Of course, this often delivers a dystopic message: that the loss of humanness as we know it will inevitably accompany an increasingly technologized world. Thus cyber subjectivity still gets portrayed in terms of wounds, gaps, and lapses of humanity (RoboCop aches at the loss of his family – more so, interestingly enough, than the loss of his penis and sexuality – and struggles to recapture whatever of Murphy he can) and this depthlessness often mirrors, in a movie like *RoboCop*, a human landscape strewn in moral, physical, and social decay. In this sense, the cyborg is not only a metonym but a metaphor for the state of human society at large: for the humans who, in *Blade Runner*, are even colder and less emotional than the replicants, and, in *RoboCop*, are the victims or managers of corporate hedonism living in a world where all life has been reified and reduced to things. Technology as encoded in the popularization of cyborg identity (and tinged, though muddied, with phallic and masculinist overlays) then is embued with multiple meanings and referents. It stands for the type of hypertechnologized world we now live in; for the embeddedness of this technology in our everyday lifestyles, identities, and skins; and for the fluctuations and dispersals of a postmodern existence, both because and apart from technology.

Exploding into New Borderlands

Violence marks all this with the signs of rupture and disorder, but the dynamics are far more ambiguous than merely nihilistic and cyborgs are subjects who perpetuate and fall victim to violence, yet are also vulnerable and resistant to damage. I read this volatility, mapped through violence both into and out of cyborg bodies, as not only plotting destruction but also emplotting construction in ways that bear a productive potential for helping viewers (and here I am thinking particularly about children) navigate, experience, or conceptualize their own way in this postindustrial world. I propose two such constructive possibilities.

First, as Appadurai has argued, in today's world where new forms of media and migrations have produced an intense level of rupture, the role played by the imagination is critical (and, according to him, stronger than ever before). As he presents it in *Modernity at Large* (1996), this role, most importantly, is cohesive: images of places here and there connect people to imaginary communities that, in this deterritorialized world, may no longer even exist. The emphasis here is how the imagination works to overcome what seems "rhizomic" and "schizoid" (1996:29) by (re)constructing the collective (in various, i.e., diasporic, forms). Yet, imagination in the sense of imagining the world and the place we (any of us) assume in it, also works the other way, I suggest, by recreating and mimicking the very sense of rupture and disconnectedness so paradigmatic of the times in which we live. Kids are drawn to violence in an imaginary format because, in part, it stimulates fracturation in their own lives and can also help, when a model of/for survival – queering the world and the self – is offered as well, for dissimulating the sense of pain and isolation that can accompany it.

How rocky life can be even for youth in America's "heartland" became apparent to me in the reactions my "Introduction to Cultural Anthropology" class (of 140 Duke undergraduates) had to the Columbine shootings. Leading a discussion the day after the shootings occurred, I was struck by how many of these Duke students identified with, if not the acts themselves, the emotions of rage and isolation they attributed to the killers. Speaking of the pressures to perform and fit in, they remembered how anxiety-provoking and lonely high school could be, particularly for those picked on for being different (queer in the most basic sense of the word). That such feelings could boil over into rage and aggression as with fights, back-biting, or "tricks" played on others was something many recalled from their own days of middle and upper school. Home was often no solace, some added, because parents tended to be "clueless" about their children's worlds: mainly where they were "in their heads" – what they thought and talked about with their friends and enjoyed in the way of music, pastimes, and games. A couple of students added that parents should learn how to communicate by not immediately rejecting their children's imaginary worlds (and thus further distancing kids) as incomprehensible, disgusting, or perverse. Being attracted to something dark like Gothic fandom (shared by the Columbine killers) did not, in and of itself, signal psychic or social pathology these students largely agreed; indeed, several admitted to similar attractions.

In cyborg violence, the world is imagined through a grim concatenation of explosions: bodies are ripped open, split apart, smashed to pieces, and reduced to pulp. And, not included in the definition given media violence by scholars like Hamilton (1998), is the fact that the "hero" is split apart as well; we see as many scenes of RoboCop battered, punctured, and splintered as we do of him whole, in control of situations, and conquering foes. In Freudian language, RoboCop often appears castrated;[22] he loses body parts, comes apart at the waist, is lain prone on a table where he is operated on by technicians, and gets multiply wounded and attacked throughout the duration of all three films.[23] This state of fluctuating powers would suggest a different kind of fantasy and spectator involvement than that usually associated with film with its fantasies of plenitude that tend to reassure and comfort viewers (in suturing over the threat of castration, for example, in Laura Mulvey's classic articulation). The interactions here seem more akin to what happens in the case of television where, as Beverle Houston has argued, viewers are kept at a "near panic" level of activity and take something like pleasure in the "terror of desire" (Houston 1984:183–184). Video games – whose main players are adolescent boys, those for whom issues of body and identity are particularly tinged with fears of castration – have been described similarly where excitement stems from imaginary battles, attacks, and killings that target not only others but also the self (Kinder 1991; see also Jenkins 1997; Piot n.d.). Cyberpunk literature too has been characterized by the same dynamic where, in authors like Bruce Sterling and William Gibson, the body becomes a "battleground," whose continual invasions and (re)inventions by mechanical alteration keep eroding any semblance of human identity – a state readers experience as the thrilling fear of what Ross has called "cyberpsychosis" (1991:161). Ross reads further into this psychic dissolution a retreat of (white) masculinity in 1980s and 1990s United States given that most of the authors and readers of the cyberpunk genre are white males.

The question, of course, is what is the relationship between experiencing psychic frenzy (Kirby 1988) in the imaginary format of a video game, cyberpunk novel, or violent cyborg movie and dealing with similar emotions in the context of "real" life – at school, for example, when one is being picked on or ignored by other kids? That identity disintegration can get expressed in dismemberment of flesh, both imaginary and "real," was brought home to me in seminar one day when a student admitted that, as a suicidal junior in high school, he had contemplated going to school and shooting all his enemies before killing himself. This story was (surprisingly) told two weeks following Columbine and by a student, who, while a fan of violent-tinged popular culture, was strongly against – as have been almost all the college-aged as well as middle- and upper-school youth I have discussed this with – the perception that media violence causes violent behavior. More than anything, he spoke of a personal disequilibrium – within himself and within the world he was living in – that became enwrapped (for whatever reason) in scenarios of violence. It is this sense of dissolution and disconnect(edness) that strikes me as increasingly common in U.S. youth today and is at work, I believe, in the fascination that bodily rupture holds for so many children in media entertainment. Rather than deny such feelings, kids must learn how to face and deal with them (his inability to do this seems more likely an explanation for my student's death plots than over-exposure to violent media) and it is here that the genre of violent cyborgs has something, I argue, to offer youth.

The constructive possibility I propose is that, in movies like *RoboCop*, viewers are being offered protagonists whose very fluctuation between states of empowerment and disempowerment, coherence and disintegration, helps children balance their own anxieties (about vulnerability) and desires (for control) in a way that refuses to get anchored in either spot. Bruno Bettelheim (1976) has made a similar argument about the value of violence and evil in fairy tales as strategies useful to kids in accepting their own feelings of aggression and impotency, and also in learning to cope with a less than gentle or perfect world.[24] Advocates of the television show, *The Mighty Morphin Power Rangers*, have countered its violence on the same grounds: that the rangers, in getting attacked, learn to confront and subsequently overcome challenges (beastly foes but also inner fears and trepidations that show the rangers in both strong and weak poses; see, for example, Seiter 1999).

Although theorists of film tend to argue that either mastery (by far the prevalent view) or masochism (the view most persuasively argued by Shaviro [1993], following Deleuze [1991], but also by others including Studlar [1988] and Silverman [1992] is the overarching effect/pleasure rendered by film, my thesis is that, in the case of violent cyborg entertainment, it is both. That is, the "unmooring of subjectivity" (1993:147) Shaviro so applauds when viewers are denied the fantasy of phallic optimism (and the illusion of intact subjectivity) is certainly at work in the genre of violent cyborgs. But though a phallicism of macho domination may get dislodged in movies like *RoboCop*, it is noteworthy that cyborgs not only undergo savage attacks, but also survive them, albeit in altered/queered form. So, unlike a film like David Cronenberg's *The Fly* where the man-turned-fly is "born in the excruciating rigors of an estrangement without hope of return" (Shaviro 1993:147), RoboCop (re)presents a violated subject whose subjectivity gets remade rather than totally wiped out. And, in this, kid viewers are given something potentially constructive for facing disruptions in their own lives: not a perfectly phallic hero who reassures with the plenitudes of mastery but a far more ambiguous character whose shifts – between life and death, viability and danger, and (bounded) identity and queerness – resonate with the volatility in children's lives and with their struggles to (somehow, if imperfectly) survive.

A second way in which the violence of cyber fantasies like *RoboCop* is potentially productive is that, in disrupting old models of phallic surety and macho heroism, new forms and formats of subjectivity arise. Out of the chopping done to phallicism, for example, a new breed of hero emerges: a cyborg whose powers are both ambiguous and bodily ambiguated unlike the cleaner, clearer male victors of old. As part machine, this warrior is far less sutured to a naturalistic male body than (most) other action heroes.[25] The fact that the (organic) man Murphy must die in order for the cyber cop to get (re)built opens the way for female viewers, as well as males, to identify with RoboCop along lines other than the traditional masculinism claimed by Springer. Pulled away from its moorings in male nature, superheroism is also broadened by organizing it in terms of flux and fragility as much as surety and performance. We see as many scenes of RoboCop battered and punctured as we do of him mastering situations and conquering foes. Power here then is truncated and the hero is less encased in phallic infallibility than vulnerable to ups and downs.

In the figure of RoboCop, superheroism is a less certain, pleasant, or manly affair. This has ramifications for both female and male viewers. Given that Hollywood has packaged heroism and phallicism almost exclusively in the bodies and identities of white men, there is reason to recognize and push the potential for cyborg movies to shatter these limits. Girls are given more a chance to see themselves as action heroes (as in *Power Rangers*) and boys are less indulged by (or challenged to live up to) the fantasy of superlative phallicism. In the disaggregation of old gender lines, cyborg warriors also bear the seeds of gender-aggregate subjects. RoboCop, for example, assumes the position of both the macho man in armored gear and take-charge mode as well as what has been the feminine or feminized position of vulnerability and passivity; he is penetrated by bullets, held down on a table, and continually made over. It is in the sites of cyber-violence, in fact, that the sights of queered subjectivity are most apparent. When RoboCop is slashed by saws or disassembled into segments, he least resembles a (hu)man and these scenes – of both mutilation and reconstitution – are continually replayed, reshot, and revisualized throughout the films.

In what gives new meaning to the term "male gaze," the destruction wrought on the body of RoboCop is lingered over as if a caress. Not unlike pornography where acts of penetration are extended and repeated via different angles, settings, and body parts to heighten impact and visibility, the attacks on RoboCop are prolonged. Viewers are thus given plenty of time to see the cyborg coming apart; that also means seeing the parts (as they variously attach/detach) themselves. As Linda Williams has written about the "frenzy of the visible" (1989:56) in pornography, the bodily zones most spectacularized are those audiences are most likely to associate with holding secrets. To "see" then is to "know." But, unlike pornography where gazing is mainly focused on female bodies, a cyborg like RoboCop is a different kind of object: a (hu)man machine we come to know, to the extent we do, through the pulsations of violence that dismantle but also dissect his body in ways that fascinate fans. So, in this cyborg, we get tropes of both an object to be looked at and a subject who moves the story and plot – stances that have (hitherto) been kept gender distinct.

Cyber fighters are also composites of multiple parts none of which definitively houses the identity or essence of the cyborg. Thus, just as there is no single center to the cyborg's host of powers, the cyborg can be put together in an assortment of ways. In the toy model I bought of RoboCop, for example, he came packaged with neurobrain, shoulder armor, chin strap, helmet, tac bomb, pistol, chest plate, pelvic cover, and leg armor. All these pieces are detachable: that highlights the costuming of RoboCop's body and its mix (up) of weapon, internal organ, and protective covering. The brain, one should note, can be as easily removed and reinserted as any other of RoboCop's movable parts. This shows how all of the cyborg comes apart, and also the promiscuity with which the different-partedness is conceived; a tac bomb is little different from a chest plate or leg, and a chin strap is as much a body-part as is a hand or an arm. The grammar of assemblage is bricolage or pastiche. Demonstrating the logic of flexible accumulation, the cyborg body is comprised of "widgets" (Clarke 1995) between which distinctions, once rigid, are now dissolved. In studying the play habits of children in today's age of "cyborg objects," Sherry Turkle (1998) has noted this plasticity in the way kids conceive the relationship between animate and inanimate things, and see their own identities as constantly morphing (as in *Power Rangers*) between different states and forms. This sense of fluidity allows children to balance a universe of disparate and changing parts (families that change members, homes that move from place to place, and so on). As Mizuko Ito (1998) has also observed in the ways children play video games, what is make-believe constantly weaves in and out of what is everyday, and closure is both imposed and disrupted as part of playing the game.

Playing with cyborgs encourages not only an attitude of flexibility towards an increasingly heterogenous and fluctuating world, but also a willingness to conceive the world and one's place in it as blended rather than anchored to singular and hegemonic essences. In my research on character trends – Power Rangers, Sailor Moon, Tamagotchi, and Pokémon – children both in the United States and Japan say they love the various iterations, changes, and hosts of characters in these play-worlds. In *Sailor Moon*, for example, the main character alternates between being a strong, courageous, transhuman superhero and a whiny, lazy, food-crazy 14-year-old girl. It is this transformative, multisided nature of Sailor Moon that delights fans and constructs her identity as something more than, and non-reducible to, either "superhero" or "girl" – an excess that cannot be definitively pinned to a singular essence.[26] *Sailor Moon* has also started a new marketing trend in what has been called "action fashion": blending what had hitherto been gender-specific – action figures for boys and fashion dolls for girls. For Sailor Moon, her accessories include clothes and jewels but also tools:[27] an accesorization that has become standard for all kinds of characters today – dinosaurs, animals, and Pokémon as well as warriors and fashion models. One effect is a bleeding of the female/male border that has accelerated in more recent trends such as Tamagotchi – the portable, digital pet lacking ostensible gender – and Pokémon – a world of human trainers and 250 monsters, all with a myriad of parts, few of which break down overtly by gender.[28] For manufacturers, of course, accessories and designs (with multiple parts, multiple characters, and multiple versions of the same hero like Batman) are made to increase sales. And with the increase in parts and toys, the desire to consume is ever more deeply produced and insinuated within the appetites of our children to play. Yet another more salutary effect to the spread of accessorized figures is, I would argue, the shifting, diversifying, and queering of the identity (particularly gendered) lines of consumer play.

Conclusion

The more I ponder the issue of violence and children's entertainment, the more complicated and messy the matter appears. Every day the newspaper reports stories about children at risk, in pain, abused, or dead. And increasingly frequent are the stories about children who are violators themselves: kids who attack others in acts that can be as shockingly casual and random as they are savage and deadly. What in a child's world, it is repeatedly asked, would propel them towards such violence? When children live in environments unsettled by war, parental neglect, or hunger the answer seems obvious. And the mass media often makes this connection: that, raised and bred in such habitats, the habit of violence comes naturally. As *Mother Jones* reported recently about children from violent homes (calculated to be 3,000,000 in the United States today), half will grow up to be abusers as adults and many mimic, while still children, the abuse they see or receive in their dealings with others (Dowling 1998). Although the tendency in such reportage on violent kids is to blame the environment rather than the child, there is also the inclination to consider children from certain environments as indelibly prone to and marked by violence.

This makes the cases of child-killings/child-killers in the heartland of America, places (once) considered rock-solid in the national imaginary, so disturbing. Such events, minuscule (even with their "shocking" rise) when compared to other forms of death, misery, and brutality at large in the United States today, have triggered what the *New York Times* has called "a search to the depths of the national soul" (Egan 1998:1). Again the question becomes: What possibly in the perpetuators' real or imaginary worlds could have incited such violence? Not surprisingly, the inclination, for many, has been to disavow connection to these incidents. The inhabitants of Springfield, Oregon, for instance, posted the words "We have done nothing wrong" on the theater marquee after Kipland Kinkel opened fire at the local school. In the commentary too on these events, the cause is often sought in something outside the local terrain – in a bug somewhere in the child's home lives or psychological make-up, or in a "lethal virus" infecting our children with an alien strain of virulent badness.

It is in this quest that media violence has been seen as a killer toxin spreading an attitude of predation in the United States that peaks in predatory kids. So too was pornography in the 1980s accused of inciting and perpetuating sexism: a behavior that today is attributed (as I think is the consensus) to a host of conditions that exceed, if also appear in, pornography. Violence is a similarly complex behavioral pattern and can be neither reduced to a singular cause nor blamed on something "foreign" that rests outside the worlds in which we live, grow up, and find (or do not find) meaning and pleasure – no matter how "normal" or "tranquil" these worlds appear. This is why it is imperative to study media violence in terms of not only its effects – with the assumption of unilineal causation from "outside" – but also the factors involved in its incredible power to engage, stimulate, transport, or resonate with children in their "inner" lives – where children go to make sense of, survive, or escape lived realities. To say this another way, media violence cannot alone be held accountable for the ruptures and rages plaguing people today. These fissures exist already and a mass media so engulfed in the production and transmission of breakage (images and stories of beings, cities, countries, and relationships broken apart, mixed up, dispersed, attacked, and recombined) is perhaps amplifying, but certainly speaking of, and to, the desires, fears, and realities people, including kids, struggle with all the time.

Not that long ago when my son left for the summer – in a familial situation tinged, as it is for many in the United States, with anxiety and hostility – he went armed with a bagful of action figures along with what has now replaced them, a CD player on which he listens to music sometimes as explosive as the cyborg scenarios he once replayed. In Adam's case, his weathering of many forms of rupture and fracture has been accompanied, and soothed, I sense, by the imaginary play he has engaged with cyborg warriors. I do not deduce from this that violent cyborgs or mass media in general are necessarily, similarly, or simply beneficial for all consumers. Far more work, of all types and from a number of perspectives, needs to be done. My only conclusion is that we need to do this work rather than be convinced, without doing so, that we already know what effect and affect media violence holds for its fans.

NOTES

1 In a recent study on media violence, Hamilton cites the following figures (drawing on Nielsen reports and Times Mirror surveys conducted in 1994): 72.8 percent of male respondents and 59.9 percent of female respondents between the ages of 18 and 34 in the United States are heavy viewers of violent entertainment (1998:55) and 80 percent of males and 68 percent of females in the same age bracket reported watching the Hollywood cyborg blockbuster, *Terminator 2* (Nielsen Media Research 1993, cited in Hamilton 1998:60).

2 As a representative study, see the National Television Violence Study that assembled three tiers of investigators (media scholars from four universities, representatives from national policy organizations, and project administration) for a three-year study of violence on television (its results are published in three annual studies beginning in 1996 with volume 1 (Wilson et al. 1996).

3 The full title of the FTC report is: "Marketing Violent Entertainment to Children: A Review of Self-Regulation and Industry Practices in the Motion Picture, Music Recording and Electronic Game Industries." The report was presented in front of the Senate Commerce Committee in September 2000 (Federal Trade Commission 2000) and is available from the FTC's website at http://www.ftc.gov. For an overview of its findings, see Hampton 2000.

4 See, for example, Richard Rhodes, "Hollow Claims About Fantasy Violence" (2000:WK:19).

5 I am using *queer* in this paper to mean the dislodging of intact demarcators of/for identity, including but not limited to gender and sexuality. This is akin to what Eve Sedgwick has described as "one of the things that 'queer' can refer to: the open mesh of possibilities, gaps, overlaps, dissonances and resonances, lapses and excesses of meaning when the constituent elements of anyone's gender, of anyone's sexuality aren't made (or *can't be* made) to signify monolithically" (1993:8). In employing queerness here to think constructively about the destructions rampant in cyborg entertainment, I concentrate more on the dimension of (gendered, transgendered) identity than of (same-sex, cross-sexed) desire which, of course, is also a central issue in queer studies/theory today.

6 My current research, which I have conducted in both Japan and the United States, is on Japanese character merchandising (*sentai* or warrior heroes, girl warriors like Sailor Moon, digital pets, and Pokémon) as it circulates in Japan and also the U.S. export market. Although I am both aware of and interested in the specificities of these two cultural markets – different traditions and mythologies of the human/machine interface and different socio-cultural contexts that situate violence, youth, and violent entertainment – my focus in this paper is on what is shared by Japan and the United States: a mass media fixation on violent cyborgs that I take to be a symptom of the late capitalist, turn-of-the-century technologization that is remaking and re-imagining the human/machine border across the world. For the structure of violent cyborgs, I look at examples from both U.S. and Japanese mass media, but to consider how this entertainment is located within the everyday lives of children, I am only interested in the United States, for reasons of space, in this paper.

7 I did individual and group interviews (that included viewing and discussing episodes of the show) with 30 children, aged 9 to 14, in Durham, North

Carolina, on *Sailor Moon*. I also did internet surveys (sending out my own survey and analyzing 100 replies from males and females ranging from age 8 to 40, mainly, though not exclusively, from the United States).

8 *Henshin* in Japanese.

9 As a transformer, Sailor Moon's identity shifts and is not consistently cyborgian. I categorize her here as a cyborg, though, because, in power-mode, she has mechanical components (tiara, moon prism power-wand) that merge with her body and self.

10 By fan, I mean someone who overtly likes the genre of cyborg action and refer here to children I have interviewed (in the United States and Japan), undergraduate students at Duke (mainly the 40 who were in a class I taught on cyborgs), and scholars writing on cyborgs.

11 The homoerotic subtheme played in Japan (in the comic book and cartoon), but was to be removed for the U.S. broadcast (before this became an issue however, the show was taken off network television).

12 In these early post-war years, a strikingly different kind of popular superhero was projected on Japanese television screens: Tetsuwan Atomu – an adorable boy/robot created with atomic powers in the futuristic time of 2026 A.D. Designed by Japan's "father" of comic artistry, Tezuka Osamu, first as a *manga* in the 1950s and then as Japan's first serialized cartoon on television starting in 1962, Tetsuwan Atomu was built as a multi-powered, multi-parted humanoid robot, whose mechanical vulnerabilities and breakdowns resemble RoboCop's composition (and decomposition) far more than they do Superman's more naturalistic (though alien) powers. The social and economic trauma Japan was experiencing in the 1950s and its blueprint for rebuilding itself as an industrial power through reliance on both technology and the industriousness of Japanese workers is crystallized in the spunky character of "Mighty Atom" – a model of cyborg identity and flexible labor that came later to the United States in the 1980s with, arguably, more unease in figures such as RoboCop.

13 A superhero like Superman was also subjected to regular attack, of course, and also displayed a "split" personality – as is true of superheroes generally – that oscillated between the vulnerable, klutzy Clark Kent and the tough, super-strong Superman. Still, the degree of attack and the incidence of damage and vulnerability are far greater in the case of RoboCop disabusing this hero of what Superman arguably possessed – an intact power-center (symbolized by his ever-ready red/blue super costume).

14 The following section is a synopsis of *RoboCop* based on my own viewing of the video.

15 That is far more common, however, in Euro-American than Japan.

16 A particularly prescient choice as the home of Fordism, now post-Fordism.

17 Significantly, there are far more cyborg and android fighters designed with overtly female bodies in Japanese mass culture. These range from the more gender-neutral or (gender-)muted power costumes worn by the girl (and boy) members of *sentai* (warrior teams) – girls in the *renja*-series, for example, that appear in the United States as *The Mighty Morphin Power Rangers* (and started in Japan in 1973) – to the school girl motif favored by *Sailor Moon* (and other comic and cartoon series such as *Gunma*, translated into English as *Battle Angel Alita*) to the femme fatale style of sexy women (adopted by the boomers in *A.D. Police Files*). These female warriors, often heroes, have a fandom of boys as well as girls in Japan. By contrast, there is a paucity of overtly female fighters, cyborgs, or heroes in children's entertainment in the United States (*Buffy the Vampire Slayer* and *Xena, Warrior Princess* are two exceptions) and, even when they do appear, it tends to be with the eroticized bodies that seem targeted to be sex objects for boys (such as Lara Croft in the popular video game, Tomb Raider); see Cassell and Jenkins (1997) on the gendering lines and debates in video games in the United States as well as Piot (n.d.). My comments on the macho prevalence in cyborg trends are to be read in this light. I agree that maleness hegemonizes the form given action characters, including cyborg warriors, in U.S. children's entertainment today. My point, however, is that this "maleness" is far more troubled, unstable, and fluctuating a category and identity than commonly perceived.

18 For important exceptions, see Fuchs 1995 and Goldberg 1995.

19 Special topics for "Anthropology and Film." Class enrollment was 40 students, almost equally mixed between females and males; about 70 percent white and the rest black, Asian-American, and international.

20 There are others who share the view I express here – that identity/identification in stories involving violence and monsters/cyborgs/hybrids is unstable and troubled (queer in my word) – including Fuchs (1995) writing about violent cyborgs, Hurley

(1995) in a provocative essay on horror films, Stone (1995) in her wonderful work on cyborgs, and Shaviro (1993), whose extension of Deleuze and Guattari (1983, 1987), in theorizing cinematic body image/pleasure is of major importance.

21 As Edelman has written (1995), desire and identity always "exceed" (in being more ambiguous and complicated than) the names/categories into which they are routinely slotted. In queerness, the fictive borders demanded by straight society are refused rather than acquiesced to, and excesses (of body/sexuality/gender/subjectivity) are accepted.

22 I use this language here only to challenge the assumption of phallic wholeness so commonly adopted in writings on violent cyborgs.

23 Twice his hand is chopped off which is a common trope: Luke Skywalker in the *Star Wars* series, the Terminator in *Terminator*, and Tetsuo in *Akira* all lose hands as well in what have been described as oedipal/phallic losses.

24 And ambivalence towards even loving caregivers. The constant figures of "good" as well as "bad" (step)mothers in *The Grimm Fairytales* allows children to psychically "split" their feelings towards mothers between love and rage, Bettelheim argued (1976).

25 Wonder Woman was a wonderful exception to the Superman era of manly superheroes though it should be noted that her creator, Dr. William Marston, intended her sexiness and boldness to feed male rather than female desire.

26 See also Susan Willis (1987) on the genre of transformer heroes and how gender gets both commodified and blended in the marketing of transformer hero toys.

27 I thank an anonymous reviewer for the terminology "jewels" and "tools."

28 Yet, driven by a market mentality that demands new products and changes all the time, the latest version (*kin, gin* [silver, gold] released in fall 1999 in Japan) has added new pokemonsters that are now genderized. If there is any consolation to this, it is that the manufacturers consider the addition of gender here to be "new."

REFERENCES

Allison, Anne. 2000[1996]. *Permitted and Prohibited Desires: Mothers, Comics, and Censorship in Japan*. Berkeley: University of California Press.

Appadurai, Arjun. 1996. *Modernity at Large: Cultural Dimensions of Globalization*. Minneapolis: University of Minnesota Press.

Balsamo, Anne. 1996. *Technologies of the Gendered Body: Reading Cyborg Women*. Durham, NC: Duke University Press.

Bataille, Georges. 1994. *Eroticism*. Mary Dalwood, trans. London: Boyars.

Bersani, Leo. 1986. *The Freudian Body: Psychoanalysis and Art*. New York: Columbia University Press.

Bettelheim, Bruno. 1976. *The Uses of Enchantment: The Meaning and Importance of Fairy Tales*. New York: Knopf.

Bok, Sissela. 1998. *Mayhem: Violence as Public Entertainment*. Reading, MA: Addison-Wesley.

Bright, Susie. 1995. *Sexwise*. Pittsburgh: Cleis Press.

Cannon, Angie. 1998. Answers Abound, Yet Culprits Complex. *The News and Observer*. May 31:19A, 20A.

Cassell, Justine, and Henry Jenkins, eds. 1997. *From Barbie to Mortal Kombat: Gender and Computer Games*. Cambridge, MA: MIT Press.

Clarke, Adele. 1995. Modernity, Postmodernity and Reproductive Processes, ca. 1890–1990, or "Mommy, Where Do Cyborgs Come from Anyway?" In *The Cyborg Handbook*. Chris Gray, ed. Pp. 139–156. New York: Routledge.

Clover, Carol J. 1992. *Men, Women, and Chain Saws: Gender in the Modern Horror Film*. Princeton, NJ: Princeton University Press.

Deleuze, Gilles. 1991. *Masochism: Coldness and Cruelty*. Jean McNeil, trans. New York: Zone Books.

Deleuze, Gilles, and Félix Guattari. 1983. *Anti-Oedipus*. Robert Hurley, Mark Lane, and Helen Lane, trans. Minneapolis: University of Minnesota Press.

Deleuze, Gilles, and Félix Guattari. 1987. *A Thousand Plateaus*. Brian Massumi, trans. Minneapolis: University of Minnesota Press.

Dowling, Claudia. 1998. Violence Lessons. *Mother Jones* 23(4):32–41.

Edelman, Lee. 1995. Queer Theory: Unstating Desire. *GLQ* 2:343–346.

Egan, Timothy. 1998. From Adolescent Angst to School Killings. *New York Times*. June 14:1, 20.

F.A.C.T. Book Committee, ed. 1992. *Caught Looking: Feminism, Pornography, and Censorship*. East Haven, CT: LongRiver Books.

Federal Trade Commission. 2000. *Marketing Violent Entertainment to Children: A Review of Self-Regulation and Industry Practices in the Motion Picture, Music Recording and Electronic Game Industries*. September 11. Washington, DC: Federal Trade Commission.

Fuchs, Cynthia. 1995. "Death Is Irrelevant": Cyborgs, Reproduction, and the Future of Male Hysteria. In *The Cyborg Handbook*. Chris Gray, ed. Pp. 281–300. New York: Routledge.

Goldberg, Jonathan. 1995. Recalling Totalities: The Mirrored Stages of Arnold Schwarzenegger. In *The Cyborg Handbook*. Chris Gray, ed. Pp. 233–254. New York: Routledge.

Hamilton, James. 1998. *Channeling Violence: The Economic Market for Violent Television Programming*. Princeton, NJ: Princeton University Press.

Hampton, Howard. 2000. Blood and Gore Wars. *Film Comment* 36:30.

Haraway, Donna Jenne. 1991. *Simians, Cyborgs, and Women: The Reinvention of Nature*. New York: Routledge.

Harvey, David. 1989. *The Condition of Postmodernity: An Enquiry into the Origins of Cultural Change*. Cambridge, MA: Basil Blackwell.

Houston, Beverle. 1984. Viewing Television: The Metapsychology of Endless Consumption. *Quarterly Review of Film Studies* 9(3):183–195.

Hurley, Kelly. 1995. Reading Like an Alien: Posthuman Identity in Ridley Scott's Alien and David Cronenberg's Rabid. In *Posthuman Bodies. Judith Haberstam and Ira Livingstone*, eds. Pp. 203–224. Bloomington: Indiana University Press.

Ito, Mizuko. 1998. Inhabiting Multiple Worlds: Making Sense of SimCity 2000 TM in the Fifth Dimension. In *Cyborg Babies: From Techno-sex to Techno-tots*. Robbie Davis-Floyd and Joseph Dumit, eds. Pp. 301–316. New York: Routledge.

Jameson, Fredric. 1982. Progress versus Utopia: or, Can We Imagine the Future? *Science Fiction Studies* 9:147–158.

Jameson, Fredric. 1984. Postmodernism, or the Cultural Logic of Late Capitalism. *New Left Review* 146:53–92.

Jenkins, Henry. 1997. Video Games are Good For You (Interview). *Next Generation* 29:8–13, 161–162.

Kinder, Marsha. 1991. *Playing with Power in Movies, Television, and Video Games: From Muppet Babies to Teenage Mutant Ninja Turtles*. Berkeley: University of California Press.

Kipnis, Laura. 1992. Male Desire and (Female) Disgust: Reading Hustler. In *Cultural Studies*. Lawrence Grossberg, Cary Nelson, and Paula Treichler, eds. Pp. 373–391. New York: Routledge.

Kirby, Lynne. 1988. Male Hysteria and Early Cinema. *Camera Obscura* 17:113–131.

Nielsen Media Research. 1993. Nielsen Television Index: Index programs by DMA, November 1993. New York: Nielsen Media Research.

Penley, Constance. 1991. Time Travel, Primal Scene, and the Critical Dystopia. In *Close Encounters: Film, Feminism, and Science*. Constance Penley, Elisabeth Lyon, Lynn Spigel, and Janet Bergstrom, eds. Pp. 67–84. Minneapolis: University of Minnesota Press.

Pfeil, Fred. 1990. *Another Tale to Tell: Politics and Narrative in Postmodern Culture*. London: Verso.

Piot, Charles. n.d. *Heat on the Street: Video Violence and American Teen Culture*.

Rhodes, Richard. 2000. Hollow Claims About Fantasy Violence. *The New York Times*. September 17: WK:19.

Ross, Andrew. 1989. *No Respect: Intellectuals and Popular Culture*. New York: Routledge.

Ross, Andrew. 1991. *Strange Weather: Culture, Science and Technology in the Age of Limits*. London: Verso.

Rubey, Dan. 1997. Not So Long Ago, Not So Far Away. *Jump Cut* 41:2–130.

Sedgwick, Eve Kosofsky. 1993. *Tendencies*. Durham, NC: Duke University Press.

Seiter, Ellen. 1999. Power Rangers at Preschool: Negotiating Media in Child Care Settings. In *Kids' Media Culture*. Marsha Kinder, ed. Pp. 239–262. Durham, NC: Duke University Press.

Shaviro, Steven. 1993. *The Cinematic Body*. Minneapolis: University of Minnesota Press.

Silverman, Kaja. 1992. *Male Subjectivity at the Margins*. New York: Routledge.

Springer, Claudia. 1993. Muscular Circuitry: The Invincible Armored Cyborg. *Cinema* 18:87–101.

Stone, Allucquere Rosanne. 1995. *The War of Desire and Technology at the Close of the Mechanical Age*. Cambridge, MA: MIT Press.

Studlar, Gaylyn. 1988. *In the Realm of Pleasure: Von Sternberg, Dietrich, and the Masochistic Aesthetic*. Urbana: University of Illinois Press.

Turkle, Sherry. 1998. Cyborg Babies and Cy-Dough-Plasm: Ideas about Self and Life in the Culture of Simulation. In *Cyborg Babies: From Techno-sex to Techno-tots*. Robbie Davis-Floyd and Joseph Dummit, eds. Pp. 317–329. New York: Routledge.

Williams, Linda. 1989. *Hard Core: Power, Pleasure and the "Frenzy of the Visible."* Berkeley: University of California Press.

Willis, Susan. 1987. Gender as Commodity. *The South Atlantic Quarterly* 86(4):403–419.

Wilson, Barbara, Dale Kunkel, Dan Litz, James Potter, Ed Donnerstein, Stacy Smith, Eva Blumenthal, and Mike Berry. 1996. *National Television Violence Study 1*. Thousand Oaks, CA: Sage Publications, Inc. Multimedia.

MULTIMEDIA WORKS CITED (FILMS)

Cameron, James, dir. 1984. *Terminator*. Orion Pictures/Hendale FilmCorporation/Pacific Western.

Cameron, James, dir. 1991. *Terminator 2*. Carolco Pictures/LightstormEntertainment/Pacific Western/Guild.

Carpenter, John, dir. 1978. *Halloween*. Falcon International.

Cronenberg, David, dir. 1986. *The Fly*. Brooksfilms/20th Century Fox.

Dekker, Fred, dir. 1993. *Robocop 3*. Orion Pictures.

Kershner, Irvin, dir. 1990. *Robocop 2*. Orion Pictures.

Lucas, George, dir. 1977. *Star Wars*. Lucas Film Ltd.

McTiernan, John, dir. 1988. *Die Hard*. 20th Century Fox/Gordon Co./Silver Pictures.

Otomo, Katsuhiro, dir. 1988. *Akira*. Akira Committee Co.

Scott, Ridley, dir. 1982. *Blade Runner*. Warner/The Ladd Co./Blade Runner Partnership.

Tsukamoto, Shinya, dir. 1988. *Tetsuo, the Iron Man*. Kaijyu Theater (Fox Lorber/Image).

Verhoeven, Paul, dir. 1987. *Robocop*. Orion Pictures.

2

Everything You Ever Wanted To Know about Assimilation but Were Afraid To Ask

Marcelo M. Suárez-Orozco

As if by centennial design the first and last decades of the twentieth century were eras of large-scale immigration (see figures 2.1 and 2.2). During the first decade of the twentieth century, the United States saw the arrival of what was then the largest wave of immigration in history when a total of 8,795,386 immigrants, the vast majority of them European peasants, entered the country. By the 1990s, the wave of "new immigration" (which began in 1965) peaked when about a million new immigrants were arriving in the United States each year. By 1998 the United States had over 25 million immigrants, setting a new historic record.[1]

Two dominant features characterize this most recent wave of immigration: its intensity (the immigrant population grew by 30 percent between 1990 and 1997) and the somewhat radical shift in the sources of new immigration: up to 1950, nearly 90 percent of all immigrants were Europeans or Canadians; today over 50 percent of all immigrants are from Latin America, and 27 percent are from Asia (see table 2.1).

The recent U.S. experience is part of a broader – indeed, global – dynamic of intensified transnational immigration. As we enter the twenty-first century, the worldwide immigrant population is over 100 million people – plus an estimated 20 to 30 million refugees. And these numbers reveal only the tip of a much larger immigration iceberg; by far the majority of immigrants and refugees remain within the confines of the "developing world" in individual nation-states. China, for example, has an estimated 100 million internal migrants.[2]

It is not surprising, then, that in recent years there has been renewed interest in basic research and policy in the field of immigration. While there is now robust scholarly activity on some aspects of immigration – for example, its economic causes and consequences – the scholarship on other important facets is somewhat anemic. For example, we know comparatively little about the long-term adaptations of immigrant children – the fastest-growing sector of the child population in the United States. Data and conceptual work on their health, schooling, and transition to the world of work are quite limited.[3] So is the work on the cultural processes of change generated by large-scale immigration. This is in part because labor economists, demographers, and sociologists have set the tone of the current research agenda – while anthropologists, psychologists, legal scholars, and scholars of the health sciences have played a more modest role.

Large-scale immigration is at once the cause and consequence of profound social, economic, and cultural transformations.[4] It is important to differentiate analytically between the two. While the claim has been made that there are powerful economic interests in having a large pool of foreign workers (a major cause of large-scale immigration), immigration nevertheless generates anxieties and at times even fans the fires of xenophobia (a major consequence of large-scale immigration). Two broad concerns have set the parameters of the debate over immigration scholarship and policy in the United States and Europe: the economic and the sociocultural consequences of large-scale immigration.

Recent economic arguments have largely focused on (1) the impact of large-scale immigration on the wages of native workers (Do immigrants depress the wages of native, especially minority, workers?), (2) the fiscal implications of large-scale immigration (Do immigrants "pay their way" taxwise, or are they a burden, consuming more in publicly funded services than they contribute?), and (3) the redundancy of immigrants, especially poorly educated and low-skilled workers, in new knowledge-intensive economies that are far less labor-intensive than the industrial economies of yesterday.[5]

Reducing the complexities of the new immigration to economic factors can, of course, be limiting. Indeed, there is an emerging consensus that the economic implications of large-scale immigration are somewhat ambiguous. Research shows that immigrants generate benefits in certain areas (including worker productivity) and costs in others (especially in fiscal terms). Furthermore, we must not lose sight of the fact that the U.S. economy is so large, powerful, and dynamic that, ideologues aside, immigration will neither make nor break it. The total size of the U.S. economy is on the order of $7 trillion; immigrant-related economic activities are a small portion of that total (an estimated domestic gain on the order of $1 to $10 billion a year, according to a National Research Council study).[6]

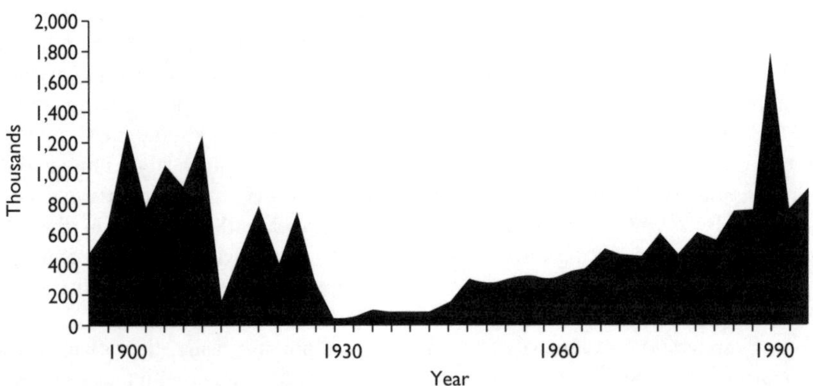

Figure 2.1 Immigrants admitted: fiscal years 1900–1996

Source: Adapted from U.S. Department of Justice, Immigration and Naturalization Service, *Statistical Yearbook of the Immigration and Naturalization Service* (Washington, DC: G.P.O., 1998).

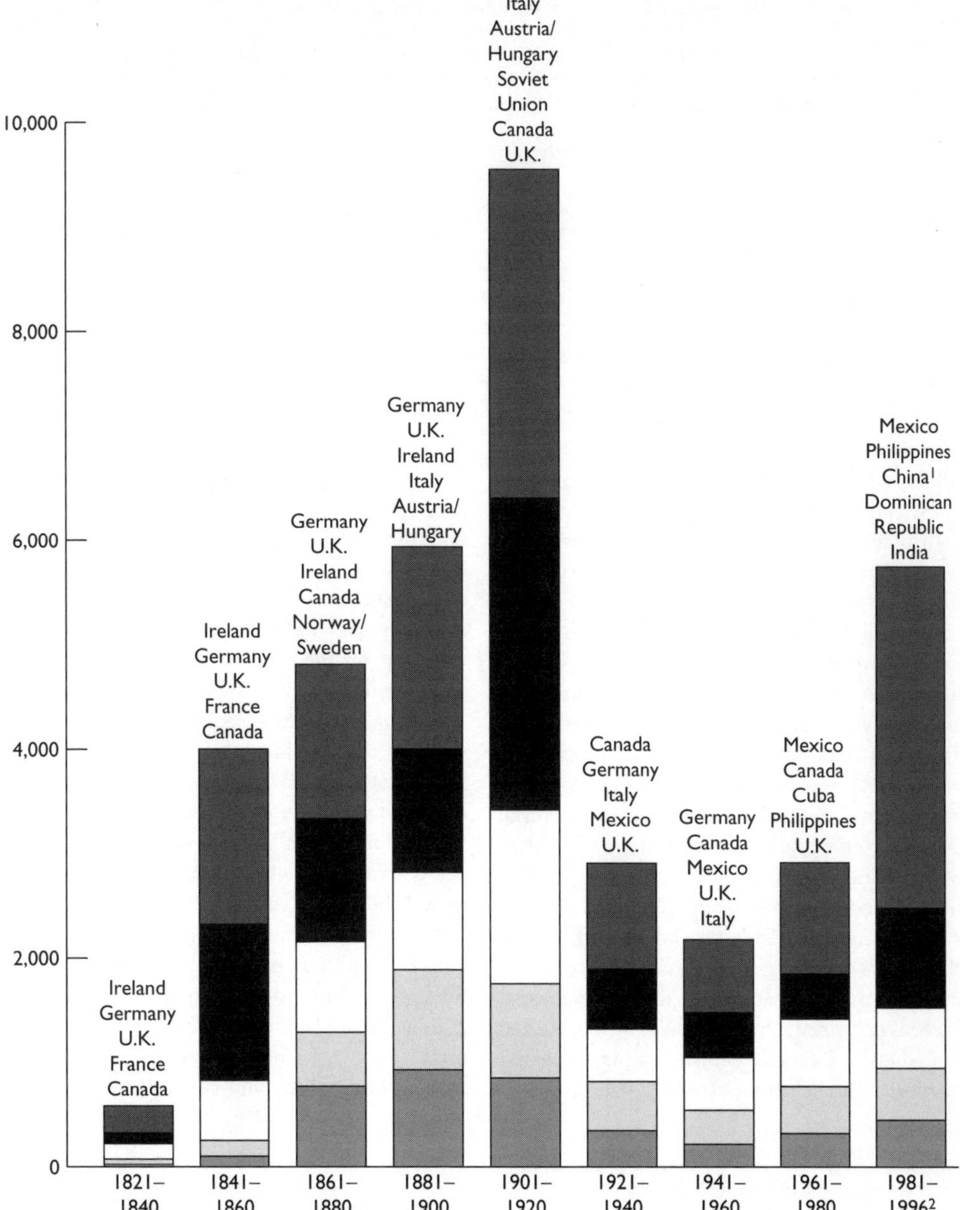

Figure 2.2 Immigrants admitted: country of origin, top five countries

[1] Includes People's Republic of China and Taiwan.

[2] 16-year period.

Source: Adapted from U.S. Department of Justice, Immigration and Naturalization Service, *Statistical Yearbook of the Immigration and Naturalization Service* (Washington, DC: G.P.O., 1998).

Table 2.1. Foreign-born as a percentage of the total U.S. population

	1880	*1900*	*1920*	*1950*	*1960*	*1970*	*1980*	*1990*	*1997*
% foreign born	13.3	13.6	13.3	6.9	5.4	4.7	6.2	8.6	9.3*

*1998 foreign-born population = 25,208,000

Percentage of foreign-born by region of origin

	1880	*1920*	*1950*	*1980*	*1997*
Europeans	97	93.6	89.3	49.6	17
Asians	1.6	1.7	2.65	18	27
Latin Americans	1.3	4.2	6.3	31	51

Source: Harvard Immigration Project, 2000.

The fact that the most recent wave of immigration is comprised largely of non-European, non-English-speaking "people of color" arriving in unprecedented numbers from Asia, the Caribbean, and Latin America (see table 2.2 and figure 2.3) is at the heart of current arguments over the sociocultural consequences of immigration. While the debates over the economic consequences of immigration are largely focused on the three areas of concern discussed above, the debate over the sociocultural implications is somewhat more diffused. Some scholars have focused on language issues, including bilingual education (Are they learning English?). Others examine the political consequences of large-scale immigration (Are they becoming American in letter and in spirit?). Still others focus on immigrant practices that are unpalatable in terms of the cultural models and social practices of the mainstream population (the eternal issues here are female genital-cutting, arranged marriages, and, in Europe especially, the veil).

Rethinking Assimilation

Old ideas about immigrant "assimilation" and "acculturation" – first articulated to make sense of the experiences of the transatlantic migrants of a century ago – have naturally been dusted off and tried out on the new arrivals. But in this case, applying the old to the new is not simply a reflex, a kind of intellectual laziness. Rather, I think it suggests that thinking about immigration in the United States is always, explicitly or implicitly, a comparative exercise: the here and now of the "new immigration" versus what, for lack of a better term, we might call the "mythico-historic" record.[7] This is a record in which equal parts of fact, myth, and fantasy combine to produce a powerful cultural narrative along the following lines: poor but hard-working European peasants, pulling themselves up by their bootstraps, willingly gave up their counterproductive old-world views, values, and languages – if not their

Table 2.2. Region of birth of foreign-born population

Year	*Total*	*Europe*	*Asia*	*Africa*	*Oceania*	*Latin America*
1900	10,341,276	8,881,548	120,248	2,538	8,820	137,458
1960	9,738,091	7,256,311	490,996	35,355	34,730	908,309
1970	9,619,302	5,740,891	824,887	80,143	41,258	1,803,970
1980	14,079,906	5,149,572	2,539,777	199,723	77,577	4,372,487
1990	19,767,316	4,350,403	4,979,037	363,819	104,145	8,407,837

Source: Adapted from U.S. Bureau of the Census, Current Population Reports, Series P23–195, *Profile of the Foreign-Born Population in the United States: 1997* (Washington, DC: G.P.O., 1999).

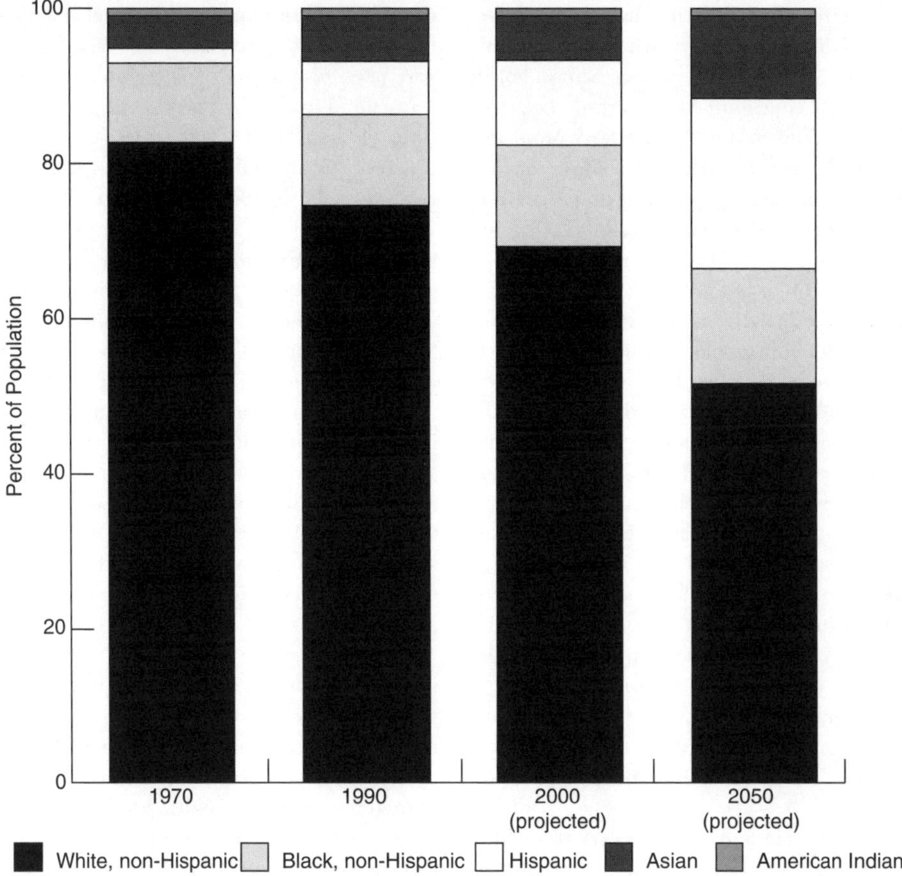

Figure 2.3 Racial/ethnic composition of the population

Source: U.S.Bureau of the Census, Current Population Reports (Washington, DC: G.P.O., 1996).

accents! – to become prosperous, proud, and loyal Americans.[8]

Because the United States is arguably the only postindustrial democracy in the world where immigration is at once history and destiny, every new wave of immigration reactivates an eternal question: How do the "new" immigrants measure up to the "old"? This was asked one hundred years ago when the "new" immigrants were Irish, Italians, and Eastern Europeans and the "old" immigrants were English (see figure 2.2). The recurring answer to that question is somewhat predictable. New immigrants *always* fail the comparative test by falling short of the mythico-historic standards set by earlier immigrants. Hence, the most basic rule governing public attitudes about immigration: we love immigrants at a safe historical distance but are much more ambivalent about those joining us now.[9]

It is hardly surprising, then, what questions many are asking today: Are the new immigrants of color recreating the structures of the foundational mythico-historic narrative – the grammar of which was articulated in Irish, Italian, and Eastern European accents on the streets and docks of the Lower East Side of Manhattan one hundred years ago? Or is today's unprecedented racial and cultural diversity – think of the over one hundred languages now spoken by immigrant children in New York City schools – generating an entirely new script? Is what we hear today an incomprehensible Babelesque story, which is not only unlike anything we have heard before but is quite likely to contribute to our already polarized race relations and chronic "underclass" problems? Will today's new arrivals turn out to be like our mythical immigrant ancestors and assimilate, becoming loyal and proud Americans? Or, conversely, will they by the sheer force of their numbers redefine what it is to be an American?

Much of the analytic – as well as the emotional – framework for approaching the topic of immigration was developed as the then-young nation was in the process of metabolizing the great transatlantic European immigration wave of a century ago. Ideas about "assimilation" and "acculturation," terms often used interchangeably, were first introduced in the social sciences to examine the processes of social and cultural change set in motion as immigrants began their second journey: their insertion into mainstream American life.[10] The basic theme in the narratives of "assimilation" and "acculturation" theories that came to dominate the social sciences predicted that immigration sets in motion a process of change that is directional, indeed unilinear, nonreversible, and continuous.

The direction or aim of the process was said to be "structural assimilation" (typically operationalized in terms of social relations and participation in the opportunity structure) and "acculturation" (typically operationalized in terms of language, values, and cultural identifications) into what was, implicitly or explicitly, the prize at immigration's finish line: the middle-class, white, Protestant, European American framework of the dominant society.[11] The process as it was narrated in the social-science literature seemed to follow neatly the van Gennepian structural code: *separation* (from social relations and from participation in the opportunity structure of the country or culture of origin), *marginality* (residential, linguistic, economic, especially during the earlier phases of immigration and especially acute among the first generation), and, finally, a generation or two after immigration, *incorporation* into the social structures and cultural codes of the mainstream.

The process of change was said to be nonreversible in that once an immigrant group achieved the goals of acculturation and structural assimilation, there was, so to speak, "no going back." This is in part because scholars of immigrant change conceptualized it as a dual process of gain (new culture, participation in new social structures) and loss (old culture, old social structures). The process was said to be continuous because it took place transgenerationally. The immigrant generation (outsiders looking for a way in), the second generation (Americanized insiders), the third and fourth generations (the "Roots" generation in search of "symbolic ethnicity"), and so on all had their assigned roles in this telling of the immigrant saga.

The dominant narratives of immigrant assimilation were structured by three reasonable assumptions. I will call them the "clean break" assumption, the "homogeneity" assumption, and the "progress" assumption. These assumptions, I suggest, need reexamination in light of some of the distinct features characterizing the latest wave of immigration.

First, immigration was theorized to take place in clearly delineated waves (versus ongoing flows) between two relatively remote, bounded geopolitical and cultural spaces. Immigrants left country "A" to settle permanently in country "B." When immigrants chose to return to their country of origin, and large numbers did, it was again seen as a permanent move.[12] The norm, however, was that immigrants leaving Ireland or Eastern Europe were not supposed to look back. This is hardly surprising, since the very idea of immigration was to look forward to a new start and better opportunities in a new country. The renaming rituals at Ellis Island, when immigrants traded – some voluntarily, others involuntarily – exotic names for "Americanized" versions, signified the beginning of a new life. A "clean break" was needed before the process of Americanization could begin.

The second assumption was that immigrants would, in due course, over two or three generations, join the mainstream of a society dominated by a homogeneous middle-class, white, European American Protestant ethos.[13] While American society was never homogeneous, "the color line" being a defining feature of its landscape, it was never assumed that the African-American culture played a significant factor in the immigrant equation. When assimilation was debated it went without saying: its very point was to join mainstream culture.

The third assumption dominating thinking about immigrant assimilation was structured by a powerful teleological reflex: immigration is about uniform progress, about going from "good" (first generation) to "better" (second generation), to "best" (third and fourth generations). The immigrant's journey to success was the stuff of the American dream. *Ragtime*, the acclaimed Broadway musical, gives artistic form to this basic idea: the Russian family moves from the misery of the shtetl to glamorous Hollywood in one generation – assimilation in fast-forward, so to speak. Taken together with the two previous assumptions, a coherent narrative unfolds: as immigrants give up their old ways, and they assimilate to middle-class, white European American Protestant culture, they find enormous rewards.

The "Clean Break" Assumption: A Critique

It may no longer be useful to assume that immigration takes place between remote, neatly bounded geopolitical spaces, where a "clean break" is, even if not desired, inevitable. Indeed, in recent years, anthropologists and sociologists have claimed that what is novel about the "new immigrants" is that they are actors on a transnational stage.[14] The relative ease and accessibility of mass transportation (1.5 billion airline tickets were sold last year) and the new globalized communication and information technologies make possible a more massive back-and-forth movement of people, goods, information, and symbols than ever before.[15] Compared to Mexican or Dominican immigrants today, the Irish and Eastern European immigrants of last century – even if they had wanted to – simply could not have maintained the level and intensity of contact with the "old country" that we are now witnessing.[16] Furthermore, the new immigration from such places as Latin America and the Caribbean can be best characterized as an uninterrupted "flow" rather than neatly delineated "waves" typical of the earlier European transatlantic immigration. This ongoing, uninterrupted migratory flow is said to "replenish" constantly social practices and cultural models that would otherwise tend to be "lost" to assimilation.[17] Indeed, in certain areas of the Southwest, Latin American immigration is generating a powerful infrastructure dominated by a growing Spanish-speaking mass media (radio, television, and print), new market dynamics, and new cultural identities.[18]

Another relevant feature of the new transnational framework is that even as they enmesh themselves in the social, economic, and political life in their new lands, immigrants remain powerful protagonists in the economic, political, and cultural spheres back home.[19] With international remittances estimated at nearly $100 billion per annum, immigrant remittances and investments have become vital to the economies of most countries of emigration. A U.S.-Mexican Binational Study on Immigration estimates that remittances to Mexico were the "equivalent to 57 percent of the foreign exchange available through direct investment in 1995, and 5 percent of the total income supplied by exports."[20]

Politically, immigrants are emerging as increasingly relevant actors with influence in political processes both "here" and "there." Some observers have noted that the outcome of the most recent Dominican presidential election was largely determined in New York City – where Dominicans are the largest group of new immigrants. Likewise, Mexican politicians – especially those of the opposition – have recently "discovered" the political value of the seven million Mexican immigrants living in the United States. The new Mexican dual nationality initiative – whereby Mexican immigrants who become nationalized U.S. citizens would retain a host of political and other rights in Mexico – is also the product of this emerging transnational framework.[21]

Because of a new ease of mass transportation and new communication technologies, immigration is no longer structured around the "sharp break" with the country of origin that once characterized the transoceanic experience. Immigrants today are more likely to be at once "here" *and* "there," articulating dual consciousness and dual identities and, in the process, bridging increasingly unbounded national spaces.[22]

The "Homogeneity" Assumption: A Critique

It may no longer be useful to assume that immigrants today are joining a homogeneous society dominated by the middle-class, white, European American Protestant ethos.[23] The new immigrants are entering a country that is economically, socially, and culturally unlike the country that absorbed – however ambivalently – previous waves of immigrants. Economically, the previous large wave of immigrants arrived on the eve of the great industrial expansion in which immigrant workers and consumers played a key role.[24]

Immigrants now are actors in a thoroughly globalized restructured economy that is increasingly fragmented into discontinuous economic spheres. Some have characterized the new post-industrial economy in terms of the "hourglass" metaphor. On one end of the hourglass there is a well-remunerated, knowledge-intensive economic sphere that has recently experienced unprecedented growth. On the other end, there is a service economy where low-skilled and semiskilled workers continue to "lose ground" in terms of real wages, benefits, and security. Furthermore, in the new economy there are virtually no bridges for those at the bottom of the hourglass to move into the more desirable sectors. Some scholars have argued that unlike the low-skilled industry jobs of yesterday, the kinds of jobs typically available today to low-skilled new immigrants do not offer serious prospects of upward mobility.[25]

Another defining aspect of the new immigration is the intense social segregation between new immigrants of color and the middle-class, white, European American population. While immigrants have always concentrated in specific neighborhoods, we are witnessing today an extraordinary concentration of large numbers of immigrants in a handful of states in large urban areas polarized by racial tensions. Some 85 percent of all Mexican immigrants in the United States reside in three states (California, Texas, and Illinois). As a result of an increasing segmentation of the economy and society, large numbers of low-skilled immigrants "have become more, not less, likely to live and work in environments that have grown increasingly segregated from whites."[26] These immigrants have, by and large, no meaningful contact with the middle-class, white, European American culture. Rather, their point of reference is more likely to be co-nationals, co-ethnics, or the African-American culture.

But perhaps the lethal blow to the homogeneity assumption comes from what I call a "culture of multiculturalism." Rather than face a "relatively uniform 'mainstream'" culture,[27] immigrants today must navigate more complex and varied currents. The cultural models and social practices that we have come to call multiculturalism shape the experiences, perceptions, and behavioral repertoires of immigrants in ways not seen in previous eras of large-scale immigration. A hundred years ago there certainly was no culture of multiculturalism celebrating – however superficially and ambivalently – ethnicity and communities of origin. Indeed, the defining ritual at Ellis Island was the mythic renaming ceremony when immigration officers – sometimes carelessly and sometimes purposefully – renamed new arrivals with more Anglicized names, a cultural baptism of sorts. Others chose to change their names to avoid racism or anti-Semitism, or simply to "blend in." Hence, Israel Ehrenberg was reborn as Ashley Montague, Meyer Schkolnick was reborn as Robert Merton, and Issur Danielovitch Demsky was reborn as Kirk Douglas.[28]

Immigrants today enter social spaces where racial and ethnic categories are important gravitational fields – often charged with important political and economic implications. The largest wave of immigration into the United States took place largely after the great struggles of the civil rights movement.

In that ethos, racial and ethnic categories became powerful instrumental as well as expressive vectors. By "expressive ethnicity" I refer to the subjective feeling of common origin and a shared destiny with others. These feelings are typically constructed around such phenomena as historic travails and struggles (as in the case of the Serbian sense of peoplehood emerging from their defeat five centuries ago at the hands of the Ottmans in the Battle of Kosovo), a common ancestral language (as in the case of the Basques), or religion (as in the case of the Jews in the Diaspora).[29]

By "instrumental ethnicity," I mean the tactical use of ethnicity. In recent years, "identity politics" has become a mode of expressive self-affirmation as well as instrumental self-advancement. This is in part because ethnic categories have become a critical tool of the state apparatus. Nation-states create categories for various reasons, such as to count people for census, taxation, and apportionment for political representation. Ethnic categories as generated by state policy are relevant to a variety of civic and political matters; furthermore, they are appropriated and used by various groups for their own strategic needs.

Pan-ethnic categories such as "Asian American" and "Hispanic" are largely arbitrary constructions created by demographers and social scientists for purposes of data development, analysis, and policy. The term "Hispanic," for example, was introduced by demographers working for the U.S. Bureau of the Census in the 1980s as a way to categorize people who are either historically or culturally connected to the Spanish language. Note that "Hispanic," the precursor to the more au courant term Latino, is a category that has no precise meaning regarding racial or national origins. Indeed, Latinos are white, black, indigenous, and every possible combination thereof. They also originate in over 20 countries as varied from each other as Mexico, Argentina, and the Dominican Republic.[30]

For large numbers of new arrivals today, the point of reference seems to be the cultural sensibilities and social practices of their more established co-ethnics – i.e., Latinos, Asians, Afro-Caribbeans – rather than the standards of the increasingly more remote middle-class, white, Protestant European Americans.

The "Progress" Assumption: A Critique

The foundational narratives of immigrant assimilation typically depicted an upwardly mobile journey. The story was elegant in its simplicity: the longer immigrants were in the United States, the better they would do in terms of schooling, health, and income. As Robert Bellah once noted, "The United States was planned for progress," and each wave of immigrants was said to recapitulate this national destiny. This assumption needs rethinking in light of new evidence. A number of scholars from different disciplines using a variety of methods have identified a somewhat disconcerting phenomenon. For many new immigrant groups, length of residency in the United States seems to be associated with *declining* health, school achievement, and aspirations.[31]

A recent large-scale National Research Council study considered a variety of measures of physical health and risk behaviors among children and adolescents from immigrant families – including general health, learning disabilities, obesity, and emotional difficulties. The NRC researchers found that immigrant youths tend to be healthier than their counterparts from nonimmigrant families. These findings are "counterintuitive in light of the racial and ethnic minority status, lower overall socioeconomic status, and higher poverty rates of many immigrant children and families." The NRC study also found that the longer immigrant youths are in the United States, the poorer their overall physical and psychological health. Furthermore, the more "Americanized" they became, the more likely they were to engage in risky behaviors such as substance abuse, unprotected sex, and delinquency (see figure 2.4). While the NRC data are limited, they nevertheless should be cause for reflection.[32]

In the area of education, sociologists Ruben Rúmbaut and Alejandro Portes surveyed more than 5,000 high-school students in San Diego, California, and Dade County, Florida. Rúmbaut writes:

> an important finding supporting our earlier reported research is the *negative* association of length of residence in the United States with both GPA and aspirations. Time in the United States is, as expected, strongly predictive of improved English reading skills; but despite that seeming advantage, longer residence in the United States and second generation status [that is, being born in the United States] are connected to declining academic achievement and aspirations, net of other factors.[33]

In a different voice, Reverend Virgil Elizondo, rector of the San Fernando Cathedral in San Antonio, Texas, articulates this same problem: "I can tell by looking in their eyes how long they've been here. They come sparkling with hope, and the first

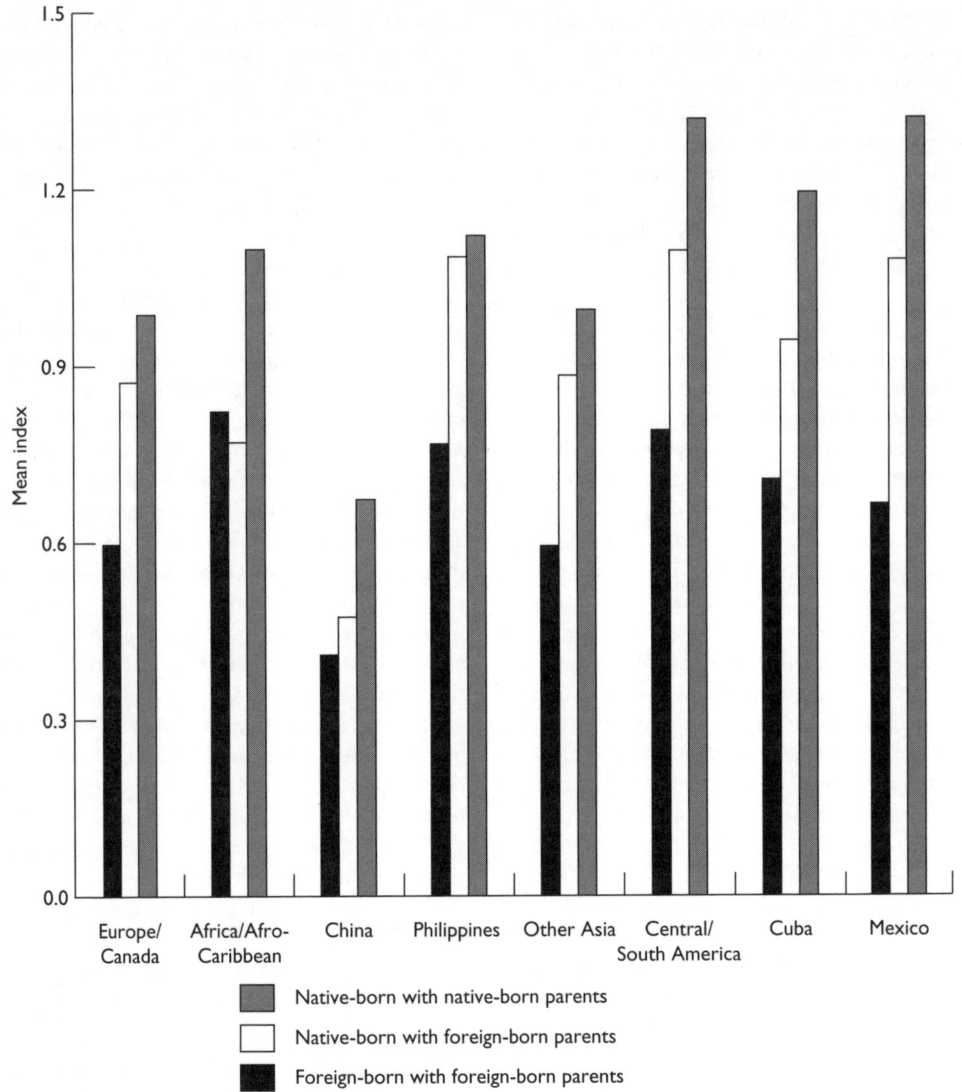

Figure 2.4 Mean risk behavior by ethnic group and immigrant status

Source: Adapted from National Research Council, *From Generation to Generation: The Health and Well-Being of Children in Immigrant Families* (Washington, DC: National Academy Press, 1998), 84.

generation finds hope rewarded. Their children's eyes no longer sparkle."[34]

A number of scholars are currently exploring the problem of decline in schooling performance, health, and social adaptation of immigrant children. Preliminary research suggests that several factors seem to be implicated. The various forms of "capital" that the immigrant families bring with them – including financial resources, social class and educational background, psychological and physical health, as well as social supports – have a clear influence on the immigrant experience.

Legal status (documented versus undocumented immigrant), race, color, and language also mediate how children and families manage the upheavals of immigration. Economic opportunities and neighborhood characteristics – including the quality of schools where immigrants settle, racial and class segregation, neighborhood decay, and violence – all contribute significantly to the adaptation process. Anti-immigrant sentiment and racism also play a role. These factors combine in ways that seem to lead to very different long-term outcomes. Until better longitudinal data are available, it is no longer safe to assume that immigration inevitably leads to measurable progress.

Indeed, it may be wise to think about what is taking place today in the United States as two very distinct migratory formations – formations that have different causes and generate divergent outcomes. In the long term, these distinct dynamics may turn out to be quite different from what we have seen in the field of immigration before.

Utopia

One migratory formation is made up of highly educated, highly skilled workers drawn by the explosive growth in the knowledge-intensive sectors of the economy. These immigrants thrive. They are among the best-educated and most skilled people in the United States. Immigrants today are overrepresented in the category of people with doctorates. Fully half of all entering physics graduate students in 1998 were foreign-born.[35] Thirty-two percent of all scientists and engineers working in California's famed Silicon Valley are immigrants.[36] Roughly a third of all Nobel Prize winners in the United States have been immigrants. In 1999, all (100 percent!) U.S. winners of the Nobel Prize were immigrants. Perhaps with the exception of the highly educated immigrants and refugees escaping Nazi Europe, immigrants in the past tended to be more uniformly poorly educated and relatively unskilled than they are today.[37]

These immigrants are likely to settle in safe middle-class suburban neighborhoods – the kinds of neighborhoods that tend to have better schools. Their children, not surprisingly, are outperforming native-born children in terms of grades, as winners of the nation's most prestigious science competitions, and as freshmen in the nation's most exclusive colleges – two of the three top Intel Science prizes in March of 2000 went to immigrant youths. These highly educated and skilled immigrants are rapidly moving into the more desirable sectors of the U.S. economy, generally bypassing the traditional transgenerational modes of immigrant status mobility.[38] Never in the history of U.S. immigration have so many immigrants done so well so fast. For them, immigration means Utopia realized.

Distopia

The other migratory formation is made up of large numbers of poorly educated, unskilled workers – many of them in the United States without proper documentation (i.e., as illegal aliens). These immigrants come to survive – some are escaping economies that more or less "broke" during global restructuring; others are escaping violence or war. They are workers drawn by the service sector of the U.S. economy where there seems to be an insatiable appetite for foreign workers. They typically end up in poorly paid jobs that offer no insurance or basic safeties and no promise of upward mobility.

These immigrants tend to settle in areas of deep poverty and racial segregation. Concentrated poverty is associated with the "disappearance of meaningful work opportunities."[39] Youngsters in such neighborhoods are chronically underemployed or unemployed and must search for work elsewhere. In such neighborhoods, with few opportunities in the formal economy, underground or informal activities tend to flourish. These kinds of economies often involve the trade of illegal substances and are associated with gangs and neighborhood violence. This ethos is the primary point of reference for many poor immigrant children of color today.

When poverty is combined with racial segregation, the outcomes can be devastating: no matter what their personal traits or characteristics, people who grow up and live in environments of concentrated poverty and racial isolation are more likely to become teenage mothers, drop out of school, achieve only low levels of education, and earn lower adult incomes.[40]

One hundred years ago, low-skilled immigrant workers with very little formal schooling could, through floor-shop mobility, attain living wages and a comfortable lifestyle. Today's global economy is unforgiving of immigrants without skills and credentials. Furthermore, low-skill service jobs not only lead nowhere in the status hierarchy but also fail to provide for the basic needs of a family. Indeed, new research suggests that among new immigrants, a general pattern of declining returns on education means that with more schooling they will be getting fewer rewards in the post-educational opportunity structure than ever before in the history of U.S. immigration.[41] The high-school graduate who bypasses college and enters the workforce with no special skills has only a limited advantage over the high-school dropout.[42]

Poor, low-skilled immigrants of color have few options but to send their children to schools located in drug-, prostitution-, and gang-infested neighborhoods.[43] All too many immigrant schools can only be characterized as sites overwhelmed by a "culture of violence."[44] Many newly arrived immigrant youths find themselves deeply marginalized in toxic schools that offer inferior education.[45]

In the long term, many immigrant youths of color coming from low-skilled and poorly educated backgrounds will face serious odds. Intense segregation, inferior schools, violent neighborhoods, structural and interpersonal racism – all co-conspire to snuff the immigrants' most precious asset: hope and optimism about the future.[46]

Culture and Assimilation: Concluding Thoughts

This latest wave of immigration has rekindled the eternal American debate about the long-term consequences of large-scale immigration. Some worry about the economic implications, while many others have focused on its cultural implications. I turn now to some of these cultural concerns because, I think, they rest on a somewhat flawed understanding of culture.

Analytically, it is sometimes useful to differentiate between two broad spheres of culture: "instrumental culture" and "expressive culture." By instrumental culture, I mean the skills, competencies, and social behaviors that are required successfully to make a living and contribute to society. By expressive culture, I mean the realm of values, worldviews, and the patterning of interpersonal relations that give meaning and sustain the sense of self. Taken together, these qualities of culture generate shared meanings and understandings, and a sense of belonging. In sum, the sense of who you are and where you belong is deeply patterned by these qualities of culture.

In the instrumental realm, there is arguably a worldwide convergence in the skills that are needed to function in today's global economy. Whether in Los Angeles, Lima, or Lagos, the skills that are needed to thrive in the global economy are in fundamental respects the same. These include communication, higher-order symbolic and technical skills as well as habits of work, and interpersonal talents that are common in any cosmopolitan setting.

Immigrant parents are very much aware that if their children are to thrive they must acquire these skills. Indeed, immigration for many parents represents nothing more, and nothing less, than the opportunity to offer children access to these skills. Indeed, we have yet to meet an immigrant parent who tells us that he does not want his daughter to learn English or to acquire the skills and work habits that will prepare her for a successful career whether in the United States or "back home."

While immigrant parents encourage their children to cultivate the "instrumental" aspects of culture in the new setting, they are decidedly more ambivalent about their children's exposure to some of the "expressive" elements of culture in the new land. During the course of our research, it has not been difficult to detect that many immigrant parents strongly resist a whole array of cultural models and social practices in American youth culture that they consider highly undesirable. These include cultural attitudes and behaviors that are anti-schooling ("school is boring") and anti-authority, the glorification of violence, and sexually precocious behaviors. Many immigrant parents reject and resist this form of acculturation.

Hence, I claim that the incantation of many observers – "acculturate, acculturate, acculturate" – needs rethinking. If acculturation is superficially defined as acquiring linguistic skills, job skills, and participation in the political process, then there is a universal consensus on these shared goals. If, on the other hand, we choose a broader definition of assimilation and acculturation as also including the realm of values, worldviews, and interpersonal relations, then a worthy debate ensues.

The first issue that needs airing is the basic question of "acculturating to what?" American society is no longer, if it ever was, a uniform or coherent system. Given their diverse origins, financial resources, and social networks, immigrants end up gravitating toward very different sectors of American society. While some are able to join integrated well-to-do neighborhoods, the majority of today's immigrants come to experience American culture from the vantage point of poor urban settings. Limited economic opportunities, toxic schools, ethnic tensions, violence, drugs, and gangs characterize many of these settings. The structural inequalities found in what some social theorists have called "American Apartheid" are implicated in the creation of a cultural ethos of ambivalence, pessimism, and despair. Asking immigrant youths to give up their values, worldviews, and interpersonal relations to join this ethos is a formula for disaster.[47]

For those immigrants who come into intimate contact with middle-class mainstream culture, other trade-offs will be required. As our data suggest, immigrant children of color perceive that mainstream Americans do not welcome them and, indeed, disparage them as not deserving to partake in the American dream.[48] Identifying wholeheartedly with a culture that rejects you has its psychological costs, usually paid in the currency of shame, doubt, and even self-hatred.

But even if the new immigrants were unambivalently embraced by middle-class mainstream Americans, it is far from clear that mimicking their behaviors would prove to be in the long term an adaptive strategy for immigrants of color. Mainstream middle-class children are protected by social safety nets that give them leeway to experiment with an array of distopic behaviors that can include drugs, sex, and alcohol. On the other hand, for many immigrant youths, without robust socioeconomic and cultural safety nets, engaging in such behaviors is a high-stakes proposition in which one mistake can have lifelong consequences. While a white middle-class youth caught in possession of drugs is likely to be referred to counseling and rehabilitation, an immigrant youth convicted of the same offense is likely to be deported.

The current wave of immigration involves people from fantastically diverse and heterogeneous cultural backgrounds. Beneath surface differences, a common grammar can be identified among groups as culturally distinct from each other as Chinese, Haitian, and Mexican immigrants. The importance of family ties, the importance of hard work, and optimism about the future are examples of shared immigrant values.[49]

These three realms are aspects of culture that become highlighted and come to the fore in the process of immigration. Consider, for example, the case of strong family ties among immigrants. Many immigrants come from cultures in which the family system is an integral part of the person's sense of self. These family ties play a critical role in family reunification – an important force driving new immigration. Furthermore, once immigrants settle, family ties are accentuated because immigration poses many emotional and practical challenges forcing immigrants to turn to one another for support.[50]

Hard work and optimism about the future are likewise central to the immigrant's *raison d'être*. The immigrant's most fundamental motivation is to find a better life. Immigrants tend to view hard work as essential to this project. The fact that many immigrants will do the impossible jobs that native workers simply refuse to consider is an indication of just how hard they are willing to work. Immigrant family ties, work ethic, and optimism about the future are unique assets that should be celebrated as adding to the total cultural stock of the nation.

Immigration generates change. The immigrants themselves undergo a variety of transformations. Likewise, the immigration process inevitably changes the members of the dominant culture. In the United States today we eat, speak, and dance differently from the way we did 30 years ago, in part because of large-scale immigration. But change is never easy. The changes brought about by the new immigration require mutual calibrations and negotiations.

Rather than advocating that immigrant children abandon all elements of their culture as they embark on their uncertain assimilation journey, a more promising path is to cultivate and nurture the emergence of new hybrid identities and bicultural competencies.[51] These hybrid cultural styles creatively blend elements of the old culture with those of the new, unleashing new energies and potentials.[52]

The skills and work habits that are required to thrive in the new century are essential elements of assimilation. Immigrant children, like all children, must develop this repertoire of instrumental skills. At the same time, maintaining a sense of belonging and social cohesion with their immigrant roots is equally important. When immigrant children lose their expressive culture, social cohesion is weakened, parental authority is undermined, and interpersonal relations suffer. The unthinking call for immigrant children to abandon their culture can only result in loss, anomie, and social disruption.

The model of unilinear assimilation – in which the bargain was straighforward: please check all your cultural baggage before you pass through the Golden Gate – emerged in another era.[53] The young nation, then, was eager to turn large numbers of European immigrants into loyal citizen workers and consumers. It was an era of nation-building and bounded national projects.[54]

But even then, accounts of immigrants rushing in unison to trade their culture for American culture were greatly exaggerated. German Americans, Italian Americans, and Irish Americans have all left deep cultural imprints in the molding of American culture. Even among fifth-generation descendants of the previous great wave of immigration, symbolic culture and ethnicity remain an emotional gravitational field.[55]

But beyond the argument that maintaining the expressive elements of culture is symbolically important and strategic from the point of view of social cohesion, there is another point worth considering. In the global era, the tenets of unilineal assimilation are no longer relevant. Today there are clear and unequivocal advantages to being able to operate in multiple cultural codes – as anyone working in a major (and now not-so-major) corporation knows. There are social, economic, cognitive, and aesthetic advantages to being able to move across cultural spaces. Dual consciousness has its instrumental and expressive advantages. Immigrant children are in a position to maximize that unique advantage. While many view their cultural – including linguistic – skills as a threat, I see them as precious assets to be cultivated.

A renowned historian once said the history of the United States is in fundamental respects the history of immigration.[56] Throughout history, U.S. citizens have ambivalently welcomed newcomers. The fear then, as now, focused on whether the immigrants would contribute to the American project. The gift of hindsight demonstrates just how essential immigration has proven to the making and remaking of the American fabric.

However, with diversity comes conflict and dissent. Working through frictions in the public sphere by reasoned debate and compromise is central to the idea and practice of democracy. Immigrant children are uniquely poised to play a significant role in the remaking of American democracy. In the era of multiculturalism and transnationalism, their bicultural experiences and skills prepare them well to be the cultural brokers able to find the common ground.

NOTES

1 See, for example, *Profile of the Foreign-Born Population in the United States: 1997* (Washington, DC: U.S. Bureau of the Census, Current Population Reports, 1999).

2 See, for example, Erik Eckholm, "For China's Rural Migrants, an Education Wall," *New York Times*, December 12, 1999:A8.

3 See, for example, Carola Suárez-Orozco and Marcelo M. Suárez-Orozco, *Children of Immigration* (Cambridge, MA: Harvard University Press, 2000).

4 Theorists of immigration have argued that transnationalized labor-recruiting networks, family

reunification, and changing cultural models and expectations about, for example, what is an acceptable standard of living are all powerfully implicated in generating and sustaining new migratory flows. Wars nearly always generate large-scale immigration: World War II gave birth to the Mexican *bracero* program, which started the largest wave of immigration to the United States in history. Without the Cold War, there would not be today over a million Cuban Americans in the United States. The Southeast Asian Diaspora is the product of the war in Indochina. The million or so Central Americans who now make the United States their home arrived following the intensification of the U.S.-backed counterinsurgency campaigns in El Salvador, Guatemala, and Nicaragua of the 1980s.

5 A great deal of energy has gone into assessing the economic consequences of immigration, and the research findings are somewhat ambiguous. Indeed, they are often contradictory – some economists claim that the new immigrants are a burden to taxpayers and an overall negative influence on the U.S. economy; others suggest that they continue to be an important asset. A recent study on the economic, demographic, and fiscal effects of immigration by the National Research Council concludes: "immigration produces net economic gains for domestic residents." National Research Council, *The New Americans: Economic, Demographic, and Fiscal Effects of Immigration* (Washington, DC: National Academy Press, 1997), 3. For another overview of immigrants and the economy, see George Borjas, *Heaven's Door: Immigration Policy and the American Economy* (Princeton, NJ: Princeton University Press, 1999).

6 National Research Council, *The New Americans*, 5.

7 Suárez-Orozco and Suárez-Orozco, *Children of Immigration.*

8 For a recent exquisite treatment of this narrative, see Riv-Ellen Prell, *Fighting to Become Americans: Jews, Gender, and the Anxiety of Assimilation* (Boston: Beacon Press, 1999). Consider also the introductory paragraph on a recent *New York Times* story on the families of vice-presidential candidate Senator Joseph Lieberman and his immigrant wife, Mrs. Hadassah Lieberman, a child of Holocaust survivors: "They came over on wobbling merchant marine ships, refugees with a few valises apiece that contained all they owned in the world. Rebuilding from scratch – they had, after all, lost their homes and most of their closest kin – they worked at low-paying jobs in dingy dress factories, luncheonettes, dry-goods stores. For many, it was too late for any grander aspirations. Their children would redeem their expectations." Joseph Berger, "Mrs. Lieberman's Story, and Others," *New York Times*, August 13, 2000:A26.

9 Suárez-Orozco and Suárez-Orozco, *Children of Immigration.*

10 See, inter alia, Robert E. Park and Ernest W. Burgess, *Introduction to the Science of Sociology* (Chicago: University of Chicago Press, 1965); Milton M. Gordon, *Assimilation in American Life: The Role of Race, Religion, and National Origins* (New York: Oxford University Press, 1964); and Richard Alba and Victor Nee, "Rethinking Assimilation Theory for a New Era of Immigration," *International Migration Review* 31 (Winter 1997).

11 The process of change was said to be unilinear in that all new arrivals would be expected to undergo roughly the same process of change.

12 See, for example, Jose C. Moya, *Cousins and Strangers: Spanish Immigrants in Buenos Aires, 1850–1930* (Berkeley: University of California Press, 1998) and Michael Piore, *Birds of Passage: Migrant Labor and Industrial Societies* (New York: Cambridge University Press, 1971).

13 See, for example, Alejandro Portes, ed., *The New Second Generation* (New York: Russell Sage, 1996).

14 See Peggy Levitt, "Transnationalizing Civil and Political Change: The Case of Transnational Organizational Ties between Boston and the Dominican Republic," Ph.D. dissertation, Massachusetts Institute of Technology, 1996; "Commentary," in Marcelo M. Suárez-Orozco, ed., *Crossings: Mexican Immigration in Interdisciplinary Perspectives* (Cambridge, MA: David Rockefeller Center for Latin American Studies and Harvard University Press, 1998); Linda Basch, Nina Glick Schiller, and Cristina Szanton Blanc, *Nations Unbound: Transnational Projects, Postcolonial Predicaments and Deterritorialized Nation-States* (Basel, Switzerland: Gordon and Breach Science Publishers, 1994).

15 Borrowing the delicious words of Luís Rafael Sanchez, many new immigrants today live neither here nor there but rather in "la guagua aérea" – the air bus.

16 See Ricardo Ainslie, "Cultural Mourning, Immigration, and Engagement: Vignettes from the Mexican Experience," in Suárez-Orozco, ed., *Crossings: Mexican Immigration in Interdisciplinary Perspectives.*

17 See David G. Gutierrez, "Ethnic Mexicans and the Transformation of 'American' Social Space: Reflections on Recent History," in Suárez-Orozco,

ed., *Crossings: Mexican Immigration in Interdisciplinary Perspectives.*

18 Since 1990, while the Hispanic population in the United States grew by more than 30 percent, its buying power has grown by more than 65 percent, to about $350 billion in 1997. This is changing the way business is conducted in many parts of the country.

19 Wayne Cornelius, "The Structural Embeddedness of Demand for Mexican Immigrant Labor," in Suárez-Orozco, ed., *Crossings: Mexican Immigration in Interdisciplinary Perspectives*; and Jorge Durand, "Migration and Integration," ibid.

20 See Binational Study, *Migration Between Mexico and the United States* (Washington, DC: U.S. Commission on Immigration Reform, 1998). Cornelius, however, argues that over time Mexican immigrants in the United States are less likely to invest in capital improvements in the communities they emigrated from. In fact, he argues that a new feature of the Mexican experience in the United States is that as Mexican immigrants become increasingly rooted in the U.S. side of "the line," they mainly go back to these communities for rest and relaxation. See Cornelius, "The Structural Embeddedness."

21 Culturally, immigrants not only significantly reshape the ethos of their new communities but are also responsible for significant social transformations "back home." Peggy Levitt has argued that Dominican "social remittances" affect the values, cultural models, and social practices of those left behind. See Levitt, "Transnationalizing Civil and Political Change."

22 Basch, Schiller, and Blanc, *Nations Unbound.*

23 I concur with Alejandro Portes when he argues that we can no longer assume that new immigrants will assimilate into a coherent mainstream.

24 John Higham, *Send These To Me: Jews and Other Immigrants in Urban America* (New York: Atheneum, 1975).

25 Portes, *The New Second Generation.*

26 Roger Waldinger and Mehdi Bozorgmehr, eds., *Ethnic Los Angeles* (New York: Russell Sage Foundation, 1996).

27 Portes, *The New Second Generation.*

28 Lawrence J. Friedman, *Identity's Architect: A Biography of Erik H. Erickson* (New York: Scribner, 1999).

29 Lola Romanucci-Ross and George DeVos, *Ethnic Identity: Creation, Conflict, and Accommodation*, 3rd edn (Walnut Creek, CA: Alta Mira Press, 1995).

30 Nor do these categories address the sensibilities rooted in history and generation in the United States. A Latina can be a person who is the descendant of the original settlers in what is today New Mexico. Her ancestors spoke Spanish – well before English was ever heard in this continent. Her family has resided in this land before the United States appropriated the Southwest territories. She is considered a Latina just as is a Mayan-speaking new arrival from Guatemala who crossed the border last week. Likewise, the term Asian brings together people of highly diverse cultural, linguistic, and religious backgrounds. A Chinese Buddhist and a Filipino Catholic are both considered Asian American though they may have very little in common in terms of language, cultural identity, and sense of self.

31 See Grace Kao and Marta Tienda, "Optimism and Achievement: The Educational Performance of Immigrant Youth," *Social Science Quarterly* 76 (1) (1995), 1–19; National Research Council, *From Generation to Generation: The Health and Well-Being of Children in Immigrant Families* (Washington, DC: National Academy Press, 1998); Ruben Rúmbaut, "The New Californians: Comparative Research Findings on the Educational Progress of Immigrant Children," in Ruben Rúmbaut and Wayne Cornelius, eds., *California's Immigrant Children* (San Diego, CA: Center for U.S.-Mexican Studies, University of California, San Diego, 1995); Laurence Steinberg, B. Bradford Brown, and Sanford M. Dornbusch, *Beyond the Classroom: Why School Reform Has Failed and What Parents Need to Do* (New York: Simon & Schuster, 1996); and Carola and Marcelo Suárez-Orozco, *Transformations: Immigration, Family Life and Achievement Motivation among Latino Adolescents* (Stanford, CA: Stanford University Press, 1995).

32 The data reported is largely cross-sectional panel data – some of it self-reported. Better-quality longitudinal data is now needed to develop a more clear sense of the factors leading to these worrisome trends. See National Research Council, *From Generation to Generation.* Quote from ibid., 159.

33 Rúmbaut, "The New Californians."

34 Quoted in Roberto Suro, *Strangers Among Us: How Latino Immigration is Transforming America* (New York: Alfred Knopf, 1998), 13.

35 See "Wanted: American Physicists," *New York Times*, July 23, 1999:A27. Of course, not all of these foreign-born physics graduate students are immigrants – some will indeed return to their countries of birth while others will surely go on

to have productive scientific careers in the United States.

36 See AnnaLee Saxenian, *Silicon Valley's New Immigrant Entrepreneurs* (San Francisco, CA: Public Policy Institute of California, 1999). I am thankful to Professor Michael Jones-Correa of the department of government at Harvard University for alerting me to this important new study.

37 See, for example, George Borjas, "Assimilation in Cohort Quality Revisited: What Happened to Immigrant Earnings in the 1980s?" *Journal of Labor Economics* 13(2) (1995), 211–245.

38 See Waldinger and Bozorgmehr, *Ethnic Los Angeles.*

39 William Wilson, *When Work Disappears: The World of the New Urban Poor* (New York: Vintage Books, 1997).

40 Douglas Massey and Nancy Denton, *American Apartheid* (Cambridge, MA: Harvard University Press, 1993).

41 See Dowell Myers, "Dimensions of Economic Adaptation by Mexican-Origin Men," in Suárez-Orozco, ed., *Crossings: Mexican Immigration in Interdisciplinary Perspectives*, 188.

42 See Richard Murnane, *Teaching the New Basic Skills: Principles for Educating Children to Thrive in a Changing Economy* (New York: Martin Kessler Books, Free Press, 1996).

43 In one such site, one of our research assistants found that boys sneak out of school at noon to watch pornographic films at a shop across the street from the school. Many of these schools are dilapidated and unkempt. Violence is pervasive. In an elementary school, a young girl was found raped and murdered on school premises. In another, an irate parent stabbed a teacher in front of her students. In yet another school, just days after the Columbine incident, a cherry bomb was set off as one of our research assistants was conducting an interview. In many schools there is tremendous ethnic tension. In one of our sites, students regularly play a game they call "Rice and Beans" (Asian students versus Latino students) that frequently deteriorates into physical violence. In many sites immigrant students report living in constant fear; they dread lunch and class changes as the hallways are sites of confrontation and intimidation, including sexual violence.

44 An ethnographic study of a number of immigrant schools in Miami found that three factors were consistently present in schools with "cultures of violence." First, school officials tended to deny that the school had problems with violence or drugs. Second, many of the school staff members exhibited "non-caring" behaviors toward the students. Third, the schools took lax school-security measures. See Michael Collier, "Cultures of Violence in Miami-Dade Public Schools," working paper of the Immigration and Ethnicity Institute, Florida International University, November 1998.

45 These schools affect the opportunities and experiences of immigrant children in several immediate ways. They tend to have limited resources. Classrooms are typically overcrowded. Textbooks and curricula are outdated; computers are few and obsolete. Many of the teachers may not have credentials in the subjects they teach. Clearly defined tracks sentence students to noncollege destinations. Lacking English skills, many immigrant students are often enrolled in the least demanding and competitive classes that eventually exclude them from courses needed for college. These schools generally offer few (if any) Advanced Placement courses that are critical for entry in many of the more competitive colleges. The guidance counselor–student ratio is impossibly high. Because the settings are so undesirable, teachers and principals routinely transfer out in search of better assignments elsewhere. As a result, in many such schools, there is little continuity or sense of community. Children and teachers are often preoccupied with ever-present violence and morale is often very low.

46 For a superb but somewhat pessimistic study of how "persistent, blatant racial discrimination" along with inferior schools in high-crime neighborhoods is implicated in the transgenerational decline of West Indian immigrants in New York City, see Mary Waters, *Black Identities: West Indian Immigrant Dreams and American Realities* (Cambridge, MA: Harvard University Press, 1999).

47 Massey and Denton, *American Apartheid.*

48 See Carola Suárez-Orozco, "Identities Under Siege," in Antonius Robben and Marcelo M. Suárez-Orozco, eds., *Cultures Under Siege: Collective Violence and Trauma* (New York: Cambridge University Press, 2000).

49 For an overview of recent research on immigration and family ties, see Ruben Rúmbaut, "Ties that Bind: Immigration and Immigrant Families in the United States," in Alan Booth, Ann C. Crouter, and Nancy Landale, eds., *Immigration and the Family: Research and Policy on U.S. Immigrants* (New Jersey: Lawrence Erlbaum, 1996). See also Suárez-Orozco and Suárez-Orozco, *Transformations: Immigration, Family Life and Achievement*

Motivation Among Latino Adolescents and Celia Falicov, *Latino Families in Therapy: A Guide to Multicultural Practice* (New York: Guilford, 1998). For an overview of immigrant optimism and achievement orientation, see Grace Kao and Marta Tienda, "Optimism and Achievement: The Educational Performance of Immigrant Youth," *Social Science Quarterly* 96 (1995), 1–19.

50 See Suárez-Orozco and Suárez-Orozco, *Children of Immigration*.

51 I concur with Teresa LaFromboise and her colleagues on the need to reconceptualize what they call the "linear model of cultural acquisition." See Teresa LaFromboise et al., "Psychological Impact of Biculturalism: Evidence and Theory," in Pamela Balls Organista, Kevin M. Chun, and Gerardo Marin, eds., *Readings in Ethnic Psychology* (New York: Routledge, 1998).

52 Margaret Gibson articulates a theoretical argument on immigrant transculturation and a calculated strategy of "accommodation without assimilation" in her study of highly successful Sikh immigrants in California. See Margaret Gibson, *Accommodation without Assimilation: Sikh Immigrants in an American High School* (Ithaca, NY: Cornell University Press, 1988). For a theoretical statement on the psychology of ethnic identity and cultural pluralism, see Jean S. Phinney, "Ethnic Identity in Adolescents and Adults: Review of Research," in Organista, Chun, and Marin, eds., *Readings in Ethnic Psychology*.

53 By unilinear assimilation I mean the idea that various immigrant groups have followed roughly a single path of assimilation.

54 Bounded national projects is a counterpoint to the idea that today transnationalism means, inter alia, that nations are becoming increasingly enmeshed or "unbounded," to borrow Linda Basch's word. Basch, Schiller, and Blanc, *Nations Unbound*.

55 See, for example, Nathan Glazer and Daniel Patrick Moynihan, *Beyond the Melting Pot* (Cambridge, MA: MIT Press, 1970).

56 Oscar Handlin, *The Uprooted* (Boston: Little, Brown, 1951).

3

Dousing the Fire or Fanning the Flames: The Role of Human Relations Practitioners in Intergroup Conflicts

Judith Goode

Ester[1] was sent to an emergency meeting to "represent her people" (Puerto Ricans) by her white parish priest, an active participant in a local human relations consortium. The meeting was called to promote local unity in the aftermath of two interracial youth murders.[2] The assembled group was comprised of leaders from the many human relations organizations in Philadelphia and local residents who had voluntarily given up their evening because they wanted to prevent additional violence and build community relations in the rapidly changing neighborhood. When one white speaker mentioned racism in relation to the fact that the Puerto Rican youths had yelled "Let's get whitey" before the murder, an angry Puerto Rican woman shouted, "Puerto Ricans are *victims* of oppression. We cannot be racist; only white people can be racist." Ester joined with her fellow Puerto Ricans in the angry shouting that ensued. She did this despite the presence of white community members with whom she had close personal ties.

Ester was a 38-year-old single mother who was born on the island where she lived until the age of 8. Her best friends were both white and Puerto Rican. The godparent of her children was an Italian-American neighbor and the children of both households moved freely back and forth between them playing, sharing meals, and sleeping. In her activist parish, Ester maintained a large network of both white and Puerto Rican friends who had lent her money to buy her house. She talked about her affection for and reliance on her friends, saying "They are always there for me." The multiracial parish was engaged in many campaigns to stem local decline. In this moment, Ester's identity as a Puerto Rican and her loyalty to the multiracial coalition of poor people were split. Ester looked a little embarrassed as she chose sides against her assembled white friends.

The Puerto Rican speaker was referring to the logic of structural racism which recognizes the historic institutionalization of white privilege and racial exclusion in the United States. Her white working-class neighbors who implicitly reject this structural argument which implicates them, see racism as located in individual beliefs and actions. To them, both murders followed the logic of revenge killing and were equally motivated by racial bias. These whites were tired of being viewed by the middle-class human relations experts and the media as the primary repositories of racism in the city.

This is but one example of the racially infused conflicts that are occurring in declining urban neighborhoods throughout the United States (Gregory 1998; Hartigan 1999; Rieder 1985; Sanjek 1998).[3] At the meeting, once structural racism was evoked, Ester had no choice but to identify with Puerto Ricans as victims of racism. At the same time, her white friends had no space in which to speak. In public spaces like this healing event, whites are often silenced by an oversimplified rhetoric of structural racism which ignores the role of class and power in creating hegemonic beliefs and practices. This event, like many others, produced a setback for the collective actions of the poor multiracial coalition.

Ester's personal ambivalence illustrates the contradictory relationships and identities which pervade impoverished changing neighborhoods in Philadelphia. As poor whites and minorities increasingly live together in places from which capital investment and public services have been withdrawn, they sometimes forge relationships of trust and interdependence across racial lines like Ester and her white friends. They are developing new politicized subjectivities as poor residents facing common oppressive constraints. Yet while they live in a time and place in which material inequality is rapidly growing, racialized identities and discourses are dominant in the public sphere. Racialized discourses are deployed pervasively, stereotypically, and divisively in public arenas, precluding any analysis of the ways in which race and class intersect in particular local formations. Yet as Hartigan (1999:279) demonstrates in his analysis of three Detroit neighborhoods, classed nuances and differences in spatial locations create varying significance for white racialness. He says: "The particular contours of spatial formations, with their distinct racial and class compositions, informs the discursive modes through which the significance of racialness is assessed, manipulated and negotiated." Such distinct circumstances can create openings or foreclose options for cross-racial, class-based collective action against the continued production of poverty.

The priest's action in sending Ester to represent her group is one example of the liberal public multicultural sensitivity developed by the institutions of government and civil society in the wake of the civil rights movement and the large wave of post-1965 immigration. Anthropologists and other social scientists have recently turned considerable attention to the nature of the U.S. racial hierarchy, the future of race and ethnic relations, and the intersection of race and class in the United States (Gregory and Sanjek 1994; Omi and Winant 1994). Anthropological contributions both broaden the context of this discussion and present the complexity, nuance, and variety in the way racial processes play out on the ground. Breadth is developed by placing these issues in a comparative world context which incorporates both postcolonial and national myths within a context of transnational movements of capital and labor (Basch et al. 1994; Williams 1989, 1993), or by examining how race, class, and ethnicity historically intersect in U.S.

discourses of nation-building (Brodkin 1998; Chock 1995; Dominguez 1995; Ignatiev 1995; Roediger 1990). Nuance and variety are also demonstrated through ethnographic studies of residential localities, particularly those experiencing rapid changes in racial, ethnic, and class composition as a result of economic decline or gentrification (Anderson 1990; Goode and Schneider 1994; Gregory 1998; Hartigan 1999; Horton 1995; Lamphere 1992; Portes and Stepick 1993; Rieder 1985; Sanjek 1998; Williams 1988).

In this literature about local conflict, little has been said about the role played by a new group of experts, the human relations specialists, like the white priest who sent Ester to the community meeting. These experts are usually agents of institutions of civil society such as clergy, or social service professionals such as teachers and social workers. They are charged with preventing or healing the local racial and anti-immigrant conflict which accompanies rapid, large-scale neighborhood turnover. Clergy draw their legitimacy from their moral authority while helping professionals draw theirs from presumed control of the technologies of psychological intervention to reform or educate morally flawed or "ignorant" people. Their practices are based on the assumption that racism is a problem of individuals to be eradicated through knowledge, moral reform, and/or therapeutic treatment of damaged egos.

In this essay, I will examine the role of such practitioners using ethnographic material from two communities. The data are drawn primarily from the Philadelphia Changing Relations Project.[4] Between 1988 and 1990, a team of 14 anthropologists engaged in fieldwork in two Philadelphia neighborhoods. For a two-year period, everyday activities on the block, in schools, and on the shopping strip, as well as activist campaigns in community organizations and special events (neighborhood celebrations and healing events in the wake of disruptive incidents) were observed. Community leaders and members of over 50 households were interviewed. Since 1990, as a member of the board of several community organizations, I have continued to keep track of continuity and change.

I argue that the new practices designed to treat inter-group conflict have had the unintended effect of undercutting the development of informal cross-racial local relationships like Ester's. The ironic result is that activities designed to reduce tensions have instead interfered with people's active and ongoing constructions of common interests. While the white working class generally projects an internalized sense of white privilege and is hostile toward overt discussions of racism and cultural nationalism, which they see as blaming them, some whites have forged a sense of common subjectivity based on class with neighbors of color. These have the potential to be sustained through collective political struggles since grassroots activism can, in some cases, engender the kind of local political spaces in which, as Gregory (1998) states, "people through collective actions render power visible and recognize themselves as political subjects." These actions enable poor whites to transcend dominant racial and ethnic assumptions. These moments of insight are fragile and difficult to sustain over time. The following examples illustrate what happens when powerful institutions, in an attempt to deal with racial tension, resort to dominant ethnic, racial, and multicultural constructions which leads to the reassertion of racialized identities.

I will demonstrate that it is through these human relations practices that experts interpret, transmit, and enforce simplified nation-building narratives and new state categories to local communities. At the same time, they fail to take into consideration the ways in which local decline produced by political and economic restructuring affects boundary formation and discourses of difference as they mask the larger political and economic power relationships which underlie local conflict. While decline has the potential to harden racial and ethnic boundaries, at the same time, as we see here, it can foster the development of intimate cross-racial ties in order to cope with everyday life, and sometimes can lead to collective demands on the state. In these cases, as the neighborhoods became targets of programs to quell racial disturbances, the very state discourses invoked to heal rifts actually perpetuated current hegemonic constructions of race and ethnicity to further emphasize naturalized difference, thus interfering with emerging politicized class identities.

The Setting

Once the largest manufacturing center in the United States, Philadelphia has been more affected than comparable cities by post-1970 economic restructuring.[5] The service economy based on health care and higher education upon which the city's wellbeing rests today is vulnerable to volatile shifts in state funding. Since the 1980s, the major urban development strategy has been the move to commodify the city as a tourist landscape of consumption for the new corporate professional and managerial classes (Ruben 2001; Zukin 1995) This tourist strategy and related development policy has encouraged gentrification which has further dislocated poor people and shrunk the pool of available affordable housing.

Philadelphia has played a major role in most of the critical population shifts in U.S. history. The city flourished as the major industrial center for most of the last century, making it an important destination for the immigration waves of the 19th and early 20th centuries (Adams et al. 1991). Initially racialized and excluded from the mainstream, the descendants of these immigrants were "whitened" after World War II as they entered the new middle-income groups created by organized labor and the expansion of the credentialed professional/managerial and technical class[6]. The city was also a significant point of new settlement for rural southern blacks who moved into a declining and segregated economy during the waves of migration between 1915 and 1960 (Adams et al. 1991).

The downturn in the local economy of today has reduced the role of the city as an immigrant destination. Philadelphia has been a minor destination for the new wave of Latin American, Caribbean, and Asian immigrants in relation to other cities. However, in the context of overall population loss, new immigrants are significant local populations (Goode and Schneider 1994). These populations are entering a racially divided city which is now 6 percent Hispanic and 3 percent Asian with the remaining 90 percent divided relatively equally between whites and blacks.

Hit hard by postwar suburbanization and extensive white flight, the population of the city is highly segregated residentially (Goldstein 1986). The eastern part of the city is predominantly white and the western zone predominantly black, a pattern which gradually emerged during the postwar population movements of black in-migration and white flight. The increasingly impoverished neighborhoods in this study are places where this color line was broken in the 1970s as the once white working-class neighborhoods connected to local industries were destabilized and materially devastated by economic restructuring. Corporate and state decisions produced household downward mobility and economic insecurity through plant closings and the loss of middle-income unionized jobs. New jobs in the service economy became bifurcated as either high-end professional-managerial or low-wage unskilled, part-time, and temporary work. Actions by banks, realtors, and state agencies further increased instability, housing abandonment, and blight through mortgage redlining, public housing and refugee resettlement policies, and realtor practices such as flight-inducing blockbusting. These neighborhoods now accommodate poor whites who cannot afford to relocate, blacks who have moved eastward in the wake of destruction of their housing stock, and new immigrants.

Olney in the north was for a long time a destination for the aspiring middle-class whites moving northward from the industrial heartland to the first rung of better housing stock. While it has experienced massive turnover in the past decade, it still houses a stream of newcomer upwardly mobile populations. Today, however, these aspiring middle-class populations are African Americans and immigrants from over 40 countries. As a group, the remaining downwardly mobile whites are poorer than Asians and Latinos who broke the color line and joined them, a fact which, as we will see, complicates the understanding of race and class. However, households are getting poorer across all populations. (Goode 1998).

In contrast, Kensington is one of the city's poorest neighborhoods. An industrial mill town since the early 1800s, Kensington's experience with plant closings accelerated in the 1960s. By the 1970s related actions of financial and government institutions had produced visible urban blight, the destruction of the private real estate market, and increased housing abandonment.

Those who could afford to leave moved out of the area. The church congregations and civic associations they had sustained died out. Today, Kensington houses the poorest whites and Latinos in the city (Goode and Schneider 1994). The bulk of Latino institutions are in Kensington. In the 1980s new residents also included increasing numbers of blacks, Southeast Asian refugees placed by agencies, and some Korean and Palestinian merchants.

The color line had been guarded previously in these two neighborhoods by incidents of harassment and vandalism. In the 1970s there were many conflict incidents when the first racial minority households moved in. Today there are still some incidents of violence like the murders referred to above. There are also pockets of active nativists organized into formal organizations and informal gangs who respond to "move-ins." In addition to the small but active number of visible racist/nativists, downward mobility across racial lines has generated less visible interracial and interethnic tensions produced through private discourses of racial resentment (Adams et al. 1991; Goode and Schneider 1994). For example, some established residents close ranks and use racial rhetoric to strengthen preexisting social boundaries in order to defend their sense of seniority and "ownership" of local public spaces. They feel resentment because in many cases immigrants/people of color are better off economically. This does not fit the historically formed ideology of naturalized white superiority which allowed poor whites to displace their abjection onto poor minorities (DuBois 1992[1934]; Roediger 1990.) The success of racial minorities is resented and explained through a belief that immigrants and native-born blacks receive special benefits from an unfair state.

At the same time, many immigrants maintain strong structures of mutual aid and retain their native language for everyday social interaction. They often participate in cultural identity movements which anticipate and defend against white racist actions. Mobilizing for collective action to bid for power, they develop discourses of cultural nationalism which can deploy essentialist and naturalized ideas about race and ethnicity. This essentialism frequently produces assertions of their own collective moral superiority. Rather than advocating an end to hierarchy and inequality, one woman, when asked what she had learned in a multicultural workshop, said: "I learned that one day [my group] may get to be on top." Simultaneously but separately, Puerto Ricans, Koreans, and Afrocentrists talked about their morally superior family structures and communal values and talked against the allegedly selfish, individualistic values of whites.

Nonetheless, there are also dynamics developing in these neighborhoods which push people toward a common identity as neighbors. Philadelphia is a city of row houses. It is important to note that these two neighborhoods differ from others in which ethnographers have studied race relations (Gregory 1998; Merry 1986; Rieder 1985; Sanjek 1998). Separate populations are not clustered on mono-racial blocks or high-rise housing projects interacting warily in shared and contested public spaces and institutions. Instead, especially in Olney, the blocks we studied were themselves residentially integrated. It is ironic that these mixed neighborhoods which are seen by suburbanites as hotbeds of racial conflict were actually settings for much more everyday interracial collaboration than the segregated settlements and workplaces of the suburbs.

Developing Intimacy, Empathy, and Trust

Day-to-day community life in many instances can engender multiracial harmony in many of the following ways. However, as Ester's example demonstrates, it is difficult to transform these personal understandings into interventions in public discourse or political action which contradicts the hegemonic discourses about U.S. social categories. In fact, the very actions of state governance, economic policy, and hegemonic discourses of difference often interfere with the conversion of these emerging relations of trust into political identities and actions. As Steven Gregory states, "Hegemony works less on the hearts and minds of the disempowered than on their ability to articulate and exercise a political identity able to realize the social force necessary to change the order of power relations" (Gregory 1998:246).

Our fieldwork demonstrated that these neighborhoods contained many strong bonds of intimacy, empathy, and trust which crossed such socially constructed boundaries as those between poor whites and people of color, or new immigrants and established citizens. For example, intermarried households are common in the communities, and these mixed families feel at home in schools and churches. Sally, a white woman married to a black man, worries about having to move, "Where else can I move in the city where my kids don't get called names? There's nothing they need to feel out of place about here. There are so many other children of intermarriage." Anna, a white woman, describes the warm relationship that developed with the family of her black son-in-law after a rocky start. Linda jokes, "You can't call me prejudiced, all my nieces and nephews [children of her two sisters] are black and Latino."

Meaningful neighborhood exchanges were also common. Elena, a young Nicaraguan, and Ann, a 70-year-old daughter of Eastern European immigrants, spend their days together. Elena drives her older neighbor Ann everywhere in return for English language lessons on the stoop. Carmen, a woman from Colombia, is arranging for her sister to deliver an almost new sofa to her neighbor Pat in return for the "many times she helped me out." Many neighbors are engaged in critical social exchanges like babysitting. Carol babysits for seven mothers on her block. They include "Spanish [street term for Latino], Turkish, Indian, and from the islands [Haitian]...a real United Nations. My mother said, you have everyone but an Oriental. I told her it wouldn't be long. My Korean neighbor is pregnant." Carol often talks about how the common interest in the children's welfare brings the women close together as they share intimate details of their everyday lives. Ester talks about her intimate conversations with white neighbors about problems with ex-spouses, "I've learned their men are just like ours. We're just the same." Mary talks about how her Latino neighbors watch her daughters as they move throughout the neighborhood. "If they get into trouble, I would hear right away. They really watch out for us." In many cases, these relationships do not merely lead to a view that the friend is a rare and exceptional member of their race, but provide entrée into intimate and increasingly shared social worlds of extended families and celebratory events.

Through friendship, some whites become sensitized to the ways in which people of color encounter overt racism daily, and develop strong empathy for their situation. For example, Anita, an Olney descendant of turn-of-the-century European immigrants, often described her indignation about the way one of her husband's workmates in a public transportation job, a black woman and close friend of the family, faced discrimination from customers. We see this process discussed as well in Zavella (2001).

Several conditions foster the move from bonds of intimacy and common subjectivity to active political struggle. First, the context of the neoliberal withdrawal of public services (school overcrowding, loss of security, recreation infrastructural maintenance) engenders grievances against state and market practices producing a potential for community action to wrest improvements in quality of life from the state. Secondly, many of these households had succumbed to pressure for white flight. They describe being "run out" of North Philadelphia a generation ago as a result of realtor-induced panic. They talk about resisting panic flight and digging in their heels to save their institutions through incorporating minority residents as political allies.[7]

Ongoing constructions of common subjectivity among diverse new neighbors creates a potential site for mobilizing to confront the state. Most of this organizing is done by women through "activist mothering" (Naples 1998:11–12), defined as "political activism as a central component of mothering", in which women "draw on traditional female identities to justify taking revolutionary action to improve the community and the lives of their families."[8] These activities emerge from friendship cliques, informal block groups, and formal institutions and contribute to a sense of common subjectivity as beleaguered neighbors. In Philadelphia these took the form of campaigns for child safety, demands for playgrounds and new recreation programs, protest movements in response to school overcrowding, and actions to get the city to close and seal drug houses. In many instances, these place-based, child-oriented oppositional activities also serve to move these women from personal feelings of empathy and trust to action through politicized identities as poor mothers confronting the state.

Staughton Lynd (2000:21) recently critiqued those who wish to bring about anti-racist ideological change in workers' movements by "preaching door to door." He stated, "Racism too will be transformed by experience and struggle...As workers' *actions* change in response to the need for solidarity in which the survival of each depends on the survival of all, *attitudes* will change also." Many local campaigns, first engendered by common subjectivity, not only produced new demands on the state, but disrupted the old racial order. With increased awareness and anger at the racialized discourses directed against their neighbors, several whites severed relationships with racist relatives, intervened publicly against racial statements and joined anti-racist movements. For example, in Kensington, we had known Mary for a year when her house burned down. The relatives of Mary and her husband urged them to move away from the increasingly Latino neighborhood. One of them, referring to the neighborhood, said, "It's not going down anymore; it already went when Hispanics moved in." Yet the family, engaged in several local community campaigns, told their relatives to leave them alone, decided to stay, and bought another house a block away. Such new deracialized identities in turn moved the political struggles forward.

Candy provides one example of this shift. Candy, angered by the threats to the safety of her children on the streets, organized a successful block organization with Puerto Rican, Vietnamese, Brazilian, and Palestinian neighbors. The group has met monthly for several years. It demanded that the city close a drug house and provide recreational facilities. As a result of this activity, Candy convinced her husband to stay in the neighborhood and continued to play a significant role in local cross-racial political campaigns (Goode 1998; Goode and Schneider 1994). Loretta tells a similar story. During a crisis in her family, a Latina neighbor became "like a sister" to her. Their children are best friends. She was horrified by the way her own extended family talked about "that Hispanic boy," whom she sees as a fictive nephew and who was allowed to come in without knocking and to stay for meals or a sleepover. Her white kin and friends have been exhorting Loretta to leave the neighborhood for years. Yet Loretta, a mother of four, like many other white residents is attached to place. She has actively created bonds with her new neighbors of different backgrounds. She has been active in the home and school association and her parish for years. She does not drive and finds the local shopping strip to be convenient for everything. She felt she had to cut herself off from her racist relatives. She led parents from different backgrounds to organize and sustain a protest against school district practices of bussing children of color out of the mixed neighborhood in order to integrate a more solidly white community.[9] She devoted two years to a campaign to foster new school construction and maximum integration. The campaign ultimately succeeded in attaining limited court-ordered construction.[10] Loretta says, "Look at what we can do if we just stick together and fight for what's best for our kids. It took a lot of work to get us all together, especially the mothers that don't speak good English, but we were all being pushed around by the school district; so we had to do something."

Human Relations Specialists and their Discourses

In a city full of public and quasi-public agencies working against racism and violence, the human relations experts representing institutions of civil society respond quickly to racial incidents through formal programs. Seeking local stability and order they are either willfully ignorant or fearful of the many actual and potential cross-racial networks and activities which are developing informally on the ground to demand resources.

Philadelphia had a long history of inter-group violence, such as anti-Catholic riots perpetrated in Kensington by the Protestant English textile workers against Irish immigrants in the early eighteenth century. The significant antebellum population of free African Americans continued to grow during and after the Civil War (DuBois 1992 [1934]). The majority of Ignatiev's examples of Irish riots against blacks use Philadelphia-based incidents. Southern and Eastern European Slavic and Jewish migration at the turn of the twentieth century again produced significant nativist and religious or race-based violence. In 1947, the immediate postwar period, and in the early days of the civil rights movement, the first, and still active, human relations institution in the country called the Fellowship Commission was created to deal with racial incidents. These efforts were spearheaded and sustained by strong Quaker, Jewish, and African American organizations separately and in collaboration. A publicly funded Human Relations Commission soon followed.

Throughout fieldwork, the ethnographic team encountered a dense network of organizations and programs engaged in teaching tolerance to reduce conflict and to defuse tensions when incidents did occur.[11] They came to train local leaders and the growing network of citywide public and non-profit agencies for crisis intervention which had recently developed. Over the two years of formal fieldwork, we went to over 20 agency- or university-sponsored citywide and neighborhood "trainings," which featured the same keynote speakers and facilitators, both white and black.

While the cases discussed below occured in local community organizations, the major focus of human relations activity were civil institutions such as schools, hospitals, and workplaces as well as institutions of criminal justice. The purpose of the training was to smooth over conflicts and misunderstandings which interfered with institutional goals. In addition, several crisis intervention networks in the city which had developed to counter gang and drug activity also became players in the human relations network. It was during this period that "diversity" or "multicultural" training was being formally institutionalized. In the communities, students of all ages, teachers, clergy, policemen, and social workers were all experiencing human relations/multicultural training.

Who was doing the training and what were their credentials? Most of those who worked in this field were self-taught and learned through on-the-job experience, perhaps a few brief packaged workshops and some courses in group dynamics and intercultural communication. They were often promoted from the ranks of workers in hospitals, the police department, crisis intervention outreach workers, and the school district to be experts in race and multiculturalism. When we began fieldwork in 1988, two of the well-known trainers had just left their institutional employers (the school district and a hospital) to set themselves up as private consultants. Both were self-taught experts. One, a former teacher, had been promoted to a high-level school district job training teachers in multiculturalism; his sessions were reported to be entertaining and "great fun." The other was a former hospital social worker who thought her experience dealing with families from different backgrounds and her own attendance at training workshops had prepared her well. Now that the corporate world had become interested in diversity training as a form of social control and conflict prevention for their employees, these two individuals each set up shop as independent consultants hoping for more lucrative corporate contracts, but still willing to service the developing demand of the school district and health-care institutions for diversity expertise.[12] The expensive nature of these trainings was captured in the comment of a professional staff member of a community-based non-profit organization when she decided to use a large part of a neighborhood human relations grant (see below) to hire a pricey corporate diversity trainer to provide a local workshop. As she exhorted local leaders of the organization to come, she said, "You are getting quite a bargain; corporations pay hundreds of dollars a day for this workshop and you are getting it for nothing."

Discourses of Difference

Recent theorizing about race and class formations illustrate the contingent nature of racial hierarchies and discourses of difference. As a "nation of immigrants," U.S. nation-building narratives focus on creating unity out of diversity. Prior to World War II, U.S. national unity was promoted through institutional policies of Anglo-conformity and assimilation. At the same time, racializing ideas and practices were used to exclude economically exploited populations such as former slaves and exploited labor migrants from inclusion in the unified nation.[13] Recent scholarship helps us understand the ways in which race, class, and politics were intertwined in earlier moments of history such as the nineteenth-century formation of the industrial working class (Ignatiev 1995; Roediger 1990) and the postwar period of suburbanization (Brodkin 1998; Sacks 1994). Each significant shift produced new discourses of inclusion and exclusion.

Human relations practitioners do not employ an understanding of historic contingency in their programs. Instead they use one of two widely accepted national narratives. The first is a liberal pluralist multicultural understanding which ignores class and figures race as a kind of ethnic identity. This model is individualistic, superficial, and diverts attention away from the structural economic conditions and power relations between the state and neighborhoods that shape institutional racism while focusing on a myth of structural equality and individual blame.

The second mode of understanding race and class is more progressive. This model attends to the structural conditions that produce poverty and class stratification. However, it tends to conflate race and class, implicitly assuming that most blacks and Latinos are poor or working-class, while most white people are middle-class. While this assumption has a significant degree of empirical support in the aggregate,[14] this view is limited in the insights it provides into the actual dynamics of multiracial poor and working-class communities.

The post-civil rights narratives deployed in some of the following cases reflects new discursive relationships promulgated by the state. The civil rights movement called attention to the history of race-based exclusion and demanded redress. As a result, OMB Directive 15 (1977) brought race explicitly and officially into the picture as the state reified five categories of difference largely for the purpose of collecting information to monitor civil rights remedies. Four categories were considered racial (black, white, Asian/Pacific Islander, American Indian) while one, Hispanic, was designated ethnic (based on shared culture and language). Some discursive uses of official racial categories further conflated race and class. They located the source of all social disadvantage in race, further muting the significance of class position, and fostered a view of class homogeneity within racial categories.

In the 1970s, as the state funded bicentennial celebration activities, the liberal narrative of cultural pluralism was institutionalized partly to counteract the negative historical reading of racial oppression. The new narrative focused on national heritages and interpreted the United States as a nation of immigrant groups within a context of equality of opportunity, with each group making positive cultural contributions to the "mosaic" or "tapestry" that is the nation. Rather than extol Anglo-conformity or assimilation, each group was valued for its difference, and encouraged to highlight its contributions to the nation. In asserting the equivalent cultural value of each group the hierarchy of worthiness based on race or class was effectively denied (Dominguez 1995; Williams 1989, 1993). In fact, Steinberg (1981) asserts that the very revival of the new ethnic pluralism on the part of European-origin groups occurred partly to deny the structural racism revealed through the civil rights movement. The shift to an emphasis on culture (ethnic, national-origin heritage) rather than race allowed each ethnic group to claim both valuable cultural contributions of "difference" and equivalent histories of struggle and suffering. The mosaic or tapestry model was institutionalized during the bicentennial celebrations in the 1970s which funded the organization of groups, museums, and celebrations based on national-origin identities (Goode 1998).

Over time, official OMB racial categories have been appropriated by the cultural pluralism discourse to become semi-official categories of multiculturalism: African American, Asian American, Native American, Hispanic, and European American. In this usage whites are not placed in opposition to excluded people demanding rights but are included as just another category representing different but equivalent, unranked cultural/behavioral traits.

Since Philadelphia served as the national location for bicentennial celebrations, museums and multicultural festivals proliferated in the 1970s and remain today as part of downtown life. Constituent groups of the U.S. mosaic are represented by ethnic museum exhibits, cultural performance groups, ethnic foods, and folkloric crafts. These festivals can be seen as part of the culture and arts industry which is being developed to turn the city center into a landscape of consumption attracting the commerce of overconsuming suburbanites, urban gentry, and tourists. For these diversity-seeking populations, such events fill the same desire for authenticity and exotica that is filled by the proliferation of international travel, new restaurant cuisines, and shopping venues such as the retail chain called Anthropologie. They allow the new professional and managerial classes to become cosmopolitan participants in the new global world scene liberated from the soulless modernity of bureaucratic work as well as from racism and the fear of otherness.

This is an important part of the liberal pluralist multiculturalism which was invoked to deal with neighborhood conflict in the city, as formerly white neighborhoods became racially mixed. Human relations specialists prided themselves in their knowledge and politically correct discussions of race. Fearing disorder from what they perceived as irrational, unruly masses of white working-class racists, they responded to conflict incidents with a repertoire of therapeutic interventions but little local knowledge. Human relations specialists, clergy, and teachers who valued cosmopolitan multicultural consumption in their private lives thought it to be only common sense that similar events invoking a liberal pluralist mosaic of equivalent cultural differences would resolve conflict caused by the ignorant fear of the "Other" in poor multiracial neighborhoods. Teaching about official categories of racial and ethnic difference and exposing people to exotic cultural performances and aestheticized commodities through "multicultural appreciation" would end this fear.

The following cases illustrate how these healing events interfere with local political struggles and their promise for transcending racialized political identities. Instead, when faced with the simplified anti-racist discourse, activists like Ester are forced to choose a side, while the cultural pluralist events not only promote a false ideology of equality which hides the actual sources of inequality, but simultaneously allow space for covert messages of difference and hierarchy to creep in through the reification and naturalization of racial and ethnic difference in the name of pluralism.

Healing Events

The overwhelming preference for multicultural performances was illustrated by one citywide initiative, the Neighborhood Human Relations Project (NHRP) which distributed several hundred thousand dollars to fund such programming.[15] The administrator of NHRP often expressed unlimited faith in such folklore-based programs to solve local problems: "People will eat each other's food and enjoy each other's culture and tensions will melt away. They will know how to understand each other." Avoiding race and power, such festivals limited culture to aesthetic domains. They avoided confronting those cultural stereotypes connected to moral conflict zones of family structures and work ethics. Demonstrating the desire for consuming exotic commodities, one workshop sponsor urged the audience to approach multicultural situations "as if you are going into a museum looking for treasures." Another spoke of "the adrenaline rush I get when I hear other languages on the street and see the crafts in store windows."

These remedies totally ignored: (1) the material structures of inequality produced by late capitalism; (2) the ideological structures of institutionalized racism which conflate race and class; and (3) the contradictions between the ideology of white privilege/superiority and the poverty and downward mobility of poor whites. In so doing, they ignore the existence of poverty and continue to produce the anger and displaced abjection which trigger most conflict incidents. In the following analysis of several events, I will illustrate the ways in which the simplistic narratives deployed by institutional agents are contested by residents while at the same time they continue to disrupt the developing sense of collective agency in the face of increasing poverty. We can see that, while intending to avoid distinctions in race and power, multicultural celebrations often subtly pointed out such differences. The attempt to display equivalent cultural components only called attention to the actual differences in each group's place in the hierarchy, further separated people into categories, and did not address any of the material or ideological roots of racial discrimination and poverty.

An Olney parish festival

One activist parish in Olney was the site of many campaigns for neighborhood improvement. As the neighborhood changed, the parish recruited new members along racial/ethnic lines by offering mass in several languages and by creating separate clubs and musical groups for each newcomer population. While informal activities such as volunteering in the parish school, or participating in clean-up and beautification programs, created friendships, formal activities channeled people into separate groups. The parish, faced with these self-inflicted divisions, tried to create unity through multicultural appreciation days which ultimately exacerbated boundaries and produced contradictions and resistance.

Half of the parish membership consisted of established residents, descendants of turn-of-the-century European immigrants. The other half was comprised of newcomers to the neighborhood: native-born blacks and immigrants from Puerto Rico, Colombia and Central America, Korea, Laos, Portugal, South Asia, and the Caribbean. Long-term parishioners had expressed some resentment about the special events and masses for new immigrants. They complained that, while new parishioners dressed better, drove newer cars and brought expensive video cameras and cellphones to events, they did not donate time as volunteers or contribute to the many necessary parish fundraising drives.

As a tide of NHRP-funded multicultural events flooded Olney in the wake of an incident (see below), the clergy decided that a parish celebration of cultural difference was what was needed to create unity. The unity festival intended to promote the idea that we are all descendants of immigrants who have struggled in the U.S. Yet by treating populations differently, the event further inscribed a line between "whitened" turn-of-the-century immigrants and newcomers, who were treated as "subordinated subnationals" (Williams 1989). Ultimately, the priest's attempts to organize the event according to the national narrative of cultural pluralism was ultimately contested by both new immigrants and established residents.

The celebration was typical of most local multicultural events. Held in the main public spaces of the parish school, the day's activities included a fair held in the gym and playground where different ethnic groups offered games of chance similar to those offered at school and community fairs. Immigrant groups sponsored games from their home countries. Individuals and families traveled from booth to booth in the early morning. The main attractions were the communal events which occurred in the large school auditorium/lunchroom. In the morning, women set the eating tables and organized the presentation of food at food tables around the perimeter. The midday meal was followed by a formal sequence of cultural performances on stage.

Two priests had organized the event. National identities characteristic of bicentennial pluralism were ascribed to descendants of European immigrants. In contrast, blacks and new immigrant groups were lumped together in the large panethnic categories of post-1970s multiculturalism. These categories ignored national identity and lumped immigrant populations as Asians, Hispanics, etc. Ironically, these usages reversed people's self-constructed identities. National labels were used for those for whom they were no longer salient and denied to recent immigrants for whom national origin was central.

In these former white working-class neighborhoods, national identity had ceased to be salient to descendants of turn-of-the-century immigrants. In the postwar period, the strong circumscription of marriage of descendants of turn-of-the-century immigrants to those of the same national origin gave way to broader intermarriage among all white Catholics (Goode 1998). At the same time, "whiteness" had been extended to these former immigrants and their descendants in reaction to their shared (as opposed to segregated) war experiences, the federally aided creation of new white middle-class suburbs, and reactions to the civil rights movement. The formerly "not quite white" saw themselves as patriotic white Americans rather than immigrants with national-origin identities. At anti-racist workshops, many individuals refused to provide ethnic labels on their name tags and often joked about their hybrid ancestry as they rejected the old nationality labels which in this context marked them as other.[16]

The organizers, in emphasizing the national origins of established Americans, were reflecting their experience with bicentennial national discourses which placed Anglo-European sending nations at the center of the national origin myth. Knowing nothing about the nation-states of other regions which had sent forth the bulk of post-1965 immigrants, the "race"-based OMB panethnic categories were used for new immigrants. They were simple and convenient. Yet treating old and new immigrants differently contradicted the narrative of equivalence and further underscored differences between unmarked whiteness and racially marked others.

The preparation for the festival inadvertently itself reinforced differences between newcomers and established white residents, as no attempt was made to encourage established parishioners to relinquish their "insider" status. At a planning meeting attended by white women regulars accustomed to running parish celebrations, these women were allowed to organize themselves in customary fashion. At the same time, the priest in charge took responsibility for paternalistically organizing those he called "the ethnics" (immigrants). He selected brokers he knew from each immigrant group and contacted them by phone, precluding any contact between them and other participants. The priest's constant use of the gloss "the ethnics" for immigrants also marked their separateness, as did the encouragement of the use of native language and exotic costumes and practices. Festival organizers encouraged exoticism in the cultural performances of new immigrants, thus exaggerating difference. After a performance, they criticized a South Asian Indian and a Puerto Rican group for singing songs in English instead of their native languages. In both cases, the people had been subjects in English-speaking colonial situations and were indeed reflecting cultural practices from their homelands.

The event ultimately became a series of segregated components. The early morning set-up was dominated by established women who were used to controlling the kitchen space in the hall. Two Latina women had begun to participate in these kitchen activities during the year and were developing relations with the oldtimers. While they helped out today, they were marked as other by queries and comments about their cuisine depicted by whites as "spicy" or "too hot," separating their dishes from the Americanized dishes these women had prepared.

At the event, clergy ran into resistance from European American groups when the women removed the nationality signs and flags (Polish, Irish, German, Italian) placed on the tables by the clergy and put up a hastily constructed American flag. As they had worked together in the rectory kitchen over the years to prepare food events, the long-term parishioners had developed an integrated "American" menu which incorporated common Anglo, Italian, and Central European elements that were now part of the national cuisine. The same foods – different kinds of sausages, deli meats in gravy and sauce, and mayonnaise salads (coleslaw, potato salad, and macaroni salad) – were always prepared collectively the night before in the rectory kitchen, reflecting the pattern of avoidance of ethnic markers. As they prepared the food, women often referred to similarities between particular national cuisines, commenting on how sausages or cabbage could be found across them all. In contrast, the immigrant groups' food contributions were prepared in people's homes and were highly marked in style and content.

At the same time, new immigrants from Puerto Rico, Colombia, Nicaragua, Guatemala, El Salvador, and Mexico, for whom nationality was critical, tore down the large Hispanic banner which the priests had placed on one table and ran home for flags and other items of national pride as they strongly asserted homeland identities. Such national identities remain central for immigrants increasingly living in and imagining futures in transnational social fields. In addition, as Basch et al. (1994) demonstrate, for many Caribbean peoples, strong national identities are deployed to avoid racialization as blacks. In Philadelphia, many non-Puerto Rican Latinos, growing numbers from the Dominican Republic, Colombia, and elsewhere use national identities to avoid being identified as Puerto Ricans, who are also stigmatized as both stateless (colonized) and underclass. We frequently were told by individuals from South and Central America that Puerto Ricans should be ashamed of their commonwealth status (as opposed to national independence), that Puerto Rican women were "too attractive" (overtly sexual), and that Puerto Ricans "just don't know how to behave" (Goode 1998; Goode and Schneider 1994: 83).

The event reinforced boundaries in other ways as well. As newcomer groups brought their dishes in, there was some jockeying for the best locations in table space. There had also been some competition over the sequence of performance times. At the festival itself, people clustered at their own game booths and food tables. They also tended to leave after their own group had performed. Moreover, several of the more well-to-do immigrant groups invested significant resources in costumes and props for their performance, thus reinforcing the resentment of less well-off established whites. In spite of this, the event, in marking "the ethnics" as different served to underscore white ownership of the parish and reinforced boundaries, both self-ascribed and imposed.

The festival developed by the activist parish was based on the common template of multicultural appreciation: the mosaic notion of equivalent aesthetic cultures promulgated by local elites through the Neighborhood Human Relations Project. The failure of this simplified narrative to encompass the complexities and contradictions of group relations in everyday life led to a covert invocation of differences between groups by treating white established residents differently from immigrants. The latter were placed in panethnic rather than national categories, called "the ethnics" by the organizer, and treated as subordinates needing paternalistic care in the preparation and planning phase. These actions both undermined contact and reinscribed divisions. While there were subtle cues like the elaborateness of costumes and stage sets which depicted some newcomer groups as well-to-do, the priests' willful ignoring of the intertwined class and race issues which underlay parish tensions left the fissures at most exacerbated or at least intact. For a parish developing collective neighborhood activism, this was an unfortunate outcome.

A Struggling Kensington CDC

Another set of problems, some similar and some different, emerged when an activist Community Development Corporation (CDC) in Kensington organized a cultural pluralist festival under the auspices of the NHRP. In this instance, the NHRP assumptions forced the same problems resulting from constructing descendants of turn-of-the-century European immigrants in terms of national origin rather than as white Americans. In contrast, Latino leaders also used their understandings of race and cultural nationalism to create an opposition between whites and racial minorities.

The CDC served a territory with a mixed Puerto Rican, white, and black constituency. The group was attempting to gain rights to local abandoned or tax delinquent homes in order to rehabilitate and rent them. It was working hard to overcome an earlier local reputation as an organization "for Puerto Ricans only." In order to change this image, the new executive director, a Puerto Rican professional and activist, had worked to integrate the board which now represented the mixed make-up of the community. She worked daily with poor whites and African Americans to collectively improve local living conditions. The organization had accepted NHRP money in the way underfunded non-profits often accept targeted external resources. They hoped the funds could be used to partially aid their core agenda. In this case they hoped to fund some local women who worked as volunteers. The money came with an expectation of a multicultural appreciation festival.

When no local household members identified themselves through the hyphenated national origin identities of the pluralist mosaic, Irish-born priests in a local mission for the homeless came to the rescue with a food display of colcannon, a potato and cabbage dish, and soda bread. The multicultural mosaic model also engendered a major controversy over the language of the flyers. To symbolize unity in diversity, the flyer, written in English, also included the word "welcome" in 11 languages, which symbolically represented both turn-of-the-century and current immigrants.

In actuality there were only two languages used in public settings: English and Spanish. The sponsoring community group ran all of its meetings in both languages. It was customary for all flyers posted locally to be bilingual. Angered by the absence of expected English–Spanish parity, some Spanish-speakers rejected this false symbolic representation of the neighborhood as a multi-lingual mosaic and wanted the flyers to represent the bilingual social reality. At one event-planning meeting, a local activist diverted the entire meeting to an argument about the flyer. "No Latino will come to this event if you don't have flyers in Spanish as well as English. This is a Spanish-speaking area and people have a right to expect all information to be in their language." The CDC leader explained that it was too late to change the flyers and that they were in keeping with the pluralist message of the event.

The event also caused conflict on the board of the community-based organization because it diverted so much time and energy from the central housing activism of the group. As one woman activist explained, "I can't waste my time on this stuff when we've got all these people desperate for a roof over their heads." Several festival workers withdrew their labor from the festival. At the eleventh hour, much of the grant was used to hire a professional human relations expert, a middle-class African American woman with downtown festival experience, to manage the event. She brought in the upscale museum exhibits, quasi-professional performance groups, vendors, and public relations outlets which had become commonly used in upscale festivals. The event shifted from one which served the local community and dealt with relevant local issues to a standardized display of the American mosaic. The only Asian dance group represented a nation which was not represented among local residents. This reflected the reification and naturalization of the panethnic category of Asianness, which led to the belief that any Asian could represent all Asians. The Solidarity-oriented display of locally resident Polish refugees was negatively received by several in attendance because it differed from the traditional costumed Polish dance performances used to represent Polish Americans in Philadelphia.

The bulk of those who ultimately attended the event were craft vendors, university students, and professionals from around the city. These were the self-selected diversity-seekers and consumers of authentic cultural commodities who were responsible for promoting this type of experience. Many residents stood sullenly on their porches around the square on which the event took place but never ventured over. They complained about the noise and the outsiders who were invading their space. Many were aware of all the contestation about the festival. Moreover, the craft and food booths recruited by the hired multicultural specialist sold expensive items aimed at the upscale diversity-seekers. The festival appealed to "downtown" multiculturalists for whom these festivals provide moments of safe passage into Philadelphia's impoverished communities transformed for the moment into interesting sites of cultural diversity to be enjoyed and experienced and used to satisfy voyeuristic curiosity.

While the poor whites were relegated to pluralist national heritage categories, elements of anti-racist, anti-imperialist discourses organized another component of the festival in which all people of color were constructed as oppressed while whites were implicitly on the other side. In the Spanish space of West Kensington which is dominated by Puerto Rican institutions, leaders trace their oppression to the imperialist U.S. state which colonized them after the war with Spain in 1898. Racism is talked about not only in terms of skin color but in terms of exclusions based on language (English vs. Spanish), citizenship status (voluntary vs. colonized) and poverty. In all these polarities, whites are seen as opposed to Puerto Ricans and associated with the negative actions of the U.S. state. In narratives of everyday life, distrust of whites and fear of racist actions is carried over in a careful marking of spaces and institutions as white-controlled and threatening or non-white and safe for Latinos (Goode 1998).

This anti-racist, anti-imperialist ideology has been an important part of the mobilization of the Puerto Rican civil rights movement since the Young Lords movement in the 1970s (Whalen 1998). Political solidarity resulted in a successful series of actions, including a voting rights lawsuit to redraw a state senatorial district, campaigns for fairness in the criminal justice system, and hearings before the Human Relations Commission about the under-representation of Latinos in public sector jobs. Yet each victory required cross-racial alliances as the next step. For example, while court-enforced legislative redistricting created the first Puerto Rican-dominated electoral district, the bulk of elected officials depend on alliances with both whites and blacks in the political party structure. These alliances have culminated in greater presence of Latinos in the regime of the mayor, John Street, who was elected in 1999.

In high-poverty Kensington, Korean merchants and Palestinian merchants and landlords played important economic roles while whites, Latinos, and blacks shared poverty. This local reality refuted the simplistic opposition between powerful whites and powerless minorities. Why did the CDC leadership insist on inserting this race-based construction of power into the festival? First and foremost, this was a way of resisting the way in which the NHRP pluralism theme totally ignored the salience of race in discourses of difference. While sticking to the pluralist mandate in the contested issue of language for the flyers, the leadership added on this segment to counteract the hegemonic ideology of pluralist equality.

Secondly, this was an attempt to reach out to the economically powerful local Koreans and Palestinians to solicit feelings of solidarity with them through depicting shared victimization by U.S. oppression. The organizers invited several Koreans and Palestinians to participate by donating food, goods, and performances. The Koreans and Palestinians, seeing themselves as entrepreneurs whose success separated them politically and economically from neighborhood residents, declined. At the event, these populations were nevertheless represented by films shown during the event which depicted their nations of origin as victims of U.S. imperialism. In attempting to use this pluralist event to communicate a broader political message, the anti-racist framework pushed whites out of collective solidarity with poor Latinos (and blacks) and into the category of those who needed to confront their complicity in U.S. racism and imperialism.[17]

The CDC learned an important lesson from the festival, which engendered a lot of local criticism. Residents complained that the performances and exhibits were not interesting to them. One white church group who had been actively involved with the CDC pulled away. Another group of recent Polish refugee families also felt that their exhibit had been maligned and withdrew from collaborative activities. In the weeks after the event, several meetings were held to critique it. The following year, after much reflection about the festival, a simple neighborhood fair occurred. All references to diversity and narratives of cultural difference were removed. Events to celebrate the neighborhood's strength and projects still occur a decade later.

These celebrations of multiculturalism fail to address the threat of racial incidents in these changing communities. They appeal to human relations specialists who enjoy the consumption of diversity because they avoid direct confrontations of race and power. In their practice, such events not only fail to achieve their goals but they backfire, reinforcing categories of difference and creating situations in which anti-racist, anti-imperialist rhetoric is deployed in contexts in which the target is not the state or capital but their fellow community members.

This case demonstrates that attempts to use U.S. narratives of difference based on liberal pluralism are not merely ineffective; they also disrupt the fragile cross-racial political alliances developing in these neighborhoods. The CDC festival is an example of how a cross-race class mobilization was disrupted.

Conflating class and race

If liberal pluralist events do not work because they ignore race and class, what happens when professionals confront race directly? Here again liberal state and civil authorities (e.g. human relations specialists, clergy, and teachers) argue for therapeutic psychological interventions aimed at presumed low self-esteem in poor people whose racist acting out was attributed to psychological inadequacies. While liberal pluralism sees the flawed individual to be ignorant and the cure to be cross-cultural aesthetic experience, anti-racist workshops see the individual flaw as low self-esteem and the primary therapy involves workshop training directed at rebuilding egos coupled with teaching self-censorship, conflict resolution skills and the transfer of other skills for self-governance (Cruikshank 1993). Experts used generic methods and ignored the ways in which local events underpinned conflict, allowing no opening for local knowledge and understanding.

A shared repertoire of generic "one-size-fits-all" techniques is employed based on the assumption that, once "processed," the individual's behaviors and attitudes will be transformed. Rooting out the racism of poor and working-class whites appealed to human rights specialists because it displaced the responsibility for racism from institutions of power to individuals of a lower class and required no structural change.

Over the course of the two years of fieldwork, we observed over 20 of these workshops. The goal was to "get inside" individuals clustered in small, artificially constructed groups, by "opening them up" through ice-breaking games and role play exercises which would instantly improve understanding and empathy. Individuals were asked to make contact either literally (through touching) or figuratively through self-revelatory games. The key was to get people to develop self-esteem. Yet they had to do this in the face of the obvious class disdain of workshop presenters. Human relations workers corrected the speech of participants and ascribed personal flaws to those white residents who did not dress well and who used dated and tainted group labels like Oriental and Negro. This implicit class contempt is what had helped to produce white working-class racism, through displaced abjection, in the first place.

At one professional's vaunted workshop which was identically performed in three different localities, the audience was exhorted to "Say uh oh to the uh oh," meaning that by carefully self-censoring one's thoughts, one could eliminate racism. The message was that we are all flawed individuals who can be cured by rooting out our internal evil. The historical and structural processes which had nurtured the roots of this evil currently and in earlier periods were totally ignored.

Recall the earlier examples of how poor whites who engaged in close relationships or political struggle with people of color often developed a consciousness of the way race works against their neighbors. The following example illustrates the development of such a consciousness in two Olney residents and the ways it was stifled within the context of a mobilization against realtor practices. The campaign was being organized by a group of liberal clergy, teachers, and social service workers who saw racism as a disease of poor whites.

In Olney in the late 1980s, the number of realtors operating in the community had increased from four to 20 as illegal techniques to promote sales played on fears of racial turnover and loss of property values.[18] In an effort to monitor and fight against these illegal tactics, these organizers, who were not residents of the neighborhood, were trying to organize the neighborhood. However, they were unaware of the growing and significant interracial networks of women described above. Furthermore, they viewed all poor white residents as ignorant and unreasonable and all people of color as powerless victims.

Yet in Olney, even more than in high-poverty Kensington, the class relations between whites and non-whites did not fit the national narrative that conflates race and class location. Whites were poorer than many influential people of color who were significant players in the local economy and political structure. In fact, the residential turnover the group observed was not occurring as a result of white flight since most of the whites remaining could not afford to leave. It was more a result of moves to the suburbs by upwardly mobile people of color. In addition many new immigrants were active as realtors and landlords. Their actions were contributing to the turnover.

The issue of differential investment power had underpinned a major conflict over Korean language signs which occurred several years before. The shopping strip, a major center of local social life, had been significantly transformed by immigrant investment. This led to restricted access to much of the space on the strip. Residents were being increasingly excluded from important public space as the result of the expansion of a Korean-only sector of retail and wholesale stores which were locked and only opened for Korean customers.[19] Citywide Korean business organizations whose political contributions gave them access to city government had gone directly to city agencies for permission to erect Korean-language street signs marking this space as Koreatown. Local residents saw this as a new example of their powerlessness in controlling meaningful community space. Local civic groups saw control of local space as their bailiwick and were angry at being bypassed. Clearly the economic and political clout of an immigrant group which didn't play by local rules was resented.

On the day that the *Philadelphia Inquirer* ran an article headlined "Olney to Become Koreatown," the signs were vandalized. The article highlighted the Korean business leaders intent to make the area a Korean service center for Korean merchants and customers from throughout the Middle Atlantic. The street signs had been requested to orient merchants from out of town. Ignoring the economic and political issues which clearly undergirded these actions, city human rights specialists had responded with multicultural festivals and training in self-esteem and conflict resolution.

At the same time, less powerful local Korean merchants whose outlets depended on a mixed customer base were angry at not being consulted by citywide Korean leaders. Rosemary, active in the local merchant association, had developed close relationships with several of these merchants. While Korean merchants had until now belonged to a separate local organization, Rosemary talked to several Korean store owners whom she saw as facing the same struggles against larger-scale businesses as native-born local owners. She brought two of them onto the board of the local merchant association. She spoke up for these local merchants at the public meetings in the wake of the crisis, describing them as part of the community. She said later, "I took a lot of heat at that meeting but I couldn't sit there and let them be blamed. These guys are working for the community and they belong here as much as I do." She had spoken to all levels of merchants and often spoke in private about the difference between the powerful actors in the citywide business group whom she saw as responsible for the incident and the locally embedded merchants with whom she had a great deal in common.

Linda was another local resident for whom the sign incident was a watershed. Linda was a gregarious, sympathetic person. Her problematic marriage to a man who tried to limit her contact with non-whites did not deter her from crossing boundaries every day. Her experience as a local day-care provider for diverse parents on the block, her church work as a lay home visitor, and service as a committee person for a political party all involved her in home visits with her multiracial neighbors, providing health-care referrals, spiritual aid, and constituent service. She counted dozens of minority and immigrant families in her personal network and had an active social life involving constant celebrations of family life-cycle events. Unlike the sponsors of diversity festivals, she understood the actual diversity of immigrant cultural practices. Both Rosemary and Linda daily crossed boundaries between racially defined populations and between established residents and newcomers in activities which they interpreted as building community in the face of economic and political pressures. They saw the locally embedded Korean merchants and struggling immigrant households as sharing their stake in the local community.

The professionals organizing the anti-realtor movement saw things differently. In discussions about strategy, race and class were conflated. All people of color were stereotyped as struggling and powerless in contrast to white residents: "Immigrants are powerless, they live in a world where decisions of power are made every day without them." "They come with the clothes on their backs and live on one bag of rice a year." There was no recognition that some immigrants had the resources to manipulate local real estate markets and create political power.

In an interview with one of the local clergy who later took a role in the anti-realtor campaign, I asked what he thought of the local community leadership's views of the sign incident which condemned the vandalism as inappropriate and uncivil, but saw the grievance as justifiable and related to issues of local vs. elite power. He responded, "That's true of course, but it is not important. We cannot do anything here if we do not root out the racism in these people first." He did not see that common struggles for the community might be ultimately more useful in ending racism. Nor did he see that failing to listen to the analysis of local white leaders while at the same time bringing in programs that pointed the finger at their racism would create resentment.

Rosemary and Linda became active in the anti-destabilization campaign after the non-resident organizers requested an endorsement for the campaign from the major civic umbrella organization. Before this request was made, as they strategized about confronting the civic group, the organizers talked about their expectation that they would either be physically ejected or verbally shouted down by a racist rabble. They were very surprised to find that the local white residents wanted to preserve a mixed population as much as they did. The campaign for ethical real estate practices was unanimously endorsed and Linda and Rosemary were recruited as volunteers. The two were experts in local life. They had a keen understanding of local power and control. Aware that an immigrant realtor/landlord was acting to encourage people to move from a cluster of blocks in which he had an interest, they wanted to include his actions in the group's agenda for intervention. This ran counter to the campaign leaders' construction of all immigrants as powerless and the view that criticizing any action by people of color revealed the psychologistic disease of racism. At one meeting the women presented the issue but were ignored. At the next meeting, their comments were silenced by statements like "We can't talk about [immigrant realtors], it's too close to racism." The two women left the meeting early and never came back. After they left, one of the men said, "They were so good during the Korean sign incident, but tonight you could see their fundamental racism." Everyone nodded their heads in agreement. It was as if they were relieved to find their diagnosis of racism had been confirmed.

The two women had been publicly critical of the behavior of a racially different immigrant. The leaders saw their role as protecting powerless immigrants from white racists. They reacted accordingly. This had a fatal consequence. The all-white, all-male leadership of the real estate action group continually worried about the racial inclusiveness of their organization. While they talked constantly about their enjoyment of diversity in the neighborhood, they had no close relationships with local people of color. Instead, they sought endorsements from the citywide leaders of the appropriate minority categories: a Latino councilman, a Korean business broker, etc. These were people who were publicly visible and accessible through their staffs. The symbolic use of their names by the campaign had limited use. In the case of the business broker who was heavily involved in sales contributing to turnover on the strip, it was even hypocritical.

The campaign needed workers to sustain it. It could have served as a major action bringing people together across racial boundaries to support their common local commitment. Yet instead, white women activists whose developed political subjectivity had crossed racial boundaries were cast as flawed, racist individuals rather than as women whose intensive and extensive relationships within interracial social networks were essential to a successful campaign. The best opportunity for recruiting local residents of color to the campaign would have been through Rosemary and Linda. Now they felt driven out of the mobilization. The anti-realtor campaign was an ideal vehicle for a class-based, cross-racial movement to prevent real estate brokers from promoting population turnover, which was a factor that weakened the formation of block organizations and local campaigns for better schools and city services. The organizers, conflating race and class, ignored the relative class positions of the white residents and the people of color from whom they recruited endorsements. This ultimately undermined the emergence of class politics as well as local participation in the campaign.

Conclusion

As these cases show, the resort to "experts" who specialize in human relations has produced a repertoire of superficial, mass-produced solutions which deny the significance of the workings of race and power throughout U.S. history and their particular dynamics in local situations. Middle-class professionals, whose expertise is based on nothing more than their lived experience and status as "respectable" members of society, demonstrate great certainty in their superior knowledge and moral superiority. Yet, at the same time, they are willfully ignorant of the contingent nature of the historically structured racial formation in the United States and the lived experience of those in the local situations which they target. This allows them to displace racism onto the white working class and regard themselves as free from personal racism. They abhor any conflict and disorder which challenge the status quo. They prefer technologies of social control and regimes of rebuilding egos which reinforce their superordinate positions and sense of self. Contradictorily they claim to be building self-esteem in the working class in spite of their condescending practices, such as correcting vocabulary and grammar. They advocate the consumption of multicultural (read exotic) aesthetics as a road to understanding diversity, which reflects both their desire to consume diversity as a mark of cosmopolitan class status and the expanding availability of multicultural commodities.

We must be wary of the discourses of difference constructed by powerful civic institutions which deny the significance of poverty and racial inequality in their desire to discursively create a myth of equality through aesthetic cultural equivalence. We must also avoid the pitfalls of over-reliance on simplistic oppositions between whites and peoples of color which conflate racial and class dynamics and allow the middle class to take on an aura of moral superiority which belies the realities of community life. Similarly, we must avoid the discourse of individual blame which defines racism as a personal condition created by ignorance, fear, and low self-esteem and that seeks to "cure" it through festivals and workshops while ignoring the role of the state and capital in creating the structures which shape both material realities and corresponding social constructions.

Yet the rhetorical thrusts of those who are aware of the historical formation of structural racism are also counterproductive in the public sphere. Returning to Ester's forced identity choice which opened this essay, we can see that Ester felt compromised by the discrepancy between the Puerto Rican rhetoric of racism and her own new politicized subjectivity as part of a multiracial coalition engaged in a local struggle for a better life. There is no question that Ester had experienced acts of racism throughout her life and that, structurally, race persists in making the overall material conditions of life for poor people of color generally worse than they are for whites. It is understandable that Ester would overcome her ambivalence to side with outspoken Latino activists. The Latina speaker engaged in "getting whites to understand their racism" had a worthy and necessary goal.

As Lynd's comments about action and experience indicate, this rhetorical tactic at public events parallels those of the organizers whom Lynd criticizes who expect to change people "by preaching door to door." It fails to convince these poor whites that they should be scapegoats for all local problems. Instead of relying on "experts" in multiculturalism, we must look toward strengthening the role that common political struggle itself plays in the transformation of people's political identities in the hope of ultimately strengthening this struggle. The possibility of effective poor people's political action requires cross-racial alliance-building at every level. To enable this, we must create a new multiculturalism that goes beyond simplistic beliefs in equal opportunity and cultural relativity, and class-evasive oppositions of white and other. Such a turn requires attention to both historically contingent and locally nuanced class and power relations and the development of a critique which allows cross-group alliances to flourish.

NOTES

1 All personal names have been changed to pseudonyms.

2 In the summer of 1988, two killings, one month apart, involving groups of white and Puerto Rican teenagers filled the local media. In the first case, the perpetrators were Puerto Rican and the victim white. In the second, it was the reverse. A full discussion of the nuances of these incidents can be found in Goode and Schneider (1994: 195–206).

3 Contrasting but related processes also occur in gentrifying neighborhoods such as those studied by Anderson (1990) and Williams (1993).

4 The Philadelphia Changing Relations Project was part of the national Changing Relations Project supported by the Ford Foundation. It was comprised of six city projects using ethnographic data to look at the changing relations between new immigrants and established residents within each of these cities (Bach 1993; Lamphere 1992; Lamphere et al. 1994).

5 Seventy-five percent of all manufacturing jobs disappeared in the two decades between 1955 and 1975 (Adams et al. 1991) through plant closings or relocation of work to the suburbs, sunbelt or out of the country. Summers and Luce (1988) show that more jobs left for the suburbs in Philadelphia than in 42 comparable U.S. cities. Withdrawal of federal aid also hit this city harder than comparable urban areas. In 1979, 25.5 percent of the budget came from federal aid. By 1988, this had dropped to 7.5 percent (Goode and Schneider 1994:30–1.).

6 Brodkin (1998) and others have pointed to the way in which federal policies related to the GI Bill and federally insured mortgages excluded blacks and contributed to the increasing racial divide.

7 In spite of the quick resolution of conflict as a result of the intervention of black politicians who were part of the new reform democratic coalition, the 1964 riots in North Philadelphia triggered white working-class flight to the older streetcar suburbs further north like Olney. Having experienced panic sales and the loss of "community," residents vowed not to succumb to panic again. This was aided by the "respectability" of the aspiring middle-class people of color who were moving in.

8 For the past two decades, there has been a growing literature on women as community-builders and political activists making demands for concessions by the state in an era when it has withdrawn services from poor communities (Bookman and Morgen 1988; Susser 1981). Many had learned political organizing skills as participants in the Civil Rights and Welfare Rights movement (Piven and Cloward 1979) as well as the Community Action Program (CAP) of the War on Poverty: poor white women (Susser 1981), African American women (Hyatt 1997; Naples 1998; Stack 1996), Latino women (Naples 1998; Pardo 1998). Like these women, the women we encountered from different racial categories in Philadelphia were also creating alliances to promote their family and community interests.

9 The cash-strapped school district had responded to overcrowded schools in these neighborhoods in a way which did not cost money but actually produced income. Instead of rehabilitating buildings to add local space and preserve residentially integrated schools, they bussed children (a one-hour trip) to a distant all-white area to integrate those schools and bring in desegregation moneys.

10 Instead of building new buildings, the district converted older local structures into annexes for existing schools.

11 Philadelphia has long supported groups promoting tolerance. As the seat of the Society of Friends, the legacy of William Penn's "city of brotherly love" is frequently referred to as a tradition. The city created one of the first human relations commissions (1952), and even before, in 1947, an active Fellowship Commission was formed to promote racial tolerance. During our fieldwork, we encountered dozens of locally generated programs which emerged from the civil rights era tied to the Urban League, Urban Coalition, the Society of Friends, the Cardinal's Commission on Human Relations, and the Jewish Community Relations Council, etc.

12 While there was no professional accrediting organization, certificates such as those one received for attending classes and workshops at institutions such as the Multicultural Training Institute at Temple University were used to demonstrate competence.

13 For further discussion of this, see Goode (2001), Merry (2001), and Takaki (1979).

14 According to Massey and Denton (1993), the black poverty rate is two to three times the white rate. However, in the neighborhoods described in this essay, the upwardly mobile blacks who have broken the color line tend to have higher levels of income and education than the downwardly mobile whites they have joined. The same is true for immigrant Latino and Asian households.

15 The funding for the NHRP projects came from a consortium of developers and corporate leaders who were active in many of the city's public–private partnerships with strong interests in urban peace. The program was administered by the Urban League.

16 People married before World War II often spoke about pressures to marry within national heritage groups. One woman with Irish ancestry spoke about her husband's German-origin family never accepting her. Murray Dubin (1996) describes the frequent comments about the first "mixed" marriage between an Irish man and a non-Irish woman in another area. For several

generations, Italian-origin peoples maintained regional endogamy emphasizing Sicilian, Calabrese or Abruzzese origin. (Goode et al. 1984). Couples married after the war did not experience these pressures. For white Catholics who belonged to a nationality parish, early social life took place in social spaces with common national origins. However, archdiocesan high schools were fed by all the nationality parish schools and had a major effect on these early practices of national endogamy. On this day, joking banter about being "one-eighth Irish, one-eighth Italian and one-eighth Polish and gosh knows everything else" was frequently heard.

17 Blacks were often seen by Latinos as similar to whites. As far as their contacts with city agencies was concerned, blacks had a lot of power in the political system and held many visible public jobs. They were seen as more successful in taking advantage of affirmative action mechanisms. In the festival, they also were not present as participants but were represented by museum exhibits.

18 The increase in realtors was accompanied by increasing reports of churning activities to increase sales, which violated Human Relations Commission rules: unreasonable solicitation through postcards and phone calls, the use of references to and photos of people of color, steering clients to particular blocks and away from others, and excessive use of sale signage.

19 One community leader reported knocking on the door of a Korean dress store while soliciting advertisements for a local publication. She was told, "This store is for Koreans only and besides you cannot afford our clothes." This single comment reinforced her feeling of exclusion from her local space and her sense of class resentment.

REFERENCES

Adams, Carolyn, David Bartelt, David Elesh, Ira Goldstein, Nancy Kleniewski and William Yancey. 1991. *Philadelphia: Neighborhoods, Division and Conflict in a Postindustrial City*. Philadelphia: Temple University Press.

Anderson, Elijah. 1990. *Streetwise: Race, Class and Change in an Urban Community*. Philadelphia: University of Pennsylvania Press.

Bach, Robert. 1993. *Changing Relations: Newcomers and Established Residents in U.S. Communities*. New York: Ford Foundation.

Basch, Linda, Nina Glick Schiller, and Cristina Szanton Blanc. 1994. *Nations Unbound*. Langhorne, PA: Gordon & Breach.

Bookman, Ann and Sandra Morgen, eds. 1988. *Women and the Politics of Empowerment*. Philadelphia: Temple University Press.

Brodkin, Karen. 1998. *How Jews Became White Folks and What This Says about Race in America*. New Brunswick, NJ: Rutgers University Press.

Chock, Phyllis. 1995. Culturalism: Pluralism, Culture and Race in the Harvard Encyclopedia of American Ethnic Groups. In Virginia Dominguez, ed., *(Multi) Culturalisms and the Baggage of "Race." Let's Get Our Act Together: Dealing with Race in the Context of Mobilizing for Neighborhood Action*. Theme issue. *Identities*. 1(4):301–324.

Cruikshank, Barbara. 1993. Revolutions Within: Self-Government and Self-Esteem. *Economy and Society* 22(3):327–343.

Dominguez, Virginia, ed. 1995. *(Multi)Culturalisms and the Baggage of "Race"*. Theme issue. *Identities* 1 (4):297–446.

Dubin, Murray. 1996. *South Philadelphia: Mummers, Memories and the Melrose Diner*. Philadelphia: Temple University Press.

DuBois, W. E. B. 1992[1934]. *The Philadelphia Negro*. Philadelphia: University of Pennsylvania Press.

Goldstein, Ira. 1986. The Wrong Side of the Tracts: A Study of Residential Segregation in Philadelphia. Ph.D. dissertation. Temple University.

Goode, Judith. 1998. The Contingent Construction of Local Identities: Koreans and Puerto Ricans in Philadelphia. *Identities* 5(1):33–64.

Goode, Judith. 2001. Teaching against Cultural Essentialism in Anthropology. In Ida Susser and Thomas Patterson, eds., *Cultural Diversity in the United States: A Critical Reader*. Oxford: Blackwell.

Goode, Judith, Karen Curtis and Janet Theophano. 1984. Meal Formats, Meal Cycles and Menu Negotiations in the Maintenance of an Italian-American Community. In Mary Douglas, ed., *Food and the Social Order*. New York: Russell Sage.

Goode, Judith and JoAnne Schneider. 1994. *Reshaping Ethnic and Racial Relations in Philadelphia: Immigrants in a Divided City*. Philadelphia: Temple University Press.

Gregory, Steven. 1998. *Black Corona*. Princeton: Princeton University Press.

Gregory, Steven and Roger Sanjek, eds. 1994. *Race*. New Brunswick, NJ: Rutgers University Press.

Hartigan, John Jr. 1999. *Racial Situations: Class Predicaments of Whiteness in Detroit*. Princeton: Princeton University Press.

Horton, John. 1995. *The Politics of Diversity*. Philadelphia: Temple University Press.

Hyatt, Susan Brin. 1997. Policy in a Post-Welfare Landscape: Tenant Management Policies, Self-Governance and the Democratization of Knowledge in Great Britain. In Sue Wright and Chris Shore, eds., *The Anthropology of Policy*. London: Routledge.

Ignatiev, Noel. 1995. *How the Irish Became White*. New York: Routledge.

Lamphere, Louise, ed. 1992. *Structuring Diversity*. Chicago: University of Chicago Press.

Lamphere, Louise, Alex Stepick and Guillermo Grenier, eds. 1994. *Newcomers in the Workplace: Immigrants in a Restructuring Economy*. Philadelphia: Temple University Press.

Lynd, Staughton. 2000. Overcoming Racism. *Monthly Review* 51:16–23.

Massey, Douglas and Nancy Denton. 1993. *American Apartheid: Segregation and the Making of the Underclass*. Cambridge, MA: Harvard University Press.

Merry, Sally. 1986. *Urban Danger*. Philadelphia: Temple University Press.

Merry, Sally Engle. 2001. Racialized Identities and the Law. In Ida Susser and Thomas C. Patterson, eds., *Cultural Diversity in the United States: A Critical Reader*. Oxford: Blackwell.

Naples, Nancy A. 1998. *Grassroots Warriors: Activist Mothering, Community Work and the War on Poverty*. New York: Routledge.

Omi, Michael and Howard Winant. 1994. *Racial Formation in the United States. From the 1960s to the 1980s*. New York: Routledge.

Pardo, Mary S. 1998. *Mexican American Women Activists: Identity and Resistance in Two Los Angeles Communities*. Philadelphia: Temple University Press.

Piven, Frances Fox and Richard Cloward. 1979. *Poor People's Movements: Why They Succeed and How They Fail*. New York: Vintage Books.

Portes, Alejandro and Alex Stepick. 1993. *City on the Edge: The Transformation of Miami*. Berkeley: University of California Press.

Rieder, Jonathan. 1985. *Canarsie: The Jews and Italians of Brooklyn Against Liberalism*. Cambridge, MA: Harvard University Press.

Roediger, David. 1990. *The Wages of Whiteness: Race and the Making of the American Working Class*. London: Verso.

Ruben, Matthew. 2001. Suburbanization and Urban Poverty under Neoliberalism. In Judith Goode and Jeff Maskovsky, eds., *The New Poverty Studies: The Ethnography of Power, Politics and Impoverished People in the United States*. New York: New York University Press.

Sacks, Karen Brodkin. 1994. How Did Jews Become White Folks? In S. Gregory and R. Sanjek, eds., *Race*. New Brunswick, NJ: Rutgers University Press.

Sanjek, Roger. 1998. *The Future of Us All: Race and Neighborhood Politics in New York*. Ithaca, NY: Cornell University Press.

Stack, Carol. 1996. *Call to Home: African Americans Reclaim the Rural South*. New York: Basic Books.

Steinberg, Stephen. 1981. *The Ethnic Myth: Race, Ethnicity and Class in America*. New York: Athaneum.

Summers, Anita and Thomas Luce. 1988. *Economic Report on the Philadelphia Metropolitan Area, 1988*. Philadelphia: University of Pennsylvania Press.

Susser, Ida. 1981. *Norman Street*. New York: Columbia University Press.

Takaki, Ron. 1979. *Iron Cages: Race and Culture in 19th-Century America*. New York: Knopf.

Whalen, Carmen. 1998. Bridging Homeland and Barrio Politics: The Young Lords in Philadelphia. In Andres Torres and Jose Velasquez, eds., *The Puerto Rican Movement: Voices from the Barrio*. Philadelphia: Temple University Press.

Williams, Brackette. 1989. A Class Act: Anthropology and the Race to Nation Across Ethnic Terrain. *Annual Review of Anthropology* 18:401–444.

Williams, Brackette. 1993. The Impact of the Precepts of Nationalism on the Concept of Culture. *Cultural Critique*. Spring volume.

Williams, Brett. 1988. *Upscaling Downtown: Stalled Gentrification in Washington, DC*. Ithaca, NY: Cornell University Press.

Zavella, Patricia. 2001. The Tables are Turned: Immigration, Poverty and Social Conflict in California Communities. In Judith Goode and Jeff Maskovsky, eds., *The New Poverty Studies: The Ethnography of Power, Politics and Impoverished People in the United States*. New York: New York University Press.

Zukin, Sharon. 1995. *The Culture of Cities*. Oxford: Blackwell.

Part II

Church, Family, and the Dynamics of Post-Civil Rights Migration

4

What it Means to be Christian: The Role of Religion in the Construction of Ethnic Identity and Boundary among Second-Generation Korean Americans

Kelly H. Chong

In both sociological and historical investigations of immigrant groups in America, the important role played by ethnic religion in the lives of immigrants and their communities has received considerable attention. Numerous studies, both of the earlier European groups and of the more recent "new" immigrant groups,[1] have documented in particular ethnic religion's role in the adjustment process of immigrants, and in maintaining group identity and culture (Dolan 1972; Fenton 1988; Gjerde 1986; Haddad and Lummis 1987; Lucas 1955; Miller 1977; Mol 1976; Palinkas 1982; Rutledge 1985; Smith 1978; Swierenga 1991; Williams 1988).

Despite such a rich body of literature, studies of ethnic religion and its role and impact on the *second* generation have been less extensive. One possible reason for this is the earlier dominance of the assimilationist paradigm which, based primarily on the experiences of the "old" turn-of-the-century European immigrant groups, has tended to postulate a second-generation rejection of ethnicity and religion (cf. Hansen 1952; Herberg 1955). However, not only have recent theoretical developments rendered such linear perspectives of ethnicity unviable, evidence from some contemporary ethnic groups suggests that ethnic religion may be playing a far greater role in the lives of second-generation members than was supposed for earlier European immigrant groups. Based on an ethnographic study of a contemporary second-generation ethnic group, Korean-American Christians in Chicago, the aim of this paper is to reexamine the role of the ethnic church for the second generation. In particular, the investigation will focus on the role played by ethnic religion in the construction and maintenance of second-generation ethnic identity and boundary.[2]

Since the influx of Korean immigrants into the US in the 1970s and 1980s, the Korean-American community has become distinguished by the vitality of its ethnic religious life. With close to 75–80 percent (Hurh and Kim 1990) of the immigrant community professing Protestant church affiliation, various studies have attempted to explain the uncommonly high rate of ethnic church participation by Koreans (Choy 1979; Han 1994; I. Kim 1981, 1995; Patterson 1988; Hurh and Kim 1990). However, what has been even more notable about the Korean-American community has been the apparent vitality of ethnic Christian institutions among the community's second-generation members. Second-generation Korean Americans display a high level of ethnic religious participation compared with many other ethnic groups,[3] a pattern which appears paradoxical since many members of the group have achieved a considerable level of economic and "cultural" integration[4] into the mainstream society.[5] This presents a challenge to theories which link the loosening of ethnic ties with upward mobility (Warner 1953; Whyte 1943). Furthermore, as Stephen Warner (1990) has observed, religious participation of Korean Americans tends to be accompanied by an unusually high degree of ethnic identity and consciousness, suggesting that indeed, ethnic church participation may be strongly linked to the issue of ethnicity for these Korean Americans.

In pursuing this investigation, this paper has two major goals. First, by exploring a range of subjective factors motivating the church members' religious participation in the ethnic church, I seek to ascertain some of the major reasons for this particular pattern of ethnic religious participation, especially as it relates to Korean-American group status within American society. Second, by means of participant observation, in-depth interviews, and analyses of rhetoric within the churches, I explore and describe the various ways by which the ethnic church contributes to the construction and support of ethnic identity and consciousness among second-generation members. This will be accomplished particularly by examining the significance of the ethnic church as both a social and religious institution, and how these two dimensions interrelate with regard to ethnic identity.

The main thesis of this paper is that Christianity in the Korean-American community, more specifically conservative/evangelical Protestantism, plays a powerful role in the construction, support, and reinforcement of Korean ethnic identity/boundary in second-generation members. As an institutional vehicle for the cultural reproduction and socialization of the second generation, this is accomplished in the ethnic church by ideologically legitimizing and defending a set of core traditional Korean values and forms of social relationships which I argue constitute the main components of the second-generation ethnicity.

I also argue that the strong sense of ethnic identity and exclusivity observed among second-generation church-goers reflect a form of defensive ethnicity against their perceived "marginal" status within American society as a non-white minority group. Thus, despite its role as a vehicle for the cultural interests of the first generation, the paradoxical appeal of the Korean ethnic church for many second-generation members lies in its capacity to provide a kind of "refuge" from this sense of marginalization, and along with it, positive social identity and group empowerment.

The Korean ethnic church, however, is by no means an ideologically monolithic institution. Through a brief illustration of some intergenerational and gender conflicts within the churches, I also demonstrate certain tensions inherent in this process of ethnic reproduction, tensions expressive of ideological challenges by the second generation. By offering an insight into the ethnic and religious life of this particular second-generation group, I hope to contribute to a better understanding of the continuing relevance of ethnic religion in contemporary America, as well as the role religion plays in the general process of cultural pluralization and ethnicization. In addition, I hope to bring about an improved understanding of the ethnic experience of some contemporary non-white minority ethnic groups, whose experiences of acculturation and assimilation differ in significant ways from earlier European immigrant groups.

Theoretical Perspective

Ethnicity and the second generation

Reflecting on the experiences of turn-of-the-century European immigrants, Marcus Lee Hansen (1952), the eminent historian of immigrants, proclaimed in 1937 "the principle of the third-generation interest." Observing that "what the son wishes to forget the grandson wishes to remember," Hansen juxtaposed in this principle the ethnically "returning" third generation to the "fleeing" second generation, who, eager for assimilation and acceptance by the larger society, would try mightily to reject its ethnicity.

Since the 1960s, such perspectives on the intergenerational assimilation process have come under much criticism, particularly for ignoring the crucial issue of the historical and situational context which would differentiate the experiences not only of each generation but of each immigrant group (Glazer 1990; Archdeacon 1990). Other scholars, such as Nahirny and Fishman (1965), have called attention to the salience of second-generation ethnicity. Based on their data on Jews, Nahirny and Fishman show that despite the second-generation members' eagerness to reject some aspects of their cultural heritage – such as language and traditional customs – they retain some important forms of ethnic identification. These are "abstract values" and "ideals" that ostensibly *symbolize* their ancestral heritage, as opposed to the "old ways" and lived "realities" that comprise the "tangible ethnicity" of the first generation.

Nahirny and Fishman's characterization of Jewish second-generation ethnicity, however, raises some questions. To what extent can this view of second-generation ethnicity – very similar to Gans's (1979) concept of the third/fourth-generation "symbolic" ethnicity in which ethnicity is expressed by the "symbols" and "feelings" of being ethnic without the need for "practiced culture" – hold for other ethnic groups, especially non-white groups, whose situational context may differ from earlier immigrants? In particular, to what extent can the inherited, "tangible" elements of traditional ethnicity be excluded as a possible form of second-generation ethnicity?

To a large degree, the problem of conceptualizing second-generation ethnicity is not simply an issue of intergenerational ethnicity but a question of how to conceptualize ethnicity in general. In the social sciences, the classic "primordialist" perspective on ethnicity has come under much recent challenge by what I shall refer to as the "developmental" perspective. Whereas the "primordialist" perspective (Geertz 1963; Isaacs 1975) views ethnicity as a form of primordial attachment defined by and based on inherited and unalterable "given" attributes, such as shared ancestry and culture, the "developmental" perspective (Glazer and Moynihan 1963; Roosens 1989; Sarna 1978; Yancey, Ericksen, and Juliani 1976) seeks to understand ethnicity more as an emergent phenomenon, a form of social organization designed to achieve ends for a group of people and an adaptive response to external forces. Deemphasizing the cultural component as a basis of ethnic formation, this view focuses on ethnicization as being driven by the particular status and position of different groups within a particular society.

Viewing ethnicity more as a situationally driven and transformable phenomenon, the developmental perspective avoids some of the shortcomings of the primordialist perspective. However, in its focus on the interest-and situation-driven *motivations* for ethnic mobilization, the developmental perspective fails sufficiently to take into account the salience of primordial factors in ethnic mobilization and the definition of ethnic identity. That is, it cannot explain why interests are pursued through ethnic cohesion rather than by some other forms of solidarity (McKay 1982).

I believe that the best way to think about ethnicity is an approach which integrates the two perspectives. While ethnicity must be seen as a dynamic, emergent cultural construction arising in response to external conditions over time, ethnic identity must also not be understood simply as a "collective fiction," but as a construction which "incorporates, adapts, and amplifies preexisting communal solidarities, cultural attributes, and historical memories" (Conzen et al. 1992). In other words, whatever the motivation for ethnic mobilization, it must be recognized that a group's rationale and basis for its identity can often be primordial in nature, based on a belief in elements of shared or inherited culture.[6]

In examining the ethnicity of second-generation Korean-American church-goers, my aim will be to use this integrative approach to understand how the cultural attributes of the Korean ethnic group are being appropriated and utilized by church members in the process of ethnic boundary construction and group self-definition, and the role religion plays in this process. As opposed to the "transplanted" ethnicity of the first generation, ethnicity for the second generation will be seen primarily as an emergent concept which incorporates, appropriates, and in part reshapes the cultural attributes of the first generation in ways which are more than simply "abstract" or "symbolic."

Religion and ethnic identity

The question of the relationship between religion and ethnic identity involves two important related issues. First, how is religion, as a basis of identity, related to ethnic identity, and second, *how* does religion support ethnic identity and cohesion? Regarding the first issue, although religion has long been recognized for its close relationship to ethnic identity, the exact nature of the intersection between the two has not always been clear. It appears that religion can interact with ethnicity in one of two ways: either as identical to or precedent to ethnic identity, or as ancillary to ethnic identity (Williams 1988:12–13). Literature on various early European immigrant groups tends to emphasize the former. For example, William Galush (1977) points to the inseparable link between the identity of Polish immigrants and Roman Catholicism. Henry S. Lucas (1955), in his study of Dutch Calvinists, asserts that Dutch Calvinists "stick together not primarily on the bases of ethnicity or nationalism but on the basis of their religion."

Evidence from more recent groups, such as Asian Indians (Williams 1988), however, demonstrates that the two do not have to be identical. Williams (1988), for instance, describes how immigrants can use different aspects of their various religions to develop *new* patterns of group identity, such as ethnic or national identity, in the new society. This not only clearly shows how religious identity can be subordinate to the imperatives of other forms of group identity, but, more importantly, how it can be used to support the creation or maintenance of other types of group identities. It is also clear that, depending on the relative contributions of cultural and situational interest factors, religion reinforces ethnic identity to varying degrees for different groups (Lewins 1978:20).

In studying second-generation Korean Americans, the concept of ethnic religion as a vehicle for the development and maintenance of ethnic identity is particularly salient, first, because unlike in many ethno-religious groups, Christian identity cannot be considered an inherent part of Korean ethnic identity, and second, because, as will be argued, Christianity and its institutions are important in supporting an *emerging* sense of second-generation ethnic identity. In other words, the development of, and commitment to, Christian identity often coincides with the emergence of a stronger ethnic identity in the second generation.

Regarding the issue of *how* religion supports and reinforces ethnicity, this paper focuses on the concepts of sacralization (Mol 1976) and legitimation (Weber 1963) as the main explanatory tools for understanding the role of religion in supporting ethnic identity. In his theorizing about religion in group life, Weber has emphasized the ethical and legitimating functions of religion, as well as its role as a vehicle of protest, while Mol has more recently given attention to the issue of religion and identity with his concept of religion as the sacralization of identity, "the process by means of which man has pre-eminently safeguarded and reinforced...a complex of orderly interpretations of reality, rules, and legitimations, which provides identity" (Mol 1976:15). While these thinkers have used these concepts to explore the relationship of religion to identity in general, I will examine how they can be used to consider the ways in which religion supports *ethnic* identity. For instance, religion can serve as a powerful means of sacralizing or legitimizing the immigrant's ethnic identity, insofar as it legitimates the various aspects of the immigrant's sense of shared culture and solidifies the immigrant's commitment to her/his ethnic identity.

Method and Data

The analysis for this study is based on fieldwork conducted in two Korean-American ethnic churches in the Chicago area in 1995, consisting of participant observation and in-depth interviews with lay members and church leaders. The first church, my primary research site which I will call the Chicago Church from here on, is located in a northern suburb of Chicago. It is one of the largest and oldest Korean Presbyterian churches in the Chicago area with a membership of approximately 1,600 people. The leader of the church, a male pastor who founded the church about 20 years ago, is assisted by a group of elders, deacons, several assistant pastors, and four youth pastors who lead the youth congregation with which this study is concerned. The second church, to be called the South Park Church, is a smaller Korean Methodist church that mainly serves a small middle-class community in the southside of Chicago.

The Chicago Church was chosen as the primary site for my research for two reasons. First, because it is one of the largest churches in Chicago, it provides a good sampling size. And although I make no claims about this church as a "typical" Korean ethnic church, it is not so atypical as to make it unique. Second, because it is large and relatively affluent, this church is one of the few churches in Chicago that possesses a separate second-generation congregation, allowing me to better isolate the dynamics of the second-generation interaction. This second-generation congregation, which is further subdivided into the Young-Adult Congregation (with about 70 listed members) and the Youth Congregation for teenage members (with about 100 members) is also one of the largest in Chicago. The South Park Church, although much smaller in size with about 100 members, also has a separate second-generation congregation totaling about 40 people.

At the Chicago Church, most of my interviews were conducted with members of the Young-Adult Congregation, although some interviews were conducted with members from the Youth Congregation as well as the Adult Congregation. The interviews, in-depth and both semi-structured and unstructured, were conducted in both churches through a random sampling of people listed in the congregation roster and through the "snowball" method. My participation observation consisted of "sitting in" on Sunday services and Bible study classes, and of participating in numerous church-related activities. The total number of interviews was 62. A number of interviews were also conducted with a group of non-Christian second-generation members to observe the variations in responses regarding the issue of ethnic identity.

Motivation for Ethnic Church Involvement

My first task in investigating the role of the Korean ethnic church for second-generation members was to try to determine why these members would choose to attend the ethnic church. In many ways, the members of the two churches are typically representative of second-generation Korean Americans of that age group; they are ostensibly well acculturated, highly educated, and upwardly mobile. The members, who range in age between 17 to 33 years old, are mostly attending or have graduated from four-year colleges, and are employed in professional occupations such as business, law, medicine, social services, or education. A majority are American-born, and speak little or no Korean. Religious services, as well as most informal conversations, are thus carried out in English. All of the interviewees also appear to be quite committed religiously, and profess a strong faith in God. About half come from Christian families, but confess that they did not become "real" Christians until after high school. All of them admit to being converted, "born again," or recommitted to Christianity as young adults.

Nevertheless, when asked to explain why they attend a Korean church, what is most striking about the members' responses is the great importance they place on the "social" and "cultural" reasons for coming to a Korean church. Most of the members respond that being able to maintain social networks with other Korean Americans or to "keep up" the Korean culture and language are just as important as, if not more important than, "religious" reasons for attending the Korean church. Tina,[7] a 28-year-old married member, confessed:

> Why do I come to a Korean church? Well, it's not strictly for religious reasons, but cultural. Part of the reason is to keep some contact with the Korean community because it's our only source of cultural identity. It's also important to our parents – this is not the most important factor, but one of the important factors. Another thing is that we think about the next generation. Our kids will have the same exposure if we have contact with the Korean community.

According to another member:

> The first thing that attracts people is fellowship, a sense of closeness. It's trying to find a group that's comfortable. Lots of kids from white areas come to church to relate to Korean friends. There is a sense of comfort in being with other Koreans or Asians because there's an understanding in terms of background. For example, all Asian parents are strict.[8] Korean Americans have an unspoken understanding that we've all been there, like experiences of prejudice.

Although it is obvious that the desire for ethnic community and fellowship serves as a primary motivation for participating in the ethnic church, an even more striking aspect of their responses, however, is the degree to which participation seems to be driven not only by a simple need for ethnic fellowship, but also by a powerful desire to *preserve* their ethnicity and culture, not only for themselves, but for posterity. For instance, most report that even though as Christians they could in principle worship anywhere, they would choose to worship only in Korean churches in order to maintain their ethnic culture not only for themselves, but for their future children.

What are some of the explanations behind this intense attachment to ethnic identity and culture? While some proponents of the developmental perspective of ethnicity emphasize the importance of political or economic ends in the goal of ethnic formation, others, such as Sarna (1978), view "ethnicization" as a response to *adversity* and *ascription* of a particular group, where ethnic unity, ascribed by outsiders, is accepted "as part of the defense against prejudice and hostility" (Sarna 1978:374). Given the central emphasis church-goers place on adversity and ascription in describing their experiences, Sarna's view may be a good starting point for understanding the particularly strong ethnic attachment of second-generation Korean-American church members.

One of the first things revealed by my interviews was the existence of relatively strong perceptions of racism, prejudice, and discrimination by church members, which most attribute to their race and color. Most respondents describe having developed this awareness in young adulthood, mainly in college and through work experiences. Most members also relate that this awareness served as a prelude to major crises of identity, spurring on, in many cases, a loss of confidence regarding the possibility of complete assimilation for themselves and their posterity. According to Tom, a youth pastor in the Chicago Church:

> I think American society is most outrageous and unjust. It's still so racist. No matter how hard we try to prove ourselves, there's always a barrier in the minds of white Americans. They have a superiority complex. You know, like the recent racist remarks by that senator against Judge Ito. They don't know what minorities go through. It's never on equal footing....I didn't realize prejudice and discrimination growing up, but since college and up you see a lot more discrimination. Once I started to notice, I saw it everywhere. There is a *lot*. US is *not* a melting pot. We've got a lot of problems.

As another 29-year-old respondent put it:

> Hey, let's face it. It's clear I'm not apple pie. You are always going to look like you are not apple pie. I just want to be proud of where I am from and where my parents are from. I am adjusting to the situation I am in.

For most of them, these identity crises become a significant catalyst for their decision to become involved in the ethnic church, which organization subsequently serves as an important vehicle in their efforts at ethnic "rediscovery." For many, church participation becomes a prelude to a genuine religious "conversion." For those who were already "Christians," such point of crisis seems often to lead to a renewed commitment to religion, or to a "born again" experience. As described by a female church member:

> I used to go to church, nominally though, when I was growing up, but when I went to college, I decided not to hang around with any Koreans. But I found that friendships with Americans were shallow and not very satisfying. So I ended up spending a lot of time with Koreans. In church, I found God. Although I have some problems with Korean churches, I get a lot out of it. In church, I felt my ethnicity affirmed. There, it was OK to be Korean.

Second-generation Korean ethnic identity

If the second-generation Korean-American ethnicity can thus be seen, in large part, as situationally driven, what, then, is the nature of this ethnic identity? In dealing with this question, it is useful to investigate the nature of symbolic boundaries church-goers draw to distinguish themselves as a group from the outside world, which is an intrinsic part of the process of constructing self-identity (Lamont 1992). According to Barth (1969), cultural contents of ethnic dichotomies are of two orders – *overt signals or signs*, the diacritical features that people look for and exhibit to show identity, which often include features such as dress, language, house-form, or general style of life; and *basic value orientations*, the standards of morality and excellence by which performance is judged (Barth 1969:14). Although the criteria which the second-generation members employ to define group boundary and membership at the most general level consist of the former, namely race, nationality, and language, I argue in this paper that one of the most important markers of second-generation ethnicity, and those for which the role of the ethnic church becomes relevant and essential, consists of these "basic value orientations."

Race, an involuntary and ascriptive marker, is considered by Korean Americans to be one of the most central features of identity which separates them from the dominant Anglo society. However, one of the most significant ways in which the second-generation members within the church articulate their ethnic identity is through the appropriation of certain elements of "practiced culture," that is, values and standards of traditional Korean morality. These values, ubiquitously invoked in their discourse about their Korean identity, consist of a set of core traditional Korean Confucian values – most significantly, filial piety, respect for parents, family-centeredness, and work ethic.

> My Korean values include respect for elders, emphasis on education. Another thing I love about Korean culture is its family-orientedness. I adore my parents. And I really like how children take care of their parents.

> Of course, I'm Korean physically. Also I'm different from most Americans in that I go out of my way to help my parents. Is that a Korean thing? Americans don't care about parents. For example, when I was working, I would tell my boss I couldn't travel because I had to help out my parents' business at home. I really don't mind doing it because they work like dogs. Korean values also include respect for the elderly.

Compared to non-church-goers, the church members display a considerably higher degree of attachment to these Korean values and standards of morality, which are appropriated by them as highly salient criteria of their Korean ethnic identity and as self-defined markers for signaling membership and exclusion. Indeed, the more "religious" a member, the more embracing s/he tends to be of the traditional values espoused by the parents. The non-church-goers, although they may hold generally to these values, are not as strict in their interpretation of or adherence to them. Furthermore, compared with non-church respondents, the church members hold far more strictly to traditional Korean views regarding sexual morality and gender relations, displaying a much more critical stance toward American culture and values[9] such as individualism and liberal sexual morality. According to Gina, a devout church member:

> It's very important for me to cherish my Korean culture. I think Koreans in general have a better value system than Americans, like having respect for parents. American kids "dis" their parents and I think that kind of thing is at the root of a lot of problems in this society. You know, my parents strove to send me to school. So being Korean is having a sense of obligation. Also having self-sacrifice, I guess. It's also having a certain work ethic. To tell you the truth, I think Americans are lazy in general. They just do what needs to be done, and no more. And Americans, they do whatever they want to do. They have a gluttonous life-style. Their sexual morality is going down the drain. I don't believe in pre-marital sex. We have more respect for elders. We are more conservative, believe in rules.

And while the non-church members tend to believe much more in "making decisions for oneself" rather than blindly obeying parents, the church members express little objection to the hierarchy and authority of the Korean culture, actually indicating a preference for its "clear rules" over values of individualism.

The Ethnic Church: The Site of Cultural Reproduction and Socialization

The major significance of the Korean ethnic church for the second generation lies, then, not only in its capacity to strengthen and reinforce ethnic identity by supporting general aspects of "culture (food, language, and customs)," but through its capacity to provide reinforcement for value orientations. Aside from the cultural functions of the ethnic church, Christianity is above all a system of values and ethics, and it is through the power of this ethical dimension, and the way it interrelates with the Korean system of values, that a powerful sense of group consciousness and boundary is forged among the second generation.

Despite variations in their degrees of religious commitment,[10] I have found that most church-goers take their Christian faith and identity very seriously, displaying a deep commitment to God and to Christian values and worldview. And as is revealed in the following response by Tina regarding the meaning of her faith, the beliefs these church-goers hold are of a conservative/fundamentalist worldview.[11]

> I believe in Christ, that He is our Lord. I believe in His salvation of us. I believe that all the history about the fall and redemption is central to Christianity. Once you respect that Christ is a redeemer, these have consequences for life....It means serving through the church. I think some of it is trying to filter out the impact of what one's exposed to in secular messages. We often receive contradictory messages. It's having hopefulness. It's a form of happy encouragement....It means that you have eternal life. It also means that you believe that God really is the creator of earth, He has dominion over your life. And believing you have a distinct, different purpose....I guess it means filtering out popular culture, abiding by the Ten Commandments.... Things like living your life so you're fulfilling God's ambition. If I wanted to be rock star, I don't think I'll be fulfilling God's wish. You know, I had a friend in college living with a guy – this is definitely against being a Christian.

However, when one closely examines their discourse about religious faith and identity, seemingly one of classic conservative Christian rhetoric, what is striking is the extent to which this discourse seems to be resonant of their discourse about Korean identity. For instance, one often finds that some of the principal traditional Korean values, such as filial piety, are prominently reflected in their discourse about their Christian values and faith.

> Q: What does it mean for you to be Christian? What does it mean to "live by the word of God?"
>
> A: Trying to live like the Christ did, trying to live holy. How you act toward the ones you love, and loving your enemies. Bible also tells you to respect your parents.
>
> A: Being Christian means loving God, loving others. Don't smoke, drink, or party. Be obedient to parents.
>
> A: Church made me into a good person. Like respecting elders. My attitude toward sex. That we should cherish family.
>
> A: Christian values include don't smoke, drink, do drugs. Be more merciful. Also it includes obeying my parents. God gave me these parents for a reason. We should also treat our elders better. That would be a Christian thing to do.

Aside from filial piety, values related to family and sexual conduct also appear indistinguishable as Korean or conservative Christian morality. And sometimes, as illustrated in the following remark by a 25-year-old member, the boundaries of conservative Christian identity and those of Korean ethnic identity appear as virtually fused.

> There are many truths in the American society. Because of that, there is no value system. Everything and anything is permissible. So we lose common dignity, respect, and people end up getting absorbed in their own little worlds. People used to live by Christian virtues, knew definite right or wrong. Now, kids are being killed, and are killing their parents. All because the parents don't have any values to give them. People are encouraged to be open-minded so they lose definition. Koreans have a better value system, like the way Christianity used to be.

Focusing on the Chicago Church, I explore in the following pages the ways in which second-generation ethnic identity and boundary are reinforced and constituted within the Korean church through its relationship with conservative Christianity.[12] Through an investigation both at the level of institution and rhetoric, I focus on how this reinforcement occurs through a general process of cultural transmission within the church and by the way traditional Korean values are legitimized and sacralized through their identification with conservative Christian morality.

Cultural transmission: institutional

Institutionally, cultural transmission at the Chicago Church begins with the structure and organization of the church itself, which is governed by two major principles: gender and age-based hierarchy. In the manner of the traditional Korean church, the Chicago Church is organized in a vertical, male-dominated, hierarchical structure, headed by a male pastor who wields considerable authority and power, and governed by a large group of elders, all of whom are male. As in the majority of the Korean ethnic churches, women are not only prohibited from the position of pastorship in the Chicago Church, but female members of the church cannot become elders, although they are allowed to become deaconesses. Such fundamental gender inequality and separation is reflected in daily tasks and activities as well; the division of responsibility within the church, both among the first and the second generations, tends to fall generally along gender lines, with women usually taking on all of the traditional female activities, like cooking, cleaning, and serving. With regard to leadership positions, female deacons are usually given responsibilities for those departments of the church commonly considered "soft," such as education, library, and Korean language, while "hard" departments, such as finance and preaching, are maintained under male leadership.

Aside from the gender hierarchy, the hierarchy of authority in the church is also strictly age-based, the dynamics of which can be observed not only within the first-generation congregation, but between the first and the second generations and within the second generation. In the Chicago Church, as in most of the other Korean churches, the second-generation ministry is unquestionably subordinate to the authority of the first generation, and governed by an authoritarian style of leadership. According to a youth leader of the church:

> One of the important cultural aspects of the Korean church is its authoritarian aspect – father knows best. Don't disobey the father 'til he dies. Every older person in the church has absolute authority over the younger person. In the Korean context, these family father-figures have absolute authority in every area of your life. In Christianity, this is not necessarily true. So all this is more cultural than religious or Christian.

Another church member observed that, "We are never equal [the first and the second generation]. We always have to do what they say. A lot of ideas we have are too radical for the head pastor to deal with. We are seen as 'rocking the boat.'"

This general organizational framework, with its embodiment of the sacred core of traditional Korean values and principles of social relationships – authoritarianism and gender/age hierarchy – can be considered the most general level at which the ethnic socialization of the second-generation members, which begins in the home, is continued. While these ethnic values may be embraced or accepted to varying degrees by the second generation, becoming a "serious" Christian on the part of the second generation does seem to entail a serious acceptance of all the cultural aspects of the church. As one former churchgoer observed of Korean-American Christians: "The more you believe in God, the more Korean you tend to be."

The second level at which Korean culture is transmitted and reinforced among the second generation is that of social interaction. Through a variety of unwritten norms, rules, and codes of conduct which are transmitted and perpetuated at the level of everyday social interaction, and through the strong, unspoken expectation within the church that everyone conform to these rules, the normative socialization of the second-generation members is further realized. According to one respondent:

> This church has all these rules. When you're in the church, you have to play by these rules. It's an influence from the first generation. What kind of message are we giving to the kids? Well, that you have to become Korean to become Christian.

The rules of behavior such as those related to the "deference to elders," for example, are the ones to which everyone strictly adheres; even within the second generation itself, the younger members must display a behavior of respect and deference to older members, no matter how much older.

Another striking aspect of the social culture among second-generation members is the adherence to traditional gender roles in male–female interaction. In the course of everyday social interaction, one can observe a great effort on the part of the female members to display "proper" traditional feminine behavior, such as behaving in a polite, subdued, and non-aggressive manner. As one former church member remarked, "Korean girls [within the church] tend to be more appeasing, to not want to cause trouble, not assert themselves," being typically "quiet, passive." Proposing that this conservatism probably comes from being a Korean woman as much as it does from being a Christian, Laura, a 23-year-old graduate student, remarked:

> Girls are definitely supposed to act a certain way. I'm friends with a lot of guys. That bugs them. In Korean churches, male/female separation is a very big deal. You know, all the etiquette, sitting in a certain way....Like, I would go to church, and they can't deal with me because I have a lot of guy friends and I'm very friendly. These women come up to me and say you have to be mean to the guys or they'll all ask you out. Isn't it the Christian thing to be nice? That's not a Christian mentality, that's a Korean mentality....The gender role, it's in a lot of little things. The way Koreans think bugs me. For example, if I'm outgoing, they automatically stereotype me. I guess I'm supposed to be a perfect little Korean girl. They think I'm not very deep, a flitty social butterfly.

Further evidence of adherence to traditional gender roles is also revealed in the way women and men tend to segregate themselves spatially in social situations. Bible classes are also strictly gender-segregated.

As important markers of ethnic, as well as of religious identity and boundary, these norms and rules of conduct are reproduced within the church among the second generation through enormous pressures to conform. One respondent observed:

> Yeah, [Korean] Christians are all preppy, and conservative. You have no freedom. You have to dress a certain way, act a certain way. You have to greet adults in a certain way. It seems to me that in American churches, you have much more freedom.

Susan, who no longer attends Korean churches because she is very "dissatisfied" with "superficial" and "hypocritical" aspects of the Korean church, related the following:

> If you go to church, it's great because everyone is second-generation Korean American; they speak English but they are also Korean. But, I found many of them very hard to socialize with. There were certain standards that were created there – within the church group but outside the religious aspect – like ways of speaking, standards of behavior. Second, the way you looked – they were all very preppy, appearance-conscious people. The standard of behavior I saw was like, don't question anything. Everyone has to be the same, think and look the same. Everyone looked so proper and superficial. Being a free thinker, I was always questioning them, their religion, but that was taboo. And another standard of behavior was the way everyone worshipped – singing the songs fervently, loudly, with passion. You listen to sermons and in little groups, you paraphrase what is said in the Bible, and agree and write down everything the group leader said. It appeared that you didn't question. There was severe pressure to conform.

Indeed, one of the highly notable things about the social atmosphere of the Chicago Church is its inwardness; the church members do not appear particularly open to newcomers in general, tending to behave in a very "cliquish" manner.

As a "little ethnic world" for these Korean Americans, one major criterion for membership in this group seems to be conformity to the traditional Korean manners of conduct within the church and to the values that underlie them. In addition to being a Christian, an individual must conform to these rules of conduct, or one is not considered a member. It appears that the underlying message is indeed, that one "must become Korean to become Christian."

Cultural transmission: rhetorical

It is clear that the church is institutionally an important arena for the transmission and maintenance of traditional Korean values. However, another fascinating aspect of this process is the way the religious dimensions of Christianity interact with Korean culture to provide legitimation for Korean culture and values, thereby supporting a sense of Korean ethnic identity and group consciousness. While various studies have amply documented the existence and importance of the "ethnic" functions of the Korean church (Han 1994; Hurh and Kim 1984; Min 1992), very few studies have closely examined the relationship of the "religious" functions of the church to the matter of ethnicity, tending to separate the "cultural/ethnic" and "religious" dimensions of the church. In this section, by examining the nature and strategies of persuasive religious discourse, or rhetoric, within the churches, I show how the ethnic and religious aspects of the church are irrevocably interrelated in supporting and reinforcing ethnic identity and consciousness.

Religious language is employed by the speaker to give an interpretation of reality (Palinkas 1982: 248). The persuasive or rhetorical quality of that language allows for that interpretation to be shared by others: "An agreed-upon and commonly held interpretation of reality is a prerequisite for social identity. It is also the constructive link with personal identity" (Mol 1976:67). Thus, by looking at religious language and strategies of discourse, we can deconstruct the various ways in which it helps form, symbolically, a sense of identity in the listeners.

In discussing Chinese Christian churches in the U.S., Lawrence Palinkas (1982, 1989) speaks of the process of "identification" between the Christian and Chinese worldviews which occurs in the rhetoric of the pastor, whereby through the use of various rhetorical devices such as the use of kinship terms, anecdotes, and analogy relating Christian principles to Chinese examples, the pastor establishes an identification between the Chinese and Christian worldview, helping to resolve the identity conflict of the immigrants. Within the second-generation congregation of the two Korean ethnic churches, I found a similar process of identification to be occurring. Through a selective use and interpretation of the Bible during sermons or Bible instruction, a kind of unity and identification are established directly between Korean values/worldviews and Christian values/worldviews, providing a powerful religious sanction and legitimation for traditional Korean morality and "way of life."

For example, one of the most commonly stressed themes in sermons and Bible study in the churches is that of "obedience" or "submissiveness." In one Bible study class I observed for a group of junior high-school boys, the theme of instruction was termed "developing a submissive mind." Despite the fact that humility is a classic Christian virtue, what was distinctive about the approach of this class was its single-minded devotion to fostering an obedient attitude, and that the primary goal of the instruction lay in applying this supposedly Christian virtue of submissiveness to what appeared to be a rather unquestioning obedience to parents. For instance, after a study of a biblical passage designed to demonstrate the principles of obedience to Jesus Christ, the Bible study instructor pontificated:

> Do you listen to your parents? Are you submissive to your parents? How can Jesus Christ's example teach us how to be more obedient to our parents? God has to be within you for you to be motivated to be obedient. To obey God and to have Him in you is to obey your parents!

Eun-Young Kim (1989), in her study of a group of Christian college students in California, has made a similar observation that the "theme of total surrender" is one of the most frequently used rhetorical devices in sermons, and that the analogy of God and humans to fathers and children is one of the most frequently used metaphors. She says, "In the sermons, it is repeatedly emphasized that one should surrender completely to God's authority and power, and should learn humiliation and humbleness" (p. 16).

Related closely to filial piety and obedience, another theme also frequently emphasized is that of generational continuity, as the following passage from a sermon at the South Park Church clearly helps to demonstrate. Relating to his audience how he happened to arrive at his calling, the minister stated:

> Do you know why I became a minister? I used to say facetiously it was because I had nothing else to do. I thought I was privileged. I was told I had special talents, and that I was the "hope"...but soon, however, my understanding of my calling went through major revisions. It started when I began to feel that there was a foggy area that didn't explain why I became a minister. However, after a while, I realized that becoming a minister had nothing to do with me!! My father came from North Korea, the only one in my family who came to the south after the Korean War. I bet my grandfather up in North Korea, who was a devout Christian, prayed every day and night for his kid. And what better fruit for their prayer than for their grandchild to become a minister? So I realized my calling had to do with my grandparents, and I felt connected to them. They were involved in one of the biggest decisions in my life. What is the point of all this? That we are all connected to people who had gone before us and to those who will come after us. What our ancestors did had tremendous effect on us and what we do. And when you see children, you know what you see and do influences them too.

With filial obedience as an undercurrent theme as well, the central message of this sermon is that God was not the only source of the pastor's calling toward the ministry, but that the wishes of his ancestors were just as vital. By subtly weaving the desirability of piety and Christian devotion with the message of filial devotion, the point is made that not only is being filial being a good Christian but that being a good Christian amounts to being filial.

In the Bible study classes for girls, the themes of obedience and submission are emphasized as well. However, whereas the boys' classes tend to relate the themes to larger social, political, and historical examples, the lessons in the girls' classes are illustrated mostly through references to exemplary behaviors of prominent biblical heroines whose conduct also demonstrates the related feminine virtues of self-sacrifice, chastity, purity, devotion, self-control, and perseverance. For instance, in one junior high-school girls' class I observed, the topic of the study was the life of the female biblical heroine Anna,[13] whose heroism consisted of spending her long life in celibate devotion to God after the loss of her husband at a young age. After reviewing with the students the virtues of her life, the most important of which is Anna's choice of celibacy in the service of God after her husband's death, the instructor remarked:

> Of course, these days and age, getting remarried is OK, but the point of this story is that to serve God, it's easier to do it when you are alone. Once Anna lost her husband, she decided to devote her life to this single thing. She spent all her time at the temple, fasting and praying. How did God use her? She was a pure, holy vessel God spoke through.

This example is rich with implications. Although one can argue that the virtues and principles inculcated here, such as devotion and chastity, represent some of the traditional Christian principles, the selection of a heroine whose devotion to God is demonstrated by chastity, especially through a refusal of remarriage, is significant. For women in the pre-modern Korean Confucian society, chastity and a life-long devotion to one's husband and his family were considered two of the cardinal female virtues; women who lost their husbands were discouraged from remarrying and were expected to spend the rest of their lives in the service of the in-laws (Deuchler 1992). Although the instructor here recognizes the inapplicability of such principles in the present day and age, the subtle and underlying message extolling the virtues of such behavior is definitely present, and not lost on the students. The virtue of single-minded devotion, if not to one man, then to God, is also an important message here. The idea of purity, which Anna was able to acquire by not getting remarried, is of course also central.

Ideology of Korean Christian identity and boundary maintenance

The church, however, does much more than transmit, reinforce, and legitimize traditional cultural elements which help to support a sense of ethnic identity. It is also instrumental in consolidating group unity and powerfully catalyzing a sense of exclusive group identity and consciousness in its members by helping to create strict boundaries against the outside world.

Aside from the process of religious legitimation and validation, I have found that the strengthening of collective unity, which often leads to an exclusionary group mentality and delineating of strict boundaries, is achieved through a kind of ideological "fusion" of Korean and Christian group identities and consciousnesses. More specifically, a sense of strong ethnic group unity and exclusivity is achieved by portraying Koreans as a "special" group of Christians, in particular as a "better" and more "true" type of Christian than those found in society at large. Moving beyond the emphasis placed on Korean values in sermons and the validation of those values as Christian, one also finds in religious discourse the idea that Korean values, as superior to the values of the larger society, are actually *more consistent* with Christian values and principles, so that Koreans are better, or suited to be better, Christians. For instance, the argument is often made that traditional Korean values such as respect for elders are more consistent with Christian values than "American individualism" (Min

1992:1384) – so that *Korean* Christians as a group stand apart from the rest of the society.

This stance is commonly demonstrated in the rhetoric that Korean Christians, as a morally superior group, have a duty to "save" and "improve" American society, although it is not always clear how this is to be done. One of the youth pastors put it this way.

> I think Korean Americans are called in a particular way by God. God calls particular people to work through. The responsibility of Korean Americans is to renew the Kingdom of God in America, help better its morality and value system. Morality in the U.S. is declining. Korean Americans have a special place in a struggle against that. I believe that God works through marginalized people. They can see the real problems of society. Korean Americans are sometimes too busy trying to be successful but they can contribute a lot to this. We still have the tradition of respecting elders, taking care of children.

Going further, a special sense of group identity and unity is achieved, both for the first and the second generations, by reinforcing a sense of nationhood and nationalism; Korea as a nation has been chosen by God to "save" the world and Koreans have a special "mission" in America and the world. A first-generation female deacon explained.

> God chooses nations to move the world. You know, Christianity came from Europe to Korea as Korea was ending. God uses Koreans. To me, we're called. I think He chose us for the kingdom of God. That's why so many Korean kids go to the seminary. Maybe God's raising up Korean children. Look at America. Their generation is gone to me. They're not very effective. If Billy Graham's gone, God will choose someone else but we won't have that strong evangelists for while. Maybe Koreans will be it.

Indeed, another common way Korean ethnic churches contribute to maintaining Korean ethnic identity is by bringing church members' attention to their homeland in many different ways. One common theme is the reunification of Korea.

In delineating a group boundary which is both religious and Korean, an opposition is erected not just between Christians and non-Christians, but between Korean Christians and the "larger" society in general, including other Christians. Charging that American society has "turned against" the principles of true Christianity, this opposition is expressed most clearly in visceral critiques of American society which seem to crop up ubiquitously in sermons. The following is an excerpt from a first-generation sermon.

> Since the middle of the 20th century American society has suffered from its highest development of materialist civilization, which on the other hand has brought forth the corruption of religious and moral life.... The materialistic progress of American society has not produced a paradise. On the contrary, it has caused wholesale social problems – labor unrest, racial conflicts, the busing issue, prostitution, traffic congestion, and juvenile delinquency, and drug addiction.... The fundamental reason for all these social problems derives from the degradation of moral life among Americans. Is it right that the fetishism of material progress gives rise to a belief that moral life is an individual matter? Is it right that moral education should be excluded from the curriculum of elementary schools? ... Materialistic civilization bases its existence on the premise that the human brain can solve all the problems. This kind of civilization means idolatry. Miracles will happen at the moment we liberate ourselves from idolatry and return to God (I. Kim 1981: 205–206).

Creating a boundary which is as much ethnic as religious, this critique of American society as a chaotic, degenerate, and morally decaying place becomes the pivotal point at which the unity between Korean and Christian values is effected.

This analysis suggests that a crucial element in Korean Christian ideology, and one which becomes especially salient and meaningful in the drawing of group boundaries and mobilizing collective identity and consciousness, is the role of the conservative/fundamentalist ideology and worldview. In this fusion of Christian and Korean worldviews, the rationale for boundary maintenance becomes one of conservative morality, which is articulated in its critique against the "moral decay" of society, including sexual immorality, extreme individualism, relativism, and lack of family values and discipline. This phenomenon, then, provides some explanation for the particularly conservative, if not fundamentalist, orientations of most Korean ethnic churches in the U.S., which are known, regardless of denominational affiliation, for their conservative theological orientations. In sum, theological conservatism, in addition to the cultural conservatism of the church, is vital to maintaining group cohesion; the important cultural function of the Korean ethnic church is intertwined with and supported in key ways by the church's theological orientation.

Despite its considerable success in socializing the second generation, the Korean ethnic church, however, is by no means an ideologically monolithic institution. Within the church, there exist a variety of ideological tensions between the two generations. These reveal that the socialization process of the second generation does not occur without a considerable level of conflict and tension. The following section will briefly consider these problems.

Intergenerational and Gender Conflict

The first major source of intergenerational conflict lies in the second generation's ambivalence toward the basic cultural norms of the church. In spite of their internalization of many of the basic ethnic cultural norms, there nevertheless exists a considerable amount of contestation and questioning of these norms on the part of second-generation members, which, in effect, represents a challenge to first-generation authority. For many, particular areas of tension involve the authoritarianism of the first-generation leadership, and the church's quietistic orientation. According to one member:

> At the church, the decisions are made unilaterally, usually by the pastor. It's totally undemocratic. The idea of working as a team is an anathema. There is not enough emphasis on lay leadership. Because of its top-down structure, it does not know how to tap into the gifts of various people within the church. The church does not value people's gifts, which, I think, is an important biblical value. Instead, it places scriptural emphasis on the wrong things. For example, they justify this top-down leadership by emphasizing a servant–leadership relationship in the Bible.

Charging the church as being "culturally" rather than "biblically mediated," this state of affairs is seen by many as being overly reflective of Korean culture. As one evidence of its inwardness and lack of social consciousness, Joseph, a youth pastor at the Chicago Church, points out what he sees as the church's insensitivity to racial issues and problems, as well as its lack of cultural and racial openness. He says:

> Mainly, there is a total misreading of the scripture, in the context, audience, and needs. The leadership does not value biblical priority, such as having openness and sensitivity. There are lots of things that should be biblical priorities that are not fully lived out in the church, like authenticity as Christians, character, integrity, things that should not just be assumed for Christians. And evangelization is fine, but it should involve everybody, not just Koreans, and people of other countries too.

He also makes the critique that, despite its relative wealth, the church does very little for the community in which it is located, allocating most of its budget for internal purposes, especially those directed at maintaining the prestige and size of the church. Others criticize the tendency of the churches toward schisms, caused in many cases by the struggles for "status and power" within the churches. As one member sees it, the crux of the problem is that there is "more Koreanization of Christianity than vice versa."

Furthermore, one of the major ways in which the "cultural problem" of the ethnic church is expressed is through the members' struggle between their Korean and Christian identities; many feel that the cultural aspects of the Korean church hinder them from becoming "true" Christians. One member put it this way:

> Many Korean Americans understand Christian faith through the grid of the Korean culture. And sometimes this can be negative, like, it is not about being Christian at all. People get very hypocritical. It becomes about "putting your best foot forward" at the church, turning around, and then being like everyone else. I don't like the way Korean culture has influenced what it is to be Christian.

According to another member:

> You know, many of them [church-goers] can't distinguish between Koreanness and Christianity. Their idea of Christianity is bound up within the Korean church. To them, their image of God is often their pastor. So when they reject Korean culture, Christianity often goes along with it.

Within the context of intergenerational conflict, the ambivalence, however, is more pronounced typically for the female church members. For them, the "conservative" Korean values regarding women can translate into even greater tensions with the norms of the ethnic church and into a greater sense of clash between their "Korean" and "American" value systems and identities. One of the obvious reasons for this is that the Korean female members are subject to an additional dimension of hierarchalization: female subordination. The following is a response by Rachel, a married American-born member in her twenties.

> In the church, two cultures [Korean and Christian] coincide, like the aspect of obedience and submission. Women are definitely second-class citizens. There are many who don't think women should be in positions of authority. Yeah, the submissive/ obedience aspect. This means that you don't have any rights. As a Korean or as a Korean American, our relationship tends to be hierarchical, with elders and authority figures. You are expected to obey. Even in the second generation, there's segregation between men and women....Christianity reinforces the idea that you serve – Christian life is one of service. There's a lot of reinforcement of this in church. But it's always the women who serve. And when you get married things really change for women. My observation is that before I got married, I led a very different life. Now I've absorbed a lot of cultural norms. When I was single, people didn't expect as much as they do now. Once you're married, they expect you to be more conforming, like being more serving, domestic. Before it was less of a social blunder if I happened not to think of doing something. Now, there's less forgiveness....Being Korean is a struggle with where to draw the line in being less important than men.

She adds, "You know, for women, the issues are deeper. Because let's face it, men have always had it easier in the Korean culture."

Discussion and Conclusion

Through the study of two Korean Protestant ethnic churches, this paper has attempted to reexamine the issue of second-generation ethnicity in the context of a contemporary non-white ethnic group, and the role ethnic religion plays in the construction, support, and reinforcement of this ethnic identity. I have tried to show that one major significance of the Korean ethnic church, more specifically the evangelical/conservative Protestant church, lies in its capacity to help construct and reinforce in the second generation certain forms of "tangible" ethnicity, namely key traditional morality and values inherited from the first generation. This is accomplished within the Korean ethnic church by providing a powerful religious basis for the legitimation and sacralization of some of these traditional ethnic values and moral standards, which serve as decisive markers for the members' sense of emerging Korean identity. Although by no means identical to the first-generation ethnicity, such appropriated "primordial" values and moral standards, fused in significant ways with conservative/fundamentalist Christian values, become central to the articulation of the second generation's often highly exclusive sense of group identity.

This study has found that, in their quest for ethnic church involvement, the church members are motivated to a great extent by their sense of marginalization from the larger society. The belief on the part of many Korean Americans that complete assimilation is not possible because of their race and physiognomy generates an intense drive toward ethnic identity, sought often through the ethnic church. Thus, in spite of a great deal of ambivalence and conflict held by many Korean Americans toward the ethnic church, the first-generation church remains crucial for the second-generation members as one of the few institutions in the Korean-American community that is able to effectively provide a significant sense of belonging and group identity. And while it is clear that the church functions as a powerful instrument of legitimation for the ethnic interests of the first generation, it is important for the second generation as a vehicle of group empowerment through its capacity to confer positive value on group identity and to enable the members to challenge the negative group-image and stereotypes imposed by the larger society. In this way, the church serves a classic "double function": as an apology and legitimation for the status quo, but also as a means of empowerment, protest, and liberation for the socially subordinate group (McGuire 1983; Solle 1984). Or as one church member put it: "In church, you play by Korean rules, not God's rules. But I get a lot out of it. I get a lot of support. I feel a sense of peace and Christ provides a sense of bond between people."

These findings have important theoretical implications for the issues of second-generation ethnicity and religion. First, the findings regarding the nature and the process of the construction of Korean-American second-generation ethnicity point to a need to revise traditional perspectives on second-generation ethnic identity and the intergenerational assimilation process, most of which have been based on the experiences of earlier European immigrant groups. For a contemporary ethnic group like Korean Americans, the data suggest that the issue of race is highly salient as a determinant of their ethnic experience and expectations of assimilation. In challenge to earlier theories which postulate that second-generation members, eager for assimilation and acceptance, would attempt to overthrow the legacies of their ethnic identity and religion especially as they move up the economic ladder, the Korean-American case has demonstrated that, when faced with sufficient levels of subjective barriers to assimilation, many will attempt to cope with the problems of marginality by attempting to reclaim their ethnicity and and by constructing highly defensive forms of ethnic identity.[14]

Second, the findings of this study highlight the need to modify earlier views regarding the role of ethnic religion for the second generation, while lending support to perspectives which emphasize the continuing vitality of religion in America, especially for ethnic groups. Contrary to the secularization theory, religion continues to flourish in America because religion has always been, and remains, a fundamental expression of subcultural identity in a pluralist society (Warner 1993). While this role of religion has always had a special pertinence for the first-generation immigrants, this paper has shown that ethnic religion can continue to play a highly significant role for the second generation as a source of and support for emergent ethnic identity and group cohesion. Furthermore, in our increasingly multicultural environment where ethnicity has become an ever more socially acceptable mode of expressing group identity, this function of religion has become even more salient.

The other important insight of this paper, however, is the significance and relevance of *conservative* Protestantism in successfully generating and maintaining this kind of ethnic group cohesion. Various scholars have noted that the strengths and vitality of contemporary evangelicalism can be attributed to its "strictness," which confers strong social bonds and cohesion among the church members (Kelley 1972; lannaccone 1994). It is my contention that Christian conservatism, both through its peculiar resonance with traditional Korean values and its ability to help articulate a clear sense of group boundary and identity, is crucial to the ethnic project of the Korean church regarding the second generation. The conservative Protestant ideology of the Korean church, through its reference to the unchanging, divine laws which dictate standards of strict ethics and morality for the members of the group, has proven quite effective as a form of legitimation for strict, exclusive ethnic group identity in the second-generation church members. In contrast, scholars such as Steve Bruce (1983) have remarked on the relative ineffectiveness of liberal Protestantism in generating such group cohesion. As Bruce (1983:68) puts it, "The liberal insistence on reason as filter for revelation produces a variety of problems in social reproduction. In a pluralist society, denial of an objective and unchanging source of revelation invites diversity and the consequent problems of maintaining cohesion and commitment."

The challenges posed by second-generation members toward the ethnic church, however, raise questions about the future of the Korean ethnic church. In this paper, I suggest that the future of the ethnic church will depend largely on the future assimilation experiences of Korean Americans. To be sure, the assimilation path for an ethnic group depends on a variety of factors besides race. Other relevant factors can include the class character of a group, larger cultural orientation toward ethnic diversity, and, as recently stressed by scholars such as Gans (1992), economic conditions of the society that can facilitate or impede upward mobility. However, by demonstrating the problematic assimilation experiences even of a largely middle-class, upwardly mobile ethnic group like the Korean Americans, this paper has attempted to show the extent to which the effects of race can be powerful in outweighing the effects of economic conditions and even class character of a group on the assimilation process. If, in the future, Korean Americans are successful in achieving a sense of full assimilation, it is possible that Korean Protestant churches will live out their usefulness for the second generation. If not, the Korean ethnic church, in its current or in modified forms, will remain a viable institution for many members of the second, or even third generation seeking certainties of identity and a sense of belonging in American society.

NOTES

1 Much of immigrant literature on earlier turn-of-the-century European immigrant groups refers to these groups as "new," in opposition to the "old" first Puritan settlers in America. In this paper, however, "new" immigrants will refer to non-white groups predominantly from the Third World whose influx began after the liberalized provisions of the 1965 Immigration Act. "Old" immigrants in turn will refer to turn-of-the-century immigrant groups who were overwhelmingly European and white. This is consistent with the categories and terminologies set out in Portes and Rumbaut's (1990) *Immigrant America: A Portrait*.

2 I include as second-generation all those who have been born in the U.S. and those who arrived in the States before the age of 5. For the purposes of comparison, my study included interviews with a few church members who came to the U.S. between the ages of 6 and 10, but I did not see any noticeable differences between the two groups in terms of their sense of ethnic identity. For the sake of brevity, I will sometimes refer to the second-generation group simply as "Korean Americans." If speaking about the first generation, I will specify it as such.

3 As far as I am aware, there are no formal statistics on the rate of second-generation ethnic church participation in existence. My statement is based on personal estimates provided by various church leaders in the Chicago Korean community, all of whom concur that the rate of second-generation ethnic church participation up to the age of 17 is about 65 percent to 70 percent, a very high proportion of the teenage population. They also agree that the rate declines somewhat among the college population, at least during the initial years of college, although the estimates for this vary.

4 I use here the terms defined by Milton M. Gordon (1964: 70) in his classic study, *Assimilation in American Life: The Role of Race, Religion, and National Origins*. In this work, he defines "cultural" assimilation, or "acculturation," as "change of cultural patterns to those of host society, including religious belief and observance" which would be followed, if not occur simultaneously with "structural" assimilation – a "large-scale entrance into cliques and clubs, and institutions of host society, on primary group level." It is not clear where Gordon would place "economic" integration, that is, integration into the labor and work structure of the society, so I will employ this as a separate analytic category.

5 Although no comprehensive economic or social statistics on the second-generation members *per se* exist, most of my interviewees are enrolled in or have attended "elite" four-year private universities or colleges around the country, and those with jobs hold professional positions in such occupations as corporate-business, law, medicine, social services, or secondary-school teaching, placing them safely within the ranks of the middle or upper-middle class. In keeping with their class status, the respondents are also geographically dispersed, and generally do not reside in ethnic enclaves.

6 In fact, cultural interests or primordial sentiments themselves can become an important *motivation* for ethnicization, and these cultural interests can interact in complex ways with other types of interests, whether economic or political, to constitute the motivations and definitions for ethnic formation and mobilization.

7 All the names in this paper have been changed to protect the privacy of the informants.

8 There is often an expression of shared sense of cultural similarity with other "Asians" as well, which usually means Chinese or Japanese – those nations with strong Confucian cultural traditions. Although I did not sense a particularly strong degree of "pan-Asian" feelings among Korean Americans,

pan-Asian sentiments are sometimes expressed and mobilized in opposition to the "dominant" white group. Among Asians however, my sense is that particularistic ethnic sentiments based on nationalities remain predominant, as is the case among Korean Americans.

9 For the church-goers too, however, the responses were not without criticism related to Korean "culture." Some recognize that such an authoritarian value system also has its costs, like loss of individualism. According to one respondent, for example; "You know, Koreans can be like automatons. They have less independent thought because they are too influenced by their parents. There has to be some kind of a balance I think – there has to be respect for your parents and some independent thought."

10 Balch (1985:28) distinguishes three levels of religious involvement: "recruitment," "conversion," and "commitment." Recruitment refers to "joining a group," conversion means a change in belief and personal identity, and commitment refers to "the level of intensity of participation." This framework works well for categorizing the levels of church participation and involvement in both Korean churches.

11 Some of the central features of this conservative/fundamentalist belief system include a belief in Jesus Christ as personal savior, in His fall and redemption, and in a stance of non-accommodation toward secular culture. I have also found that most members adhere to some variant of biblical literalism.

12 Much evidence, gathered both from my interviews and from observations over the years, suggests that Korean parents tend to possess relatively negative feelings about assimilation; most Korean parents do not view complete Americanization as a desirable goal, remaining adamant about the importance of preserving the Korean "race," as clearly expressed in their efforts to prevent intermarriage in their children. It is my view that the Korean ethnic church, one of whose major purposes lies in deterring the process of assimilation in the second generation, constitutes the second most important arena of ethnic socialization, next to the home.

13 The story of widow Anna is found in Luke, 2: 36–38.

14 The current assimilation trajectory of Korean Americans has been characterized by Hurh and Kim (1984:27) as "adhesive adaptation," a situation where a group "would be Americanized both culturally and socially, but to a limited extent (especially in social dimension), and such Americanization would not replace or weaken any significant aspect of Korean traditional culture and social networks."

REFERENCES

Archdeacon, T. J. 1990. Hansen's hypothesis as model of immigrant assimilation. In *American Immigrants and their Generations: Studies and Commentaries on the Hansen Thesis after Fifty Years*, ed. P. Kivisto and D. Blanck, 42–63. Urbana and Chicago: University of Illinois Press.

Balch, R. W. 1985. What's wrong with the study of new religions and what we can do about it. In *Scientific Research of New Religions: Divergent Perspectives*, ed. B. K. Kilbourne, 24–39. Proceedings of the Annual Meeting of the Pacific Division of the American Association for the Advancement of Science, and the 59th Meeting of the Rocky Mountain Division, San Francisco: AAAS.

Barth, F. 1969. Introduction. In *Ethnic Groups and Boundaries: The Social Organization of Cultural Differences*, ed. F. Barth, 9–38. Boston, MA: Little, Brown, & Co.

Bruce, S. 1983. Identifying conservative Protestantism. *Sociological Analysis* 44:65–69.

Choy, B. Y. 1979. *Koreans in America*. Chicago: Nelson-Hall.

Conzen, K. N., D. A. Gerber, E. Morawska, G. E. Pozzeta, and R. J. Vecoli. 1992. The invention of ethnicity: A perspective from the U.S.A. *Journal of American Ethnic History* 29:3–41.

Deuchler, M. 1992. *The Confucian Transformation of Korea: A Study of Society and Ideology*. Cambridge, MA: Harvard University Press.

Dolan, J. P. 1972. Immigrants in the city: New York's Irish and German Catholics. *Church History* 41:354–368.

Fenton, J. Y. 1988. *Transplanting Religious Traditions: Asian Indians in America*. New York: Praeger.

Galush, W. J. 1977. Faith and fatherland: Dimensions of Polish-American ethnoreligion, 1875–1975. In *Immigrants and Religion in Urban America*, ed. R. Miller and T. D. Marzik, 84–102. Philadelphia, PA: Temple University Press.

Gans, H. 1979. Symbolic ethnicity: The future of ethnic groups and cultures in America. *Ethnic and Racial Studies* 2:1–20.

Gans, H. 1992. Second generation decline: Scenarios for the economic and ethnic futures of the post-1965

American immigrants. *Ethnic and Racial Studies* 15:173–192.

Geertz, C. 1963. The integrative revolution: Primordial sentiments and civil politics in new states. In *Old Societies and New States: The Quest for Modernity in Asia and Africa*, ed. C. Geertz, 105–157. New York: Free Press of Glencoe.

Gjerde, J. 1986. Conflict and community: A case study of the immigrant church in America. *Journal of Social History* 19:681–697.

Glazer, N. 1990. Hansen's hypothesis and the historical experience of generations. In *American Immigrants and their generations: Studies and Commentaries on the Hansen Thesis after Fifty Years*, ed. P. Kivisto and D. Blanck, 104–112. Urbana and Chicago: University of Illinois Press.

Glazer, N., and D. P. Moynihan. 1963. *Beyond the Melting Pot: The Negroes, Puerto Ricans, Jews, Italians, and Irish of New York City*. Cambridge, MA: MIT Press.

Gordon, M. 1964. *Assimilation in American Life: The Role of Race, Religion, and National Origins*. Oxford: Oxford University Press.

Haddad, Y. Y., and A. T. Lummis. 1987. *Islamic Values in the United States: A Comparative Study*. New York: Oxford University Press.

Han, G. S. 1994. *Social Sources of Church Growth: Korean Churches in Homeland and Overseas*. Lanham, MD: University Press of America.

Hansen, M. L. 1952. The third generation in America. *Commentary* 14 (November): 492–500.

Herberg, W. 1955. *Protestant—Catholic—Jew: An Essay in American Religious Sociology*. New York: Doubleday.

Hurh, W. M., and K. C. Kim. 1984. *Korean Immigrants in America*. Rutherford, NJ: Fairleigh Dickinson University Press.

Hurh, W. M., and K. C. Kim. 1990. Religious participation of Korean immigrants in the United States. *Journal for the Scientific Study of Religion* 29:19–34.

Iannaccone, L. R. 1994. Why strict churches are strong. *American Journal of Sociology* 99:1180–1211.

Isaacs, H. R. 1975. Basic group identity: The idols of the tribe. In *Ethnicity*, ed. N. Glazer and D. P. Moynihan, 29–52. Cambridge, MA: Harvard University Press.

Kelley, D. M. 1972. *Why Conservative Churches are Growing*. New York: Harper & Row.

Kim, E. Y. 1989. In search of self: Young Korean Americans in California and the ethnic church. Paper presented at the Sixth National Conference of the Association for Asian-American Studies, Hunter College, 1–3 June, New York.

Kim, I. 1981. *New Urban Immigrants: The Korean Community in New York*. Princeton, NJ: Princeton University Press.

Kim, I. 1995. Korean immigrant churches in the United States. *Yearbook of American and Canadian Churches 1995*, ed. K. B. Bedell. Nashville, TN: Abingdon Press.

Lamont, M. 1992. *Money, Morals, and Manners: The Culture of the French and American Upper-middle Class*. Chicago, IL: University of Chicago Press.

Lewins, F. W. 1978. Australia: Religion and ethnic identity. In *Identity and Religion*, ed. H. Mol, 19–38. Beverley Hills, CA: Sage Publications.

Lucas, H. S. 1955. *Netherlanders in America: Dutch Immigration to the United States and Canada, 1789–1950*. Ann Arbor: University of Michigan Press.

McGuire, M. B. 1983. Discovering religious power. *Sociological Analysis* 44:1–10.

McKay, J. 1982. An exploratory synthesis of primordial and mobilizationist approaches to ethnic phenomena. *Ethnic and Racial Studies* 5:395–420.

Miller, R. M. 1977. Introduction. *Immigrants and Religion in Urban America*, ed. R. M. Miller and T. D. Marzik, xi–xxii. Philadelphia, PA: Temple University Press.

Min, P. G. 1992. The structure and social functions of Korean immigrant churches in the United States. *International Migration Review* 26:1370–1394.

Mol, H. 1976. *Identity and the Sacred: A Sketch for a New Social-scientific Theory of Religion*. New York: Free Press.

Nahimy, V. C., and J. A. Fishman. 1965. American immigrant groups: Ethnic identification and the problem of generations. *Sociological Review* 13:311–326.

Palinkas, L. A. 1982. Ethnicity, identity, and mental health: The use of rhetoric in an immigrant Chinese church. *The Journal of Psychoanalytic Anthropology* 5:235–258.

Palinkas, L. A. 1989. *Rhetoric and Religious Experience: The Discourse of Immigrant Chinese Churches*. Fairfax, VA: George Mason University Press.

Patterson, W. 1988. *The Korean Frontier in America*. Honolulu: University of Hawaii Press.

Portes, A., and R. G. Rumbaut. 1990. *Immigrant America: A Portrait*. Berkeley: University of California Press.

Roosens, E. E. 1989. *Creating Ethnicity: The Process of Ethnogenesis*. London: Sage.

Rutledge, P. J. 1985. *Role of Religion in Ethnic Self-identity*. Lanham, MD: University Press of America.

Sarna, J. D. 1978. From immigrants to ethnics: Towards a new theory of ethnicization. *Ethnicity* 5:370–378.

Smith, T. L. 1978. Religion and ethnicity in America. *American Historical Review* 83: 1155–1185.

Solle, D. 1984. The Christian–Marxist debate of the 1960s. *Monthly Review* 36 (July–August):20–26.

Swierenga, R. 1991. Religion and immigration behavior. In *Belief and Behavior*, ed. P. Vandermeer, 164–188. New Brunswick, NJ: Rutgers University Press.

Warner, R. S. 1990. The Korean immigrant church in comparative perspective. Paper presented at the colloquium on The Korean Immigrant Church: A Comparative Perspective, Princeton Theological Seminary, 16–18 February, Princeton, NJ.

Warner, R. S. 1993. Work in progress toward a new paradigm for the sociological study of religion in the U.S. *American Journal of Sociology* 98:1044–1093.

Warner, W. L. 1953. *American Life*. Chicago, IL: University of Chicago Press.

Weber, M. 1963. *The Sociology of Religion*. Boston, MA: Beacon Press.

Whyte, W. F. 1943. *Street Corner Society: The Social Structure of an Italian Slum*. Chicago, IL: University of Chicago Press.

Williams, R. B. 1988. *Religion and Immigrants from India and Pakistan*. Cambridge: Cambridge University Press.

Yancey, W. L., E. P. Ericksen, and R. N. Juliani. 1976. Emergent ethnicity: A review and reformulation. *American Sociological Review* 41:391–403.

5

"The Normal American Family" as an Interpretive Structure of Family Life among Grown Children of Korean and Vietnamese Immigrants

Karen Pyke

The use of monolithic images of the "Normal American Family" as a stick against which all families are measured is pervasive in the family wars currently raging in political and scholarly discourses (Holstein & Gubrium, 1995). The hotly contested nature of these images – consisting almost exclusively of White middle-class heterosexuals – attests to their importance as resources in national debates. Many scholars express concern that hegemonic images of the Normal American Family are ethnocentric and that they denigrate the styles and beliefs of racial–ethnic, immigrant, gay–lesbian, and single-parent families while encouraging negative self-images among those who do not come from the ideal family type (Bernades 1993; Dilworth-Anderson, Burton, and Turner 1993; Smith 1993; Stacey 1998; Zinn 1994). Yet we still know little about how the Family ideology shapes the consciousness and expectations of those growing up in the margins of the mainstream. This study examines the accounts that grown children of Korean and Vietnamese immigrants provide of their family life and filial obligations. The findings suggest that public images of the Normal American Family constitute an ideological template that shapes respondents' familial perspectives and desires as new racial–ethnic Americans.

Family Ideology as an Interpretive Structure

Images of the Normal American Family (also referred to as the Family) are pervasive in the dominant culture – part of a "'large-scale' public rhetoric" (Holstein and Miller 1993:152). They are found in the discourse of politicians, social commentators, and moral leaders; in the talk of everyday interactions; and in movies, television shows, and books. Smith (1993:63) describes these ubiquitous images as an "ideological code" that subtly "inserts an implicit evaluation into accounts of ways of living together." Such images serve as instruments of control, prescribing how families ought to look and behave (Bernades 1985). Most scholarly concern centers on how this ideology glorifies and presents as normative that family headed by a breadwinning husband with a wife who, even if she works for pay, is devoted primarily to the care of the home and children. The concern is that families of diverse structural forms, most notably divorced and female-headed families, are comparatively viewed as deficient and dysfunctional (Fineman 1995; Kurz 1995; Stacey 1998). Scholars concerned about the impact of such images point to those who blame family structures that deviate from this norm for many of society's problems and who suggest policies that ignore or punish families that don't fit the construct (e.g., Blankenhorn 1995; Popenoe 1993, 1996).

In addition to prescribing the structure of families, the Family ideal contains notions about the appropriate values, norms, and beliefs that guide the way family members relate to one another. The cultural values of "other" families, such as racial–ethnic families, are largely excluded. For example, prevailing family images emphasize sensitivity, open honest communication, flexibility, and forgiveness (Greeley 1987). Such traits are less important in many cultures that stress duty, responsibility, obedience, and a commitment to the family collective that supersedes self-interest (Chung 1992; Freeman 1989). In further contrast to the traditional family systems of many cultures, contemporary American family ideals stress democratic rather than authoritarian relations, individual autonomy, psychological well-being, and emotional expressiveness (Bellah, Madsen, Sullivan, Swidler, and Tipton 1985; Bernades 1985; Cancian 1987; Coontz 1992; Skolnick 1991). Family affection, intimacy, and sentimentality have grown in importance in the United States over time (Coontz 1992), as evident in new ideals of fatherhood that stress emotional involvement (Coltrane 1996).

These mainstream family values are evident in the therapeutic ethic, guiding the ways that those who seek professional advice are counseled and creating particular therapeutic barriers in treating immigrant Asian Americans (Bellah et al. 1985; Cancian 1987; Tsui and Schultz 1985). Family values are also widely disseminated and glorified in the popular culture, as in television shows like *Ozzie and Harriet*, *Leave It To Beaver*, *The Brady Bunch*, *Family Ties*, and *The Cosby Show*, many of which are rerun on local stations and cable networks (Coontz 1992). Parents in these middle-class, mostly White, television families are emotionally nurturing and supportive, understanding, and forgiving (Shaner 1982; Skill 1994). Indeed, such shows tend to focus on the successful resolution of relatively minor family problems, which the characters accomplish through open communication and the expression of loving concern. Children in the United States grow up vicariously experiencing life in these television families, including children of immigrants who rely on television to learn about American culture. With 98 percent of all U.S. households having at least one television set, Rumbaut (1997:949) views TV as an immense "assimilative" force for today's children of immigrants. Yet, he continues, it remains to be studied how their world views are shaped by such "cultural propaganda." The images seen on television serve as powerful symbols of the "normal" family or the "good" parent – and they often eclipse our appreciation of diverse family types (Brown and Bryant 1990; Greenberg, Hines, Buerkel-Rothfuss and Atkin 1980). As the authors of one study on media images note, "The seductively realistic portrayals of family life in the media may be the basis for our most common and pervasive conceptions and beliefs about what is natural and what is right" (Gerbner, Gross, Morgan, and Signorielli 1980:3). Family scholars have rarely displayed analytic concern about the emphasis on emotional expressiveness and affective sentimentality that pervades much of the Family ideology, probably because the majority – who as middle-class, well-educated Whites live in the heartland of such values – do not regard them as problematic. As a result, this Western value orientation can seep imperceptibly into the interpretive framework of family research (Bernades 1993; Dilworth-Anderson et al. 1993; Fineman 1995; Smith 1993; Thorne and Yalom 1992).

The theoretical literature on the social construction of experience is an orienting framework for this study (Berger and Luckmann 1966; Holstein and Gubrium 1995). According to this view, cultural ideologies and symbols are integral components of the way individuals subjectively experience their lives and construct reality. The images we carry in our heads of how family life is supposed to be frame our interpretation of our own domestic relations. This is evident in the different ways that Korean and Korean American children perceived their parents' childrearing behavior in a series of studies. In Korea, children were found to associate parental strictness with warmth and concern and its absence as a sign of neglect (Rohner and Pettengill 1985). These children were drawing on Korean family ideology, which emphasizes strong parental control and parental responsibility for children's failings. In this interpretive framework, parental strictness is a positive characteristic of family life and signifies love and concern. Children of Korean immigrants living in the United States, on the other hand, viewed their parents' strictness in negative terms and associated it with a lack of warmth – as did American children in general (Pettengill and Rohner 1985). Korean American children drew on American family ideology, with its emphasis on independence and autonomy, and this cast a negative shadow on their parents' strict practices.

Although pervasive images of the Normal American Family subtly construct Asian family patterns of interaction as "deviant," countervailing images of Asians as a "model minority" are also widely disseminated. News stories and scholarly accounts that profile the tremendous academic success among some immigrant Asian children or describe the upward economic mobility observed among segments of the Asian immigrant population credit the cultural traditions of collectivist family values, hard work, and a strong emphasis on education. Such images exaggerate the success of Asian immigrants and mask intraethnic diversity (Caplan, Choy, and Whitmore 1991; Kibria 1993; Min 1995; Zhou and Bankston 1998). Meanwhile, conservative leaders use model minority images as evidence of the need to return to more traditional family structures and values, and they blame the cultural deficiency of other racial minority groups for their lack of similar success, particularly African Americans and Latinos (Kibria 1993; Min 1995; Zhou and Bankston 1998). The model minority construct thus diverts attention from racism and poverty while reaffirming the Family ideology. In the analysis of the accounts that children of immigrants provided of their family life, references to such cultural images and values emerged repeatedly as a mechanism by which respondents gave meaning to their own family lives.

Korean and Vietnamese Immigrant Families

This study focuses on children of Vietnamese and Korean immigrants because both groups constitute relatively new ethnic groups in the United States. Few Vietnamese and Koreans immigrated to the United States before 1965. However, from 1981 to 1990, Korea and Vietnam were two of the top five countries from which immigrants arrived (*Statistical Yearbook* 1995, table 2: pp. 29–30). Thus adaptation to the United States is a relatively new process for large groups of Koreans and Vietnamese, one that is unassisted by earlier generations of coethnic immigrants. The children of these immigrants, located at the crossroads of two cultural worlds, offer a good opportunity to examine the familial perspectives and desires of new racial-ethnic Americans.

Most in-depth study of children of immigrants examines only one ethnic group, which makes it difficult to know which aspects of adaptation are shared with other ethnic groups and which are distinct. Studying only one Asian ethnic group also contributes to a tendency to over-generalize the findings to all Asian ethnic groups. Thus this study was designed to compare two Asian ethnicities so that ethnic differences and similarities could be noted. The author selected Koreans and Vietnamese because, in addition to being new American ethnic groups, their economic status and pathways to immigration differ. Whereas Koreans have immigrated voluntarily, in search of better economic opportunities and educations for their children, most Vietnamese arrived as political refugees or to rejoin family members, some doing so after spending time in Vietnam's prisons or "re-education camps" (Gold 1993; Hurh 1998; Kibria 1993; Min 1998). Vietnamese immigrants have been, overall, less educated and from more rural and poorer backgrounds than Korean immigrants. Only 12 percent of first-generation Vietnamese heads of household have a college degree, compared with 45 percent for Koreans (Oropesa and Landale 1995). Family socioeconomic status is important to the study of adaptation because it affects the kinds of neighborhoods where immigrant children grow up and attend school (Zhou 1997). However, equally important are the cultural practices that organize family relationships, including parental values and childrearing practices, and the expectations that parents have of their children. It is here that ethnic differences among Koreans and Vietnamese appear more subtle.

Due to the relatively short history of massive Asian immigration, Asian American family research has been fragmented and limited. As Uba (1994) points out, most of the research has been descriptive rather than explanatory, has focused on Chinese Americans and Japanese Americans, and has given little attention to between-group differences. Thus the empirical picture of Korean and Vietnamese family systems is incomplete. What we do know is that the philosophical values of Chinese Confucianism have influenced the traditional family systems of Korea and Vietnam. These values emphasize solidarity, hierarchal relations, and filial piety (Kibria 1993; Hurh 1998; Min 1998; Sue and Morishima 1982). Confucianism provides a firm set of rules about how family members are supposed to behave toward one another (Cha 1994; Chung 1992; Kim and Choi 1994; Min 1998; Zhou and Bankston 1998). Priority is placed on family interests over individual desires and needs in order to maintain stability and harmony. Status distinctions guide the way in which members are to interact with one another. Younger members are expected to display respect, deference, and obedience to elders (including to older siblings, especially brothers), and wives are expected to show the same to their husbands and parents-in-law. Children – including adult offspring – are forbidden from expressing dissenting opinions or confronting parents, which is viewed as disrespectful (Chung 1992; Kibria 1993; Min 1998; Pettengill and Rohner 1985). Emotional expressiveness, including displays of affection, is discouraged, while self-control is emphasized (Hurh 1998; Uba 1994). Family ties and roles are central from birth until death, with a strong emphasis on family devotion. In general, parents are expected to rely on their children's support in later life. Confucianism assigns the care and financial support of aging parents to the eldest son and his wife, who are expected to live under the same roof as the parents. Korean and Vietnamese cultures also derive from Confucianism a respect for the well educated, and education is considered the primary means for social mobility. This undergirds the great importance that many Asian parents place on their children's education (Min 1998; Zhou and Bankston 1998). The economic hardships of many immigrant parents strengthen their emphasis on the education of their children, who they expect to forge success in the United States (Kibria 1993; Min 1998).

There are, of course, ethnic differences between Korean and Vietnamese families, as well as differences in the degree to which they conform to traditional family practices. Although the comparative research is scant, Confucianism appears to have a stronger influence on the traditional family system in Korea than in Vietnam. For example, in Vietnamese families there is a greater tendency for siblings to pool resources in providing filial care rather than relying on the elder son alone, which might be related to their poorer economic circumstances. Additionally, Vietnamese women are permitted stronger kinship ties to their family of origin upon marriage than are Korean women, who are expected to live with their in-laws if they marry an elder son (Hurh 1998; Kibria 1993).

Although more research is needed that closely examines Asian ethnic differences in family practices, the existing literature reveals patterns of similarities among the family systems of Koreans and Vietnamese that differentiate them from American family patterns. The role prescriptions, family obligations, hierarchal relations, lack of emotional expressiveness, and collectivist values associated with the traditional family systems of Korea and Vietnam contrast sharply with the emphasis on individualism, self-sufficiency, egalitarianism, expressiveness, and self-development in mainstream U.S. culture (Bellah et al. 1985; Cancian 1987; Chung 1992; Hurh 1998; Kim and Choi 1994; Min 1998; Pyke and Bengtson 1996; Tran 1988; Uba 1994). Immigrant children tend to quickly adopt American values and standards, creating generational schisms and challenges to parental control and authority. That parent–child conflict and cultural gaps exist in many Asian immigrant families is well documented (Gold 1993; Freeman 1989; Kibria 1993; Min 1998; Rumbaut 1994; Zhou and Bankston 1998; Wolf 1997). However, no study to date has closely examined the cultural mechanisms at play in this process. This study begins that task.

Method

The data are from an interview study of the family and social experiences of grown children of Korean and Vietnamese immigrants. Respondents were either located at a California university where 47 percent of all undergraduates are of Asian descent (Maharaj 1997) or were referred by students from that university. In-depth interviews were conducted with 73 respondents consisting of 34 Korean Americans (24 women, 10 men) and 39 Vietnamese Americans (23 women, 16 men). Both parents of each respondent were Korean or Vietnamese, except for one respondent, whose parents were both Sino-Vietnamese. Respondents ranged in age from 18 to 26 and averaged 21 years. Only one respondent was married, and none had children.

Respondents were either born in the United States (second generation) or immigrated prior to the age of 15 (1.5 generation), except for one Vietnamese American woman who immigrated at 17. The foreign-born accounted for 77 percent of the sample and immigrated at an average age of 5 years. The remaining 23 percent were born in the United States. Most respondents in this sample spent their entire adolescence in the United States, and a majority lived in the United States for most, if not all, of their childhood. Eight percent of the Vietnamese American respondents were born in the United States, compared to 38 percent of Korean American respondents (see table 5.1 for gender and ethnic differences). All study participants were college graduates or students and all resided in California, where one-third of U.S. legal immigrants arrive and 45 percent of the nation's immigrant student population lives (Zhou 1997). Thus the sample overrepresents those who are academically successful. Because the respondents have endured sustained exposure to assimilation pressures from the educational system, higher levels of assimilation were expected in this sample than in the larger immigrant population. As a result, these respondents were perhaps more likely to invoke American cultural ideals in describing their family life than a more representative sample that included the less educated and those who immigrated at older ages.

The author gathered the 73 individual interviews analyzed here in the preliminary phase of

Table 5.1. Sample Characteristics

Ethnicity	*n*	*Average age (years)*	*Foreign-born (%)*	*Average age at immigration (years)*
Korean American women	24	21	62	5
Korean American men	10	21	60	7
Vietnamese American women	23	21	96	5
Vietnamese American men	16	22	81	5
Total for sample	73	21	77	5

data collection for a larger ongoing project sponsored by the National Science Foundation (#SBR-9810725). The larger study includes a sample of 184 who participated in individual and focus group interviews. Only the initial phase of data collection was designed to prompt respondents' extensive descriptions of family life. The purpose of the larger study is to compare the dynamic complexities and structural contexts of adaptation and ethnic identity among children of immigrants, with special attention to their subjective experiences in mediating different cultural worlds. Because ethnic identity development differs for males and females (Espiritu 1997; Waters 1996), I also stratified the sample by gender.

As previously discussed, I stratified the sample by ethnicity, as well, in order to compare the effects of structural and cultural factors on adaptation processes. Despite Korean and Vietnamese distinctions in socioeconomic status, pathways to immigration, and cultural practices, I did not observe ethnic differences relevant to the central focus of this analysis. Although this is surprising, ethnic differences in the specific areas of family life that I was investigating are probably relatively subtle, particularly from the viewpoint of American children of Asian immigrant parents. More specifically, because respondents relied on American family ideology in giving meaning to their domestic relations, their focus was on how immigrant family life differs from the American ideal rather than from other Asian ethnic groups. This can blur ethnic distinctions and serve as a basis for shared personal experiences across ethnic groups. In fact, the rise of an Asian American ethnic identity among Asian-origin individuals is believed to result, in part, from the shared experiences of growing up American in an Asian home (Kibria 1997).

Gender differences observed in these data focused on the nature of respondents' criticisms of parents, with females complaining that parents grant more freedom and respect to sons. Males also complained of strict parents, but, when asked, acknowledged receiving more respect and freedom than sisters. These observed differences are not central to this analysis and are presented elsewhere (Pyke and Johnson 1999).

A five-page interview guide with open-ended questions and follow-up probes concerning the familial and social experiences of respondents directed the intensive interview process. All respondents were asked what being a child of immigrants was like, how they think immigration affected their family, what their parents were like when the respondent was growing up, what communication was like with their parents, what their parents' marriage was like, how close they feel to their parents, whether they ever felt embarrassed by their parents, whether they ever deceived their parents, what kinds of things their parents would do to get them to obey, whether they have ever disappointed their parents in any way, how they would change their parents if they could change anything about them they wanted, what kinds of assistance they plan to provide for their parents, and how they feel about providing assistance. The author conducted about one-third of the interviews, and several trained student assistants conducted the remainder. The student assistants took a qualitative methods course with the author, in which they learned interviewing skills and conducted practice interviews. They also received extensive training and practice with the interview guide prior to collecting project data. Most trained student interviewers were children of Asian immigrants near in age to the respondents. They were therefore able to establish rapport with respondents, and they typically received candid responses, as revealed by respondents' frequent use of colloquialisms and profanity in interviews. Interviews were conducted in 1996 and 1997 and lasted between 1½ and 3 hours. They were tape-recorded and transcribed for analysis.

This research began with the general goal of learning about the subjective family experiences of children of Asian immigrants. I used a grounded research approach that emphasized an inductive method of generating explanation from the data (Glaser and Strauss 1967; Strauss and Corbin 1990). Except for the general assumption that respondents are active agents in the construction of their family experiences, I imposed no apriori assumptions, hypotheses, or specific theoretical frames on the research process. This allowed unanticipated data to emerge. Interviews focusing on family dynamics were conducted until a point of saturation was reached, as indicated by the recurring nature of the data and the emergence of clear trends (Ambert, Adler, Adler, and Detzner 1995; Glaser and Strauss 1967).

The overwhelming majority of respondents provided negative descriptions of their parents and upbringing in at least one domain, such as discipline, emotional closeness, or communication; only a small minority provided wholly positive accounts. Despite such intergenerational strain or distance, most respondents were strongly committed to caring for their parents in later life. In order to more closely examine the interview data, and thus to uncover deeper layers of understanding to these prominent patterns, two research assistants coded data into topical categories that corresponded with the questions asked. These coded segments were extracted for ease in theoretical sorting. I then analyzed the data, moving back and forth between emerging theoretical categories of the extracted data and the full interviews in order to check the validity of the findings. Because I am a native-born White American and wanted both to guard against the introduction of personal bias in the analysis and to acquire greater awareness of ethnic meanings, I shared my interpretive understanding of the data with Asian American students and student assistants. I then incorporated their insights into the analysis.

During the analysis, I noted recurring references in one form or another to notions about so-called normal families. Respondents used such references for one purpose only – as a point of contrast to life in their families. Three categorical expressions of this theme emerged in the data: (a) comparisons with television families; (b) comparisons with families of non-Asian friends; and (c) contrasts with specific family behavior or characteristics described as normal or American. I did not anticipate the importance of such family imagery when I devised the interview guide; thus I never asked respondents about family life on TV or among friends, or what they regarded as a normal or ideal family. Rather this theme emerged unexpectedly in the interviews. The unprompted and recurring nature of these references indicates their importance as resources in respondents' construction of their family experiences. In the following discussion, I present a sample of the qualitative data, in the form of quotes, to illustrate the observed patterns (Ambert et al, 1995). Respondents chose the pseudonyms used here.

Results

I examine two ways in which respondents commonly used the typification of American family life as a contrast structure against which behavior in immigrant Asian families was juxtaposed and interpreted (Gubrium and Holstein 1997). When describing relations with their parents, most respondents provided negative accounts of at least one aspect of their relationship, and they criticized their parents for lacking American values that emphasize psychological well-being and expressive love. Recurring references to a narrow Americanized notion of what families ought to look like were woven throughout many such accounts. However, when respondents described the kinds of filial care they planned to provide for their parents, the respondents switched to an interpretive lens that values ethnic family solidarity. In this context, respondents' references to notions of the Normal American Family became a negative point of comparison that cast their own immigrant families, and Asian families in general, in positive terms.

Viewing parental relations through an Americanized lens

Respondents were asked to fantasize about how they would change their parents if they could change anything about them that they wanted to change. The three areas of desired change that respondents mentioned most often reveal their adoption of many mainstream American values. They wished for parents who: (a) were less strict and gave them more freedom; (b) were more liberal, more open-minded, more Americanized, and less traditional; (c) were emotionally closer, more communicative, more expressive, and more affectionate. These three areas are interrelated. For example, being more Americanized and less traditional translates into being more lenient and expressive. A small minority of respondents presented a striking contrast to the dominant pattern by describing, in terms both positive and grateful, parents who had liberal attitudes or Americanized values and parenting styles.

The communication most respondents described with parents focused on day-to-day practical concerns, such as whether the child had eaten, and about performance in school and college, a major area of concern among parents. Conversations were often limited to parental directives or lectures. For the most part, respondents were critical of the emotional distance and heavy emphasis on obedience that marked their relations with their parents. Chang-Hee, an 18-year-old who immigrated from Korea at 8, provided a typical case. When asked about communication, she disparaged her parents for not talking more openly, which she attributed to their being Asian. Respondents typically linked parental styles with race and not with other factors such as age or personality. Like many other respondents, Chang-Hee constructed an account not only of her family relations, but also of Asian families in general.

> To tell you the truth, in Asian families you don't have conversations. You just are told to do something and you do it.... You never talk about problems, even in the home. You just kind of forget about it and you kind of go on like nothing happened. Problems never really get solved. That's why I think people in my generation, I consider myself 1.5 generation, we have such a hard time because I like to verbalize my emotions....[My parents] never allowed themselves to verbalize their emotions. They've been repressed so much [that] they expect the same out of me, which is the hardest thing to do because I have so many different things to say and I'm just not allowed.

Some respondents volunteered that their parents never asked them about their well-being, even when their distress was apparent. Chang-Hee observed, "If I'm sad, [my mom] doesn't want to hear it. She doesn't want to know why. ...She's never asked me, 'So what do you feel?'" This lack of expressed interest in children's emotional well-being, along with the mundane level of communication, was especially upsetting to respondents because, interpreted through the lens of American family ideology, it defined their parents as emotionally uncaring and distant.

Several respondents longed for closer, more caring relationships with their parents that included expressive displays of affection. Thanh, a married 22-year-old college student who left Vietnam when she was 6, said, "I'd probably make them more loving and understanding, showing a bit more affection.... A lot of times I just want to go up and hug my parents, but no, you don't do that sort of thing."

Research indicates that the desire for greater intimacy is more common among women than men (Cancian 1987). Thus it was surprising that many male respondents also expressed strong desires for more caring and close talk – especially from their fathers, who were often described as harsh and judgmental. Ralph, 20, a Korean American man born in the United States, said:

> My dad, he's not open. He is not the emotional type. So he talks...and I would listen and do it. It's a one-way conversation, rather than asking for my opinions....I would think it'd be nicer if he was...much more compassionate, caring, because it seems like he doesn't care.

Similarly, Dat, a 22-year-old biology major who left Vietnam when he was 5, said:

> I would fantasize about sitting down with my dad and shooting the breeze. Talk about anything and he would smile and he would say, "Okay, that's fine, Dat." Instead of, you know, judge you and tell me I'm a loser....

A definition of love that emphasizes emotional expression and close talk predominates in U.S. culture (Cancian 1986). Instrumental aspects of love, like practical help, are ignored or devalued in this definition. In Korean and Vietnamese cultures, on the other hand, the predominant definitions of love emphasize instrumental help and support. The great divide between immigrant parents who emphasize instrumental forms of love and children who crave open displays of affection was evident in the following conversation, which occurred between Dat and his father when Dat was 7 or 8 years old. Dat recalled, "I tried saying 'I love you' one time and he looked at me and said, 'Are you American now? You think this is *The Brady Bunch*? You don't love me. You love me when you can support me.'" These different cultural definitions of love contributed to respondents' constructions of immigrant parents as unloving and cold.

The family as a contrast structure in the negative accounts of family life

Many of the images of normal family life that respondents brought to their descriptions came in the form of references to television families or the families of non-Asian American friends. Although these monolithic images do not reflect the reality of American family life, they nevertheless provided the basis by which respondents learned how to be American, and they served as the interpretive frame of their own family experiences. By contrasting behavior in their immigrant families with mainstream images of normalcy, the respondents interpreted Asian family life as lacking or deficient. Dat referred to images of normal family life in America, as revealed on television and among friends, as the basis for his desire for more affection and closeness with his father:

> Sometimes when I had problems in school, all I wanted was my dad to listen to me, of all people. I guess that's the American way and I was raised American.... That's what I see on TV and in my friends' family. And I expected him to be that way too. But it didn't happen.... I would like to talk to him or, you know, say "I love you," and he would look at me and say, "Okay." That's my ultimate goal, to say, "I love you." It's real hard. Sometimes when I'm in a good mood, the way I show him love is to put my hands over his shoulders and squeeze it a little bit. That would already irritate him a little.... You could tell. He's like, "What the fuck's he doing?" But I do it because I want to show him love somehow. Affection. I'm an affectionate person.

Similarly, Hoa, a 23-year-old Vietnamese American man who immigrated at age 2, referred to television in describing his own family: "We aren't as close as I would like... We aren't as close as the dream family, you know, what you see on TV. Kind of like... *Leave It To Beaver*. You know, stuff I grew up on."

Paul, a 21-year-old Korean American born in the United States, also criticizes his father, and Asian fathers in general, in relation to the fathers of friends and those on television:

> I think there is somewhat of a culture clash between myself and my parents. They are very set on rules – at least my father is. He is very strict and demanding and very much falls into that typical Asian father standard. I don't like that too much and I think it is because... as a child, I was always watching television and watching other friends' fathers. All the relationships seemed so much different from me and my father's relationship.... I guess it's pretty cheesy but I can remember watching *The Brady Bunch* reruns and thinking Mike Brady would be a wonderful dad to have. He was always so supportive. He always knew when something was wrong with one of his boys. Whenever one of his sons had a problem, they would have no problem telling their dad anything and the dad would always be nice and give them advice and stuff. Basically I used what I saw on television as a picture of what a typical family should be like in the United States. I only wished that my family could be like that. And friends too – I used to see how my friends in school would be in Little League Baseball and their dad would be like their coaches or go to their games to cheer their sons on and give them support. I could not picture my father to be like that kind of man that I saw on TV, or like my friends' fathers.

Respondents did not refer to non-Asian American friends who had distant, conflict-ridden family relationships. Yet many respondents likely did have contact with such individuals. It appears as though respondents see only in ways permitted by the Family ideology. That is, as Bernades argued, "the image or idol of 'The Family' rather than the reality of people's lives is taken as the object of attention" (1985:288). Looking at "American" families through this ideological lens determines which families are "seen." Those that do not fit the cultural imagery are not seen or are viewed as atypical. "Atypical" families are not referenced in these accounts, even though, in actuality, they are probably closer to the empirical reality of American family life. Friends whose families do comply, on the other hand, loom large as symbols that verify the existence of the Family ideal.

In comparison to this ideal, even parents who had adopted more American parenting practices fell short. For example, the parents of Mike, 22, who had immigrated to the United States from Vietnam as an infant, were less strict than the parents of most respondents. Nevertheless, Mike said:

> My parents were really easy. They let me hang out with my friends, they had no problem with me sleeping over or other people sleeping over. So having friends in high school wasn't hard at all, and going out wasn't a problem at all. It was just, you know, you go over to your friend's house and he just talks to his parents about everything. So I got a little bit jealous. You know, I wished I could talk to my parents about stuff like that but I couldn't.

Sometimes respondents simply made assumptive references to normal or American families, against which they critically juxtaposed Asian immigrant families. Being American meant that one was a member of the Normal American Family and enjoyed family relations that were warm, close, and harmonious. Being Asian, on the other hand, meant living outside such normality. Thuy, a 20-year-old Vietnamese American woman who had immigrated when 13, said:

> If I could, I would have a more emotional relationship with my parents. I know they love me, but they never tell me they love me. They also are not very affectionate. This is how I've always grown up. It wasn't really until we came to the United States that I really noticed what a lack of love my parents show. *American* kids are so lucky. They don't know what it's like to not really feel that you can show emotion with your own parents.

Similarly, Cora, 20, a Korean American woman born in the United States, remarked:

> I would probably want [my parents] to be more open, more understanding so I could be more open with them, 'cause there's a lot of things that I can't share with them because they're not as open-minded as *American* parents....'Cause I have friends and stuff. They talk to their parents about everything, you know?

When asked how he was raised, Josh, 21, a Vietnamese American man who immigrated when 2, responded by calling up a construction of the "good" American Family and the "deficient" Asian Family. He said, "I'm sure that for all *Asian* people, if they think back to [their] childhood, they'll remember a time they got hit. *American* people, they don't get hit."

Respondents repeatedly constructed American families as loving, harmonious, egalitarian, and normal. Using this ideal as their measuring stick, Asian families were constructed as distant, overly strict, uncaring, and not normal. In fact, respondents sometimes used the word "normal" in place of "American." For example, Hoa, who previously contrasted his family with the one depicted in *Leave It To Beaver*, said, "I love my dad but we never got to play catch. He didn't teach me how to play football. All the stuff a *normal* dad does for their kids. We missed out on that." Thomas, 20, a Korean American who arrived in the United States at age 8, said, "I always felt like maybe we are not so normal. Like in the real America, like Brady Bunch normal....I always felt like...there was something irregular about me." Similarly, after describing a childhood where she spoke very little to her parents, Van, 24, who immigrated to the United States from Vietnam at 10, began crying and noted, "I guess I didn't have a *normal* childhood." To be a normal parent is to be an American parent. Asian immigrant parents are by this definition deficient. Such constructions ignore diversity within family types, and they selectively bypass the social problems, such as child abuse, that plague many non-Asian American families. It is interesting, for example, that respondents did not refer to the high divorce rate of non-Asian Americans (Sweet and Bumpass 1987) to construct positive images of family stability among Asian Americans. This may be because, applying an Americanized definition of love, many respondents described their parents' marriage as unloving and some thought their parents ought to divorce.

Respondents relied on the Family not only as an interpretive framework, but also as a contrast structure by which to differentiate Asian and American families. This juxtaposition of American and Asian ignores that most of the respondents and the coethnics they describe are Americans. "American" is used to refer to non-Asian Americans, particularly Whites. The words "White" and "Caucasian" were sometimes used interchangeably with "American." Indeed, the Normal American Family *is* White. This Eurocentric imagery excludes from view other racial minority families such as African Americans and Latino

Americans. It is therefore not surprising that racial-ethnic families were not referenced as American in these interviews. In fact, respondents appeared to use the term "American" as a code word denoting not only cultural differences but also racial differences. For example, Paul, who was born in the United States, noted, "I look Korean but I think I associate myself more with the *American race*." The oppositional constructions of Asian and American families as monolithic and without internal variation imply that these family types are racialized. That is, the differences are constructed as not only cultural but also racially essential and therefore immutable (Omi and Winant 1994). By defining American as White, respondents revealed the deep-seated notion that, as Asian Americans, they can never truly be American. Such notions dominate in mainstream depictions of Asian Americans as perpetual foreigners. For example, in a speech about foreign donations, Ross Perot read the names of several Asian American political donors and commented, "So far we haven't found an American name" (Nakao 1996). When respondents centered Whites as a point of reference in these accounts, they reaffirmed the marginalized position of racial-ethnic minorities in the Family ideology and in U.S. culture writ large.

These data illustrate how Eurocentric images of normal family relationships promulgated in the larger society served as an ideological template in the negative accounts that respondents provided of their immigrant parents. However, as described next, when respondents discussed their plans for filial care, they presented positive accounts of their immigrant families.

Maintaining ethnic values of filial obligation

Respondents were not consistent in their individual constructions of Asian and American families as revealed in their interviews. When discussing future plans for filial care, most respondents positively evaluated their family's collectivist commitment to care. Such an interpretation is supported by model minority stereotypes in mainstream U.S. culture that attribute the success enjoyed by some Asian immigrants to their strong family values and collectivist practices (Kibria 1993; Zhou and Bankston 1998).

The majority of respondents valued and planned to maintain their ethnic tradition of filial care. For example, Josh, who criticized his parents (and Asian parents in general) for using physical forms of punishment, nonetheless plans to care for his parents in their old age. He said, "I'm the oldest son, and in Vietnamese culture the oldest son cares for the parents. That is one of the things that I carry from my culture. I would not put my parents in a [nursing] home. That's terrible." In contrast to White Americans who condition their level of filial commitment on intergenerational compatibility (Pyke 1999), respondents displayed a strong desire to fulfill their filial obligation and – especially among daughters – were often undeterred by distant and even conflict-ridden relations with parents. For example, after describing a strained relationship with her parents, Kimberly, 20, who came to the U.S. from Vietnam when 7, added, "I would still take care of them whether I could talk to them or not. It doesn't matter as long as I could take care of them." Similarly, in Wolf's study of 22 grown children of Filipino immigrants, respondents who complained of tension and emotional distance with parents nonetheless experienced family ties and responsibilities as a central component of their daily lives and identities (1997).

Most respondents expected to begin financially supporting their parents prior to their elderly years, with parents in their fifties often regarded as old. A few respondents had already begun to help out their parents financially. Many planned on living with parents. Others spoke of living near their parents, often as neighbors, rather than in the same house, as a means of maintaining some autonomy. The tradition of assigning responsibility for the care of parents to the eldest son was not automatically anticipated for many of these families, especially those from Vietnam. Respondents most often indicated that responsibility would be pooled among siblings or would fall exclusively to the daughters. Several said that parents preferred such arrangements, because they felt closer to daughters. Although the tendency for daughters to assume responsibility for aging parents is similar to the pattern of caregiving common in mainstream American families (Pyke and Bengston 1996), several respondents noted that such patterns are also emerging among relatives in their ethnic homeland.

The importance of collectivism as an expression of love

Respondents typically attributed their future caregiving to reciprocation for parental care in the past and a cultural emphasis on filial respect and support. Yet the enthusiasm and strong commitment that pervades their accounts suggests that they are motivated by more than obligation. For example, Vinh, 26, a graduate student who immigrated from Vietnam at age 5, said about his parents:

> They are my life. They will never be alone. I will always be with them. When I was growing [up] as a child, my parents were always with me. And I believe...when you grow up, you should be with them; meaning, I will take care of them, in my house, everything. Your parents didn't abandon you when you were a kid. They did not abandon you when you [were] pooping in your diaper. Then when they do, I will not abandon them....Whatever it takes to make them comfortable, I will provide it. There is no limit.

Unable to express love via open displays of affection and close talk, filial assistance becomes a very important way for adult children to symbolically demonstrate their affection for their parents and to reaffirm family bonds. Blossom, 21, who immigrated to the United States from Korea when 6, described the symbolic value of the financial assistance her father expects. She said, "Money is not really important, but it's more about our heart that [my dad] looks at. Through money, my dad will know how we feel and how we appreciate him." Remember that Dat's father told him, "You love me when you can support me." Because instrumental assistance is the primary venue for expressing love and affection in these immigrant families, adult children often placed no limits on what they were willing to do. For example, John, 20, who immigrated from Vietnam when 3, remarked "I'm willing to do anything (for my parents), that's how much I care."

Parental financial independence was not always welcomed by those children who gave great weight to their role of parental caregivers. For example, it was very important to Sean, 19, an only child, to care for his Sino-Vietnamese parents. Sean, who planned to become a doctor, commuted from his home to a local university. He said, "I want my parents to stay with me. I want to support them....I'll always have room for my parents....When I get my first paycheck, I want to support them financially." As reflected in the following exchange with the interviewer, Sean viewed his parents' retirement plan with some hurt.

> SEAN: They have their own retirement plan, and they keep track of it themselves, so they're all prepared for me to be the disobedient son and run away.
>
> INTERVIEWER: Is that how you feel?
>
> SEAN: Yes I do....Or if I don't succeed in life, they'll be taken care of by themselves.
>
> INTERVIEWER: So is that how you see their retirement plan, as a kind of symbol that they're...?
>
> SEAN: They're ready for me to mess up.

The emotional centrality of family ties is also apparent in Sean's description of his hurt when his father – who worries that the time Sean spends away from home studying or at his job is pulling him away from the family – occasionally tests his son's commitment by suggesting that he leave the family home and "fly away." With tear-filled eyes, Sean explained:

> It hurts me because I've never had that idea to fly away....I don't want to go and that's what hurts me so bad. I mean, I could cry over things like that. And this is a 19-year-old kid that's crying in front of you. How seldom do you get that?

The family as a contrast structure in the positive accounts of filial obligation

Many respondents distinguished their ethnic collectivist tradition of filial obligation from practices in mainstream American families, which they described as abandoning elderly parents in retirement or nursing homes. The belief that the elderly are abandoned by their families is widespread in U.S. society and very much a part of everyday discourse. Media accounts of nursing home atrocities bolster such views. Yet most eldercare in the U.S. is not provided in formal caregiving settings but by family members (Abel 1991). Nonetheless, respondents used this tenacious myth as a point of contrast in constructing Asian American families as more instrumentally caring. For example, Thuy, who previously described wanting a "more emotional relationship" with her parents, like "American kids" have, explained:

> With the American culture, it's...not much frowned upon to put your parents in a home when they grow old. In our culture, it is a definite no-no. To do anything like that would be disrespectful....If they need help, my brother and I will take care of them, just like my mom is taking care of her parents right now.

Similarly, Hien, 21, a Vietnamese American woman who arrived in the U.S. as an infant, noted, "I know a lot of non-Asians have their parents go to the nursing homes...but I personally prefer to find a way of trying to keep them at home."

Mike, who wished he could talk to his parents the way his friends do to theirs, plans to care for his Americanized parents even though they have told him they do not want him to. He was not alone in remaining more committed to filial care than his parents required him to be. He said:

> They tell me to just succeed for yourself and take care of your own family. But [referring to filial care] that's just how the Vietnamese culture is. Here in America, once your parents are old, you put them in a retirement home. But not in my family. When the parents get old you take care of them. It doesn't matter if they can't walk, if they can't function anymore. You still take care of them.

When discussing relationships with their parents, respondents used the Family as the ideological raw material out of which they negatively constructed their parents as unloving and distant. However, when the topic changed to filial care, respondents switched to an ethnic definition of love that emphasizes instrumental support and that casts a positive and loving light on their families. As Katie, 21, a Korean American woman born in the United States, observed:

> When you say that you are close to your parents here in America. I think most people would take that as you are affectionate with your parents, you hang out with them, you can talk to them about anything... more of a friendship thing. But Korean families are not like that....They do not get close to their children like that. They are not friends with them. The kids of Korea do not open up with their parents. Their parents are really their *parents*....But still, no matter what, they are very close. Here in America... Caucasians don't take care of their parents like we do. They just put them in an old people's home and that's it. It's like they say, "You are too old for me. I don't need you anymore and I'm just going to put you here 'cause it's convenient for me and you'd be in the way anyway...." And in that way, Americans are *not* close to their parents. So it really depends on how you define the word "close" – the answer changes. [Note that the words "Caucasian" and "American" are used synonymously here, as previously discussed.]

In describing their plans for parental care, respondents turned their previous construction of Asian and American families on its head. In this context the Family was constructed as deficient and uncaring, while the families of respondents – and Asian families in general – were described as more instrumentally caring and closer. Respondents' view of American families as uncaring should not be interpreted as a departure from mainstream family ideology. There has been much concern in the public discourse that today's families lack a commitment to the care of their elders and children (e.g., Popenoe 1993; see Coontz 1992:189–191). Indeed, the pervasive criticism that "individualism has gone haywire" in mainstream families – bolstered by references to the solidarity of model minority families – provides ideological support for ethnic traditions of filial care. That is, children of immigrants do not face ideological pressure from the dominant society to alter such practices; rather, they are given an interpretive template by which to view such practices as evidence of love and care in their families. In fact, U.S. legislative attempts to withdraw social services from legal immigrants without citizenship, with the expectation that family sponsors will provide such support, structurally mandate collectivist systems of caregiving in immigrant families (Huber and Espenshade 1997). In other words, the dominant society ideologically endorses and, in some ways, structurally requires ethnic immigrant practices of filial care. Filial obligation thus serves as a site where children of Korean and Vietnamese immigrants can maintain their ethnic identity and family ties without countervailing pressure from the mainstream.

Discussion

Interweaving respondents' accounts with an analysis of the interpretive structure from which those accounts are constructed suggests that the Family ideology subtly yet powerfully influences the children of immigrants, infiltrating their subjective understandings of and desires for family life. Respondents relied on American family images in two ways. When discussing their relations with parents and their upbringing, respondents used the Family ideology as a standard of normal families and good parents, leading them to view their immigrant parents as unloving, deficient, and not normal. However, when respondents discussed filial care, a complete reversal occurred. Respondents referred to negative images of rampant individualism among mainstream American families, specifically in regard to eldercare, to bolster their positive portrayals of the instrumental care and filial piety associated with their ethnic families. Thus the Family ideology was called upon in contradictory ways in these accounts – in the denigration of traditional ethnic parenting practices and in the glorification of ethnic practices of filial obligation.

Findings from this study illustrate how a narrow, ethnocentric family ideology that is widely promulgated throughout the larger culture and quickly internalized by children of immigrants creates an interpretive framework that derogates many of the ethnic practices of immigrant families. As others have argued, the cultural imposition of dominant group values in this form of "controlling images" can lead minorities to internalize negative self-images (Espiritu 1997). That is, racial-ethnic immigrants can adopt a sense of inferiority and a desire to conform with those values and expectations that are glorified in the mainstream society as normal. Indeed, many respondents explicitly expressed a desire to have families that were like White or so-called American families, and they criticized their own family dynamics for being different. Rather than resist and challenge the ethnocentric family imagery of the mainstream, respondents' accounts reaffirmed the Normal American Family and the centrality of White native-born Americans in this imagery. This research thus reveals a subtle yet powerful mechanism of internalized oppression by which the racial-ethnic power dynamics in the larger society are reproduced. This is a particularly important finding in that racial-ethnic families will soon constitute a majority in several states, causing scholars to ponder the challenge of such a demographic transformation of the cultural and political hegemony of White native-born Americans (Maharidge 1996). This study describes an ideological mechanism that could undermine challenges to that hegemony.

This research also uncovered an uncontested site of ethnic pride among the second-generation respondents who drew on mainstream images of elder neglect in their positive interpretation of ethnic filial commitment. As previously discussed, the belief that mainstream American families abandon their elders is tenacious and widespread in the dominant society, despite its empirical inaccuracy. This negative myth has been widely used in popular discourse as an example of the breakdown of American family commitment, and it sometimes serves as a rallying cry for stronger "family values." Such cries are often accompanied by references to the family solidarity and filial piety celebrated in the model minority stereotype. Thus the mainstream glorification of ethnic filial obligation, as contrasted with negative images of abandoned White American elders, provided respondents with a positive template for giving meaning to ethnic practices of filial care. The mainstream endorsement of filial obligation marks it as a locale where respondents can maintain family ties and simultaneously produce a positive self-identity in both cultural worlds. This might explain why some respondents were steadfastly committed to filial care despite parental requests to the contrary.

It remains to be seen, however, whether these young adults will be able to carry out their plans of filial obligation. It is likely that many will confront barriers in the form of demanding jobs, childrearing obligations, geographic moves, unsupportive spouses, competing demands from elderly in-laws, and financial difficulties. Furthermore, parents' access to alternative sources of support such as Social Security and retirement funds could diminish the need for their children's assistance. Some research already finds that elderly Korean immigrants prefer to live on their own and are moving out of the homes of their immigrant children despite the protests of children, who see it as a public accusation that they did not care for their parents (Hurh 1998). Although this research examined first-generation immigrant adults and their aging parents, it suggests a rapid breakdown in traditional patterns of coresidential filial care that will likely be reiterated in the next generation. Future research is needed to examine these dynamics among second-generation immigrants, to look at how they will cope with inabilities to fulfill ethnic and model minority expectations of filial obligation, and to assess the impact of any such inabilities on their ethnic identity.

This study makes a unique contribution to the small and largely descriptive literature on Asian immigrant families. Rather than simply reiterating as descriptive data the accounts of family life offered by respondents, I examined the ideological underpinnings of those accounts. In so doing, I uncovered a subtle process by which White hegemonic images of the Family infiltrate the ways that children of immigrants think about their own family lives. Although scholars have often assumed that the prescriptive and moralistic characteristics of the Family are hurtful to those whose families do not comply, the findings presented here provide an empirical description of how such ideology negatively biases the family accounts of children of immigrants. It must be noted, however, that because the sample in the study was demographically predisposed to higher levels of assimilation, the respondents are probably more likely than a less assimilated sample to view their families through an Americanized lens. This suggests the need for further study of how variations in acculturation levels affect the accounts that children of immigrants provide of their family lives.

A broader sample of families that do not conform with images of the Normal American Family also needs to be investigated. This sample should include native-born racial minorities and children of single parents, as well as immigrants. Studying a broader sample will allow greater understanding of whether narrow cultural notions of a normal family life influence the subjective experience of diverse groups of children growing up in the margins of the mainstream. It is particularly important, as family scholars begin to respond to the burgeoning numbers of ethnically and structurally diverse family forms, that researchers generate culturally sensitive interpretive frameworks that do not automatically and unconsciously perpetuate existing notions that certain family types and practices are inferior. The effort to develop such frameworks requires researchers to examine not only the values and assumptions they bring to their analyses (Dilworth-Anderson et al. 1993), but also the values and assumptions that respondents bring to their accounts. To summarize, this study suggests the need for family researchers to analytically bracket as problematic the ideological structures that shape the empirical accounts of family life we rely upon in our research.

REFERENCES

Abel, E. K. 1991. *Who Cares for the Elderly?* Philadelphia: Temple University Press.

Ambert, A., Adler, P., Adler, P., and Detzner, D. 1995. Understanding and evaluating qualitative research. *Journal of Marriage and the Family* 57:879–893.

Bellah, R. N., Madsen, R., Sullivan, W. M., Swidler, A., and Tipton, S. 1985. *Habits of the Heart.* San Francisco: Harper & Row.

Berger, P. L., and Luckmann, T. 1966. *The Social Construction of Reality.* New York: Doubleday.

Bernades, J. 1985. "Family ideology": Identification and exploration. *Sociological Review* 33:275–297.

Bernades, J. 1993. Responsibilities in studying post-modern families. *Journal of Family Issues* 14:35–49.

Blankenhorn, D. 1995. *Fatherless America.* New York: Basic Books.

Brown, D., and Bryant, J. 1990. Effects of television on family values and selected attitudes and behaviors. In J. Bryant, ed., *Television and the American Family* (pp. 253–274). Hillsdale, NJ: Erlbaum.

Cancian, F. M. 1986. The feminization of love. *Signs* 11:692–708.

Cancian, F. M. 1987. *Love in America*. New York: Cambridge University Press.

Caplan, N., Choy, M. H., and Whitmore, J. K. 1991. *Children of the Boat People: A Study of Educational Success*. Ann Arbor: University of Michigan Press.

Cha, J. 1994. Aspects of individualism and collectivism in Korea. In U. Kim, H. C. Triandis, Ç. Kâğitçibaşi, S. Choi, and G. Yoon, eds., *Individualism and Collectivism: Theory, Methods, and Applications* (pp. 157–174). Thousand Oaks, CA: Sage.

Chung, D. K. 1992. Asian cultural commonalities: A comparison with mainstream American culture. In S. Furuto, R. Biswas, D. Chung, K. Murase, F. Ross-Sheriff, eds., *Social Work Practice with Asian Americans* (pp. 27–44). Newbury Park, CA: Sage.

Coltrane, S. 1996. *Family Man*. New York: Oxford University Press.

Coontz, S. 1992. *The Way We Never Were*. New York: Basic Books.

Dilworth-Anderson, P., Burton, L. M., and Turner, W. L. 1993. The importance of values in the study of culturally diverse families. *Family Relations* 42:238–242.

Espiritu, Y. L. 1997. *Asian American Women and Men*. Thousand Oaks, CA: Sage.

Fineman, M. A. 1995. *The Neutered Mother, the Sexual Family, and Other Twentieth Century Tragedies*. New York: Routledge.

Freeman, J. M. 1989. *Hearts of Sorrow: Vietnamese-American Lives*. Stanford, CA: Stanford University Press.

Gerbner, G., Gross, L., Morgan, M., and Signorielli, N. 1980. *Media and the Family: Images and Impact*. Washington, DC: White House Conference on the Family, National Research Forum on Family Issues. (ERIC Document Reproduction Service No. ED 198 919).

Glaser, B. G., and Strauss, A. L. 1967. *The Discovery of Grounded Theory*. New York: Aldine.

Gold, S. J. 1993. Migration and family adjustment: Continuity and change among Vietnamese in the United States. In H. P. McAdoo, ed., *Family Ethnicity* (pp. 300–314). Newbury Park, CA: Sage.

Greeley, A. 1987 (May 17). Today's morality play: The sitcom. *New York Times*, p. H1.

Greenberg, B. S., Hines, M., Buerkel-Rothfuss, N., and Atkin, C. K. 1980. Family role structures and interactions on commercial television. In B. S. Greenberg ed., *Life on Television: Content Analyses of U.S. TV Drama* (pp. 149–160). Norwood, NJ: Ablex.

Gubrium, J. F., and Holstein, J. A. 1997. *The New Language of Qualitative Method*. New York: Oxford University Press.

Holstein, J. A., and Gubrium, J. F. 1995. Deprivatization and the construction of domestic life. *Journal of Marriage and the Family*, 57:894–908.

Holstein, J. A., and Miller, G. 1993. Social constructionism and social problems work. In J. A. Holstein and G. Miller, eds., *Reconsidering Social Constructionism* (pp. 151–172). New York: Aldine De Gruyter.

Huber, G. A., and Espenshade, T. J. 1997. Neo-isolationism, balanced-budget conservatism, and the fiscal impacts of immigrants. *International Migration Review* 31:1031–1054.

Hurh, W. M. 1998. *The Korean Americans*. Westport, CN: Greenwood Press.

Kibria, N. 1993. *The Family Tightrope: The Changing Lives of Vietnamese Americans*. Princeton, NJ: Princeton University Press.

Kibria, N. 1997. The construction of "Asian American": Reflections on intermarriage and ethnic identity among second-generation Chinese and Korean Americans. *Ethnic and Racial Studies* 20:523–544.

Kim, U., and Choi, S. 1994. Individualism, collectivism, and child development: A Korean perspective. In P. Greenfield and R. Cocking, eds., *Cross-Cultural Roots of Minority Child Development* (pp. 227–257). Hillsdale, NJ: Erlbaum.

Kurz, D. 1995. *For Richer, for Poorer*. New York: Routledge.

Maharaj, D. 1997 (July 8). E-mail hate case tests free speech protections. *Los Angeles Times*, pp. A1, A16.

Maharidge, D. 1996. *The Coming White Minority: California Eruptions and America's Future*. New York: New York Times Books.

Min, P. G. 1995. Major issues relating to Asian American experiences. In P. G. Min, ed., *Asian Americans* (pp. 38–57). Thousand Oaks, CA: Sage.

Min, P. G. 1998. *Changes and Conflicts: Korean Immigrant Families in New York*. New York: Allyn & Bacon.

Nakao, A. 1996 (November 17). Asians' political image marred: Fund-raising probes' timing "unfortunate." *The San Francisco Examiner*, p. A1.

Omi, M., and Winant, H. 1994. *Racial Formation in the United States*. New York: Routledge.

Oropesa, R. S., and Landale, N. S. 1995. *Immigrant Legacies: The Socioeconomic Circumstances of Children by Ethnicity and Generation in the United States*. (Working Paper 95–01R). Population Research Institute, The Pennsylvania State University, State College.

Pettengill, S. M., and Rohner, R. P. 1985. Korean-American adolescents' perceptions of parental control, parental acceptance–rejection and parent–adolescent conflict. In I. R. Lagunes and Y. H. Poortinga, eds., *From a Different Perspective: Studies of Behavior across Culture* (pp. 241–249). Berwyn, IL: Swets North America.

Popenoe, D. 1993. American family decline, 1960–1990: A review and appraisal. *Journal of Marriage and the Family*, 55:527–555.

Popenoe, D. 1996. *Life without Father: Compelling New Evidence that Fatherhood and Marriage are Indispensable and for the Good of the Children and Society*. New York: Martin Kessler/Free Press.

Pyke, K. D. 1999. The micropolitics of care in relationships between aging parents and adult children: Individualism, collectivism, and power. *Journal of Marriage and the Family*, 61:661–672.

Pyke, K. D., and Bengtson, V. L. 1996. Caring more or less: Individualistic and collectivist systems of family eldercare. *Journal of Marriage and the Family*, 58:379–392.

Pyke, K. D., and Johnson, D. 1999 (November). *Between Two Faces of Gender: The Incongruity of Home and Mainstream Cultures among Sons and Daughters of Asian Immigrants*. Paper presented at the Annual Meeting of the National Council of Family Relations, Irvine, CA.

Rohner, R. P., and Pettingill, S. M. 1985. Perceived parental acceptance–rejection and parental control among Korean adolescents. *Child Development* 56:524–528.

Rumbaut, R. G. 1994. The crucible within: Ethnic identity, self-esteem and segmented assimilation among children of immigrants. *International Migration Review* 28:748–794.

Rumbaut, R. G. 1997. Assimilation and its discontents: Between rhetoric and reality. *International Migration Review* 31:923–960.

Shaner, J. (1982). Parental empathy and family role interactions as portrayed on commercial television. *Dissertation Abstracts International* 42:3473A.

Skill, T. (1994). Family images and family actions as presented in the media: Where we've been and what we've found. In D. Zillmann, J. Bryant, and A. C. Huston, eds., *Media, Children, and the Family* (pp. 37–50). Hillsdale, NJ: Erlbaum.

Skolnick, A. 1991. *Embattled Paradise: The American Family in an Age of Uncertainty*. New York: Basic Books.

Smith, D. E. 1993. The standard North American family: SNAF as an ideological code. *Journal of Family Issues* 14:50–65.

Staccy, J. 1998. The right family values. In K. Hansen and A. Garey, eds., *Families in the U.S.* (pp. 859–880). Philadelphia: Temple University Press.

Strauss, A., and Corbin, J. 1990. *Basics of Qualitative Research*. Newbury Park, CA: Sage.

Sue, S., and Morishima, J. K. 1982. *The Mental Health of Asian Americans*. San Francisco: Jossey-Bass.

Sweet, J. A., and Bumpass, L. 1987. *American Families and Households*. New York: Russell Sage Foundation.

Thorne, B., and Yalom, M. 1992. *Rethinking the Family: Some Feminist Questions*. Boston: Northeastern University.

Tran, T. V. 1988. The Vietnamese American family. In C. H. Mindel, R. W. Habenstein, and R. Wright, Jr., eds., *Ethnic Families in America: Patterns and Variations* (pp. 276–299). New York: Elsevier.

Tsui, P., and Schultz, G. 1985. Failure of rapport: Why psychotherapeutic engagement fails in the treatment of Asian clients. *American Journal of Orthopsychiatry* 55:561–569.

Uba, L. 1994. *Asian Americans: Personality Patterns, Identity, and Mental Health*. New York: The Guilford Press.

U.S. Immigration and Naturalization Service. 1997. *Statistical Yearbook of the Immigration and naturalization service, 1995*. Washington, DC: U.S. Government Printing Office.

Waters, M. C. 1996. The intersection of gender, race, and ethnicity in identity development of Caribbean American teens. In M. C. Waters ed., *Urban Girls: Resisting Stereotypes, Creating Identities* (pp. 65–81) New York: New York University Press.

Wolf, D. 1997. Family secrets: Transnational struggles among children of Filipino immigrants. *Sociological Perspectives* 40:457–482.

Zhou, M. 1997. Growing up American: The challenge confronting immigrant children and children of immigrants. *Annual Review of Sociology* 23:63–95.

Zhou, M., and Bankston, III, C. 1998 *Growing Up American: How Vietnamese Children Adapt to Life in the United States*. New York: Russell Sage Foundation.

Zinn, M. B. 1994. Feminist rethinking of racial–ethnic families. In M. B. Zinn and B. T. Dill, eds., *Women of Color in U.S. Society* (pp. 303–314). Philadelphia: Temple University Press.

6

"I Really Do Feel I'm 1.5!": The Construction of Self and Community by Young Korean Americans[1]

Kyeyoung Park

> It is a peculiar sensation, this double-consciousness, this sense of always looking at one's self through the eyes of others, of measuring one's soul by the tape of a world that looks on in amused contempt and pity. One ever feels his twoness – an American, a Negro; two souls, two thoughts, two unreconciled strivings; two warring ideals in one dark body, whose dogged strength alone keeps it from being torn asunder.[2]

As W. E. B. Du Bois posited the existence of a duality within Afro-American life, the same duality may be found within Korean American life, in particular among the 1.5-generation Korean Americans. The 1.5-generation Korean Americans, *ilchŏm ose*, are different from the first generation, *ilse*, or second generation, *ise*:

> [A]ll I was trying to say to my aunt in Korean one night was that I couldn't do the dishes because I had some cuts in my fingers. At that moment, my aunt joked, "Lord, David cannot speak Korean or English. What is he going to do?" Everyone laughed except me. I stomped into my room with anger and frustration.... A dark cloud of shame and disgrace hung over my head that night.[3]

Since the turn of the century, generational discourse within the Asian American community has been dominated by the Japanese American community, *issei, nisei*, and *sansei*. The official definition of generation centers around birthplace, such as U.S.-born or foreign-born. Immigrants become the first generation and their children the second generation. However, generation is not the same as nativity. Korean immigrants distinguish between different segments of the first generation. In this article, I focus on the Korean immigrant community's cultural construction of the 1.5 generation. Although biologically the notion of a "1.5" generation is absurd, the sociocultural characteristics and psychological experiences of the pre-adult immigrant are distinct from those of either the first- or second-generation ethnic American.[4]

More than three-quarters of Korean immigrants are post-1965, many immigrating on family reunification provisions. The Korean immigrant community includes many child immigrants who are often called the 1.5ers, or what is called *ilchŏm ose* within the Korean American community, the term first used in the 1970s (of both Los Angeles and New York Korean American communities) and popularized by community leaders such as Professor Eui-young Yu and Bong Hwan Kim, former director of Korean Youth and Community Center. In the early 1980s, it was K. W. Lee, the editor of the *Korea Times English Edition*, who first wrote about the 1.5 generation Korean Americans (hereafter KA). He suggests an analogy of "twilight" in locating the 1.5 generation in the context of Korean American history. To him, this conception has been employed for pragmatic reasons and is a "transitional" cultural phenomenon before the numerical dominance of the second generation within the KA community.[5]

In my view, the term *ilchŏm ose* was also influenced by a term, used in Hawaiian Japanese American communities, "knee-high" generation. Later, Won Moo Hurh's definition paid attention to their demographic characteristics; that is, immigration at a young age – to be exact, early and middle adolescence, between 11 and 16 years old. In anthropological and ethnological senses, a particular division of labor within the Korean immigrant family designates some children to be linguistic and cultural brokers while remaining loyal to the family and ethnic community. It may be true that demographic and other sociocultural characteristics (i.e., family/community structure) contributed to popularity of this term of *ilchŏm ose*, in my analysis, political reasons also played a certain part. For instance, Bong Hwan Kim, a 1.5-generation Korean American community leader himself, said:

> [T]hey understand both the first generation perspective yet have access to the mainstream culture and its institutions.... The second generation are more assimilated into the mainstream of American culture and are relatively disassociated from immigrant Korean Americans and community-based institutions. It is the 1.5 generation that I believe represents the most promise for effective leadership.[6]

In other words, KA community expects some 1.5ers to be bridge-builders with the rest of American society in political and other arenas, a task which cannot be done satisfactorily by the current immigrants due to their linguistic, cultural, and other barriers.

In sociological literature, Rumbaut and Ima called foreign-born youths who immigrated to the United States before age 12 the "one-and-a-half generation."[7] Although many have made references to the 1.5 generation as a useful concept, no one has done research on the process and meanings of 1.5-generation Asian Americans' identity construction compared to the first or the second generation. This article is the first empirical article on any 1.5-generation group.

In my research, I tried to analyze the following questions. How do Korean Americans (1.5 or second generation) define the 1.5 generation? How does the 1.5 generation relate to Korea or the U.S.? How do they explore questions of nation, race, gender, and other categories of "imagined community"? How do they talk about their position in this multiethnic society? What are the implications of invoking the notion of "1.5"? How do they come to terms with the identity issue? What important strategies are employed?

According to the 1990 census, U.S.-born Korean Americans constitute about 28 percent of the community, and the proportion of non-adults (people under age 18) among total Korean Americans has been high, about 31 percent. The Korean American community's definition and meanings of 1.5ers are more inclusive and complex than the demographic ones given by Rumbaut or Hurh. Accordingly, I pay attention to the various ways 1.5ers are defined and debated within the Korean American community. For instance, by the early 1990s in New York City, *ilchŏm ose* meant those Korean Americans who came to the U.S. after finishing junior high or high school. However, at the same time in Los Angeles, the term referred to much younger children, for instance, those immigrants who finished their grade school education in Korea. Or, those who immigrated to the U.S. before age 5 are considered second generation. Immigration between the ages of 6 and 10 places one as 1.7 generation; between 11 or 12, 1.5 generation; between 13 and 14, 1.2 generation. After graduating high school, one is classified as the first generation. On the other hand, I am sometimes classified as 1.5, instead of the first generation, although I immigrated to the U.S. from Korea as an adult.

Shu-mei Shih situates the 1.5 generation in an ambiguous and often antagonistic relationship to both first- and second-generation Korean Americans. They are neither "Korean," "American," nor "Korean American," while at the same time all three. The simultaneity of their being "neither/nor" and "both/all" distinguishes the 1.5 generation from both immigrant Koreans and American-born Korean Americans.[8]

I support the view that the category 1.5 generation, though widely used within the Korean American community, has been largely subsumed under the rigid definitions of first, second, and third generation in Asian American discourse.

On the other hand, the sociological literature on the "new second generation" contemplates whether today's children of immigrants will follow their European predecessors and move steadily into the middle-class mainstream, or if their ascent in mobility will be blocked, causing them to join children of earlier black and Puerto Rican migrants. According to the "segmented assimilation" thesis developed by Portes and his colleagues, assimilation has continued to serve as a norm of immigration adaptation, but that its outcomes have become segmented:[9] "either confinement to permanent underclass memberships or rapid economic advancement with deliberate preservation of the immigrant community's values and solidarity."[10]

The theory asks us to assess how well 1.5- or second-generation Korean Americans will fare in the contemporary context of a restructured economy, or what is called an "hourglass" economy. Similarly, a number of empirical studies have examined the relationship between levels of ethnic identification and school performance among high-school students. Studies by Gibson and Ogbu, Zhou and Bankston III, and Rumbaut and Ima have consistently supported the view that second-generation and immigrant children's strong ethnic attachment and ethnic identity are positively correlated with their motivations, academic performance, and behavioral traits conducive to successful academic performance.[11]

Equally important, such segmented adaptations described between ethnic groups have also been observed within a single ethnic group, ethnic neighborhood, or even within a single family.[12] In the film, *My Family*, Francis Ford Coppola beautifully portrays how each child, even within the Sanchez family, attempted to resolve identity issues and conflicts differently, representing a spectrum from *Cholo* to Anglicized, from bilingual to Spanish-speaking to English-only-speaking, from assimilated youth to gang member.

However, I do not use this set of literature on segmented adaptation for my operational model in this article, because it is mostly concerned with school performance and economic adjustments at the labor market. Instead, I will analyze the process of identity formation in terms of collective agency. From a member's own perspective, the term 1.5-generation Korean Americans is a highly conscious category with complex meanings invoking certain responsibilities.

In addition to my research based on participant observation of the Los Angeles Korean American community, in the fall of 1995, I conducted ethnographic interviews[13] with 117 Korean American adults who were born and/or grew up in the U.S.[14] Except twenty-five who were born in the U.S., most of my interviewees were born in Korea but grew up in the U.S. The majority of interviewees were in their twenties or early thirties, at the beginning stage of their career, and mostly working as professionals such as engineers, teachers, social workers, community workers, preachers, designers, and as professionals in media/entertainment, finance, or high-technology-related fields. Interviewees also included store owners, clerks, graduate students, homemakers, the unemployed, gangsters, professional golfers, and CEOs.[15] Interviewees were located through churches, community organizations, and various personal networks. Interviews often took one or two or more hours and were transcribed later on.

The following topics were the focus of the life history interviews: immigration and work history; different experiences over life course (childhood and adolescence, college, and present); different experiences over different social settings such as home, school, church, neighborhood, workplace, and community; ethnic/racial and gender identities shaped in part by parents' attitudes; experiences with prejudice/discrimination and coping strategies; ethnic vs. non-ethnic friendship networks and dating patterns; nature of activities in different social settings; attitudes and practices of ethnic culture; meanings of Koreatown; and perspectives on Korean American experiences and the Korean American community.

Visiting Koreatown (K-town)

For many first-generation Korean immigrants, Koreatown, commonly known as "K-town," has become a center of their economic and social/political activities as well as residential area. David observed how 1.5ers use K-town:

> At 9:30 p.m., three friends and I [David], all 1.5ers, who came to the U.S. as a child, drove to K-town in Los Angeles. All of us speak Korean moderately, meaning we can communicate in Korean with our parents, but we prefer to speak English. In the car, Tyus[16] was sitting beside me in the passenger seat, and Sedale and Nick were sitting in the back. It took forty minutes to get to K-town because we were lost in the dense fog.

These three young Korean Americans are demographically near second generation but culturally 1.5 generation. As reported about other ethnic groups of the second generation, they feel more comfortable with English, despite being bilingual.

> As soon as we hit the road, I sensed the excitement of my friends just conversing and joking around. They started using black slang like, "What up, dog?" (Tyus), "What up, nigga?" (Sedale), and "What you gettin' into tonight, fool?" (Tyus). All of us started laughing. I managed to squeeze in one myself, "Hey now." Sedale, particularly, liked telling nasty guy jokes. For instance, he talked about homosexuality. He said to Tyus, "Do you feel lonely tonight, Tyus?" Sedale was getting touchy with Tyus by rubbing Tyus' legs and arms. Tyus responded with disgust, "C'mon stop it. I'm serious!" All of us except Tyus started laughing real hard. Then, Sedale asked a hypothetical question, "What would you do if a gay guy came up to you to suck his penis for a million dollars?" Everybody said, "Hells no." Somehow the topic moved to girls. Sedale said that one has to get them young, like sixteen, because the old ones are not good. He clarified that the young ones are tender and fresh. The others seemed to disagree. One stated that sixteen-year-old girls are too young, and said dating them would be child molestation.

We notice, here, that they also use certain black slang in their moments of leisure. Here, some hegemonic notions of gender and sexuality are debated.

> Sedale kept getting excited about the $3.50 per pitcher special and a whole chicken that we were going to have at Bulldog's Café. Prior to going to the café, we stopped by a Mexican burrito place near K-town. This was around ten. Nick, Sedale, and Tyus had the carne asada burritos with horchata [a sweetened rice drink]. Sedale constantly praised the place for its great tasting food, especially the burritos. He informed me that many Koreans stop by here to eat. As a matter of fact, I saw two Korean females with one male Korean eating at a table. They looked like they were in their mid-twenties. Tyus felt a little uncomfortable being there, since he is originally from an area where there is not a considerable minority population other than Asian, the city of Cerritos.[17] On the other hand, Sedale mentioned that he grew up in a Latino environment; therefore, he stated he was used to it, and he was "down with them." He also talked about the secret sauce that made the burritos so tasty. When they were done eating, Sedale insisted on doing the "second round," going to Bulldog's Café to drink. Tyus softly hummed a Korean popular song soon after.

In multiethnic K-town, they stopped by a Mexican Burrito place. Sedale, who grew up in a multiethnic neighborhood, is able to enjoy food and culture other than Korean. In the following, at a Korean café, these youngsters attribute seniority, singing, heavy drinking, and a close, bonded relationship to aspects of Korean culture. More importantly, they're aware of being racialized and ethnicized as Asian or Korean American.

> At 10:20, we arrived at the café. Immediately upon entering, we were checked for our IDs. The Korean security guard checked all of us. I recognized our server, a Korean female in her late twenties, dressed in black. The music was loud. There was a DJ playing popular Korean songs. He was in his early twenties.... After about five minutes, we were served beer. Sedale insisted on pouring beer for Tyus because he was the oldest (by a month), then me and then Nick (the youngest). Sedale called on Tyus to make a toast.... Nick encouraged Tyus to drink, "C'mon, this beer is water. You can't live without water, right? Drink up, Tyus." Tyus was forced to drink up due to pressure from Nick and Sedale.... I asked Sedale, "Do you find yourself to be more Korean or American?" He replied, "Of course, more Korean. No matter how much you look in the mirror, it'll tell you you're Korean, regardless. I'm Korean." Then, I asked him what kind of friends he associates with and what he does with them. "Basically, drinking," he said, and also added that "one cannot completely assimilate into American culture. There is only a certain degree. One must take the good of American and other cultures." Somebody made the "salad-bowl" analogy. Sedale then grabbed Tyus' head by his forearm and insisted that Tyus go sing...[18]

In the above description, these mostly second-generation Korean American young men show some command of the Korean language. Second, they exhibit influence from the cultures of other minorities, evidenced by their use of black slang and preference for Mexican food. That is partly because some grew up in the inner city and partly because others identify themselves with minority youth and their style. Third, they struggle with different ideologies of love, sex, and sexuality in Korean and American cultures. Fourth, they continue to practice alleged aspects of Korean culture, such as the importance of seniority,[19] a close, bonded relationship, compulsive drinking, and singing. Some are familiar with Korean popular songs.[20] Fifth, these young people struggle with the issue W. E. B. Du Bois called "double consciousness," among African Americans.[21] In other words, the problem of being American without sacrificing their Koreanness. Finally, they identify strongly with Koreans despite their biculturalism.

Learning from the Media and Visiting Korea

David Moon, a graduate from UCLA, has grown up under the influence of hip hop since junior high. Radio and television were the main purveyors of hip hop shaping his acculturation into American life. He writes:

> Some of the rap artists I enjoyed listening to on the radio were L.L. Cool J, Kool Mo Dee, N.W.A., Ice-T, Public Enemy, Too Short, KRS-one, and Big Daddy Kane.[22] The rap songs covered many facets of urban life, particularly for African Americans. Back then, discussions of such issues did not relate to me, since I did not reside in an urban area nor was I African American. However, my amusement came from the music's "attitude," the poetic style of lyrics, funk, and rhythmic sound. Synthesized beats of the music created the "hippity-hoppity" rhythms that were very energetic. Therefore, to me, dancing to the rhythms of this music was new, unique, and fun. I would go to my friend's house after school every day, and we'd try to copy the latest dance moves by Bobby Brown and M.C. Hammer (both popular and admired dancing figures) shown in their music videos.

Before long his style of speaking English started to change, at least among his peers: he was acquiring the grammatical and intonation style used by hip hop artists (or in the general sense, black English):

> To demonstrate, if I were to say "hi" to someone in hip hop language, I'd say, "What up, g?" Also, if I wanted to say, "That's a nice car," I'd say, "Man, check out that dope lookin' fly set of wheels." And if I wanted to say "I'm not stupid" in the hip hop language, I'd say "Yo, I ain't no fool." My peers wondered why I spoke in this manner....One reason to justify this acculturation to hip hop was my general need to belong and to identify with a particular culture during my formative adolescent years. And the hip hop culture filled my need.

Hip hop culture made popular the style of wearing baggy clothing.

> My introduction to this fashion came from the rap music videos and *Soul Train* (a television dance show)...a loose fit became the "right" fit. One of my favorite types of clothing was the thick, athletic, hooded sweatshirts. When worn, I had the convenience of covering my head with the hood which created a certain type of look that, in my opinion, portrayed a certain attitude to others, somewhat dark and mysterious. I valued that look, because it gave me the tough and fearful image that most teenage boys sought in high school. [Some students of mine asserted that otherwise few young Asian American men can receive respect outside their ethnic group.] For me, being tough in high school as a teenager was important for getting respect and friends...There is even a distinct walking form that is popularized in hip hop behavior. This walk is quite difficult to execute. One must reach relaxation from the chest down to the feet while creating a strut that slightly hops from one foot to another. One can sense the relaxed but tough attitude of the walker, similar to the attitudes displayed in rap music. Since I had my body in tune for dancing, I did not have an arduous time learning the walk.[23]

The existing literature points out that some children of immigrants who grew up in the inner city fall into the category of underachieving minority youth. Factors of class and geography as well as the racialization process contribute to such identification. However, it is important to note that David didn't grow up in the inner city or become part of the underachieving. Some Korean Americans, like David, feel camaraderie with African Americans and Latinos, partly because they are sensitive to the discrimination encountered by racial minorities in the U.S. and partly because other minorities provide role models in fighting racism. Thus, the model of adaptation undertaken by these Korean Americans is more complex than existing models might suggest.[24] Media also played an important role in defining minority youth culture. Perhaps David's case was not common; however, his case points to the fact that it is not accurate to think of Korean American identity formation only in relation to white, middle-class life ways. It is also problematic to view immigrant minority attraction to African American culture as detrimental to school performance. Issues of gender seem to play an important role in the coming of age of minority youth, as David seeks answers to his struggle with masculinity from African American men.

Similarly, 1.5-generation Korean American identity formation may involve traveling to Korea. In this process, some come to demystify the images and identities of Korea and the U.S. Sean, a 22-year-old student at UCLA, came to the U.S. at the age of 3 in 1977. He considers himself to be second generation demographically, but a 1.5er Korean American culturally. Throughout his life, Sean took pride in Koreans as hardworking, God-fearing, and honest. Instilled by his father, this view was undoubtedly biased. Sean perceived the contradiction most vividly during the Seoul Olympics boxing match. A judge took a bribe and awarded the gold medal to an undeserving Korean fighter. This incident shamed Koreans as a whole. Sean was embarrassed to be Korean. He wondered how Korea could have done that while hosting the nations of the world. His original pride in being a Korean was broken, and he concluded that Koreans were selfish. Further disillusionment came with the collapse of a department store in Seoul.[25] Many innocent lives were lost as a result of shoddy construction.[26]

Native-Born 1.5 Generation

A 24-year-old female clinical research coordinator who came to the U.S. at the age of 4 in 1975 sees herself as near-second-generation demographically, but 1.5er culturally. At home she speaks English to her brother, but Korean to her parents. At work she only speaks English. At church and with her friends she also speaks only English. She never really thought about the question of ethnicity at any great length. Basically all of her friends were white and she wanted to fit in by acting "white." But she reminded the interviewer, John Yi, that this was 20 years ago when there were not so many Asians around. However, now she is proud to be Korean and wants to learn more about her culture. She was never aware of being treated differently because of her ethnicity. She adds that then she was not aware of it. Although many 1.5er Korean Americans shared the transformative experience of first "acting white" and then later affirming their Korean heritage, a few had the contrary experience: they grew up in multiethnic Koreatown and struggled to get along with whites later on. Still others recognized the many different cultural strands in their Korean American experience.

Similarly, Jenny is a U.S.-born, 22-year-old auditor/accountant who explains clearly the hybridity in the making of Korean American culture. According to her:

> I have gone through several identity crises. I haven't necessarily come up with a conclusion, and it's definitely a struggle to juggle two cultures. You have to think about what makes your identity. Is it your appearance, where you grew up...? If it's where I grew up, then I'm American. If it's where my parents came from, then I'm Korean. If it's my values, then I'm American. I juggle all these things in my mind. I'm glad I grew up knowing different ethnicities and I'm glad that I know Caucasians. I like my experience – I've seen a lot of Koreans who have only been surrounded by Koreans, so I feel very lucky to have gone through both experiences. In childhood, I practiced more of my American identity, whereas in college (UCLA), it was my Korean identity.[27] I really feel that I am both and you can be both. That's a part of being American. We are a melting pot of different cultures and people.

Regarding her definition of Korean American culture, she said there are aspects of American and Korean cultures in Korean American culture. In addition she explained how she practices Korean American culture:

> I would say, in the Korean subculture, a typical conversation would consist of someone talking about American movies, American actors, American politics, while also talking about Korean music, Korean videos, and Korean church (she is a church member). I think a Caucasian or a recent Korean immigrant would get lost in this conversation. In terms of Korean culture, I try to show respect toward elders. I like both Korean and American food. If I had to live with just one, I wouldn't be able to choose. In terms of language, I'm a lot more

comfortable in English, but I do want to learn more Korean.

Here we sense that Korean American cultural traits are practiced mostly as broader repertoires of consumption.[28] Korean Americans also seem to hold mystified notions of American society, for instance, not realizing that "diligence and hard work" are also an important element in American culture. Her suggestion for the future of the Korean American community is:

> I think Korean Americans should be just that: Korean American. I see Koreans sometimes getting wrapped up in Korean Power – it's almost like a separatist attitude. If you live in America, you are American also. If you want to be recognized more by America, then you should have more contact with other Americans. I think there's a danger in getting wrapped up in your own Koreanness. That will only lead to further discrimination and maintain the preconceived notions that others have. But if we, Korean Americans, are more dispersed and take part in the American community, we can have more influence in this country.[29]

In discussions about Korean American identity, the aspect of religious identity, such as Christianity, plays a significant, perhaps overly significant role. A 26-year-old male, a youth pastor, came to the U.S. at the age of 7 in 1977. In the following conversation with the interviewer, Jane Kim, he expresses his view:

J: How's it affected you overall? Socially, culturally, being a Korean American?

P: Does it matter, the Christian aspect?

J: It seems like the Christian aspect neutralizes everything.

P: Yeah, so many ways...I like the fact that I have two cultures. Like you said, taking the good from both cultures. I like that. Um...it's taught me to be more sensitive to other cultures and I could hang out with Koreans because of their customs and similarities. It's something I like to do.

J: Do you feel part of the Korean American communities?

P: Mostly through church. Yeah. That's what I have to say. But I'm not very familiar with Korean Americans who don't go to church, but I wish I could be. I could reach out to them. Not only reach out but just realize where they are.

J: Do you have any suggestions for the Korean American community?

P: Other than turning to God, I guess really there's nothing that solves all the problems, but having a good sense as a Christian first of all and then being comfortable with the fact that you're a Korean American.

On the one hand, there is concern among churches that Korean American Christianity will not continue in the next generation. On the other hand, there are reports that some 1.5-generation Korean Americans at elite institutions become very religious and fundamentalist, and abandon school in order to pursue fundamentalist missionary work.

Foreign-Born 1.5 Generation

Korean Americans who came to the U.S. at a later age than the above group but still as adolescents discussed their take on Korean American identity. A 26-year-old male, an associate engineer, came to the U.S. at the age of 12 in 1981. He told the interviewer, John Yi:

> I consider myself a 1.5 generation Korean American due to the fact that I immigrated at the age of twelve. There is no way I could consider myself second generation. I am not completely comfortable with Koreans or whites and I do not have absolute mastery over the Korean or English language.
>
> Therefore, I am caught right in the middle of the two cultures, which I consider the 1.5 generation situation. The telling incident for me was when I was filling out an application in Korean and I could not understand everything it said.
>
> This shattered my notion that I was fluent in the Korean language.

He generally associates with Koreans, but more with 1.5-generation Koreans than with the first generation. In addition, he feels he has reaped the benefits of life in America. He has received a good education, achieved a comfortable lifestyle, and most importantly, he has found God. He became a Christian after immigrating and it changed his whole life. He reveals:

> Although I have never been the victim of anti-Asian violence, I have been attacked by racial slurs throughout my junior high and high school years. I have been called everything from a "chink" to a "dog eater." This racism has caused me to associate only with Koreans because I feel rejected by

whites....Nevertheless, I used to be overly proud of Korea, but after learning about the injustices that occur over there, I feel sorry for the oppressed Koreans.

Also, I disliked America at first, but I have grown to appreciate the freedom available in the U.S. Now I think of Koreans as more narrow-minded and bossy. On the contrary, I feel that Americans are more polite, friendly, and warm due to my interactions with them since immigrating.[30]

In this way, 1.5-generation Korean Americans constantly modify their understanding of Korean and American cultures and arrive at more complex and realistic pictures of Korea and the U.S.

Another male, a 23-year-old manager of his parents' photo store, who has lived in Japan, came to the U.S. at the age of 9 in 1981. He acknowledged his struggle with three different cultures and advocated Korean pride as a defense mechanism:

I totally struggle with my identities sometimes. It's hard sometimes because I think in three languages. And the social situation I'm in dictates which language I'll be thinking in. For example, my girlfriend is Japanese, so I think in Japanese when I'm around her, or when I think about her, I think in Japanese. But some of my Korean friends and I talk in Korean, and at those times I don't think in Japanese at all. The other thing is when a certain idea pops into my head, it's most naturally expressed in one of the languages I'm familiar with. Like with you [Korean-speaking Chinese American researcher Mark Cheng], I can speak Konglish. It's natural that way....However, I don't feel like I'm really part of the Korean American community because I'm not really active in political issues or community activities. That doesn't mean I don't feel like I'm Korean. Anyway, more Koreans who are out of school should devote more time and resources to the Korean American community. It's important for us to tell the next generations who are born here not to lose their Koreanness. They shouldn't get white-washed. They should also be damn proud that they're Korean and not wish that they were white or anything else. It's that Koreanness that gives a sense of identity and security.[31]

Construing Self through Constructing Community

A 25-year-old male *T'aekwŏndo* instructor, with an MA degree from Harvard, came to the U.S. at the age of 7 in 1977. He speaks English 80 percent of the time in public, but at home he speaks Korean 95 percent of the time. According to interviewer Mark Cheng, he is fed up with too much identity talk and argues for the importance of community involvement:

These days I identify myself more and more as an individual, avoiding identifying with this or that community. Before it was more of a Korean thing, now more of an international thing...focusing too much on one's ethnicity often leads to a narrow, warped conception of the world. There's nothing more to it than that...I don't struggle with my identity. I think too many Korean Americans spend too much time and personal energy struggling with identity. There are so many more important sociopolitical issues they should struggle with (given limited time and energy). Introspection is necessary but not sufficient. Nevertheless, I've faced hostility because of my ethnicity...things like racial comments...I responded by either straight out confronting the person or ignoring them.

As far as Korean American social and cultural practices are concerned, he listed: language, social conventions, food, music, and friendship and other social ties, and drawing the best from both sides for whatever suits the particular situation. He added his comments on the Korean American experience:

Korean Americans (at least the 1st generation) are to be commended for their sacrifices. Thus far, their sweat and blood have and should continue to define Korean American identity. I explain my Korean American identity as a continuation or evolution of their experience. My generation has to build on the experiences of our predecessors, but we're also bound to improve relations between Koreans and non-Koreans, instead of just wanting to be left alone.[32]

Michelle, a 22-year-old female, came to the U.S. at the age of 8 in 1982 and grew up in Monterey Park, along with lots of Filipinos and Latinos at a Catholic school. She now works at a law firm. Her discussion of the 1.5 generation is somewhat elaborate and she argues for the 1.5er as a "bridge-builder":

I was literally the 1.5. A lot of my friends came here when they were one or two [years old]. I think they are second generation. They don't know anything about their culture, they don't have any memories of Korea. Even though it's of my childhood, I still have it…I think 1.5 are people who are really stuck in between. Not "too Koreanized," but I really do feel I'm 1.5, you know? I really feel that the Korean community needs more 1.5 generation people who know not just people who speak Korean, but who have experience in the American society that could really be a bridge…I guess I don't mind when people say, "I'm Korean American." That's fine, too, but when they are like my cousin who grew up in a Caucasian neighborhood and try to emphasize that they're American, that gets to me…I guess being American is in a sense accepting diverse cultures around me…[33]

Besides the important conception of the 1.5er as "bridge-builder," it is evident that different social spaces shape different racial/ethnic consciousness and overall understandings of American culture.

A similar view has been aired by Grace; a 30-year-old female director of public relations who represents the station KSCI-TV Channel 18. She came to the U.S. at the age of 11 in 1977. She speaks and writes Korean as well as English. She is happy to work here and has a high level of interest in issues that impact Asian Pacific Americans, newly arrived immigrants – including people from European countries and South American countries – and also women's issues. She also has lived in European countries. Growing up in Monterey Park with Anglos as well as third- and fourth-generation Japanese Americans, she remembers that at school her three brothers and herself were the only ones who couldn't speak English.[34] The teachers did not know what to do with them since when tested in math, the siblings were far above their grade level, but when tested in English, they did poorly.

She has been quite active in and outside of the Korean American community. She sits on the community advisory board with what she calls an Anglo-affluent group of women whose husbands are in corporate America. She is also on the board of the Korean American scholarship foundation and is a founding member of the Koreatown YMCA. She is also a founding member and former president of WORK (Women's Organization Reaching Koreans) and several other groups including the Korean American Museum. She was asked whether she faced personal hostility or discrimination (glass ceiling, etc.) because of her race or ethnicity. Her response was:

Well, I faced racial discrimination immediately upon arriving in this country, and it came from those little white kids who were making fun of me because I looked so different. As I got older and as I began working full-time, I often wondered, why does my boss think that I cannot deal with Anglo groups? Why am I being boxed in? You know. Or why do I feel like I am being boxed in? Let's deal with the ethnic media; for example, why don't I get the opportunity to deal with reporters from the mainstream media outlets…I still face racist remarks. What I try to do, even when I hear it in the form of a joke, is to make it a point to tell people that it should not be said. And I think most people appreciate that. It's not that I want to confront them with anything but you should never joke about someone's race, gender, or sexual preference…

She characterized the Korean American experience in the following way:

The Korean American experience has been one that has been very, very fortunate. It has been a blessing, a blessed experience. We, as a group of immigrants, were very lucky to have come at the end of the civil rights movement led by Martin Luther King, Jr. And in all the atrocities our Japanese and Chinese counterparts, many, many years before, have [had] experienced here.…(Then, does she at times still struggle with her identity?) No, I don't let myself struggle with that anymore. I think that I have been through enough struggling. Now I am quite comfortable being who I am and what I am. I think I have come to terms with the fact that I am very different. Not only are my facial features very different but my thinking is very different. I have very high self-esteem so I don't struggle with self-identity anymore.

The interviewer, Natalie Lee, a Chinese American, asked whether she feels part of the Korean American community.

I feel very much a part of the Korean community. I feel like I grew up with the community. As I said, I have been doing community work for the last twenty years and I have been very fortunate. A lot of people whom I started out with when I was young are now in very influential positions because they have stuck to the community for the last twenty years…I feel a sense of responsibility to the Korean

> American community, and actually to the Republic of Korea for gaining the same kind of economic and political stature as Japan and China. Someday in whatever role I can play as a Korean American, I would like to play a role in that....One example is that in the Chinese community there are organizations like the Organization of Chinese Americans, and in the Japanese there is the Japanese American Citizens' League. Granted that these two communities have had three or four generations who have lived and died in this country, we, too, as Korean Americans should form such a national group that could symbolically, if nothing else, raise those concerns that impact Korean Americans.[35] We don't have that voice, we have a great void right now...

Finally, the interviewer asked "What generation do you consider yourself?"

> I consider myself to be a 1.5, and 1.5 generation people are an island themselves. Because we are really neither, if you really looked at us. It's kind of flattering to say I'm bicultural, it sounds really nice and all. But when you really cut to the chase, you're neither. I can't say that I am totally American. For example, I cannot live on an American diet for a whole month. I assure you, I cannot. I don't even want to find out if I could. And I like the luxury of being able to choose what I want and when I want. But oftentimes it's very lonely because people have different expectations. The older Koreans, the first generation Korean men in their fifties and sixties, have a different expectation for the 1.5 generation than they do of the second generation, who were born here. Because they can immediately excuse them, "Aye, it's okay, you were born here. They don't know anything about Korean culture and tradition." Well 1.5 is treated differently.[36]

It should be kept in mind that it might be a minority who can perform a true "bridge-building" role like the above interviewee.[37] Nevertheless, it is also true that many of them do perform such functions in the family and community, in a broader sense of "bridge building."

Interpretation

Portes and his colleagues' segmented assimilation thesis gives us ways of looking at Korean American ethnic identity formation in practical and material dimensions, whereas other studies on ethnic identity have been dematerialized, or tend to reify ethnic identity.[38] It is important to note that within the Korean American community, the term 1.5-generation Korean American has been adopted and popularized not in order to feel good about Korean or Korean American culture, but to achieve certain objectives and invoke a certain historical consciousness.

The existing sociological literature points out the bifurcated and polarized nature of "segmented assimilation" among children of immigrants. Fernandez-Kelly and Richard Schauffler maintained that the outcome of assimilation depends on a series of toponimical – that is, socially and physically situated – factors: internal differentiation by class, type of reception, quality of resources, degree of spatial concentration, and length of time in the area of destination. For instance, the experience of gainers such as Cubans shows that a welcoming reception in areas of destination – including government initiatives to facilitate immigrant adaptation – can have long-term benefits.[39]

Recognizing the importance of such historical circumstances in shaping the bifurcated and multiple nature of segmented assimilation among children of immigrants, I ask, what categories of social inequality further contribute to the above toponomical factors? First of all, cultural geography is important in that these Korean Americans are located in the oldest and largest Korean American and Asian American community, different from the Midwest where there are few Korean Americans. In short, the school and labor market performance of these children of Korean immigrants fit into the modified linear theory either through mainstream or ethnic economy; however, their identity formation does not neatly correspond to their location in the labor market. The causal factors have much to do with the workings of race / gender / class variables. Growing up with some kind of prejudices, many 1.5er KAs develop a milder form of Du Boisian double consciousness as a reference to and a confirmation of the existence of ambiguities and vacillations between assimilationist and nationalist tendencies in Korean American life. Therefore, some 1.5er Korean Americans from suburbs associate themselves with African Americans or Latinos, as they are subjected to racialization or genderization processes in the U.S. In their appearances, for instance, there are traces of African American men's style or Latina dress/hair style. In the discussion on the racial construction of Asian American manhood, Espiritu noted that "whereas the evil Oriental stereotype marks Asian American men as the white man's enemy, the stereotype of the sexless Asian sidekick-Charlie Chan, the Chinese laundryman, the Filipino houseboy – depicts Asian men as devoted and impotent, eager to please."[40] More importantly, it speaks to the increasing number of young Korean Americans who identify themselves with other inner-city racial minorities politically.

In other words, as far as questions of race, gender / sexuality, and politics (to a lesser extent, language) are concerned, young Korean Americans are influenced by other racial minorities. However, as far as school and labor market performances are concerned, their strategy is grounded in their immigrant minorities' lives as well as in (white) middle-class lifestyles. For instance, most are encouraged to do better than white classmates, because they are of Korean descent and are a racial minority. Also this strategy of identifying with other minorities is an alternative model to the conventional one in which Korean Americans identify mostly with suburban middle-class whites; this alternative model can be found among some Korean Americans, but not all. My analysis may be applied to other second-generation Asian Americans and is certainly generational, but it is beyond the scope of this article to say whether this phenomenon is American.

Economically speaking, as seen in the 1990 census, my data indicates that many 1.5er Korean Americans enter the so-called mainstream economy. However, this does not mean they shed their cultures, as also reported in several works.[41] The disjuncture between the economic location and the dynamic process of identity formation should be foregrounded. Not only are they situated in the post-Fordist economy, but the mainstream economy itself goes through much transformation, due to the restructuring of the American economy and the discovery of multiethnicity as a new source of consumers.[42]

Among 1.5er Korean Americans, identities are fluid and constantly evolving to some extent. More importantly, in this process some come to demystify their images and identities of Korea and the U.S. and develop a more complex understanding of two nations. Many become overly Koreanized or Americanized at different times. Others hold stereotypical, mythologized, or ritualistic understandings of either Korean or American cultures. On the other hand, the process of identity formation among these Korean Americans is situational and complex, and yet contradictory and compartmentalized. It is also time-, space-, and speaker-specific. Many indicate adopting categories of American (often meaning white American), Asian American, and Korean American, as they go through grade school, high school, and college: "from bleached back to the original color." Consequently, Korean American phenomena indicate the importance of "hybridity" and "third space," as well as "multiplicity" and "heterogeneity" in identity formation.

Although the linguistic dimension is an important element, biculturalism (as operating in two culturally coded systems of behavior with different assumptions and logic, different practices and outcomes) and multiculturalism (or transculturalism) seem to be the most significant criteria in defining 1.5-generation Korean Americans. Therefore, I define the 1.5-generation Korean Americans culturally, as people of Korean descent who came to the U.S. as minors (infants, children, or adolescents), or are U.S.-born, and who practice aspects of biculturalism/multiculturalism involving Korean and American cultures, often with conflict. At the same time, many develop aspects of "double consciousness" due to contradictions between Americans and Koreans. They often turn to Christianity, and some are seriously concerned about the political future of the Korean American community as "bridge-builders."

On the other hand, 1.5ers do not have unique characteristics. In other words, 1.5ers should not be defined by any inherent cultural attributes, but by cultural organization, following Barth's suggestion that we study "the ethnic boundary that defines the group, not the cultural stuff that it encloses."[43] Therefore, in this article, I have paid attention to the way the concept of "1.5er" is constructed and mobilized for certain purposes and in its specific context. Such a high level of valorization of the term 1.5er has much to do with the political expectation within the Korean

American community for 1.5ers to be "bridge-builders."

This article reveals a smoother process than expected of hybrid Korean American identity formation among 1.5ers. Conversely, it also speaks to the lack of critical consciousness. Accordingly, I see two different kinds of cosmopolitanism among 1.5-generation Korean Americans: yuppie cosmopolitanism and marginalized cosmopolitanism. People in the first category are content with consuming Korean as well as American commodities and engaging in aspects of social relationships as part of their yuppie mainstream background. People in the second category, including artists and intellectuals as well as gangsters, are on the edge and still feel alienated, perhaps suspicious of both cultures. Future research is needed concerning the second category.

Given the understanding that "not all hybridities are equal or the same," it is important to look into the conditions for the production of hybridities. As Dirlik put it, "the emergence of Pacific Asian economies as key players in the global economy has had a transformative effect on the Asian American self-image, as well as on the perceptions of Asian Americans at large...the most visible effect may be the elevation of Asian American status vis-à-vis other minority groups....".[44] The changing structure of the global political economy and the emergence of transnationalism, including the rise of the Pacific Rim and Korea as the world's twelfth economic power, as well as the post-civil rights racial structure in the U.S. are the context in which this young generation of Korean Americans develops its sense of self and community. Also, new images of Asian Americans have further contributed to their position. Since the 1960s, the "unassimilable Orientals" have transformed into "successful model minorities." In addition, through the 1992 LA riots, many of these 1.5er Korean Americans went through racialization and politicization.

At this point, my interviewees remain at various levels of "practicing" the community. Many are content with consumption-oriented ethnicity/culture (e.g., enjoying the Korean food, music/dance/art and other popular cultural aspects, speaking the language, etc.). Others are satisfied with being members of "geographies of ethnicity," for instance, cultivating Korean family/kin and friends and other social relationships, going to Korean church, language school, and other functions and participating in community events. Only a few are concerned about "producing and practicing" the communities (caring about the political future of the communities). For these individuals, working for the Korean American community inevitably entails a broader vision of social justice.

In this process, becoming a member of the ethnic community often becomes a first step to resolving the question of one's identity or selfhood. Therefore, what is significant for increasing numbers of Korean American youth is not the struggle with the issue of identity but the formation of the Korean American community, starting with family, friends, and church. In that process, they go beyond an ethnic-specific interest and work towards building relations with other people of color, the oppressed, disadvantaged, and despised. They feel comfortable with their self-identity as they create a more inclusive community and struggle toward political empowerment of the Korean and minority communities. Politics, if addressed at all, is often treated as a distinct, relatively autonomous arena of urban life. By the same token, politics is rarely considered a social process implicated in the formation and reformulation of urban Korean American identities.[45] From this perspective, the identity of Korean Americans in the United States has everything to do with politics.[46]

At this point, the second generation Korean American experience seems to be subsumed under the category of the 1.5 generation. As they attempt to find solidarity with 1.5ers, they feel their predicament isn't different from 1.5ers metaphorically. In the future, increasing numbers of the second generation might contribute to the formation of a different perspective.

NOTES

1 In this article Korean Americans means the first generation as well as U.S. born second generation. I sometimes use Korean immigrants interchangeably with Korean Americans.

2 W. E. B. Du Bois, *The Souls of Black Folk: Essays and Sketches* (New York: Signet, 1969 [1903]), 45.
3 Fieldnote, by David Moon, 1996.
4 Won Moo Hurh, The "1.5 generation": A Paragon of Korean-American Pluralism. *Korean Culture* (Spring 1990), 21.
5 Personal communication with K. W. Lee, October 28, 1997.
6 Bong Hwan Kim, Issues of Community-Based Joint Economic Ventures. In *Multiethnic Coalition Building in Los Angeles*, Eui-young Yu and Edward Chang, ed. (Los Angeles: Institute for Asian American and Pacific Asian Studies, California State University, Los Angeles, 1995), 152.
7 Ruben G. Rumbaut and K. Ima, *The Adaptation of Southeast Asian Refugee Youth: A Comparative Study* (Washington, DC: U.S. Office of Refugee Resettlement, 1988).
8 Shu-mei Shih, Feminist Diaspora and the Nation: Theresa Hak-Kyung Cha's *Dictee* and Myung Mi Kim's *Under Flag*. Paper presented at the conference on "Transnational Korea: Division and Diaspora" at University of Southern California, 1995, 3.
9 Alejandro Portes and Min Zhou, The New Second Generation: Segmented Assimilation and its Variants. *Annals of the American Academy of Political and Social Sciences*, 530 (November 1993), 74–96. See also Min Zhou, Segmented Assimilation: Issues, Controversies, and Recent Research on the New Second Generation. *International Migration Review* 31 (1997), 975–1008.
10 Min Zhou, Growing Up American: The Challenge Confronting Immigrant Children and Children of Immigrants. *Annual Review of Sociology* 23 (1997), 63–95, esp. 75.
11 Margaret A. Gibson and John Ogbu, eds., *Minority Status and Schooling: A Comparative Study of Immigrant and Involuntary Minorities* (New York: Garland, 1991); Min Zhou and C. L. Bankston III, *Growing Up American: The Adaptation of Vietnamese Children in American Society* (New York: Russell Sage Foundation, 1998); Rumbaut and Ima, *The Adaptation of Southeast Asian Refugee Youth*.
12 Ruben Rumbaut, The Crucible Within: Ethnic Identity, Self-Esteem, and Segmented Assimilation among Children of Immigrants. *International Migration Review* 28:4 (1994), 754.
13 Ethnographic interviews indicate open-ended, thematic and phenomenological interviews, in contrast to psychological or attitudinal interviews.
14 So far some research has been conducted among the student population of Korean Americans. This reflects a general trend in which research on the children of immigrants has been done in the area of the sociology of education.
15 The overall reaction to my research has been positive, though there were some mixed reactions. For example, a 25-year-old female billing clerk who came to U.S. at the age of 5 was not happy about the research. She identifies herself as a 1.5 generation Korean American; however, she feels that asking questions and making people reveal their experiences with racism and discrimination put up barriers between ethnicities when Korean are trying to blend in. In contrast, most enjoyed the interview because it raised a lot of important issues for them.
16 All the names of the interviewees have been changed, except public figures or community leaders.
17 In the 1990 census, the Asian Pacific population is 45.2 percent of the populations of Cerritos.
18 Field note, by David Moon, November 20, 1995.
19 At Sunnyhill High School, in Orange county, teachers informed me that it's a difficult issue to reduce tension over proper use of honorifics among Korean American students of different generations.
20 This reflects a new relationship that Korean Americans have with Korea in the changing global context, due to new modes of communication and technology.
21 Du Bois, *Souls of Black Folk*, chapter 1.
22 Similarly, according to filmmaker Spike Lee, an increasing number of middle-class suburban white youth stated that their favorite music was Snoop Dogg, Wu-Tang Clan, and Puff Daddy, *New York Times*, October 13, 1998.
23 Field note, by David Moon, January 12, 1996.
24 Pyong Gap Min and Rose Kim, eds., *Struggling for Ethnic Identity: Young Asian American Professionals* (Walnut Creek, CA: Alta-Mira Press, 1999).
25 The collapse of the "Sampoong" department store in the most affluent neighborhood in Korea in 1995 challenged many Koreans to problematize the ideology of development and modernity.
26 Interview by David Moon, January 12, 1996.
27 As of 1999, Asian American students make up the largest racial group among freshmen and there are more than 3,000 Korean American students on the UCLA campus.
28 I owe Henry Em for this insight.
29 Interview by Susanna F. Cha, 1995.
30 Interview by John Yi, 1995.
31 Interview by Mark Cheng, 1995.
32 Ibid.

33 Interview by Annette Kim, 1995.

34 As of 1997, Monterey Park became a predominantly Chinese immigrant community, as described vividly by John Horton, *The Politics of Diversity: Immigration, Resistance, and Change in Monterey Park, California* (Philadelphia: Temple University Press), 1995.

35 Actually, there are such organizations; however, they have yet to address issues concerning Korean Americans nationwide.

36 Interview by Natalie Lee, 1995.

37 Eui-Young Yu and K. W. Lee reminded me of this important point.

38 There are some exceptions. For Filipino American youth, see Yen Le Espiritu, The Intersection of Race, Ethnicity, and Class: The Multiple Identities of Second-Generation Filipinos. *Identities* 1:2–3 (1994), 249–273, and Diana Wolf, Family Secrets: Transnational Struggles among Children of Filipino Immigrants. *Sociological Perspectives* 40:3 (1997), 457–482. For Chinese and Korean American young adults, see Nazli Kibria, The Construction of "Asian American": Reflections on Intermarriage and Ethnic Identity among Second-Generation Chinese and Korean Americans. *Ethnic and Racial Studies* 20:4 (1997), 77–86. See also Min and Kim, *Struggling for Ethnic Identity*.

39 Patricia Fernandez-Kelly and Richard Schauffler, Divided Fates: Immigrant Children in a Restructured U.S. Economy. *International Migration Review* 28:4 (1994), 663, 676, and 686.

40 Yen Le Espiritu, *Asian American Women and Men: Labor, Laws, and Love* (Thousand Oaks, CA: Sage Publications, 1997), 91.

41 See Portes, ed., *The New Second Generation* (New York: Russell Sage Foundation, 1996) and Min and Kim, *Struggling for Ethnic Identity*.

42 Personal communication with Pyong Gap Min, October 22, 1997.

43 Fredrik Barth, ed., *Ethnic Groups and Boundaries* (Boston: Little Brown, 1969), 14–15.

44 Arif Dirlik, Asians on the Rim: Transnational Capital and Local Community in the Making of Asian America. *Amerasia Journal* 22:3 (1996), 3.

45 Stephen Gregory made the seminal argument in his *Black Corona: Race and the Politics of Place in an Urban Community* (Princeton, NJ: Princeton University Press), 1998.

46 I am referring to a group, not to the personal identity of Korean Americans.

Part III

Consumption, Class, and Traditions of Negotiation and Investment

7

Challenging Traditional Marriage: Never Married Chinese American and Japanese American Women

Susan J. Ferguson

Marriage rates are declining in the United States, and more people are either living alone or cohabiting outside of marriage (Mintz and Kellogg 1988; Waite 1995). The high rate of divorce, the decline in fertility, and the timing and incidence of first marriage have dramatically influenced these changes in marriage patterns (Rodgers and Thornton 1985; Sweet and Bumpass 1987). One of the most striking changes in recent years is the increasing number of people who are either delaying or rejecting marriage. In 1997, for example, the median age at first marriage was 25.0 years for women and 26.8 years for men (U.S. Bureau of the Census 1997). Moreover, during the past four decades the proportion of never married women and men has increased substantially. Between 1960 and 1997, among persons 30 to 34 years of age, the rates of nonmarriage tripled to 19.6 percent for women and more than doubled to 30.3 percent for men (Saluter 1990:2; U.S. Bureau of the Census 1997). These data reveal that many individuals are spending the majority of their adult years unmarried. This demographic shift away from traditional heterosexual marriage affects family formation patterns, housing arrangements, and the economic and social well-being of individuals.

This demographic shift also has unique gender implications, especially since research shows that marriage often has significant, but contrary, effects on women and men: Never married men have higher mortality rates than married men (Hu and Goldman 1990), while never married women enjoy greater mental and physical health than other women (Keith 1989). Moreover, Umberson (1987) found that married men are less likely to be excessive drinkers or participants in risk-taking behaviors than are single men. Marriage also has been found to affect the career mobility and wages men and women receive. For example, never married men are less likely than married men to be hired and promoted (Schoen 1991), while never married women are seen as more committed to their careers by some employers (Bradsher 1989; Houseknecht, Vaughan, and Statham 1987). In addition, Daniel (1995) found that married men received a wage premium for being married compared to the wages received by single men. Married women, on the other hand, especially European American women and women with children, were found to pay a wage penalty for being married when compared to single women. Being never married, however, can also have negative economic consequences for women, including reducing their access to dual incomes, insurance, and other financial benefits of heterosexual marriage (Becker 1976; Blau and Ferber 1986; Smith 1994). Thus, the costs and benefits of marriage differ for women and men.

These inconsistent consequences and perceived benefits of heterosexual marriage raise interesting research questions concerning the never married.[1] In particular, we need more information about the people who are delaying first marriage or not marrying at all and about the causes and consequences of nonmarriage for women, men, and people from different racial and ethnic groups. In the research literature, *never married* is primarily a demographic construct, where it is assumed that marriage is the normal adult status, since more than 90 percent of the population in the United States eventually marries. A person is characterized as never married until he or she marries for the first time. While it is true that potentially a person can marry at any time during adult life, one is categorized as never married until he or she does marry. Thus, being never married is not necessarily considered to be a permanent state or a stigmatized social status. Instead, those who never marry are considered to be qualitatively different from those who do marry. That is why family researchers and demographers prefer to use the term *never married* instead of the terms *single* or *unmarried*, because *single* could convey one of four marital statuses: never married, divorced, separated, or widowed. Moreover, many demographers and family scholars often use different age markers when they study never married populations. Since most people marry for the first time in their twenties or thirties, researchers will often use the age marker of 35 years to distinguish the never married who have the highest probability of marrying from those who are older. Demographers often choose an older age marker, such as 55 years and older, to identify those never married women who are beyond their childbearing years. These age categorizations not only reveal different assumptions about the normality of marriage and the linkage of marriage to fertility in the research, but they also indicate that different stages in the life course of adults may be affecting their desires or opportunities to marry. Specifically, existing research on the causes of nonmarriage includes economic, demographic, and cultural explanations. Many theories address marriage market variables, such as the gender ratio (Guttentag and Secord 1983; Lichter et al. 1992), economic status (Becker 1973, 1976), and age differentials of potential spouses (Coale and McNeil 1972; Dixon 1971; Kiernan and Eldridge 1987; Rindfuss and Sweet 1978). This study builds on these explanations of the never married, but it attends more closely to the issues of gender, race and ethnicity, culture, and attitudinal changes toward heterosexual marriage (Ferguson 1993, 1995). In brief, never married Asian American women present one of the most interesting research groups because they challenge many assumptions about gender, race and ethnicity, and marriage.

One of the most commonly held assumptions about Asian American women is that they have high rates of marriage. Historically, the marriage rates of Asian women in China and Japan have been very high, leading to almost universal female marriage. These higher rates of marriage among Chinese and Japanese women are primarily due to arranged marriages, patrilocal household formation, and the centrality of the family as the primary religious, social, and economic unit (Cornell 1984; De Vos 1984; Hajnal 1965; Pelzel 1970; Watkins 1984). Until recently, Chinese and Japanese women have had few available social roles or economic means for survival other than marriage. Although this historical background might well lead to high marriage rates in the United States among Chinese Americans and Japanese Americans, earlier research, in fact, revealed that native-born Chinese American and Japanese American women have lower rates of marriage than do native European American women (Ferguson 1993, 1995). Even foreign-born Chinese American and Japanese American women have significant rates of nonmarriage. These high rates of nonmarriage are surprising, not only because of the historically high frequency of female marriage in China and Japan, but also because of the elevated incidence of interracial marriage in the United States, especially for Japanese American women (Sung 1990; Takagi 1994).

Contemporary research on never married women has examined some racial differences in U.S. marital patterns. Marriage rates and the experience of marriage vary between racial ethnic groups. For instance, some researchers argue that nonmarriage among African American women causes them to be impoverished (Moynihan 1986; Murray 1984), while others argue that living in poverty is what causes many African American women not to marry (Stack 1974; Wilson 1987). Wilson's research, for example, emphasizes the economic "unattractiveness" of some African American males because of their high unemployment and incarceration rates. In contrast, instead of focusing on poverty, research on never married European American women emphasizes the influence of education and careers on marital status (Cherlin 1980; Mare and

Winship 1991). One problem with this research on U.S. never married women is that it primarily compares African Americans and European Americans, excluding other racial and ethnic groups such as Asian Americans. Moreover, previous studies on never married women often assume U.S. black and white populations to be homogeneous, thus ignoring intraracial heterogeneity (Bennett, Bloom, and Craig 1989; Lichter, LeClere, and McLaughlin 1991; Schoen and Kluegel 1988). For example, variation in socioeconomic status within each racial group is not always controlled for in marriage research, although some researchers have argued that social class may be as significant as race (Wilson 1987). This research on Chinese American and Japanese American women expands our understanding of the never married beyond this Black-white dichotomy.

Changing Marital Behavior

The purpose of this study is to investigate the changing marital behavior of Chinese Americans and Japanese Americans by examining how factors such as age, nativity, family background, educational attainment, and careers affect women's opportunities and desires to marry. In particular, the in-depth interviews examine why Chinese American and Japanese American women have moved away from traditional cultural and familial expectations concerning marriage. Why do Chinese American and Japanese American women have the second highest rates of nonmarriage among all U.S. racial ethnic groups?[2] Researchers have examined the increasing rate of nonmarriage among European Americans and African Americans. This study examines the prevalence of and reasons for being never married among heterosexual Chinese American and Japanese American women, because the marital behavior of Asian Americans has not been as thoroughly investigated as that of other U.S. racial ethnic groups.

Since earlier research also has not adequately explored the experience of being never married or the changing attitudes toward marriage, especially in light of greater educational and career opportunities for women and the declining social stigma of being never married,[3] this study emphasizes the attitudinal and lifestyle characteristics of never married Chinese American and Japanese American women. Most important, this study breaks new ground by focusing on the respondents' decisions and explanations for their never married status. What particular individual choices and structural constraints influence a woman's decision to delay marriage or never marry? Research has documented an increasing female resistance to marriage as other life opportunities become available, such as access to higher education and careers (Gerson 1985; Goldscheider and Waite 1986; Havens 1973). Building on this research, I hypothesize that some of the factors that have affected the decisions of never married Chinese American and Japanese American women are their educational attainment, their career aspirations, and the presence of familial demands on the daughter's labor, either in a family business or caring for an elderly parent. All of these potential explanations are supported by earlier research (Ferguson 1993, 1995; Gerson 1985; Goldscheider and Waite 1986; Havens 1973; Salaff 1976, 1981).

In addition, building on feminist theories of family and gender roles, I hypothesize that some Chinese American and Japanese American women are hesitant to marry Asian men who may want more traditional wives. Hunt and Hunt (1987) argue that a cultural lag exists between the changing domestic roles of women and men in U.S. society. Specifically, women are positively embracing their new work and family roles, while men are resisting the increasing independence of women in the workplace and the greater demands placed on men in the home. Sociological research has documented this cultural lag between white ethnic women and men (Gerson 1985; Hochschild 1989). The cultural lag in gender roles could be even greater among Asian Americans, causing some Chinese American and Japanese American women to resolve this work and family conflict by not marrying. Unfortunately, little research has examined how changing gender roles are affecting Asian American families and women's decisions to marry.

I further propose that changes in gender roles among Asian Americans are complicated by race and ethnicity, socioeconomic background, and immigrant history. Yanagisako, for example, argues that second- and third-generation Japanese Americans believe that marriage should be based on romantic love, not duty; that the conjugal bond takes precedence, not the filial bond; and that marriages should have greater emotional intensity, verbal communication, and flexibility in the sexual division of labor than that which existed in their parents' and grandparents' marriages (1985:122). These views contrast with those of the first generation, which believed that marriage was a mandatory obligation enmeshed in other family relationships. Thus, different age groups and generations of women may have different reasons for not marrying, especially if they are experiencing conflicting social norms concerning work, family, and marital expectations. The interview data explore these familial and cultural expectations concerning marriage.

Method

This study uses in-depth, semistructured interviews with both native- and foreign-born Chinese American and Japanese American women to ascertain the influence that family background, socioeconomic factors, and individual attitudes have on their marital status. A pilot study was conducted during the summer of 1996 when five never married Chinese American and Japanese American women were interviewed in the Bay Area of Northern California. Three additional never married Asian American women were interviewed in January 1997 in San Diego, California. After completing these initial eight interviews, the interview schedule was shortened and modified. Respondents then were asked a series of open- and close-ended questions pertaining to their experiences and decisions concerning marriage and family life. In addition, questions also focused on how their family backgrounds and occupational plans have affected their attitudes toward marriage and their personal decisions about whether to marry. Before each interview, all of the respondents were screened regarding their age, marital status, racial ethnic origin, and sexual orientation.[4] The resulting face-to-face interviews required about two hours to complete, with some interviews lasting up to three hours. The interviews were tape-recorded for future transcription, and field notes were recorded after each interview.

As of August 1998, I had interviewed 62 never married Chinese American and Japanese American women. These interviews were conducted primarily in the Bay Area of California, but interviews also occurred in Northern and Southern California. Most of the interviews took place in the respondents' homes or at their workplaces. The initial sample of respondents was obtained via snowball or convenience sampling. Colleagues in California gave me the initial list of names of never married Asian American women or names of contacts within either the Chinese American or Japanese American communities. Phone calling from this initial list of contacts resulted in several dozen interviews. Moreover, at the end of each interview, each respondent was asked to recommend additional participants. I also contacted more than 100 Asian American organizations and placed ads in *Asian Week*, an Asian American newspaper. From these contacts, the word about my research continued to spread, with additional Asian American newspapers, such as *Nikkei West* and the *Hokubei Mainichi*, running stories; announcements also were placed in church bulletins, in the Asian American community calendar, and in newsletters of various organizations.

The sample consists of 62 never married women: 30 Chinese American women, and 32 Japanese American women. Twelve of the 14 foreign-born respondents are of Chinese descent, and 11 of these women constitute the first-generation American women in this study. Of the remaining 19 Chinese American women, 9 are second generation in that their parents immigrated to the United States, 9 are third generation because their grandparents immigrated, and 1 is fourth generation because her great-grandparents immigrated. Of the 32 Japanese American women, 9 are second generation, or Nisei, because their parents immigrated; 22 are third generation, or Sansei, because their grandparents immigrated; and 1 respondent is fourth generation, or Yonsei, because her great-grandparents immigrated to the United States. All of the women in the current sample are English speakers, but many also speak Chinese or Japanese as their first or second language, depending on whether they were raised with the language in the home or if they went to Chinese or Japanese language school when they were growing up.

The ages of the never married women in the sample range from 33 to 80 years, with an average age of 46.65 years.[5] The sample also is a highly educated one with an average educational attainment of 17.94 years, or some graduate work. Only 1 of the 62 respondents had only a high-school education. Almost all of the respondents described themselves as middle-class, even though they may have grown up in a lower socioeconomic class. The mean annual income of the nonretired respondents is $43,278, with most of the respondents working full-time in professional or clerical positions. The sample includes doctors, nurses, lawyers, teachers, counselors, secretaries, computer analysts, and corporate employees. Twelve of the 62 respondents are retired (19.4 percent), but most of these women continue to work either part-time for pay or for the community, doing volunteer work in churches and social service agencies.

Findings

Why are these Chinese American and Japanese American heterosexual women never married? How do their families of origin affect their desire to marry? Or, are these women who really wanted to marry but for a number of reasons were unable to pursue that ideal? Preliminary findings reveal that the women in the sample express various sentiments about the desirability of marriage. All of the respondents were asked directly if they wanted to marry when they were younger and, if given the opportunity, would they want to be married now. The answers to these two questions characterize four clusters of women within the sample. The first group of women (n = 20, or 32.3 percent) said that they wanted to marry when they were younger, and given the opportunity, they would still like to marry now. These women were typically younger, in their thirties and forties, and many still hoped to find a suitable mate with whom to marry and have kids. The second group of women (n = 18, or 29.0 percent) said they wanted to marry when they were younger, but they did not want to marry now. These women preferred to remain never married for the rest of their lives. Most of these women were older than 45; they described themselves as being past the usual age of thinking about marriage and children,[6] and they were comfortable with living alone. This group is similar to the women in South's (1991) research, where he finds that as women get older, marriage is less desirable because they perceive marriage as costly to their freedom and overall happiness. The third group of women (n = 10, or 16.1 percent) said that they never wanted to marry and would prefer to remain never married for the rest of their lives. Most of these women did not date or have serious boyfriends. These never married women also stated that they never wanted to have children. Since having children is the expected outcome of marriage in both the Chinese American and Japanese American communities, women who knew that they did not want to have children often avoided marriage altogether. The fourth and final group of women (n = 14, or 22.6 percent) are a cluster of respondents who felt ambivalent about getting married either in the past or present. Thus, the never married respondents in this sample express diverse sentiments concerning the desirability of marriage.

Given this diversity, what were some of the reasons that Chinese American and Japanese American women gave as to why they remained never married or why marriage was not desirable to them? The women stated a variety of reasons for being never married. In this article, I address four of the factors affecting the respondents' never married status that consistently appeared across many of these women's diverse stories: their parents' marriages, their status as eldest daughters, their educational goals, and the perceived lack of appropriate suitors. These four factors were emphasized by a majority of the respondents to have affected their decisions and opportunities to marry.

Parents' marriages

One of the most important factors in my study of Chinese American and Japanese American never married women is the effect the parents' marriages had on the respondents' views of marriage. More than two-thirds of the respondents said that their parents' marriages profoundly influenced their desire to marry. The overwhelming majority ($n = 48$, or 77.4 percent) described their parents' marriages as very unhappy and conflictual. Similar to findings in Glenn's (1986) and Yanagisako's (1985) research, several of the respondents expressed concern that their parents' marriages were based on duty and obligation instead of on romantic love. Many of the respondents' parents had arranged marriages ($n = 24$, or 38.7 percent) or, at minimum, traditional Asian marriages where the father is the patriarch and the mother is subservient to him. For example, when I asked one respondent, a 38-year-old, second-generation Chinese American, why she had not married, she responded by saying,

> I think it's because I want to find the right person, I didn't want to end up like how my parents were. They weren't compatible, it was a fixed marriage for them....[Not] compatible in that my mom is reserved and my dad is pretty outgoing. Just different thinking, their personalities aren't even the same.

When I asked another respondent, a 40-year-old, third-generation Japanese American, whether her parents' marriage affected her desire to marry, she replied,

> I think in some ways yes, I've seen that particularly my mother has not had an ideal life, meaning that it hasn't been peaches and cream. She hasn't been treated like a queen and a princess. She has had to work very hard domestically and taking care of my father as if my father is a child. And in viewing that, in many ways, I've seen my mother as my dad's servant in some regards. Now they have a very good marriage and it works, and they do care for each other. But in terms of a choice for me, I don't want to have to serve a man like my mother has. That's not my choice, that's not what I would want to do.

In many of the respondents' parents' marriages, especially in those that were arranged, the husband is much older than his wife, and in a few cases, Chinese men may actually have second wives and families. This practice was common among older Chinese immigrants who may have wives and families in China, and then had second wives and families in the United States (Glenn 1983; Ishii-Kuntz 1997; Wong 1995). The age disparity was mentioned by several respondents to be a problem in their parents' marriages. One respondent, a 38-year-old, second-generation Chinese American, said that her parents' age difference made for an unhappy marriage. When I asked her how her parents met, she replied,

> It was formally arranged. The only thing I know is he [her father] was in the U.S. in the Navy at the time and then somehow it got arranged. I don't really know how. They didn't really talk about it, but I think it was family that arranged it. Dad went back to China and got married to my mom and brought her here to the U.S....There was a big age difference. When my dad passed away he was 73 and my mom was only 58. [He was] 14 or 15 years older.

Another respondent, a 40-year-old, second-generation Chinese American, answered the following when I asked her directly why she had not married:

> That's a really good question. I think there are a lot of factors involved. One is that my mother's marriage was arranged, she married my father when she was 19 and he was 31, a 12-year age difference. I think that particular age difference is significant. I really didn't feel that my mother was that happy in marriage, she wasn't a very happy person. And I thought that marriage was really oppressive to her and that I thought she was smarter than my father was but that because the wife had to sort of take the back-seat role, she really subordinated herself. And she wasn't able to really develop her own natural talents and skills and capacities. So I thought that was a big shame, and I really felt like marriage was the reason that she wasn't able to do all that. And I always felt she should have divorced my dad.

It is significant that this respondent would comment that she felt her mother should divorce her father. Only 2 of the 62 respondents' parents' marriages ended in divorce, even though most of the marriages were reported to be unhappy and, at times, abusive.[7] This finding is not surprising, given that divorce is highly stigmatized among older generations of Chinese Americans and Japanese Americans (Glenn 1994:136; Salaff 1981; Wong 1995). Most of my respondents reported that divorce brings shame and dishonor to the family, or as one respondent, a 33-year-old, third-generation Japanese American, explained,

> Shame is associated with divorce...because it's a failure, and I think the extended family views it that way, that it is a failure whether or not you were young or informed when you walked into the marriage – if it fell apart, then you failed and there is always that – you failed.

Another respondent, a 49-year-old, third-generation Japanese American further explained that divorce was almost a taboo subject growing up. One just did not talk about it. She says,

> When I was growing up, I thought that Japanese Americans never divorced, and if they did, that was something you didn't talk about. I don't know why but I thought there was something shameful about it. As were hysterectomies, because my mother wouldn't talk about that kind of surgery. So divorce was sort of like that.

Several respondents made clear that while divorce was entirely unthinkable for older generations, including their parents, grandparents, and aunts and uncles, divorce was beginning to occur among their cousins or among the younger generations of Chinese Americans and Japanese Americans. Thus, a generational shift in family cultural values, especially in the stigmatization of divorce, is evident among Chinese American and Japanese American families. This finding is consistent with the generational family value shifts discussed by other family scholars in Japanese American and Chinese American families (Glenn 1986; Nishi 1995; Wong 1995; Yanagisako 1985). However, the respondents in this study also consistently reported that they were raised with the value that *marriage is a lifelong relationship that one is expected to endure*. Since divorce was not an option for the majority of the respondents' parents, the women in these marriages were expected to endure, and in many cases, they did endure alcoholism, opium addiction, gambling, and verbal or physical violence. Most of the respondents' parents' marriages endured until the death of one of the spouses. Thus, many of the respondents said that they did not want marriages like their mothers'.

Gender and birth order

Another significant factor that has affected the respondents' view of family and their never married status is their gender and sibling birth order. At least 35 of the 62 respondents were the eldest daughters in their families of origin. Being the eldest daughter meant additional responsibilities and social roles. Salaff (1976, 1981), in her study of working daughters in Hong Kong, states that filial piety is a driving force in ensuring that never married daughters dedicate their labor to their families of origin. Salaff further argues that it is expected that daughters learn to serve the men in their families, including their fathers and brothers, and that unmarried daughters live at home with their parents until marriage.

For some female respondents in this study, being the eldest daughter in their families meant taking on the child-care responsibilities for younger siblings or working to help support the family. One respondent, a 34-year-old, first-generation Chinese woman, was sent to the United States at the age of 12 to learn English, to go to school, and to eventually secure employment that would enable the rest of the family to emigrate. She was the eldest daughter and, therefore, was expected to establish herself in the United States and then help her younger siblings and family. I asked her to explain why her family sent her first to the United States.

> Well, I was born in Hong Kong. But at the age of two I moved to an island in the Caribbean called Aruba. And I spent up my youth there, until I was 12. My father wanted me to have an American education and to settle down here, if possible, and that's why I was sent here. I lived with his, his sister, my aunt... in North Beach, San Francisco.

This respondent was able to get an American education and secure employment. However, she is still struggling to obtain permanent residency in the United States. I asked her when the rest of her family moved to the United States and she explained that her mother moved to California five years ago.

> Well, before my mother, actually my sisters moved, moved out first. And, I think that happened in my teen years, rather than, before I hit 20, yes....That, I guess was a big adjustment because I had to share my tiny room with my two sisters....And, and another event that I remember my father died...when I was in my twenties....Yeah, and I, I skipped one semester of school to go back [to Aruba] to help out in the business there, while he was under hospital care.

The heavy burden of being the eldest daughter defines this young Chinese woman's life. Not only was this respondent expected to be the lead link in setting up a chain migration to the United States for the rest of her family, but she also was expected to sacrifice her education and personal goals to help in the family business back in Aruba.

For other respondents, whether they were eldest daughters or just female offspring who remained unmarried, it meant that they were expected to take care of their aging parents until their deaths. The following respondent, a 58-year-old, first-generation Chinese American woman, lived with her father in his home until his death. She said she did not leave her father's home until she was 36 years old, after he died.

> I lived two years away, then came back home. It's very Chinese that you don't move out of your house unless you marry, that's for my generation, but nowadays when kids pack up and leave, they can. [Back then] it was expected that you would stay home because a woman living on her own, that was not appropriate.

In fact, 11 additional respondents (19.4 percent) were currently living with their parents or had lived with them until their parents died. While most of these respondents were age 47 or older, some younger respondents also commented that they were expected to live at home or take care of aging parents. One 34-year-old, foreign-born Chinese woman said that she was expected to move back in with her mother after her mother immigrated to the United States. The respondent had lived independently for a few years and did not want to move back in with her mother. She related,

> Before my mother came here, I lived on my own. My aunt in the meantime has passed away, too. And after my aunt passed away, I lived on my own for several years and when my mother came, she came with my brother. So my brother lived with her for a while, but my brother went back to Hong Kong to work, so my mother wanted me to move in with her....And I was so, I mean, I liked living by myself and I really – you know, didn't want to move in with her. Or, move in with anybody. So, I balked for a long time, but you know, finally I gave in and it was a big adjustment, moving in with my mother.

For many women, living with one's parents as an adult meant a loss of independence, in general, and more specifically, it meant less social freedom to date and have intimate relationships with men. For others, the responsibility of caring for an elder parent or parents, in addition to working full-time, meant that there was little time or energy left to socialize.

A few of the respondents commented that being the eldest daughter meant that they took the brunt of their mother's or father's abuse, while the other children, especially the boys, were spared. In fact, one respondent told me that in Chinese culture, boys are the preferred children because they are seen as bringing wealth into the family, while daughters are seen as more costly because they take wealth out of the family. This finding also is reported in the literature on the gender socialization of Chinese children: Since family lineage was maintained and inherited by sons, boys were given preferential treatment over girls (Ishii-Kuntz 1997:118). Thus, many of the respondents reported that they knew their mothers and/or fathers were disappointed with the respondents' gender. And in a couple of families, the daughters were expected to help care for brothers who had health problems or who acted out. For example, when I asked one respondent, a 33-year-old, third-generation Japanese American, what her major memories from childhood were, she said, "Actually, most of the major events in my childhood revolved around my brother hurting himself and us going to the hospital and that was about it." Other respondents talked about the brothers who received special attention from their parents because, as one mother said to her only daughter, "Well, he is my only son." In many of these families, sacrifices were made to give the sons the greater advantage at the expense of the daughters.

While some of the respondents admired their fathers and a few reported being very close to their fathers, most described their fathers as distant and difficult to please. Many of the respondents also perceived their mothers as being strict and setting high standards for their children. Several respondents, especially the Chinese American women who had mothers who were raised in China, commented on the cultural clash between their mothers' generation and their own. One respondent, a 40-year-old, second-generation Chinese American, described her relationship with her mother as fairly conflictual:

> [My relationship with my mother was] conflictual, really so. It's sort of known throughout everyone that knew us that it's the classic cultural clash textbook case. When I was about 8 or 9 years old, my mother threatened to send me here to San Francisco to a boarding school so that I could learn more [Chinese] filial piety. I was not sufficiently obedient. I was out of control in her view. And she threatened that. She didn't actually follow through with her threat but she got some books for me on filial piety and she made me read them. That stuff is like: when you are a girl, you obey your father; when you are a wife, you obey your husband; when you are an old woman, you will obey your eldest son – that kind of stuff. First and foremost, you obey your parents. So we really clashed. Then my teenage years were really terrible because we had knock-down drag-out fights.

As Wong (1995:69) explains, filial piety was a Confucian family value that included duty, obligation, the importance of the family name, service, and self-sacrifice to elders. This principle was taught to children at a very young age and was continually reinforced. In this study, many respondents of both Chinese and Japanese descent reported conflicts with their mothers either in regard to changing cultural values around gender roles or in their decisions to date men their mothers did not find suitable. As adults, many respondents reported that they kept their mothers at arm's length by refusing to share much intimate information about their lives with them.

Educational expectations

One way daughters felt pressured by their parents was to live up to the ideals of working hard and becoming educated. Education is highly valued in both Chinese American and Japanese American cultures (Chan 1991; Daniels 1988; Nishi 1995; Wong 1995). High standards of educational excellence placed a great deal of pressure on these respondents. They were expected to do well at everything they tried, especially at school. As one 58-year-old, first-generation Chinese American woman said of her father,

> He tried to raise us in traditional Chinese fashion. He didn't want me to play sports. For Chinese you should be studying, you shouldn't be out playing. He encouraged me to go to school and study. I shouldn't waste my time playing.

However, many of the respondents also were expected *not* to take pride in their hard work. Every success was either downplayed or labeled as not being good enough. Several respondents talked about feeling torn between these two contrary cultural expectations. They should do well, but at the same time, they should not take pride in their success.

The other cultural conflict that respondents described was the expectation to be good wives and mothers and also to be well educated. Without exception, most of the respondents said that they were expected to get an education before they married. Almost all of the respondents grew up knowing that they were expected to go to college *and* to marry well. The reality of doing both was nearly impossible for many of these women because going to school often involved working to financially support themselves through college, and after college, they were expected to get started on their careers. A 48-year-old, first-generation Chinese American woman made the following comment about trying to fulfill both expectations:

> I think that was hard growing up in my age group [with] a social factor that states you should get married and have kids. But, on the other hand, my father sent us all to college to get educated so that if we wanted a career and a profession that we could do it. So how do you mix both?

Similarly, another respondent, a 33-year-old, foreign-born Chinese American woman, said that in her family, women were expected to be both wives and mothers and to get a good education.

> In my family, I think my parents are the ones that kind of encouraged me to go to medical school. My mom never got to finish college so actually, in my family, they pushed me to get the education. No [women are] not just wives and mothers, they really want us to be as well educated as we can. They think it's giving us an opportunity that they never had.

For the older respondents in the study, going to college was unique for women of their generation. Their families saw education as a vehicle to increase employment opportunities and the social status of their children. However, obtaining a college education and, in many cases, advanced graduate training, also meant the respondent had to focus more time on working her way through school rather than on dating and social relationships.

One 74-year-old, first-generation Chinese American woman said that her parents had considered marrying her off at 18 years of age after being approached by the local matchmaker. Most Chinese women of her generation would have been getting married at this age. Fortunately, her mother refused the match after seeing the photos of the proposed suitor, and she told the matchmaker that her daughter wanted to go to college. However, the family had no funds to send the daughter to school. Traditionally, only boys were sent to school.

> [In Chinese culture] they want them [the daughters] to work, you know, and they help the boys [go to school]....Well they used to, all the girls work...put the boy through college. But my mother said that [if] I wanted [to go to college], she said, well, she told me that, you know, she said we couldn't help you, because your dad's so old. But if you wanna go, you can go, we were not, we're not gonna [help you], you can put your self through, you know.

This respondent devoted most of her young life to putting herself through college and then finding a teaching job. She said she had no time for dating in college or after she began working; instead, whatever time remained after work was devoted to taking care of her elderly parents. This respondent lived at home, taking care of her parents until they died.

Similarly, several older women said that completing their education and getting good jobs was their primary goal, and they assumed that relationships and marriage would come later. A 49-year-old, third-generation Japanese American described her view:

> Through the beginning of college, my image of myself was that by this time, I would have my Ph.D. in biology/biochemistry and I would do research, but of course, I would get married. It was always there that I would get married, because that was what I saw around me. And yeah, I was aiming a little higher than most people I saw, with getting a Ph.D., but I would get married and have a couple of kids.

Moreover, getting a college education opened up career opportunities not available to other women of the same time period. Of course, at the time, career mobility in many professions meant being unmarried. Several respondents said that they would not have been considered for professional advancements or travel if they had married. In other professions, being never married was the expected norm, especially in teaching and nursing.

For the younger respondents, a college education was assumed since childhood regardless of the social class background of the family. The family would sacrifice to ensure that the children went on to school. One respondent, a 40-year-old Chinese American woman, said that because she grew up in poverty, the pressure to go to college was even stronger for her and her brother. The entire family worked as migrant farm workers harvesting fruit and nut crops in California.

> In a word, basically my mother said to us that if we didn't go to college we would end up like this [in poverty]. You will end up working like us. That put the fear of God in us. My brother, my sister, and I all completed college, but my sister and my brother completed undergrad but they didn't go on. I was the only one that went on.

This respondent went on to law school and is now working as an attorney in San Francisco. However, this change in social status is the result of years of hard work and saving enough money to go to college. She describes her working childhood as follows:

> I guess the other thing that sort of overall characterizes my childhood is that I started working on the farm stuff when I was 4. I was the fastest fruit cutter in all the county because by the time I was 6 years old people would come in from San Francisco to watch me cut fruit. What we did is we would take apricots and cut them in half, take the pit out, and then lay the two halves on a tray and fill up the tray. They would then take the tray and put sulfur on it and put it outside and you would get dried apricots, that's what we did.... My earnings went into an account which my mother kept for me for college. She didn't take the money and spend it on the family. That was the overall view, every summer we had to do that. My brother and I both, and we also had to pick fruit so we would be on pick crews for walnuts.... We had to do that every summer as kids. I don't know where we got the energy because we were up and ready to work by 7:00 a.m.

For this particular respondent, the hard work she encountered in childhood, coupled with her parents' strong expectations for educational attainment, influenced her to attend college and law school. Working hard and saving money for college were expected by children who came from poor and working-class families in this sample.

Middle-class families also stressed getting an education, especially for obtaining professional careers. The importance of education in affecting the timing and occurrence of marriage was discussed by many of the respondents during the interview. For example, when asked what the current expected age of marriage is in the Chinese American and Japanese American communities, all of my respondents said the expected age of first marriage is in one's mid- to late twenties, or maybe early thirties, after one has completed their college education and worked a few years. Thus, cultural expectations within the Chinese American and Japanese American communities for women to complete their education and have careers have effectively delayed marriage for many women in this study. Researchers have found a similar pattern in other racial ethnic groups of women, where the increased number of years of educational attainment and higher occupational career goals have either delayed marriage or lowered the probability of many women marrying during their lifetimes (Gerson 1985; Goldscheider and Waite 1986; Havens 1973).

Lack of appropriate suitors

The final factor that was consistently mentioned by the respondents as affecting their marital status was the perceived lack of appropriate suitors. In fact, more than 46 of the 62 respondents (74.2 percent) specifically identified this to be one of the primary reasons they had not married. The pool of suitors was so limited, according to many respondents, because their families placed restrictions on the types of men they could date and marry. Especially when they were younger, interracial dating was strictly prohibited, and many women commented on how they were expected to marry within their Asian ethnic groups, a nearly impossible expectation for women who grew up in all-white neighborhoods.

The racial ethnic preferences of their parents and extended family were made very clear to the respondents; these women knew they were supposed to marry a "good" Chinese American or Japanese American boy. "Good" also meant the boy came from a respectable Asian family and that he had an education and, hopefully, a professional career. The appropriate social status of suitors was assumed, as implied in the Chinese saying one respondent shared with me: "A bamboo door to a bamboo door and a wooden door to a wooden door." A bamboo door signified someone of a lower social status. Thus, when these women were younger, their parents stressed marriage with someone of their same social status and racial ethnic backgrounds. As the women aged and remained unmarried, some of the parents became more flexible concerning their views of interracial dating and marriage. However, many of the respondents reported that the timing and opportunity to meet available men became much harder as they grew older.

Strong parental expectations for the respondents to marry within their racial ethnic groups also may be one reason why these women did not marry European American men, which, in general, is a relatively frequent occurrence among

Asian American women. More specifically, Japanese Americans outmarry (i.e., marry spouses of different racial or ethnic backgrounds) at a rate that is between 40 and 50 percent of all marriages (Takagi 1994:157), and Chinese Americans outmarry at a rate of 27 percent of all marriages (Glenn 1994:137; Sung 1990), with the majority of these outmarriages occurring between Asian American women and European American men. Glenn (1994) argues that this gendered pattern of intermarriage reflects racial differences in the construction of gender. Citing research by Weiss (1974), Glenn states that Asian American women outmarry more than Asian American men because:

> Asian women are judged more attractive by white standards of femininity than Asian men [are] by white standards of masculinity. Some Asian female students stated that they liked being associated with white men because in U.S. society white men have power. However, another factor may ironically be the patriarchal family system that emphasizes male lineage. Chinese American sons may be under more pressure from parents to marry within the group to continue the family line. This interpretation is consistent with the pattern in earlier times in which parents opposed their sons marrying an American-born Chinese and arranged marriages with Chinese-born women to ensure a docile daughter-in-law. (1994:138)

Thus, the respondents in this study may be caught in multiple binds concerning marrying men from within their own racial ethnic groups. On one hand, they typically have parents who encourage intramarriage. On the other hand, these Asian American women may desire European American men because, in U.S. society, these men are perceived to have higher social status and power, and white men also may be perceived to be less traditional than Asian American men. In addition, Asian American women also may know that Asian American men are not only being pressured to marry within their racial ethnic groups but may even be pressured to marry a foreign-born woman or, at minimum, a more traditional woman. Since the respondents tend to be more educated and career-focused than the average woman, and since the respondents also are critical of the traditional marriage arrangements of their parents, these respondents know they do not want to be traditional Asian wives or "docile" daughters-in-law.

Several respondents commented that dating Asian American men was difficult because of different gender role expectations between Asian American men and women. As suggested by many social scientists (Gerson 1985; Hochschild 1989; Hunt and Hunt 1987), in U.S. society, a cultural lag exists between the changing gender roles and expectations of men and women. According to the respondents, this cultural lag appears to be even more pronounced for Asian American men and women because the women are seeking more egalitarian relationships with men who will share household and child-care responsibilities, while the men are seeking more traditional women who will be subservient like their mothers. One respondent, a 47-year-old, second-generation Chinese American woman, said that traditional gender role expectations among Asian men were the primary reason that she did not marry.

> I don't know if there is a stereotype of what an Asian woman should be among men. I don't know what today's expectations of men are of Asian women. If it's traditional, I think we're in deep shit....But I'm not sure. It certainly [is] what I grew up with and probably a lot of why I'm not married today. Because the men that I dated in high school and college were very traditional males. The expectation is that you will get married, take my name, have my kids, and you are going to be the good little wife. No, I don't think so, there is something more for me out there.

Another respondent, a 49-year-old, third-generation Japanese American, made a similar comment about dating men from her own racial ethnic group:

> The Japanese American guys would treat me perhaps the way they would treat their mothers. They would take me for granted, these were the guys who would have other relationships while they were with me; I would be totally enamored with them, but they would be dominant. I would fall into my mother's role, which has no substance, and the guy would be like my father, who sort of ran things and determined how things were. I was very uncomfortable with this, in a way it was natural for me to fall into this, but on the other hand, this was when the

women's liberation started at Berkeley in 1969, when I graduated from college. I was aware that this was not the way you were supposed to be and it was sad.

This perception of Asian and Asian American men being more traditional in their gender role expectations continues today. Commenting on why there were so many Asian men who were not married, a 38-year-old, third-generation Chinese American woman offered the following:

> I think a lot of it has to do with their expectations, maybe. And, kinda being caught between old-world and new-world. Like one of my Japanese friends, um, he's, he's 40, nearly, gonna be 40. And he's never been married, and he wants a wife to do all those traditional things, like cook, clean, and all of that kind of stuff, and he wants her to have a career too. I said, "Are you nuts?" I said, "No, if she's gonna have a full-time career, you hire a housekeeper. And you guys share the workload on the rest." And he's like, "No."

Another respondent, a 47-year-old, second-generation Chinese American, said that it is harder for Asian American women to find mates than it is for European American women:

> I think for Asian women it is different than for white women. I don't really know why but I do think there is a difference. I also think that there are times that if I didn't have the relationship that I have now, that if I could have the relationship I would prefer, I would prefer to have it with somebody that is Asian. I think that what we [Asian women] find is that a lot of Asian males, at least the general sense that I get, is that they are too rigid and too stereotyped.

This respondent continues by commenting on how difficult it is to meet Asian American men and on the vast cultural differences between the native-born and foreign-born Chinese. She explains,

> I think it is harder for Asian women to meet other Asian males. It depends on the circle of the individual groups that you are in. Most of us, we are Americans, we don't consider ourselves Asian Americans, we consider ourselves American Asians. Americans who just happen to be Asian. And I think that social group of other Asian men, I don't even know where you even begin to find them.... When I went to school there were not that many Asian Americans around. Among Chinese I think it is a lot more difficult because you are two groups of Chinese. I don't know how it is among the Japanese, or other Asian groups, but among the Chinese, you have what we call FOB [fresh off the boat] and ABC [American-born Chinese]. So there is a real split in that group. Neither group likes each other. When I grew up that was the way it was, I think today it is still that way. And there is a real separation. There is now a real difference among the Hong Kong Chinese who are coming to the United States and who are starting to live in the U.S. I think that there are real biases among how they socialize among men and women. If [you] are going to speak to those women who are Hong Kong-born and American-born Chinese, you'll find a different and separate world. The women are different, our lifestyles are different. Culturally we may share experiences, but we are not the traditional Japanese or Chinese female by a long shot.

Not only is there a shortage of eligible Asian American men to marry, but the newer Asian immigrants are not necessarily appropriate suitors either. The cultural and gender differences between men and women, and between the native and foreign-born, are vast. Not only did most of the respondents voice a concern about Asian and Asian American men being more traditional than men from other racial ethnic groups, but they also described great difficulties in meeting men, in general, who were eligible to date. As the women get older, they report that it becomes even harder to meet men. Thus, if a Chinese American or Japanese American woman wants to marry within her racial ethnic group, she may have difficulty finding potential partners.

Conclusion

To conclude, Chinese American and Japanese American heterosexual women are not marrying for a variety of reasons. The four most significant factors are the effect of their parents' marriages, their status as eldest daughters, their pursuit of higher educational attainment, and the lack of eligible suitors. Many of the respondents reported that their parents' traditional marriages and their filial duties as the eldest or only daughter negatively shaped their views of marriage and, for some, their desire to have children. The respondents said repeatedly that they did not want marriages like their parents' and that they did not have positive role models for marriage when they were growing up. These family-of-origin factors were compounded by the pressures most of the respondents felt to obtain an advanced education and to marry a "good" Chinese American or Japanese American man. Most of the women talked about the difficulties they felt in trying to fulfill both of these expectations. Instead, for many of these never married women, college and graduate school opened up work opportunities and avenues to independence that would have been contradicted by marrying more traditional Asian men. For others, they were still hoping to balance the cultural contradictions between their family upbringing, their educational attainment and careers, and their relationship options with men.

This study begins to fill critical gaps in the research literature on the never married. Not only does it provide more information on why Chinese American and Japanese American women have high rates of nonmarriage (two under-researched groups in the never married literature), but it also provides insight into how gender, social class, race and ethnicity, and sexuality intersect with a complexity of other factors to shape women's choices and nonchoices about marriage and family. In particular, this study highlights how cultural dynamics, especially in regard to generational differences that arise from immigration experiences and adaptation to the U.S. culture, contribute to decisions concerning marriage and family life. The women are constrained by and provided different opportunities based on the historical context of their generation and immigrant history.

Another significant contribution of this study is that it gives voice to individual women to describe their perceptions and experiences as never married people. It is noteworthy that the respondents in this study have lived full and varied lives as never married Chinese American and Japanese American women. While about 25 (40 percent) of the 62 women expressed some regret at not being married, for most of those women, their regret was primarily about not having children and not about being never married per se. Instead, most of these never married women were happy with the decisions they made and were living rich and fulfilling lives. Most were economically successful, immersed in a community of friends and family, and actively involved in their work or community projects. Thus, these never married women are not only challenging the traditional marriages of their parents and the cultural expectations to marry within the Chinese American and Japanese American communities but also are challenging the pro-marriage norms and gender role expectations of the dominant culture. As such, we have much to learn from these women, and how, by never marrying, their lives are changing the assumptions we can make about the meaning and experience of family in the United States.

NOTES

1 Until 1970, the never married had rarely been studied as a distinct marital status category. Most early work tended to combine all single persons (i.e., the widowed, divorced, separated, and never married) into one category to compare those who were married with those who were not (see Stein 1981). Family scholars now know that each of these marital statuses has unique effects on individual and collective lives. However, while the divorced, widowed, and separated have been extensively researched, social scientists have been slow to study the lives of the never married.

2 Previous research has shown that African American women have the highest rates of nonmarriage. Chinese American and Japanese American women have the next highest rates, while European American women have the lowest rates of nonmarriage of these four racial ethnic groups (see Ferguson 1993, 1995).

3 Since the 1970s, most of the research on the never married has been quantitative. Some studies involve complex demographic models that have attempted to estimate the risk or "hazard" of not marrying over a cohort of individuals' lifetimes (Coale and McNeil 1972; Das Gupta 1975; Dixon 1971; Kiernan and Eldridge 1987; Rodgers and Thornton 1985). Other studies have attempted to estimate the costs and benefits of marriage or the "attractiveness" of spouses from certain population subgroups in a localized marriage market (Bennett, Bloom, and

Craig 1989; Lichter, LeClere, and McLaughlin 1991; Lichter et al. 1992; Oppenheimer 1988; Schoen and Kluegel 1988; Wilson 1987). While these quantitative studies provide useful information about some of the socioeconomic factors that predispose some individuals to delay or reject marriage, their statistical projections and macrolevel analyses often fall short in describing the complexity of variables, especially individual attitudes and values, that might better explain marriage decisions. This study builds on the only two interview studies done on never married women: Barbara Levy Simon's (1987) *Never Married Women* and Katherine R. Allen's (1989) *Single Women/Family Ties: Life Histories of Older Women*. While both of these works primarily provide insight into the lives of elderly white women who have never married, they do not examine the reality of nonmarriage for diverse racial and ethnic groups, especially Asian American women, and for women who are younger, in their thirties, forties, or fifties.

4 The desired respondent was to be 35 years or older, Chinese American or Japanese American, and self-identified as either bisexual or heterosexual. Thus, before each interview, respondents were screened via telephone and again at the interview by reading a cover letter that described the research and the desire to interview bisexual and heterosexual women only. If a respondent self-identified as younger than 35, as multiracial, or as lesbian, she was screened from the sample. Only 1 of the 62 respondents self-identified as bisexual; all of the remaining respondents identified as heterosexual. It is possible that the sample may contain more lesbians and bisexuals if these women felt uncomfortable disclosing their sexual identity to the researcher. However, given my sense of these 62 women after detailed discussions about their intimate relationships with men, and the effort to screen all respondents at two different points before the interview began, I think the likelihood is probably fairly low that many of these respondents self-identified as lesbian. Possibly one or two may be lesbian, but for whatever reason, they would not self-identify or name this aspect of themselves, if they were aware of it. Five of the 62 respondents (including two respondents from the pilot interviews) were younger than 35 at the time of the interview.

5 While a woman potentially can marry at any time during her adult life, most researchers begin to consider a woman to be never married after the age of 35. At this age, a woman is 10 years past the median age of 25 for first marriage for women in the United States (U.S. Bureau of the Census 1997). That is not to say, however, that a woman older than 35 will remain unmarried for the duration of her life. Instead, as she ages, the probability of her marrying decreases substantially. For my study, I was interested in interviewing women primarily older than 35, when women are typically beyond the college and graduate school years.

6 In my study, most respondents reported that the expected age of first marriage and having children in both the Chinese American and Japanese American communities was during a woman's mid- to late twenties. As a woman progressed into her thirties and remained never married, she often felt increasing pressure from her family and community to marry. Many respondents articulated that it was expected that they would marry and have children and that if they waited too long into their thirties to marry they might not be able to have children. Moreover, almost all of the respondents said they were raised not only to see children as the goal of marriage but to see having children outside of marriage as highly problematic.

7 In her research, Chow (1996) found that numerous Chinese women reported hidden histories of family violence, especially wife abuse, as well as desertion and divorce, which often resulted in their disillusionment, despair, and even mental breakdown.

REFERENCES

Allen, Katherine R. 1989. *Single Women/Family Ties: Life Histories of Older Women*. Newbury Park, CA: Sage.

Becker, Gary S. 1973. A theory of marriage, part I. *Journal of Political Economy* 81:813–846.

Becker, Gary S. 1976. *The Economic Approach to Human Behavior*. Chicago: University of Chicago Press.

Bennett, Neil G., David E. Bloom, and Patricia H. Craig. 1989. The divergence of Black and white marriage patterns. *American Journal of Sociology* 95:692–722.

Blau, Francine D., and Marianne A. Ferber. 1986. *Economics of Women, Men, and Work*. Englewood Cliffs, NJ: Prentice Hall.

Bradsher, Keith. 1989. Do married men fare better career-wise? *Sunday Republican*, December 31: E1, E5.

Chan, Sucheng. 1991. *Asian Americans: An Interpretive History*. Boston: Twayne.

Cherlin, Andrew. 1980. Postponing marriage: The influence of young women's work expectations. *Journal of Marriage and the Family* 42:355–365.

Chow, Esther Ngan-Ling. 1996. Family, economy, and the state: A legacy of struggle for Chinese American women. In *Origins and Destinies: Immigration, Race, Ethnicity in America*, ed. Silvia Pedraza and Ruben G. Rumbaut. Belmont, CA: Wadsworth.

Coale, A. S., and D. R. McNeil. 1972. The distribution by age of the frequency of first marriage in a female cohort. *Journal of the American Statistical Association* 67:743–749.

Cornell, Laurel L. 1984. Why are there no spinsters in Japan? *Journal of Family History* 9:326–339.

Daniel, K. 1995. The marriage premium. In *The New Economics of Human Behavior*, ed. M. Tommasi and K. Jerulli. Cambridge, UK: Cambridge University Press.

Daniels, Roger. 1988. *Asian America: Chinese and Japanese in the United States since 1850*. Seattle: University of Washington Press.

Das Gupta, Prithwis. 1975. A method of computing period rates of spinsterhood and childlessness from census data applied to the United States. *Social Biology* 22:134–143.

De Vos, George. 1984. Religion and family: Structural and motivational relationships. In *Religion and the Family in East Asia*, ed. George De Vos and Takao Sofue. Berkeley: University of California Press.

Dixon, Ruth B. 1971. Explaining cross-cultural variations in age at marriage and proportions never marrying. *Population Studies* 25:215–233.

Ferguson, Susan J. 1993. "Old Christmas cake" or independent women? Never married Chinese American and Japanese American women. Ph.D. diss., Department of Sociology, University of Massachusetts, Amherst.

Ferguson, Susan J. 1995. Marriage timing of Chinese American and Japanese American women. *Journal of Family Issues* 16(3):314–343.

Gerson, Kathleen. 1985. *Hard Choices: How Women Decide about Work, Career, and Motherhood*. Berkeley: University of California Press.

Glenn, Evelyn Nakano. 1983. Split household, small producer and dual wage earner: An analysis of Chinese-American family strategies. *Journal of Marriage and the Family* 45:35–46.

Glenn, Evelyn Nakano. 1986. *Issei, Nisei, War Bride: Three Generations of Japanese American Women in Domestic Service*. Philadelphia: Temple University Press.

Glenn, Evelyn Nakano, with Stacey G. H. Yap. 1994. Chinese American families. In *Minority Families in the United States: A Multicultural Perspective*, ed. Ronald L. Taylor. Englewood Cliffs, NJ: Prentice Hall.

Goldscheider, Frances Kobrin, and Linda J. Waite. 1986. Sex differences in the entry into marriage. *American Journal of Sociology* 92:91–109.

Guttentag, Marcia, and Paul F. Secord. 1983. *Too Many Women? The Sex Ratio Question*. Beverley Hills, CA: Sage.

Hajnal, John. 1965. European marriage patterns in perspective. In *Population in History*, ed. D. V. Glass and D. E. C. Eversley. London: Arnold.

Havens, Elizabeth M. 1973. Women, work and wedlock: A note on female marital patterns in the U.S. *American Journal of Sociology* 78:975–981.

Hochschild, Arlie. 1989. *The Second Shift: Working Parents and the Revolution at Home*. New York: Viking.

Houseknecht, Sharon K., Suzanne Vaughan, and Anne Statham. 1987. The impact of singlehood on the career patterns of professional women. *Journal of Marriage and the Family* 49:353–366.

Hu, Yuanreng, and Noreen Goldman. 1990. Mortality differentials by marital status: An international comparison. *Demography* 27:233–250.

Hunt, Janet G., and Larry L. Hunt. 1987. Male resistance to role symmetry in dual-earner households: Three alternative explanations. In *Families and Work*, ed. Naomi Gerstel and Harriet Engel Gross. Philadelphia: Temple University Press.

Ishii-Kuntz, Masako. 1997. Chinese American families. In *Families in Cultural Context: Strengths and Challenges in Diversity*, ed. Mary Kay DeGenova. Mountain View, CA: Mayfield.

Keith, Pat M. 1989. *The Unmarried in Later Life*. New York: Praeger.

Kiernan, Kathleen E., and Sandra M. Eldridge. 1987. Age at marriage: Inter and intra cohort variation. *British Journal of Sociology* 38:44–63.

Lichter, Daniel T., Felicia B. LeClere, and Diane K. McLaughlin. 1991. Local marriage markets and the marital behavior of Black and white women. *American Journal of Sociology* 96:843–867.

Lichter, Daniel T., Diane K. McLaughlin, George Kephart, and David J. Landry. 1992. Race and the retreat from marriage: A shortage of marriageable men? *American Sociological Review* 57:781–799.

Mare, Robert D., and Christopher Winship. 1991. Socioeconomic change and the decline of marriage for Blacks and whites. In *The Urban Underclass*, ed. Christopher Jencks and Paul E. Peterson. Washington, DC: Brookings Institution.

Mintz, Steven, and Susan Kellogg. 1988. Coming apart: Radical departures since 1960. In *Domestic Revolutions: A Social History of American Family Life*. New York: Free Press.

Moynihan, Daniel Patrick. 1986. *Family and Nation*. San Diego, CA: Harcourt, Brace, Jovanovich.

Murray, Charles. 1984. *Losing Ground*. New York: Basic Books.

Nishi, Setsuko Matsunaga. 1995. Japanese Americans. In *Asian Americans: Contemporary Trends and Issues*, ed. Pyong Gap Min. Thousand Oaks, CA: Sage.

Oppenheimer, Valerie K. 1988. A theory of marriage timing. *American Journal of Sociology* 94:563–591.

Pelzel, John C. 1970. Japanese kinship: A comparison. In *Family and Kinship in Chinese Society*, ed. Maurice Freedman. Stanford, CA: Stanford University Press.

Rindfuss, Ronald R., and James A. Sweet. 1978. The pervasiveness of postwar fertility trends in the United States. In *Social Demography*, ed. Karl E. Taeuber, Larry L. Bumpass, and James A. Sweet. New York: Academic Press.

Rodgers, Willard L., and Arland Thornton. 1985. Changing patterns of first marriage in the United States. *Demography* 22:265–279.

Salaff, Janet W. 1976. The status of unmarried Hong Kong women and the social factors contributing to their delayed marriage. *Population Studies* 30:391–412.

Salaff, Janet W. 1981. *Working Daughters of Hong Kong: Filial Piety or Power in the Family?* Cambridge, UK: Cambridge University Press.

Saluter, Arlene F. 1990. Marital status and living arrangements: March 1989. *Current Population Reports*, series P-20, no. 455. Washington, DC: U.S. Bureau of Census.

Schoen, Robert. 1991. Unpublished dissertation work at the Population Studies Center, University of Michigan, Ann Arbor.

Schoen, Robert, and James R. Kluegel. 1988. The widening gap in Black and white marriage rates: The impact of population composition and differential marriage propensities. *American Sociological Review* 53:895–907.

Simon, Barbara Levy. 1987. *Never Married Women*. Philadelphia: Temple University Press.

Smith, J. P. 1994. Marriage, assets, and savings. Working paper, RAND, Santa Monica, CA.

South, Scott J. 1991. For love or money? Socioeconomic determinants of the expected benefits from marriage. Paper presented at Annual Meetings, American Sociological Association, Cincinnati, Ohio.

Stack, Carol. 1974. *All Our Kin: Strategies for Survival in a Black Community*. New York: Harper & Row.

Stein, Peter J., ed. 1981. *Single Life: Unmarried Adults in Social Context*. New York: St. Martin's.

Sung, Betty Lee. 1990. *Chinese American Intermarriage*. Staten Island, NY: Center for Migration Studies.

Sweet, James A., and Larry L. Bumpass. 1987. The never-married. In *American Families and Households*, ed. J. A. Sweet and L. L. Bumpass. New York: Russell Sage.

Takagi, Dana Y. 1994. Japanese American families. In *Minority Families in the United States: A Multicultural Perspective*, ed. Ronald L. Taylor. Englewood Cliffs, NJ: Prentice Hall.

Umberson, D. 1987. Family status and health behaviors: Social control as a dimension of social integration. *Journal of Health and Social Behavior* 28:306–319.

U.S. Bureau of the Census. 1997. Marital status and living arrangements: March 1997. *Current Population Reports*, series P-20, no. 468. Washington, DC: Government Printing Office.

Waite, Linda J. 1995. Does marriage matter? *Demography* 32(4):483–507.

Watkins, Susan Cotts. 1984. Spinsters. *Journal of Family History* 9:310–325.

Weiss, Melford. 1974. *Valley City: A Chinese Community in America*. Cambridge, MA: Schenkman.

Wilson, William J. 1987. *The Truly Disadvantaged: The Inner City, the Underclass, and Public Policy*. Chicago: University of Chicago Press.

Wong, Morrison G. 1995. Chinese Americans. In *Asian Americans: Contemporary Trends and Issues*, ed. Pyong Gap Min. Thousand Oaks, CA: Sage.

Yanagisako, Sylvia Junko. 1985. *Transforming the Past: Tradition and Kinship among Japanese Americans*. Stanford: Stanford University Press.

8

Cultural Citizenship as Subject-Making: Immigrants Negotiate Racial and Cultural Boundaries in the United States[1]

Aihwa Ong

In the fall of 1970, I left Malaysia and arrived as a freshman in New York City. I was immediately swept up in the antiwar movement. President Nixon had just begun his "secret" bombing of Cambodia. Joining crowds of angry students marching down Broadway, I participated in the "takeover" of the East Asian Institute building on the Columbia University campus. As I stood there confronting policemen in riot gear, I thought about what Southeast Asia meant to the United States. Were Southeast Asians simply an anonymous mass of people in black pajamas? Southeast Asia was a far-off place where America was conducting a savage war against "communism." American lives were being lost, and so were those of countless Vietnamese, Cambodians, Laotians, and others. This rite of passage into American society was to shape my attitude toward citizenship. As a foreign student I was at a disadvantage, ineligible for most loans, fellowships, and jobs. My sister, a naturalized American, could have sponsored me for a green card, but the bombing of Cambodia, symptomatic of wider disregard for my part of the world, made American citizenship a difficult moral issue for me.

Much writing on citizenship has ignored such subjective and contradictory experiences, focusing instead on its broad legal-political aspects. For instance, Thomas Marshall (1950) defines citizenship as a question of modernity, but he identifies it primarily in terms of the evolution of civil society and the working out of the tensions between the sovereign subject and solidarity in a nation-state. Other scholars have pointed to the contradiction between democratic citizenship and capitalism – the opposition between abstract, universalistic rights and the inequalities engendered by market competition, race, and immigration (Hall and Held 1989; Portes and Rumbaut 1990). But these approaches seldom examine how the universalistic criteria of democratic citizenship variously regulate different categories of subjects or how these subjects' location within the nation-state and within the global economy conditions the construction of their citizenship. Indeed, even studies of citizenship that take into account the effects on it of capital accumulation and consumption have been concerned with potential strategies for political change to remake civil society (Yudice 1995). Seldom is attention focused on the everyday processes whereby people, especially immigrants, are made into subjects of a particular nation-state.

Citizenship as Subjectification

Taking an ethnographic approach, I consider citizenship a cultural process of "subject-ification," in the Foucauldian sense of self-making and being-made by power relations that produce consent through schemes of surveillance, discipline, control, and administration (Foucault 1989, 1991). Thus formulated, my concept of cultural citizenship can be applied to various global contexts (see Ong 1993; Ong and Nonini 1997), but in this paper I will discuss the making of cultural citizens in Western democracies like the United

States. Philip Corrigan and Derek Sayer (1985), in their analysis of the state as a cultural formation, speak of "governmentality," by which they mean the state's project of moral regulation aimed at giving "unitary and unifying expression to what are in reality multifaceted and differential experiences of groups within society" (1985:4–5). This role of the state in universalizing citizenship is paradoxically attained through a process of individuation whereby people are constructed in definitive and specific ways as citizens – taxpayers, workers, consumers, and welfare dependents.

This notion of citizenship as dialectically determined by the state and its subjects is quite different from that employed by Renato Rosaldo (1994), who views cultural citizenship as the demand of disadvantaged subjects for full citizenship in spite of their cultural difference from mainstream society.[1] While I share Rosaldo's sentiments, his concept attends to only one side of a set of unequal relationships. It gives the erroneous impression that cultural citizenship can be unilaterally constructed and that immigrant or minority groups can escape the cultural inscription of state power and other forms of regulation that define the different modalities of belonging. Formulated in this manner, Rosaldo's concept of cultural citizenship indicates subscription to the very liberal principle of universal equality that he seeks to call into question.

In contrast, I use "cultural citizenship" to refer to the cultural practices and beliefs produced out of negotiating the often ambivalent and contested relations with the state and its hegemonic forms that establish the criteria of belonging within a national population and territory. Cultural citizenship is a dual process of self-making and being-made within webs of power linked to the nation-state and civil society. Becoming a citizen depends on how one is constituted as a subject who exercises or submits to power relations; one must develop what Foucault (cited by Rabinow 1984:49) calls "the modern attitude," an attitude of self-making in shifting fields of power that include the nation-state and the wider world.

Furthermore, in analyzing the pragmatic struggle towards an understanding of cultural citizenship, one must attend to the various regulatory regimes in state agencies and civil society. Michel Foucault (1991) notes that in modern Western democracies control of subjects is manifested in rituals and rules that produce consent; "governmentality" refers to those relations that regulate the conduct of subjects as a population and as individuals in the interests of ensuring the security and prosperity of the nation-state. A major problem with Corrigan and Sayer's (1985) approach is its restriction to the state sector, ignoring civil institutions and social groups as disciplinary forces in the making of cultural citizens. Indeed, it is precisely in liberal democracies like the United States that the governmentality of state agencies is often discontinuous, even fragmentary, and the work of instilling proper normative behavior and identity in newcomers must also be taken up by institutions in civil society. For instance, hegemonic ideas about belonging and not belonging in racial and cultural terms often converge in state and nonstate institutional practices through which subjects are shaped in ways that are at once specific and diffused. These are the ideological fields within which different criteria of belonging on the basis of civilized conduct by categorically distinguishable (dominant) others become entangled with culture, race, and class (Williams 1991:2–29).

Race, Class, and Economic Liberalism

My approach constitutes an intervention into the conventional theorizing of American citizenship solely in terms of racial politics within the framework of the nation-state (Omi and Winant 1986; Gregory and Sanjek 1994). What is urgently needed is a broader conception of race and citizenship shaped by the history of European imperialism. African slavery and colonial empires were central to the making of modern Western Europe and the Americas. Encounters between colonizers and the colonized or enslaved gave rise to the view that white-black hierarchies are homologous with levels of civilization, a racist hegemony that pervades all areas of Western consciousness (Memmi 1967; Fanon 1967; Alatas 1977; Said 1978; Nandy 1983; Gilman 1985; Stoler 1995). These historically specific ideologies, Western European in origin, order human groupings distinguished by real and alleged biological features into status hierarchies that become the bases of various forms of discrimination and exclusion in Western democracies (Domínguez 1986; Miles 1989; Gilroy 1987; Williams 1989, 1991; Hall 1992; Gregory and Sanjek 1994).

Recently, however, scholars claim that there has been a distinct shift in dominant Western European exclusionary practices whereby cultural rather than racial difference is used to justify calls for banning immigrants (Stolcke 1995). Paul Gilroy, however, maintains that if we take race as a political rather than a biological category, newer discourses of marginalization in Britain focus on the "distinctive culture" of blacks without discarding racism (1987:109, 149). He calls the discourse of cultural difference a new racism that is more diffused but still racist even though state policies, informed by sympathetic liberalism, combat the kind of crude, neofascist racism that characterized earlier forms of discrimination in Britain (pp. 148–50). What Gilroy fails to mention, from his British vantage point, is how U.S. racial discourses, long interwoven with notions of cultural difference as in Patrick Moynihan's notion of "black pathology," may have influenced the biological-cultural shift in discourses of marginal or ineligible citizenship on the other side of the Atlantic.

Thus this race-versus-culture construction of exclusionary discourses is, albeit unintentionally, a red herring. Nevertheless, leading U.S. scholars such as Michael Omi and Howard Winant (1986) continue to study the shifting constructions of racial politics without reference to normative performance or schemes of cultural assessment. Gilroy cautions that "'race' is a political category that can accommodate various meanings which are in turn determined by struggle....racial differentiation has become a feature of institutional structures – legal subjectivity of citizenship – as well as individual action" (1987:38). A fuller understanding of racism and its embeddedness in notions of citizenship requires an examination of racial concepts and their uses in liberal ideologies and cultural practices.

Another lacuna in theories of racism and citizenship is the effect of class attributes and property rights on citizenship status (see Harrison 1991). As we shall see, the interweaving of ideologies of racial difference with liberal conceptions of citizenship is evident in popular notions about who deserves to belong in implicit terms of productivity and consumption. For instance, in the postwar United States, neoliberalism, with its celebration of freedom, progress, and individualism, has become a pervasive ideology that influences many domains of social life. It has become synonymous with being American, and more broadly these values are what the world associates with Western civilization. There is, however, a regulatory aspect to neoliberalism whereby economics is extended to cover all aspects of human behavior pertaining to citizenship. An important principle underlying liberal democracy emphasizes balancing the provision of security against the productivity of citizens. In other words, neoliberalism is an expression of the biopolitics of the American state as well as setting the normative standards of good citizenship in practice. In the postwar era, such thinking has given rise to a human-capital assessment of citizens (Becker 1965), weighing those who can pull themselves up by their bootstraps against those who make claims on the welfare state. Increasingly, citizenship is defined as the civic duty of individuals to reduce their burden on society and build up their own human capital – to be "entrepreneurs" of themselves (Gordon 1991:43–45). Indeed, by the 1960s liberal economics had come to evaluate nonwhite groups according to their claims on or independence of the state. Minorities who scaled the pinnacles of society often had to justify themselves in such entrepreneurial terms. A rather apt example was the 1990s nomination of Clarence Thomas to the Supreme Court of the United States, a move widely viewed as the token appointment of an African American to the powerful white-dominated institution. In his confirmation hearings, Judge Thomas painted himself as a deserving citizen who struggled out of a hardscrabble past by "pulling himself up by his bootstraps." The can-do attitude is an inscription of ideal masculine citizenship; its legitimating power was more than sufficient to overcome the ugly stain of sexual harassment that plagued the judge's confirmation.

Attaining success through self-reliant struggle, while not inherently limited to any cultural group, is a process of self-development that in Western democracies becomes inseparable from the process of "whitening." This racializing effect of class and social mobility has evolved out of historical circumstances whereby white masculinity established qualities of manliness and civilization itself against the "Negro" and the "Indian" (Bederman 1993). Inspired by W. E. B. Du Bois's work on race and class (1977), David R. Roediger (1991) argues that the 19th century was the formative period of "whiteness" among the working classes in a slave-owning republic. "Whiteness was a way in which workers responded to a fear of dependency on wage labor and to the necessities of capitalist work discipline" (1991:13). The Revolutionary ideal of masculine independence found in black slavery and "hireling" wage labor was a convenient other. The black population was viewed as embodying "the preindustrial, erotic, careless style of life the white worker hated and longed for" (pp. 13–14). "The Negro" as a "contrast conception" or "counterrace" is a legacy of white–black relations under slavery and Emancipation that " 'naturalizes' the social order" (Copeland 1939:179).[2]

Although one need not imagine a contemporary synchrony of views on intrepid individualism, the white man, and deserving citizenship, the convergences and overlaps between hegemonies of race, civilization, and market behavior as claims to citizenship are too routine to be dismissed. Hegemonies of relative racial contributions often conflated race and class, as, for example, in the polarizing contrast between the "model minority" and the "underclass" (Myrdal 1944), both economic terms standing for racial ones. As I will show, the different institutional contexts in which subjects learn about citizenship often assess newcomers from different parts of the world within given schemes of racial difference, civilization, and economic worth. Because human capital, self-discipline, and consumer power are associated with whiteness, these attributes are important criteria of nonwhite citizenship in Western democracies. Indeed, immigrant practices earlier in the century also subjected immigrants from Europe to differential racial and cultural judgments (see, e.g., Archdeacon 1983). The racialization of class was particularly evident in the construction of Irish-American (and Southern European) immigrants whose whiteness was in dispute (Roediger 1991:14). This racializing logic of class attributes is applied even to current flows of immigrants from the South and East who seem obviously nonwhite; discriminatory modes of perception, reception, and treatment order Asian immigrants along a white–black continuum. Although immigrants come from a variety of class and national backgrounds, there is a tendency, in daily institutional practices, towards interweaving of perceived racial difference with economic and cultural criteria, with the result that long-term residents and newcomers are ideologically constructed as "the stereotypical embodiments" of ethnicized citizenship (Williams 1989:437).

Of course, these processes of implicit racial and cultural ranking do not exhaust the conditions that go into processes of subjectification as citizens. It is worth keeping in mind that when we attend to the pragmatic construction of belonging, we see that official racial categories are reproduced by everyday American activities of inclusion and exclusion, separating the civilized from the primitive. Constance Perin (1988) has described such attempts at maintaining symbolic coherence in the face of ambiguities and keeping fears at bay as "drawing lines" against the culturally deviant. Racial oppositions are not merely the work of discriminatory laws and outright racists but the everyday product of people's maintenance of their "comfort level" of permissible liberal norms against the socially deviant newcomers who disturb that sense of comfort. Again, such encoding of white–black oppositions in behavioral and discursive strategies also saturates everyday life in other liberal, white-dominated societies, such as Britain and New Zealand (Gilroy 1987; Wetherell and Potter 1993). I will present ethnographic accounts of interactions between key institutions and newcomers, the drawing of lines against Asian others, and the struggles over representations that are part of the ideological work of citizen-making in the different domains of American life.[3] While I will be dealing with the making of immigrants into American citizens, I maintain that the processes of explicit and implicit racial and cultural ranking pervading institutional and everyday practices are but a special case of similar constructions in Western democracies in general.

New Asian Immigrants in Metropolitan Countries

When I moved from Massachusetts to California in the early 1980s, I was struck by the range of peoples from the Asia-Pacific region at a time when the scholarly literature defined Asian Americans as people largely of Chinese, Japanese, and Korean ancestry. (Filipinos were then viewed simply as Pacific Islanders.) Global conflicts and economic restructuring were important reasons that the 1980s were an especially turbulent era, bringing a renewed influx of refugees from Latin America, Africa, and Asia into metropolitan countries. It was not unusual to see Mayan Indians, still wrapped in their colorful clothes, working in English gardens or sarong-clad and turban-wearing Laotians shopping in the neighborhood market. The withdrawal of U.S. troops from mainland Southeast Asia and the later invasion of Cambodia by Vietnam caused waves of refugees to flee, by way of refugee camps, to Australia, Western Europe, and the United States. Other waves of war refugees left Sri Lanka, Afghanistan, Ethiopia, and Central America for the same destinations. Concurrent diasporas of an economic nature introduced poor workers as well as wealthy investors from Africa and Asia into Europe and North America. These massive waves of immigrants from the metaphoric South radically challenged liberal conceptions of citizenship in Western Europe and the United States.

The San Francisco Bay area was one of the major sites of resettlement for refugees from all over the Third World, the majority of whom were Southeast Asians.[4] Most arrived in two waves: in the aftermath of the communist takeover of Saigon in 1975 and following the Vietnamese invasion of Cambodia in 1979. At about the same time, another flow of immigrants, mainly professionals and upper-middle-class people seeking investments in stable markets in the West, arrived from Southeast Asia and India. The combined impact of these flows greatly exceeded that of earlier arrivals from Asia, increasing the Asian population in America by 80 percent to 6.88 million by the end of the decade. Asians are "far and away the most rapidly growing minority in the country" (*New York Times*, February 24, 1991). They have fanned out across the country to establish sizable Asian American communities outside the Chinatowns of the east and west coasts, spreading to the southern states and the Midwest. There are Vietnamese fishing villages in Texas, Cambodian crab farmers in Alabama, and Asian professionals in fields such as electronics, medicine, and mathematics. The number of Chinese restaurants has increased in smaller towns all over the country. In major cities such as Queens, Houston, and Los Angeles, investments by Koreans and Chinese immigrants have raised real estate prices to stratospheric levels (see, e.g., *Wall Street Journal*, January 15, 1991).

The new Asian demographics are so striking that today Asians make up a third of the population of San Francisco and 30 percent of the student body at the University of California, Berkeley. Overall, the Bay Area, with a population of over 6 million, has "emerged as the Western Hemisphere's first genuine Pacific metropolis," with one out of every five residents being of Asian background (*San Francisco Chronicle*, December 5, 1988). The increasing importance of the economic boom in Asia and the influx of Pacific Rim capital as well as boat people into the Western democracies make Asian immigration a highly charged issue that is framed differently from the issue of immigration from other parts of the world.

The changing demographics in California have changed the terms of debate on immigration and multiculturalism not just for the state but for the whole country. What will the United States as a Pacific country look like? Throughout the 1980s, the rising waves of Asian newcomers were exceeded by the influx of Central American refugees and migrant workers (Portes and Rumbaut 1990:44–46). Against the background of forecasts that whites will become just one more minority in California by the year 2000, there has been a backlash by political forces controlled or influenced by white voters. In 1986 an initiative was passed declaring English the state's official language; in 1994 another initiative called for the denial of health and educational services to illegal immigrants (mainly from Latin America). Both measures appeared to set limits to the increasing cultural and economic diversity of the state's population.

The measures reflect nationwide concerns about immigration from south of the border as well as from non-European countries. Nevertheless, there is discrimination among different categories of immigrants by national origin and by class. In a stunning move, the regents of the University of California system recently banned affirmative-action programs in admissions and hiring, setting off a national debate on official sponsorship of multiethnic representation in different areas of society. But what appear to be attempts to make all immigrants adhere to standardized, "color-blind" norms are in fact attempts to discriminate among them, separating out the desirable from the undesirable citizens according to some racial and cultural calculus. For instance, politicians such as House Speaker Newt Gingrich have declared affirmative action unfair to whites *and* Asians (*San Francisco Chronicle*, July 31, 1995). California's Governor Pete Wilson has been quoted as saying that affirmative action promotes "tribalism," a code word for colored minorities that presumably excludes Asian Americans (*San Francisco Chronicle*, July 23, 1995). In the debate, Asian Americans have been referred to as "victimized overachievers" – "victimized," that is, by other immigrants and minorities presumably not certified as "overachievers."[5] Such discourses "whiten" Asian Americans while using them as a "racial wedge" between whites and minority "tribals." The fight over affirmative action is an excellent example of "whitening" and "blackening" processes at work, where racial difference or skin color is variously encrusted with the cultural values of a competitive society. As Thomas Archdeacon has observed, "ethnicity is a dynamic force that keeps America's national, racial, and religious groups in constant flux" (1983:242). The continuing influx of immigrants keeps ethnic formation unstable, merging and diverging in ways that break up racial components (see Lowe 1991), but ethnic identities are also inscribed by elite discourses as to where and how different populations are included in or excluded from mainstream society. Indeed, since explicit statements including Asian Americans in the dominant sector of society have been so rare, very few Asian Americans protest the image of them as victimized overachievers in the anti-affirmative-action discourses. Despite this silent acquiescence, the image of Asian overachievers is an ideological misrepresentation of the diversity among Asian populations in the country. Indeed, the Californian media have distinguished two categories of Asian Americans: the "model minority" Chinese immigrants from Hong Kong, Taiwan, China, and Vietnam and the new underclass represented by Cambodians and Laotians. The bifurcated model follows the formula of academics and policymakers who use national origin as the basis of ethnic identity among immigrants (Portes and Rumbaut 1990:141–42). If, as I have suggested, we think of ethnicities as dynamic formations constructed out of the everyday processes of inclusion and exclusion, how do we account for the bifurcation of Asian immigrants into these two categories? How do different modalities of regulation use gender stereotypes in configuring race, nation, and citizenship privileges whereby differing groups are accorded cultural normativity or deviance in relation to white masculinity?[6]

I will examine institutional practices that differently receive and socialize Asian immigrants depending on their gender, position within racial hierarchies, and class and consumption. Drawing on ethnographic research, I will explore the ways in which Cambodian refugees, on the one hand, and affluent Chinese cosmopolitans, on the other, explore the meanings and possibilities of citizenship in California. By contrasting Asian groups from different class backgrounds I hope to show how despite and because of their racialization as Asian Americans, they are variously socialized by and positioned to manipulate state institutions, religious organizations, civilian groups, and market forces inscribing them as citizens of differential worth.

Disciplining Refugees in an Age of Compassion Fatigue

The moral imperative to offer refugees shelter has been a hallmark of U.S. policy since 1945, breaking from earlier policies that privileged race, language, and assimilation above concerns about human suffering (Loescher and Scanlan 1986:210). During the cold war, refugees from communist regimes were treated with special kindness because of the ideological perception that they had undergone great suffering as symbolic or literal "freedom fighters" (p. xviii). This policy continued more or less even after the United States ended its intervention to prevent the spread of communism in Indochina, setting off waves of boat people fleeing Vietnam. In 1979, tens of thousands of Cambodians fled to the Thai border after the Vietnamese invasion of Kampuchea. President Carter, in the spirit of his human rights campaign, signed a refugee act to increase immigration quotas for them. Between 1975 and 1985, almost 125,000 Cambodians arrived in the United States. Anticommunist ideology and opportunities for making political capital in Congress dictated a system of "calculated kindness" whereby Southeast Asian and Cuban refugees were favored over those from Haiti, El Salvador, and Chile (pp. 213–15). But the shadow of the U.S. defeat in the Indochina conflict hung over the reception of these war refugees. Furthermore, they arrived at a time when the country was suffering from an economic recession, and many Americans became worried about scarce housing, jobs, welfare needs, and competition from immigrants. Rioting by Mariel Cuban refugees contributed to the image of "difficult migrants" (p. 217). Compassion fatigue quickly set in, and a climate of antagonism greeted the increasing influx of refugees of color from Asia, Latin America, and Africa.

From the beginning, a political ambiguity dogged Cambodian refugees because of the immigration authorities' suspicion that many Khmer Rouge communist-sympathizers managed to slip through screening by the Immigration and Naturalization Service (INS) and gain entry to the country (Golub 1986; Ngor 1987). This morally tainted image was accompanied by the perception of Cambodian refugees as mainly peasants, unlike the boat people, who were by and large unambiguously anticommunist Sino-Vietnamese and middle-class, despite significant numbers of fishermen and peasants among them. Cambodians in refugee-processing camps were quickly separated out as destined for lower-class status. At the Philippine Refugee Processing Center, classes trained U.S.-bound Cambodians to be dependent on Americans, who dealt with refugees only from their positions as superiors, teachers, and bosses (Mortland 1987:391). One teacher charged that, from the very beginning, training programs were "ideologically motivated to provide survival English for entry-level jobs" in the United States (Tollefson 1990:546). Khmers were socialized to expect limited occupational options and taught subservient behavior, as well as a flexible attitude towards frequent changes of jobs which would help them adapt to cycles of employment and unemployment. Thus, the camp training of Cambodian refugees as dependent on Americans and as potential low-wage workers initiated the minoritization process even before they set foot in the country. This ideological construction of Khmers as a dependent minority channeled them into the same economic situations as other refugees from poor countries: "Policy and ideology underlying the [Overseas Refugees Training Program] ensure that refugees serve the same function as African Americans and Latinos" (p. 549).

Furthermore, once immigrants arrived in the country, whatever their national origin or race, they were ideologically positioned within the hegemonic bipolar white–black model of American society. The racialization of Southeast Asian refugees depended on differential economic and cultural assessment of their potential as good citizens. Although all relied on refugee aid for the first two years after their arrival, Cambodians (together with Laotians and Hmongs) found themselves, by acquiring an image of "welfare-dependent" immigrants, quickly differentiated from the Vietnamese, who had arrived in this country out of the same war. Cambodian and Laotian immigrants were ethnicized as a kind of liminal Asian American group that has more in common with other poor refugees of color like Afghans and Ethiopians than with the Vietnamese. They were often compared to their inner-city African American neighbors in terms of low-wage employment, high rates of teenage pregnancy, and welfare-dependent families.

As mentioned earlier, the transfer of racial otherness from one minority group to another in order to draw the lines of social and economic citizenship has a historical precedent in the differentiation between whites and blacks after Emancipation. The symbolic link between blackness and "preindustrial license" was even transferred to Irish immigrants, who were considered by some to be part of "a separate caste or 'dark' race" (Roediger 1991:107, 133–34). The ideological formation of whiteness as the symbol of ideal legal and moral citizenship today continues to depend upon the "blackening" of less desirable immigrants. Immigrants situated closer to the black pole are seen as at the bottom of the cultural and economic ranking. A Vietnamese social worker said to me,

> Most of the Khmers are not highly educated. They were farmers and their tendency is to be lazy.... So with the income they receive from welfare right now it is easy for them to be lazy. They are not motivated to go to work...they find some way to get out of [the training and language program].... They do not want to improve their skills here.... Maybe the young people will grow up here and become educated and want to change.

This man was partly expressing his frustration over the difficulty of getting the Cambodian refugees to sign up for job training in electronic assembly work, car mechanics, child care, and janitorial work but also revealing his own ethnic bias against Cambodians.

By 1987, well over half of the 800,000 Indochinese refugees in the country had settled down in California, and there was widespread fear that there would be "perpetual dependence on the welfare system for some refugees" (*New York Times*, April 27, 1987). This positioning of Cambodians as black Asians is in sharp contrast to the model-minority image of Chinese, Koreans, and Vietnamese (including Sino-Vietnamese), who are celebrated for their "Confucian values" and family businesses. Although there have been racist attacks on Vietnamese fishermen in Texas and California and exploitation of Vietnamese workers in chicken-processing plants in the South, the general perception of them is as possessed of "can-do" attitudes closer to the white ideal standards of American citizenship.[7] It is therefore not surprising that Cambodians are almost always referred to as "refugees" whereas Vietnamese refugees are viewed as immigrants. Regardless of the actual, lived cultures of the Khmers before they arrived in the United States, dominant ideologies clearly distinguish among various Asian nationalities, assigning them closer to the white or the black pole of American citizenship.

As I will show, the disciplining of the welfare state, combined with the feminist fervor of many social workers, actually works to weaken or reconstitute the Cambodian family. My own research on the welfare adjustments of Khmers, described below, may seem to reinforce the hegemonic picture of their dependency, but my goal is actually a critique of the effects of the welfare system as it operates now in an increasingly low-waged, service-oriented economy. Earlier generations of poor immigrants have managed to establish basic security for their families through blue-collar employment (Komorovsky 1967). The welfare system continues to operate by withdrawing support from families with a single wage-earner, whereas for most poor immigrants like the Cambodians, part-time and unsteady low-wage employment are needed to supplement welfare aid. Like ghetto blacks and poor Puerto Rican immigrants, Cambodians are in a continual struggle to survive in a low-wage economy in which they cannot depend on earnings alone and, despite their organizational skills, everyday problems of survival and social interventions often adversely affect family relations and dynamics (Harrington 1962; Valentine 1971; Stack 1974).

Within the refugee population, there are frequent reports of marital conflict, often attributed to the suffering and dislocation engendered by war and exile. However, I maintain that most of the tensions are exacerbated by the overwhelming effort to survive in the inner city, where most of the Cambodian refugees live. Many of the men, with their background in farming and inability to speak English, cannot make the leap into job training and employment in the United States. Their wives often lose respect for them because of their inability to make a living and their refusal to share "women's" household and child-care chores at home. Cambodian customs regarding family roles and gender norms have become if not irrelevant at least severely undermined as men fail to support their families and wives become more assertive in seeking help. Relations between husband and wife, parents and children have come to be dictated to a significant degree not by Khmer culture as they remember it but by pressing daily concerns to gain access to state resources and to submit to the rules of the welfare state.

Male informants complain that "in America, men feel they have lost value because they are no longer masters in their own families." A *kru khmer* (shaman) who is often consulted by unhappy couples noted that "money is the root cause of marital problems in the United States." Welfare has become a system which provides families with material support and women with increased power and a bargaining position vis-à-vis their husbands and children. The shaman explained:

> For instance, most of us who came to the United States are recipients of welfare assistance; the majority of us are supported by the state. It is usually the wife who gets the welfare check but not the husband. She is the one who takes care of the kids. But when she receives the check, her husband wants to spend it. When she refuses, and wants to keep the money for the children, that's what leads to wife abuse.

Some Khmer men lash out at their wives, perhaps to restore the sense of male privilege and authority they possessed in Cambodia. In many instances, they beat their wives in struggles to gain control over particular material and emotional benefits. Besides fights over welfare checks, the beatings may be intended to compel wives to resume their former deferential behavior despite their newly autonomous role in supporting the children. Many women try to maintain the male-dominated family system despite the threats and abuse. A woman confided:

> There are many cases of wife abuse. Yes, everyone gets beaten, myself included. But sometimes we have to just keep quiet even after a disagreement. Like in my case, I don't want to call the police or anything. As the old saying goes, "It takes two hands to clap. One hand cannot sound itself." I just shed a few tears and let it go. If it gets out of hand, then you can call the police. But the men still think more of themselves than of women. They never lower themselves to be our equals.

This acknowledgment of a shift in the balance of domestic power, linked to dependency on state agencies, indicates that Khmer women do not think of themselves as passive victims but are aware of their own role in marital conflicts. The speaker seems to imply that she tolerates the occasional beating because men cannot adjust to their change in status and she always has the option of calling the police. Like their counterparts among European immigrants in the early-20th-century United States, Cambodian women are often caught in their "double position" as victims of wife abuse and guardians of their children (Gordon 1988:261); they stand up to their husbands in order to ensure their children's economic survival.

Some women who can manage on their own with welfare aid abandon their spouses. A social worker reported cases involving couples over 65 years old in which the wives kicked their husbands out and then applied for SSI (Supplementary Security Income). Informants told me that there were Cambodian women who, having fallen in love with American co-workers, left their husbands and even their children; this was something, they claimed, that happened in Florida and Long Beach, not in their own community. Speaking of her former neighbors, a woman noted that many Cambodian women had left their husbands because they "look down on them...for not working, for not being as clever as other men." They felt free to do so because Aid to Families with Dependent Children (AFDC) supported them and their children in any case. In an optimistic tone, she continued, "That's why Khmer women are very happy living in America, because they now have equal rights.... We can start up business more easily here. If we want to work, we can pay for day care."

One of the indirect effects of the welfare system is to promote rather complex strategies for manipulating and evading rules, thus affecting household composition. Cambodian households, often composed of mother–child units, routinely pool incomes from different sources, and many households depend on a combination of different welfare checks received by family members and both part- and full-time employment. Through the pooling of income from multiple sources, household heads hope to accumulate savings to buy a home outside the violent neighborhoods in which many live. As has been reported among inner-city blacks, such strategies for coping with the welfare system increase the networking among female kin and neighbors but contribute to the shifting membership of households (Stack 1974:122–123).

Many Khmers seek to prolong the time they can receive welfare support by disguising the age of children and by concealing their marital status and income-generating activities. In some cases, young girls who become pregnant are allowed to keep their babies so that the latter can receive financial aid that helps to support the entire family. Many girls who get pregnant marry the fathers of their babies but fail to register their change of status in order to avoid revealing that their husbands are working and thus forfeiting their chance to get AFDC for the babies. For instance, Madam Neou[8] lived with two sons, seven daughters, and a son-in-law in her one-bedroom apartment. Her eldest daughter was 18 and pregnant. She had married her boyfriend according to Khmer ceremonies but had not registered her marriage, and therefore she continued to receive her General Assistance (GA) check. Her husband, who worked in a fast-food restaurant, disguised the fact that they were living together by giving a false address. They hoped to have saved enough money by the time their GA stipends ended to move out and rent a home of their own. Thus, although parents try to discourage their daughters from having premarital sex, they also tolerate and support those who do become pregnant. Not all pregnant girls get married or receive their mothers' support. However, those who do marry are taken in to enable them to save on rent and perhaps continue to accumulate welfare benefits so that they can ultimately become an independent household.

Social workers are frustrated by the mixed motivations and strategies that, in their view, promote teenage pregnancy. A social worker complains about Cambodians "working the system" and says that young girls "become pregnant again and again and have no time to go to school." However, it appears that peer pressure and street culture are primarily responsible for the few pregnancies in girls younger than 16 (well below the average marriage age of 18 for women in Cambodia before the upheavals of war and diaspora). In one case, a social worker intervened and advised a Khmer mother to let her recently married daughter use contraceptives so that she could continue to go to school and have a career later on. However, the girl's husband, who was employed as a mechanic, refused to practice family planning and wanted her to get on welfare. They lived with her mother in exchange for a small monthly payment. The social worker threatened to expose the mother's strategy of combining welfare checks across households, thus exercising the disciplinary power of the state that threatens family formation among people at the mercy of the welfare system and a chronic low-wage market. The withdrawal of welfare support at a point in young people's lives when they are first breaking into the labor market thus compels poor families to scheme to prolong welfare dependency so that they can save towards economic independence. The dual structure of supporting poor mothers, on the one hand, while disciplining chronic underemployment, on the other, contributes to a particular minoritization process of Cambodian refugees that is not so very different from that experienced by other poor people of color (Valentine 1971; Stack 1974). Welfare policy promotes the "blackening" of the underprivileged by nurturing and then stigmatizing certain forms of coping strategies.

An academic cottage industry on refugee affairs, ignoring the disciplinary effects of the welfare state and the low-wage economy, has emerged to provide cultural explanations for the presumed differential economic and moral worth of different Asian immigrant groups. Cambodians (together with Hmongs and Laotians) are identified as culturally inferior to Vietnamese and Chinese and thus to be targeted for "civilizing" attention by state agents and church groups. In a report to the Office of Refugee Settlement, social scientists elaborated a "sociocultural" portrait of Khmers (and Laotians) as more "Indian" than "Chinese" among the "Indochinese" (Rumbaut and Ima 1988:73) – a term that is itself the creation of French imperialism. This artifact drew upon the anthropological model of the "loosely structured" society (Embree 1950), noting that Cambodians were more individualistic, prone to place feelings and emotions above obligations, and likely to use Americans as role models than the Vietnamese (who were "more Chinese") (p. 76) – in other words, Cambodians were more deferential and susceptible to socialization by U.S. institutions than groups that possessed Confucian culture. Cambodians were viewed as "affectively oriented"; their "love of children" and "non-aggressive" behavior seem in implicit contrast to the "more pragmatic" Vietnamese. This moral discrimination among Asian groups becomes a diffused philosophy that informs the work of agencies dealing with immigrants, thus demonstrating that in mechanisms of regulation, hierarchical cultural evaluations assign different populations places within the white–black polarities of citizenship.

The disciplinary approach to Cambodians often takes the form of teaching them their rights and needs as normative lower-class Americans. In the Bay Area, the refugee and and social service agencies are driven by a feminist ethos that views immigrant women and children as especially vulnerable to patriarchal control at home. Implicit in social workers' training is the goal of fighting Asian patriarchy – "empowering" immigrant women and "teaching them their rights in this country," as one lawyer-activist explained. Perhaps influenced by essentializing statements that Khmers are "more prone to divorce and separation" than the Vietnamese (Rumbaut and Ima 1988:75–76), service workers tend to view the Khmer family as rife with patriarchal domination and violence. At the same time, service agents working with Cambodians frequently complain about their "primitive culture," especially as expressed in male control and a tendency to be swayed by emotions rather than by rationality and objectivity.

This ideological construction often puts Sam Ngor, a Cambodian social worker, in the uncomfortable position of being caught between his sympathy for the plight of Cambodian men and the social worker's implicit unfavorable comparison of them with white men. At a Cambodian self-help group meeting, Sam was trying to explain why a married couple gave contradictory accounts of their conflict. He noted that there was a difference between "oral and literate cultures"; in oral cultures, "people always change their minds about what happened" (presumably, in a literate society they do not).[9] Furthermore, in a literate society like the United States, men can be jailed for abusing their wives and children. Covert smiles lit up the faces of the women, while the men looked down. The man fighting with his wife crossed his arms and said, "I respect her, but it is she who controls me."

Indeed, Cambodian men complain that service workers are not only eager to interfere in their family affairs but favor women and children over men in domestic battles. Another social worker notes that "often, among refugees of all nationalities, men have lost their place in society. They don't like to ask for help, and it seems they've lost control over their families. Women tend to ask for help more." Sam added that both the welfare system and affirmative action favored women of color over men, so that the former had easier access to resources and jobs.

Some Khmer women, emboldened by service workers and the disciplining of refugee men, routinely call for outside intervention in settling domestic disputes. In one example, Mae, a woman in her thirties, called the police after claiming that her husband, an alcoholic, had hit her. A few days later she came to the self-help group and wanted assistance in getting him released from jail. She insisted that the policeman had misunderstood her and that she had never claimed that she was abused. Meanwhile, she called her husband in jail, boasting that she would try to "free" him if he promised, when he came out, to stop drinking and to attend the self-help group regularly. Mae's husband, it was reported, charged her with delusions of power: "I think that the judge is the one who will decide to release me, but she thinks she is the one who is controlling the situation. She thinks that by telling the police that I did not beat her she is securing my release." A couple of months later, Mae dropped the charges, and her husband was set free and prevailed upon by the group to join Alcoholics Anonymous. Although the marriage remained rocky, Mae apparently had manipulated the police, the self-help group, and the court system to discipline her husband. A neighbor reported that Mae's daughter said she wanted her mum to be in jail and her dad home. Public interventions in such domestic battles implicitly devalue men of color while upholding white masculinity, as presented by police and judge, as the embodiment of culturally correct citizenship and privilege.

Engendering Religious Modernity

Beyond the domain of the welfare state, institutions such as the church also construct commonsensical understandings of different ways and claims of belonging in Western democracies. Church groups are vital agents in converting immigrants into acceptable citizens, since they have always played a major role in sponsoring, helping, and socializing newcomers to Western culture, whether in the colonies or in the metropolitan centers.[10] In Northern California, the Church of the Latter-day Saints (LDS, or the Mormon church) shapes cultural citizenship by promoting white middle-class masculinity as the standard of civilization and class property to displaced Third World populations. In this civilizing mission, the LDS church has been perhaps more thorough and successful than other churches which also came to the aid of refugees and poor immigrants flowing north in the 1980s.

Harold Bloom refers to the LDS church as an "American original" in that it is homegrown, post-Christian, and ultimately a religion of the manly self, one that seeks salvation and freedom through individual struggles rather than through the community (1992:28–36).[11] Although ignored or feared by liberals, it is very much part of the religious mainstream and has pervasive influence throughout the United States and increasingly in Europe. Its basic goal is to establish the Kingdom of God in the world by the millennium. It is one of the fastest-growing religions in the world and by the year 2020 may dominate the western United States and large areas of the Asia-Pacific world through mass recruitments of both the living and (through postmortem baptism) the dead (Bloom 1992:122; see also Gordon 1994).[12]

Mormonism promotes a modernity that makes middle-class respectability accessible to the displaced and the poor who are socially ambitious in new metropolitan contexts. Originally a church of outsiders in frontier conditions, the LDS church has become very adept at recruiting outsiders into the mainstream by ordering peoples of color into specific racial, gender, and class hierarchies with the hope of achieving social success as represented by white masculinity. This modus operandi depends on the rule of colonial difference, which represents the other as "inferior and radically different" (Chatterjee 1993:33) but with the hope of being socialized to dependency on Anglo-Saxon hegemony. Early Mormon doctrines linked depravity and sin with dark-skinned peoples; a history of denying black men ordination to priesthood (crucial to salvation) was ended only in the late 1970s, when the church vigorously expanded its missionizing activities overseas (Bringhurst 1981). The church's initial hesitation over "African-like" Melanesians soon gave way to a greater flexibility towards peoples of color in Africa and the Asia-Pacific region when it became clear that their recruitment would be the most important part of the drive to become a worldwide, multiethnic religion (p. 194). This new tolerance for multiracial and mixed-race recruits, however, operates as an alibi for the church's insistent invocation and mapping of barbaric others in relation to white Mormons (Gordon 1994).

In the San Francisco Bay Area as elsewhere, the LDS church is divided into separate wards for different ethnic/racial groups such as Chinese, Vietnamese, Samoans, Cambodians, and blacks. This mapping of ethnic and racial difference is in relation to moral leadership by white men, who embody American goals of freedom, self-reliance, and individual responsibility. The Mormon masculine ideal is clean-cut, in conservative business suit and tie and often armed with a briefcase. For disadvantaged newcomers, the church must represent a ladder to the American dream, but first they have to learn the steps leading to economic success, moral superiority, and salvation by overcoming the stigma of racialized male inferiority. On Sunday mornings, little Cambodian boys and girls attend Sunday school at the Mormon temple. One teacher wrote "I MUST OBEY" on the blackboard right next to a poster of a kneeling Jesus Christ's "Agony in the Garden." Many children and their parents find the church a more effective institution for teaching English than the state-sponsored English as a Second Language classes. Such instruction, especially for the very young, provides the context wherein the church can prize the young away from their parents and culture and integrate them into the structure of white authority.

The church regularly engages in the symbolic violence that uses "primitive" difference as a way to appropriate the moral authority of parents and realign young Cambodians with the church hierarchy. White Anglo-American supremacy is defined in opposition to the pathologized sexuality of subaltern figures as represented by the patriarchal Asian families and unmasculine Asian men. Such native embodiments of deviant sexual norms make them ripe for salvation by the white church. The bishop told me that he had two specific goals regarding his Cambodian converts, both attempts to correct what he considered their dysfunctional heterosexuality. One was to help Khmer women who had had their marriages arranged for them by their parents when they were teenagers in Cambodia. Perhaps oblivious to the irony, he claimed that the church was a critical agent in fighting the patriarchy of Cambodian culture and teaching Asians about marriage as a partnership. His second goal was to promote an ideal nuclear family headed by a white man. A white supremacist ideology not only defines the Khmers as racially inferior and sexually deviant but also suggests their redemption through the conjoining of white (male) and nonwhite (female) bodies, a particular intertwining of race and sex that, while seemingly promoting multiracial diversity, reproduces white–nonwhite asymmetry in the Mormon order.

The LDS church appeals to young, displaced people because it sometimes becomes the key vehicle for their making the transition to white middle-class culture. Mormon missionaries not only teach American English but also instruct youngsters in the acquisition of other social and bodily skills that will win respect from Americans. For some young immigrant women, the path is through a white marriage. There is something enormously appealing to refugee girls seeking acceptance in the clean-cut young men in business suits who visit their homes and seek to convert them. Mormonism represents upward mobility into a white world where outsiders will be spiritually accepted, though still as racial others. Young Cambodian female converts report that they like the Mormon teachings of "young women's values," including chastity, modesty, and self-discipline. A young woman I will call Vanna confessed,

> Being Mormon helps me to operate better in the U.S. When I was in high school, many Khmer girls married in the twelfth grade, about half of them to older Khmer guys whose jobs were not so good. They got pregnant or simply married to get away from strict parents who wouldn't let them out of the house, but they then found that it was worse in marriage. The husbands won't let them out; they are jealous about other guys, and worried about having no control.

The strict Mormon morality is appealing not only because it seems to echo Cambodian values for female virgins but also because it helps Cambodian girls to attain social mobility. By maintaining sexual purity, female converts avoid teenage pregnancy and early marriage to Khmer men, most of whom are working-class. Mormon lessons in balancing self-control with an affectionate personality socialize the young women to old-fashioned American values of emotion-work that prepare them for their future roles as loving wives and mothers. For instance, Vanna said that she was busy attending college and not dating. She wanted to wait and marry a returned missionary (a young Mormon man who has finished serving his two years as a missionary and is considered ready for marriage). "I really like the Mormon idea of being married for eternity. There is less divorce among Mormons. As far as sex is concerned, being Mormon and being Asian are the same – not to have sex before marriage. You have to be morally clean; it applies to the men too." The respectability, sexual allure, and moral purity attributed to white masculinity burnish the image of minority men who have comparable social and cultural capital. Says Vanna,

> It is more than likely that I'd marry a Caucasian. I want someone who is well-educated, doesn't smoke and drink, and who respects me for who I am. I find Caucasian and Chinese men more attractive than Khmer, for example, the tall Chinese guys who look Caucasian, who are light-skinned and more into American traditions like dating, whereas Khmer men hardly do that, like my brothers-in-law.

The latter also had working-class jobs such as glass manufacturing and packaging. In Vanna's eyes, the pursuit of middle-class status appears to be inseparable from marrying white men. Only through a marital relationship with white masculinity can she cross over the obstacles to the privileges of class and American citizenship.

The Mormon church, then, represents a disciplinary system providing an alternative modality of belonging which, more explicitly than state agencies, employs racialized masculinity in structuring class, gender, and citizenship ideals. Even as the church teaches recruits the self-discipline and entrepreneurship of American success, these attitudes are cast within the framework of white patronage or domination. Immigrant subjectivities, especially those of young girls seeking acceptance, are influenced by socializing processes that racialize gender and class through definitions of pathological (Khmer) and normalized (white) gender and sexuality. Thus Mormon Khmers are the latest in a historical process whereby the labor regimes of immigrants produce a conflation of race and class with the result that ambitious members of minorities often marry out of their community into the white community (see, e.g., Yanagisako 1985). Do affluent Chinese immigrants to California, arriving with capital and credentials, experience other ways of "whitening" and its limits?

Chinese Cosmopolitans: Class, Property, and Cultural Taste

In Northern California, the so-called Hong Kong money elite resides in an exclusive community on the flank of the San Francisco Peninsula mountain range. All the homes in this suburb cost over a million dollars. The choicest are set into the hillsides, with mountains as a backdrop and a view of the bay. Mansions in an Asian-Mediterranean style stand amidst clearings where few trees remain unfelled. This was a sore point with locals, along with the fact that many of the houses were paid for in hard cash, sometimes before the arrival of their new occupants. The driveways are parked with Mercedes Benzes, BMWs, and even a Rolls Royce or two.

The *feng-shui* ("wind-water" propitious placement) of the place is excellent. Fleeing the impending return of Hong Kong to China's rule or merely seeking to tap into U.S. markets, overseas Chinese crossed the Pacific to make this former white enclave their new home. Led initially by real estate agents and later by word of mouth, the influx of wealthy Chinese from Hong Kong, Taiwan, and Southeast Asia has spread to cities and upscale communities all over the state and the country. While many of the newcomers are well-educated professionals who work in the Silicon Valley, an increasing number are property developers, financiers, and industrialists who work on both sides of the Pacific.[13] Their presence has changed the social landscape of suburban California, increasing the number of shopping malls (called "Pacific Renaissance" and "Pacific Rim") and sophisticated restaurants that serve a predominantly Asian clientele (see also Fong 1994). Thus, in addition to being the destination of Third World refugees and migrant workers, U.S. cities are fast becoming the sites of overseas Asian investment and settlement.

What kinds of processes are making such cosmopolitan subjects into citizens? Although the affluent immigrant Chinese appear to be able to evade disciplining by the state, they are not entirely free of its citizenship requirements, on the one hand, and local mediations over what being part of the imagined American community (or the Northern Californian version of it) is all about. Unlike the vast majority of Cambodian refugees, the Chinese investor-immigrants and professionals are "transnational cosmopolitans" who strategically manage meaning as they negotiate and contest the shifting discursive terrains in the world economy (Hannerz 1990; Ong 1993; Ong and Nonini 1996). However, these self-styled "astronauts" – so called because they spend so much time shuttling back and forth across the Pacific (Ong 1993) – are not always as attuned to the cultural norms of particular Californian locales as they are to the transnational opportunities opened up by globalization. Two examples will show that there are cultural limits to the ways in which they can negotiate the hegemonic production of Chineseness in California and the local values about what constitutes civilized conduct and appropriate citizenship.

Family biopolitics and parachute kids

The key motivation and predicament of the transnational strategies of affluent Chinese are their families. Although immigrant businessmen and investors are willing to shuttle back and forth across national borders themselves, locating their children in California is a major priority. These plans are the outgrowth of what, borrowing from Foucault, I have called "family biopolitics" (Ong 1993). The heads of wealthy Chinese families manifest a biopolitical instrumentality in governing the conduct of family members in the interest of ensuring the security and prosperity of the family as a whole. Family biopolitics constitute members' sense of moral worth in terms of relations within the family. Parents instill in their children self-discipline in education, work, and consumption – habits that foster the steady accumulation of economic and symbolic capital – that contributes to the family's prosperity and honor. For instance, the term "utilitarian familialialism" has been applied to the normative and practical tendencies whereby Hong Kong Chinese families place family interest above all other individual and social concerns (Lau 1983:72). As part of such family governmentality, the middle and upper-middle classes in Hong Kong and Taiwan deploy family members abroad to obtain universally certified educational degrees and eventually green cards for the entire family. By relocating some members in California the family maximizes opportunities for overseas business expansion while attempting to evade the governmentality of the home country. However, despite the flexibility afforded them by transnational capitalism, emigrant business families do not fully escape the disciplining of the host country.

At the moment, immigration law has changed to allow for an "investor category" whereby would-be immigrants can obtain a green card in return for a million-dollar investment that creates at least ten jobs. On Wall Street there have been seminars on how to obtain U.S. citizenship through real estate investment and acquisition. A sponsor urges Asian Americans to "think of your relatives in Asia. If they invest $1 million in you, they get a green card and you get a new business" (*Wall Street Journal*, February 21, 1991). The new citizenship law thus constructs the affluent Chinese newcomer as a *homo economicus*, an economic agent who is a "manipulable man, a man who is perpetually responsive to modifications in his environment" (Gordon 1991:43). Perceived as economic agents of choice, overseas Chinese immigrants will nevertheless be disciplined by citizenship criteria and manipulated in their deployment of capital. However, even super-rich would-be immigrants refuse to be subjected to such controls on their investments, perhaps because they are ultimately more susceptible to capitalist instrumentality than to state biopolitics.

A more common strategy for gaining residence rights is to send children to U.S. high schools and colleges. For instance, Alex Leong, a middle-aged executive from a Hong Kong-based finance company, confided that his father always told him, "Your future is really going to be outside Hong Kong. So you should be educated outside, as long as you maintain some Chinese customs and speak Chinese." Since the 1960s an entire generation of middle-class and upper-middle-class Chinese students from Hong Kong and Taiwan has embarked upon overseas education in the United States, seeking educational certifications and residence rights that will eventually enable their families to settle here. Parents visit their children to buy homes, set up bank accounts, and assess the local real estate. Upon graduation the sons may open up a U.S. branch of their family company. Thus, after graduating from Berkeley and the University of Wisconsin business school, Alex joined his father's business by setting up a San Francisco office. Because Alex is not yet a citizen, his parents plan to retire in Vancouver, where residential rights can be purchased with a smaller investment of C$300,000. He expects that eventually they will join him in the Bay Area.

The practice of sending young children to school in California has given rise to another image of affluent Chinese immigrants. Taiwanese parents favor sending children to U.S. high schools because they hope that they will give them a better chance (than in Taiwan) of gaining entry to college, while earning residence rights in the United States. Furthermore, children in the United States provide a chance to invest in property and establish a home base against political instability in Asia. However, sometimes the attempts to coordinate family biopolitics with the disciplining requirements of citizenship undermine carefully constructed plans of business travel, children's education, and managing a transpacific lifestyle. Some 40,000 Taiwanese teenagers have been left to fend for themselves in California while their parents pursue business interests in Asia. Many of these youngsters live with their siblings in expensive homes, sometimes equipped with Asian servants. These so-called parachute kids have the run of the house and manage household finances like adults. One 17-year-old girl, who first arrived when she was 13, has been acting as parent to her younger sisters. Their parents drop by periodically from Taiwan. She is worried that her sisters will be quite lost when she goes to college. Other teenagers have developed a consumerist, laid-back attitude that both critiques and reinforces the *homo economicus* image of their parents. Some youngsters freely spend their parents' large allowances. Newspapers report a Taiwanese brother-and-sister pair, both high-school students near Los Angeles, spending their free time shopping in malls and frequenting restaurants and karaoke bars. The girl, who dons the latest Valley Girl fashions, calls her father "the ATM machine" for issuing money but nothing else. The boy expresses his resentment more directly: "If they're going to dump me here and not take care of me, they owe me something. That is my right" (*Straits Times*, June 26, 1993). The effect of a transnational strategy of economic and cultural consumption has been to split up the much-vaunted Chinese family unit, with family biopolitics dictated in large part by accumulation concerns that oblige business couples to spend their time overseas while abandoning their children to develop a sense of individualistic rights and bravado. Some of the children have shoplifted, joined local Chinese gangs, or created problems in school, drawing the attention of the social services. By and large, however, it is the disciplining of accumulation strategies that produces a sense of global citizenship and contingent belonging for the business-immigrant family.

Affluent transnational Chinese in California are caught up in the dialectic of embedding and disembedding (Giddens 1990) in the international economy, a process which enables them to escape to some extent the disciplining of the state because of their flexible deployment of capital but not within the locality where their families are based. The flexibility of Chinese professionals shifting back and forth across the Pacific thus contradicts local notions of belonging as normative American citizens. Even compared with the proverbial restless Californians, the new Chinese immigrants are footloose cosmopolitans. As the following incident shows, the attenuated sense of a primary link to a particular society comes up against an American class ethos of moral liberalism.

Bad taste or the homeless in an affluent neighborhood?

Whereas poor Asians are primarily disciplined by state agencies, affluent Chinese immigrants, as home-buyers and property developers, have encountered regulation by civic groups upset at the ways in which their city is being changed by transnational capital and taste. In wealthier San Franciscan neighborhoods, residents pride themselves on their conservation consciousness, and they jealously guard the hybrid European ambiance and character of particular neighborhoods. In their role as custodians of appropriate cultural taste governing buildings, architecture, parks, and other public spaces, civic groups routinely badger City Hall, scrutinize urban zoning laws, and patrol the boundaries between what is aesthetically permissible and what is intolerable in their districts. By linking race with habitus, taste, and cultural capital (Bourdieu 1984), such civic groups set limits to the whitening of Asians, who, metaphorically speaking, still give off the whiff of sweat despite arriving with symbolic starter capital.

Public battles over race/taste have revolved around the transformation of middle-class neighborhoods by rich Asian newcomers. At issue are boxy houses with bland facades – "monster houses" – erected by Asian buyers to accommodate extended families in low-density, single-family residential districts known for their Victorian or Mediterranean charm. Protests have often taken on a racialist tone, registering both dismay at the changing cultural landscape and efforts to educate the new arrivals to white upper-class norms appropriate for the city. While the activists focus on the cultural elements – aesthetic norms, democratic process, and civic duty – that underpin the urban imagined community, they encode the strong class resentment against large-scale Asian investment in residential and commercial properties throughout the city (see Mitchell 1997). A conflict over one of these monster houses illustrates the ways in which the state is caught between soothing indignant urbanites seeking to impose their notion of cultural citizenship on Asian nouveax riches while attempting to keep the door open for Pacific Rim capital.

In 1989 a Hong Kong multimillionaire, a Mrs. Chan, bought a house in the affluent Marina district. Chan lived in Hong Kong and rented out her Marina property. A few years later, she obtained the approval of the city to add a third story to her house but failed to notify her neighbors. When they learned of her plans, they complained that the third story would block views of the Palace of Fine Arts as well as cut off sunlight in an adjoining garden. The neighbors linked up with a citywide group to pressure City Hall. The mayor stepped in and called for a city zoning study, thus delaying the proposed renovation. At a neighborhood meeting, someone declared, "We don't want to see a second Chinatown here." Indeed, there is already a new "Chinatown" outside the old Chinatown, based in the middle-class Richmond district. This charge thus raised the specter of a spreading Chinese urbanscape encroaching on the heterogeneous European flavor of the city. The remark, with its implied racism, compelled the mayor to apologize to Chan, and the planning commission subsequently approved a smaller addition to her house.

However, stung by the racism and the loss on her investment and bewildered that neighbors could infringe upon her property rights, Chan, a transnational developer, used her wealth to mock the city's self-image as a bastion of liberalism. She pulled out all her investments in the United States and decided to donate her million-dollar house to the homeless. To add insult to injury, she stipulated that her house was not to be used by any homeless of Chinese descent. Her architect, an American Chinese, told the press, "You can hardly find a homeless Chinese anyway" (*Asia Week*, May 6, 1995). Secure in her overseas location, Chan fought the Chinese stereotype by stereotyping American homeless as non-Chinese, while challenging her civic-minded neighbors to demonstrate the moral liberalism they professed. Mutual class and racial discrimination thus broke through the surface of what initially appeared to be a negotiation over normative cultural taste in the urban milieu. A representative of the major's office, appropriately contrite, remarked that Chan could still do whatever she wanted with her property; "We just would like for her not to be so angry." The need to keep overseas investments flowing into the city had to be balanced against neighborhood groups' demands for cultural standards. The power of the international real estate market, as represented by Mrs. Chan, thus disciplined both City Hall and the Marina neighbors, who may have to rethink local notions of what being enlightened urbanites may entail in the "era of Pacific Rim capital" (Mitchell 1996).

Other Chinese investor-immigrants, unlike Mrs. Chan, try to negotiate the tensions between local and global forces and to adopt the cultural trappings of the white upper class so as to cushion long-term residents' shock at the status change of the racial other, until recently likely to be a laundry or garment worker. Chinese developers who live in San Francisco are trying harder to erase the image of themselves as "economic animals" who build monster houses, as well as the perception that they lack a sense of civic duty and responsibility. They try to maintain their Victorian homes and English gardens, collect Stradivari violins and attend the opera, play tennis in formerly white clubs, and dress up by dressing down their nouveau riche appearance. I have elsewhere talked about the limits to cultural accumulation of Chinese gentrification in Western metropolitan circles (Ong 1992). Perhaps realizing the limits to how they can be accepted through these whitening practices, some Chinese investors are for the first time making significant philanthropic contributions outside the old Chinatown. I interviewed a surgeon who was the first Chinese American to sit on the board of the city symphony.

When he complained about the lack of Chinese contributions to the symphony, I had to remind him that there were hardly music lessons in Chinatown or other poor urban schools.

But the effort to funnel Pacific Rim money upwards continues. Hong Kong-based companies are making generous donations to major public institutions such as universities and museums. Leslie Tang-Schilling (her real name), the daughter of a Hong Kong industrialist, married into a prominent San Franciscan family, and a commercial developer in her own right, leads the move to soften the hard-edged image of Chinese investor-immigrants. The Tang family name is emblazoned on an imposing new health center on the Berkeley campus. Other overseas Chinese and Asian businesses have donated large sums to the construction of buildings devoted to chemistry, life sciences, computer science, and engineering. An East Coast example is the gift of $20 million to Princeton University by Gordon Wu, a Hong Kong tycoon whose money could perhaps better have benefited long-neglected universities on the Chinese mainland.

Whereas an earlier generation of overseas Chinese tycoons went home to build universities in China, today Asian investors wish to buy symbolic capital in Western democracies as a way to ease racial and cultural acceptance across the globe. Like earlier European immigrant elites looking for symbolic real estate, overseas Chinese donors show a preference for "hardware" (impressive buildings bearing their names) over "software" (scholarships and programs that are less visible to the public eye).[14] The difference is that subjects associated with Third World inferiority have scaled the bastions of white power.[15] Such showcase pieces have upgraded Asian masculinity, layered over the hardscrabble roots of the Asian *homo economicus*, and proclaimed their arrival on the international scene. Nevertheless, there are limits to such strategies of symbolic accumulation, and white backlash has been expressed in a rise in random attacks on Asians. By placing an Asian stamp on prestigious "white" public space, the new immigrants register what for over a century – one thinks of the plantation workers and railroad men, maids and garment workers, gardeners and cooks, shopkeepers and nurses, undocumented workers laboring in indentured servitude, whether in the colonies or in cities like New York and Los Angeles – has been a space of Asia-Pacific cultural production within the West.[16]

Are the New Asians Asian Americans?

Through an ethnographic examination of cultural citizenship as subjectification and cultural performance, I argue that the ideological entanglements of race and culture operate both to locate and to marginalize immigrants from the metaphorical South and East. This approach thus suggests that while "cultural fundamentalism" may have replaced racism in rhetorics of exclusion (Stolcke 1995), in practice racial hierarchies and polarities continue to inform Western notions of cultural difference and are therefore inseparable from the cultural features attributed to different groups. I maintain that the white – black polarities emerging out of the history of European-American imperialism continue to shape attitudes and encode discourses directed at immigrants from the rest of the world that are associated with racial and cultural inferiority. This dynamic of racial othering emerges in a range of mechanisms that variously subject nonwhite immigrants to whitening or blackening processes that indicate the degree of their closeness to or distance from ideal white standards.

The contrasting dynamics of the subjectification experienced by new immigrants demonstrate the critical significance of institutional forces, both domestic and international, in making different kinds of minorities. Cambodian refugees and Chinese business people did not arrive as ready-made ethnics. Through the different modes of disciplining – the primacy of state and church regulation in one and the primacy of consumption and capitalist instrumentality in the other – Cambodian refugees and Chinese immigrants are dialectically positioned at different ends of the black – white spectrum. The racialization of class, as well as the differential othering of immigrants, constitutes immigrants as the racialized embodiments of different kinds of social capital.

Thus, the category "Asian American" must acknowledge the internal class, ethnic, and racial stratifications that are both the effect and the product of differential governmentalities working on different populations of newcomers. It must confront the contradictions and instabilities within the imposed solidarity and temporary alliances of what has been prematurely called an "Asian American panethnicity" (Espiritu 1992). The two new Asian groups represent different modalities of precarious belonging – one as ideologically blackened subjects manipulating state structures in order to gain better access to resources and the other expressing an ultramodern instrumentality that is ambivalently caught between whitening social practices and the consumer power that spells citizenship in the global economy. They are thus not merely new arrivals passively absorbed into an over arching Asian American identity,[17] nor can they be easily subsumed within the inter-Asian coalitions that emerged among college students in the 1960s or united simply on the basis of having been treated "all alike" as biogenetic others sharing a history of exclusion (Chan 1991:xiii). The entanglement of ideologies of race, culture, nation, and capitalism shapes a range of ethnicized citizenship in different fields of power. Given all these factors, the heterogeneity and instability of Asian American identities (Lowe 1991) suggest that a dramatic shift in coalitions may cut across racial lines – for example, Asian-Anglo partnerships in business or linkages between Cambodian and other refugees of color in dealing with the welfare state.

I end by returning to the moral predicament of my own passage into American society. Twenty years later, and only after the birth of my first child (whose father is a fourth-generation Japanese- and Spanish-speaking Chinese American) did I feel ready to mark my long apprenticeship in cultural citizenship by becoming a legal citizen. I continue to view the term "Asian American" with ambivalence, as much for its imposed racialized normativity as for what it elides about other-Asians/other-Americans and for what it includes as well as excludes within the American scheme of belonging. One learns to be fast-footed, occasionally glancing over one's shoulder to avoid tripping over – while tripping up – those lines.

The unbearable lightness of being a nonwhite American means that the presumed stability and homogeneity of the Asian American identity must, in this era of post-civil rights politics (Takagi 1994)[18] and globalization, be open to the highly particularized local reworkings of global forces. In California these forces have been dramatically played out in domestic, racial terms as well as in transnational, class ones, foreshadowing the reconfiguration of citizenship in the West in the new global era.

NOTES

1 According to Rosaldo (1994:57), cultural citizenship is "the right to be different (in terms of race, ethnicity, or native language) with respect to the norms of the dominant national community, without compromising one's right to belong, in the sense of participating in the nation-state's democratic processes. The enduring exclusions of the color line often deny full citizenship to Latinos and other people of color. From the point of view of subordinate communities, cultural citizenship offers the possibility of legitimizing demands made in the struggle to enfranchise themselves. These demands can range from legal, political and economic issues to matters of human dignity, well-being, and respect."

2 I thank Brackette Williams for discussing these points with me and supplying the references.

3 A recent volume, *Structuring Diversity* (Lamphere 1992), provides ethnographic cases of encounters between newcomers and U.S. urban institutions. The focus of these case studies is on the integration of immigrants into dominant American society. My approach views such encounters and practices as relations of power that constitute varied minoritization processes and foster differential understandings of cultural citizenship among different groups of newcomers.

4 In 1988, the Bay Area was the third-most-favored destination for legal immigrants, after New York and Los Angeles. Nearly 41,000 immigrants arrived in the Bay Area that year, 60 percent of them Asian (*San Francisco Chronicle*, July 6, 1989).

5 Some Asian American professionals have protested being put into the position of a "racial bourgeoisie" – a buffer class between whites and other minorities (*San Francisco Chronicle*, August 22, 1995).

6 Cynthia Wong Sau-ling (1992:111–12) employs the concept "ethnicizing gender" to describe a parallel racializing process whereby "white ideology assigns selected gender characteristics to various ethnic

others," for example, in representations of effeminized Asian men and ultrafeminized Asian women.

7 See Kelly (1980), Nicholson (1989), Welaratna (1993), and Ong (1995 a, b) for studies of how, after their arrival in the United States, Southeast Asian refugees are differently socialized in a range of institutional contexts to the requirements of the dominant white culture. Gail Kelly's (1980) concept of "internal colonialism" to describe the "schooling" of blacks, Native Americans, and immigrant communities as a generic colonized labor force is too general to capture the complex and contingent discriminations among different categories of immigrants.

8 All the names of informants are fictive to protect their privacy.

9 The notion of Khmer culture as "oral" – despite a literate history (based on Sanskrit, Hinduism, and Buddhism) stretching back to the 9th-century Khmer kingdom that built Angkor Wat and Angkor Thom, among other monuments (see Chandler 1983) – is part of the misconception that Khmers are a "primitive" people.

10 For an example of churches socializing colonized populations to Western values, see Schieffelin (1981), for an example of churches socializing Asian immigrants, see Hirata (1979).

11 Harold Bloom, like others before him (see, e.g., Whalen 1964), considers the LDS church a post-Christian "American religion" in that it is non-monotheistic, has no absolutely formal creeds, and rejects creationism, believing instead in a material and contingent God found within the believer. Its indigenous American roots are reflected in the romantic quest for oneself, freedom, progress, and even immortality (1991:40–42, 113–115).

12 In the Mormon church, the family rather than the individual is the "unit of exaltation." The destiny of the Latter-day Saints is godhood. Baptism for the dead is a way to "save" ancestors, and spirit children are produced by Mormon couples so that these family members can join their living Mormon descendants in the "eternal progression" towards godness (Bloom 1992:121–123).

13 Of course, the influx into the United States of poor, working-class Chinese from the mainland and Southeast Asia, many in difficult and illegal conditions, continues. For a feminist perspective on Chinese emigration, see Ong (1995c). With the growing influx of affluent and professional Chinese, the image of the Pacific Rim male executive is eclipsing somewhat the image of the Chinese laundry worker and illegal alien (see Ong 1993).

14 The Malaysian Chinese philanthropist Tan Kah Kee is famous for building Xiamen University and many other public works in Fujian, China, the land of his birth. Today his U.S.-educated children are organizing a campaign to contribute to the chemistry building on the Berkeley campus.

15 Of course, in making donations to public buildings, Asian American nouveaux riches are merely replicating a long immigrant tradition cultivated by Irish, Italian, and Jewish immigrants who made good. The Chinese newcomers to the Bay Area are following in the footsteps of the Hearsts, the Aliotos, and the Haases. However, for the first time we are seeing the nonwhite arrivals scaling the social heights with wealth gained in the international economy and causing reluctant, minimal adjustments in the domestic racial hierarchy. For an anthropological study of a major American family dynasty and the symbolic boundaries of wealth, see Marcus (1992). For an account of the Chinese diaspora within the context of global flexible accumulation, see Ong and Nonini (1997). Finally, for an interesting comparison with another highly successful non-European immigrant community, Cubans in Florida, see Portes and Stepick (1993).

16 I am paraphrasing the title of a volume edited by Rob Wilson and Arik Dirlik (1996).

17 The construction of which, as Sylvia Yanagisako (1993) has noted, is ideologically dominated by the history of male Chinese railroad workers, thus marginalizing or excluding the experiences of women and of other Asian groups.

18 Takagi defines "post-civil rights politics" as the struggle of multiethnic groups beyond the old black-white framework, marked by the tendency for racial interests to be disguised by social and economic language and for solutions to racial problems to be sought in class terms (1994:237–239).

REFERENCES

Alatas, Syed Hussein. 1977. *The Myth of the Lazy Native*. London: Cass.

Archdeacon, Thomas J. 1983. *Becoming American: An Ethnic History*. New York: Free Press.

Becker, Gary C. 1965. A theory of the allocation of time. *Economic Journal* 75:493–517.

Bederman, Gail. 1993. Civilization, the decline of middle-class manliness, and Ida B. Wells's anti-lynching campaign (1892–94). In *Gender in American*

History since 1890, ed. Barbara Melosh. Pp. 207–239. New York: Routledge.

Bloom, Harold. 1992. *The American Religion: The Emergence of the Post-Christian Nation*. New York: Simon & Schuster.

Bourdieu, Pierre. 1984. *Distinction: A Social Critique of the Judgement of Taste*. Cambridge, MA: Harvard University Press.

Bringhurst, Newell G. 1981. *Saints, Slaves, and Blacks: The Changing Place of Black People within Mormonism*. Westport, CT: Greenwood Press.

Chandler, David P. 1983. *A History of Cambodia*. Boulder, CO: Westview Press.

Chatterjee, Partha. 1993. *The Nation and its Fragments: Colonial and Postcolonial Histories*. Princeton: Princeton University Press.

Copeland, Lewis C. 1939. The Negro as a contrast conception. *In Race Relations and the Race Problem: A Definition and an Analysis*, ed. Edgar T. Thompson. Pp. 152–179. Durham: Duke University Press.

Corrigan, Philip, and Derek Sayer. 1985. *The Great Arch: English State Formation as Cultural Revolution*. London: Basil Blackwell.

Domínguez, Virginia. 1986. *White by Definition: Social Classification in Creole Louisiana*. New Brunswick: Rutgers University Press.

Du Bois, W. E. B. 1977[1935]. *Black Reconstruction in the United States, 1860–1880*. New York.

Embree, John F. 1950. Thailand – a loosely structured social system. *American Anthropologist* 52:181–193.

Espiritu, Yen LE. 1992. *Asian American Panethnicity: Bridging Institutions and Identities*. Philadelphia: Temple University Press.

Fanon, Frantz. 1967. *Black Skin, White Masks*, trans. C. L. Markman. New York: Grove Press.

Fong, Timothy P. 1994. *The First Suburban Chinatown: The Remaking of Monterey Park, California*. Philadelphia: Temple University Press.

Foucault, Michel. 1989. The subject and power. In *Michel Foucault: Beyond Structuralism and Hermeneutics*, ed. H. L. Dreyfus and P. Rainbow. Pp. 208–228. Chicago: University of Chicago Press.

Foucault, Michel 1991. On governmentality. In *The Foucault Effect*, ed. G. Burchell, C. Gordon, and P. Miller. Pp. 87–104. Chicago: University of Chicago Press.

Giddens, Anthony. 1990. *Modernity and Self-identity*. Stanford: Stanford University Press.

Gilman, Sander. 1985. *Difference and Pathology: Stereotypes of Sexuality, Race, and Madness*. Ithaca: Cornell University Press.

Gilroy, Paul. 1987. *"There Ain't no Black in the Union Jack": The Cultural Politics of Race and Nation*. Chicago: University of Chicago Press.

Golub, Stephens. 1986. *Looking for Phantoms: Flaws in the Khmer Rouge Health Screening Process*. Washington, DC: U.S. Committee for Refugees.

Gordon, Colin. 1991. Governmental rationality: An introduction. In *The Foucault Effect*, ed. G. Burchell, C. Gordon, and P. Miller. Pp. 1–51. Chicago: University of Chicago Press.

Gordon, Linda. 1988. *Heroes of their Own Lives: The Politics and History of Family Violence*. New York: Penguin.

Gordon, Tamar. 1994. Constructing authenticities and modernities at the Polynesian Cultural Center. Paper presented at the American Anthropological Association meetings, Atlanta, November 30-December 3.

Gregory, Steven, and Roger Sanjek, ed. 1994. *Race*. New Brunswick: Rutgers University Press.

Hall, Catherine. 1992. *White, Male, and Middle-class: Explorations in Feminism and History*. London: Polity Press.

Hannerz, Ulf. 1990. Cosmopolitans and locals in world culture. In *Global Culture: Nationalism, Globalization, and Modernity*, ed. Mike Featherstone. Pp. 237–252. London: Sage.

Harrington, Michael. 1962. *The Other America*. New York: Macmillan.

Harrison, M. L. 1991. Citizenship, consumption, and rights: A comment on B. S. Turner's theory of citizenship. *Sociology* 25:215–218.

Hirata, Lucie Cheng. 1979. Free, indentured, enslaved: Chinese prostitutes in nineteenth-century America. *Signs* 5:3–29.

Kelly, Gail P. 1980. The schooling of Vietnamese immigrants: Internal colonialism and its impact on women. In *Comparative Perspectives on Third World Women: The Impact of Race, Sex, and Class*. Pp. 276–296. New York: Praeger.

Komorovsky, Mirra. 1967. *Blue-Collar Marriage*. New York: Vintage Books.

Lamphere, Louise, ed. 1992. *Structuring Diversity: Ethnographic Perspectives on the New Immigration*. Chicago: University of Chicago Press.

Lau, Siu-Kai. 1983. *Society and Politics in Hong Kong*. New York: St. Martin's Press.

Loescher, Gil, and John A. Scanlan. 1986. *Calculated Kindness: Refugees and America's Half-open Door: 1945 to the Present*. New York: Free Press.

Lowe, Lisa. 1991. Heterogeneity, hybridity, and multiplicity: Masking Asian American differences. *Diaspora* 1:24–44.

Marcus, George E., with Peter D. Hall 1992. *Lives in Trust: The Fortunes of Dynastic Families in Late Twentieth-century America*. Boulder, CO: Westview Press.

Memmi, Albert. 1967. *The Colonizer and the Colonized*, trans. Howard Greenfield. New York: Beacon Press.

Miles, Robert. 1989. *Racism*. London: Routledge.

Mitchell, Katharyne. 1997. Transnational subjects: The constitution of the cultural citizen in the era of Pacific Rim capital. In *Ungrounded Empires: The Cultural Politics of Modern Chinese Transnationalism*, ed. A. Ong and D. Nonini. New York: Routledge. In press.

Mortland, Carol. 1987. Transforming refugees in refugee camps. *Urban Anthropology* 16:375–404.

Myrdal, Gunnar. 1944. *An American Dilemma: The Negro Problem and Modern Democracy*. New York: Harper & Row.

Nandy, Ashis. 1983. *The Intimate Enemy: Loss and the Recovery of Self under Colonialsm*. Delhi: Oxford University Press.

Ngor, Haing. 1987. *A Cambodian Odyssey*. New York: Macmillan.

Nicholson, Barbara. 1989. The influence of culture on teaching Southeast Asian paraprofessionals: A challenge to social work education. *Journal of Teaching in Social Work* 3:73–86.

Omi, Michael, and Howard Winant. 1986. *Racial Formation in the United States: From the 1960s to the 1990s*. New York: Routledge & Kegan Paul.

Ong, Aihwa. 1993. On the edges of empires: Flexible citizenship among cosmopolitan Chinese. *Positions* 1:745–778.

Ong, Aihwa. 1995a. Making the biopolitical subject: Khmer immigrants, refugee medicine, and cultural citizenship in California. *Social Science and Medicine* 40:1243–1257.

Ong, Aihwa, 1995b. Mother's milk in war and diaspora. *Cultural Survival Quarterly* 19:61–64.

Ong, Aihwa. 1995c. Women out of China: Travelling theories and traveling tales in postmodern feminism. In *Women Writing Culture*, ed. R. Behar and D. Gordon. Pp. 350–372. Berkeley: University of California Press.

Ong, Aihwa, and Don Nonini, eds. 1997. *Ungrounded Empires: The Cultural Politics of Modern Chinese Transnationalism*. New York: Routledge.

Perin, Constance. 1988. *Belonging in America: Reading between the Lines*. Madison: University of Wisconsin Press.

Portes, Alejandro, and Ruben G. Rumbaut. 1990. *Immigrant America: A Portrait*. Berkeley: University of California Press.

Portes, Alejandro, and Alex Stepick. 1993. *City on the Edge: The Transformation of Miami*. Berkeley: University of California Press.

Rabinow, Paul, ed. 1984. *The Foucault Reader*. New York: Pantheon.

Roediger, David R. 1991. *The Wages of Whiteness: Race and the Making of the American Working Class*. London: Verso.

Rosaldo, Renato. 1994. Cultural citizenship in San Jose, California. *Polar* 17:57–63.

Rumbaut, Ruben G. and Kenji Ima. 1988. *The Adaptation of Southeast Asian Youth: A Comparative Study*. (Final report to the Office of Refugee Settlement, U.S. Department of Health and Human Services, Family Support Administration.) Washington, DC: Office of Refugee Settlement.

Said, Edward. 1978. *Orientalism*. New York: Pantheon.

Schieffelin, Edward. 1981. Evangelical rhetoric and the transformation of traditional culture in Papua New Guinea. *Comparative Studies in Society and History* 23:150–156.

Stack, Carol. 1974. *All our Kin: Strategies for Survival in a Black Community*. New York: Harper & Row.

Stolcke, Verena. 1995. Talking culture: New boundaries, new rhetorics of exclusion in Europe. *Current Anthropology* 36:1–24.

Stoler, Ann L. 1995. *Race and the Education of Desire*. Durham: Duke University Press.

Takagi, Dana Y. 1994. Post-civil rights politics and Asian-American identity: Admissions and higher education. In *Race*, ed. Steven Gregory and Roger Sanjek. Pp. 229–242. New Brunswick: Rutgers University Press.

Tollefson, J. W. 1990. Response to Ranard and Gilzow: The economics and ideology of overseas refugee education. *TESOL Quarterly* 24:543–555.

Valentine, Charles A. 1971. Deficit, difference, and bicultural models of Afro-American behavior. *Harvard Educational Review* 41(2).

Welaratna, Usha. 1993. *Beyond the Killing Fields: Voices of Nine Cambodian Survivors in America*. Stanford: Stanford University Press.

Wetherell, Margaret, and Jonathan Potter. 1993. *Mapping the Language of Racism: Discourse and the Legitimation of Exploitation*. New York: Columbia University Press.

Whalen, William J. 1964. *The Latter-Day Saints in the Modern-Day World*. New York: John Day.

Williams, Brackette F. 1989. A class act: Anthropology and the race across ethnic terrain. *Annual Review of Anthropology* 18:401–444.

Williams, Brackette. 1991. *Stains on my Name, War in my Veins: Guyana and the Politics of Cultural Struggle*. Durham: Duke University Press.

Wilson, Rob, and Arif Dirlik, eds. 1996. *The Asia/Pacific as Space of Cultural Production*. Durham: Duke University Press.

Wong Sau-Ling, Cynthia. 1992. Ethnicizing gender: An exploration of sexuality as sign in Chinese immigrant culture. In *Reading the Literatures of Asian America*, ed. S. G. Lim and A. Ling. Pp. 111–129. Philadelphia: Temple University Press.

Yanagisako, Sylvia J. 1985. *Transforming the Past: Tradition and Kinship among Japanese Americans*. Stanford: Stanford University Press.

Yanagisako, Sylvia. 1993. "Transforming Orientalism: Gender, nationality, and class in Asian American Studies," in *Naturalizing Power*. Edited by S. Yanagisako and C. Delaney. Stanford: Stanford University Press.

Part IV

The Politics and Perils of Assimilation

9

More than "Model Minorities" or "Delinquents": A Look at Hmong American High School Students

Stacey J. Lee

The first Southeast Asian refugees arrived in the United States in 1975, and within ten years the popular press identified Southeast Asian youth as "the new whiz kids" (Brand 1987). Conspicuously absent from these reports were Hmong American youth, whose academic difficulties bumped up against the popular "model minority" image (Walker-Moffat 1995). The first Hmong arrived in the United States as refugees from Laos over 25 years ago. Early scholarly and popular descriptions of Hmong refugees emphasized the differences between Hmong culture – described as rural, preliterate, patriarchal, and traditional – and mainstream American culture (e.g., Donnelly 1994; Fass 1991; Rumbaut and Ima 1988; Sherman 1988). These cultural differences were explained as the root of many of the social and economic problems Hmong refugees faced in the United States. For example, cultural barriers were identified as the reason behind the high dropout rates among Hmong refugee students in middle and high school (Cohn 1986; Goldstein 1985). Hmong girls, in particular, experienced high dropout rates, which were traced back to the Hmong cultural practices of early marriage and early childbearing (Goldstein 1985; Rumbaut and Ima 1988; Walker-Moffat 1995).

While the early research on Hmong refugees painted a grim picture of Hmong student achievement, much of the recent research has highlighted the success of Hmong American students. Several researchers have argued that Hmong students as a group have overcome their early difficulties and are now managing to do well in school despite high rates of poverty, low levels of parental education, and the cultural practice of early marriage among teens (Call and McNall 1992; Dunnigan, Olney, McNall, and Spring 1996; Hutchinson 1997; Hutchinson and McNall 1994; Rumbaut 1995). Scholars attribute the success of Hmong American students to the support of the immigrant community, family support, and adherence to traditional values such as respect for elders (Hutchinson 1997; Rumbaut 1995). Thus, in contrast to earlier portrayals of Hmong culture as problematic, current scholarship characterizes it as a positive influence on student achievement. In his recent study on Hmong students in Wisconsin, Hutchinson (1997) concluded that "Hmong youth will be more successful in their educational careers than any other immigrant or refugee group to ever come to the United States" (p. 1). It would appear that Hmong American students have joined the ranks of the model minority.

Although many Hmong American students appear to be successful, there is evidence that some Hmong youth are exhibiting serious adjustment problems. Truancy, rising dropout rates, and delinquency among teens have been identified by researchers as some of the major concerns within Hmong American communities (Faderman 1998; Thao 1999; Walker-Moffat 1995). These problems have not gone unnoticed by the popular press, which has highlighted the rise of Southeast Asian gangs (e.g., Ingersoll 1999; Kifner 1991). The academic literature and the popular press convey a perception that Hmong American youth fall into two opposite groups: high-achieving model minorities, and delinquents, truants, and gang members.

Research on other Southeast Asian ethnic groups suggests that dropping out of school, truancy, and other forms of resistant behavior are more common among second-generation than first-generation youth (Rumbaut 1995; Zhou and Bankston 1998). Some researchers argue that the youth who experience trouble in school and with the law are those who have become disconnected from their families and culture and therefore become over-Americanized (Rumbaut 1995; Zhou and Bankston 1998). In his research on Hmong youth in Chicago, Thao (1999) asserts that youth who are over-Americanized are particularly vulnerable to gang involvement. Similarly, the popular explanation the media advances suggests that second-generation youth have lost their culture. One newspaper article, for example, referred to the rise in Southeast Asian gangs as evidence of the "cultural growing pains" (Ingersoll 1999:1) within immigrant communities. Such analysis, of course, oversimplifies the reasons youth engage in resistant behavior. This analysis assumes that "American" culture is inherently dangerous and that Hmong culture can protect its youth from harm. Furthermore, it places Hmong-ness and American-ness into mutually exclusive categories.

Other researchers have observed the impact of race, social context, and economic opportunities on the adjustment of second-generation youth (Ima 1995; Portes 1995, 1996; Portes and Rumbaut 1996; Suárez-Orozco and Suárez-Orozco 1995). Portes asserts, "There are three features of the social contexts encountered by today's newcomers that create vulnerability to downward assimilation. The first is color, the second is location, and the third is the absence of mobility ladders" (1995:73). The strength of this selection of work is that it considers the impact of structural forces on student adjustment.

In this article, I explore the way economic forces, relationships with the dominant society, perceptions of opportunities, family relationships, culture, and educational experiences affect Hmong American students' attitudes toward school. Specifically, I compare the way 1.5-generation and second-generation Hmong American students respond to education.[1] Additionally, I focus attention on variations within each group. The following questions provide the focus for this piece: How do Hmong American students view education? Do responses to education vary between 1.5-generation and second-generation students? I pay particular attention to how the forces inside and outside of school affect attitudes toward education.

Data for this article was collected as part of a one and one-half academic year ethnographic study of Hmong American students at a Wisconsin public school, University Heights High School (UHS).[2] I visited UHS three days per week on average for three to five hours at a time. The primary means of data collection were participant observation of Hmong students in the high school (e.g., in classrooms, during lunch periods, during study hall, and during extracurricular activities) and interviews with Hmong students and school staff. Interviews lasted from one to three hours and were taped when possible. I also analyzed school documents, observed Hmong parents at meetings organized by the school district, and conducted participant observation at local Hmong community events. Although there are many places in the article where I provide verbatim quotes from interviews and describe individuals in detail, at other times I speak more generally about a group. My decision to speak generally reflects an effort to protect the identity of individuals who revealed sensitive information that they did not want traced back to them.

Located in a mid-size city in Wisconsin, UHS enjoys an excellent reputation in the city and the state. Mr. Schenk, the school social worker, explained that the faculty and staff at UHS are proud of its high academic standards and many consider UHS to be a "public prep school":

> It is a public school that has many, many qualities of a private prep school. It services a population in the community that are primarily university families or university-connected families, professional families. And then...about a fourth of...the student population...are special populations: African Americans, Asian Americans...probably...somewhat less a percentage of poor kids. But it really is...in terms of the traditions, in terms of the way it views itself, it's

really kind of a prep school. It is invested in the academic standards...the quality of the students, in terms of the high achieving, it has a really broad selection....And so it is kind of a secondary image, a secondary school, trying to become like a university, which it is very close to. Then I think that if you are looking for a sort of prep school attitude toward academics...that is what would capture University Heights High – a public prep school.

UHS enrolled 2,023 students during the 1999–2000 academic year, with 29 percent of these students classified as students of color and 14 percent listed as receiving free or reduced lunch. Several members of the staff commented that the percentage of students of color and lower-income students had grown significantly in the last 20 years. A significant portion of the student population still comes from middle-class and professional families who live in the neighborhood of the school. Although there has been an increase in the diversity of the student population, Mr. Schenk's comments suggest that the school continues to reflect the culture of the middle-class students.

Since UHS and the school district classify all students of Asian descent into one category, "Asians," it was difficult to attain an exact count of the Hmong students. According to estimates by various school staff, there were 54 Hmong students enrolled at UHS during the 1998–1999 school year and approximately 65 enrolled during the 1999–2000 school year.[3] Most of the Hmong students were from low-income families and received free or reduced lunch. Many lived in low-income housing in the poorer sections of the city.

With few exceptions, Hmong American students at UHS were acutely aware of issues of identity and typically used ethnicity, race, gender, age, generation, and marital status to situate others. In my first encounters with Hmong students I was typically asked the following: "Are you Hmong?" "Where were you born?" and "Are you married?" As a third-generation Chinese American woman, I share a panethnic/racial identity with the Hmong students. This helped to facilitate our initial conversations, but the fact that I am not Hmong still branded me an ethnic outsider. Because the Hmong students saw me as an outsider they were initially very cautions around me. Many of my informants, for example, would switch to speaking Hmong when discussing potentially sensitive topics (e.g., marriage, funerals, ritual healing, etc.). Two of my primary informants hid their married status from me for several months until they felt that I was trustworthy. Significantly, these young women hid their married status from school officials, for fear of moral and even legal judgment.

Similarly, in her research on Hmong immigrants in Wisconsin, Koltyk (1998) discovered that most Hmong go to great lengths to protect their culture from the gaze and criticism of outsiders. Koltyk (1998) explains, "As the Hmong have learned that aspects of their culture seem primitive or offensive to many Americans, they have become reluctant to talk to outsiders about them" (p. 14). By keeping their secrets and sharing aspects of my Chinese cultural background, I was eventually able to gain the trust of many students, though they remained cautious in new situations.

"There are two groups of Hmong students at UHS"

During my first week at UHS, Mrs. Her, one of the Hmong bilingual resource specialists, informed me that there were basically two groups of Hmong students at UHS. Using language that could best be described as diplomatic, she referred to the first group as the English as a Second Language (ESL) students and the second group as the "Americanized" students. She explained that the ESL students were "newcomers" and the Americanized students were born in the United States, and that the Hmong student population at UHS had shifted over two decades. In the 1980s, Hmong American students were all first-generation, while today they are mostly second-generation. While ESL students were the norm in the 1980s, most Hmong American students at UHS today are in mainstream classes. Mrs. Her elaborated by saying that the newcomers "still keep and value Hmong traditions," and that the Americanized students had adopted more American ways. She added that the two groups of students had very different relationships to schooling. She explained:

> We don't have problems with those ESL kids. Because, they are, I don't know, they seem, maybe they're not Americanized...so they are still thinking, like they said they are still, let's say, good kids. So they are working hard and trying to graduate from UHS. The other problems, I think the problem that most of the Hmong students face are students who are in the mainstream – they are facing truancy.

Like many scholars (Thao 1999; Zhou and Bankston 1998), Mrs. Her points to the negative impact of Americanization on student achievement. In a later interview, Mrs. Her stated that Hmong parents divided Hmong youth into the "good kids" and the "bad kids":

> The good kid will go back to the culture, whether it's a boy or a girl. When they come back home, they will, I guess help the parents, [by] doing housework, chores. I guess [they] dress differently too....A normal kid...practicing some traditional culture, and going to school, attending school, getting good grades, will be...good, a good child, a good boy or girl. And also, I guess doing what the parents want them to do....And, so the opposite is when the kids start to rebel or talk back to the parents, not obeying. And then wearing the baggy clothes, not attending school. Those are the bad kids.

At a school district-sponsored meeting for Southeast Asian parents, several Hmong parents stated (through interpreters) that they were afraid that they were losing their children to the American culture. Some parents explained that while their children were "good kids" they feared that "bad Hmong kids" at school would influence their children. Like Mrs. Her, these parents viewed students' wearing baggy clothes as the first sign of trouble. In this regard, Mrs. Her and the parents were in agreement: they all identify "good kids" and "bad kids" by their clothes, their relationship with adults, and their attitudes toward school.

The Hmong students at UHS also emphasized the differences between ESL and Americanized students. In my one and one-half academic years at UHS, the social boundaries between the 1.5-generation and second-generation groups of students were rarely crossed at school. Students in one group would admit to having cousins in the other group, but they maintained their distance. While 1.5-generation students were more likely to participate in the school's Asian Club, second-generation students dominated the school's Hmong Club. While the Asian Club included students from various Asian ethnic groups (e.g., Chinese, Tibetan, Vietnamese, Hmong, etc.), all members of the Hmong Club were ethnically Hmong. When I asked 1.5-generation students why they chose to participate in the Asian Club instead of the Hmong Club, they explained that they wanted to be in a club that emphasized teaching others about their culture. These students suggested that the members of the Hmong Club were more interested in parties than in their culture. My observations of the Hmong Club revealed that its members were interested in organizing parties and other social events, but they were also interested in participating in a club where they could express their own identities. Although these second-generation students did not see themselves as being traditional, they participated in the club because they were proud of being Hmong.

Several 1.5-generation students reported that their parents warned them to stay away from "bad kids" who were "too Americanized." Echoing the sentiments of the parental generation, a 1.5-generation student compared the two groups like this: "We are more traditional. We speak Hmong and know the Hmong culture. The others speak more English – they want to be cool. They don't follow what adults say." For their part, second-generation Hmong students ridiculed 1.5-generation students for being too "traditional" and "old-fashioned." They even used derogatory terms such as *FOB* or *FOBBIES* (i.e., Fresh Off the Boat) to describe 1.5-generation students. A second-generation student described 1.5-generation students like this: "FOBs don't care about clothes. They are stingy about clothes. They dress in out-of-date 1980s-style clothes. American-born Hmong are into clothes and cars."

1.5-Generation Students

During lunch hours, members of the 1.5 generation can be found sitting with other foreign-born Asians at the edge of the cafeteria. The more academically successful 1.5-generation students cluster in one group, and those who are struggling academically sit together in another. Observers are likely to hear 1.5-generation students speaking a combination of Hmong and English. Typical topics of conversations include family and school. Born in Thailand or Laos, most of these students have been in the United States for three to eight years. Those who remember life before the United States stress that things are better here than in their native countries. This dual frame of reference is typical of immigrant children and allows them to persist in the face of difficulties in the new country (Ogbu 1993; Suárez-Orozco 1989; Suárez-Orozco and Suárez-Orozco 1995). In describing the significance of the dual frame of reference, Ogbu (1993) writes:

> The immigrants often compare themselves with the standard of their home country or with their peers "back home" or in the immigrants' neighborhood. When they make such a comparison they usually find plenty of evidence that they have made significant improvements in their lives. (p. 100)

In terms of cultural expression (e.g., dating, language), 1.5-generation students appear to many to be "traditionally Hmong." Mrs. Her described 1.5-generation students as "not Americanized," suggesting a kind of cultural purity. Although most 1.5-generation students live by their parents' rules, the Hmong culture has not remained static. Even as relative newcomers, 1.5-generation students and their families have made cultural adjustments in response to life in the United States. One of the biggest of these adjustments is their increased support for the education of girls and women (Goldstein 1985; Koltyk 1998; Lee 1997). Furthermore, while 1.5-generation students in this study follow their parents' ways out of respect, many assert that that they will raise their own children in "Hmong *and* American ways." Such attitudes suggest a more complex embracing of Hmong culture than is evident at first glance.

Perceptions of education

From their parents, 1.5-generation students have acquired a "folk theory of success" that links education to social mobility (Ogbu 1993), a concept typical among immigrants from many cultures (Gibson 1988; Suárez-Orozco 1989). Many students who participated in this research study diligently because they, like their parents, believe that education is the route to ascending the socioeconomic ladder of American society. Most students dream of going to college or vocational school after graduating from high school. It is not uncommon to find members of the 1.5 generation studying in groups before school and during lunch. Some students seek out other hard-working foreign-born Asians as friends and study companions. Friendly competition over test scores on the latest French or chemistry test helps to further motivate the students. Many 1.5-generation students are well aware that UHS has a reputation for being an excellent school with high academic standards. In comparing UHS to schools in Thailand or Laos, they conclude that the educational opportunities in the United States are far superior and consider themselves to be fortunate to be attending such a school.

May, a sophomore, dreams of becoming a doctor. She firmly believes that as a woman her educational opportunities are greater in the United States than they would have been in Laos. Furthermore, she maintains that UHS is a particularly good school:

> This is a really good school. At this school if you want to be a success you can. There are harder and better classes here than at other schools. I feel lucky to go to school here and I tell my sister that she is lucky she will be coming here.

Family obligations

Like other immigrant children, 1.5-generation Hmong youth report having significant family responsibilities that they must juggle along with their schoolwork (Portes and Rumbaut 1996; Song 1999). Many Hmong students at UHS are responsible for interpreting for their parents, driving their parents to appointments, performing various household chores, and even working to help support the family. Jackson, a senior in high school, misses school occasionally because he has to drive his parents to appointments. Cha, a sophomore, must work at a local supermarket in order to earn money to help support his mother, who is living on disability insurance. Cha explained, "It is my job to take care of my mother…my father is in Laos." Girls, in particular, are often expected to help cook, clean, and take care of younger siblings. May wakes up at 6:15 a.m. and helps her younger siblings get ready for school. She catches the bus at 7:00 a.m. and meets her friends to study in the school cafeteria for an hour before school starts. After a full day of academic classes, she attends an after-school tutoring program for academically talented students from disadvantaged backgrounds until 7:00 p.m. When she gets home, she cooks dinner and then helps her siblings with their homework before doing her own homework. By the time she goes to bed at midnight she is exhausted. Jackson, Cha, May, and others perform this caring work because they feel obliged to their parents and because they believe it is the right thing to do. Despite the fact that the traditional parent–child relationships are reversed within these families, parental authority is preserved.

In describing the conditions necessary to maintain parental authority, Portes and Rumbaut write:

> Parental authority is maintained in those admittedly rare instances where little acculturation takes place in either generation. More commonly, that authority is preserved where sufficient resources exist to guide second-generation acculturation. These resources are of two kinds: first, parental education, allowing the first generation to "keep up" with their children's learning and to monitor its course; second, ethnic bonds, creating incentives for youth to comply with community norms and to combine them with American cultural patterns. (1996:240–241)

Although the parents of 1.5-generation students have little formal education, most 1.5-generation students report that their parents have close ties to the Hmong community that support parental authority. May, for example, reports that the Hmong community monitors her actions and that this prevents her from straying from her parents' ways. May's parents' ability to maintain their authority also derives from their willingness to make certain cultural accommodations. In describing her parents, May says, "They are traditional, but they want me to go to college." May is quick to point out that her parents' support for her education distinguishes them from some Homong parents, who fail to support higher education for their daughters. Because her parents support her dreams for higher education, she perceives them as reasonable. This judgment leads her to follow their rules with little resistance.

Although students rarely complained about their family responsibilities, it is important to note that family obligations can interfere with students' educational pursuits. In her research on Hmong college students, for example, Ngo (2000) discovered that students often had to choose between their education and their family responsibilities. In my study, students explained that family obligations often had to come before homework, which ultimately affected their grades. Cha, for example, explained that after work and household chores, he was often too tired to do his homework. Similarly, early marriage and childbearing can create obstacles for young women. Many immigrant parents now believe that their daughters should wait until after graduating from high school to get married, but there are still some parents who encourage their daughters to marry while in high school. On the subject of early marriage, Dunnigan et al. (1996) recently concluded that "early marriage and childbearing do not appear to serve as an impediment to young Hmong adults' pursuit of education" (p. 206). Unlike these researchers, I am less optimistic about the impact of early marriage on the educational persistence of Hmong girls. Although most parents value education for their daughters, once girls are married, the decision to pursue education is in the hands of their in-laws. Furthermore, even when in-laws support the idea of education it is often difficult for young women to successfully pursue an education when they are responsible for the care of the in-laws' family.

During my research at UHS, I learned about three girls who were pressured into getting married. The experiences of my respondents serve as cautionary tales regarding the impact of early marriage on the pursuit of education. One student explained that although she did not want to get married, she ultimately agreed to the marriage out of feelings of obligation to her parents. Her in-laws and parents have all agreed that she should be allowed to go to college when she graduates from high school, but her increased family obligations often interfere with her studies. This young woman now splits her time between her parents' house, where she continues to help cook and care for her siblings, and her in-laws' house, where she also cooks and cleans. Given the increase in her family responsibilities, she now fears that she will not be able to earn the grades to win a scholarship to go to school, but she has not given up. Such stories serve as a warning to researchers who would too blithely dismiss the impact of early marriage on girls.

Although my data suggests that early marriage may negatively affect girls' education, I would caution schools not to condemn early marriage. Early marriage is a highly political issue and one about which the Hmong community is very sensitive. The fact that many married Hmong girls at UHS choose to hide their married status suggests that they are well aware of the fact that school authorities would condemn their status. By condemning early marriage, schools may inadvertently be asking students to choose between their education and their families.

ESL as a safe space

Although UHS has an excellent reputation among the White, middle-class population of the city, some people of color have criticized the school for overlooking the specific needs of students of color. The ESL program at UHS, however, is led by a team of educators dedicated to serving students who are English-language learners.[4] Most 1.5-generation students are enrolled in the ESL program, which offers courses in ESL, social studies, science, and math. The school offers guided-study courses to help students make the transition from ESL to mainstream classes. In addition to these course offerings, the department employs part-time bilingual resource specialists to assist with tutoring and translations, as well as a special guidance counselor to help students select courses. In ESL classes students are encouraged to draw on their cultural experiences. They are also afforded the freedom to develop their English-language skills without fear of being ridiculed by mainstream students (Olsen 1997). Students who are 1.5 generation reported that they felt more comfortable talking in their ESL classes than in their mainstream classes. In short, the ESL program provides a safe space for its students in a large and often intimidating school. Ms. Heinemann, the chair of the ESL department during the 1998–1999 school year, believes that the mission of the ESL program is to teach students the academic and cultural skills to make the transition to mainstream classes. In her words:

> I think we're teaching language and culture, including the culture of an American high school and how to access that. I'm very concerned about holding kids separate because, for their learning, they need to be in contact with peers. And I think for our society, if we don't have different groups mixing at the high school level, some of those groups will never mix. So, for those two reasons, I've worked really hard to try to create joint courses between departments.

Despite the efforts of the ESL program to integrate ESL students into the mainstream of the school, ESL and former ESL students remain socially segregated from mainstream students. Several 1.5-generation students complained about the social environment of the school, where it is difficult to make "American" friends. Although they are frustrated by this, most of them also emphasize that they are getting superior educational opportunities in the United States. Many 1.5-generation students report having close relationships with their ESL teachers, which further confirms their faith in the American educational system. May, for example, said she even felt comfortable talking to Mrs. Heinemann about "private things."

Contrary to the model minority stereotype, most 1.5-generation students were not high achievers. In fact, achievement among 1.5-generation students ranged from high to low, with the majority passing their classes with average grades. According to some school personnel, a growing minority of ESL students are falling into a pattern of chronic truancy.

Mr. Thao, a bilingual resource specialist, explained that some students begin skipping classes because they cannot keep up with the material. According to Mr. Thao, these students are often overlooked because they are quiet and teachers assume that they are working hard. Unfortunately, these students do not receive the assistance they need in order to survive academically. Thus, the emerging stereotype of the hard-working, quiet model minority works against the students' best interests. Their quiet demeanor serves as a reminder that resistance to schooling is not always expressed through direct confrontation. Other chronic truants, however, have come to the attention of school authorities for engaging in what is characterized as "negative behaviors." Sam, like other 1.5-generation students who are chronically truant, began skipping classes because he could not understand the material. Since becoming a chronic truant he has been suspended for fighting on more than one occasion. According to the tenth-grade principal, the most recent suspension came after Sam hit a White student for calling him a derogatory name. Although the principal was sympathetic to Sam, he could not make exceptions to the rules regarding fighting.[5] For Sam, the suspension served to confirm his suspicions that UHS is a racist institution. Unlike the higher achieving ESL students, Sam cannot console himself with dreams of higher education because his high-school grades are low. For students like Sam, UHS is a social and academic minefield. What is significant about Sam's case is that he only began to skip his classes after he had struggled academically. Skipping classes was a way for him to avoid further embarrassment and frustration caused by his academic difficulties. Students like Sam do not begin skipping classes out of a desire to resist authority or out of a rejection of school. Unfortunately, Sam's truancy exacerbated his academic difficulties and got him into other trouble.

At the other end of the spectrum are the few students who are successful enough to make the honor roll. Interestingly, the students with the highest educational aspirations and the highest levels of achievement (e.g., grade point average) are girls. They are also the most likely to participate in after-school tutorial programs for academically successful students, and to be identified by teachers as exceptionally hard workers. In my previous work on Hmong American college women, I discovered that high achievement among Hmong women was in part a response to cultural norms regarding gender, which have been described as patrilinear and patriarchal (Donnelly 1994; Lynch 1999; Rumbaut and Ima 1988). In describing the role of Hmong women in Laos, Donnelly (1994) wrote, "Ultimately, each woman worked under the command of men of her own household – under her husband if married, under her father and brothers if unmarried, under her son if aged" (p. 32). Gender roles in Laos were also shaped by the agricultural lifestyle. For example, women were encouraged to marry as teens and bear many children, who could then work on the farm (Lynch 1999). Hmong American girls and women perceive the United States as a place where they have the chance to gain gender equality. Hmong American women explained that Hmong men could get respect with or without an education, but education was one of the only ways for women to gain freedom (Lee 1997). May, for example, is a high-achieving sophomore who works hard in school because she wants "a good life where I won't have to work as hard as my mother." May's mother works two jobs, maintains the family's vegetable garden, and takes care of the house.

Second-Generation Students

> For the young, there is no going back. For better or worse, they are Americans. (Faderman 1998:88)

At lunchtime, large groups of second-generation students gather at tables in the cafeteria. All American-born students are welcome, but the students they refer to as "FOBs" (1.5-generation Hmong American students) are not. After eating their lunch, some students run outside for a smoke while others stay inside and talk or study.

Although they proudly assert their American-born status, second-generation youth also express a strong sense of ethnic solidarity. Those who are active in extracurricular clubs choose to participate in the school's Hmong Club. During the 1999–2000 academic year, for instance, the Hmong Club had a difficult time finding an advisor. At one point a teacher suggested that the

Hmong Club merge with the Asian Club, but the students dismissed this idea as being out of the question. The students explained that they wanted their own club. When I asked why they chose to participate in the Hmong Club, the girls responded by saying, "I love the Hmong people" and "I can relate to Hmong people."

In interviews, second-generation students consistently asserted that getting an education is important because it leads to a good job. Despite these professed beliefs regarding the instrumental value of education, their actual responses to education vary. Within the second generation are students who work hard, do well in school, and plan on going to college, and others who are chronically truant and on the brink of failing most of their courses. Like some of the 1.5-generation students who are chronic truants, some second-generation students begin skipping classes because of academic difficulties. For these students, truancy does not reflect a rejection of education but is a response to feelings of inadequacy and embarrassment. One such student, for example, stated that he hated going to class "because it makes me feel stupid." Other second-generation students begin to skip classes because of intergenerational conflicts at home. Still other second-generation students skip classes because they doubt that education will lead to social mobility.

Intergenerational conflicts

Second-generation students routinely complain that their parents are too strict and do not understand life in the United States. According to them, immigrant parents want their American-born children to be "more traditional." However, second-generation youth, born and educated in the United States, inhabit a world apart from their immigrant parents. While many immigrant parents only speak Hmong, most second-generation youth are more fluent in English. Intergenerational conflict between immigrant parents and their American-born teens reflects the tension over how each group imagines the future of Hmong America. Like students of the 1.5 generation, many second-generation students are expected to perform caring work (e.g., interpreting and driving) and household chores. In second-generation families, however, these role reversals often lead to the weakening of parental authority. Portes and Rumbaut (1996) assert that the loss of parental authority is directly related to the fact that the parental generation has not acculturated at the same rate as their children. According to Portes and Rumbaut (1996), this "generational dissonance occurs when second-generation acculturation is neither guided nor accompanied by changes in the first generation. This situation leads directly to role reversal in those instances when first generation parents lack sufficient education or sufficient integration into the ethnic community to cope with the outside environment and hence must depend on their children's guidance" (p. 241). It is important to point out that second-generation students are not rejecting their Hmong backgrounds. Rather, they are trying to redefine what it means to be Hmong in the United States. Intergenerational conflict between immigrant parents and their American-born teenagers reflects the tension over how each group imagines the future of Hmong America.

One of the most common conflicts between parents and adolescents revolves around the issue of dating. Girls, in particular, lament that they are forbidden to spend time alone with boys. Jane, for example, complains that "it is so stupid. Parents think that if you are alone with a guy, you are fooling around." Many girls report that their parents expect their dates to come to the house to visit with the entire family, an idea that most second-generation girls find appalling. Many parents also prefer arranged marriages, while their second-generation daughters dream of marrying someone of their own choice. In an effort to circumvent their parents' rules, many second-generation youth have turned to the Internet as a way to meet members of the opposite sex. Adolescents report that it is becoming very common for young people to meet on the Internet in Hmong chatrooms. Once adolescents have established a relationship over the Internet, they go to considerable effort to arrange clandestine face-to-face meetings (Lee 2001).

Another source of tension between second-generation youth and their parents involves the way teenagers dress. Many Hmong parents consider what their American-born children wear to be a sign of gang membership. Mrs. Her describes the way the adult Hmong community view youth who wear baggy clothes: "The kids start wearing the different clothes. Big clothes, loose clothes, baggy clothes. So they [Hmong adults] will start to call those kids 'gang'." Second-generation youth report that their parents learn about the dangers of Asian gangs from the television and from the larger Hmong community. The local school district has also tried to educate Hmong parents about the dangers of gangs. This attention to gang prevention contributes to the tension between parents and second-generation youth. For example, I attended a school district-sponsored meeting for Southeast Asian parents that focused on gangs. The day after this meeting, several students complained that such meetings stir up trouble by leading parents to believe that gangs are more prevalent than they actually are. Hope, a sophomore in high school, complained:

> They look at us as some bad kids. They call us some "little gang bangers" 'cause [of] the people around us, the way we dress and stuff....People started dressing all baggy and they don't like it. People, like the old folks, they just say that we've forgotten our language a little bit, [and] we have a little bit, but then we still carry our traditions and stuff around.

Hope explains that she would like to learn more about her culture and history, but she finds communication with her parents frustrating. She asserts that she is proud of being Hmong, but she does not agree with all Hmong traditions. She understands that her clothes make her "look like a thug" in her parents' eyes, but she maintains that she and her friends are not in gangs. Because of their clothing, however, Hmong elders and many school authorities assume that she and her friends are involved with gangs. Criticized by adults, many second-generation students like Hope cling more tightly to their peers and turn away from adults.

Hmong immigrant parents view the changing family roles, their children's desire for increased independence, and their children's clothes as evidence that they are losing their second-generation children to "American ways." Research shows that immigrant parents have responded to the situation by trying to further control all aspects of their children's lives. Suárez-Orozco and Suárez-Orozco (1995) discovered that Latino immigrant parents may "over-restrict the activities of the children and attempt to minimize the host country's influence" (p. 65). Similarly, some Hmong parents attempted to control all aspects of their children's lives. Many second-generation Hmong American youth respond to their parents' hyper-control by resisting parental authority. Resistance may come in the form of direct confrontation (e.g., talking back to parents) or in the form of indirect challenges to parental authority (e.g., sneaking around). Toua, a junior at UHS, has had problems with truancy for the past two years. She explains that she skips class because "school is the only time we can hang out with our friends." When she is not in school, Toua and her friends are expected to be at home helping with the chores, but at school she and her friends have figured out that they can control their own time. Thus, truancy is an indirect way to circumvent their parents' control.

Toua and Hope are examples of students who experience significant conflict with their parents. This intergenerational conflict is related to differences in opinion regarding how to respond to life in the United States. In other cases, however, the intergenerational conflict is less severe. Moua, for example, explains that her parents are "traditional, but not real traditional," and they are "strict, but not super strict." Although they do not really approve of the clothes their second-generation children wear, Moua's parents do allow their children to pick their own clothes. They have also allowed their oldest daughter to go away to college in California. Although many Hmong parents now support higher education for their daughters, most expect their daughters to attend colleges near home. The fact that Moua's parents have been willing to make compromises has, paradoxically, helped to limit the intergenerational conflict within the family and helped to maintain parental authority.

"All Americans are rich"

In contrast to the generally hopeful attitude of the 1.5 generation, most second-generation students are somewhat cynical about life in the United States, where ongoing experiences with poverty have contributed to their cynicism about opportunities. Unlike immigrants, second-generation youth do not have a dual frame of reference (Ogbu 1993). All they know is life in the United States and they want to be treated like other Americans. They cannot relate to what their parents say about life in Laos. They are more likely to compare themselves to their White, middle-class peers than to relatives in Thailand or Laos. Based on their observations at UHS and the images from the media, second-generation students have concluded that most Whites are wealthy. Moua, for example, moved to Wisconsin from California with her parents because they heard that there were greater economic opportunities in Wisconsin. Moua imagines that the typical White family is economically well off and supportive. She says:

> When I think of the mainstream I think of a White family I guess. As both parents working...have really good jobs and maybe one kid or two kids, three at the most. And the kids are doing house chores and everything, they, like, have good grades and even when the girl grows up, the woman, the mom has a good job like a doctor or something. And the father supports the girl – she may go to college to be a doctor or major in business or something and the dad totally supports it.

Moua's father works at two jobs and her mother works one full-time job and takes in sewing. During her senior year Moua worked part-time on weekends to save money to attend community college. Students like Moua compare themselves to their White, middle-class peers, which makes them painfully aware that they are poor. For example, when I asked her why she did not participate in class discussions in her philosophy class, Moua said her experiences were "less interesting" than those of "White kids who have traveled all over." Another student, Toua, lives with her mother and two siblings in low-income housing. Her father died unexpectedly a few years ago. Toua bitterly expresses her resentment about being poor. She complained, "I hate being poor. ...All Hmong people are poor and live in shabby houses." Toua and many of her peers have concluded that money is the most important thing in the United States, and they dream of being rich.

Some second-generation students see education as the route out of poverty. Like many immigrant youth, these students cling to a folk theory of success that links education to social mobility. Moua, for example, graduated from UHS with a B average. She plans to earn her associate's degree and then transfer to the local university to earn her bachelor's degree. Moua's parents have encouraged her and her two older siblings to pursue higher education in order to get better jobs. Other second-generation youth, however, have begun to question whether education will lead to social mobility. Like other working-class and poor youth, many second-generation youth do not see how academic subjects will help them get a job (Eckert 1989; Willis 1977). Furthermore, they question whether it makes sense to spend time in high school when they can be earning money at a job. Some chronic truants hold on to the belief that a high-school diploma is important, but they have clearly prioritized their part-time jobs over their schooling. "G," for example, should be a senior in high school, but she has only earned enough credits to be a sophomore. "G" explains that her part-time job is more important than school because she earns money to buy herself clothes and to travel to Hmong soccer tournaments in cities throughout the Midwest.[6] She has dropped out of high school, but she still hopes to earn her high-school equivalency degree.

"They think we are all lazy and on welfare"

Second-generation students complain that non-Hmong people mock their culture and stereotype them as lazy welfare recipients with big families. Tim, a senior in the class of 1999, complained that "a lot of Americans think all Asians eat dogs and cats. We don't. They think Hmong are all on welfare. We aren't." Other students tell stories about being treated like gang members by store clerks, police officers, and others. Second-generation students are unwilling to overlook instances of racism and discrimination. Sia, a graduate of the class of 1999, explains her distrust of White people:

> For me, I feel, I just feel like some White people neglect me. I mean as much as I try to be nice to them, give them respect, they don't give it back to me. Why should I even bother with them? Because I feel like I really don't need people like that....I mean, if you're not Asian like me, you don't understand where I'm coming from either. Like White people, I mean, they may say they do, but I don't see it. They don't really know how it feels.

Sia's distrust for White people extends to White teachers as well. During her senior year in high school Sia was having serious family problems and she almost flunked out of school. When I suggested that she tell her teachers or counselors about her problems, she refused because she did not trust them to treat her problems with respect. Many second-generation Hmong American students at UHS share a similar distrust of teachers. One semester there was a rumor that one of the vice-principals had made racist comments about Hmong students. Although the students were angry about the alleged comment, most were not shocked to hear that a school authority might have made racist comments. Previous experiences inside and outside of school led students to be suspicious of White authority figures.

Most second-generation students were in ESL classes during elementary and middle school, but have been mainstreamed at UHS. Unlike the ESL students who have a somewhat sheltered experience at UHS, students in the mainstream find themselves in an impersonal and highly competitive culture. Mr. Schenk, like other faculty and staff who work closely with students of color, points out that the culture of UHS reflects and favors those same White, middle-class students. Furthermore, they assert that the needs of poorer students and students of color are often sacrificed to protect the interests of White, middle-class students. Mr. Burns, one of the vice-principals, says:

> I think...any time you have...this diverse group, this heterogeneous culture...I think just by default, there's some pecking order to that. And I think that exists here at UHS. I mean...we have a diverse student population....I think there's still...some sort of elemental power relative to those subsets.... There has to be some sort of...system in place, or some sort of order by which...things are [done]...at the school. And I think that exists here at UHS. For example...I think the school is very responsive to... our talented students, the ones who are honor students. It doesn't necessarily mean that the school isn't responsive to the students at the other end of the spectrum. But, you know, the school is set up in a sense to be very responsive to the kids...who are achieving.

What Mr. Burns does not say here is that the majority of "honor students" at UHS are White. His comments do suggest, however, that lower-achieving students and students who are outside of the mainstream experience a kind of benign neglect at UHS.

Despite these conditions, some second-generation students manage to survive and even thrive at UHS. Each semester a few second-generation students earn high enough grades to make the honor roll. Most of these "successful" students had been identified as "good" students by their elementary school teachers, and they had maintained good relationships with their teachers into high school. The majority of the second-generation students, however, become disconnected from school. They complain that they cannot relate to the curriculum or their teachers. As noted earlier, many question whether classes like algebra, chemistry, or Shakespeare can lead to a job. Tim, for example, believes that the vocational high school he attended when his family lived in California was superior to UHS because it offered job skills. He explains:

> My school in California gave a lot of electives and stuff. Back there, they give you vocational classes already and everything. So, you know what part of the field you're going to go into already and get experience and all that. Here is just really academic classes and stuff like that. So I would say I like it there a lot better than here.

Many students also distrust their teachers, assuming that they are racist or at the very least critical of Hmong culture. As mentioned earlier, girls who are married hide their marital status from school authorities. Referring to the impact of isolation of Hmong American students, Mr. Schenk says,

> Every kid that I have talked to, whether they are sort of these hard gang members or whomever, that are Hmong, they feel like this place just doesn't fit them.

> If you listen to the actual words, you know, "the teacher doesn't like me," "I don't have any place to go," "I don't like the principals," "if I am in the hall somebody's..." it is all about whether or not they are invited or included in some way. Those are the words. Whether they are angry or whether they are depressed or sad or whatever, those are still the words and the words have to do with being included or excluded.

Several second-generation students remarked that the content of their classes is simply boring and that they crave a curriculum that reflects their culture and history. They asserted that they would take any class that focused on Hmong culture. Hope, a chronic truant who failed ninth grade, said that she would welcome a class in Hmong culture, history, or language so she could learn about "her people." When she was in elementary school she took Hmong language classes at the community center. She still uses some of that Hmong when she participates in Hmong chatrooms.

Like the low-achieving 1.5-generation students, some second-generation students start skipping class because they're having academic difficulties. These students often hide their problems until it becomes apparent to teachers that their grades are dropping and they are failing exams. By that time, of course, much of the damage is already done. Some low-achieving students have internalized their shame and simply accept that they are "stupid." Jane, for example, is one year behind in school because she failed her sophomore year. When she revealed this to me she said sarcastically that it was "the Hmong way" to be at least one year behind.

Many UHS educators blame students for their own academic problems. Some members of the staff have concluded that Hmong American students simply lack motivation. One guidance counselor came to this conclusion after comparing Southeast Asian students with East Asian students.[7] She says, "An East Asian student might be number three in the class and going to Yale, but the Southeast Asians aren't very motivated." What this counselor fails to recognize and address, however, is the possibility that the school may or may not be doing something to affect underachievement among some Hmong youth. The fact that some Asians are successful proves to her that success is possible for Asians at UHS. The fact that many of the East Asians are from highly educated backgrounds is not factored into the equation of their success – the perception is that their success is just an issue of motivation.

Other UHS educators assume that Hmong students' cultural differences create problems for them. Although cultural issues no doubt play a role, many educators use the cultural explanation to free themselves of responsibility for guiding these students toward achievement at UHS. According to many of these educators, cultural issues are the responsibility of the ESL department. Most second-generation Hmong are not in ESL, but as soon as they have problems they are referred there. It should be noted that this is not an official school policy, but rather an unofficial practice.

Ms. Heinemann, the chair of ESL, complained that the school often abdicates responsibility for culturally different students. She argues that

> the school needs to recognize the population of students who are born and educated here and still don't feel part of the mainstream curriculum, the mainstream school activities....I don't think those students should be counted as ESL students, because that makes them more different, that separates them more. They don't want that.

Ms. Heinemann's comments are echoed in the words of second-generation students themselves, who say that they do not want to be in ESL and that ESL is just for "FOBs." Kim, a senior, complained, "They always put Hmong students in ESL, which is racist. My cousin was put in ESL here and he doesn't even need it. I told him not to let them do that."

As in the 1.5-generation group, there are second-generation students who begin to skip classes in response to academic difficulties. Although second-generation Hmong students speak about the importance of education, some are beginning to question whether education is the most efficient method of achieving social mobility. In short, second-generation students' attitudes regarding education are shaped by their experiences inside and outside of school. Intergenerational relationships, experiences with racism, economic circumstances, relationships with school authorities, and academic achievement all influence their reactions to school.

Conclusions

The Hmong American students at UHS embody a complexity that challenges simplistic representations of Hmong youth as either model minorities or juvenile delinquents. Additionally, descriptions of Hmong students as either traditional or Americanized fail to fully appreciate the extent to which those who are described as traditional have acculturated and those who are described as Americanized have maintained a distinct identity as Hmong Americans. Although Mrs. Her and many Hmong students at UHS characterized Hmong students as falling into two distinct groups – 1.5-generation students, who are traditional (i.e., "good kids"), and second-generation students, who are Americanized (i.e., "bad kids") – my data suggests a more complex picture.

Although 1.5-generation youth are characterized as being traditional, some of them embrace aspects of mainstream American society and many indicate that they will raise their children to follow both Hmong and American ways. On the other hand, while second-generation students appear to be Americanized (e.g., in their clothes and language), most continue to identify strongly as Hmong. There are high-achieving and hard-working students in both the 1.5-generation and second-generation groups, and there are chronic truants in both groups. While intergenerational conflict between second-generation youth and their parents is common, some second-generation youth, like their 1.5-generation counterparts, obey their parents' authority with little resistance. One significant difference between 1.5-generation and second-generation students concerns their respective responses to racism. While both groups complained about the way non-Hmong people treat them, 1.5-generation students were more willing to overlook instances of discrimination and to focus on the positive aspects of life in the United States.

My ethnographic data challenges work that suggests a simplistic one-to-one relationship between the maintenance of traditional culture and high achievement, and Americanization and low achievement and delinquency (Hutchinson 1997; Thao 1999). Arguments regarding the positive impact of traditional culture on achievement underestimate the extent of cultural transformation in the Hmong community. Hmong culture, like all cultures, is fluid and dynamic. What researchers describe as traditional is in fact a culture that has changed and adapted in response to external conditions.

Rather than seeing the maintenance of traditional culture as being at the root of success, my data suggests that it is the practice of "accommodation and acculturation without assimilation" (Gibson, 1988: 24) that supports success. This strategy involves conforming to certain rules of the dominant society (i.e., accommodation) and making certain cultural adaptations while maintaining the group's own cultural identity (pp. 24–25). The experiences of 1.5-generation and second-generation students suggest that their parents' willingness and ability to adopt aspects of the dominant culture are directly related to their ability to maintain aspects of the Hmong culture. May (1.5-generation) and Moua (second-generation), for example, accept their parents' authority because their parents have made certain cultural adjustments. In other words, my data suggests that academic success is the result of both cultural transformation and cultural preservation.

Although Hmong culture certainly plays a role in school achievement, a sole focus on the role of culture in achievement fails to adequately consider the impact of structural forces on students' attitudes toward education. My data supports the previous research that points to the impact of racism and economic opportunities on students' responses to school and their perceptions of life opportunities (Portes 1995; Suárez-Orozco and Suárez-Orozco 1995). Second-generation youth, in particular, had long-term experiences with racism and poverty that challenged their faith in education. These students are not resisting school because they are Americanized, but because they do not perceive school to offer real opportunities.

Additionally, my research highlights the significance of the local school culture in the lives of these students and in their levels of school achievement. Unlike many poor immigrants and second-generation youth, the Hmong American youth in my study attend a relatively well-funded school with a reputation for academic excellence. Despite this reputation and perhaps even because of it, students of color and those from other marginal categories often fall through the cracks and fail to see themselves as part of the larger community of the school. The one major exception to this is the ESL program, which serves as a major source of support for many 1.5-generation students. For second-generation students there is no comparable source of support or inclusion.

To make these students full citizens in the schools that are intended to serve them, a number of things are necessary: educators who understand and respect their culture and the difficulties they face in their homes as they try to straddle the gulf between their culture and the larger American society; a curriculum that reflects their history; and a sense of inclusion in the school community at large. In sum, the school success or failure of 1.5- and second-generation Hmong students does not hinge on any one thing, but rather on a marriage of both external and internal forces.

NOTES

1 The term *1.5 generation* is used to describe foreign-born individuals who arrive in the United States as children and are largely educated and socialized in the United States (see Portes 1996).

2 The names of the school and of individuals quoted are pseudonyms.

3 School staff estimated the number of Hmong students at UHS by searching the school roster for Hmong surnames.

4 It is important to point out that not all teachers in the ESL program were equally dedicated and/or qualified to work with ESL students. For example, two teachers had reputations among the students for being "nice, but too easy." Other ESL teachers criticized these "easy teachers" in hushed tones. Furthermore, some of the very dedicated ESL teachers complained that their efforts to improve the ESL program were often thwarted by school district regulations.

5 According to the school district's conduct and discipline plan, middle- and high-school students charged with hitting another student are subject to suspension.

6 Hmong soccer and volleyball tournaments are popular among 1.5- and second-generation youth. Like the Hmong New Year celebrations, the sports tournaments offer Hmong American youth an opportunity to meet and socialize with other Hmong youth. While most 1.5-generation youth report attending tournaments with their parents, second-generation youth attend with families or peers.

7 At UHS, the Southeast Asian category includes Hmong, Cambodian, Vietnamese, and Laotian students, while the East Asian category includes Chinese and Korean students.

REFERENCES

Brand, D. 1987 (August 31). The new whiz kids. *Time*, pp. 42–51.

Call, K., and McNall, M. 1992. Poverty, ethnicity and youth adjustment: A comparison of poor Hmong and non-Hmong adolescents. In W. Meeus, M. de Goede, W. Kox, and K. Hurrelmann, eds., *Adolescence, Careers, and Cultures* (pp. 373–392). Berlin, NY: Degruyter.

Cohn, M. 1986. Hmong youth and the Hmong future in America. In G. Hendricks, B. Downing, and A. Deinard, eds., *The Hmong in transition* (pp. 197–201). Staten Island, NY: Center for Migration Studies.

Donnelly, N. 1994. *Changing Lives of Refugee Hmong Women*. Seattle: University of Washington Press.

Dunnigan, T., Olney, D., McNall, M., and Spring, M. 1996. Hmong. In D. W. Haines, ed., *Refugees in America in the 1990s: A Reference Handbook* (pp. 191–212). Westport, CT: Greenwood Press.

Eckert, P. 1989. *Jocks and Burnouts: Social Categories and Identity in the Highschool*. New York: Teachers College Press.

Faderman, L. 1998. *"I begin my life all over": The Hmong and the American Experience*. Boston: Beacon Press.

Fass, S. 1991. *The Hmong in Wisconsin: On the Road to Self-Sufficiency*. Milwaukee: Wisconsin Policy Research Institute.

Gibson, M. 1988. *Accommodation without Assimilation: Sikh Immigrants in an American High School*. Ithaca, NY: Cornell University Press.

Goldstein, B. 1985. Schooling for Cultural Transitions: Hmong Girls and Boys in American High Schools.

Unpublished doctoral dissertation, University of Wisconsin, Madison.

Hutchinson, R. 1997. *The Educational Performance of Hmong Students in Wisconsin*. Thiensville: Wisconsin Policy Research Institute.

Hutchinson, R., and McNall, M. 1994. Early marriage in a Hmong cohort. *Journal of Marriage and Family* 56:579–590.

Ima, K. 1995. Testing the American dream: Case studies of Southeast Asian refugee students in secondary schools. In R. Rumbaut and W. Cornelius, eds., *California's Immigrant Children: Theory, Research, and Implications for Educational Policy* (pp. 191–208). San Diego: Center for U.S.-Mexican Studies.

Ingersoll, B. 1999 (November 19). Cultural growing pains. *Wisconsin State Journal*, pp. 1A, 3A.

Kifner, J. 1991 (January 6). Immigrant waves from Asia bring an underworld ashore. *New York Times*, p. 11A.

Koltyk, J. 1998. *New Pioneers in the Heartland: Hmong Life in Wisconsin*. Boston: Allyn & Bacon.

Lee, S. 1997. The road to college: Hmong American women's pursuit of higher education. *Harvard Educational Review* 67:803–831.

Lee, S. J. 2001. Transforming and exploring the landscape of gender and sexuality: Hmong American teenaged girls. *Race, Gender and Class* 8(2):35–46.

Lynch, A. 1999. *Dress, Gender, and Cultural Change: Asian American and African American Rites of Passage*. New York: Berg.

Ngo, B. 2000. Obstacles, Miracles, and the Pursuit of Higher Education: The Experiences of Hmong American College Students. Unpublished master's thesis, University of Wisconsin, Madison.

Ogbu, J. U. 1993. Variability in minority school performance: A problem in search of an explanation. In E. Jacob and C. Jordan, eds., *Minority Education: Anthropological Perspectives* (pp. 83–107). Norwood, NJ: Ablex.

Olsen, L. 1997. *Made in America: Immigrant Students in our Public Schools*. New York: New Press.

Portes, A. 1995. Segmented assimilation among new immigrant youth: A conceptual framework. In R. Rumbaut and W. Cornelius, eds., *California's Immigrant Children: Theory, Research, and Implications for Educational Policy* (pp. 71–76). San Diego: Center for U.S.-Mexican Studies.

Portes, A. 1996. *The New Second Generation*. New York: Russell Sage Foundation.

Portes, A., and Rumbaut, R. 1996. *Immigrant America: A Portrait* (2nd edn.) Berkeley: University of California Press.

Rumbaut, R. 1995. The new Californians: Comparative research findings on the educational progress of immigrant children. In R. Rumbaut and W. Cornelius, eds., *California's Immigrant Children: Theory, Research and Implications for Educational Policy* (pp. 17–69). San Diego: Center for U.S.-Mexican Studies.

Rumbaut, R., and Ima, K. 1988. *The Adaptation of Southeast Asian Refugee Youth: A Comparative Study*. Washington, DC: U.S. Office of Refugee Resettlement.

Sherman, S. 1988. The Hmong: Laotian refugees in the land of the giants. *National Geographic* 174:586–610.

Song, M. 1999. *Helping Out: Children's Labor in Ethnic Businesses*. Philadelphia: Temple University Press.

Suárez-Orozco, M. 1989. *Central American Refugees and U.S. High Schools: A Psychosocial Study of Motivation and Achievement*. Stanford, CA: Stanford University Press.

Suárez-Orozco, M., and Suárez-Orozco, C. 1995. The cultural patterning of achievement motivation: A comparison of Mexican, Mexican immigrant, Mexican American, and non-Latino White American students. In R. Rumbaut and W. Cornelius, eds., *California's Immigrant Children: Theory, Research, and Implications for Educational Policy* (pp. 161–190). San Diego: Center for U.S.-Mexican Studies.

Thao, P. 1999. *Hmong Education at the Crossroads*. New York: University Press of America.

Walker-Moffat, W. 1995. *The Other Side of the Asian American Success Story*. San Francisco: Jossey-Bass.

Willis, P. E. 1977 *Learning to Labor: How Working Class Kids Get Working Class Jobs*. New York: Columbia University Press.

Zhou, M., and Bankston, C. L. 1998. *Growing up American: How Vietnamese Children Adapt to Life in the United States*. New York: Russell Sage Foundation.

10

"We Don't Sleep Around Like White Girls Do": Family, Culture, and Gender in Filipina American Lives

Yen Le Espiritu

> I want my daughters to be Filipino especially on sex. I always emphasize to them that they should not participate in sex if they are not married. We are also Catholic. We are raised so that we don't engage in going out with men while we are not married. And I don't like it to happen to my daughters as if they have no values. I don't like them to grow up that way, like the American girls.
>
> Filipina immigrant mother

> I found that a lot of the Asian American friends of mine, we don't date like white girls date. We don't sleep around like white girls do. Everyone is really mellow at dating because your parents were constraining and restrictive.
>
> Second-generation Filipina daughter

Focusing on the relationship between Filipino immigrant parents and their daughters, this article argues that gender is a key to immigrant identity and a vehicle for racialized immigrants to assert cultural superiority over the dominant group. In immigrant communities, culture takes on a special significance: not only does it form a lifeline to the home country and a basis for group identity in a new country, it is also a base from which immigrants stake their political and sociocultural claims on their new country (Eastmond 1993:40). For Filipino immigrants, who come from a homeland that was once a U.S. colony, cultural reconstruction has been especially critical in the assertion of their presence in the United States – a way to counter the cultural Americanization of the Philippines, to resist the assimilative and alienating demands of U.S. society, and to reaffirm to themselves their self-worth in the face of colonial, racial, class, and gendered subordination. Before World War II, Filipinos were barred from becoming U.S. citizens, owning property, and marrying whites. They also encountered discriminatory housing policies, unfair labor practices, violent physical encounters, and racist as well as anti-immigrant discourse.[1] While blatant legal discrimination against Filipino Americans is largely a matter of the past, Filipinos continue to encounter many barriers that prevent full participation in the economic, social, and political institutions of the United States (Azores-Gunter 1986–87; Cabezas, Shinagawa, and Kawaguchi 1986–87; Okamura and Agbayani 1997). Moreover, the economic mobility and cultural assimilation that enables white ethnics to become "unhyphenated whites" is seldom extended to Filipino Americans (Espiritu 1994). Like other Asians, the Filipino is "always seen as an immigrant, as the 'foreigner-within,' even when born in the United States" (Lowe 1996:5). Finally, although Filipinos have been in the United States since the middle of the 1700s and Americans have been in the Philippines since at least the late 1800s, U.S. Filipinos – as racialized nationals, immigrants, and citizens – are "still practically an invisible and silent minority" (San Juan 1991:117). Drawing from my research on Filipino American families in San Diego, California, I explore in this article the ways racialized immigrants claim through gender the power denied them by racism.

My epigraphs, quotations of a Filipina immigrant mother and a second-generation Filipina daughter, suggest that the virtuous Filipina daughter is partially constructed on the conceptualization of white women as sexually immoral. This juxtaposition underscores the fact that femininity is a relational category, one that is co-constructed with other racial and cultural categories. These narratives also reveal that women's sexuality and their enforced "morality" are fundamental to the structuring of social inequalities. Historically, the sexuality of racialized women has been systematically demonized and disparaged by dominant or oppressor groups to justify and bolster nationalist movements, colonialism, and/or racism. But as these narratives indicate, racialized groups also criticize the morality of white women as a strategy of resistance – a means of asserting a morally superior public face to the dominant society.

By exploring how Filipino immigrants characterize white families and white women, I hope to contribute to a neglected area of research: how the "margins" imagine and construct the "mainstream" in order to assert superiority over it. But this strategy is not without costs. The elevation of Filipina chastity (particularly that of young women) has the effect of reinforcing masculinist and patriarchal power in the name of a greater ideal of national/ethnic self-respect. Because the control of women is one of the principal means of asserting moral superiority, young women in immigrant families face numerous restrictions on their autonomy, mobility, and personal decision-making. Although this article addresses the experiences and attitudes of both parents and children, here I am more concerned with understanding the actions of immigrant parents than with the reactions of their second-generation daughters.

Studying Filipinos in San Diego

San Diego, California has long been a favored area of settlement for Filipinos and is today the third-largest U.S. destination for Filipino immigrants (Rumbaut 1991:220).[2] As the site of the largest U.S. naval base and the Navy's primary West Coast training facility, San Diego has been a primary area of settlement for Filipino navy personnel and their families since the early 1900s. As in other Filipino communities along the Pacific Coast, the San Diego community grew dramatically in the 25 years following passage of the 1965 Immigration Act. New immigration contributed greatly to the tripling of San Diego county's Filipino American population from 1970 to 1980 and its doubling from 1980 to 1990. In 1990, nearly 96,000 Filipinos resided in the county. Although they made up only 4 percent of the county's general population, they constituted close to 50 percent of the Asian American population (Espiritu 1995). Many post-1965 Filipino immigrants have come to San Diego as professionals – most conspicuously as health-care workers. A 1992 analysis of the socioeconomic characteristics of recent Filipino immigrants in San Diego indicated that they were predominantly middle-class, college-educated, and English-speaking professionals who were more likely to own than rent their homes (Rumbaut 1994). At the same time, about two-thirds of the Filipinos surveyed indicated that they had experienced racial and ethnic discrimination (Espiritu and Wolf 2001).

The information on which this article is based comes mostly from in-depth interviews that I conducted with almost one hundred Filipinos in San Diego.[3] Using the "snowball" sampling technique, I started by interviewing Filipino Americans whom I knew and then asking them to refer me to others who might be willing to be interviewed. In other words, I chose participants not randomly but rather through a network of Filipino American contacts whom the first group of respondents trusted. To capture the diversity within the Filipino American community, I sought and selected respondents of different backgrounds and with diverse viewpoints. The sample is about equally divided between first-generation immigrants (those who came to the United States as adults) and Filipinas/os who were born and/or raised in the United States. It is more difficult to pinpoint the class status of the people I interviewed. To be sure, they included poor working-class immigrants who barely eked out a living, as well as educated professionals who thrived in middle- and upper-class suburban neighborhoods. However, the class status of most was much more ambiguous. I met Filipinos/as who toiled as assembly workers but who, through the pooling of income and finances, owned homes in middle-class communities. I also discovered that class status was transnational, determined as much by one's economic position in the Philippines as by that in the United States. For example, I encountered individuals who struggled economically in the United States but owned sizable properties in the Philippines. And I interviewed immigrants who continued to view themselves as "upper-class" even while living in dire conditions in the United States. These examples suggest that the upper/middle/working-class typology, while useful, does not capture the complexity of immigrant lives. Reflecting the prominence of the U.S. Navy in San Diego, more than half of my respondents were affiliated with or had relatives affiliated with the U.S. Navy.

My tape-recorded interviews, conducted in English, ranged from three to ten hours each and took place in offices, coffee shops, and homes. My questions were open-ended and covered three general areas: family and immigration history, ethnic identity and practices, and community development among San Diego's Filipinos. The interviewing process varied widely: some respondents needed to be prompted with specific questions, while others spoke at great length on their own. Some chose to cover the span of their lives; others focused on specific events that were particularly important to them. The initial impetus for this article on the relationship between immigrant parents and their daughters came from my observation that the dynamics of gender emerged more clearly in the interviews with women than in those with men. Because gender has been a marked category for women, the mothers and daughters I interviewed rarely told their life stories without reference to the dynamics of gender (see Personal Narratives Group 1989:4–5). Even without prompting, young Filipinas almost always recounted stories of restrictive gender roles and gender expectations, particularly of parental control over their whereabouts and sexuality.

I believe that my own personal and social characteristics influenced the actual process of data collection, the quality of the materials that I gathered, and my analysis of them. As a Vietnam-born woman who immigrated to the United States at the age of 12, I came to the research project not as an "objective" outsider but as a fellow Asian immigrant who shared some of the life experiences of my respondents. During the fieldwork process, I did not remain detached but actively shared with my informants my own experiences of being an Asian immigrant woman: of being perceived as an outsider in U.S. society, of speaking English as a second language, of being a woman of color in a racialized patriarchal society, and of negotiating intergenerational tensions within my own family. I do not claim that these shared struggles grant me "insider status" into the Filipino American community; the differences in our histories, cultures, languages, and, at times, class backgrounds, remain important. But I do claim that these shared experiences enable me to bring to the work a comparative perspective that is implicit, intuitive, and informed by my own identities and positionalities – and with it a commitment to approach these subjects with both sensitivity and rigor. In a cogent call for scholars of color to expand on the premise of studying "our own" by studying other "others," Ruby Tapia argues that such implicitly comparative projects are important because they permit us to "highlight the different and *differentiating* functional forces of racialization" (1997:2). It is with this deep interest in discovering – and forging – commonalities out of our specific and disparate experiences that I began this study on Filipino Americans in San Diego.

"American" and Whiteness: "To me, American means white"

In U.S. racial discourse and practices, unless otherwise specified, "Americans" means "whites" (Lipsitz 1998:1). In the case of Asian Americans, U.S. exclusion acts, naturalization laws, and national culture have simultaneously marked Asians as the inassimilable aliens and whites as the quintessential Americans (Lowe 1996). Excluded from the collective memory of who constitutes a "real" American, Asians in the United States, even as citizens, remain "foreigners-within" – "non-Americans." In a study of third-and later-generation Chinese and Japanese Americans, Mia

Tuan (1998) concludes that, despite being long-time Americans, Asians – as racialized ethnics – are often assumed to be foreign unless proven otherwise. In the case of Filipinos who emigrated from a former U.S. colony, their formation as racialized minorities does not begin in the United States but rather in a "homeland" already affected by U.S. economic, social, and cultural influences (Lowe 1996:8).

Cognizant of this racialized history, my Filipino respondents seldom identify themselves as American. As will be evident in the discussion below, they equate "American" with "white" and often use these two terms interchangeably. For example, a Filipina who is married to a white American refers to her husband as "American" but to her African American and Filipino American brothers-in-law as "black" and "Filipino," respectively. Others speak about "American ways," "American culture," or "American lifestyle" when they really mean *white* American ways, culture, and lifestyle. A Filipino man who has lived in the United States for 30 years explains why he still does not identify himself as American: "I don't see myself just as an American because I cannot hide the fact that my skin is brown. To me, American means white." A second-generation Filipina recounted the following story when asked whether she defined herself as American:

> I went to an all-white school. I knew I was different. I wasn't American. See, you are not taught that you're American because you are not white. When I was in the tenth grade, our English teacher asked us what our nationality was, and she goes how many of you are Mexican, how many of you are Filipino, and how many of you are Samoan and things like that. And when she asked how many of you are American, just the white people raised their hands.

Other Asian Americans also conflate *American* and *white*. In an ethnographic study of Asian American high-school students, Stacey Lee reports that Korean immigrant parents often instructed their children to socialize only with Koreans and "Americans." When asked to define the term *American,* the Korean students responded in unison with "White! Korean parents like white" (Lee 1996:24). Tuan (1998) found the same practice among later-generation Chinese and Japanese Americans: the majority use the term *American* to refer to whites.

Constructing the Dominant Group: The Moral Flaws of White Americans

Given the centrality of moral themes in popular discussions on racial differences, Michele Lamont (1997) has suggested that morality is a crucial site to study the cultural mechanisms of reproduction of racial inequality. While much has been written on how whites have represented the (im)morality of people of color (Collins 1991; Marchetti 1993; Hamamoto 1994), there has been less critical attention to how people of color have represented whites.[4] Shifting attention from the otherness of the subordinate group (as dictated by the "mainstream") to the otherness of the dominant group (as constructed by the "margins"), this section focuses on the alternative frames of meaning that racially subordinate groups mobilize to (re)define their status in relation to the dominant group. I argue that female morality – defined as women's dedication to their families and sexual restraint – is one of the few sites where economically and politically dominated groups can construct the dominant group as other and themselves as superior. Because womanhood is idealized as the repository of tradition, the norms that regulate women's behaviors become a means of determining and defining group status and boundaries. As a consequence, the burdens and complexities of cultural representation fall most heavily on immigrant women and their daughters. Below, I show that Filipino immigrants claim moral distinctiveness for their community by re-presenting "Americans" as morally flawed, themselves as family-oriented model minorities, and their wives and daughters as paragons of morality.

Family-oriented model minorities: "White women will leave you"

In his work on Italian immigrant parents and children in the 1930s, Robert Anthony Orsi (1985) reports that the parents invented a virtuous Italy (based on memories of their childhood) that they then used to castigate the morality of the

United States and their U.S.-born or -raised children. In a similar way, many of my respondents constructed their "ethnic" culture as principled and "American" culture as deviant. Most often, this morality narrative revolves around family life and family relations. When asked what set Filipinos apart from other Americans, my respondents – of all ages and class backgrounds – repeatedly contrasted close-knit Filipino families to what they perceived to be the more impersonal quality of U.S. family relations.[5] In the following narratives, "Americans" are characterized as lacking in strong family ties and collective identity, less willing to do the work of family and cultural maintenance, and less willing to abide by patriarchal norms in husband/wife relations:

> American society lacks caring. The American way of life is more individual rather than collective. The American way is to say I want to have my own way. (Filipina immigrant, 54 years old)

> Our [Filipino] culture is different. We are more close-knit. We tend to help one another. Americans, ya know, they are all right, but they don't help each other that much. As a matter of fact, if the parents are old, they take them to a convalescent home and let them rot there. We would never do that in our culture. We would nurse them; we would help them until the very end. (Filipino immigrant, 60 years old)

> Our [Filipino] culture is very communal. You know that your family will always be there, that you don't have to work when you turn 18, you don't have to pay rent when you are 18, which is the American way of thinking. You also know that if things don't work out in the outside world, you can always come home and mommy and daddy will always take you and your children in. (Second-generation Filipina, 33 years old)

> Asian parents take care of their children. Americans have a different attitude. They leave their children to their own resources. They get baby sitters to take care of their children or leave them in day care. That's why when they get old, their children don't even care about them. (Filipina immigrant, 46 years old)

Implicit in negative depictions of U.S. families as uncaring, selfish, and distant is the allegation that white women are not as dedicated to their families as Filipina women are to theirs. Several Filipino men who married white women recalled being warned by their parents and relatives that "white women will leave you." As one man related, "My mother said to me, 'Well, you know, don't marry a white person because they would take everything that you own and leave you.' " For some Filipino men, perceived differences in attitudes about women's roles between Filipina and non-Filipina women influenced their marital choice. A Filipino American navy man explained why he went back to the Philippines to look for a wife:

> My goal was to marry a Filipina. I requested to be stationed in the Philippines to get married to a Filipina. I'd seen the women here and basically they are spoiled. They have a tendency of not going along together with their husband. They behave differently. They chase the male, instead of the male, the normal way of the traditional way is for the male to go after the female. They have sex without marrying. They want to do their own things. So my idea was to go back home and marry somebody who has never been here. I tell my son the same thing: if he does what I did and finds himself a good lady there, he will be in good hands.

Another man who had dated mostly white women in high school recounted that when it came time for him to marry, he "looked for the kind of women" he met while stationed in the Philippines: "I hate to sound chauvinistic about marriages, but Filipinas have a way of making you feel like you are a king. They also have that tenderness, that elegance. And we share the same values about family, education, religion, and raising children."

The claims of family closeness are not unique to Filipino immigrants. For example, when asked what makes their group distinctive, Italian Americans (di Leonardo 1984), Vietnamese Americans (Kibria 1993), South Asian Americans (Hickey 1996), and African Americans (Lamont 1997) all point proudly to the close-knit character of their family life. Although it is difficult to know whether these claims are actual perceptions or favored self-legitimating answers, it is nevertheless important to note the gender implications of these claims. That is, while both men and women identify the family system as a tremendous source of cultural pride, it is women – through their unpaid housework and kin work – who shoulder the primary responsibility for maintaining family closeness. As the organizers of family rituals, transmitters of homeland folklores, and socializers of young children, women have been crucial for the maintenance of family ties and cultural traditions. In a study of kinship, class, and gender among California Italian Americans, di Leonardo argues that women's kin work, "the work of knitting households together into 'close, extended families,'" maintains the family networks that give ethnicity meaning (1984:229).

Because the moral status of the community rests on women's labor, women, as wives and daughters, are expected to dedicate themselves to the family. Writing on the constructed image of ethnic family and gender, di Leonardo argues that "a large part of stressing ethnic identity amounts to burdening women with increased responsibilities for preparing special foods, planning rituals, and enforcing 'ethnic' socialization of children" (1984:222). A 23-year-old Filipina spoke about the reproductive work that her mother performed and expected her to learn:

> In my family, I was the only girl, so my mom expected a lot from me. She wanted me to help her to take care of the household. I felt like there was a lot of pressure on me. It's very important to my mom to have the house in order: to wash the dishes, to keep the kitchen in order, vacuuming, and dusting and things like that. She wants me to be a perfect housewife. It's difficult. I have been married now for about four months and my mother asks me every now and then what have I cooked for my husband. My mom is also very strict about families getting together on holidays, and I would always help her to organize that. Each holiday, I would try to decorate the house for her, to make it more special.

The burden of unpaid reproductive and kin work is particularly stressful for women who work outside the home. In the following narrative, a Filipina wife and mother described the pulls of family and work that she experienced when she went back to school to pursue a doctoral degree in nursing:

> The Filipinos, we are very collective, very connected. Going through the doctoral program, sometimes I think it is better just to forget about my relatives and just concentrate on school. All that connectedness, it steals parts of myself because all of my energies are devoted to my family. And that is the reason why I think Americans are successful. The majority of the American people they can do what they want. They don't feel guilty because they only have a few people to relate to. For us Filipinos, it's like roots under the tree, you have all these connections. The Americans are more like the trunk. I am still trying to go up to the trunk of the tree but it is too hard. I want to be more independent, more like the Americans. I want to be good to my family but what about me? And all the things that I am doing. It's hard. It's always a struggle.

It is important to note that this Filipina interprets her exclusion and added responsibilities as only racial when they are also gendered. For example, when she says, "the American people they can do what they want," she ignores the differences in the lives of white men and white women – the fact that most white women experience similar competing pulls of family, education, and work.

Racialized sexuality and (im)morality: "In America...sex is nothing"

Sexuality, as a core aspect of social identity, is fundamental to the structuring of gender inequality (Millett 1970). Sexuality is also a salient marker of otherness and has figured prominently in racist and imperialist ideologies (Gilman 1985; Stoler 1991). Historically, the sexuality of subordinate groups – particularly that of racialized women – has been systematically stereotyped by the dominant groups.[6] At stake in these stereotypes is the construction of women of color as morally lacking in the areas of sexual restraint and traditional morality. Asian women – both in Asia and in the United States – have been racialized as sexually immoral, and the "Orient" – and its women – has long served as a site of European male power fantasies, replete with lurid images of sexual license, gynecological aberrations, and general perversion (Gilman 1985:89). In colonial Asia in the nineteenth and early twentieth centuries, for example, female sexuality was a site for colonial rulers to assert their moral superiority and thus their supposed natural and legitimate right to rule. The colonial rhetoric of moral superiority was based on the construction of colonized Asian women as subjects of sexual desire and fulfillment and European colonial women as the paragons of virtue and the bearers of a redefined colonial morality (Stoler 1991). The discourse of morality has also been used to mark the "unassimilability" of Asians in the United States. At the turn of the twentieth century, the public perception of Chinese women as disease-ridden, drug-addicted prostitutes served to underline the depravity of "Orientals" and played a decisive role in the eventual passage of exclusion laws against all Asians (Mazumdar 1989:3–4). The stereotypical view that all Asian women were prostitutes, first formed in the 1850s, persisted. Contemporary American popular culture continues to endow Asian women with an excess of "womanhood," sexualizing them but also impugning their sexuality (Espiritu 1997:93).

Filipinas – both in the Philippines and in the United States – have been marked as desirable but dangerous "prostitutes" and/or submissive "mail-order brides" (Halualani 1995; Egan 1996). These stereotypes emerged out of the colonial process, especially the extensive U.S. military presence in the Philippines. Until the early 1990s, the Philippines, at times unwillingly, housed some of the United State's largest overseas airforce and naval bases (Espiritu 1995:14). Many Filipino nationalists have charged that "the prostitution problem" in the Philippines stemmed from U.S. and Philippine government policies that promoted a sex industry – brothels, bars, and massage parlors – for servicemen stationed or on leave in the Philippines. During the Vietnam War, the Philippines was known as the "rest and recreation" center of Asia, hosting approximately ten thousand U.S. servicemen daily (Coronel and Rosca 1993; Warren 1993). In this context, *all* Filipinas were racialized as sexual commodities, usable and expendable. A U.S.-born Filipina recounted the sexual harassment she faced while visiting Subic Bay Naval Station in Olongapo City:

> One day, I went to the base dispensary.…I was dressed nicely, and as I walked by the fire station, I heard catcalls and snide remarks being made by some of the firemen.…I was fuming inside. The next thing I heard was, "How much do you charge?" I kept on walking. "Hey, are you deaf or something? How much do you charge? You have a good body." That was an incident that I will never forget. (Quoted in Espiritu 1995:77)

The sexualized racialization of Filipina women is also captured in Marianne Villanueva's short story "Opportunity" (1991). As the protagonist, a "mail-order bride" from the Philippines, enters a hotel lobby to meet her American fiancé, the bellboys snicker and whisper *puta* (whore): a reminder that U.S. economic and cultural colonization in the Philippines always forms a backdrop to any relations between Filipinos and Americans (Wong 1993:53).

Cognizant of the pervasive hypersexualization of Filipina women, my respondents, especially women who grew up near military bases, were quick to denounce prostitution, to condemn sex laborers, and to declare (unasked) that they themselves did not frequent "that part of town." As one Filipina immigrant said,

> Growing up [in the Philippines], I could never date an American because my dad's concept of a friendship with an American is with a G.I. The only reason why my dad wouldn't let us date an American is that people will think that the only way you met was because of the base. I have never seen the inside of any of the bases because we were just forbidden to go there.

Many of my respondents also distanced themselves culturally from the Filipinas who serviced U.S. soldiers by branding them "more Americanized" and "more Westernized." In other words, these women were sexually promiscuous because they had assumed the sexual mores of white women. This characterization allows my respondents to symbolically disown the Filipina "bad girl" and, in so doing, to uphold the narrative of Filipina sexual virtuosity and white female sexual promiscuity. In the following narrative, a mother who came to the United States in her thirties contrasted the controlled sexuality of women in the Philippines with the perceived promiscuity of white women in the United States:

> In the Philippines, we always have chaperons when we go out. When we go to dances, we have our uncle, our grandfather, and auntie all behind us to make sure that we behave in the dance hall. Nobody goes necking outside. You don't even let a man put his hand on your shoulders. When you were brought up in a conservative country, it is hard to come here and see that it is all freedom of speech and freedom of action. Sex was never mentioned in our generation.

> I was 30 already when I learned about sex. But to the young generation in America, sex is nothing.

Similarly, another immigrant woman criticized the way young American women are raised: "Americans are so liberated. They allow their children, their girls, to go out even when they are still so young." In contrast, she stated that, in "the Filipino way, it is very important, the value of the woman, that she is a virgin when she gets married."

The ideal "Filipina," then, is partially constructed on the community's conceptualization of white women. She is everything that they are not: she is sexually modest and dedicated to her family; they are sexually promiscuous and uncaring. Within the context of the dominant culture's pervasive hypersexualization of Filipinas, the construction of the "ideal" Filipina – as family-oriented and chaste – can be read as an effort to reclaim the morality of the community. This effort erases the Filipina "bad girl," ignores competing sexual practices in the Filipino communities, and uncritically embraces the myth of "Oriental femininity." Cast as the embodiment of perfect womanhood and exotic femininity, Filipinas (and other Asian women) in recent years have been idealized in U.S. popular culture as more truly "feminine" (i.e., devoted, dependent, domestic) and therefore more desirable than their more modern, emancipated sisters (Espiritu 1997:113). Capitalizing on this image of the "superfemme," mail-order bride agencies market Filipina women as "'exotic, subservient wife imports' for sale and as alternatives for men sick of independent 'liberal' Western women" (Halualani 1995:49; see also Ordonez 1997:122).

Embodying the moral integrity of the idealized ethnic community, immigrant women, particularly young daughters, are expected to comply with male-defined criteria of what constitute "ideal" feminine virtues. While the sexual behavior of adult women is confined to a monogamous, heterosexual context, that of young women is denied completely (see Dasgupta and DasGupta 1996:229–231). In the next section, I detail the ways Filipino immigrant parents, under the rubric of "cultural preservation," police their daughters' behaviors in order to safeguard their sexual innocence and virginity. These attempts at policing generate hierarchies and tensions within immigrant families – between parents and children and between brothers and sisters.

The Construction(s) of the "Ideal" Filipina: "Boys are boys and girls are different"

As the designated "keepers of the culture" (Billson 1995), immigrant women and their behavior come under intensive scrutiny both from men and women of their own groups and from U.S.-born Americans (Gabbacia 1994:xi). In a study of the Italian Harlem community from 1880 to 1950, Orsi reports that "all the community's fears for the reputation and integrity of the domus came to focus on the behavior of young women" (1985:135). Because women's moral and sexual loyalties were deemed central to the maintenance of group status, changes in female behavior, especially that of growing daughters, were interpreted as signs of moral decay and ethnic suicide and were carefully monitored and sanctioned (Gabbacia 1994:113).

Although details vary, young women of various groups and across space and time – for example, second-generation Chinese women in San Francisco in the 1920s (Yung 1995), U.S.-born Italian women in East Harlem in the 1930s (Orsi 1985), young Mexican women in the Southwest during the interwar years (Ruiz 1992), and daughters of Caribbean and Asian Indian immigrants on the East Coast in the 1990s (Dasgupta and DasGupta 1996; Waters 1996) – have identified strict parental control on their activities and movements as the primary source of intergenerational conflict. Recent studies of immigrant families also identify gender as a significant determinant of parent–child conflict, with daughters more likely than sons to be involved in such conflicts and instances of parental derogation (Rumbaut and Ima 1988; Woldemikael 1989; Matute-Bianchi 1991; Gibson 1995).

Although immigrant families have always been preoccupied with passing on their native culture, language, and traditions to both male and female children, it is daughters who have the primary burden of protecting and preserving the family.

Because sons do not have to conform to the image of an "ideal" ethnic subject as daughters do, they often receive special day-to-day privileges denied to daughters (Haddad and Smith 1996:22–24; Waters 1996:75–76). This is not to say that immigrant parents do not place undue expectations on their sons; rather, these expectations do not pivot around the sons' sexuality or dating choices.[7] In contrast, parental control over the movement and action of daughters begins the moment they are perceived as young adults and sexually vulnerable. It regularly consists of monitoring their whereabouts and forbidding dating (Wolf 1997). For example, the immigrant parents I interviewed seldom allowed their daughters to date, to stay out late, to spend the night at a friend's house, or to take an out-of-town trip.

Many of the second-generation women I spoke to complained bitterly about these parental restrictions. They particularly resented what they saw as gender inequity in their families: the fact that their parents placed far more restrictions on their activities and movements than on their brothers'. Some decried the fact that even their younger brothers had more freedom than they did. "It was really hard growing up because my parents would let my younger brothers do what they wanted but I didn't get to do what I wanted even though I was the oldest. I had a curfew and my brothers didn't. I had to ask if I could go places and they didn't. My parents never even asked my brothers when they were coming home." As indicated in the following excerpt, many Filipino males are cognizant of this double standard in their families:

> My sister would always say to me, "It's not fair, just because you are a guy, you can go wherever you want." I think my parents do treat me and my sister differently. Like in high school, maybe 10:30 at night, which is pretty late on a school night, and I say I have to go pick up some notes at my friend's house, my parents wouldn't say anything. But if my sister were to do that, there would be no way. Even now when my sister is in college already, if she wants to leave at midnight to go to a friend's house, they would tell her that she shouldn't do it.

When questioned about this double standard, parents generally responded by explaining that "girls are different":

> I have that Filipino mentality that boys are boys and girls are different. Girls are supposed to be protected, to be clean. In the early years, my daughters have to have chaperons and curfews. And they know that they have to be virgins until they get married. The girls always say that is not fair. What is the difference between their brothers and them? And my answer always is, "In the Philippines, you know, we don't do that. The girls stay home. The boys go out." It was the way that I was raised. I still want to have part of that culture instilled in my children. And I want them to have that to pass on to their children.

Even among self-described Western-educated and "tolerant" parents, many continue to ascribe to "the Filipino way" when it comes to raising daughters. As one college-educated father explains,

> Because of my Western education, I don't raise my children the way my parents raised me. I tended to be a little more tolerant. But at times, especially in certain issues like dating, I find myself more towards the Filipino way in the sense that I have only one daughter so I tended to be a little bit stricter. So the double standard kind of operates: it's alright for the boys to explore the field but I tended to be overly protective of my daughter. My wife feels the same way because the boys will not lose anything, but the daughter will lose something, her virginity, and it can be also a question of losing face, that kind of thing.

Although many parents discourage or forbid dating for daughters, they still fully expect these young women to fulfill their traditional roles as women: to marry and have children. A young Filipina recounted the mixed messages she received from her parents:

> This is the way it is supposed to work: Okay, you go to school. You go to college. You graduate. You find a job. *Then* you find your husband, and you have children. That's the whole time line. *But* my question is, if you are not allowed to date, how are you supposed to find your husband? They say "no" to the whole dating scene because that is secondary to your education, secondary to your family. They do push marriage, but at a later date. So basically my parents are telling me that I should get married and I should have children but that I should not date.

In a study of second-generation Filipino Americans in northern California, Diane Wolf (1997) reports the same pattern of parental pressures: Parents expect daughters to remain virgins until marriage, to have a career, *and* to combine their work lives with marriage and children.

The restrictions on girls' movement sometimes spill over to the realm of academics. Dasgupta and DasGupta (1996:230) recount that in the Indian American community, while young men were expected to attend faraway competitive colleges, many of their female peers were encouraged by their parents to go to the local colleges so that they could live at or close to home. Similarly, Wolf (1997:467) reports that some Filipino parents pursued contradictory tactics with their children, particularly their daughters, by pushing them to achieve academic excellence in high school but then "pulling the emergency brake" when they contemplated college by expecting them to stay at home, even if it meant going to a less competitive college, or not going at all. In the following account, a young Filipina relates that her parents' desire to "protect" her surpassed their concerns for her academic preparation:

> My brother [was] given a lot more opportunity educationally. He was given the opportunity to go to Miller High School that has a renowned college preparatory program but [for] which you have to be bussed out of our area.[8] I've come from a college prep program in junior high and I was asked to apply for the program at Miller. But my parents said "No, absolutely not." This was even during the time, too, when Southside [the neighborhood high school] had one of the lowest test scores in the state of California. So it was like, "You know, mom, I'll get a better chance at Miller." "No, no, you're going to Southside. There is no ifs, ands, or buts. Miller is too far. What if something happens to you?" But two years later, when my brother got ready to go on to high school, he was allowed to go to Miller. My sister and I were like, "Obviously, whose education do you value more? If you're telling us that education is important, why do we see a double standard?"

The above narratives suggest that the process of parenting is gendered in that immigrant parents tend to restrict the autonomy, mobility, and personal decision-making of their daughters more than that of their sons. I argue that these parental restrictions are attempts to construct a model of Filipina womanhood that is chaste, modest, nurturing, and family-oriented. Women are seen as responsible for holding the cultural line, maintaining racial boundaries, and marking cultural difference. This is not to say that parent–daughter conflicts exist in all Filipino immigrant families. Certainly, Filipino parents do not respond in a uniform way to the challenges of being racial-ethnic minorities, and I met parents who have had to change some of their ideas and practices in response to their inability to control their children's movements and choices:

> I have three girls and one boy. I used to think that I wouldn't allow my daughters to go dating and things like that, but there is no way I could do that. I can't stop it. It's the way of life here in America. Sometimes you kind of question yourself, if you are doing what is right. It is hard to accept but you got to accept it. That's the way they are here. (Professional Filipino immigrant father)

> My children are born and raised here, so they do pretty much what they want. They think they know everything. I can only do so much as a parent. ...When I try to teach my kids things, they tell me that I sound like an old record. They even talk back to me sometimes....The first time my daughter brought her boyfriend to the house, she was 18 years old. I almost passed away, knocked out. Lord, tell me what to do? (Working-class Filipino immigrant mother)

These narratives call attention to the shifts in the generational power caused by the migration process and to the possible gap between what parents say they want for their children and their ability to control the young. However, the interview data do suggest that intergenerational conflicts are socially recognized occurrences in Filipino communities. Even when respondents themselves had not experienced intergenerational tensions, they could always recall a cousin, a girlfriend, or a friend's daughter who had.

Sanctions and Reactions: "That is not what a decent Filipino girl should do"

I do not wish to suggest that immigrant communities are the only ones in which parents regulate their daughters' mobility and sexuality. Feminist scholars have long documented the construction, containment, and exploitation of women's sexuality in various societies (Maglin and Perry 1996). We also know that the cultural anxiety over unbounded female sexuality is most apparent with regard to adolescent girls (Tolman and Higgins 1996:206). The difference is in the ways immigrant and nonimmigrant families sanction girls' sexuality. To control sexually assertive girls nonimmigrant parents rely on the gender-based good girl/bad girl dichotomy in which "good girls" are passive, threatened sexual objects while "bad girls" are active, desiring sexual agents (Tolman and Higgins 1996). As Dasgupta and DasGupta write, "the two most pervasive images of women across cultures are the goddess and whore, the good and bad women" (1996:236). This good girl/bad girl cultural story conflates femininity with sexuality, increases women's vulnerability to sexual coercion, and justifies women's containment in the domestic sphere.

Immigrant families, though, have an additional strategy: they can discipline their daughters as racial/national subjects as well as gendered ones. That is, as self-appointed guardians of "authentic" cultural memory, immigrant parents can attempt to regulate their daughters' independent choices by linking them to cultural ignorance or betrayal. As both parents and children recounted, young women who disobeyed parental strictures were often branded "non-ethnic," "untraditional," "radical," "selfish," and "not caring about the family." Female sexual choices were also linked to moral degeneracy, defined in relation to a narrative of a hegemonic white norm. Parents were quick to warn their daughters about "bad" Filipinas who had become pregnant outside marriage.[9] As in the case of "bar girls" in the Philippines, Filipina Americans who veered from acceptable behaviors were deemed "Americanized" – as women who have adopted the sexual mores and practices of white women. As one Filipino immigrant father described "Americanized" Filipinas: "They are spoiled because they have seen the American way. They go out at night. Late at night. They go out on dates. Smoking. They have sex without marrying."

From the perspective of the second-generation daughters, these charges are stinging. The young women I interviewed were visibly pained – with many breaking down and crying – when they recounted their parents' charges. This deep pain, stemming in part from their desire to be validated as Filipina, existed even among the more "rebellious" daughters. One 24-year-old daughter explained:

> My mom is very traditional. She wants to follow the Filipino customs, just really adhere to them, like what is proper for a girl, what she can and can't do, and what other people are going to think of her if she doesn't follow that way. When I pushed these restrictions, when I rebelled and stayed out later than allowed, my mom would always say, "That is not what a decent Filipino girl should do. You should come home at a decent hour. What are people going to think of you?" And that would get me really upset, you know, because I think that my character is very much the way it should be for a Filipina. I wear my hair long, I wear decent makeup. I dress properly, conservative. I am family oriented. It hurts me that she doesn't see that I am decent, that I am proper and that I am not going to bring shame to the family or anything like that.

This narrative suggests that even when parents are unable to control the behaviors of their children, their (dis)approval remains powerful in shaping the emotional lives of their daughters (see Wolf 1997). Although better-off parents can and do exert greater controls over their children's behaviors than do poorer parents (Wolf 1992; Kibria 1993), I would argue that all immigrant parents – regardless of class background – possess this emotional hold on their children. Therein lies the source of their power: As immigrant parents, they have the authority to determine if their daughters are "authentic" members of their racial-ethnic community. Largely unacquainted with the "home" country, U.S.-born children depend on their parents' tutelage to craft and affirm their ethnic self and thus are particularly vulnerable to charges of cultural ignorance and/or betrayal (Espiritu 1994).

Despite these emotional pains, many young Filipinas I interviewed contest and negotiate parental restrictions in their daily lives. Faced with parental restrictions on their mobility, young Filipinas struggle to gain some control over their own social lives, particularly over dating. In many cases, daughters simply misinform their parents of their whereabouts or date without their parents' knowledge. They also rebel by vowing to create more egalitarian relationships with their own husbands and children. A 30-year-old Filipina who is married to a white American explained why she chose to marry outside her culture:

> In high school, I dated mostly Mexican and Filipino. It never occurred to me to date a white or black guy. I was not attracted to them. But as I kept growing up and my father and I were having all these conflicts, I knew that if I married a Mexican or a Filipino, [he] would be exactly like my father. And so I tried to date anyone that would not remind me of my dad. A lot of my Filipina friends that I grew up with had similar experiences. So I knew that it wasn't only me. I was determined to marry a white person because he would treat me as an individual.[10]

Another Filipina who was labeled "radical" by her parents indicated that she would be more open-minded in raising her own children: "I see myself as very traditional in upbringing but I don't see myself as constricting on my children one day and I wouldn't put the gender roles on them. I wouldn't lock them into any particular way of behaving." It is important to note that even as these Filipinas desired new gender norms and practices for their own families, the majority hoped that their children would remain connected to Filipino culture.

My respondents also reported more serious reactions to parental restrictions, recalling incidents of someone they knew who had run away, joined a gang, or attempted suicide. A Filipina high-school counselor relates that most of the Filipinas she worked with "are really scared because a lot of them know friends that are pregnant and they all pretty much know girls who have attempted suicide." A 1995 random survey of San Diego public high schools conducted by the Federal Centers for Disease Control and Prevention (CDC) found that, in comparison with other ethnic groups, female Filipino students had the highest rates of seriously considering suicide (45.6 percent) as well as the highest rates of actually attempting suicide (23 percent) in the year preceding the survey. In comparison, 33.4 percent of Latinas, 26.2 percent of white women, and 25.3 percent of black women surveyed said they had suicidal thoughts (Lau 1995).

Conclusion

Mainstream American society defines white middle-class culture as the norm and whiteness as the unmarked marker of others' difference (Frankenberg 1993). In this article, I have shown that many Filipino immigrants use the largely gendered discourse of morality as one strategy to decenter whiteness and to locate themselves above the dominant group, demonizing it in the process. Like other immigrant groups, Filipinos praise the United States as a land of significant economic opportunity but simultaneously denounce it as a country inhabited by corrupted and individualistic people of questionable morals. In particular, they criticize American family life, American individualism, and American women (see Gabbacia 1994:113). Enforced by distorting powers of memory and nostalgia, this rhetoric of moral superiority often leads to patriarchal calls for a cultural "authenticity" that locates family honor and national integrity in the group's female members. Because the policing of women's bodies is one of the main means of asserting moral superiority, young women face numerous restrictions on their autonomy, mobility, and personal decision-making. This practice of cultural (re)construction reveals how closely the conduct of private life can be tied to larger social structures.

The construction of white Americans as the "other" and American culture as deviant serves a dual purpose: It allows immigrant communities both to reinforce patriarchy through the sanctioning of women's (mis)behavior and to present an unblemished, if not morally superior, public face to the dominant society. Strong in family values, heterosexual morality, and a hierarchical family structure, this public face erases the Filipina "bad girl" and ignores competing (im)moral practices in the Filipino communities. Through the oppression of Filipina women and the denunciation of white women's morality, the immigrant community attempts to exert its moral superiority over the dominant Western culture and to reaffirm to itself its self-worth in the face of economic, social, political, and legal subordination. In other words, the immigrant community uses restrictions on women's lives as one form of resistance to racism. This form of cultural resistance, however, severely restricts the lives of women, particularly those of the second generation, and it casts the family as a potential site of intense conflict and oppressive demands in immigrant lives.

NOTES

1 Cordova 1983; Sharma 1984; Scharlin and Villanueva 1992; Jung 1999.
2 Filipino settlement in San Diego dates back to 1903, when a group of young Filipino *pensionados* enrolled at the State Normal School (now San Diego State University).
3 My understanding of Filipino American lives is also based on the many conversations I have had with my Filipino American students at the University of California, San Diego, and with Filipino American friends in the San Diego area and elsewhere.
4 A few studies have documented the ways racialized communities have represented white Americans. For example, in his anthropological work on Chicano joking, José Limón (1982) reports that young Mexican Americans elevate themselves over whites through the telling of "stupid American" jokes in which an Anglo American is consistently duped by a Mexican character. In her interviews with African American working-class men, Michele Lamont (1997) finds that these men tend to perceive Euro Americans as immoral, sneaky, and not to be trusted. Although these studies provide an interesting and compelling window into racialized communities' views of white Americans, they do not analyze how the rhetoric of moral superiority often depends on gender categories.
5 Indeed people around the world often believe that Americans have no real family ties. For example, on a visit to my family in Vietnam, my cousin asked me earnestly if it was true that American children put their elderly parents in nursing homes instead of caring for them at home. She was horrified at this practice and proclaimed that, because they care for their elders, Vietnamese families are morally superior to American families.
6 Writing on the objectification of black women, Patricia Hill Collins (1991) argues that popular representations of black females – mammy, welfare queen, and Jezebel – all pivot around their sexuality, either desexualizing or hypersexualizing them. Along the same line, Native American women have been portrayed as sexually excessive (Green 1975), Chicana women as "exotic and erotic" (Mirande 1980), and Puerto Rican and Cuban women as "tropical bombshells...sexy, sexed and interested" (Tafolla 1985:39).
7 The relationship between immigrant parents and their sons deserves an article of its own. According to Gabbacia, "Immigrant parents fought with sons, too, but over different issues: parents' complaints about rebellious sons focused more on criminal activity than on male sexuality or independent courtship" (1994:70). Moreover, because of their mobility, young men have more means to escape – at least temporarily – the pressures of the family than young women. In his study of Italian American families, Orsi reports that young men rebelled by sleeping in cars or joining the army, but young women did not have such opportunities (1985:143).
8 The names of the two high schools in this excerpt are fictitious.
9 According to a 1992 health assessment report of Filipinos in San Francisco, Filipino teens have the highest pregnancy rates among all Asian groups and, in 1991, the highest rate of increase in the number of births as compared with all other racial or ethnic groups (Tiongson 1997:257).
10 The few available studies on Filipino American intermarriage indicate a high rate relative to other Asian groups. In 1980, Filipino men in California recorded the highest intermarriage rate among all Asian groups, and Filipina women had the second-highest rate, after Japanese American women (Agbayani-Siewert and Revilla 1995:156).

REFERENCES

Agbayani-Siewert, Pauline, and Linda Revilla. 1995. Filipino Americans. In *Asian Americans: Contemporary Trends and Issues*, ed. Pyong Gap Min, 134–168. Thousand Oaks, CA: Sage.

Azores-Gunter, Tania Fortunata M. 1986–87. Educational Attainment and Upward Mobility: Prospects for Filipino Americans. *Amerasia Journal* 13(1):39–52.

Billson, Janet Mancini. 1995. *Keepers of the Culture: The Power of Tradition in Women's Lives.* New York: Lexington.

Cabezas, Amado, Larry H. Shinagawa, and Gary Kawaguchi. 1986–87. New Inquiries into the Socioeconomic Status of Philipino Americans in California. *Amerasia Journal* 13(1):1–21.

Collins, Patricia Hill. 1991. *Black Feminist Thought: Knowledge, Consciousness, and the Politics of Empowerment*. New York: Routledge.

Cordova, Fred. 1983. *Filipinos: Forgotten Asian Americans, a Pictorial Essay, 1763–1963*. Dubuque, Iowa: Kendall/Hunt.

Coronel, Sheila, and Ninotchka Rosca. 1993. For the Boys: Filipinas Expose Years of Sexual Slavery by the U.S. and Japan. *Ms.* November/December: 10–15.

Dasgupta, Shamita Das, and Sayantani DasGupta. 1996. Public Face, Private Space: Asian Indian Women and Sexuality. In *"Bad Girls/Good Girls": Women, Sex, and Power in the Nineties*, ed. Nan Bauer Maglin and Donna Perry, 226–243. New Brunswick, NJ: Rutgers University Press.

di Leonardo, Micaela. 1984. *The Varieties of Ethnic Experience: Kinship, Class, and Gender among California Italian-Americans*. Ithaca, NY: Cornell University Press.

Eastmond, Marita. 1993. Reconstructing Life: Chilean Refugee Women and the Dilemmas of Exile. In *Migrant Women: Crossing Boundaries and Changing Identities*, ed. Gina Buijs, 35–53. Oxford: Berg.

Egan, Timothy. 1996. Mail-Order Marriage, Immigrant Dreams and Death. *New York Times*, May 26, 12.

Espiritu, Yen Le. 1994. The Intersection of Race, Ethnicity, and Class: The Multiple Identities of Second Generation Filipinos. *Identities* 1(2–3):249–273.

Espiritu, Yen Le. 1995. *Filipino American Lives*. Philadelphia: Temple University Press.

Espiritu, Yen Le. 1997. *Asian American Women and Men: Labor, Laws, and Love*. Thousand Oaks, CA: Sage.

Espiritu, Yen Le, and Diane L. Wolf. 2001. The Paradox of Assimilation: Children of Filipino Immigrants in San Diego. In *Ethnicities: Children of Immigrants in America*, ed. Ruben Rumbaut and Alejandro Portes. Berkeley: University of California Press; New York: Russell Sage Foundation.

Frankenberg, Ruth. 1993. *White Women, Race Matters: The Social Construction of Whiteness*. Minneapolis: University of Minnesota Press.

Gabbacia, Donna. 1994. *From the Other Side: Women, Gender, and Immigrant Life in the U.S., 1820–1990*. Bloomington: Indian University Press.

Gibson, Margaret A. 1995. Additive Acculturation as a Strategy for School Improvement. In *California's Immigrant Children: Theory, Research, and Implications for Educational Policy*, ed. Ruben Rumbaut and Wayne A. Cornelius, 77–105. La Jolla: Center for U.S.-Mexican Studies, University of California, San Diego.

Gilman, Sander L. 1985. *Difference and Pathology: Stereotypes of Sexuality, Race, and Madness*. Ithaca, NY: Cornell University Press.

Green, Rayna. 1975. The Pocahontas Perplex: The Image of Indian Women in American Culture. *Massachusetts Review* 16(4):698–714.

Haddad, Yvonne Y., and Jane I. Smith. 1996. Islamic Values among American Muslims. In *Family and Gender among American Muslims: Issues Facing Middle Eastern Immigrants and their Descendants*, ed. Barbara C. Aswad and Barbara Bilge, 19–40. Philadelphia: Temple University Press.

Halualani, Rona Tamiko. 1995. The Intersecting Hegemonic Discourses of an Asian Mail-Order Bride Catalog: Pilipina "Oriental Butterfly" Dolls for Sale. *Women's Studies in Communication* 18 (1):45–64.

Hamamoto, Darrell Y. 1994. *Monitored Peril: Asian Americans and the Politics of Representation*. Minneapolis: University of Minnesota Press.

Hickey, M. Gail. 1996. "Go to College, Get a Job, and Don't Leave the House without Your Brother": Oral Histories with Immigrant Women and their Daughters. *Oral History Review* 23(2):63–92.

Jung, Moon-Kie. 1999. No Whites: No Asians: Race, Marxism and Hawaii's Pre-emergent Working Class. *Social Science History* 23(3):357–393.

Kibria, Nazli. 1993. *Family Tightrope: The Changing Lives of Vietnamese Immigrant Community*. Princeton, NJ: Princeton University Press.

Lamont, Michele. 1997. Colliding Moralities between Black and White Workers. In *From Sociology to Cultural Studies: New Perspectives*, ed. Elisabeth Long, 263–285. New York: Blackwell.

Lau, Angela. 1995. Filipino Girls Think Suicide at Number One Rate. *San Diego Union-Tribune*, February 11, A-1.

Lee, Stacey J. 1996. *Unraveling the "Model Minority" Stereotype: Listening to Asian American Youth*. New York: Teachers College Press.

Limón, José E. 1982. History, Chicano Joking, and the Varieties of Higher Education: Tradition and Performance as Critical Symbolic Action. *Journal of the Folklore Institute* 19(2/3):141–166.

Lipsitz, George. 1998. *The Possessive Investment in Whiteness: How White People Profit from Identity Politics*. Philadelphia: Temple University Press.

Lowe, Lisa. 1996. *Immigrant Acts: On Asian American Cultural Politics*. Durham, NC: Duke University Press.

Maglin, Nan Bauer, and Donna Perry. 1996. Introduction. In *"Bad Girls/Good Girls": Women, Sex, and Power in the Nineties*, ed. Nan Bauer Maglin and

Donna Perry, xiii–xxvi. New Brunswick, NJ: Rutgers University Press.

Marchetti, Gina. 1993. *Romance and the "Yellow Peril": Race, Sex, and Discursive Strategies in Hollywood Fiction*. Berkeley: University of California Press.

Matute-Bianchi, Maria Eugenia. 1991. Situational Ethnicity and Patterns of School Performance among Immigrant and Nonimmigrant Mexican-Descent Students. In *Minority Status and Schooling: A Comparative Study of Immigrant and Involuntary Minorities*, ed. Margaret A. Gibson and John U. Ogbu, 205–247. New York: Garland.

Mazumdar, Suchetta. 1989. General Introduction: A Woman-Centered Perspective on Asian American History. In *Making Waves: An Anthology by and about Asian American Women*, ed. Asian Women United of California, 1–22. Boston: Beacon.

Millett, Kate. 1970. *Sexual Politics*. Garden City, NY: Doubleday.

Mirande, Alfredo. 1980. The Chinano Family: A Reanalysis of Conflicting Views. In *Rethinking Marriage, Child Rearing, and Family Organization*, ed. Arlene S. Skolnick and Jerome H. Skolnick, 479–493. Berkeley: University of California Press.

Okamura, Jonathan, and Amefil Agbayani. 1997. *Pamantasan:* Filipino American Higher Education. In *Filipino Americans: Transformation and Identity*, ed. Maria P. Root, 183–197. Thousand Oaks, CA: Sage.

Ordonez, Raquel Z. 1997. Mail-Order Brides: An Emerging Community. In *Filipino Americans: Transformation and Identity*, ed. Maria P. Root, 121–142. Thousand Oaks, CA: Sage.

Orsi, Robert Anthony. 1985. *The Madonna of 115th Street: Faith and Community in Italian Harlem, 1880–1950*. New Haven, CT: Yale University Press.

Personal Narratives Group. 1989. Origins. In *Interpreting Women's Lives: Feminist Theory and Personal Narratives*, ed. Personal Narratives Group, 3–15. Bloomington: Indiana University Press.

Ruiz, Vicki L. 1992. The Flapper and the Chaperone: Historical Memory among Mexican-American Women. In *Seeking Common Ground: Multidisciplinary Studies,* ed. Donna Gabbacia. Westport, CT: Greenwood.

Rumbaut, Ruben. 1991. Passages to America: Perspectives on the New Immigration. In *America at Century's End,* ed. Alan Wolfe, 208–244. Berkeley: University of California Press.

Rumbaut, Ruben. 1994. The Crucible Within: Ethnic Identity, Self-Esteem, and Segmented Assimilation among Children of Immigrants. *International Migration Review* 28(4):748–794.

Rumbaut, Ruben, and Kenji Ima. 1988. *The Adaptation of Southeast Asian Refugee Youth: A Comparative Study*. Washington, DC: U.S. Office of Refugee Resettlement.

San Juan, E., Jr. 1991. Mapping the Boundaries: The Filipino Writer in the U.S. *Journal of Ethnic Studies* 19(1): 117–131.

Scharlin, Craig, and Lilia V. Villanueva. 1992. *Philip Vera Cruz: A Personal History of Filipino Immigrants and the Farmworkers Movement*. Los Angeles: University of California, Los Angeles Labor Center, Institute of Labor Relations, and Asian American Studies Center.

Sharma, Miriam. 1984. Labor Migration and Class Formation among the Filipinos in Hawaii, 1906–46. In *Labor Immigration under Capitalism: Asian Workers in the United States before World War II,* ed. Lucie Cheng and Edna Bonacich, 579–611. Berkeley: University of California Press.

Stoler, Ann Laura. 1991. Carnal Knowledge and Imperial Power: Gender, Race, and Morality in Colonial Asia. In *Gender at the Crossroads of Knowledge: Feminist Anthropology in the Postmodern Era,* ed. Micaela di Leonardo, 51–104. Berkeley: University of California Press.

Tafolla, Carmen. 1985. *To Split a Human: Mitos, Machos y la Mujer Chicana*. San Antonio, TX.: Mexican American Cultural Center.

Tapia, Ruby. 1997. Studying Other "Others." Paper presented at the Association of Pacific Americans in Higher Education, San Diego, CA, May 24.

Tiongson, Antonio T., Jr. 1997. Throwing the Baby out with the Bath Water. In *Filipino Americans: Transformation and Identity,* ed. Maria P. Root, 257–271. Thousand Oaks, CA.: Sage.

Tolman, Deborah L., and Tracy E. Higgins. 1996. How Being a Good Girl Can Be Bad for Girls. In *"Bad Girls/ Good Girls": Women, Sex, and Power in the Nineties,* ed. Nan Bauer Maglin and Donna Perry, 205–225. New Brunswick, NJ: Rutgers University Press.

Tuan, Mia. 1998. *Forever Foreigners or Honorary Whites? The Asian Ethnic Experience Today*. New Brunswick, NJ: Rutgers University Press.

Villanueva, M. 1991. *Ginseng and Other Tales from Manila*. Corvallis, OR: Calyx.

Warren, Jenifer. 1993. Suit Asks Navy to Aid Children Left in Philippines. *Los Angeles Times,* March 5, A3.

Waters, Mary C. 1996. The Intersection of Gender, Race, and Ethnicity in Identity Development of Caribbean American Teens. In *Urban Girls: Resisting Stereotypes, Creating Identities,* ed. Bonnie J. Ross Leadbeater and Niobe Way, 65–81. New York: New York University Press.

Woldemikael, T. M. 1989. *Becoming Black American: Haitians and American Institutions in Evanston, Illinois*. New York: AMS Press.

Wolf, Diane L. 1992. *Factory Daughters: Gender, Household Dynamics, and Rural Industrialization in Java*. Berkeley: University of California Press.

Wolf, Diane L. 1997. Family Secrets: Transnational Struggles among Children of Filipino Immigrants. *Sociological Perspectives* 40(3):457–482.

Wong, Sau-ling. 1993. *Reading Asian American Literature: From Necessity to Extravagance*. Princeton, NJ: Princeton University Press.

Yung, Judy. 1995. *Unbound Feet: A Social History of Chinese Women in San Francisco*. Berkeley: University of California Press.

11

College and Notions of "Asian American": Second-Generation Chinese and Korean Americans Negotiate Race and Identity

Nazli Kibria

> The traditional college years, the late teens through the mid-twenties, are years of extraordinary maturation and growth. These are the years when many young people leave home, often for the first time, meet very different kinds of people (also often for the first time), come upon previously unheard ideas, and have the opportunity, and indeed the task, of defining for themselves and others who they are – what they think, the values they hold, their place in a world beyond the one in which they grew up.[1]

As evident to even perhaps the most casual observer, Asian American students respond in highly varied ways to the challenges and opportunities for self-exploration that are offered by the complex racial environments of contemporary U.S. college campuses. Drawing on materials from a qualitative study of post-college, second-generation Chinese and Korean Americans, in this article I explore negotiations of race and identity during the college years, focusing on the development of approaches to the "Asian American" concept, in particular its meaning and significance as a basis of affiliation and community. My analyses focus on those persons who had for the most part, not been involved in pan-Asian organizations and activities during college. While pan-Asian organizations are present on most college campuses today, many Asian American students do not participate or become affiliated with them.

While the institutional and political development of the Asian American concept has been extensively studied, we know far less about how the rank and file of those who are widely viewed as "Asian American" understand and respond to this notion. That is, the "public" dimensions of pan-Asian ethnicity have been more extensively studied than its "private" aspects.[2] This is particularly so when it comes to the large segment of Asian Americans who are generally detached or uninvolved in pan-Asian activity, networks or organizations. Yet an exploration of the experiences of such persons can provide important insights into the opportunities and constraints that surround the development of pan-Asian coalition and community.

Race, Asian Americans, and the Post-Civil Rights Campus

The post-civil rights college campus is one in which issues of race have been prominent. The decades since the 1960s have seen a rise in the numbers of racial minority students attending college.[3] While this increase has not been uniform across types of institutions or affected minority groups equally, it is nonetheless one that has transformed the overall racial composition of the college population. Drawing on a 1991 report issued by the American Council on Education, Paul Loeb notes that "students of color presently number 1 out of 6 at four-year colleges and 1 out of 5 if you count two-year community colleges."[4] Asian American students have been an important part of this development. According to Hune and Chan, in 1994, Asian Pacific Americans constituted 4.8 percent of those obtaining bachelor's degrees.[5] Between 1984 and 1995, the numbers of Asian Pacific Americans enrolled in higher education institutions rose 104.5 percent, with comparable figures of 5.1 percent for whites, 37 percent for African Americans and 104.4 percent for Hispanics. Students of Asian origin have also been an important part of the growth in the foreign student population on U.S. college campuses.[6]

Reflecting this rise in minority student presence, the college campus has been an important arena for larger societal debates on questions of racial equity and integration. Issues of race, for example, have been at the core of controversies over curriculum and course content as well as faculty hiring and student admissions policies. These controversies appear as "hot buttons" in a campus environment that some describe as highly polarized along racial lines.[7] There are, for example, disturbing reports of widespread harassment and violence against minority students.[8] After describing the hostilities experienced by Black students following the acquittal of O. J. Simpson (a verdict that was viewed by Blacks and whites in sharply divergent ways), a 1995 *New York Times* article concludes: "The overall picture of racial relations on campus is one that seems to get more brittle as time goes by."[9] Racial polarization among students is also suggested by what has been described as "balkanization." That is, in ways that violate the expectations of integration, some observe that the current trend is for students to engage in social activities that are divided along racial lines. Whether it is in terms of the campus organizations that they join or those with whom they spend their spare time, students stick to their own racial groups:

> A quick glance at the local eateries on campus is more suggestive of segregation than integration. Blacks sit with blacks, whites sit with whites, Asians sit with Asians, each group clustered at separate tables.[10]

Asian Americans have been positioned within these currents of racial controversy in complex and at times seemingly contradictory ways. Particularly important here has been the image of Asians as a "model minority," a group that is culturally predisposed to socioeconomic achievements. In educational settings, this stereotype is tied to the assumption that Asians are good students, an idea that is supported by several general indicators of high academic performance among Asian American students.[11] As analyzed by Dana Takagi, the example of Asian Americans – as a minority group that is successful through merit – has thus often been used to support arguments in favor of ending affirmative action in college admissions. As a result of this perception, Asian Americans are less likely to experience the label of "undeserving" that is often applied to minority students. In other words, while Black and Latino students may be resented and even condemned for having reputedly been admitted due to preferential policies and not merit, the same charge is less likely to be made of Asian American students, given their reputation for academic excellence. Among the potential consequences of this positioning are tensions and feelings of distance between Asian American and other racial minority students, as well as their differing attitudes on such issues as affirmative action.[12] Related to this is the possibility of greater uncertainty among Asian American students in comparison to those of other minority groups about the prevalence of racism on college campuses.

However, the construction of Asian Americans as "meritorious" does not mean that they have been immune from racial hostility on college campuses. The reputation of Asians for academic achievement means that they are not only applauded but also feared and resented. In selective colleges and universities for example, the significant presence of Asian-origin students has elicited hostility, in ways that echo the hysterical fears of a "yellow invasion" that marked the environment in which laws to halt Asian immigration were enacted in the late nineteenth–early twentieth century. Anxieties about an "Asian takeover" are reflected in the appearance, in informal student cultures, of such phrases as "Made in Taiwan" to refer to MIT and "University of Caucasians living among Asians" to refer to UCLA. Asian students are also resented for generating competition in the struggle for grades. They are the "damned curve raisers," making the academic game more difficult for everyone else. In short then, racial hostility towards Asian-origin students often takes as an explicit focus the problems created for others by their academic achievements.

Besides these broad racial currents, there are also the racialized images of the "typical Asian student" that are part of contemporary campus life. For Asian American students, these images are an important part of the context within which negotiations of identity take place. While quite varied in certain respects, these images affirm an understanding of "Asianness" as embodying qualities or traits that are deeply contradictory to U.S. culture's emphasis on individuality. More generally, there is an affirmation of the "foreignness" of Asians, or their location outside of what is prototypically "American."

The reputation of Asians as academic achievers is tied to the popular image of Asian students as "nerdy" – extremely studious, serious, shy, mathematically inclined and lacking in social skills and outside interests. The "Asian nerd" embodies qualities that are fundamentally antithetical to individuality. There is a routine or machine-like quality to academic achievements here, as highlighted by the charge that Asian students are "good but not exceptional."[13] In other words, while competent in a routine sense, Asian students lack the edge of individual spark and creativity that could lead them into exceptional achievement. The idea of "foreignness" is also deeply embedded in this image. The deficient social skills, passivity and orientation towards math and technical subjects that are part of the image suggest a certain lack of comfort and familiarity with the norms and expectations of U.S. culture.

In recent years, there has developed another, seemingly contradictory Asian student image, one that while perhaps specifically associated with foreign students from Asia, affects Asian Americans as well. This is the image of the frivolous and well-to-do Asian student who is "cliquey" and focused on parties and conspicuous consumption. Folded into this image are other popular stereotypes of Asian cultural behavior. This includes the idea of Asians as group-oriented, driven by the dictates of conformity to group life. Thus the party-oriented Asian student is obsessed with the display of material goods (e.g., clothes, cars) that will gain him or her status within the clique. The particular markers that are part of this status game can be viewed as further affirmations of the foreign status and nature of Asian students. That is, in their character and substance, the markers (e.g., a particular style of clothing) are seen as off cue or not in sync with what is "culturally American." Also embedded in this image is the association of Asian culture with gender traditionalism. That is, the Asian cliques are marked by a culture of gender traditionalism that supports male dominance and enforces separate standards for men's and women's behavior. In essence, these notions affirm "foreignness" – the Asian-origin student is an outsider to what is "American."

For many Asian Americans, college is a time when they first come to seriously consider the notion of "Asian American" and its relationship to themselves. Here it is important to bear in mind that college students have been critical to the history and development of the Asian American movement. The movement was organized on college campuses in the 1960s by young U.S.-born Asian American activists who were inspired by the civil rights struggles of the time.[14] The founders of the movement defined an ideology of pan-Asianism which has continued to provide a basic framework for the organization and activities of pan-Asian American groups. In essence, "Asian American" is defined here as a signifier of a strategic political community, one that is driven by the shared racial interests of persons of Asian origin in the U.S. as well as a larger struggle against racism.[15]

Among the legacies of this history is the widespread presence on campuses of pan-Asian student associations that aim to bring together students of varied Asian ethnic origin for political and social events. Some colleges and universities have also developed courses and programs in Asian American Studies, and student centers devoted to Asian Americans. For Asian-origin students, such forums offer an opportunity to explore the concept of "Asian American" and become exposed to the ideology of pan-Asianism, often for the first time in their lives. For those students who choose to do so, perspectives on "Asian American" are likely to be shaped in important ways by this ideology.

The development of Asian American institutions and forums on college campuses has been supported by the rising numbers of Asian American students. It has also been encouraged more generally by the prominence of racial issues on campuses as described earlier. Asian American groups and organizations have been part of the discourse and debate that surrounds these issues. Ironically however, the potential for a strengthened pan-Asian campus presence has also coincided with increasing questions and concerns about the limited involvement of Asian American students in pan-Asian groups. Often cited here is the growing ethnic and generational heterogeneity of the Asian American population. In the 1960s, the Asian-origin college population was largely U.S.-born and of Japanese or Chinese origin. Today, however, reflecting the demographic shifts experienced by the Asian American population since the immigration reforms of 1965, it includes many first-generation persons as well as students from a wide range of Asian ethnic backgrounds. These developments can make the possibility of organizing along ethnic lines (e.g., Chinese American, Korean American) both more feasible and attractive than pan-Asian activity. This is particularly so for first-generation students, for whom ethnic loyalties and a sense of connection to the historically rooted conflicts and enmities between Asian societies are likely to be sharper than that among U.S.-born Asians.

However, even for those students who remain distant from formal pan-Asian activity, the college years are likely to be a time of encounters with the Asian American concept and reflection about what it means for identity and community. For one thing, regardless of whether or not one chooses to be involved, pan-Asian groups and organizations are a visible part of campus life. It is also the case that the notion of "Asian American" has become an established part of the discourse that surrounds racial issues in the contemporary U.S. Thus, while an Asian-origin student may very well avoid pan-Asian activities on campus, she or he is nonetheless likely to confront the idea of "Asian American" in some fashion.

Methods

The materials presented here are drawn from 64 in-depth interviews with Chinese Americans and Korean Americans in the Los Angeles and Boston areas. The study was limited to 1.5- and second-generation Chinese and Korean Americans between the ages of 21 and 40. I define this group to include those who are the children of immigrants, and have been born and/or raised in the U.S. since the age of 12 or earlier. Interviewees were asked to talk about the role and meaning of their racial and ethnic affiliations in such life spheres as work, family and neighborhood over the life course. The interviews, which lasted from one-and-a-half to four hours, were tape-recorded and later transcribed. Informants were initially located through the membership lists and referrals of a variety of churches, professional and social clubs, and college and university alumni associations. The sample was expanded through "snowballing," whereby informants were asked for referrals to others who fit the criteria for inclusion in the study.

In terms of family of origin, the social background of the sample was varied. Some, for example, had grown up in working-class or small business families while others were from professional upper-middle class homes. However, the majority of the sample was college-educated. Fifty-five of the 64 informants had Bachelor's degrees from four-year colleges or universities, and in some cases, graduate or professional degrees as well. Of these 55 persons, 23 had attended public institutions (i.e., state/city colleges or universities), while 32 had been to private ones. Two of the others interviewed had obtained two-year Associates degrees from community colleges. Of the remaining informants, two had never attended college and five had attended but had left before completing their undergraduate degrees. The sample included persons who had attended college in the period ranging from 1975 to 1995, with a large number clustered in the 1980s.

A wide range of specific colleges and universities was represented in the experiences of the sample. Although concentrated on the east and west coasts, there was also diversity in the regional location of the institutions. These variations are important given the tremendous differences in racial environments across institutions. For example, institutions differ in the relative numbers of minority students, and more specifically of students of Chinese, Korean, and other Asian origin. Related to this are the variations across institutions with respect to policy on issues of race and multiculturalism. Reflecting these variations, those of my informants who had attended college in the 1980s and 1990s and in California were most likely to have found themselves on campuses with a significant Asian American student presence as well as Asian American Studies programs and centers. As I have mentioned, my analyses here focus on the segment of informants who indicated a lack of involvement in pan-Asian organizations during their college years. This segment constituted a majority of 41 out of the sample of 64 persons.

Identity Negotiations and Perspectives on "Asian American"

The second-generation Chinese and Korean Americans' accounts of their college years revealed several different perspectives on "Asian American." In what follows I explore these perspectives, focusing on the processes – the events, circumstances, decisions and negotiations that surrounded them. While the narratives tended to be dominated by one perspective over another, it was also the case that they often appeared in shifting and overlapping ways in the accounts of individuals.

The "comfort" of Asian American friendships

Among the accounts of social life during the college years were those that involved the development of a primary friendship network composed mainly of Asian Americans of varied ethnicities, usually of Japanese, Chinese, and Korean origin. For some, this development was one that overlapped with participation in organized pan-Asian groups and events on campus. My focus here, however, is on the experiences of those who remained uninvolved in such activities, despite an Asian American social circle.

Few informants spoke of their Asian American social circle as the outcome of a highly conscious decision or choice. Instead, the immediate response most often offered was that it had "just happened." In their view, underlying this "natural" course of events were the special ties of Asians. These derived from the commonalities of race and culture among Asians, and the shared experiences and personal histories implied by them. That is, because Asians had a shared racial identity in the U.S., they had all experienced certain things – being racially labeled and lumped together as "Asian," and being stereotyped as "nerdy," "foreign," and so forth. Related to this, there was the shared experience of feeling the sting of racial rejection from others, particularly from whites. It was also felt that Asian Americans shared common experiences that derived from the values that had been part of their upbringing – an emphasis on education, family and work. In short, the conception of "Asian American" embedded in this account was that of a community of shared worldview or understanding, stemming from the commonalities of race and culture. Given all of this, it was not surprising that friendships with Asian Americans had "just happened."

Wai Han, a Chinese American, had attended a state college in California in the mid-1980s. In speaking of how her college friendship circle had been primarily Asian American, she refers at first to being extremely busy, with the pressures of both classes and jobs. Friendships with others required some active effort, in contrast to those with Asian Americans that developed in a natural, almost organic fashion. She felt that there was a greater sense of social ease and receptivity among Asian Americans:

> I was working, and didn't have a lot of time. I lived at home part of the time. My friends were from classes. They were all Asian. I mean not just Chinese, but Korean, Japanese. It wasn't planned, it just happened. I've noticed that Asians are more receptive to me in terms of friendships.

Rather than something that had "just happened," for George, a Korean American, a pan-Asian social circle had developed in active response to the college environment. George spoke of how he had found white students at the Ivy League University he had attended in the 1970s to be stand-offish and unreceptive to him. In contrast, relationships with Asian American students were easy and comfortable. He felt this was in part because of family backgrounds that had been marked by the common values of education and family:

> I found myself mainly with Asian American friends. In fact there were three of us who were really close and they used to call us the Three Musketeers. Interestingly, one guy was Chinese American, the other was Japanese American, and of course I was Korean American. Maybe it's because——University is such an old, conservative and white place. But we felt more comfortable with each other. I found a lot of the students snobbish, unfriendly. Asian Americans tend to have more in common, you know. They have similar views on education and family. Similar family experiences like pressure from parents to do well when you're growing up.

As suggested by George's words, the negotiation of Asian stereotypes was part of his involvement in an Asian American friendship network. For George, the "Asian nerd" stereotype was part of a general environment of hostility towards racial minorities, one that only strengthened the bonds of his Asian American friends. The stereotypes, then, contributed to his understanding of "Asian American" as a community of solidarity against racism. But there were also other ways in which the stereotypes were negotiated and incorporated into notions of "Asian American." Several informants with pan-Asian friendship networks spoke of how the stereotypes of Asian students as "nerdy" and party-oriented were more applicable to the Chinese or Korean groups on campus. This was, they felt, because of the large numbers of first-generation as well as foreign student Chinese and Koreans that were part of these ethnically bounded groups. Creating a pan-Asian friendship network was a means to differentiate oneself from these groups and by extension, the stereotypes and connotations that were a part of them. This was because those who were part of pan-Asian friendship networks tended to be second- or later-generation Asian Americans. Meg, for example, spoke of avoiding the Chinese crowds on campus even as she "hung out" with Asian Americans. A Chinese American, she had attended a private university in California in the early 1990s:

> I've thought about this before. I think it would have been good for me to have had a variety of friends. But psychologically...I didn't feel comfortable around Caucasians. I felt more in control of the situation when I was with other Asians. There's a common background there with Asians. The other day my friends and I were talking about how whenever we got together, we always asked each other about how our parents were, how the family was, that kind of thing. And how that just wouldn't be a normal topic of conversation for whites. Also, all our growing-up experiences were the same...you can't date until you're this age, or your parents disapprove of you dating this type, that type. We all understood that. My girlfriends especially. (What was the ethnic background of your friends? Were they Chinese, or...) Oh no. It was real mixed. There was like a Chinese student crowd, and there was the CSA (Chinese Students Association). I guess I could have been involved but I felt a lot more comfortable with Asians. A lot of the Chinese crowd was not very Americanized. They're very different from me. More into the group thing, the material thing. You know, parties and stuff. I wouldn't fit in.

Meg's words highlight the ways in which consciousness of generational divisions was often an important aspect of understandings of "Asian American" among these informants. But the variable of generation was asserted not simply to achieve distance from the Asian stereotypes. It was, more generally, implicated in efforts to construct a more nuanced and selective understanding of the special ties of Asians. That is, discussion of the greater comfort and ease of relationships with Asians was punctuated with comments about how these were more likely to be felt with some Asians and not others. Sandra, for example, viewed the second-generation experience – that of growing up in the U.S. as a child of Asian immigrants – to be a vital aspect of the shared personal history and worldview of Asian Americans. A Korean American, Sandra had attended a private women's college in the mid-1980s. It is important to note that the working-class Asian immigrant history that she invokes is homogenizing of the realities of socioeconomic diversity among contemporary Asian immigrants:

> I would say the whole immigrant experience really brought us closer together. It's like they know what it's like to have parents who do not speak the language fluently, who are handicapped...culturally and verbally. And they know what it's like to see their parents working seven days a week and in these often dangerous settings or very kind of blue-collar work like dry cleaning. So I think that common experience ties us together.

Although in far more muted or less explicit ways, informants also recognized differences of Asian ethnic background in their discussion of the natural ties of Asian Americans. Due to similarities in physical characteristics as well as overlaps of history and culture, especially a tradition of Confucianism, this bond was far more pronounced among persons of East Asian descent. This point was made by George, a Korean American. As described earlier, George's closest friends in college had been Chinese American and Japanese American:

> Of all the Asian groups, Koreans, Japanese and Chinese have the most in common. (In what way?) Everybody gets us mixed up; they can't tell us apart. (That doesn't happen with a Vietnamese or Filipino?) It can happen, but it's less likely, especially if you're talking about Asians looking at each other. It's much easier I think to tell a Korean from a Filipino person than Chinese. It's also that there are common roots for Koreans, Japanese and Chinese if you go way back. Like our writing is from the same family. And the cultures are based on Confuciansm.

What I have described above are accounts of the college years that are marked by a sense of identification with "Asian American" as an affiliation, despite non-involvement with organized pan-Asian activity. This lack of involvement was reflected in important ways in the understandings of "Asian American" articulated here. While race and racism were widely acknowledged as part of the special bond of Asians, these ideas did not always translate into recognition of the shared political interests of Asian Americans or a conception of Asian American as signifying a strategic, political community. Also differentiating these perspectives from the ideology of pan-Asianism is the idea of a pan-Asian culture, in particular the shared Asian values of family and education. Mindful of the realities of diversity among Asian Americans, the Asian American movement has been critical of efforts to construct "Asian American" as a cultural community.

There was an elasticity to the notion of pan-Asian community articulated here. That is, while informants spoke of these bonds as encompassing Asian Americans in general, they also at times made distinctions. As I have described, generational divisions, especially that between immigrant and second-generation persons, were a particularly prominent distinction. For the second-generation Chinese and Korean Americans, "Asian American community" emerged out of a central experience and identification with the U.S., one that those who had not grown up elsewhere did not fundamentally share.

"Asian American" as an artificial construct

Some of the second-generation Chinese and Korean Americans spoke of their college social life with reference to a friendship circle that was primarily Chinese American or Korean American. Participation in Chinese or Korean organizations on campus could be part of these accounts, but not necessarily so. This pattern of ethnically oriented social involvements, somewhat more prevalent among the Korean Americans than Chinese Americans,[16] meant that perspectives on "Asian

American" were forged here in contrast and often in opposition to understandings of Chinese or Korean American as a basis of identity and community. In essence, "Asian American" was understood here as a weak and relatively insignificant basis of identity and community – a construct that was artificial and externally imposed, masking the more natural ties and solidarity of specific ethnic groups, such as Chinese or Koreans. For some, the activities of pan-Asian organizations on campus only highlighted the contrived character of Asian American community. For a variety of reasons, they felt distant from the political agenda of these organizations, and did not see their interests and ideas to be represented by them.

While, in some accounts, a pattern of friendships with fellow ethnics was continuous with social life before college, for others it was something new. In the latter case informants often spoke of how college had for them been a time of exploring and coming to terms with their Chinese or Korean identity. The presence on campus of significant numbers of Chinese and Korean Americans both allowed and encouraged such explorations. Often mentioned here was the experience of encountering for the first time, fellow ethnics who were U.S.-born and/or raised and who thus contradicted the Asian stereotypes. That is, they were not "nerdy," "foreign" or "traditional" in their attitudes towards men and women. Thus as in the case of the earlier accounts, negotiations of identity were marked by the Asian stereotypes and the use of generation to achieve distance from them. We see this in the account of Susan, a Korean American who had attended a state college in California in the early 1980s:

> When I started going to—— I was really anti-Korean because I thought all Korean men or boys were really chauvinistic and domineering like my dad. Or really wimpy and nerdy. And I didn't really have respect for Korean girls because my sense was they didn't have any ambition in life. They just wanted to marry right and to gossip about clothes, boys, that type of thing. They weren't conscious about other things that were going on. I don't know where I got this idea but I was really dissatisfied with Korean women. So I had this stereotype of Korean women and I used to tell myself: I'm not going to hang out with Koreans when I get to college because they're so narrow-minded and they only speak Korean and they don't assimilate. But then once I got there I met Koreans and they encouraged me to join their Korean student organizations and stuff. I realized that it was kind of a bonding that almost comes natural. I think I realized my identity and I also realized that not all the Korean kids fit the stereotype. There were Korean kids just like me who grew up in predominantly white neighborhoods, and had a lot of white friends. They weren't all nerdy or chauvinistic. We could relate to whites really well. (So your friends in college were mainly Korean American?) Yeah, I mean there were so many Korean Americans there that I didn't need to go beyond that. I mean I had a lot of friends. I did have some Chinese and Japanese friends I met through a pre-law Asian students group. But still, with Koreans it's different, I feel like there's a natural attraction.

In Susan's account, the meaning and significance of friendships across Asian groups is assessed in contradistinction to Korean ones. In this comparison, intra-Asian bonds come up short, appearing weak and insignificant. For Jeff, a Korean American who had attended a private university in the Northeast in the early 1990s, intra-Asian ties were not only weak in comparison to ethnic ones but also had an aura of falsity about them. For him, the transition to a primarily Korean American social circle had taken place during college. It had been triggered by a growing sense of discomfort and alienation from the predominantly white social groups around which he had initially organized his social life. Also important to note is that Jeff's perspective on racial issues had been deeply affected by the 1992 Los Angeles riots, during which his parents' small business had been seriously damaged:

> I would say that the first time that I started feeling a close bond with Koreans was in college. It's funny because when I started, in my freshman year, I joined a white fraternity and I was fairly active. I didn't really participate in any of the Korean functions, and I guess the Koreans called me whitewashed. Then I had a good friend who was part of that Korean clique. By my second year I kind of assimilated into the Korean crowd. (What happened with the fraternity?) I was less and less involved. I was one out of three Asians in a very large organization, and it felt strange. It was subtle, but I don't

> think I was accepted. So my friends were pretty much Korean in college and it's been that way since then. I find it's more comfortable. (Is that also the case with Asian Americans from other groups? Do you have other Asian friends?) No, not really. I mean I had acquaintances in college who were Chinese, that kind of thing. I can't say I had more in common with them than whites or blacks or whatever. It's a mistake to think there's any real bond going on there. We speak different languages, have different perspectives.
>
> I was in college during the riots. I remember reading right after the riots about how the Chinese and Japanese communities in L.A. were just...unfazed. I mean it didn't concern them – it was a Korean problem. You know, I just don't see that there's too much in common going on there. Why do we have to go around pretending that Asian Americans are the same?

The resentment felt by Jeff about what was felt to be the pretense of Asian American unity was echoed by several informants. Some referred to encounters with pan-Asian groups and activities in which the fiction of Asian American community was made sharply visible to them. This was the case for Terry, a Chinese American who had attended a state college in California in the early 1980s. Unlike the accounts described so far, for Terry, a pattern of Chinese American friendships was not new, but something with which she had grown up, having been raised in the Chinatown areas of San Francisco and Los Angeles. Terry draws on her exposure to an Asian American student organization and its internal tensions as a point of contrast for highlighting the cultural and other similarities of Chinese in comparison to Asians in general. It is of note that she also qualifies this notion of a natural Chinese bond by recognizing generational divisions among Chinese, and demarcating her sense of ethnic affinity to American-born Chinese in particular:

> Most of my friends were Chinese, I felt more comfortable socially with Chinese. (How about Asian friends, I mean from other Asian groups?) I did have some Asian friends in college who were not Chinese. At first I went to the Asian Students Association. But it was very political. One group would say: we're not getting represented, we want a voice. I couldn't get into it, I couldn't see the point. I find it less stressful with Chinese; I'm talking mainly American-born Chinese. We have the same history, we grew up with the same superstitions, foods.

Several informants echoed the general sense of discomfort voiced by Terry about the pan-Asian organizations on campus. Some complained of the "radical" political agenda of the pan-Asian groups. Their own sense of dissonance and distance from the progressive politics of Asian American groups only confirmed the fake, contrived character of "Asian American" as a basis of identity and community. We see this in the words of Bill, a Chinese American who had attended a private university in California in the early 1980s. Bill had found the progressive political agenda of the pan-Asian groups on campus to be unconvincing and in fact distasteful. While he was not very interested in the Chinese student groups either, in the latter half of his college career he found himself with a "Chinese clique." Besides connoting a certain economic glamor, Chinese ties were natural and primordial – rooted in blood:

> In college I stayed away from Chinese for a long time. I mean I didn't go looking for Chinese. The Chinese Students Association was not very interesting to me. Neither were the Asian student groups. They were too crazy. Always spouting off about oppression. I really think this whole Asian thing is overplayed. In the last couple of years I got into a Chinese clique. It was a change – I'd spent all this time avoiding Chinese. And then it seemed kind of exciting. China is such a booming area economically. I felt kind of drawn to it. I think it's like they say, being Chinese is in your blood.

The pattern of ethnic social involvements described above was one that provided the social context for an understanding of "Asian American" as peripheral if not false or artificial as a basis of identity and community. It was a community of fellow Chinese or Korean Americans rather than a pan-Asian American one that provided the means for coping with the social challenges of college life. As was true of the understandings described in the previous section, here too, talk of the "natural" bond of Chinese and Koreans was constantly punctuated with qualifications, in particular that of the distinction between immigrant and second-generation persons.

"Asian American" as stifling to individuality

The last accounts that I turn to are distinguished by a lack of connection to Asian, Chinese or Korean American communities on campus. Some informants (especially those who went to college before the 1980s) explained this absence with reference to a lack of opportunity, or the presence of very small numbers of fellow ethnics or Asian Americans on campus. More often though, what was related was an active rejection of the available opportunities to make these connections. "Asian American" was understood here as a force that stood in opposition to individuality and the exercising of freedom and choice with respect to affiliation and identity. This was so in two ways. First, Asian American communities were seen to collectively embody qualities and traits that were antithetical to individualism. These included the stereotypical qualities of clannishness, group conformity and gender traditionalism. Second, individuality was challenged by the very fact of prescribed membership. That is, the fact that one was expected to belong to Asian American group(s), regardless of how one felt about it, was stifling. As we will see, informants experienced this expectation of belonging as emanating not just from non-Asians but also from within the Asian American communities on campus.

For Gordon, a Chinese American, the expectations of Asian friendship were particularly troubling. Students of Asian origin on campus responded to his refusals to join them by labeling him as "banana" – someone striving to be white and denying his true heritage. The significance of this expectation as well as his discomfiture about it were only compounded by the reaction of his white friends who teased him about belonging to the "Asian crowd." Thus the dynamics of these expectations, along with his negative impressions (e.g., close-minded, serious) of the Asian student groups meant that the very idea of the Asian American community made him feel claustrophobic:

> It was very strange at——University because that was the first time that I was surrounded by other Asian people. And it was kind of funny but I felt uncomfortable with it. (How did it make you feel uncomfortable?) I never really looked at myself as Asian. Well I never really looked at myself as anything, you know growing up in this white suburb. When I got there I was solicited to join the Korean Club and the Chinese Club and the Asian Club. But I had never grouped myself in Asian or Chinese or anything like that. And so it was just something new. I met a lot of them and it really turned me off. It's the close mindedness to the point where they kind of shun out other people. It's kind of mean to say, but I didn't enjoy being with them. They were – they were typically Asian. They were – they were not very fun. They were very serious.
>
> (Were these people mainly Asian immigrants? Or were they raised here?) Both, I didn't see a huge difference there. I would get a lot of flak, from both sides. The Asian group, they would give me a hard time...hey, why aren't you hanging out with us? Are you a "banana"? My friends [white] would kid around about it, and ask me why I wasn't hanging out with the Asians. They were joking, they knew I wouldn't fit in with the Asians.

As suggested by Gordon's response to my question about differences between immigrant and U.S.-born Asian students, distinctions among Asians did not figure heavily in his understandings of Asian American community. What becomes clear here is the quality of fluidity that surrounds the stereotypes, in particular their shifting ability to apply to both pan-Asian boundaries and the ones contained with it. We see this in the words of Ben, who like many others voiced a sense of repulsion to the "cliquey" and conformist character of Asian campus communities. He begins by speaking of his experience with Korean students, but then slips into talking about Asians in general. Ben had attended a private university in the Northeast for a year in the early 1990s, before dropping out and joining the armed services:

> These Korean guys came up to me and said, why aren't you hanging out with us? Why aren't you part of the gang, the Korean posse? I was thinking, are we still in high school? A Korean posse? Is this for real? It was too stifling, I didn't want to be part of some group. I think it's important for people to be themselves. You always see these Asian people in a group, everything's a group.

For women in particular, an aversion to "traditional," male-dominant gender roles often marked their accounts of why they had steered clear of the Asian, Chinese or Korean communities on campus. This was suggested by Katherine, a Korean American who had attended a private university in the Northeast in the early to mid-1980s. Katherine begins by speaking specifically of her experiences with the Korean Students Association, but then moves on to Asians in general. What she felt to be the male chauvinism of the Asian men, along with the general emphasis on group activity, led her to stay away from the Asian groups:

> I had a really broad group of friends. We had a rooming group of ten women and we looked like the United Nations. Puerto Rican, Japanese American, Jewish American, a woman from Seattle, two Black women from the South. I did find though that I couldn't hang out with Koreans who were in Korean groups; that wouldn't work for me. I went to the Korean Student Association meetings and I felt like they were pointless. The men pretty much led the meetings. Basically I really like Asian women and I don't really get along with Asian men. There are few Asian men who are willing to let down all preconceptions about women, I've even seen that with a lot of really liberal, well-educated Asian guys. And I seem to break a lot of the stereotypes about Asian women. In any case, the whole group thing drove me nuts.

While Katherine's concerns about gender traditionalism focused on the behavior of Asian men, for Jane they centered around impressions of the women who were part of the Chinese student groups on campus. According to her, not only were the women deferential to men but also frivolous in nature, focused on ostentatious material displays. As a student from a modest financial background, Jane was particularly offended by these displays. A Chinese American, she had attended a private university in California in the early 1980s:

> I was working and going to school at the same time. I had a scholarship and I felt a lot of pressure to do well. You know I had basically gone to an inner-city school, and I don't think the academic standards had been too high. I had to work really hard to get good grades. I was on scholarship, but financially it was still not easy. So socially I wasn't all that active, until about my third year. My close friends were people I met in class. Pretty much Caucasian. (Did you join any Asian or Chinese student groups?) No. I did have a Chinese friend who dragged me to a couple of meetings and a dance organized by a Chinese group. It was a real turn-off. I was almost offended in some ways. It was a big status thing, expensive clothes, cars. And I didn't like the whole male-female dynamic. It was too much like the delicate Asian flower waiting for the man to sweep her off her feet.

Men informants too, voiced complaints about an excessive "party focus," particularly in relation to the Chinese or Korean groups and organizations on campus. Thus Sung, a Korean American, spoke of being turned off by the "drinking club" atmosphere of the Korean Students Association on campus. He also felt no sense of connection to the Asian American organizations on campus. He did not agree with the fundamental political agenda of the organizations, and felt a lack of space for dialogue within them. All of this only enhanced his association of the idea of Asian American affiliation with conformity and the restriction of free choice. Of note is his comment that his friends were a diverse group, a point often made by informants in the course of affirming through contrast the cliquish and conformist character of the Asian groups. Diversity in friendships thus becomes a kind of proof of individuality and the ability to make choices apart from groups:

> My friends in school were really just a motley crew, and that was something I really liked. I wasn't interested in the Korean Students Association, which was a social thing. I mean it was like a drinking club, a place to find a future wife, that kind of thing. It was like a fraternity. (How about Asian American groups?) I went to a couple of Asian American meetings my first year but the agenda that they had just didn't sit well with me. I mean I couldn't get all that interested in what they had to say. They were very much oriented towards trying to frame the Asian American experience using a language or way of describing things that is similar to civil rights. There was no room for disagreement, for dialogue. You know I thought it was kind of a stretch. African Americans have been screwed in this country for a long long time. Whereas the Asians have generally been treated better.

The accounts of the informants so far are dominated by negative impressions and reactions to

Asian student groups on campus. A somewhat different perspective was provided by Connie, a Chinese American who had attended a state college in California in the late 1970s–early 1980s. Having grown up in a largely Chinese neighborhood, she saw college as an opportunity to meet people from other groups. She felt that her college experiences had taught her to feel comfortable with different kinds of people. Thus while, for her, Asian American community did not have the kinds of negative connotations that it did for the other informants described here, it was nonetheless associated with limitations, a restriction on individual choice. Once again, a racially diverse friendship network is associated with free choice in contrast to the constraints of an Asian or Chinese social circle:

> As soon as I got there, I found myself in an Asian clique. These Asian persons that I didn't know came up and invited me to sit with them in the dining hall. And every night we'd eat together and there would be this long table of about twenty Asian Americans...Japanese, Chinese. And then I decided, what's going on here, I want to meet some other kinds of people. So after my first year I kind of expanded, joined some different groups and met other people. I had some white friends for the first time in my life, and I had Hispanic friends. (How did you feel with the other, the non-Asian friends that you made? Did you feel accepted?) Oh yes, absolutely. I think it was really important for me, because I started to feel more comfortable with other people

To summarize, the perspective described here is one in which "Asian American" is understood as stifling, claustrophobic and contradictory in an essential sense to individuality. Popular stereotypes of Asian culture clearly play an important role in shaping and giving form to such understandings. Also important was the sense of pressure felt by informants to belong to pan-Asian, Chinese or Korean communities on campus. Resisting these pressures was a means to affirm one's individuality.

Conclusions

This article highlights the diversity of social patterns and experiences among second-generation Chinese and Korean Americans during the college years. This diversity is not surprising, given the range of backgrounds, resources and specific college contexts involved. At the same time, my materials also suggest some ways in which experiences are shaped by a common racial context. These include racialized constructions of persons of Asian descent as "foreign," as captured by popular stereotypes of the "typical Asian student." These stereotypes entered into the identity negotiations of my informants in powerful yet varied ways, affirming different understandings of "Asian American." For some it provided the basis for an understanding of Asian American as a community of solidarity while for others it was an affiliation that violated identity choice. Moving across these variations was a common response – a tendency to deflect the stereotypes onto immigrant or foreign national Asians. My findings thus highlight the ways in which these stereotypes contribute to and play on immigrant versus later-generation fissures in Asian American communities.

Those who are the focus of this article were disengaged from pan-Asian student organizations and activities during their college years. Many specific explanations were offered for this absence of connection, ranging from a lack of time and energy to invest in extracurricular activities to disagreement with the progressive politics of the organizations. The lack of engagement was perhaps most striking among those who expressed a sense of pan-Asian connection and identification. As I have discussed, the understanding of Asian American community here was both less political (at least in an explicit sense) and more focused on issues of culture than that offered by the ideology of pan-Asianism. Some of these informants described themselves as "apolitical" while others did not find the political agenda of Asian American organizations to be of much relevance and interest. While quite tentative and diffuse in nature, a process of ethnicization of "Asian American" is suggested here. That is, there are hints of a transformation, one by which "Asian American" is seen by those who are encompassed by it as not simply an externally imposed category but a signifier of community, of shared culture and history. In invoking a pan-Asian culture, this process of ethnicization drew on ideas embedded in the model minority stereotype – in particular the presumed Asian emphasis on education and family. Also noteworthy were the ways in which distinctions of immigrant versus later-generation and East Asian versus "other Asian" were used to demarcate the boundaries of pan-Asian American community.

But while some of the second-generation Chinese and Korean Americans identified "Asian American" as a natural basis of community, most rejected it as a significant basis of affiliation and identity. For some it signified an effort to impose an artificial and fake social and political unity. Yet for others "Asian American" signified a restriction on individuality. These rejections capture the contradictions that are part of the notion of Asian American. That is, while "Asian American" has come on the one hand to signify a political strategy of empowerment, it also remains, for persons of Asian descent, a homogenizing and externally imposed category.

NOTES

1 Ruth Sidel, *Battling Bias: The Struggle for Identity and Community on College Campuses* (New York: Penguin Books, 1994), 12.
2 For a discussion of the distinction between "public" and "private" ethnicity, see Philip Kasinitz, *Caribbean New York: Black Immigrants and the Politics of Race* (Ithaca: Cornell University Press, 1992).
3 See Dana Y. Takagi, *The Retreat from Race: Asian-American Admissions and Racial Politics* (New Brunswick: Rutgers University Press, 1992) and Shirley Hune and Kenyon S. Chan, "Special Focus: Asian Pacific American Demographic and Educational Trends," in *Minorities in Higher Education*, ed. D. Carter and R. Wilson (Washington DC: American Council on Higher Education). Minority enrollment rose from 6.4 percent in 1960 to 13.8 percent in 1977. And in 1995, 11.7 percent of those obtaining bachelor's degrees were minority students, and 16.8 percent in 1994.
4 Paul R. Loeb, *Generation at the Crossroads: Apathy and Action on the American Campus* (New Brunswick: Rutgers University Press, 1994), 190.
5 According to Hune and Chan, 52, in 1995, 60 percent of Asian Pacific Americans attending college were enrolled at four-year institutions; 80 percent were in public institutions.
6 See Sidel, *Battling Bias*, 42. Asians have constituted about half of the foreign student population.
7 See Diversity Project, "An Interim Report to the Chancellor" (Berkeley: Institute for the Study of Social Change, 1989), 22.
8 Sidel, *Battling Bias*, 7–8.
9 Peter Applebome, "Nation's Campuses Confront an Expanding Racial Divide," *The New York Times*, October 25, 1995.
10 Takagi, *Retreat from Race*, 145.
11 For example, Hune and Chan, "Special Focus," 51, report better preparation and higher expectations of going to college for Asian Pacific Americans in comparison to other racial-ethnic groups.
12 The 1991 Diversity Report from the University of California at Berkeley mentions several cases in which the assessment of Black and Chicano/Latino students as undeserving and having received admission through preferences, was made by Asian American students. The report also cites survey results showing sharp disrepancies between the support of affirmative action between Asian American and other minority students. Thus 12.1 percent of Asian American students surveyed said that they "definitely" agreed with the underrepresented ethnic minority policy. This was in contrast to 61.5 percent of Blacks, 40.6 percent of Chicanos, 40.2 percent of Latinos, and 35.7 percent of Native Americans.
13 Deborah Woo, "The 'Overrepresentation' of Asian Americans: Red Herrings and Yellow Perils," in *Race and Ethnic Conflict*, ed. Fred Pincus and Howard Ehrlich (Boulder: Westview Press, 1994), 314–326.
14 Yen Le Espiritu, *Asian American Panethnicity: Bridging Institutions and Identities* (Philadelphia: Temple University Press, 1992).
15 Nazli Kibria, "The Construction of 'Asian American': Reflections on Intermarriage and Ethnic Identity among Second-Generation Chinese and Korean Americans," *Ethnic and Racial Studies* 20:4 (1997), 77–86.
16 Possible explanations for this discrepancy include the greater heterogeneity of the Chinese American population in comparison to Korean Americans, in terms of nationality, class and generation.

Part V

More than Consumption: Experiencing Gender, Class, and Race

12

Sexual Minorities and the New Urban Poverty

Jeff Maskovsky

Paulie (sometimes Paulina)[1] sat across from me at a corner table at the Street Eats Diner, a greasy spoon located in the heart of Philadelphia's downtown gay neighborhood. He lit a cigarette, took a sip of coffee, and began his life story, which he told with much flamboyance and flair, in the style of the jaded drag queen:

> My name is Paulie Robertson. I'm 34 years old. I'm the youngest of seven children. I grew up in North Philadelphia in a fairly nice home, nice parents. Two-parent home until I was about 15. Then, at last, there was just mom and seven children. Went all the way through school. Graduated from school. And decided to start working. Then decided I wanted to hang with the in-crowd because those were the disco days and all that. I was 15 years old. Phony ID and everything. I would just party hard. I would go to Center City and party. I would go to West Philly to the Olympia Ballroom. Wherever the party was that's where I went. To be in with the in-crowd, that included drinking and smoking cigarettes, and smoking reefer, just a total wild, crazy life. So, that was that. Sowing my oats, not knowing whether I wanted men or women. All that good old happy stuff.

In many respects, Paulie's life history resembles that of many lesbians and gay men, particularly gay men and lesbians of color, who have come of age, and come out, in major U.S. cities. Indeed, from Paulie's point of view, coming of age was about the pursuit of sexual freedom, identity, and community:

> In the long run, we all find out exactly who we are after a little while. The in-crowd, where I was going back in those days, was where you could just go and let your hair down, and dance with other men and all that other stuff back then. You thought you were hot stuff back then. Didn't need that much money like you do now. And then I got with the transgender community, those girls in dresses. I went from the in-crowd to finding the transgender crowd, and "oh, doll, you'll look good in make-up and hair and a wig and all that." "And smoke some of this good stuff right here, and it will make you feel good, and you'll be Diana Ross." It was crazy, but it was fun.

But Paulie's story of personal liberation is also a story of social suffering. Framed through the lens of drug addiction and prostitution, Paulie tells me not only about how he became a part of Philadelphia's gay and transgender communities, but also about his descent into poverty:

> So I thought it was fun. And one thing led to another. You start off with pot. You get tired of smoking pot. Then you want to drink beer. You get tired of beer. Do you want vodka? You get tired of vodka. Then crack came along. So you want to try that too. Back again, trying to be with the in-crowd. And things just got crazier and crazier. At that time, I was working in different restaurants in town, waiting tables or bussing tables. I worked in just about every restaurant, every good restaurant in Center City, from one to another. After you start doing a drug you're scamming this one and scamming that one. You scam enough people, and then you move on to the next place. Then when I started really doing hard drugs, which was crack, then it became prostitution time, because no matter how many jobs you've had, or how much money you had coming in, if you needed to put on a skirt and go in a corner to make some money, there I was. That led to about eight or nine years...doing that. Still working two jobs, still standing on the corner turning tricks, and it was just crazy. Losing jobs and losing apartments. And mother putting you out. And all that good stuff. "Get out. Come back when you get yourself together."

Paulie's life history is but one reminder that lesbians and gay men are not immune to poverty.[2]

Indeed, while cities are traditionally described as places of sexual freedom, expression, and community for lesbians and gay men in the United States, the same political-economic developments that have facilitated the growth of these liberated communities have also caused economic deprivation and immiseration affecting a growing number of sexual minorities.

In this chapter I place poor lesbians and gay men like Paulie at the center of analysis. This focus represents a shift from current preoccupations in the field of lesbian/gay studies that privilege consumption-based theories of identity formation and, consequently, elide class-based differences *within* the categories of lesbian and gay. Specifically, I show that consumption practices and commercial contexts are central in the lives of poor sexual minorities, but they operate very differently than for middle-class lesbians and gay men. Poor lesbians and gay men form communities within commercial contexts, but these are communities of workers, not consumers. Conversely, poor lesbians and gay men adopt consumer identities, but they do so in relation to the services of the welfare state, not to an ever-expanding world of retail goods and services. The chapter ends by considering the ironic and even perverse consequences of neoliberal political developments, which include the tempered yet increasingly popular embrace of gay consumer culture, for poor sexual minorities.[3]

Consumption, What's Your Function?

Foundational works by historians, anthropologists, and other scholars have identified the importance of urban-based consumerism to the development of gay and lesbian community and politics (D'Emilio 1983; D'Emilio and Freedman 1988; Duberman et al. 1989). They have shown how sexual minority identities and politics are consolidated and transformed through social relations forged in commercialized leisure sites such as bars, clubs, and theaters (Beemyn 1997; Chauncey 1994; Newton 1993). For instance, Kennedy and Davis (1993) explore how working-class lesbian communities built around the bar culture of the 1940s and 1950s in Buffalo served as a precursor to the lesbian and gay liberation movement. It was in these bars, they argue, that lesbian identity was first consolidated and then transformed into political consciousness. This and related work in the field of lesbian/gay studies focuses on sites of commercial consumption, and for good reason: for most gay men and lesbians, workplaces were, and continue to be, sites of extreme homophobia, heterosexism, and harassment. It is only in locations outside of work, in spaces where gays and lesbians are relatively, but by no means absolutely, free from harassment, that gay and lesbian identity, community, and politics have been forged.

Yet this approach overlooks the important fact that the commercialized sites of lesbian and gay consumption – whether they be bars, theaters, or even street corners – are often workplaces as well.[4] The bars and theaters that have helped to consolidate lesbian and gay communities are sustained by the labor practices of other lesbians and gay men, who typically are of different socioeconomic status than the patrons they serve. In other words, leisure sites are social spaces that are constituted not only through the consumption practices of customers, but also through the labor practices of workers. The failure to attend to labor practices has created an uneven view of lesbian and gay community formation in lesbian/gay studies. It has prevented us from asking the following questions:

1 What role do workers play in the creation of community? How do the relations of exploitation – defined here as relations that pit low-end service workers against owners and consumers in the context of the workplace, and that are structured along class lines, with their race and gender dimensions – shape the politicization of lesbian and gay identity?
2 What happens to lesbians and gay men who cannot get work? How do they form communities and politics?
3 To what extent does the emergence of lesbian and gay consumption-based communities represent a politics of exclusion in which the poor are separated for economic and/or cultural reasons from their more affluent counterparts?
4 What is the relationship of the poor to sexual minority politics?

The remainder of this chapter discusses several examples of sexual minorities living in urban poverty in the United States – examples that have until now been largely excluded from much of the academic literature in lesbian/gay studies.

Sexual Minorities in the New Urban Poverty

The growth of lesbian and gay neighborhoods and commercial zones during the past 35 years must be viewed in connection with wider economic changes affecting cities throughout the United States. Since the 1950s and 1960s, manufacturing plants have left the major mid-Atlantic, Northeastern and Midwestern cities, first for the Sunbelt and then for other countries. This shift has had two major results. First, the number, quality, wages, and security of low-skill and semi-skilled jobs have decreased nationwide, especially in large urban centers. Second, the high-skill service and financial sector has grown to manage, coordinate, and speed up production processes that have become nationally and globally dispersed to an unprecedented degree as production has been relocated across the globe. As a result, many cities are marked by what Neil Smith (1991) calls "uneven development." In this situation, the service and finance firms cluster in central business districts, sometimes accompanied by gentrified housing for their employees, and by retail outlets that employ low-end service workers; whereas older, formerly industrial neighborhoods are marked by declining social services, decaying housing stocks, and concentrated poverty. Faced with budget deficits, declining bond ratings, declining amounts of federal assistance, and loss of population and businesses, municipal leaders have been forced to pump a disproportionate share of public resources into relatively small, targeted areas in the hopes of jump-starting their local economies. "Uneven development," says Smith (1991:5), "is social inequality blazoned into the geographical landscape, and it is simultaneously the exploitation of that geographical unevenness for certain socially determined ends" – in this case, neoliberal efforts to improve cities' images and, by extension it is hoped, their economic fortunes.

An emerging body of literature locates the development of lesbian and gay communities within the dynamic of uneven development. One strand of the literature argues that gay men – and to a lesser extent lesbians – often take advantage of economic and social opportunities in developing urban areas by becoming urban pioneers and gentrifiers. By participating as urban pioneers, some argue, they form residential and commercial enclaves that help to insulate them from many forms of anti-gay discrimination (Bell and Valentine 1995; Castells 1983; Ettorre 1978; Lauria and Knopp 1985; Levine 1979). Others have challenged the putatively progressive, identity-based premise underlying this argument to show how gay and lesbian developers and small business owners place their class interests above the interests of a community based on sexual identity. Knopp (1997), for instance, shows how gay neighborhood development in New Orleans was structured by class interests. Developers, many of whom were gay, sought to make profits by building luxury housing in a gay neighborhood. This strategy of capital accumulation pitted them against middle- and low-income gay residents, with the consequence that the community became more stratified along class lines. Similarly, Weston and Rofel (1997:40) argue for a view of class as "property relations and the division of labor [that] continuously generates class divisions" in their discussion of class struggle between lesbian workers and owners in an auto mechanic shop. These studies explore the class-based contradictions that emerge in the formation of gay and lesbian communities and politics, and they do so by approaching class not exclusively as the outgrowth of consumption practices. Rather, they connect class to sexuality by examining how sexualized identities, communities, and politics are forged in contexts shaped, first and foremost, by the objective political-economic processes that produce class relations. This view of community and politics – forged out of class and its connection to sexuality – serves as the basis in this paper for my discussion of gay and lesbian poverty.[5]

This chapter builds on Knopp's and Weston and Rofel's work to show how the economy and the state (through the provision of social welfare) have become key features in the growth of community and politics for poor lesbians and gay men. I will review several examples that describe the making of poverty for lesbians and gay men, and that highlight the importance of large-scale economic restructuring and the role of welfare state policies in shaping lesbian and gay identities, communities, and politics among the poor (Maskovsky 1999).

Gay Ghetto Service Work and the Construction of Gay Identity

I begin with a description of the work history of Drew, an African American gay man in his fifties. Unlike the migration narratives that are widespread in the literature on community-building in lesbian/gay studies, Drew did not come to Philadelphia from a small town in the Midwest. He grew up in a black neighborhood outside the city center that has been hit hard over the last 30 years by the elimination of manufacturing jobs, disastrous urban planning, and the withdrawal of social services (Adams et al. 1991 describe the political-economic developments). Drew left home at 16 in search of "community." He began hanging out on 13th Street, the heart of Philadelphia's main gay neighborhood. Several gay-oriented adult bookshops are located on the street, as is Philadelphia's largest gay bar and disco. Over the years, 13th Street has become a major site of sex work for black gays and transgender men and women. It quickly became Drew's primary site not only of community but of work. Soon after his arrival, Drew started working at a local gay bar as a female impersonator.

Drew was very successful as a professional drag queen, and eventually earned enough money and notoriety to take his show on the road. For 20 years, he toured as a headliner, and helped other young gay men by hiring them to perform with him. Despite his relative fame, however, Drew always had difficulty making ends meet. While the pay was good, expenses associated with being a professional drag queen are quite high. He had to pay the other drag queens out of his own pocket; he also incurred expenses for travel, lodging, and the materials used in making elaborate costumes. Even after 20 years, he still struggled to get by.

Eventually, Drew stopped touring. Audiences, he said, lost interest in drag, and life was too hard on the road. The young men he hired often left the road without warning, and they often stole from him. He returned to Philadelphia and performed infrequently at local gay bars, which, he complains, now prefer go-go boys to drag queens. His connections in the community got him a job as a short-order cook at the Street Eats Diner, which is less than two blocks away from where he used to hang out on 13th Street. He now makes about $250 a week, without health or retirement benefits, vacation pay, or sick leave. He has moved into a one-bedroom apartment nearby. Drew now lives on the edge of impoverishment. So long as he can keep his job, or another one like it, he will avoid total destitution, but old age with minimal social security payments (since his income was mostly off the record) will probably push him below the poverty line. Despite all this, Drew is still very positive about the gay community. He says:

> I learned to be gay on 13th Street. I brought other young ones from there with me and taught them the business. It was crazy and there was a lot of fighting, but it was just my way of giving them a little fame.

As to his work situation, he adds:

> I am the same as everyone else who comes in here [to the coffee shop] or who watches my shows, except I have a little bit more fame. The only thing that I don't like is that sometimes they don't pay you. They don't know how to run a restaurant or a bar, so they run out of money and you are out of luck.

Drew's story allows us to make a number of important points about sexual minorities in the low end of the labor market. First, his experience accords with what Weston and Rofel (1997:27–30) call "bridging the public and private" in the workplace. For Drew, as for the lesbians who worked at the garage where Weston and Rofel did fieldwork, working in a gay-owned business breaks down the binary opposition between work and leisure by bringing gay identity – so often theorized only in the context of leisure activities in the private sphere – into the public sphere of the workplace. It would be a mistake to conclude that bridging the public and the private is seamless or easy, as Weston and Rofel demonstrate. As Drew's experience confirms, the politics of the gay community masks economic inequalities in the workplace. His attitudes exemplify the uneasy coexistence of gay identity and class. By viewing himself as "just like everyone else," he deploys a universal gay identity; in nearly the same breath, however, he also recounts the relations of class exploitation that differentiate him from the white middle-class employers and clientele he serves.

Drew's story also calls into question the primacy of consumption practices in shaping lesbian and gay identity. His role as a female impersonator and his efforts to train younger gay men as apprentices provide one example of the importance of the role that workers play in the consolidation of lesbian and gay identity in commercial locales. Indeed, it is often the sex workers, bartenders, barbacks, go-go boys, go-go girls, and other performers – usually from different racial groups and class positions than the consumers they serve – who become central figures in gay and lesbian communities and struggles. In Philadelphia's downtown gay community, for instance, every politically involved lesbian and gay man knows Drew. In New York, famously, the drag queens and lesbians and gay men of color who worked at the Stonewall Inn started the riot.

Drew's story also exemplifies how many men and women of color find jobs in the low-wage, low-end service sector of the gay and lesbian economy. This is the result of wider labor market trends that are exploited by gay and lesbian business owners without a second thought as to the effect on equality and solidarity within "the community." Drew's comments suggest that he has experienced a lifetime of exploitation, including the refusal of several employers to pay him for work. In the name of the gay community, employers exercise their entrepreneurial spirit on the backs of their workers, thereby reinforcing race, class, and gender divisions within lesbian and gay communities.

Poverty and Lesbian and Gay Community Formation

But what about lesbians and gay men who, because of constraints on labor markets, spend time outside of the paid workforce? For them, the institutions of social welfare play a determining role in the formation of community. In fact, as we shall see in the following example, publicly funded service programs often form the crucible in which community is formed.

Dawn and Sandi, both African American lesbians, grew up in poor neighborhoods in Newark and Atlantic City, respectively. Hit hard by the economic crises affecting inner cities in the Northeast, Dawn and Sandi experienced family lives characterized by extreme deprivation, violence, and abuse. When Dawn was 15, she was institutionalized for a month and then thrown out of the house after her mother discovered her *in flagrante delicto* with her female babysitter. For her part, Sandi ran away from home when her father, after having initiated her into drug abuse, put pressure on her to return to high school. Both were addicted to street drugs by the time they were in their mid-teens. For decades, they worked in the informal drug economies of Newark, Atlantic City, and Philadelphia.

The quasi-institutionalized setting of publicly funded drug rehabilitation programs inadvertently provides opportunities for sexual minorities like Dawn and Sandi to form community. Dawn moved to Philadelphia to get clean. She entered the New Directions Treatment Center (NDTC), an inpatient detox program, after several other attempts to stay clean had failed. Detox was a harrowing experience for Dawn. One of its advantages, however, was forced segregation between men and women. This situation helped Dawn to get to know other women. She explains,

> For the first couple of days I laid in my own pee. I was a mess. And I had the shakes. I could hardly talk. The thing there was we don't talk to the men only 'til night. Then everyone [the women] get into a community room. And then we had the chance to talk or say what you feel about an individual so that there wouldn't be any trouble. And I didn't mind

> that part about not speaking to the men. I was real happy that the women could not talk to the men because I was gay and that only left me for them to talk to. And that was real good to me. So that stipulation didn't bother me at all. They [the men] walked on one side of the wall, and we had to walk on the other side of the wall....And in the program I learned who I was. And I learned that I wasn't really a bad person. I just never had a chance to pull it together. And I learned that I was an alcoholic. And I learned that I was also a part of gamblers anonymous. And, you know, I learned a lot about me. When I left the program I left there with more friends than I had made in my whole life, I mean, real friends.

The race, class, and gender dynamics of this situation are worth mentioning. Inside NDTC, contact between drug users – most of whom are poor black, inner-city residents – is highly regimented and severely constrained. This strategy accords with wider cultural assumptions about the inner-city poor, the so-called underclass, whose (hetero)sexuality is pathologized as one aspect of the "culture of poverty." Indeed, the sexuality of the black poor – often implicitly characterized in poverty studies as "lacking monogamy" or, worse, "hypersexual" – is viewed as a causal factor in preventing their upward mobility (e.g. Wilson 1987; for a critique of this view of "underclass" sexuality, see di Leonardo 1997). It is no surprise, then, that detox programs would segregate their client populations along gender lines.

Dawn's story shows how poor lesbians and gay men can, even under the most dire of circumstances, use the presumption of heterosexuality – based in this case on racialized and gendered categorizations of poverty – to form community within state-based institutions. Furthermore, state-based institutional contexts can also be places where lesbians and gay men actively and openly pursue relationships. In Sandi's case, she spent eight years in prison and agreed to enter rehab as a condition of her parole. She had already arrived at NDTC by the time Dawn entered the program. They met at a lesbian and gay dance sponsored by a recovery group spun off from NDTC. In order to spend more time with Dawn, Sandi volunteered to be Dawn's detox counselor a few weeks later. Thus, it was through the institutional practices associated with recovery – Narcotics Anonymous meetings, recovery dances, peer-based drug counseling – that Dawn and Sandi's intimacy was forged.

Dawn and Sandi eventually became central figures in a gay and lesbian community of poor, black recovering addicts. Their wedding was publicly recognized in a marriage ceremony in a downtown Unitarian church in March 1992. Evidence that the ceremony served as an important symbol of lesbian and gay community for the poor appeared the following month in a locally produced newsletter that is read by many low-income sexual minorities. In a commentary entitled "The Wedding of the Century," one community member wrote:

> The royal court has assembled in the great hall. The women are flawlessly dressed in their finest attire. The men are handsomely modeling two and three piece suits in colors that shame the most brilliant of rainbows. The atmosphere is charged with laughter, joy, and a sense of celebration. The crowd waits anxiously for the arrival of the bride and groom in anticipation of the wedding of the century.
>
> This is not the wedding of English Royalty or the climax of some happy ever after fairy tale, but the wedding of two lesbian women. On March 7, 1992, at 1:00, before family, friends and many well wishers, Dawn Sampson and Sandi Jones affirmed their love for each other. Their vow was to love each other with the seven types of love. The ceremony brought tears to this writer's eyes as the soloists moved the souls of the audience (which sent accolades rising to the rafters). Then we all vowed to support and nurture their union. At that moment I moved from awestruck spectator to an active participant in the support of not only a marriage but the affirmation of our Gay lifestyle itself....
>
> My sincerest thanks go to Dawn and Sandi for allowing me to be a part of their celebration of love, and for being a positive example of our gay and lesbian community. The affirmation of self experienced at their wedding was outstanding. In a world where negative forces and homophobia abound, where racism, oppression, suppression and hatred are the norm (no matter how subtly), it is truly a blessing to be a part of what binds us together and encourages our triumphant survival as Gay and Lesbian MEN AND WOMEN. (Williams 1992:5–6; emphasis in original)

Elaboration of community-building through gay marriage shows that the poor are in a contradictory relationship to the social norms that seek to justify and excuse their poverty. On the one hand, Dawn and Sandi's wedding, while it displaces popular representations of sexual minorities as outside the normative assumptions about marriage and family, can nonetheless be seen as a capitulation to the bourgeois values of marriage that are sanctioned by the very state that oppresses them. This is particularly so since the institutions of the state serve as major sites in the formation of poor sexual minority communities, and, hence, are much more implicated, in a pernicious way, in their community-building practices than in the community-building practices of their more affluent counterparts. On the other hand, this wedding challenges the representation of poor blacks as deviant and pathological members of America's underclass. Indeed, while some may interpret gay marriages like Dawn and Sandi's as further evidence of pathological familial dysfunction among the inner-city poor, the overwhelmingly affirmative tone of the article quoted above refutes the abjectness that is often considered to be the essential condition of urban poverty. Thus, the uncritical and arguably conservative embrace of gay marriage functions in this instance to disrupt the "culture of poverty" argument. It provides an important, albeit contradictory, basis for the poor who are doubly oppressed by social norms (in the sense that they are not only asked to conform to them, but their ability to conform to them is then put under intense scrutiny) to legitimatize themselves in the face of a wide array of racist and classist cultural valuations that seek to blame them for their own impoverishment.

Poverty, Sexual Politics, and Sexual Citizenship

It is often said that poor sexual minorities do not participate in lesbian and gay identity politics and, hence, are not political. However, my research in Philadelphia suggests that poor lesbians and gay men are indeed political, but the dynamics of their politicization vary significantly from those of their middle-class counterparts. Excluded from leisure activities associated with the arenas of retail-oriented consumption out of which lesbian and gay identity politics was born, the politicization of poor lesbians and gay men nonetheless relates to their consumer identities. However, for the poor, these identities are forged in relation to the services of the welfare state. A case in point is poor sexual minority participation in AIDS politics. In the following example, the intersecting history of AIDS politics and poverty provides the context in which it is possible to explore avenues for political mobilization involving poor lesbians and gay men.

In Philadelphia, competition for funding between white-led and black-led AIDS organizations has manifested itself in a political discourse pitting "black providers" against "gay providers." This discourse was framed by the state's model of structuring competing claims to political authenticity and community leadership that required the emphasis of key social markers (e.g. gay, black, Latino, women) in the name of communities affected by HIV. This selective, asymmetrical, and nonsensical emphasis on sexuality vs. race as the central political struggle affecting the provision of life-supporting AIDS services had a number of consequences for HIV-positive people, particularly the poor. The harnessing of social identities conventionally used in political mobilizations to "provider" identities has displaced a class-based discourse and allowed those who identify as "providers" (i.e. the professional staff of AIDS service organizations) to gain prominence in the political field. As a result, HIV-positive people, the vast majority of whom are poor and black, have been forced to adopt the identity of "consumers" of AIDS services in the context of battles over AIDS service provision. While the adoption of this identity tends to mask issues of poverty, deprivation, and political exclusion by treating the receipt of life-supporting health services as a matter of consumer choice, it has nonetheless fostered and sustained key forms of political action among poor PWAs [persons (living) with AIDS], such as when they demanded an adequate HIV standard of health care as their "consumer" right.

However, this situation has impeded poor sexual minorities from elaborating their demands to the state as sexualized political subjects. In fact, the emergence of consumer identities in the realm of the AIDS services system must be viewed as part of the state's effort to use service provision in combination with neoliberal ideologies of "empowerment" and "consumer choice" to promote self-regulation and to quell dissent among PWAs. One aspect of this strategy of incorporation is that consumerism works to delink gay and lesbian identity from consumer identity by linking it instead with provider identities. This makes poor people into desexualized political subjects in the language of the state. Said differently, the state effectively forces poor lesbians and gay men to sacrifice their sexual identities in order to gain access to the political process as consumers. Similarly, lesbians and gay men who rely on other public services are increasingly being recast in public discussion as consumers, thereby erasing their sexual identities at the same time as consumer-based political constituencies are formed.

Yet despite efforts by the state to desexualize poverty in AIDS politics, many poor people nevertheless continue to see themselves as gay and lesbian political subjects. For instance, many refer to themselves as lesbian and gay activists after having become involved with We The People, Philadelphia's largest coalition of HIV-positive people, and one composed predominantly of low-income people of color who are active and recovering drug addicts. One such activist, Rose Williams, spoke to a group of low-income PWAs who were attending an educational program at a local AIDS organization. She said:

> When I was in my addiction I didn't think of anyone but me. Now I think of myself and other people. I made a big change. I am proud of myself from where I've come to where I am today. I'm a lesbian, I am proud to say that. I'm one of the biggest lesbian activists in the city. I fight for us. You figure, you're black, lesbian, poor, got AIDS. They don't care about us, so you got to do it yourself. We have to empower ourselves. A couple of years ago they would have said here lies a dope fiend who would have killed anyone who got in her way. Now I joined We The People, and am an actively involved woman, helping people get food stamps, get medications, get healthcare. We all have a message, I don't know how long I will be here, but while I'm here I got something to do. My higher power has allowed me to be the type of person I am today, to try to help you help yourselves.

It is important to recognize that Rose's political subjectivity is complex. Her politicization as a lesbian is linked to her politicization as a PWA, as a recovering drug user, as a poor person, as an African American, and as a woman. This is but one example of how poor sexual minorities invent overlapping (or, to use the postmodern term, fragmentary) political identities born out of historically contingent and institutionally defined circumstances.

This leads me to make a point here about gay and lesbian citizenship, an aspect of politicization that relates to, but is not wholly subsumed under, organized political activity. Specifically, I want to elaborate on the role of state-based institutions in enabling and constraining gay citizenship in relation to AIDS. The AIDS mobilization effort of the 1980s brought about the establishment of publicly funded social services, provided through organizations formed largely by activists who had fought for their creation. Most of these organizations went through a process of professionalization, where activists developed service provision skills and certification, and developed structures to offer services following increasingly formalized standards. This process of formalization has had a contradictory effect on the promotion of gay citizenship within organizations such as these. Brown (1997) argues that AIDS organizations, formed initially as voluntary organizations located in civil society and then transformed into bureaucratized agencies of service provision, are important sites of gay citizenship because they serve as gay community-centered associations where volunteers come to participate as members of the gay political community. However, he adds, these organizations have also become bureaucratic entities that disempower citizens by treating them as "clients."

As Rose's story suggests, AIDS service organizations have, to a certain extent, become a site in the expression of gay citizenship for the poor. Moreover, in these institutional contexts, the poor, like their middle-class counterparts, face increased pressure to assume formal roles in these organizations as either clients, professional staff, or board members as these organizations receive more public money to provide social services. However, unlike their middle-class counterparts, for whom there exists a wider array of privately controlled institutional locations in which it is possible to pursue gay citizenship, and for whom it is possible to take on a number of professional or voluntary roles within state-funded organizations, the poor have fewer options. They are more reliant on public institutions, and, as these organizations become more bureaucratized, ongoing professional participation and volunteerism by middle-class gay men and lesbians is more likely than it is by the poor. Indeed, a disproportionate share of poor sexual minorities are forced into the disempowering "client" role in many AIDS organizations. This shows that gay citizenship, as it is constituted in state-funded organizations, is a particularly tricky business for the poor since it is determined, first and foremost, along class lines that are structured and reproduced by the state. Still, these organizations tend to serve as important sites of community formation for poor lesbians and gay men, even if they ultimately discourage gay citizenship by promoting clientism, or, rather, consumerism, among the poor.

Towards a Lesbian/Gay Poverty Studies

In this essay I have attempted to flesh out, albeit briefly and tentatively, the link between political-economic processes and the formation of poor people's sexual-minority identities, communities, and politics. I want to conclude by discussing the consequences of these findings for lesbian and gay studies, a field that is presently led by a queer theoretical vanguard that, while actively engaged in staking out the contours of a so-called "transgressive" political project, remains largely oblivious to the poverty amongst us. In an oft-cited queer theoretical statement on the connection between capitalism and gay identity, Michael Warner (1993:xxxi) writes:

> Gay culture in [its] most visible mode is anything but external to advanced capitalism and to precisely those features of advanced capitalism that many on the left are eager to disavow. Post-Stonewall urban gay men reek of the commodity. We give off the smell of capitalism in rut, and therefore demand of theory a more dialectical view of capitalism than many people have imagined for.

For Warner, this more "dialectical" view involves the elaboration of a politics of queer identity and theory as a challenge to "the regimes of the social" under advanced capitalism. "The social," as Warner understands it, is modernity's preeminent site of normalization, a discursive domain in which subjects are constituted as either normal or deviant. More than just defining itself against what has come to be considered "normal" behavior, queer politics and theory challenge the process of normalization itself. In this way, queer identity and theory offer the possibility of unmasking broader assumptions about the economy and the state. Warner (1993:xxvii; emphasis in the original) writes:

> The social realm, in short, is a cultural form, interwoven with the political form of the administrative state and with the normalizing methodologies of modern social knowledge. Can we not hear in the resonances of queer protest an objection to the normalization of behavior in this broad sense, and thus to the cultural phenomenon of societization? If queers, incessantly told to alter their "behavior," can be understood as protesting not just the normal behavior of the social but the *idea* of normal behavior, they will bring skepticism to the methodologies founded on that idea.

As for others for whom queer theory and politics has now become *de rigueur*, Warner envisions the politics of desire as a challenge to the dominant organization of sex and gender, which in turn, translates into a paradigmatic blow against society itself.

But do we all in fact reek of the commodity, and if so, how can the politics of desire release us from commodification as it is variously constituted under the regimes of the social? For Warner and others, gay men and lesbians reek of the commodity because we are implicated in advanced capitalism's rampant consumerism. Fair enough. But positing queer subjectivity as an alternative to gay and lesbian subjectivity is hardly a solution. As Donald Morton (1995) has argued, the queer subject is also a commodified subject, and thus is an inadequate political alternative in and of itself. He writes:

> Under the ideological regime of Queer Theory, the subject is – first, last, and always – the *subject of desire* who takes the form of Warner's "cruising" (commodified/commodifying) subject and Deleuze and Guattari's "desiring machine" and lives for the "intensities" of the moment. The queer subject is utterly distrustful (incapable?) of rational calculations which inevitably "constrain" desire. The queer subject is, in other words, the model "consuming" subject for the regime of late capitalism.

I want to extend Morton's argument by suggesting that the regime of late capitalism requires both rational and irrational "consuming" subjects. For this reason, we must specify how exactly different groups of lesbians and gay men – and other sexual minorities as well – become implicated in the political economic processes of commodification if we are to hope that our academic work may have political purchase. The above examples specify the class (as well as race and gender) dimensions of poor and working-class sexual minority experience. They therefore demonstrate the class- (and race- and gender-) specific nature of our commodified selves. Specifically, I have shown how poor and working lesbians and gay men reek of the commodity, not universally as consumers in a gay marketplace, as Warner's formulation implicitly suggests, but rather as workers who must sell their labor power to gay business owners, or as "consumers" of publicly funded social services.

The implications of this argument for lesbian and gay identity politics and queer politics are significant. It is now time for us to recognize that the liberatory dimension of lesbian and gay identity politics that was operative in decades past has been replaced in the era of neoliberalism by a politics of desire that remains uncritical of the commodification of sexual minority identities. Likewise, while queer identity may be a necessary condition for building progressive political communities, it, too, is not wholly sufficient. Whereas the challenge to normalization that is envisioned in queer theory's politics of desire does move us beyond the minoritizing strategies of lesbian and gay identity politics, it does so through a heady idealism that replaces old political boundaries within sexual minority communities with new ones. Moreover, whether one believes that gay consumer power (represented, for instance, by the Martina Navratilova Visa card or gay-oriented Budweiser ads) will lead to increased tolerance and acceptance, or that the rejection of sex or gender identity under the banner of queer politics represents a radical transgression, both positions (which, tellingly, are not necessarily mutually exclusive) encourage the creation of commercialized sexual minority subcultures. These subcultures – or, in neoliberal parlance, marketing niches – work in their own ways to mask the objective political-economic processes that fragment sexual minority communities along class lines.

This point is particularly salient in the present political context. Recent shifts in health and welfare policy – shifts designed to regulate the poor through surveillance rather than supportive services – are likely to have an increasingly negative effect on the community-building strategies of poor lesbians and gay men. Indeed, as funding for health and social services associated with the welfare state has been withdrawn, voluntary detox programs, recovery programs, subsidized housing, and other supportive social and health services have been scaled back, and public funding has been diverted towards the expansion of the prison industrial complex and the development of welfare-to-work programs. This shift places more poor people in daily contact with institutions that are, for various reasons, sites of overtly coercive state control. Concomitantly, the collective survival strategies of the poor have been undermined by these shifts in social welfare policy, which have worked in tandem with wider economic restructuring to suppress wage levels for low-end workers to near historic lows (Piven 1999). As a consequence, the poor are forced into even more dire social and economic circumstances. This pattern is likely to exacerbate tensions between various groups of poor people, particularly in the context of public institutions, with increased harassment perpetrated against poor and homeless sexual minorities a likely result.

Given this likelihood, it is vital that we make our politics more meaningful for poor and working-class sexual minorities. This requires the reversal of decades-long trends in social theory and politics that have disavowed the importance of class and avoided direct challenges to capitalism itself. We should think seriously about revisiting some of the earliest debates within lesbian/gay studies, debates that occurred in the early years of gay liberation, and that focused on the relationship between sexualized political subjects and socialism. Some may be appalled by this suggestion, viewing it as a giant step backwards. Others will see it as an opportunity to align lesbian/gay studies more closely with the working-class struggles that are once again on the move in the United States and abroad. In the current neoliberal climate, poverty is becoming invisible in both popular and academic treatments of urban life. Those of us in lesbian/gay studies should do our utmost to avoid collaborating with this new regime of disappearance. If we fail to contend with the material basis of poverty, and with the neoliberal ideologies and policies that mask increased inequalities inside and outside sexual minority communities, our work will continue to ignore poverty as an issue which an increasingly large number of sexual minorities have no choice but to face in their everyday lives. But if we meet the challenge of a lesbian/gay poverty studies, our future contains the potential for a historical realignment with the perspectives and needs of a major segment of the population in whose name we carry out our work.

NOTES

1 All of the names that appear in this chapter are pseudonyms. All place names have been changed as well.

2 A joint report published by the Policy Institute of the National Gay and Lesbian Task Force and the Institute for Gay and Lesbian Strategic Studies, authored by M. V. Lee Badgett (1999), suggests that gay men and lesbians are found across the spectrum of income distribution and may, in fact, earn less than their heterosexual counterparts. One survey discussed in the report found that approximately 20 percent of lesbians and gay men earned less than $15,000 per year (as compared to almost 12 percent of heterosexuals); another found that household income is less than $10,000 for 7 to 8 percent of lesbians and gay men (and approximately 12 percent for heterosexuals).

3 Neoliberalism is commonly characterized as the strategy that promotes the primacy of unhindered market forces as the most effective means toward achieving economic growth and guaranteeing social welfare (Sanchez-Otero 1993; Bourdieu 1999). The valorization of the market is coupled with the vilification of the welfare state to justify a range of public policies that divert public dollars from spending on social programs and insurance and use them instead to make direct subsidies to private firms. This reframing of public policies away from universal access and toward market-based models is justified as a necessary step to eliminate dependency among the poor and other marginalized groups. The economic imperatives lurking behind these policies should not be overlooked, however. Mike Davis (1986) has shown that privatization became imperative in the 1970s and 1980s, as the U.S. economy entered what became a long postwar downturn. In this period, the state's intervention is explicitly aimed at sustaining the health and growth of the private sector. Indeed, the devolution of public health and welfare from public institutions to private firms is a form of state intervention and subsidy designed to avoid the impending crisis in capital accumulation. The economic imperatives lurking behind these reform efforts are seldom discussed in policy debates. Instead, debates center around the moral and political imperative to eliminate dependency and the forms of social insurance that encourage it. Neoliberal policy, then, is a form of governance to which the poor and other groups are increasingly subjected, and the rhetoric of "reform," framed historically in the United States in terms of progress, social improvement, and mobility, is used in the present period to mask the material causes of poverty and to justify a range of new policy initiatives that subordinate poor and working people's quality of life concerns to the interest of private enterprise.

4 Neoliberalism is the post-Keynesian model of the social order that champions unhindered market forces as the most effective means towards achieving economic growth and guaranteeing social welfare (Sanchez-Otero 1993; Bourdieu 1999). At the economic level, neoliberalism became imperative in the 1970s and 1980s, as the U.S. economy entered what has become a long postwar downturn (Davis 1986). Faced with a profit squeeze, U.S. capital abrogated its "Fordist" contract with labor, downsized and relocated the manufacturing

industry to the low-wage, non-union South and Southwest and overseas, and began a political and ideological assault on civil rights, environmental and other regulations, and Keynesian policies that sought to regulate the economy with public investment.

The federal government has embraced not only the legislative agenda of corporate America but also the ideology and culture of the free market. Increasingly, the government has tried to act like a corporation; it has downsized welfare, public health care, public education and a host of other important social services, and it is threatening to privatize social security and other programs that most people consider to be a public trust. Although these changes finally led to the "restoration of profitability" among U.S. firms in the 1990s, they have also created almost unprecedented social and economic polarization in the U.S. and abroad (Henwood 2000).

Yet the political and economic imperatives lurking behind these reform efforts are seldom discussed in policy debates. Instead, debates center around the moral and political imperative to eliminate dependency and the forms of social insurance that encourage it. Neoliberal policy then is a form of governance to which the poor and other groups are increasingly subjected, and the rhetoric of "reform," framed historically in the U.S. in terms of progress, social improvement and mobility, is used in the present period to mask the material causes of poverty and to justify a range of new policy initiatives that subordinate poor and working people's quality of life concerns to the interest of private enterprise.

Although the reframing of public policies away from universal access towards market-based models is justified as a necessary step to eliminate dependency among the poor and other marginalized groups, the devolution of public health and welfare from public institutions to private firms is a reactive form of state intervention and subsidy designed to overcome the crisis in capital accumulation. Thus, while a major tenet of neoliberalism is that government regulation hinders competition and prevents the system from reaching its "natural" efficiency, the truth of the matter is that government intervention has been essential in restoring profitability. In fact, one of the most misunderstood and oft-ignored differences between neoconservatism and neoliberalism is that while the former simplistically (and ironically) rails against government from within the halls of Congress, the latter embraces ideologies of "good" government and "efficient government," acknowledging in code the state's role in promoting the "free" market.

5 This approach departs not only from the dominant understanding of sexual identity in lesbian/gay studies, but also from the typical treatment of poverty by anthropologists and other scholars and policymakers. Indeed, as economic inequality increases in the United States, old assumptions about the causes of poverty have re-emerged and are once again fueling new attacks against the poor by politicians, policy experts, and media pundits. Underlying popular and political responses to poverty in the last three decades of the century has been the well-known "culture of poverty" thesis. This thesis, originally formulated by Oscar Lewis (1966) and disseminated widely through the Moynihan report (Moynihan 1965), argues that impoverished people's antisocial cultural practices prevent their upward mobility. The "culture of poverty" thesis, although thoroughly critiqued by progressive policymakers and scholars, continues to hold sway, and indeed has been resurrected and promoted most enthusiastically in recent years both in policy circles and among large segments of the American public. A more useful approach treats poverty as a political and economic problem affecting working-class neighborhoods, communities, and workplaces. Building on the work done by social scientists who challenged Oscar Lewis' original formulation, a new generation of scholars is challenging the newest versions of the "culture of poverty" thesis. By using new theoretical approaches that situate different groups' experiences of poverty in dialectical relation to global, national, state, and local political and economic change, and in relation to the interconnected ideologies of race, class, gender, sexuality, and nation, the new poverty studies treat poverty not as a static condition but as a dynamic, historically contingent process (see Susser 1982, 1996; B. Williams 1988; Goode and Maskovsky 2001).

REFERENCES

Adams, Carolyn, David Bartelt, David Elesh, Ira Goldstein, Nancy Kleniewski, and William Yancey. 1991. *Philadelphia: Neighborhoods, Divisions and Conflict in a Post-Industrial City*. Philadelphia: Temple University Press.

Badgett, M. V. Lee. 1999. Income Inflation: The Myth of Affluence among Gay, Lesbian, and Bisexual Americans. A Joint Publication of the Policy Institute of the National Gay and Lesbian Task Force and the Institute for Gay and Lesbian Strategic Studies. URL: <http://www.ngltf.org/downloads/income.pdf> (February 6, 2000).

Beemyn, Brett. 1997. A Queer Capital. In *Creating a Place for Ourselves: Lesbian, Gay and Bisexual Community Histories*. Brett Beemyn, ed. Pp. 183–210. New York: Routledge.

Bell, David, and Gill Valentine, eds. 1995. *Mapping Desire: Geographies of Sexualities*. New York: Routledge.

Bourdieu, Pierre. 1999. *Acts of Resistance against the Tyranny of the Market*. New York: New Press.

Brown, Michael P. 1997. *Replacing Citizenship: AIDS Activism and Radical Democracy*. New York: Guilford Press.

Castells, Manuel. 1983. *The City and the Grassroots*. Berkeley: University of California Press.

Chauncey, George. 1994. *Gay New York*. Chicago: University of Chicago Press.

Davis, Mike. 1986. *Prisoners of the American Dream*. London: Verso.

D'Emilio, John. 1983. *Sexual Politics, Sexual Communities*. Chicago: University of Chicago Press.

D'Emilio, John, and Estelle B. Freedman. 1988. *Intimate Matters: A History of Sexuality in America*. New York: Harper & Row.

di Leonardo, Micaela. 1997. White Lies, Black Myths. In *The Gender/Sexuality Reader*. R. Lancaster and M. di Leonardo, eds. Pp. 53–70. New York: Routledge.

Duberman, Martin B., Martha Vicinus, and George Chauncey, eds. 1989. *Hidden from History: Reclaiming the Gay and Lesbian Past*. New York: New American Library.

Ettorre, E. M. 1978. Women, Urban Social Movements and the Lesbian Ghetto. *International Journal of Urban and Regional Research* 2(3):499–520.

Goode, Judith, and J. Maskovsky, eds. 2001. *New Poverty Studies: The Ethnography of Policy, Politics and Impoverished People in the U.S.* New York: New York University Press.

Henwood, Dong. 2000. Boom for Whom? *Left Business Observer* 93 (February):4, 7.

Kennedy, Elizabeth, and M. Davis. 1993. *Boots of Leather, Slippers of Gold*. New York: Routledge.

Knopp, Lawrence. 1997. Gentrification and Gay Neighborhood Formation in New Orleans: A Case Study. In *Homo Economicus*. A. Gluckman, and B. Reed, eds. Pp. 45–64. New York: Routledge.

Lauria, Mickey, and Lawrence Knopp. 1985. Towards an Analysis of the Role of Gay Communities in the Urban Renaissance. *Urban Geography* 6:152–169.

Levine, Martin P. 1979. Gay Ghetto. *Journal of Homosexuality* 4(4):363–377.

Lewis, Oscar. 1966. The Culture of Poverty. *Scientific American* 215(4):19–25.

Maskovsky, Jeff. 1999. Fighting for our Lives: Poverty and AIDS Politics in Neoliberal Philadelphia. Ph.D. dissertation in Anthropology, Temple University, Philadelphia.

Morton, Donald. 1995. Queerity and Ludic Sado-Masochism: Compulsory Consumption and the Emerging Post-al Queer. In *Post-Ality: Marxism and Postmodernism*, a special issue of *Transformation* 1:189–215.

Moynihan, Daniel P. 1965. *The Negro Family: The Case for National Action*. Washington, DC: U.S. Department of Labor.

Newton, Esther. 1979. *Mother Camp*. Chicago: University of Chicago Press.

Newton, Esther. 1993. *Cherry Grove*. Boston, MA: Beacon Press.

Piven, Frances Fox. 1999. Welfare Reform and the Economic and Cultural Reconstruction of Low Wage Labor Markets. *City and Society* (Annual Review): 21–37.

Sanchez-Otero, German. 1993. Neoliberalism and its Discontents. *NACLA Report on the Americas* 26 (4):18–21.

Shields, Rob, ed. 1992. *Lifestyle Shopping: The Subject of Consumption*. New York: Routledge.

Smith, Neil. 1991. *Uneven Development: Nature, Capital and the Production of Space*. Cambridge, MA: Basil Blackwell.

Susser, Ida. 1982. *Norman Street: Poverty and Politics in an Urban Neighborhood*. New York: Oxford University Press.

Susser, Ida. 1996. The Construction of Poverty and Homelessness in U.S. Cities. *Annual Review of Anthropology* 25:411–435.

Warner, Michael. 1993. Introduction. In *Fear of a Queer Planet*. M. Warner, ed. Pp. vii–xxxi. Minneapolis: University of Minnesota Press.

Weston, Kath, and Lisa B. Rofel. 1997. Sexuality, Class and Conflict in a Lesbian Workplace. In *Homo Economicus*. A. Gluckman, and B. Reed, eds. Pp. 25–44. New York: Routledge.

Williams, Brett. 1988. *Upscaling Downtown: Stalled Gentrification in Washington, DC*. Ithaca, NY: Cornell University Press.

Williams, Rodney. 1992. The Wedding of the Century. *Alive and Kicking* 6:5–6.

Wilson, William J. 1987. *The Truly Disadvantaged: The Inner City, the Underclass and Public Policy*. Chicago: University of Chicago Press.

13

Institutional Violence in the Everyday Practices of School: The Narrative of a Young Lesbian

Kathryn Herr

...institutional violence is so firmly embedded in everyday practices that it is virtually concealed from scrutiny and is rarely labeled or linked to violence.

We are growing accustomed to shocking headlines and news announcements describing the latest incidents of violence in our nation's schools. Attributing these "aberrant" acts to the vagaries of "disturbed" children and adolescents, we debate whether to put 13-year-olds on trial as adults or children, focusing on holding individuals responsible for what appear to be individual actions. Ironically, although this increased focus on youth violence highlights legitimate concerns and tragedies, our current definitions of violence also obscure our vision.

We are not accustomed to naming everyday actions that diminish human capacity as violence, and they go unrecognized, unnamed, and unchallenged. We are not shocked but, rather, give a nod of recognition to societal arrangements that seem "normal" but in reality injure those not privileged by the status quo. Drawing on an expanded notion of violence, this article explores the experiences of a young lesbian, "Elise," naming her everyday experiences in public schools as part of a continuum of violence.

Part of a larger investigation of institutional violence, the study in this article will re-examine the construction of Elise as a school "failure," one of the disproportionate number of gay and lesbian youths who drop out each year. I suggest that in actuality Elise left school because of the school's perpetuation of, and failure to interrupt, institutional violence; her failure is not an individual one but, rather, rests with the institution designed expressly for her education.

Although individuals are sometimes caught and held accountable for the violent acts they perpetrate, institutions are not typically seen as contributing to these individual actions, nor are they held responsible for their part in the cultivation of individual violence. A critical lens would suggest that institutions are, in fact, doing their part in maintaining a heterosexist status quo congruent with cultural valuing.

Multiple Layers of Violence

In their reconceptualization of violence, Van Soest and Bryant (1995) link conditions of oppression with multilayered manifestations of violence. They see individual acts of violence as intricately related to institutional practices and sociocultural beliefs and values, making the case that our institutions and value system are, in reality, fertile ground for the cultivation of individual acts of violence. This lens on violence has similarities to the case made by feminists regarding a "rape supportive culture," which provides the context for actual sexual assaults (Brownmiller 1975; Donat and D'Emilio 1992). Feminists contend that, rather than an act of sexual deviancy, "sexual assault is better understood as an act of violence, supported by prevailing cultural attitudes that condone and normalize violence against women" (White and Farmer 1992:46).

Van Soest and Bryant (1995) define violence as any act or situation in which a person is injured, whether physically or psychologically; there does not need to be a direct relationship between the perpetrators and their targets but, rather, a climate in which violence prevails and allows destructive actions to be normed and carried out in an uninterrupted fashion. This "includes any avoidable action that violates a human right in the broadest sense or that prevents the fulfillment of a basic human need" (p. 550).

Whereas individual acts of violence against gays and lesbians are those most commonly reported (Pierce and Taitano 1996), institutional violence, the focus of this article, is rarely acknowledged or recognized. Most often, institutional violence is "submerged from view so that its forms are almost completely invisible. Violence at this level includes harmful actions by societal institutions and their various organizational units that obstruct the spontaneous unfolding of human potential" (Van Soest and Bryant 1995:551). As Bourdieu (1977) points out, once a system of mechanisms is in place within an institution that ensures the reproduction of the established order, "the dominant class have only to let the system they dominate take its own course in order to exercise their domination" (p. 190). Terming this "symbolic violence," he goes on to make the case that these mechanisms relieve those in power of the direct and daily work of more "elementary forms of domination" – the direct domination of one person to another. The domination and the violence, in the form of everyday institutional practices, are then disguised from recognition and critique.

For purposes of this article, these practices of symbolic, institutional violence are considered to be a direct outgrowth of the sociocultural context in which the dominant beliefs reflect a heterosexist view or what Audre Lorde (1984) describes as a "belief in the inherent superiority of one pattern of loving and thereby its right to dominance" (p. 45). Institutionally violent practices, then, are expressions of dominant societal ideologies and function as a mechanism of social control; for example, one implicit role of societal institutions, such as schools, is to promote the pervasive ideology of heterosexism and thereby perpetuate clear constructs of maleness and femaleness (Friend 1993; Lewis and Karin 1994).

To fit into schools and society in their current form is to accept, or at least not overtly resist, traditional gender-role behaviors. Many public school classrooms and curriculums explicitly privilege married heterosexuality over other practices of sexuality (Fine 1988). Homophobia, the fear of being thought to be gay or lesbian and hatred of gays and lesbians, reinforces heterosexual privilege and sexist behaviors (Elia 1993; Friend 1993). Because, as Fine points out, public schools have "rejected the task of sexual dialogue and critique" (p. 30), homophobic structures and practices are perpetuated and go uninterrupted.

It is important to remember that what happens inside schools is not divorced from the larger sociocultural environment in which schools operate (Ball 1987, cited in Corbett 1991) and that, in fact, schools often fulfill a societal purpose in maintenance of the status quo of social arrangements. Over time, institutional violence is so firmly embedded in everyday practices that it is virtually concealed from scrutiny and is rarely labeled or linked to violence.

Becoming Someone: The Development of Identities

In their work with African Canadian youths, Dei and James (1998) make the distinction between "being," that is, the given identity inferred with being Black, and "becoming," that is, the politically aware relation to a taken-on racialized identity, experienced and negotiated within a social, cultural, and historical construction in which race has meaning in systems of power. Gender and sexuality, along with race and class differences, are subject locations that inform an individual's cultural frame of reference; they "influence how knowledge is constructed, interpreted and institutionalized" (Dei and James 1998:92).

For a young lesbian, then, what within her experiences of school helps her interrogate the societal label of being gay and moves her toward a sense of becoming lesbian, in which political agency and collective resistance are possible and probable (Dei and James 1998)? Do schools even see this as desirable for minority students, given the possibility of collective resistance that potentially comes with this defining process? Work on institutionalized racism (Herr 1999) would suggest that, in fact, schools move to quell any effort to move toward a sense of becoming, when that process challenges current cultural arrangements and practices; previous work regarding the school experience of young gay and lesbian students indicates that schools are invested in framing issues of homophobia as a private problem of the individuals involved (Herr 1997).

Miller (1991) and others offer a view of female development that they term *self-in-relation*, that is, a girl or woman knows more about herself as she relates to others. "The primary experience of self is relational, that is, the self is organized and developed in the context of important relationships" (Surrey 1991:52). Developing a sense of identity "implies both uniqueness (selfhood) and sameness (relations with/to others)" (Dei and James 1998:94).

Jordan (1997) warns that a woman's voice often will not be heard if the reality she expresses is not congruent with dominant societal values; "those in a minority position...often do not experience receptivity in the listener from the dominant culture" (p. 52). As she relates, then, to others who cannot hear her, a woman experiences a sense of invalidation that can result in withdrawal, depression, or outrage.

In addition, as Fine (1988) points out, there is, in general, an unacknowledged societal ambivalence about female sexuality. Often constructed in school curriculums as the "victim" of male sexuality, adolescent girls virtually disappear as sexual agents in their own right. This current discourse of sexual victimization silences those female voices that could generate their own socially constructed sexual messages. These possible constructions could include portraits of girls as active agents of their own sexuality as well as girls loving girls. Without these alternative scripts to the public discourse regarding female sexuality, girls are left to make meaning without the benefit of complete information and images, without the "discourse of desire" as described by Fine.

Telling Tales Out of School: Elise's Narrative

Using themes presented in Elise's narrative, I will explore the ways in which her experiences as a young lesbian in school obstructed the "spontaneous unfolding" of her human potential. We do not have a lens that lets us see this diminishment of human potential as a stepsister to other more obviously violent actions. This article makes the case that these more oblique manifestations of cultural violence lessen the capacity for life as potently as more overt means of destruction.

Elise's narrative was gathered over a period of several years. Open-ended interviews were recorded and transcribed; other ongoing conversations were documented through note-taking. In addition we presented together at a professional conference; the presentation was videotaped to use as an educational tool in university classrooms but also provides another source of data for this article.

When I first met Elise she was about to turn 17 years old. It was an important birthday for her, demarcating an opportunity to leave school "for real" and take the graduate equivalency diploma (GED). She could make official the school leave-taking behaviors that she had been practicing for several years. Barely 5 feet tall, with sparkling gray-blue eyes, this young White woman had come out as a lesbian at 14 years of age. Whereas Elise experienced great relief in being able to publicly name herself, she also had squarely located herself within the terrain of sexual minorities. Although she had earned straight As and was placed in programs for the gifted while in elementary school, Elise was failing miserably by the time she was in high school. She finally gave up the struggle and dropped out, concluding, "it wasn't my place." Currently, Elise struggles to support herself through a series of minimum-wage jobs.

Van Soest and Bryant (1995) delineate three common manifestations of institutional violence: alienation, omission, and repression. These will be defined later and tied to the literature regarding the school context for gay and lesbian students. Excerpts drawn from Elise's narratives will illuminate the link between her experiences and this reconceptualization of violence; the goal is to explore the role institutionalized school violence played in the diminishment of Elise's sense of self and her perceived capacity for schooling.

The Violence of Alienation

According to Van Soest and Bryant (1995), the violence of alienation occurs when an individual is deprived of the opportunity for emotional, cultural, or intellectual growth, ultimately influencing one's own identity and self-esteem. On the institutional level, one of the ways this manifests itself is through systematically ignoring or depreciating a student's cultural background, group or community.

The sense of gays and lesbians being invisible within the borders of the schoolyard has been well documented (Durby 1994; Rofes 1989; Sears 1993; Unks 1995), leading some to conclude that gay and lesbian youths are perhaps the most underserved of all students within our school systems (Uribe 1994). Information and positive images of gays and lesbians are routinely omitted from school curriculums (Rofes 1989; Sears 1993). As D'Augelli (1992) points out, young gays and lesbians are often "deleted" from the formal curriculum, yet the "'hidden curriculum' that devalues the existence and contributions of lesbians and gay men is quite clear" (p. 214).

The world of school is an overtly heterosexual one, as manifest in the explicit curriculum as well as in the curricular silences and taboo topics (Fine 1988). If education is, in part, about establishing a reference point for what has come before and learning a body of knowledge that helps youths frame their understanding of the world, the silences and taboos speak loudly.

In Elise's case, she could not remember ever having her experience as a lesbian included in materials she read in school, other than a line or two in a health text that defined the word *homosexuality*.

> It had about two sentences on homosexuality and I read those same two sentences over and over again, hoping to extract some hidden meaning, something from them. It said "Some people," and I believe the wording was "choose to have relationships, have sex, something, with people of the same sex; these people are called homosexuals." That was it...the stuff they were teaching in health class had absolutely nothing to do with what I was going through.

For gay and lesbian youths particularly, the exclusion from the explicit curriculum leaves them very alone as they work to make meaning of their awareness of being gay. Left without accurate information or positive role models, they are vulnerable to internalizing the culturally constructed, homophobic representations of themselves.

> I always knew that I had an attraction toward women, but I never thought of it as being normal; I thought I was the only one who ever felt like this.
>
> I mean, most heterosexual people don't think about being heterosexual – that's just the norm, so to speak. And this [being lesbian] required a lot of thought on my part. Not to say it was a choice but a lot of thought about what was wrong with me...or what I was feeling; was anybody else ever going through this?

Learning also takes place in the social spaces of schools as students move through the hallways, joking and teasing, walking portraits of the male and female roles available to them through heterosexual scripts. The vibrancy of the social scene is also an additional holding point for students otherwise tenuously attached to school. If, in a school, there is not an openly gay presence, the possibility of moving through the equivalent social culture is not available to gay youth; with no sense of belonging, the heterosexual social world actually can be a deterrent to a gay youth staying in school. In reflecting on being very alone in the midst of a heterosexual school social scene, Elise mused,

> To be alone in a bunch of heterosexual people is an uncomfortable feeling, because there really isn't

> anybody else who knows what you're going through...at least in the gay sense....I hated like feeling very uncomfortable...and I hated being there. So being gay and probably the only out person at school which was predominately heterosexual – and I did get harassed – was very difficult so I would just rather not go.

Often the only time that gays and lesbians are openly acknowledged or made visible is in the "teasing" in the hallways and this becomes the "information" available to youths. For many gay youths, the absence of positive role models is exacerbated by this climate of harassment.

> To hear gay jokes and the words *faggot* and *dyke* – that's a common thing in the halls of every school, but it's completely ignored by the teachers...I mean these are people in authority – it just kind of reinforces that this is okay. And for those kids not out of the closet, who may not even recognize what it is, that's going to reinforce their self-hatred once they realize who they are.

Schools reinforce homophobia and heterosexism through two "interrelated mechanisms of silencing" (Friend 1993:212): systemic exclusion and systemic inclusion. The former is the process of excluding positive role models, messages, and images of gays and lesbians, rendering them invisible. In systemic inclusion, when discussions regarding gays and lesbians do occur, they are consistently placed in a negative context, linking homosexuality to pathology or dangerous behaviors. These techniques of silencing help to create the climate whereby tacit approval is given for anti-gay violence to take place in school, leading to what Van Soest and Bryant (1995) would term the *violence of omission.*

Violence of Omission

Van Soest and Bryant (1995) define violence of omission as failing to help people in need or danger; at the institutional level this is manifest as a failure to intervene when people are threatened by harm that is thought to be avoidable or controllable. They trace violence of omission to a cultural belief system that accepts inequality and deprivation as normal and then collectively fails to organize against violence.

Some would argue that gays are the most hated group of people in the United States and that high schools are perhaps the most homophobic institutions in American society (Unks 1995). Lipkin (1995) points out that high schools are frequent sites for homophobic rage and violence, often inflicted on gay youths by their heterosexual peers (see also Savin-Williams 1995). Indeed some research would indicate that adolescents are more likely than any other age group to perpetuate violence against gays (Masters, Johnson, and Kolodyny 1992, cited in Unks 1995).

There is some documentation regarding the increasing levels of hate crimes perpetuated against gays (Friend 1993; Pierce and Taitano 1996); other more subtle forms of violence are difficult to quantify. Racist comments are increasingly not tolerated in schools, but remarks expressed by students or educators that are derogatory to young gays and lesbians remain largely uninterrupted (Loutzenheiser 1997).

"Queer bashing" is commonly thought of as only physical violence, but Pierce and Taitano (1996) expand the definition to include a range of behaviors "from words to wounds" all of which "share the motivation of homophobic, heterosexist hatred" with a goal of "the destruction of a significant part or the total life of a lesbian or gay person" (pp. 1–2). The practices that perpetuate queer bashing are part of everyday behaviors and, as such, often go unnoticed.

> Even if you're not out for some reason, students can tell who's gay and who's not. Even before you realize it yourself, you'll get harassed and picked on; I mean, that's just the way it is, and it can be merciless.
>
> Now that I look back on it and I can kind of process what was happening – I mean, that was just the way it was. I mean, it wasn't like "Oh, I feel harassed in school today," or "Oh, they are laughing at me, giving me a hard time," "The jocks are pushing me," or whatever. That was just the way it was....I didn't have to think about it.

But the threat of this kind of harassment grew to a kind of preoccupation that made it difficult for Elise to focus in school. The daily occurrence of the experience of harassment cumulatively made for an absorption in issues of safety that crowded out thoughts of other kinds of learning.

I'd get really paranoid, walking down the hall by myself. "Are they looking at me? Are they going to follow me? Are they going to beat me up?"...Even if they weren't, it's easy to get paranoid in that kind of situation. So it was even just that, kind of the expectation to get harassed – that was horrible. That was probably even worse than the actual harassment, knowing that at the end of the period I have to walk down the hall by my locker, and that's where all those guys stand....I'd better find somebody to walk down the halls with...it was very difficult, so I would just rather not go. And when I did go, I wasn't even paying attention.

The loss was not only to her sense of safety and feeling comfortable but also a loss as to what the school experience could be in terms of being able to concentrate academically and in the sense that high school could be fun. Elise expressed the sense of being robbed of the positive experience of school throughout all the years that she went:

In high school you watch your back; I mean it's scary and it's sad. Because when you are in high school you should be worried about flirting, getting an A in chemistry, about who you're taking to the dance. And not about if I walk across behind the gym by myself am I going to get the crap beat out of me.... So your sexuality is always a reminder that it's not a natural thing. I mean, it is a very natural thing, but it doesn't feel that way because of the consequences from people who are homophobic out there.

Violence of Repression

Violence of repression encompasses infractions of the civil, political, economic, and social rights of individuals or groups (Van Soest and Bryant 1995). On an institutional level, this would include infringements of a person or group's rights to participate, with equity, in the democratic functioning of the institution. Unks (1995) makes the case that implicit and explicit censoring of information regarding homosexuality is a breach of students' academic freedom and their civil liberties:

In a truly democratic society, the primary reason in support of studying about homosexuality in schools may be to assure freedom of thought. Societies are totalitarian to the extent that they have areas of belief and attitude that are closed to reflective examination and thought....In school – if nowhere else – our youth should sate their desire for reliable knowledge. When society, however well-intentioned, denies its youth this sort of information, it perpetuates the most insidious form of intellectual rape upon its children. (pp. 11–12)

By validating only specifically disciplined knowledge, schools function as institutions of social control and moral regulation, aimed at containing minds as well as bodies (Lewis and Karin 1994).

Without the input of basic, factual information and adult role models, gay and lesbian youths as well as heterosexual students are left to make meaning of sexual difference on their own, in a climate of silence and stigma. Elise had her own questions to answer and those of her fellow students; once she was out as a lesbian, she found herself being in the role of educating her fellow students:

The reason I did answer even their stupid questions, of course some of their questions were stupid, they didn't know any better – it's not something that they learned just like it's not something I learned anything about. So the more questions of theirs that I answered correctly or that I answered at all would be that much more information that they had that was real instead of stereotypes and false information and homophobic propaganda...and the better chance that they would go through their lives being tolerant...they'd be a lot more likely to end up tolerant.

Implications

As gay and lesbian students work to make meaning of a school world that seemingly includes no one like themselves – no visible adult, gay role models, no positive images or curriculum that would offer a window into the worlds of sexual minorities – they are in danger of concluding "that they have no future, no vision, no role models, no possibilities" (Jackson and Sullivan 1994:98). Elise states this succinctly:

In terms of knowing who I was and how my life was and how I would be happy – I mean it was amazing – I never did find it in school and I don't think it was ever there.

Many internalize the myths of oppression that would tell them that their development is abnormal and their prospects for a fulfilling personal life are slight (D' Augelli 1992). Hetrick and Martin (1987, cited in Mallon 1994) point out that the primary developmental task of gay and lesbian adolescents becomes one of adjusting to a socially stigmatized role that casts them in images injurious to positive identity development.

Many give up on school, concluding with Elise that it is "just not my place." For Elise, this realization was so ingrained that it was hard for her to imagine a school experience that would feel welcoming to her; this came into play when she briefly tried college, leaving after a month:

> I HATED IT, HATED IT! Everyone kept telling me about how different college was going to be…and I'm sure it was – I just didn't stick around long enough to tell. Because I went and it felt – the school setting and the school environment – felt really, really too familiar. And I just couldn't be there.… I'd walk across campus with my head down, not making eye contact. I didn't want to look at the frat boys because they would give me shit. I mean it's the same damn thing as in high school but bigger.

If the examination of homosexuality that Unks (1995) calls for could take place, gay and heterosexual youth would benefit. As Lipkin (1995) and Loutzenheiser (1997) point out, any education that helps eliminate prejudice is beneficial for the targets of bigotry and the bigots themselves. Our current practices in school cultivate the diminishment of those who are harassed and the harassers, but it is the former who are leaving schools in droves. They are leaving, not only without the education they deserve but also with a sense of failure.

Ultimately then, the victimization of gay and lesbian youth comes at two levels – the actual homophobia they encounter in their school and social worlds as well as the destructive myths that they have internalized (D' Augelli 1992).

> As Paulo Freire shows so well in *The Pedagogy of the Oppressed*, the true focus of revolutionary change is never merely the oppressive situations which we seek to escape, but that piece of the oppressor which is planted deep within each of us. (Lorde 1984:123)

Internalized oppression acts as a veil that keeps stigmatized groups from seeing and naming their everyday experiences as expressions of violence.

If one barometer of institutional violence is the diminishment of the "spontaneous unfolding of human potential," then Elise's words are an indictment of the institution designed to equip her to take her rightful place in society:

> It is a big blow to the self-esteem, that I couldn't hack it in high school…there's this feeling of guilt and self-doubt which was like "Okay, I couldn't handle it in high school." And because my grades did slip in high school because of…all the problems I was having, I felt like I'm dumb; I'm not good enough to do this.
>
> I personally – especially after realizing how much better things got after I got out of high school – I personally think the GED, there's nothing wrong with it. But there's still also a stigma attached to the GED…that it's kind of like the losers' way out.

When she entered school, Elise was singled out as a gifted student and placed in special programs to enhance her learning; she left school 12 years later, concluding that she was dumb, knowledge garnered through her experience as a young lesbian journeying through the schools we have designed to ensure her education. She has internalized the violence rendered to her at the hands of an educational system designed to perpetuate dominant culture.

Returning to Bourdieu's (1977) notion of symbolic violence, domination is exercised in the everyday practices of school, favoring some, diminishing others. Those who stand outside the heterosexual status quo are some of those most at risk of experiencing violence at the hands of the institution. Attributing the scars they bear, at least in part, to the educational system that fails to interrupt a discourse that diminishes them, and is silent as to who they can be, is a first step in calling attention to the established order that perpetuates a violence that goes virtually unrecognized and unchallenged.

REFERENCES

Bourdieu, P. 1997. *Outline of a Theory of Practice*. Cambridge, UK: Cambridge University Press.

Brownmiller, S. 1975. *Against our Will: Men, Women and Rape*. Toronto: Bantam.

Corbett, H. D. 1991. Community influence and school micropolitics. In J. Blase, ed., *The Micropolitics of Life in Schools: Power, Conflict and Cooperation* (pp. 73–95). Newbury Park, CA: Sage.

D' Augelli, A. R. 1992. Teaching lesbian/gay development: From oppression to exceptionality. In K. M. Harbeck, ed., *Coming Out of the Classroom Closet: Gay and Lesbian Students, Teachers and Curricula* (pp. 213–227). New York: Haworth.

Dei, G. J. S., and James, I. M. 1998. "Becoming Black": African-Canadian youth and the politics of negotiating racial and racialised identities. *Race, Ethnicity and Education* 1(1):91–108.

Donat, P., and D'Emilio, J. 1992. A feminist redefinition of rape and sexual assault: Historical foundations and change. *Journal of Social Issues* 48(1):9–22.

Durby, D. 1994. Gay, lesbian and bisexual youth. In T. DeCrescenzo, ed., *Helping Gay and Lesbian Youth: New Policies, New Programs, New Practices* (pp. 1–37). New York: Haworth.

Elia, J. P. 1993. Homophobia in the high school: A problem in need of resolution. *The High School Journal* 77(1/2):177–185.

Fine, M. 1988. Sexuality, schooling, and adolescent females: The missing discourse of desire. *Harvard Educational Review* 58(1):29–53.

Friend, R. A. 1993. Choices, not closets: Heterosexism and homophobia in schools. In L. Weiss and M. Fine, eds., *Beyond Silenced Voices: Class, Race and Gender in U.S. Schools* (pp. 209–235). Albany: State University of New York Press.

Herr, K. 1997. Learning lessons from school: Homophobia, heterosexism, and the construction of failure. *Journal of Gay and Lesbian Social Services* 7(4):51–64.

Herr, K. 1999. Private power and privileged education: De/constructing institutionalized racism. *Journal of Inclusive Education* 3(2):111–129.

Jackson, D., and Sullivan, R. 1994. Developmental implications of homophobia for lesbian and gay adolescents: Issues in policy and practice. In T. DeCrescenzo, ed., *Helping Gay and Lesbian Youth: New Policies, New Programs, New Practices* (pp. 93–109). New York: Haworth.

Jordan, J. 1997. Clarity in connection: Empathetic knowing, desire and sexuality. In J. Jordan, ed., *Women's Growth in Diversity: More Writings from the Stone Center* (pp. 50–73). New York: Guilford.

Lewis, M., and Karin, B. 1994. Queer stories/Straight talk: Tales from the school playground. *Theory into Practice* 33(3):199–205.

Lipkin, A. 1995. The case for a gay and lesbian curriculum. In G. Unks, ed., *The Gay Teen: Educational Practice and Theory for Lesbian, Gay and Bisexual Adolescents* (pp. 31–52). New York: Routledge.

Lorde, A. 1984. *Sister Outsider: Essays and Speeches*. Freedom, CA: Crossing.

Loutzenheiser, L. 1997. How schools play "smear the queer." *Feminist Teacher* 10(2):59–64.

Mallon, G. P. 1994. Counseling strategies with gay and lesbian youth. In T. DeCrescenzo, ed., *Helping Gay and Lesbian Youth: New Policies, New Programs, New Practices* (pp. 75–91). New York: Haworth.

Miller, J. B. 1991. The development of women's sense of self. In J. Jordan, A. Kaplan, J. B. Miller, I. Stiver, and J. Surrey, eds., *Women's Growth in Connection* (pp. 11–26). New York: Guilford.

Pierce, D., and Taitano, K. 1996 (February). *Violence against Lesbian and Gay People: Social Work's Response*. Paper presented at the annual meeting of NASW – New Mexico, Albuquerque, NM.

Rofes, E. 1989. Opening up the classroom closet: Responding to the educational needs of gay and lesbian youth. *Harvard Educational Review* 59(4):444–453.

Savin-Williams, R. C. 1995. Lesbian, gay male and bisexual adolescents. In A. R. D' Augelli and C. J. Patterson, eds., *Lesbian, Gay and Bisexual Identities over the Life Span: Psychological Perspectives* (pp. 165–189). New York: Oxford University Press.

Sears, J. T. 1993. Alston and Everetta: Too risky for school. In R. Donmoyer and R. Kos, eds., *At-Risk Students: Portraits, Policies, Programs and Practices* (pp. 153–172). Albany: State University of New York Press.

Surrey, J. 1991. The "self-in-relation": A theory of women's development. In J. Jordan, A. Kaplan, J. B. Miller, I. Stiver, and J. Surrey, eds., *Women's Growth in Development* (pp. 51–66). New York: Guilford.

Unks, G. 1995. Thinking about the gay teen. In G. Unks, ed., *The Gay Teen: Educational Practice and Theory for Lesbian, Gay, and Bisexual Adolescents* (pp. 3–12). New York: Routledge.

Uribe, V. 1994. The silent minority: Rethinking our commitment to gay and lesbian youth. *Theory into Practice* 33(3):167–172.

Van Soest, D., and Bryant, S. 1995. Violence reconceptualized for social work: The urban dilemma. *Social Work* 40(4):549–557.

White, J. W., and Farmer, R. 1992. Research methods: How they shape views of sexual violence. *Journal of Social Issues* 48(1):45–59.

14

Queer Pilgrimage: The San Francisco Homeland and Identity Tourism

Alyssa Cymene Howe

Introduction: My Love Waits There

The loveliness of Paris seems somehow sadly gay
The glory that was Rome is of another day
I've been terribly alone and forgotten in Manhattan
I'm going home to my city by the Bay
I left my heart in San Francisco
High on a hill, it calls to me
To be where little cable cars climb halfway to the stars
The morning fog may chill the air
I don't care
My love waits there, in San Francisco, above the blue and windy sea
When I come home to you, San Francisco, your golden sun will shine for me

"I Left My Heart in San Francisco," music by George C. Cory Jr., lyrics by Douglass Cross, sung by Tony Bennett

The crowd was silent and transfixed as Tony Bennett began to croon his rendition of "I Left My Heart in San Francisco." Surrounded by the thousands who had come to baptize the Virgin MegaStore in downtown San Francisco, Bennett concluded his ditty to much applause. The song has become a kind of unofficial anthem for the city of San Francisco since it was made popular by Bennett in the early 1960s. However, the tune was written by a gay couple having recently moved from the city (Hobica 1995:190). The links among San Francisco, queer people, and the lure of a "homeland" have been a long time in the making.

Anthropologists have, for decades, noted how places are made mythical through the telling of stories and the singing of songs. Anthropologists have also, more recently, assessed how places are made mythical through anthropologists' retellings of stories and analyses of songs (Castañeda 1996; Clifford and Marcus 1986). Because San Francisco has enjoyed a long history of mythologizing embodied in songs such as "I Left My Heart in San Francisco," the following will also add to the legacy of stories about places and how people conceive of those places. In the popular imagination, the city is often proclaimed the "world's gay and lesbian capital" (Apell 1998:94). This sense of a "capital," I will suggest, is more accurately described as a territorial "homeland." While capitals are the legislative nexuses of states, homelands offer a symbolic refuge for believers who make the pilgrimage. The focus of my discussion will be to elaborate some of the elements that foster the construction of San Francisco as a queer homeland. Borrowing from de Certeau (1984), I hope to elaborate the "scriptural economy" through which "the multiple levels and contexts of cultural-ideological productions" (Castañeda 1996:65) shape the notion of a queer homeland. Through ethnographic narratives, touristic ephemera, and gay tour guidebooks,[1] I address the following questions: How is San Francisco constructed as a pilgrimage site for the elaboration of queer identity, and how might this sense of a homeland emerge over time and through "touristic" practices? Does a queer homeland rely on "staged" authenticity, the "backstage" only available to some? Further, how might nationalist-like tropes foster the construction of a territorial homeland for a queer nation?[2] Finally, how does queer group identity differ from nationalisms that are dependent on imagined primordial conscription?

In this article, I frame the construction of a queer homeland through the phenomenon of tourism. Tourism offers a rich set of juxtapositions because the interplay between tourists and residents illustrates the complexity of creating place, locality, and a sense of homeland. I also suggest that, in the case of San Francisco, tourism is critical to creating a sense of group identity for both tourists and residents, albeit in different ways. Thus, tourism as a practice that enhances identity is fundamental to the creation of a queer homeland, which relies on "identity" for its production. I further consider the city's history as integral to its construction as a homeland for queer people, and my theoretical concerns are rendered through a historical lens. The larger theoretical issues that inform my discussion take up the discursive notions of "queer," "identity," and "place." I attempt to resituate these sometimes nebulous terms by applying them to concrete ethnographic examples. Narratives of tourists and residents, as well as the language found in tour guidebooks, suggest an emerging queer homeland that is being constructed through pilgrimage. Tour book discourse, narratives of respondents, and my own interpretive gloss all evidence a slippage among categories of "gay," "lesbian," and "queer." I focus attention on a specifically "queer" homeland in order to suggest a more complex articulation of group identity than that allowed by *gay* and *lesbian*. Queerness moves beyond homogeneous identity categorization, which, I will argue, is fundamental to the creation of a homeland in San Francisco. Thus, part of my project throughout this discussion will be to highlight the multivocality that arises in attempting to grasp the panoply of sexual identities I gloss as "queer."

I maintain a particular focus on fissures of age, gender, race, and class status within a queer whole, and I argue that these factors evidence a break in queer coherence, a rip in the umbrella term that underscores the ongoing reformulation of queerness. By mapping sex onto sites, linking gazes with voyeurs, and politicizing place, I attempt to move away from essentialized constructions of queerness. Instead, I suggest that the differential marking of bodies and queer consumption among residents and tourists illustrate a continuum of sexual fluidity that marks San Francisco itself as an explicitly queer place. This discussion is complicated by my own position as a former longtime resident and occasional tourist to the city. I recognize that my "voice" often seamlessly slips between that of activist and that of analyst. Because queers have been persecuted many times in many places, I believe that territorializing a place, a homeland, can offer a sanctuary from oppression. Although I acknowledge this slippage between the positions of advocate and anthropologist, I have chosen not to erase this dynamic but, rather, to highlight its potential to add yet another dimension in the making of a homeland.

Touring the Town: Identity Migration

Tourism considered as an economic and ideological endeavor (MacCannell 1976; Rothman 1998; Urry 1990) informs how representations of the city are constructed by the purveyors of "gay tourism" and highlights how these representations are received by both gay tourists and gay residents of San Francisco. Tourism, as a "privileged practice" (Towner 1985) of the economically endowed, is inverted when considering a distinctly marginalized group such as gays and lesbians because tourism is, as the Turners (1978) have argued, linked to older forms of pilgrimage to the world religious centers.[3] Tourism, like pilgrimage, has a "magic" that is "enhanced by group identity" (Graburn 1989:34), which may prove even more magical when it is tourism itself that congeals group identity – which I argue is the case in San Francisco's queer homeland.[4] Queer tourists leave "home," where they may not be accepted based on their sexual identity, in order to come to a "homeland" where they are accepted. The medium of tourism illustrates an uneven "emergence" of a homeland, rather than an essential, "authentic" homeland. "Staged events" (MacCannell 1976) and "pseudo-events" (Boorstin 1964) have been described as those fabrications designed to create a more "authentic" experience for "moderns" in search of escape.

However, in a pilgrimage to a queer homeland, the generalized escapism of modernity is interwoven with an acute need, at times, for queer people to literally "escape." Because the queer pilgrim does not seek an escape from the modern but, rather, an escape from oppression "back home," notions of "staged" and "pseudo-events" are less germane. Rather, I invoke Castañeda's "imagined understanding of experience" (1996:17) to illuminate how an essentialized "gay authenticity" appears in the narratives of queer tourists and residents. In the elaboration of queer identity, essentialized meanings seem to facilitate a sense of membership in a larger queer nation – "imagined" or otherwise. Queer discourses of membership resemble nationalist discourses but also depart from them, particularly when factors of gender, class, and race are brought to the fore. For queers, a "homeland" comprises many voices, built consciously and unconsciously through diverse practices over time.

Moving through History

The historical and cultural nuance of "moving" holds particular significance for an immigrant city such as San Francisco.[5] Kaplan has suggested that in narratives of "modernist exile" and "postmodern tourism," it is "modern cities, especially major ports, [that] function as crucibles where identities are formed, transformed, and fixed" (1996:31). Similarly, Weston (1998) elaborates how gay migrants from rural areas and small towns sought the anonymity of urban centers, thus facilitating the creation of a "gay imaginary."[6] According to Weston, this imaginary made San Francisco "the premier destination" for identity migrants such as gays, lesbians, and "explorers" of sexuality (1998:32) to create subjectivities based on identification with "others like me." However, many historical sequences preceded the making of the homeland and intimately informed the imagining that would follow. San Francisco's past foreshadowed the representation of the city as a place of nonconformity; this nonconformity would later be transformed into an imagined gay mecca.

Weston situates the Great Gay Migration in the 1970s and early 1980s. But it is also the case that San Francisco served as a crucible for subversive identities dating back to the city's boom era in the mid-1800s. The discovery of gold in the northern reaches of the state ushered in an age of pioneering men in search of fortune. The gold rush lured a huge, predominantly male population to San Francisco following in the wake of mission-building and the near decimation of indigenous peoples.[7] Tales of the city's early days, in the 1850s, refer to the absence of women; when a woman did appear, she was greeted by hundreds of leering men intent to gaze on the female form. Word throughout the nation was that the city was a new frontier for the entrepreneurial man willing to leave the securities of home and hearth behind. Wealth was extracted from the earth, funneled into the city, and used in the service of decadence: drinking, gambling, and carousing. Fortunes were spent in the building of railroads and the development of agriculture,[8] as immigrant laborers, primarily young Chinese men, were encouraged to lend their hands and backs to the city's growth.[9] Immigration legislation was fed by a racism that considered Chinese immigrants a viable source of labor but an inappropriate group to propagate and settle in the city. Chinese women were forbidden from immigrating to California, which served to increase the predominance of a male population. This much-disseminated "origin story" of the city is one rooted in a nearly single-gendered population with a taste for decadence. Although this alludes to a sense that heteroreproductive norms would not prevail in the city, I contend that other factors would create San Francisco's reputation as a crucible for nonconformity.

I highlight the gold rush and its effects in order to make clear that San Francisco has been associated, since its inception, with an irreverence for dominant notions of home and heteronormativity. Gold rush immigration patterns were distinct from previous Western migrations, primarily because, unlike their agricultural counterparts, large families were not necessary to "strike it rich" in California. Although white settlers in the city held more power over their destinies than the Chinese immigrants, each group comprised, for some time, males only. Shiploads of Navy men on leave heightened the reputation of the city as a locale for tattooing, drinking, and other forms of decadence. This nonconformist irreverence, or "cultural libertarianism" (Bean 1968:448), surely inspired such characters as Jack London and, later, Jack Kerouac and friends to make an intellectual and artistic refuge of the city.[10]

Queer Moments in San Francisco

In the early part of the century, San Francisco gay bars were populated by travelers from across the country, and significant political organizing began to take place in the 1950s.[11] World War II drew thousands of workers to the urban centers of the West Coast, where gay enclave communities were quickly being established (Faderman 1991). After the war the military imposed more virulent restrictions on gay personnel, and many were loaded onto "queer ships" along with other "undesirable" discharges and sent to nearby port cities such as San Francisco. Indeed, ironically, the U.S. government seems to have "sponsored a migration of the gay community" (Bérubé 1982). The burgeoning growth of gay enclave communities in the postwar era, the free speech movement, protests against U.S. involvement in Vietnam, and hippie counterculture blossoming in the Haight Ashbury District all demanded diverse freedoms. The 1967 Love Generation musical hit "San Francisco (Be Sure to Wear Flowers in Your Hair)" may have signified the full bloom of hippie culture, but gay San Francisco was already there. Indeed, Fitzgerald (1986) has suggested that the Castro, "the first gay neighborhood in the country," arose singularly from an already extant counterculture.

Countercultural tendencies informed the construction of San Francisco as a particularly hospitable locale for the thousands of gay people who flocked to the Castro District in the 1970s. However, this phenomenon must be understood as a complex set of factors, not simply the "natural" evolution of counterculture.[12] In particular, progressive ideals of "tolerance" have long defined the city's political atmosphere and form a part of the city's symbolic construction. Some have suggested that San Francisco "was America's gay capital in terms of political clout" (Newton 1993:9), marking the city as not merely a haven but an explicitly political place.[13] Progressive politics appears to be a key element in the formation of a gay homeland, and San Francisco was the first city in the nation to elect an "out" gay official.[14] Anti-gay legislation spearheaded by the religious right spread across the nation throughout the late 1970s (Vaid 1995). The establishment of the city as a sanctuary for diverse sexual identities has taken place in a larger, hostile terrain: a queer homeland is necessarily built upon uneven ground.

Questioning Queer, Imagining Identity, Politicizing Place

The complexities of a queer homeland are also revealed in the more mundane, though highly contested, constructions of discourse. In the early 1990s, the term *queer* was popularized partly because it includes gay men, lesbians, bisexuals, transgendered persons, and other "sexual radicals" (those practicing sadomasochism, bondage and discipline, etc.). *Queer*, a carefully selected discursive appropriation of a derogatory term, includes "faggots" and "fairies" as well as "lezzies" and "dykes" (Faderman 1991:300). Rendering positive those monikers that have been used to abuse is queered thinking, born from real need: "Most societies try to get rid of their deviants. Most cultures have burned and beaten their homosexuals and others who deviate from the sexual common. The queer are the mirror reflecting the heterosexual tribe's fear: being different, being other and therefore lesser, therefore sub-human, in-human, non-human" (Anzaldúa 1987:18). The term *queer* has served to rally various sexualities under one umbrella "identity," sometimes engendering political coalitions. However, *queer* is not without its problems. Often, argues Anzaldúa (1991), queer serves to erase differences of race, class, and gender within the gay community, homogenizing differing interests and identities. Further, through neutralizing difference *queer* may come to be associated with the dominant sector of the community (read: white, wealthy gay men). Despite this potential slippage, Anzaldúa ultimately chooses to use the term *queer* because other identity monikers, like *lesbian*, are likewise invested with a dominant, white history. Following Anzaldúa's caveat, I find *queer* a useful umbrella term while recognizing that all are not equally sheltered under such terms. I would argue that in the making of a queer homeland, validating difference is of critical importance. A homogeneous, one-dimensional sense of queer identity does not appear to serve the purposes of an inclusive homeland.

"Identity" as a useful category of analysis has also been widely critiqued in academic works. B. Williams (1996) has insisted that identity, especially within the frame of nationalism, must be understood as a multiply constituted construct within power relations. As an analytical concept, identity is both complex and shifting. Within people's lived experience, identity may also prove a useful tool for people's self-conceptions. Anderson's discussion of nationalism formation suggests that an imagined "deep, horizontal comradeship" (1983:7) serves as the basis of national "communities." The nation is imagined as a "natural" constellation of persons because it is understood as a limited (though elastic) sovereign group with a shared history and trajectory. By framing queer identity against a backdrop of nationalism, I find similarities: both speak to political aspirations based on a shared sense of identity. However, although membership in a nation can only in certain circumstances be chosen, membership in a queer "nation" is almost certainly chosen.[15] Further, the parameters of group identity among self-identified queers are infinitely more flexible than those of nations.[16] Although both forms of "nation" share an "imagined" continuity of identity, the queer nation is not dependent on imagined ties of blood and bone but, rather, on sexual practices, self-conscious forms of marking, and political positioning.

The gay rights movement, since its inception during the civil rights era, has often made use of nationalist and racial tropes (Phelan 1997). These have proven effective in building political coalitions and consolidating a sense of community identity. If, as Lanfant, Allock, and Bruner suggest, identity is "always in reformulation, a constant site of struggle" (1995:xi), then the process by which identity takes shape must include reworking, displacement, disruption, and reflexivity. Just as gender identity coincides with factors of race, class status, and others, so too does queer identity reflect a composite, shifting form. This formulation echoes Butler's suggestion that the "doer is constructed in and through the deed" (1990:142) and the subject is constituted by an "incomplete list" (in terms of race, class, sexuality, gender, etc.) and only comes into being as an "I", or an "identity," is named: "In other words, the enabling conditions for an assertion of 'I' are provided by the structure of signification, the rules that regulate the legitimate and illegitimate invocation of that pronoun, the practices that establish the terms of intelligibility by which that pronoun can circulate" (1990:143).

Places, too, are contested, their borders defined differently based on one's position. To highlight the notion of shifting identities in a queer homeland, I oscillate between places marked as "for women" and "for men" and those marked explicitly by race. Overt gender distinctions, at times, seem antithetical to the project of queering, steeped as they are in binaries and bodily dualisms. However, distinctions continue to be made along these lines by the people with whom I spoke and within queer guidebooks, and so I follow this gendered route. In addition to questioning divisions of gender, race, class, and so on, I hope to problematize the notion of a "queer-only" space by looking to mixed-sexuality events and venues. I find "queer only" to be a problematic parameter, given the shifting, voluntaristic characteristics of queer nationhood that I have suggested. The sites I examine in the ethnographic portion of this discussion are those that appear regularly in queer tour guidebooks. They are, therefore, defined as significant locales for queer tourists by those who market to this population. The tour books themselves render a particular conceptual map of San Francisco, highlighting some venues, events, and places while diminishing the significance of others. Although I cannot hope to bring a comprehensive analysis of all of the sociopolitical factors that go into constituting these particular sites as significant to the queer community, I offer instead an examination of these representations as they exist now, remembering that this is a particular map of the heart of queer San Francisco.

Touring a Queer Homeland

The 1998 San Francisco Pride Parade, held in mid-June on a mile-long stretch through downtown, has drawn hundreds of thousands of visitors, nearly doubling the population of the city. The rambunctious procession is led by Dykes on Bikes with revving engines and lots of leather. This group is followed by Dykes on Bicycles; taking up the rear is a new addition to the parade, a contingent of the Radical Fairies calling itself Dicks on Bikes. Over the course of the three- or four-hour event a host of queer-positive groups ride atop floats, march, and cheer their way down the parade route. The Philipino Men's Chorus, gay grandparents, Muscle Systems (a.k.a., Muscle Sisters) Gym Boys, and a female-to-male transgendered contingent are a few of the many interests represented in the course of the parade. Parties, dances, and carousing compose what is also known as "Pink Saturday." Perhaps more than any event in the city, the Pride Parade serves to consolidate and elaborate queer identity. Through "praying and playing" (Turner and Turner 1978) in the parade, participants perform an expansive queer identity. While "playing" seems obvious here,[17] "praying" comes in a form particular to a queer "nation." If prayer is understood as a shared practice that aligns individuals with a spiritual deity and the community at large, then activism serves as a form of prayer for a queer nation. Networking, strengthening political alliances, and spending time together all serve to build community and strengthen individuals' alliance with a queer whole. The values reflected in respondents' narratives speak overwhelmingly to a sense of inclusion in a greater queer community, which seems to live and breathe at events such as the Pride Parade:[18] As L. noted, "The thing about San Francisco Pride is that it's political – not just a bunch of pretty boys and girls doing their thing but floats and events and all kinds of stuff which focuses on political concerns of the community."[19] L. focused attention on the politics of the Pride event, a critical aspect of queer pilgrimage. In pilgrimage, "passengers" engage in a liminal "betwixt and between" state of being, which ends in aggregation, a return to "mundane social life" (Turner and Turner 1978:14). However, in a queer pilgrimage the return is not to a "stable state" but, rather, to one invigorated with new political possibilities. Pilgrimages of all kinds involve personal transformation,[20] and queer pilgrims returning with new political agendas may upset the "mundane social life" back home. A "transformation of the self" (Bruner 1991), or at least an attempt at transformation, then, is salient for the individual as well as the larger community, adding to the magic of liminality.

At Pride, Z. described her sense of solidarity with a greater queer whole, partly because in this setting she and her girlfriend felt "safe" to do so:

> My girlfriend and I live up in Reno, but I used to live here in the city. I've been out since I was 18, but [K.] has only come out to her sister. No one in Reno knows she's a dyke, and she feels like she can't be out at work. Her parents don't know either, but that's another story. They think that I am "a friend" even though we've been together for almost two years now! Anyhow, when we come to San Francisco all of that changes. My girlfriend is out, and I get to, finally, enjoy having a girlfriend who I can hold hands with, and smooch, and dance dirty with in public. I hate being in the closet, and that's how it is in Reno for us. Here we get to be "real." I don't know what I'd do if we didn't have the city to come to. Of course Pride is fun and crazy and there are lots of babes, so we always make it down here for this.[21]

Z.'s transformation of "self" took place during the window of liminality she enjoyed during the Pride weekend. Bruner (1991) has suggested that the tourist, despite the claims of tour books and brochures, does *not* undergo any radical transformation. However, Bruner's argument is predicated on the twin factors of economic power differentials between "the native self" and the "Western tourist" and the proposition that "most tourists are quite satisfied with their own society, most are not alienated" (1991:240). However, Z. clearly felt some form of alienation in her "own society," which she mitigated through liminal experiences in San Francisco.

In Bruner's discussion of "First World" tourists visiting "Third World" touristic sites, there is an explicit "structure of power" mandating that residents cater to the "fantasies" of tourists. However, the converse appears to operate in San Francisco. If only in terms of economics, it would not be out of line to suggest that most residents of the city (which has one of the highest costs of living in the United States) are often better economically endowed than many tourists to the city. Perhaps greater economic parity between tourists and residents lends itself to transformations. It certainly appears to foster solidarity:

> I am visiting from Germany, and we do have many gay rights groups there and events. Everyone there talks about San Francisco and about this weekend. I've been hearing about it since I was a teenager and now am finally here, amongst my people, all these beautiful gay people.[22]

> This is the biggest of all the Pride events....If you haven't been to S.F. Pride, you can't even call yourself gay![23]

The refrain of "my people,"[24] and the suggestion that one cannot be gay without having experienced San Francisco Pride, lends itself to an overt articulation of nationalist-like community identity.[25] The emphasis here is on the journey of pilgrimage and experience, rather than (imagined) primordial ties. MacCannell (1976) has described the importance of experience for the modern tourist, for whom a search for "authenticity," often "back there" in space and time, provides a unifying modern consciousness. As these narratives suggest, moderns attempt to reach the "backstages" (Goffman 1959), where "true authenticity" lies, through experience rather than commodification. While queer tourists may never find an authentic backstage – indeed, one may not exist – they do engage in the aesthetic of modernity in their quest for "a more meaningful existence somewhere else" (Kaplan 1996:64). Though modern exiles may seek the aesthetic elsewhere in order to return, rejuvenated, to their origins, this does not appear to hold true for the queer tourist. Queers, who often experience exile from, and ostracism living in, their places of origin (nation-state, community, family, and so on), here find their "return" in a pilgrimage to a homeland.[26] These narratives and the nationalist-like tropes they embody reflect the imagining of a queer homeland in San Francisco. They resonate with a sense of community: a coherent queer whole. However, this coherence is disrupted in the following examples; a queer homeland is not made, it seems, through a monolithic sense of queer identity.

Located in the Castro District is Café Flore, known to many queer San Franciscans as "Café Hairdoo,"[27] where the clientele partakes of skinless chicken breast sandwiches and espresso drinks in a sanctuary-like patio. Café Flore appears in gay guides as a premiere breakfast place for a predominately gay male crowd. *Access: Gay U.S.A.* (Apell 1998), a guide that marks each of its venues with either a male or a female symbol, lists Café Flore with a male symbol with an exclamation point next to it, suggesting that this is a "très gay" *male* site. Differentiation between male and female sites is a theme that recurs in gay tour guides, emphasizing that gender is an axis of distinction for those constructing gay touristic experiences in the form of gay guides. In a recent glossy tour guide magazine called *California: Culture's Edge* (California Cultural Tourism Commission [CCTC] 1998), published by the San Francisco Arts Commission,[28] the section oriented to queer tourists highlights sites that can be visited within a three-day period. The first day's tour is entitled "The Castro." Day two is labeled "Mostly for Women: The Mission." These designations suggest that different neighborhoods will appeal to particular genders within the queer community. However, there is something more here. "The Mission" is described as "for women," whereas "the Castro" remains the unmarked signifier. The Castro, not coincidentally, is a predominately male neighborhood. As with ethnic "unmarked categories," here the dominant gender category, male, remains the a priori category. Anzaldúa's warning that "queer" may become a homogeneous (gay, white, male) category is salient here. Although it might be argued that the Castro District has achieved the status of being "famous for being famous" (Turner and Turner 1978:12), within the queer community the Castro District is famous for being a gathering place of gay men specifically. The Castro and the Mission districts are represented as specifically gendered places for queer visitors to the city.[29] Although this does not point to fissures in queer identity per se, it does suggest distinctions in how queer identity is represented, and therefore shaped, for the queer tourist. A singular sense of queerness is elaborated and intersected by other identity factors such as class status and gender through the textual constructions of gay guidebooks.

An event on the eve of Pink Saturday speaks to these differences. The Dyke March, which attracts thousands of women to the Mission for a rally, march, and after party, is a women's event. Men are encouraged to watch and cheer but not to march. Women, whether they identify as lesbians, dykes, bi, straight, polyamorous, and so forth, parade through the streets holding signs, some semiclothed and some riding atop a gigantic ejaculating vagina. In the past, there has been debate about whether transgender people should participate in the Dyke March.[30] In the case of female-to-male transgender people, many of whom have been longtime lesbian activists, their previous gender identity and commitment to women's issues would suggest that they should march, while their current gender identity would have them on the sidelines only. For male-to-female transgender people the situation is reversed, with questions of political solidarity arising more readily than issues of gender solidarity. In either case, the debate is complex and speaks to salient distinctions within the queer community itself. A singular sense of queer identity is problematized, suggesting that qualities other than one's sexual self, such as political and gender allegiance, must be negotiated within the concept of queerness. Indeed, when noting that a woman in the Dyke March proclaimed, "There are thousands of me here!"[31] one wonders if she was speaking about women, or lesbians, or queers, or all of the above.

Similar stratifications along lines of race and class appear throughout gay tour books. *Gay U.S.A.: The Straight Talking Guide to Gay Travel* (Hobica 1995) lists topical headings that highlight ethnic identity and income levels. The Pendulum, a nightclub in the heart of the Castro, is billed under the heading "African-American and Latino Bars" as a "place for black men and the men who love them" (Hobica 1995:192). Pleasuredome, under the category "Mostly for Dancing," caters to "young men on drugs" (Hobica 1995:193), and, next to this entry, The Box is billed as "racially mixed." The "young men on drugs" at Pleasuredome may be presumed to be predominantly white because they remain unmarked by race, unlike the patrons at The Pendulum and The Box.[32] Interestingly, Pleasuredome does cater to a primarily white clientele. In any case, these representations of queer sites reflect overt distinctions based on race. Similarly, the heading "Upscale Crowd" invites queer patrons to the Alta Plaza, where suits and $7 martinis are the norm. Differentiations based on race, economic status, and gender riddle the ephemera directed toward the queer tourist. This representational tactic appears to be inclusive, acknowledging the diversity of the queer community. However, these distinctions also make clear that certain dominant categories remain unmarked.

A further line of intra-queer distinction is summarized in an anonymous on-line review of *Fodor's Gay Guide to the U.S.A.* (Collins 1997):

> Consider that on page 50 of *Fodor's Gay Guide to San Francisco* Collins says that many of SF's gay bars cater "mostly to old drunks." He then describes trying to meet someone at one of these bars: "You give him a quick tap on the shoulder, just to see if anybody is in there. And crash! He falls off his bar stool." Later Collins says that there's a bar stool in SF with your name on it, and "all you have to do is try not to fall off it." It's incredible to encounter such blatant ageism. Having just spent time in SF, I can report that one of the city's most refreshing aspects is the diversity of both age and body type in its gay population, a diversity which I've never encountered in any other American city. It's possible to feel comfortable in the Castro and other neighborhoods without being a 22-year-old man with a gym body. Collins may not perceive that as being a strength. Someone should sit Collins down, show him *The Times of Harvey Milk*, and make him read *The Mayor of Castro Street*. Then he may learn that those "old drunks" in some cases gave up their lives so that he'd have a bubble of tolerance to play in. (Anonymous 1998)

The author illuminates yet another line of distinction within the queer community based on age and body type. Ultimately the author finds San Francisco to be a particularly accepting locale for all manner of queer tourists. The comments extend the frame of queer inclusion, affirming that San Francisco is often characterized as a diverse amalgamation of queer people.

Distinctions of race, gender, class, and age are positioned alongside an oft-repeated trope of gay tour guidebooks: sex. Sex penetrates guidebooks presumably because sex, desire, and "object choice" have often been foundational for both forming queer communities and establishing identity for queer people. At the same time, a singular focus on the sexual aspect of sexual identity offers a limited scope of queerness, "essentializing" and "naturalizing" complex subjectivities. In order to distinguish between queer people's lived experience and the representation of their experience and desire in gay tour guidebooks, it is important to establish the relationship between representations of experience and lived experience itself. Although sex alone does not constitute queer identity, and political motivations are vital to constructing a queer nation, it would be foolish to obscure the "communitas" engendered through cruising and coupling. This element of queer identity is not lost on the creators of queer touristic ephemera. Overt sexual references categorize venues as places for "Cruising and Drinking," getting into "Leather," or, for the very explicit, "Sex Clubs" (Hobica 1995:243–245). The heading "*Top* Tables" (Hobica 1995:243, emphasis added) highlights restaurants that serve expensive cuisine. However, Hobica's word choice here, in the context of leather and sex clubs, invokes the age-old food/sex correlation. Using the jargon of domination and submission, Hobica manages to couple gastronomy with radical sexual positionings. "*Mostly* for Dancing" (Hobica 1995:193, emphasis added) leaves the reader wondering what else might go on here. Sexual references throughout queer tour guides, some more veiled than others, emphasize the sexual aspect of representing sexual identity. To ironically twist Graburn's (1989) "sacred and profane," one might say that what is "profane" by normative standards is in fact "sacred" to a queer homeland. Heteronormative sentiments often maintain that "homosexuals [are] deviant, immoral individuals...[who] simply live an aberrant lifestyle rather than constituting a legitimate cultural identity" (Irvine 1998:575). Thus, the overt representation of queer sexual behavior throughout these guides suggests a distinct reverence for sexual behaviors that are stigmatized in heteronormative discourses.

Discussing the representation of Amsterdam as "the Gay Capital of the World," Dahles describes the contentious debates among the city's tourism boards as to whether Amsterdam's image should be that of "history" or that of "heretics and whores" (1996:231). The representation of San Francisco as an explicitly sexual gay mecca has met with similar obstacles. The director of the San Francisco Arts Commission explained that in composing the three-day tours to be represented in *California: Culture's Edge*, he contended with individuals from the San Diego Arts Commission who did not agree that a "Pride" tour should be included in the magazine.[33] The "Pride" tour was ultimately included because, in the director's words, "I could not face my constituency in San Francisco and tell them that a gay and lesbian tour had not been included." Those creating the representations of both Amsterdam and San Francisco have grappled with the cities' sexual "stigma" and the stigma of homosexuality in particular. Both Amsterdam and San Francisco continue to be linked with sexuality in the popular imagination, often through particular sites.

Josie's Cabaret and Juice Joint is situated in the nexus of the Castro/Market Street area and packs its sunny back patio with a late breakfast crowd. Vegetarian fare constitutes the menu, and the artwork of HIV+ people covers the walls. In the evenings, campy shows and comedians entertain audiences who sip ginger ale and espresso. Josie's is consistently mentioned in gay tour guidebooks among the "10 things no self respecting gay person should miss" (Hobica 1995:189). Josie's is also consistently mentioned in nonqueer guides to the city as a "must see" that is "highly recommended."[34] Josie's appearance in a diversity of guides brings to light two issues in the construction of a queer homeland. First, the fact that Josie's appears in nonqueer guides suggests that queer entertainment and perhaps queer people themselves are considered one of the many "attractions" of the city. Queer people, in this sense, are portrayed to a nonqueer audience as suitable objects of the "tourist gaze" (Urry 1990). Gazing tourists attempt to appropriate "authentic others" in order to sidestep modernity. Perhaps the very spectacle of queer performativity, in all its flamboyance, invites a voyeuristic crowd of heterosexual gazers. Perhaps vivid performances of "queer identity" are viewed as a product to be consumed, the "sexual other" taking the place of the "primitive other." However, at times it is unclear who is gazing at whom. Is the "straight" audience the active voyeur, or are queers, in fact, staring back at the "straight other"? Moreover, can the audience be rightly characterized as entirely composed of "straights"? Probably not. Feminist film theory has deconstructed the "male gaze," and many scholars have addressed the "colonial gaze" and the "white gaze." However, a comprehensive analysis of both the "queer gaze" and the "straight gaze" has yet to be produced.

In any event, gazing on a sexual "other" seems to constitute a part of the touristic experience for both "straight" and queer tourists. The visually rich performances and ambiance at Josie's are explicitly concerned with queer issues, from overtly political one-act plays to decor made by HIV+ people.[35] The allure of a queer café, unapologetically "out" about its politics, is available to both queer and nonqueer visitors to the city. This suggests a second element in the construction of a queer homeland: that coalitions must be consciously built and maintained between queer and nonqueer people. Josie's is a safe place for a panoply of patrons; it is a place that hosts a diversity of sexualities. The representation of Josie's implies that heterogeneity is necessary to build a queer nation. Boundaries, here, become stretched to include "straight" allies.

Discussing the phenomenon of "gay space," Hodge describes the controversy about "straights" in "gay space" and suggests that queer events "should be first and foremost a safe celebration space for gays, not exclusionary like 'women's only' space...though there is sometimes a need for exclusionary spaces. Although 'straight space' is never totally straight because gays are always present whether they are 'out' about it or not" (1998).[36] The construction of a "gay space," or "queer place," is complex and here includes nonqueer allies. Josie's is represented as a nonexclusive, though no less overt, queer hub. It is a place where sexualities mix, while its status as a political venue for queer people remains. Further, Josie's is not described as an exclusively "men's" or "women's" café but, instead, is represented as open to the play of various gender and sexual identities. Although the representation of Josie's is verifiably queer, the café is not represented as monolithically so. The polymorphous inclusivity of queer identity was well spoken by a female informant whom I interviewed at Josie's.

M. identified herself as a lesbian who had recently moved to San Francisco after having visited the city many times. She recalled with some nostalgia her first trips to the city, where she felt empowered by the queer surroundings and her sense of belonging to a community. M. concluded that she felt safe as an "out" lesbian in San Francisco. This sense of safety ultimately led her to place less emphasis on her sexual identity:

> When I was in Minneapolis, and after I came out, I felt like I had to be so out all of the time. It's like I had to be superlesbian because the environment there was so different than here. I went to all the marches and rallies and was involved in organizations. It was all about being gay. Here, after a while, I just quit doing all that. Now I do political work with prison rights and animal rights. But it's like I don't have to highlight queer stuff so much anymore. So, in that way, I don't think I'm quite "as gay" now.... There I had to do dyke drag all the time, constantly proving that I was part of the community. I had to be a certain kind of lesbian: the white T-shirt, the jeans, the big black boots. So I think that San Francisco has allowed me to become a different kind of *woman*, I don't have to fit the role of superdyke here.... I can be me, a little more femme, and that's OK. (emphasis added)[37]

M.'s queer identity is here intimately linked with her political activism and gender identity. As she became less involved in queer politics, M. deemphasized her sexual identity. In representing her identity, or as Butler (1990) might have it, "performing" her identity, M. associated queerness with political activism. Her "transformation" was not sexuality-based but, rather, a gender transformation – "a different kind of woman" – intimately linked to her sexuality. M.'s words reflect that sexual identity in general, and queerness in particular, is a complex set of factors that includes shifting between various versions of the self. Her comments situate queer identity not as a monolithic essence but, rather, as a fluid set of meanings hinging on notions of sexuality and gender. Like the representation of Josie's, M. reflects the political aspect of queer nation-building. Each representation denies the notion of an essential, exclusive, queer population. In this sense, M.'s discourse and the discourses surrounding Josie's suggest a particular kind of nationalist-like rhetoric, more akin to "cultural nationalism" (Chatterjee 1993) than that described by Anderson (1983). Rather than political control of the state, a network of "insider ties" coheres this queer nation.

Red Dora's Bearded Lady, on the fringe of the Mission District, is a regular rallying point for a preliminary ride by Dykes on Bikes on the eve of the Pink Saturday "Gay Day" Parade. Co-owned by a member of the notorious punk dyke band Tribe 8,[38] the café serves steamed eggs, unlimited coffee, and vegetarian hot dogs. It maintains a community bulletin board with an abundance of queer events and workshops and hosts poetry readings, musical events, and rotating shows of local artists' work. Red Dora's is listed as a "women's café" in queer tour books and does not appear in nonqueer guides to the city. I spoke with a female cashier, whom I call S., about her interaction with queer visitors to the city.[39] She explained that queer tourists were very easy to recognize: "You know when they are a tourist because they are overwhelmed by the menu and can never decide...and they buy everything: the T-shirts, and sweatshirts, and postcards, and everything. I guess they want to show everyone back home in Iowa that they were here and went to the cool gay spots."[40] S.'s comment reflects the stereotype of tourist-dupes who are never quite comfortable in their surroundings; it also emphasizes the "insider's" acumen in recognizing queer "interlopers." Further, she refers to the consumption of queer "markers," which Red Dora's is in the business of providing. Though Red Dora's does not sell rainbow flags or pink triangle bumper stickers, it does market the punky equivalent: T-shirts that say, "I may not go down in history, but I'll go down on your sister," or a play on dive bar rhetoric, "Liquor in the front. Poker in the rear." S. seemed to relay an antipathy for queer tourists who want to buy some form of identity, a shallow reflection of themselves, that can be bandied around back home. Iowa, in her estimation, is figured as a place where one must wear one's identity; San Francisco is the place to procure this "identity." Consumption then validates and marks the "experience" of the pilgrimage. In contrast, residents of the city, "insiders," are expected to manifest some "authentic" queer self without the aid of trite symbols. Perhaps being a queer resident of the city, as opposed to a mere visitor, one is supposed to live an "essential" queer identity that is not dependent on queer trappings. Residents of the city may thus avoid purchasing "touristic" queer markers in order to avoid being mistaken for anything but "authentic" queer San Franciscans. Shenhav-Keller (1995) addresses a similar phenomenon in her analysis of purchases made by tourists in Tel Aviv's popular Maskit store. Tourists, anxious to bolster their sense of Jewish identity, actively seek the most "authentic" representations available. Residents, however, rarely purchase these icons, presumably because they are comfortable with their own "authentic" identity by virtue of residing in a Jewish state. In sum, it appears as though "insider" (Boissevain 1996) status precludes overt identity markings, queer or Jewish.

In the introduction to *Gay U.S.A.* (1995), Hobica suggests a further disruption of bounded and easily marked identity categories. He writes that in San Francisco, "unlike Boston, people don't care what you do – they don't judge. You can be a lesbian one day, bi the next and heterosexual and married a week later and no one bats an eyelash" (1995:184).[41] Hobica emphasizes that San Francisco, as a place, allows people to move between and among particular identities. The fluidity he describes echoes recent debates about the use of "identity tags," which some argue limit subjectivity (Butler 1997) and obscure the heterogeneity of queerness (Anzaldúa 1991). S.'s words and those of the tour book suggest that San Francisco allows a range of sexual identity choices not available in other places. Not only can one easily choose a sexual identity, but this identity can also be easily traded in for a new one. Unlike Boston's or perhaps Iowa's, San Francisco's cultural climate does not insist on the maintenance of strict identity categories. In other words, a queer homeland provides choice in regard to sexual identities, and these identities are flexible and changeable over time; even through shifts of sexual identity, one can retain an "authentic" queer self.

These discourses of authenticity are reminiscent of Goffman's front- and backstages, where the authentic backstage is accessible only to locals, who guard the mystique of essential identities. In the case of San Francisco, however, the "authentic" queer self is enhanced by rejecting identity labels and the overt symbols of queerness: identity markers based on circumscribed categories. I would add that this ability to remain "unmarked" while still retaining an "out" queer identity is only possible in places where queer activism and a high tolerance for "alternative lifestyles" have prevailed over time. In those places where it is dangerous to be marked as queer, there is no luxury of choice. Rich's (1986) "compulsory heterosexuality" is perhaps "queered" in San Francisco to become a form of sexual fluidity. However, this inversion is possible only after heteronormativity has been disrupted to some degree. San Francisco, in this sense, is represented as a place, unlike most places on the planet, where one can "play" with sexual identity tropes. One need not take a one-dimensional stand on the sexual self.

Conclusion: A Homeland Halfway to the Stars

Guidebooks that routinely boast that San Francisco is "the gayest city in the United States" and "gay central U.S.A." reflect many of the sentiments expressed by queer tourists in search of a homeland. San Francisco becomes constructed as a pilgrimage site for the elaboration of queer identity through emerging discourses that, though sometimes "essentialized," are continually in a state of negotiation – a negotiation that takes place between "insiders" and "outsiders" and within the rubric of "queer" itself. Queer pilgrimage does not conform to a homogeneous sense of queer identity but, rather, is mediated by other factors such as race, class status, age, and gender. Thus, queerness as an identity construct reveals itself to be flexible, fluid, and open to shifts in meaning even when queerness is employed in the very concrete process of territorializing a homeland. Unlike many trends within identity politics, the imagining of a queer nation, with a homeland located in San Francisco, suggests new avenues for articulating identity. I have argued that San Francisco does serve as an imagined homeland for queers, a nexus point for the "ideoscape" (Appadurai 1996) of a queer imaginary. However, I have also elaborated how representations of the city include a flexible set of identities, rather than a singular emphasis on a one-dimensional queer subject. The city operates as a transnational mecca for queer tourists only on the condition that it not restrict too drastically its definition of "queerness."

Nationalist-like tropes, deployed to consolidate a queer nation, are ubiquitous in the ethnographic narratives I encountered in San Francisco. Although it would be unwise to configure a queer nation as exactly equivalent to other nationalist projects, it would be equally problematic to discount the efficacy of nationalist-like discourses. It is, after all, no coincidence that the largest flagpole in the city is erected in the Castro and flies the rainbow flag. The proliferation of nationalisms around the globe underscores the need to better understand diverse articulations of nationalist-like endeavors. In particular, forms of nationalist-like sentiments that do not rely on the "imagined" ties of blood, bone, and cultural patrimony may suggest new ways of conceptualizing peoplehood based on different criteria, such as sexuality.

My intention has been to emphasize that a queer homeland may be both logically and ethically tied to touristic practices. If all of the "back homes" offered the "playing and praying" possible in San Francisco, the city might not exist as a point of queer concentration. The "mundane social life" outside of the mecca stands in stark contrast to the symbolic inversion possible in a queer homeland. Although all pilgrimages involve leaving "home" to find spiritual redemption, the unique quality of queer tourism is that a reversal of religious pilgrimage is at play. Many queer tourists leave home because it is there that they have undergone spiritual exile; a "homeland" offers the sanctuary that many "back homes" do not. Pilgrimage to San Francisco also raises the question of whether having a place for queer liminality forecloses the need to effect change in the status quo back "home." The construction of a queer homeland may thus be politically dangerous, providing a "ghetto" for the banished. Whatever the political ramifications may be, the path to a homeland seems to be built on sex and politics. San Francisco's history of nonconformity is critical here too, for neither sex nor politics prefigures a sense of peoplehood; these phenomena have occurred in other places at other times without ever creating a mecca. By gazing at and through the queer tourist, it is clear that the construction of a queer homeland is a complex and rich terrain. Through these multiple aspects of identity migration, many queers have left their hearts in San Francisco, and a homeland is still in the process of being imagined.

NOTES

1 "Ephemera," such as flyers, posters, and brochures, are transient in nature, ever changing, unarchived, and quickly disposed of. In the context of ephemeral things, I would like to highlight the likewise transient and ever-changing discourse that appears in this discussion. The tour guidebooks I have examined use, for the most part, the terms *gay* and *lesbian* rather than *queer*. Thus, these guides seem to be "oriented," or marketed, to lesbians and gays rather than "queers." However, I have chosen to elaborate on a notion of a specifically "queer homeland" rather than a "gay and lesbian homeland" because of the inclusivity of "queer" identity (bisexuals, sexual radicals, etc.), which I hope to demonstrate is fundamental to the construction of a homeland in San Francisco. Overall, there is a movement among the terminology of respondents' narratives, the language of tour books, and the conceptual framework of "queerness," creating a dynamic tension that mirrors the complexity of articulating a sense of homeland.

2 My use of "a" queer nation is distinct from the political organization Queer Nation started in April 1990 by a group of AIDS Coalition to Unleash Power, or ACT UP, organizers interested in direct actions that would address a broader range of gay and lesbian issues.

3 Tourism is considered a "privileged practice" because economic status often determines who can, or cannot, engage in touristic endeavors. Further, the practice of pilgrimage, according to the Turners (1978), arose with the dominant world religions, most of which denigrate homosexuality. Tracing the pilgrimage qualities of gays and lesbians going to San Francisco serves to upset the correlation of pilgrimage with dominant and exclusionary religions. Rather, a pilgrimage to a gay homeland might be construed as overtly anti-"religious."

4 I follow Rothman's suggestion that tourism sells "ambiance, experience, and identity…[an exchange that] is more complicated and ambiguous than a material sales transaction. A feeling is transmitted and perhaps shared; a way of living is expressed" (1998:20).

5 Rothman (1998:16) maintains that "cosmopolitan, urban affluent" coastal cities, such as San Francisco and Los Angeles, "reflexively" cater to tourism and that this tourism has taken on a form distinct from that in other places in the United States where tourism has developed.

6 Weston describes the "gay imaginary" as a participatory process wherein "the designation of lesbians and gay men as 'a people' becomes bound up with the search for sexual partners and the construction of a lesbian or gay identity" (1998:34). In other words, the "gay imaginary" does not require finding one's essential gay self but, rather, subjectivity is constructed through imagining a "we-ness." Weston contends that this imagining is generated in the urban centers where gay migrations have occurred.

7 Bean explains that "the Indian death rate was accelerated" (1968:169), primarily because of disease and starvation, as hundreds of thousands of "Americans" migrated to California. A Native American population of 30,000 in 1870 was reduced to less than 16,000 by 1900 (Bean 1968:169).

8 The development of railroads, according to Rothman (1998:47), also increased the number of resorts in the San Francisco and Monterey Bay areas, thus linking industrial expansion and touristic endeavors.

9 See Bean 1968:235–243 for a discussion of the complexities among the Workingmen's Party, California employers, and the federal government on the issue of Chinese immigrant labor.

10 The early 1950s were the time of the "San Francisco Renaissance," marked by the establishment of the Poetry Center at San Francisco State (Bean 1968:448). The beat literary movement that followed soon after has been described as a combination of a retreat from the "modern" East Coast and a seeking of "individuality" (Rothman 1998:167) that was centered in San Francisco.

11 Mona's, an all-women's bar, first opened in 1936 and catered primarily to working-class women, though middle-class lesbians vacationing in San Francisco also spent time there (Faderman 1991:107). In 1950 Mattachine, a homosexual organization begun by five gay men who had been members of the Communist Party, was active in San Francisco. Two years later, Del Martin and

Phyllis Lyon would establish the first all-lesbian organization, the Daughters of Bilitis.

12 Once a significant number of queer people had moved to the Castro and created an enclave community, their numbers continued to increase. Stephen O. Murray (1992) suggests that homosexual residential concentration and the recreational facilities that followed created a sense of community and shared experience. He goes on to describe how the development of the welfare state allowed individual gay people to move to enclave communities as they were freed from economic dependence on their families/communities of origin. However, I would add that other social factors, such as the "queer ships" noted earlier, added to the phenomenon of enclave communities.

13 Likewise, Kennedy and Davis suggest that because San Francisco was a "cosmopolitan" city, "it had the numbers to generate the politically conscious leadership of the homophile movement" (1993:115). Further, Stein (1997) finds the growth of feminist culture to be rooted in the lesbian movement that was generated through lesbian bar scenes, alternative families, and woman-centered ideals found in San Francisco from the 1970s to the 1990s.

14 Harvey Milk's election to the Board of Supervisors was applauded by the gay men living in the Castro who had formed the backbone of Milk's campaign. Milk's murder in 1978 and the acquittal of his assassin, Dan White (with the infamous "Twinkie defense"), caused a profound shudder in the gay quarter of the city.

15 I am not suggesting that sexual "orientation" is chosen but, rather, that one may choose to include oneself in a larger whole of queer "nationhood."

16 The notion of "chosen" membership in a queer nation is contentious. Historically, homosexuality has been understood, variously, as "innate"/biological or a product of socialization. Foucault (1978) has also described the social construction of the term in a historical process meant to mark certain people as "other." However, in the sense that one can choose to be "out" or not, one chooses to include oneself in a queer nation. Similarly, the feminist movement in the early 1970s advocated "voluntary" lesbianism as a way to consolidate separatist power. The more recent use of *queer*, which includes nongay/nonlesbian-identified allies, certainly speaks to the chosen nature of queer nation membership.

17 Bourdieu (1980) distinguishes critical thought from ordinary perception and activity from reflection. "Leisure" or "play" is, then, a function of privilege. My use of *play* here is more flexible than that suggested by Bourdieu. "Play" functions as *active* participation in a queer community rather than solely a practice of one's cultural capital.

18 Judith Butler (1993) has suggested that play constitutes "the matrix of identity" as players, after play, make community – much as ritual leaves in its wake "a community of believers" (Lancaster 1997:24).

19 Interview with "L.," conducted at the San Francisco Pride Parade, June 1998. L. was a 31-year-old self-identified Latina bisexual originally from Dallas who lived in Los Angeles and worked as an administrative assistant. Our interview was brief because of the context of the festivities, crowds, and so on. The brevity of this interview, however, highlights the difficulty of conducting research on gay and lesbian topics within anthropology. While funding sources are limited for many anthropological research endeavors, the lack of funding available for queer research may be particularly pronounced, thus limiting researchers' ability to conduct extensive ethnographic projects.

20 Discussing a related phenomenon in heterosexual "sex tourism," Tucker notes that "tourism clearly influences power in sexual identity and presents opportunities that may be perceived as lacking in the tourist's home environment" (1997:114), suggesting that transformations through sex(uality) tourism occur within queer and "straight" encounters.

21 Interview with "Z.," conducted at Red Dora's Bearded Lady Café, June 1988. Z. was a 32-year-old self-identified white lesbian living in Reno, Nevada, who did freelance graphic design work and frequented San Francisco, her former home.

22 Interview with "J.," conducted at the San Francisco Pride Parade, June 1998, J. was a 40-year-old male, self-identified as white and homosexual, who worked as a waiter in Hamburg, Germany.

23 Interview with "O.," conducted at the San Francisco Pride Parade, June 1998. O. was a 23-year-old male who self-identified as a black gay man. O. lived in Atlanta, Georgia, his birthplace, and worked as a financial consultant.

24 This respondent's use of "my people" is particularly interesting given that he was a German tourist who was, in San Francisco, far outside the borders of his own nation-state. Further, "my people" is reminiscent of the use of *Volk* to consolidate a sense of nationalist pride. Here, gay people are configured as the "Volk," which seems to invert

the reproductive, blood ties of the German nationalist "Volk."

25 "Pride" parades and events have become ubiquitous in many U.S. cities and abroad, which suggests, perhaps, that the Pride Parade in San Francisco is just another example of this trend. However, I maintain throughout this article that the particular qualities of San Francisco as a site of identity construction, rooted in history, politics, and so forth, make the San Francisco Pride events unique and exemplify the qualities of a homeland.

26 See Shenhav-Keller 1995 for a discussion of Jewish pilgrimage to Israel, where a parallel dynamic seems to occur: a journey "back" to a "home" land that one has never been to before. Both experiences, queer and Jewish pilgrimage, serve to disrupt easy definitions of "home" as a place of material, geographic familiarity. Rather, a homeland is a composite of symbolic and material factors: a place of we-ness, sanctuary, historical relevance, and so on.

27 Café Flore is well known as a "cruising" place for gay men in the Castro, where one's ability to coif correctly may mean the difference between a date or not. I believe that the sexualized atmosphere at Café Flore alongside a playful appropriation of stereotypes about gay men's vanity are the origins of the nickname "Café Hairdoo." However, as with all cultural products that arise in subcultures, there are no doubt multiple interpretations of the meaning of "Café Hairdoo."

28 This particular guide is distinct from others in that it reflects San Francisco's representation of "itself." It is not a commercial guide from "outside" the city.

29 The economic differences between the Castro and the Mission are significant here as well. In general, rents are less in the Mission District than in the Castro, and the income levels of residents in each neighborhood seem to correspond to this fact. Commercial venues in the Castro, for example, have tended to be more costly than those in the Mission, although this has changed in recent years as the Mission District has become gentrified.

30 This debate arose sporadically while I was active in the 1995 Dyke March planning sessions. The question never reached the level of an official agenda item in the meetings, but it was bandied about as a point of contention. In comparison with the Michigan Women's Music Festival, where the debate about (specifically male-to-female) transgender inclusion has been volatile, Dyke March concerns about transgender inclusion have been far less controversial and divisive.

31 Interview, conducted at the Dyke March, June 1998, with a 29-year-old woman who self-identified as a Jewish lesbian.

32 Here I take the position that "young men on drugs" are unmarked in comparison with racial "others" who are explicitly marked by race in the text I am assessing. However, it is important to note that often, in popular media and in stereotyping discourses, men of color are portrayed as "on drugs." I do not believe that to be the case in this particular instance, but I do acknowledge that this pervasive and damaging stereotype may be a factor in how the text of this guidebook is interpreted by readers.

33 *California: Culture's Edge* (CCTC 1998) comprises 12 different tours in the cities of San Francisco, San Diego, and Los Angeles. Consensus had to be reached on which 12 tours to include because each city was responsible for providing one tour within the stated categories. In other words, all three cities have showcased tours such as "Jewish Heritage," "Fiesta," "Mission Trail," "Jazz and Blues," and so on. Apparently, the San Diego board felt it did not have enough "Pride" sites within the city and so advocated that "Pride" not be one of the tours. Whether or not this was the actual reason the San Diego board contested the "Pride" tour is, of course, questionable. The publication was funded, in large part, by the National Endowment for the Arts, whose acceptance of homosexuality and sex-positive images has not been exemplary. Perhaps a feared loss of funding influenced the conclusions of the San Diego tourism board.

34 Though Josie's is not marked explicitly in non-queer guides as a queer venue, the lists of events and descriptions of Josie's in these guides do emphasize a nonheterosexual environment.

35 Urvashi Vaid (1995) suggests that AIDS had the effect of "outing everyone" because gay and bisexual men were dying in such large numbers in the first years of the epidemic. The queer community significantly shifted focus as energies previously spent on organizing for queer rights were now needed to combat AIDS, raise awareness, promote research, and so on. The nature of politics in the queer community underwent and continues to undergo significant changes. Vaid further suggests that the AIDS epidemic forced the queer political community to revision its goals, from a "liberation" model to a "legitimation" model. Because the medical needs around AIDS are so great, queer

organizers have needed to call on "the straight world" for assistance. This shift to obtain "conditional equality" was, according to Vaid, initiated by the AIDS crisis.

36 Michael Bronski (1984) makes a similar claim in his assertion that much of what is called "straight" culture is heavily infused with a gay sensibility: ballet, opera, Broadway, theater, art, and film have all been shaped by the talents of gay men. A similar sentiment is reflected in the film *The Celluloid Closet* (1996), created by two San Francisco gay men.

37 Interview with "M.," conducted at the Lexington Club, June 1998. M. lived in San Francisco and worked as a firefighter. She is identified as a white lesbian and was 33 years old. For detailed discussions of the distinctions between "butch" and "femme," see Case 1993, Kennedy and Davis 1993, and Stein 1997.

38 "Tribe 8" has a similar pronunciation to *tribade*, which, according to the *Oxford English Dictionary*, is "a woman who practices unnatural vice with another woman."

39 "S." did not mention nonqueer tourists during our discussion.

40 Interview with "S.," conducted at Red Dora's Bearded Lady Café, June 1998. S. worked at the café, lived nearby, and identified herself as a Jewish dyke. She is originally from Kansas.

41 It seems to me that this progression from "lesbian," to "bi," to "hetero," to "married" is not accidental. The issue of bisexuality has been raised as a concern within San Francisco queer communities. Are bisexuals "authentically" queer? Can they be trusted as political allies and potential bedfellows? More recently, however, one hears more and more about "hasbians" (former lesbians now involved in significant relationships with men). As one woman ironically put it, "Lesbians these days! If they're not sleeping with men, they're becoming men."

REFERENCES

Anderson, Benedict. 1983. *Imagined Communities: Reflections on the Origin and Spread of Nationalism*. London: Verso.

Anonymous. 1998. Review of *Fodor's Gay Guide to the U.S.A.* Electronic document, http://www.amazon.com, accessed November 22.

Anzaldúa, Gloria. 1987. *Borderlands/La Frontera: The New Mestiza*. San Francisco: Aunt Lute Books.

Anzaldúa, Gloria. 1991. To(o) Queer the Writer: *Loca, escrita y chicana*. In *In Versions: Writing by Dykes, Queers and Lesbians*. Betsy Warland, ed. Pp. 249–263. Vancouver: Press Gang.

Apell, David, ed. 1998. *Access: Gay U.S.A.* New York: Access Press.

Appadurai, Arjun. 1996. *Modernity at Large: Cultural Dimensions of Globalization*. Minneapolis: University of Minnesota Press.

Bean, Walton. 1968. *California: An Interpretive History*. 2nd edn. New York: McGraw-Hill.

Bérubé, Allan. 1982. Past Times: Unearthing the History of Gay G.I.s. *Chicago Reader* 11 (June 18):36.

Boissevain, Jeremy, ed. 1996. *Coping with Tourists: European Reactions to Mass Tourism*. Providence, RI: Berghahn Books.

Boorstin, Daniel J. 1964. From Traveler to Tourist: The Lost Art of Travel. In *The Image: A Guide to Pseudo-Events in America*. Pp. 77–117. New York: Atheneum.

Bourdieu, Pierre. 1980. *The Logic of Practice*. Stanford: Stanford University Press.

Bronski, Michael. 1984. *Culture Clash: The Making of Gay Sensibility*. Boston: South End Press.

Bruner, Edward. 1991. Transformation of the Self in Tourism. *Annals of Tourism Research* 18:238–250.

Butler, Judith. 1990. *Gender Trouble: Feminism and the Subversion of Identity*. New York: Routledge.

Butler, Judith. 1993. *Bodies that Matter: On the Discursive Limits of "Sex."* New York: Routledge.

Butler, Judith. 1997. *Excitable Speech: A Politics of the Performative*. New York: Routledge.

California Cultural Tourism Commission. 1998. *California: Culture's Edge*. Los Angeles: California Cultural Tourism Commission.

Case, Sue Ellen. 1993. Toward a Butch-Femme Aesthetic. In *The Lesbian and Gay Studies Reader*. Henry Abelove, Michèle Aina Barale, and David M. Halperin, eds. Pp. 294–306. New York: Routledge.

Castañeda, Quetzil E. 1996. *In the Museum of Maya Culture: Touring Chichén Itzá*. Minneapolis: University of Minnesota Press.

The Celluloid Closet. 1996. Robert Epstein and Jeffrey Friedman, dirs. 102 min.

Chatterjee, Partha. 1993. *The Nation and its Fragments: Colonial and Postcolonial Histories*. Princeton: Princeton University Press.

Clifford, James, and George Marcus, eds. 1986. *Writing Culture: The Poetics and Politics of Ethnography*. Berkeley: University of California Press.

Collins, Andrew, ed. 1997. *Fodor's Gay Guide to the U.S.A.* New York: Fodor's Travel Publications.

Dahles, Heidi. 1996. The Social Construction of Mokum: Tourism and the Quest for Local Identity in Amsterdam. In *Coping with Tourists: European Reactions to Mass Tourism*. Jeremy Boissevain, ed. Pp. 227–246. Providence, RI: Berghahn Books.

de Certeau, Michel. 1984. *The Practice of Everyday Life*. Minneapolis: University of Minnesota Press.

Faderman, Lillian. 1991. *Odd Girls and Twilight Lovers: A History of Lesbian Life in Twentieth-Century America*. New York: Penguin Books.

Fitzgerald, Frances. 1986. *Cities on a Hill: A Journey through Contemporary American Cultures*. New York: Simon & Schuster.

Foucault, Michel. 1978. *The History of Sexuality*, vol. 1. *An Introduction*. Robert Hurley, trans. New York: Vintage Books.

Goffman, Erving. 1959. *The Presentation of Self in Everyday Life*. Garden City, NY: Doubleday.

Graburn, Nelson H. 1989. The Sacred Journey. In *Hosts and Guests*. Valene Smith, ed. Pp. 21–36. Philadelphia: University of Pennsylvania Press.

Hobica, George. 1995. *Gay U.S.A.: The Straight Talking Guide to Gay Travel*. Chicago: First Books.

Hodge, Steven. 1998. This Way Out Radio Broadcast: Gay Space in Sydney's Mardi Gras. National Public Radio, Sydney, October 11.

Irvine, Janice M. 1998. A Place in the Rainbow: Theorizing Lesbian and Gay Culture. In *Social Perspectives in Lesbian and Gay Studies*. Peter Nardi and Beth E. Schneider, eds. Pp. 573–588. London: Routledge.

Kaplan, Caren. 1996. This Question of Moving. In *Questions of Travel: Postmodern Discourses of Displacement*. Caren Kaplan, ed. Pp. 27–64. Durham: Duke University Press.

Kennedy, Elizabeth Lapovsky, and Madeline D. Davis. 1993. *Boots of Leather, Slippers of Gold: The History of a Lesbian Community*. New York: Penguin Books.

Lancaster, Roger N. 1997. Guto's Performance: Notes on the Transvestism of Everyday Life. In *Sex and Sexuality in Latin America*. Daniel Balderston and Donna J. Guy, eds. Pp. 9–32. New York: New York University Press.

Lanfant, Marie-Françoise, John B. Allock, and Edward M. Bruner, eds. 1995. *International Tourism: Identity and Change*. London: Sage.

MacCannell, Dean. 1976. *The Tourist: A New Theory of the Leisure Class*. New York: Schocken Books.

Murray, Stephen O. 1992. The "Underdevelopment" of Modern/Gay Homosexuality in MesoAmerica. In *Modern Homosexualities: Fragments of Lesbian and Gay Experience*. Ken Plummer, ed. Pp. 29–38. London: Routledge.

Newton, Esther. 1993. *Cherry Grove, Fire Island: Sixty Years in America's First Gay and Lesbian Town*. Boston: Beacon Press.

Phelan, Shane, ed. 1997. *Playing with Fire: Queer Politics, Queer Theories*. New York: Routledge.

Rich, Adrienne. 1986. Compulsory Heterosexuality and Lesbian Existence. In *Blood, Bread, and Poetry: Selected Prose, 1979–1985*. Pp. 23–68. New York: W. W. Norton.

Rothman, Hal K. 1998. *Devil's Bargains: Tourism in the Twentieth-Century American West*. Lawrence: University Press of Kansas.

Shenhav-Keller, Shelly. 1995. The Jewish Pilgrim and the Purchase of a Souvenir in Israel. In *International Tourism: Identity and Change*. Marie-Françoise Lanfant, John B. Allock and Edward M. Bruner, eds. Pp. 143–158. London: Sage.

Stein, Arlene. 1997. *Sex and Sensibility: Stories of a Lesbian Generation*. Berkeley: University of California Press.

Towner, John. 1985. *The Grand Tour: A Key Phase in the History of Tourism*. Annals of Tourism Research 12:297–333.

Tucker, Hazel. 1997. The Ideal Village: Interactions through Tourism in Central Anatolia. In *Tourists and Tourism: Identifying with People and Places*. Simone Abram, Jacqueline Waldren, and Donald V. MacLeod, eds. Pp. 107–128. Oxford: Berg.

Turner, Victor, and Edith Turner. 1978. Introduction: Pilgrimage as a Liminoid Phenomenon. In *Image and Pilgrimage in Christian Culture*. Victor Turner and Edith Turner, eds. Pp. 1–39. New York: Columbia University Press.

Urry, John. 1990. *The Tourist Gaze: Leisure and Travel in Contemporary Societies*. London: Sage Publications.

Vaid, Urvashi. 1995. *Virtual Equality: The Mainstreaming of Gay and Lesbian Liberation*. New York: Anchor Books.

Weston, Kath. 1998. *Long Slow Burn: Sexuality and Social Science*. New York: Routledge.

Williams, Brackette. 1996. *Women Out of Place: The Gender of Agency and the Race of Nationality*. New York: Routledge.

Part VI

Policing Blackness, Authenticity, and the Soul Patrol

15

Birthdays, Basketball, and Breaking Bread: Negotiating with Class in Contemporary Black America

John L. Jackson

Party Politics, or the Two-Party System

On a particularly hot and humid summer day, Paul, an African American architect living and working in New York City, celebrated his thirty-first birthday with an extravagant party. In fact, he had two of them: the first with old friends and family members in his mother's Bedford-Stuyvesant apartment that afternoon; the second inside his friend Wilson's plush Harlem brownstone and lasting well into the wee hours of the morning. Paul scheduled these two separate parties (replete with distinct guest lists) because, as he puts it, "it's really like I have two lives." Today, he is an up-and-coming professional who hobnobs with other six-figure-salaried black Americans from across the country and jet-sets to Caribbean Islands for occasional attempts at rest and relaxation. However, before his five-year sojourn at a southern university and his well-paying position in a small architectural firm, Paul was born in a lower-income housing project, attended city public schools through twelfth grade, and spent most of his teenage years with a single mother, older sister, and younger brother in a one-bedroom apartment not more than 20 minutes away from the block where he was born and raised.

Paul's life story could easily make sense as a rags-to-riches tale of upward social mobility, one of those tales that continue to keep Americans dreaming. But what stands out about Paul's story is its interesting concretization into two separate birthday fêtes – along with his specific explanations for that double bash: "It's like I have to be two different people," he offers, shaking his head as he briskly rakes five short, stubby fingers over and through his recently trimmed, tightly curled black hair. The fingers of his other hand steady a cigarette between his lips. We're sitting across a dining room table in his girlfriend Laura's place, a nicely furnished condo just outside of the city, one of those relatively close parts of New Jersey that just seem to get more and more expensive every housing market year. Paul sits up purposefully as he speaks, checking his watch periodically for Laura's imminent return from the store.

> PAUL: So, it can just be easier to let my two parts stay apart, you know. I don't want people feeling uncomfortable around other people because they don't talk the same language, or do the same things or anything like that, so I'd just as soon keep them apart. That cuts down on the drama. It cuts down on the drama for everybody – especially myself....I got my peers from work and that environment, business and professional, the movers and the shakers, and my peeps from way back when I used to run around in the streets like a wild man. Now and then.

Paul's is an almost proverbial tale of the black middle class, ever positioned betwixt and between seemingly discrete and easily separable social worlds: the rich and the poor, the black and the white. Today many people are taking a renewed interest in the trials and tribulations of these relatively well-off African Americans.[1] Recent literature on the black middle class has been both quantitative and qualitative, charting the group's condition (in terms of occupation, residency, education, and income) vis-à-vis the white middle class, chronicling some of its members' often arduous journeys from socioeconomic slavery to freedom, and describing the cumulative impact that racism has had on even African Americans who have achieved a modicum of economic success.[2]

The black middle-class experience has received a great deal of critical attention lately. Traditionally, poor (and usually minority) communities have served as the most frequent and fecund sites for social scientific research – either because the poor are often powerless to protest or because policy-makers and politicians have been preoccupied with explaining the causes of perpetual urban poverty. Anthropologists were once major players in the academic and popular discourse on the black underclass, introducing the notion of "culture" into the debates and helping to solidify (sometimes inadvertently) or challenge the "culture of poverty" and its assertion about poor people's pathological and ghetto-specific behaviors as ultimate explanation for what keeps them trapped below the poverty line.[3]

Even with the growing interest in black middle-class lives, a good deal of important information is sometimes left out of discussions about how class affects the daily experiences of black citizens. Many people give the same party line, arguing that with affirmative action and 1960s anti-discrimination legislation, the contemporary black middle class has exercised an unprecedented residential freedom, leaving the black poor behind to fend for themselves – with little or no social interaction between the two groups. Studies based on this premise downplay the black middle class's continued relationships with lower-classed African Americans, foregrounding their estrangement as one of the major reasons for many poor blacks' inability to escape poverty. I want to focus a bit on the intraracial, class-stratified contexts wherein African Americans are forced to negotiate class differences in their everyday lives.[4] Harlem residents not only have life histories that transcend the discrete categories of "black underclass" and "black middle class," they not only live in close proximity to other residents with markedly different socioeconomic realities, they also have social interactions that cut across many class lines. In Paul's case, he recognizes and negotiates class-inflected differences within his familial and friendship networks by carving kith and kin into two discrete social groupings for his birthday celebration. He has one party for his professional friends, "the black movers and shakers...my peers," and another for his "peops,"[5] the people who know him from when he hung out in the street "like a wild man." Paul thus sets the parameters for an important distinction between "peers" and "peops" that meshes with and foregrounds class-based concerns. Peers and peops stand in as proxies for different members of his multiclassed world:

PAUL: I mean, I don't know how different they are. Just makes me feel more comfortable. Because people have very, very different kinds of lives. So they won't like the same things, talk about the same kind of things, even talk the same way, and it just, I don't know, we'll see. But people like different things. Some have Masters degrees and these kinds of things. Big deal jobs. My mom hasn't been to college. Most of my family hasn't been. This is the truth.

Of course, Paul's dualistic approach to class differences among the people he knows is hardly the only way to go about dealing with disparities in education, occupation, interests and lifestyle, tastes, speech patterns, behavior, and social experiences. These are all areas that Paul slices in half and connects to the "very, very different" attendees of his two parties. These people are almost all African American; race doesn't distinguish the groups, but class-inflected differences most certainly do. Paul invokes these class-marked differences to justify the need for two separate social gatherings in celebration of his one birthday.[6]

[...] The actual life histories and socioeconomic trajectories of several African Americans in Harlem [are] histories that, I argue, transcend crudely wrought class categories. These are folks who live, work, and play next to differently classed neighbors. These kinds of class-varied *intra*neighborhood demographics are often disregarded for a twofold geographical framework of underclass prisoners and middle-class expatriates. Recent social science research shows that differently classed African Americans are more likely than their white counterparts to share the same general areas.[7] However, as real as this geographical contiguity may be, it says little about the actual nature of the social exchanges people have across class lines. [Below] I examine a few of the actual relationships that several Harlem residents have with friends, family members, and acquaintances from different socioeconomic positions, residents forced to deal with various classes of African Americans every single day of their lives.

"The Peops" versus "the Peers"

Many of the folks who attended Paul's two get-togethers didn't even live in Harlem. The second party's attendees, "the peers," were from places like Greenwich Village, different parts of New Jersey and even California (a friend in town for the weekend). Most of the people in his first party, "the peops," lived in Brooklyn – where many of them have always lived. They grew up with Paul – a few (like his Uncle Ronny and Cousin Dee) in the same low-income housing complex that was his social world for a good portion of his life. The rest of the peops at the first party either knew Paul's family very well or were his extended family: Aunt Leslie from Brownsville, cousins from different parts of Brooklyn and the Bronx, and, especially, his 62-year-old mother, sitting like a proud matriarch on her living room sofa. Some of Paul's "running buddies" from "back then" attended as well. Jimmy, 33, is living in the same apartment he lived in when they were kids. Still with his mother, Jimmy's been unemployed for the past two years. Another old friend, Tim, also in his early thirties, talks longingly about wanting to be a firefighter, but he's currently selling "warm" electronics on the street and off the books. Devon, late thirties, was like a mentor to Paul and his other buddies when they were younger; now he's a bus driver for the city and doing "pretty damn well," in Paul's estimation, especially relative to what some of the people from their old neighborhood are doing for a living. Tim, Jimmy, Paul, and Devon don't get together often these days, at least not as much as they claim they'd like to, but whenever they do, as at his early birthday party, they still talk as if they "never missed a day," with a familiarity that belies their brief and infrequent encounters. During the peops party, the guys ended up in a kind of ad hoc rap session in the back bedroom over a foldout table and a game of cards:

JIMMY: There ain't no way we could ever, I don't think, not be tight. That just ain't possible to me. It –

PAUL: [interrupting]: We are brothers, we *are* brothers, we are family, you don't speak, you do speak, but you always thinking about family, and they know you thinking about them. You don't have to see each other every day or nothing like that to know that.

JIMMY: That's what I'm trying to say.

DEVON: Man, but it ain't like old times. I mean, we used to run tight. All day and night like that.

JIMMY: True. True. True.

PAUL: Brother's gotta work and get that paper together.

JIMMY: Make it happen.

DEVON: You gotta grow up and do your thing, no doubt, I just know we used to roll hard.

Curlicues of smoke filled the room as the men enjoyed one another's company and memories. They all talked about how close they felt to one another, but with a slight tinge of loss since their friendship's childhood dynamics (which, they claim, were more "tight" than they are now) have changed, as if the bonds that once bound them together have loosened just a bit – in ways that can't easily or fully be restored.

Paul's mother lives by herself most of the time, even though relatives from out of town, or just crashing overnight from other boroughs, often stay in this second room, where Paul, Devon, Jimmy, and Tim played cards. The hallway and living room areas, where most of the attendees mingled, glittered with party decorations taped up to the ceiling, cursive "happy birthdays" accordioned across the walls. The lights were dim; the place was dark. A record player pumped out mostly old 1960s Motown tunes and 1980s soul music. The younger kids danced enthusiastically but eventually managed to get a tape from the rap group De La Soul into a cassette deck over quite a few adult objections. Paul surveyed his well-wishers and shouted to me over a hip-hop tune's extra-heavy bass line: "I could go broke tomorrow, and they would still be there for me. They would still love me. They would still say 'that is Paul.' All the other stuff is extra."

Although three people who were at the first party also attended the second one (Paul's girlfriend, his uncle, and me), most of his family only took part in the first. When Paul got himself ready to leave for his second engagement, everyone simply kissed him, congratulated him, and offered him their best wishes. Some didn't even know that he had another party brewing for later on. Paul's Aunt Mary, an elementary school cook or custodian ("or both" – Paul's not sure), offered this response to my passing query about the other party: "Paul is a grown man. He don't have time to just be hanging with us all day. He got his own life and his own business. I'm just glad I get a chance to see him. I'm too proud." Paul's mother smilingly puts that second party in perspective: "This is where his family is. He'll tell you that. He'll tell you that himself. If you ask him, he'll tell you that."

Paul's girlfriend Laura, his Uncle Rudy, and I prepared ourselves to leave with him, informal escorts to the next shindig. In fact, Paul almost didn't tell me about this early "peops" gathering and instead had me earmarked for only the "peers" event that evening. "I just didn't think to tell you about it," he explained about my early peer-placement. Paul assured me that he thought it was a good idea that I had come along to the peops party after all: "I guess I thought, I don't know what I thought, but then I said, this might be interesting for you to see my family since you have never really seen them that much. You don't really know that part of my life."

Paul conceptualizes some of the difference between the two parties in terms of business relationships versus nonbusiness relationships, a line that is not easily crossed. He thinks Laura makes the move better than most:

> PAUL: The second one [party] we were gonna talk business, talking about making money, getting things done. It was more business. I knew we would have a good time, don't get me wrong, but we are going to be making moves as well. Wil[son] had made sure some really interesting people were gonna come. That is why Laura is so bad. That is what is so cool about her. She can roll anywhere. We can be at a hip-hop concert, at a, a play, at a business meeting, what have you, and she is perfect in all those places. That's the kind of woman you need. Someone who is just comfortable in all kinds of circles and arenas. She does that better than me.

Laura is able to bridge the peers–peops, business–nonbusiness divide rather skillfully, a talent Paul admittedly finds essential.

By the time we left the first party, the place looked well spent. It had started slowly that afternoon at about 3:00 and lasted until 9:00 – at which point Paul, Laura, and I traveled to Paul's house so that he could change clothes before we took off for round two. Rudy caught up with us there. Wilson's place was larger and several folks milled about on both floors. A soft and mellow instrumental jazz tune massaged our eardrums. Wilson, the official host, had only invited the black professionals with whom he and Paul often hang out, imposing their own brand of self-selected, self-enforced two-worldliness on Paul's social universe, a two-worldliness analogous to many social scientists' understandings of black America as bifurcated into two estranged and mutually isolated halves. However, this bifurcation isn't a function of Paul's having no access to poorer, less successful blacks. It is contingent on the fact that he does have such contact, and unavoidably so. Despite his big-digit salary and his post-baccalaureate success, Paul still has relationships with differently classed African Americans that he must think about and negotiate. That summer, those interactions had the seemingly trivial effect of forcing him to throw two separate parties for at least two "very, very different" parts of his social network. Other Harlemites' social networks show some of the same socioeconomic variety that Paul's does. I want to look at a few of these class-varied relationships to see how people describe them. Where and when were they formed? Do they create particular problems for social navigation? What do they mean to and for the people involved?

No Friends

Some of the class-stratified relationships that I found in Harlem cut across friendships, others through family ties. Some people are able to negotiate class differences while maintaining the vibrancy of the relationships in question; other people recognize class differences as an insurmountable chasm across which meaningful and substantive relationships have difficulty thriving. Sometimes, when I tried to get at the issue of friendship networks head-on, specifically querying Harlemites about their friends, many adamantly maintained that they did not have any friendships with differently classed people at all. It seemed evident, however, that some of these folks did have powerfully class-stratified social relationships – even if they were not willing to call them friendships during formal, tape-recorded interviews. Zelda was one of the first people to exemplify this very split in conspicuous ways:

JOHN: Do you know any people who are really doing well?

ZELDA: You mean like money and stuff?

JOHN: Yeah, or whatever you think doing well means.

ZELDA: I know people that are happy. Not making a lot of money, maybe, but they happy. That are doing good. I think there is a lady down the hall who works for the Board of Ed. I don't really know her. We ain't really, like, close. We speak from time to time, but I don't really know her. I try to stay out of people's business.... I figure, I don't need that aggravation.

Several months later, I first met Kate, one of Zelda's co-workers. The two hang out and "go clubbing" periodically, about "once every couple weeks or so." Kate has both a B.A. and an M.A., and she works higher up the occupational food chain at the center where Zelda works. "She's up there with the bigwigs," Zelda offers. The two women get together fairly often outside of work and have very different socioeconomic realities, but Zelda didn't initially point to Kate as an example of a friend with a markedly different socioeconomic reality – or even as a friend at all – in some of our conversations. Likewise, Janet doesn't seem to create space for class-varied friendships:

JANET: I think that I have the same friends now I've had all my life. None of them live in Harlem because I don't know many people in Harlem. Not that I couldn't have friends, but now I have acquaintances. The guys who run the store on the corner. The people who I see around the block, most of the people. But most of the people here are not my friends. I'm pretty introverted. I keep to myself. I'm not a big, "hi, hi, let's hang out" person. Especially not with somebody who might not be positive or productive, that kind of thing. Just wants to act like they are fools and want you to prove you can be a fool too. Who needs that? I got my own drama, why would I need yours?

Janet's notion of "positive" people who are "about something" serves as a kind of substitute phrasing for notions of class-related success. She's quick to admit that she is "not from the street" and doesn't want to have to pretend that she is in order for people to like her or want to be around her. Janet also claims that she doesn't really know that many people in her neighborhood. Janet's real friendship network has not changed much since she moved uptown, at least not enough to include many members from her Harlem neighborhood.

Dexter prides himself on being able to talk to anybody, but even he can make a case for his substantial relationships being class homogenous:

DEXTER: It's hectic, son. We all just wanna make it, you know what I'm saying. Living. Just living. I know people who are living what I'm living. Trying to get that paper. Paying rent and trying to keep it moving. I don't run in million dollar circles like that. Not everybody is like you, bruh.

Dexter jokes, but he is also serious (as were Zelda and Janet) when he maintains that he doesn't really have friends of different class positions. Even Paul (a person whose varied social networks I know first-hand), who talked specifically about class stratification within his social networks during subsequent discussions around the time of his two birthday parties, made a case, during one of our more formal interview sessions early in my fieldwork, for the fact that he only had friendships with people in the same socioeconomic position he occupies:

JOHN: Tell me more about your friends. Who are they, and what do they do?
PAUL: I hang out with people at work. People at the gym where I work out. People who do what I do or go places where I go, and they are mostly pretty well-off, I guess. We can relate to each other.
JOHN: Why do you think that is? That you hang out with people from work?
PAUL: We relate. You share things with people that have experienced some of the same things. You know what I'm talking about? That is important. You won't agree on everything, but you have things in common.
JOHN: Things like what?
PAUL: The job for one. Things you like to do. They'll be people you went to school with. You have those things in common. Or you just happen to do the same work.

The first time I ever met Paul face to face, I conducted the interview from which the above is excerpted. I can almost remember him saying the words. They seemed clear, precise, measured, and sensible. However, half a year later, after the birthday parties, after going back through some of this material, it stood out as problematic. Paul did have friends that he called "friends" who were not colleagues from the job, who did not share the same occupation, and who weren't even working full-time. I was able to revisit these earlier responses after the birthday parties had come and gone, asking him again about the class stratification he did not mention earlier:

JOHN: What about your boys, the ones from the party? Jimmy and those guys.
PAUL: Dev and Jimmy and those guys. I guess that is true. It's definitely true. Yeah, but I don't see them that often. I'm usually busy working.
JOHN: How often do you see them?
PAUL: Maybe once a month, but they are definitely my boys. I can't forget them.

There was a kind of pattern with respect to class and friendship networks among many of the Harlem folks with whom I spoke. Like Paul and Zelda, several other Harlemites at different points in time tended to dismiss or "forget" their contacts with people from different rungs of the socioeconomic ladder. Many people found it easy to minimize all nonfamilial relationships, often going so far as to say that they have no close friendships whatsoever – not with anybody, regardless of class differences or similarities; that it is too "dangerous" and leads to "bullshit" or "drama." Many people claimed that they choose to keep to themselves instead:

DEXTER: I don't have no friends. I know people. But all motherfuckers is triflin'. I've seen it. It's real out here. You know what I'm saying. I mean I know heads. I know heads, no doubt. And they know me. And we may talk or give each other a pound or hang for a minute, but you can't be thinking that means it's all good. That ain't what it means. Not at all.

Brandi, too, doesn't have real friends. "I'm not interested in that," she offers. "People try to use you. They try to use you like that. Then you get thrown into bullshit for some 'friend,' for 'that's my friend.' "

Brandi, Dexter, and others reiterate time and again that they don't necessarily have friends or the time to actively cultivate friendships with anyone – let alone with people of different classes. This is an interesting theme that comes out of many of my interviews and discussions with Harlemites. Folks are sometimes quick to argue that they don't have any friends at all. They don't know people of different classes very intimately and don't really have any relationships outside of their familial circles that they would characterize as particularly close. But is that the end of the story? As in Paul's case, many of my informants do have nonfamilial interactions with individuals that look and sound like friendships even though they may be hesitant in applying the term. Zelda, for example, is quick to say that she, too, is a loner:

ZELDA: I have always been the one who stayed to herself. Always. That's what I did. I still do. I just don't feel like I got to be up under somebody to be happy. I don't need that. I can have fun home. If I go out, to the movies or something, I'll take myself. That is fine. I like that. It's less problems.

Zelda's statement that friendships lead to "problems" (reminiscent of Janet's earlier equation of friendships with "drama" and Brandi's argument that friendships throw one into "bullshit" situations) would imply that she too has no friends, that she even avoids friendships. Still, Zelda has an active social life, going out every few weekends with several women from her job. "We usually, when we go out, it's like party, have a few drinks, wink at some cuties and then go home." And a couple of ladies in her "regular posse" are doing really well in terms of most socioeconomic indicators; a few are even "bigwigs" like Kate, that fairly high-level supervisor at the center. Kate hangs with Zelda all the time at work and work-related recreational activities. "We are like just running around. She is mad cool, too. And she has juice, so people always want to be kissing her ass. I don't kiss her ass, though. She's cool, but I'm not trying to kiss her ass for it."

Even if he doesn't consider them his "friends," Dexter knows just about everybody he passes on the street. The kids, the cops, the local shop owners – many even call out to him by name. But they aren't friends, he says, they are just "people you know." According to Cynthia, 32, a college graduate and office manager at a Harlem-based educational institution, a woman named Karen "used to be" a friend back when they were in high school but now is "not really" a friend. When I first met Karen, wiry and tall, she was hanging out on the corner of 133rd Street and Seventh Avenue. It was early in the afternoon, and she had on dark and dirty clothes. I had stopped there to meet Cynthia, who was connecting up with me for a visit to the Studio Museum of Harlem. Cynthia is a bit of a fledgling artist, and I figured it would be nice for her to see the exhibit, particularly since she didn't get a chance to get out to museums very much. Karen spotted Cynthia as soon as we passed by and immediately smiled.

The two women exchanged pleasantries: what was going on with families; who had seen whom; details about Cynthia's Aunt Rita moving to Atlanta with some doctor she recently married. After about three minutes, Cynthia and I took our leave of Karen and headed down the block toward 125th Street. As we walked, Cynthia and I discussed Karen a bit. Cynthia is particularly clean-cut, well-groomed, and professional-looking if one's standards are creased pant suits and beauty salon hair. And Cynthia's well-groomed look made Karen's disheveled appearance that much more noticeable. In spite of their obvious history (a history I, as yet, knew nothing about, but could sense even from their brief conversation in the street that day), Cynthia seemed a bit cold and aloof toward Karen – even a bit rude, which wasn't like her at all. I'm not sure if Karen recognized it, but I most certainly thought that I did. Cynthia was cordial and polite enough, I guess, but she kept Karen at something of a distance – possibly because she was a bit anxious about being 15 minutes late already. Even with Cynthia's purposeful social distance vis-à-vis Karen, I wanted to think that I could still glimpse, hidden beneath all of that nonchalance and indifference, a closeness and affection that Cynthia held for this woman who looked old enough to be Cynthia's mother:

CYNTHIA: She's my age. Drugs and stuff done that to her. Because she is not that old. I know she looks it though.

JOHN: That's awful.

CYNTHIA: Oh yeah. She and I used to be girls. We still cool, but I mean we used to hang hard. We were always together. She got pregnant and got hooked on smoke....She is still my girl, I guess, we do go back, but she's on some other trip now. Off the hook, you know. She's done some stupid shit too, and all that is, she needs to try to get help.

JOHN: Does she work?

CYNTHIA: No. On the street. Selling her body for a smoke. And I am like, girl, are you crazy. Her apartment is in a shambles. She has a pretty baby, Shannon. I feel so bad for that baby sometimes. That's who I feel bad for. Sometimes I'll watch her [the baby] for a bit....[S]ome people don't have money, but that is not the same thing as living in a pig pen. We never had money when I was growing up, but we still had a nice home. Clean, you know. With nice stuff. Being broke ain't the same thing as being nasty and dirty.

Cynthia voices a popular perception about the difference between being a "deserving" poor person who still has American values and being one of those freeloading, lazy, shiftless, dirty, and pig-pen-dwelling poor people who are poor because they refuse to do anything positive with their lives. At the time, Cynthia had a full-time job and a well-kept apartment. Karen was on welfare and hadn't worked full-time in years. That was especially terrible, in Cynthia's opinion, because the two women started out on the same road. Karen just veered off track. Cynthia can begin to offer the beginnings of an argument about her difference from Karen as a function of the simple things her own mother did, such as keeping their apartment clean and neat when she was a child:

CYNTHIA: Drugs will do that, I guess, but she was always not clean. And when you not clean and on drugs you just a different kind of nasty. She looked at least decent when me and you saw her. The last time I saw her before that, she was looking crazy. She just looked terrible. I mean, it makes me want to cry to think that I grew up with her. I know her family, her mom. We were all kinds of close. My mom wasn't very sociable, but she hung out with [Karen's mother]. Our parents did the same things. I can't believe it. I just thank God. I really thank God. A lot of people have fallen to the drugs and stuff. But God has been good. I just feel almost like it's my responsibility or something. I know she is like her own problem and all of that, but I just feel as though if I wasn't so busy, I would just be able to help her.

If Cynthia feels somewhat responsible for Karen because of their childhood history, Ms. Joseph feels just as responsible about Damien, her 29-year-old neighbor who is "like a nephew," someone she first got to know only a few years ago. "The first time I met Damien," she recounts, "he was the meanest looking thing. Always frowning. And one day I was just walking, and I just asked him 'what are you frowning for, you are so handsome, why you so mad and mean?' And he smiled the prettiest smile after that. And I told him that I don't ever want to see him frowning and looking mean with that smile.... And every time I see him, he's smiling now."

Ms. Joseph's relationship with Damien hasn't had the long history that Karen and Cynthia share, but she admits that it is still her biggest joy to take the little she has, some money, a little food ("I love to cook"), and share it with him. Ms. Joseph and Damien speak all the time. Sometimes, he'll carry her groceries or push her shopping cart the two blocks to her home. And they often use those times to talk:

MS. JOSEPH: He told me that he was in jail....I know he's had it rough. That's how our black men get lost in the street....You know, no father, not in school, all of those things....He's never asked me for anything, but I know he is struggling. And I don't want him to start selling those drugs and whatnot, to start getting into all of that trouble. For all I know he could already be, but I just know that I want to help him out even with a little. Not a hand-out, but just a few dollars here and there. Just to say I hope you're doing okay. I guess I don't know what it's saying, but it makes me feel good to do it.

JOHN: Good in what way? Why do you feel good? [Pause] Like, what is so good?

MS. JOSEPH: I'm being helpful. That is important. I haven't met his mother. I don't know how close he is to his mother, but I do know he is kind. I could tell that from the beginning. You can look in his eyes and see he doesn't belong on the street like one of those hoodlums.... He went to church with me a couple of times, too. I liked that. It wasn't about what I had or what he didn't have. He just came with me to worship, and none of that other stuff ain't have nothing to do with it. That's a nice thing...

JOHN: Do you know his family? Friends?

MS. JOSEPH: Mostly hoodlums, I'm sorry to say. I don't know his family. He's told me a little bit about them, but I don't think I want to say too much about that. He's had it tough. But he's a kind spirit. People see that as soon as they meet him.

Cynthia can see that she has a different lifestyle and class-based reality than Karen. And Ms. Joseph can see the same thing with respect to Damien, an ex-con who, though periodically unemployed and hanging out with "hoodlums," has still occasionally accepted Ms. Joseph's invitations to worship with her at her church. Both Cynthia and Ms. Joseph try to be helpful because, as Cynthia put it, she thinks that she should. It makes her feel good and allows her to thank God for her relative successes in life.

Zelda (who knows Ms. Joseph "by sight") also doesn't have many friends that she'd label as such. She does see a guy named Jordan all the time around her block. He isn't a friend, but he's always making passes at her. Zelda is sure that he doesn't really want "anything to be serious even though he can say that." She has a baby, she isn't making a lot of money, and she is admittedly "not bringing all that much to the table" in terms of forming a long-term relationship. Jordan is a "big professional, a big-time social worker. You know, suit and tie.... He has a good job. He is that kind. Fly." Zelda feels that his flirting with her is either just being "nice" or "trying to get a piece," but it can't be anything more substantive because of the social distance (signified by dress and occupation) that she believes separates the two of them.

The first time I met Cynthia's high-school friend Karen, Cynthia and I had just bumped into her on the street. The two women shared a very brief conversation – as if Cynthia was uncomfortable with the whole scenario, and as if Karen wanted to respect the fact that her high-school "homegirl" was walking about town on a breezy morning with a black man she didn't know who was wearing a suit and tie. When I first asked Cynthia about her friend, she had very little to say, dismissing Karen as simply "off the hook" (someone who is crazy and beyond explanation), as someone she "used to know." We ran into Karen again on another day, this time on 125th Street. Cynthia seemed a bit more comfortable as they talked and laughed at length about that crazy boy who got their other high-school friend, Liz, pregnant at 14 – and about when and if Cynthia's Aunt Rita would ever move back to New York City. The conversation ended with Cynthia sliding Karen a few dollars and a hug. Once we are out of earshot, Cynthia, unsolicited, seemed to feel the need to justify her generosity.

"At first I wouldn't give her shit," she admitted, "'cause I knew what she was doing with it, but then I said you know what. I'm just gonna pray on it and ask God to step in and just do what I can."

When I accompanied Cynthia to Karen's apartment for the first time several weeks later, any reservations Cynthia held about their closeness seemed to dissolve in the warm heat of their laughter and stories. The two joked and reminisced with one another – and were even joined in their merriment later on by Liz, the woman who had grown up with them and gotten pregnant very young. I don't know what the three women talked about that night. I only walked Cynthia over to Karen's apartment, was introduced to Liz, chatted for a minute, and then left. In those few moments, I could see that these women shared a great deal and still, despite what I had interpreted as Cynthia's attempts at downplaying their relationship, gained tremendous amounts of pleasure and enjoyment from one another. A few days later, in another discussion I had with Cynthia about her relationship with Liz and Karen, the weight of the two other women's difficult lives almost brought her to tears:

> CYNTHIA: I don't know what happened. But it's fucked up. [Pause.] They used to be my girls. I mean that was it and a bag of chips. You don't know. I feel like now that is all fucked up. They are still cool, but they are so fucked up now with all of this shit. And not just the welfare. Shit happens like that sometimes, I guess. Fine. But they are like just not trying to get out of that, they are just like accepting it and getting deeper down the hole.

When Cynthia offers that Karen and Liz "used to be my girls," she's still placing the friendship in the distant past as opposed to the very real present of, say, that joy-filled get-together where the three of them were able to catch up with one another. Cynthia isn't sure where Liz is living these days, since Liz's mother threw her out about a year ago because of all "the stupid shit she pulled." Even given this ambivalence about her relationships with these women, Cynthia is just as quick to help them out as she is to downplay the importance of such assistance and to argue against the significance of the relationships in general:

JOHN: Are they good examples of the people you grew up with? I mean, are most of your friends in the same boat that those two are in?

CYNTHIA: No. I don't have a lot of friends. They aren't really my friends, I mean, Liz used to be, and I'm not nasty to her, I feel sorry for her, but she isn't my friend. I can't do anything with her, unless I wanted to do something stupid.

One Sunday morning, I spied Cynthia and Karen through the window of a local eatery. Karen was finishing off a breakfast that Cynthia had paid for. It was only the fourth time Karen had seen me over a two-month period, but she treated me like an old friend. And I appreciated her warmth.

Weeks later, Cynthia again downplayed her relationship with Karen, describing buying Karen a meal on Sunday morning as "nothing really, I'm just like, I got some time, she is, she needs food in her belly. What? I can do that." However, Cynthia did admit that she wanted to try making their weekend breakfasts a more regular thing. She thinks that's the least she can do, especially since Karen "used to be" such a good friend.

Playing Basketball

Paul and Tim (one of Paul's "peops" from that first birthday party) are basketball buddies. They meet up at least every few weekends or so during the summer and fall months to play a little ball, usually back in the neighborhood where they grew up, and where Tim lives to this day. It's a very self-conscious thing for Paul. "I know I'm not rich," he said, swerving down Kings Highway toward the above-ground subway's rusting trestlework, "but I do see that Tim is, like, really getting his ass busted. I don't want to roll out on him just 'cause he doesn't have it all straight and narrow." Tim, about three inches taller and twenty pounds heavier than Paul, lives frugally with the mother of his third child. According to Paul, he's unemployed and "trying hard to be lazy."

Once we got to the concrete courts, it became as clear as that morning's bright sky how many steps I've lost since my days as one of the first seventh graders able to graze the metal rim on the lowest of eight basketball hoops in our neighborhood playground. On this day, Paul and Tim shared smiles and not-so-furtive chuckles at my expense as the recent years of basketball inactivity made me a decided nonfactor during our morning's basketball game. I very quickly figured out that I should step aside and stop embarrassing myself for no good reason. Leaning breathlessly against the wire-meshed backstop beneath the backboard, I watched the two men attack one another with drives and jump shots at the netless basket. Every shot was contested, every point celebrated. They played hard for two vigorous games of 21; both times Tim clawed out a hard-fought victory by only a couple of points. Eventually, two more players just beginning to hold on to their early twenties entered the basketball court and challenged Tim and Paul to a two-on-two match. They accepted, teaming up valiantly in what was ultimately a losing effort against younger and more agile foes.

After dropping Tim off at his home, Paul explained how the two men use basketball as a means of keeping their relationship viable. After a game, they'll usually get something to eat and just talk a bit. "I'm not trying to change the man," Paul insisted, his car idling anxiously in front of my West Harlem building, "just play some ball with my boy." Paul feels that Tim's main problem is simple: he needs a job. If he got one and stuck with it, Paul believes that Tim would be on the right track. Paul even once tried using his peer contacts to get both Tim and Jimmy a job about a year earlier. He called in a favor, and "they fucked it up." After that fiasco, Paul believes that his buddies aren't really ready for his help.

PAUL: I tried to push it on them, you know, big brother style. Let me hook you up, that kind of thing. They were just not there. They came late, got into shit that was just awful. If they tell me they are ready, if they come to me like, put me on, that is one thing. But that is not the same thing as trying to force someone who isn't ready.... But we'll call and touch base for a second or two. Play some ball sometimes over

> here by my place, 'cause he has no beef down here with anybody, sometimes Brooklyn, just working up a sweat.

Jordan, Zelda's "fly" social worker acquaintance, the one she thinks might possibly be just "trying to get a piece," often deals with decidedly poorer African Americans as a function of his occupation. Thus he has clear opinions about the nature of the differences that separate him from the poorer blacks in need of his professional assistance:

> JORDAN: I see poor black people, poor people, all the time. I mean I could tell you stories. People who are barely holding on, and I respect that. But sometimes, I get so frustrated, they get on the white man, but really they just aren't doing what they need to do. Not the white man. Some people are just not taking care of what they have to take care of. It's as simple as that.

Jordan's been called a "house nigger" and an "Uncle Tom" many times on the job, usually when he fails to fulfill the expectations of black people sitting on the other side of his desk. In that context, he's pretty leery of dealing with blacks as a function of the work he does. Sometimes, he even claims he wants to leave social work altogether, because "it's like they hate you for having what they don't have. Not everyone, but enough." Until he finally does decide to actually leave, though, and until he finds that new job, Jordan often tries to avoid any extended contact across class lines with the black people coming in for help:

> JORDAN: People will take advantage of you. And if you don't give them what they want they are quick to call you out your name and all that kind of shit. I just want to stay away from folks who aren't about anything. And focus on what I need for me and not what other people think of me and put on me that is really about them and not me.

Jordan's is another argument about class-based avoidance, similar in some ways to the kind that Paul used to explain why he needed to keep his two sets of guests separated. And it's also akin to Dexter's thoughts about certain kinds of people he tries to avoid every now and then. For instance, the last time Dexter had an encounter with the police, he got harassed just because he was hanging with one of his boys, Dupree, a 22-year-old whom he describes as "knee-deep in all kinds of shit." The police questioned Dexter because he was standing on the corner and just talking with Dupree. Dexter admits to feeling a little on edge even when he's just walking alongside Dupree, because "when people want to settle the score they do that irregardless of who is there in the way. I don't want to catch a stray or something, some stupid-ass way to go out." Therefore, Dexter watches his back when he walks down the street. He calls himself paranoid, but that's because he knows a few people who are living a more underground lifestyle, "living kind of foul." Dexter has a job and responsibilities on the home front, and he doesn't want to get pulled down into any street confrontations. Consequently, he tries to be careful about when and where he hangs out with Dupree. In a similar move, Ms. Joseph won't let Damien's other friends in her house, "only him," she says. She doesn't feel as comfortable with them and what they might be up to. Even Paul will play basketball with Tim only in some parks – and only on certain days:

> PAUL: We almost never do the weekend unless it's real, real early. I'm usually working and too many people are out. It's good that he isn't working because he can go whenever. I'll just drive by his place and pick him up. We'll go to a good park and throw down for a few hours and then drop him back. No fuss, no muss.

Paul believes that weekdays or "real, real early" on weekends are the safest times for the two of them to play. As for Cynthia, she can pay for Karen's meals every once in a while and give her some change, but she doesn't bandy the term *friend* about in describing that relationship, at least not very easily, distrusting the term's application to a relationship that links her to a woman she grew up with who is now not doing very well. Cynthia is clear about not wanting to spend too much of her time with Karen, at least not every day. She feels that that could put her in compromising and dangerous social settings. Just as Ms. Joseph won't trust Damien's friends and

Paul won't trust the "fuss" and "muss" of overcrowded basketball courts on weekend afternoons, Cynthia doesn't trust more than infrequent contact with Karen – even though she dreams of much more frequent exchanges.

Cynthia, Ms. Joseph, and Paul are not the only individuals with agency and intentionality in these social relationships. Karen, Damien, and Tim also have thoughts about these same interactions. And sometimes it means that they jostle over how to define the most common aspects of the lives they share. For instance, Karen seems to talk about Cynthia as a friend with much less hesitation:

KAREN: That is my girl. I swear to God that is my girl. What to say? She is my ace. That is my girl. ... We used to dress the same. I was always over her house. Every day. You kidding. I know all her business. Especially from when we was kids.

Karen is quick to call Cynthia a friend, even her "ace," and she is much more likely to place that friendship in the present tense than Cynthia sometimes is (even though Karen also calls upon a shared history to ground that current friendship). The two jostle over what definition seems most applicable for describing their lives together. They use the labels they affix to their relationship as a way of tugging on the interpersonal boundaries between them, tugging in different appellative directions. These kinds of moves are more than semantic double-talk; they provide people with the tools they use to identify their social worlds in personally acceptable ways, to assign people to very particular places within cultural landscapes designed with recourse to equations about the length of shared histories and current degrees of recognizable commonality. Paul's basketball partner, Tim, corroborates Paul's assessment that the two have a long history, but he thinks that he and Paul have different things to take care of now, his little girl cuddled in his muscular arms:

TIM: He got his thing. I got my thing. Trying to make my shit happen, too. We both got shit we doing. And he got my back from day one. You know what I'm saying. From like this big. From when we was here. [Tim places his right hand two feet from the tiled floor, palms down.] Nobody could say we ain't been doing this thing from day one.

Tim obviously thinks that the two men's common history is vitally important. It is a history that no one can take away from them, that no one can say they don't share. It is a history that they hope can give them the means to at least partially cross the class lines that might divide them.[8]

Family Ties

If interclass "friendships" are often difficult to imagine and sustain, how much more so are familial ties? In many ways, this is where class-isolationist models of black America are least helpful for understanding the ways in which race and class inform the lives of black folks today. Paul set up two class-distinct parties, at least in part, as a response to the familial ties he negotiates with relatives who are obviously near and dear to his heart, even if they are not among the "movers and shakers" invited to his second birthday gig. It is important to notice the class differences that separate branches of family trees, affecting the qualities and contours of familial relationships.[9]

One of the most obvious ways in which class carves up families is intergenerationally, as is true in Paul's case. Welfare kids turned first-generation college graduates and middle-class professionals bespeak the quickly formed and often major social distances that can strain some of the interactions between parents and their children. Paul grew up as a member of the working poor. Most of his family still is. One cousin was killed five years ago in an altercation not too far from Paul's old neighborhood. Another cousin hasn't held down a job in more than two years. An uncle who never graduated from high school has been in prison for the past six years. He tries to visit him but can't bring himself to do it all that often. It's a lot different from a few mornings of pickup basketball games on half-empty concrete courts, games where one can leave the class-inflected baggage of a demanding social milieu just out of bounds beyond the metal mesh fence, slashing and driving to the basketball hoop in momentary indifference to the many chasms that separate his life trajectory and future from his family members'. Paul takes note of the fact that even his own mother, whom he loves dearly, has a markedly different set of class realities than he does, a difference that often translates into Paul having to sacrifice some of his personal needs whenever he's around her.

PAUL: I think I'm just sensitive. I don't think I was always like that, but now I'm just out of my mind trying to make other people feel comfortable. You have to make yourself happy first, and you can't be not happy thinking that you gotta do this and that. And then it's like, where are my needs, what I need....I love my family. That isn't the thing. But sometimes I feel like we can only talk about the same two or three things. And I have to hold some of myself up. I don't want to sound selfish, but sometimes I just don't want to do that. I do it, but I don't want to have to do that all the time. I just wouldn't feel comfortable to have to do that all the time, all day and night. It isn't a good feeling.

In a sense, it was Paul's desire to "feel comfortable" that made him have two parties in the first place – and that also makes Laura (someone who can be equally comfortable with peops or peers) his ideal mate. When he can't get his interests met in some of these familial contexts, Paul feels limited and stifled. He often finds the family he loves a group with which he can't really talk at all:

PAUL: They don't understand me. They don't know what I like. Things get on my nerves that they don't even think about.

JOHN: Like what?

PAUL: Like, I don't know, stupid things, ghetto things, you know what I mean. Sometimes people want to act like they are niggers because that's all they're used to.

Cynthia loves her older brother Kenneth, and he loves her right back, unequivocally, but the two almost never have any time to speak or see one another these days. Kenneth is usually busy "running all over the place trying to make money in computers," she explains as we wait for her brother's cab to drive up to her orange brick building. As we wait, she jokes about not even remembering what he looks like because she hasn't seen him in so long. I assure her that two months probably wouldn't have aged him beyond recognition. Kenneth, during our one and only (and very brief) interview, admits that sometimes when he's only in the city for a few days, he'll not even call his baby sister, because she'll want to see him, and he'd be too rushed and probably have to disappoint her. If Cynthia felt somewhat "responsible" for Karen (someone she only equivocally calls a "friend"), Kenneth feels even more accountable to his little sister.

KENNETH: That is my heart. I love her more than anything. I want to help her, that's what I'm supposed to be doing. And she's not hurting all that bad. She's working. And I kind of trust that she's gonna be all right, but I know she can be doing better, much better, and I always tell her that. She can be where I am financially, if she just applied herself and focused.

Daniel lives fifteen minutes from his mother and brother, but there are times when he purposefully avoids them for long stretches. Getting together with them can sometimes make him depressed and discouraged, he says, especially his older brother Jay, who argues forcefully with Daniel about the merits of going to school, contending that it is little more than a waste of time and money – especially, Jay argues, since Daniel will probably just end up getting a job that isn't going to pay him much more than what he earns without a degree. Daniel refuses to let Jay dissuade him from his educational goals. Instead of fighting with his brother about the usefulness of continued schooling, Daniel tries to hang around with people who are also in school – an indication, he maintains, of the fact that they actually want to make something out of their lives. He tries to purposefully steer clear of Jay sometimes, not wanting his brother's cynicism to deter him from achieving his own dreams:

DANIEL: As much as I love him [Jay], he ain't worth a shit. He's supposed to be my flesh and blood, you know. He know what I been through and all of that and he still talks that stupidness.

JOHN: Stupidness like what?

DANIEL: Just being negative about everything, about what I do. Not positive. About school. About me writing. That ain't right. You don't do that to people, not family. You can't. That's why his ass is always begging for shit. You can't get nothing if you're doing what he's doing.

Tears appear to well up in the corners of Daniel's eyes as he voices his frustration over Jay's lack of encouragement. I stop the tape and give him a second in the bathroom. I figure that he must be more tired than anything, especially since I stopped by after one of his more arduous days – a double shift on the job along with a two-hour class session. Daniel emerges from the bathroom and decides to cut our sit-down short; he is tired and wants to get some sleep. When we speak again at the end of that week, Daniel tells me that he called his brother Jay to "curse him out" the night of the interview. Two weeks later still, the two brothers shared laughs on a train ride to visit family members in Pennsylvania. The trip reminded Daniel that his brother Jay has good moments, too. Daniel just wishes there were more of them, especially as far as offering encouragement and positive feedback is concerned.

Some people can obviously negotiate class differences within familial networks more easily than can others. Daniel's difficulty with Jay sometimes overtaxes the ties that bind them. But that is not always the case. Carl is often happy to see his less financially successful brother, Lee, a 33-year-old husband and custodial engineer at a small office building in Harlem. Carl even goes out of his way to do so, driving to Lee's home or office on a whim sometimes just to check in on him. Carl gives Lee money to "help keep him together" as Lee struggles to sustain his family of four on a job that pays hardly more than minimum wage. Carl also tries to give his brother emotional support. That, he says, is most important:

CARL: I love that man. He's *my* role model. He's beautiful. The most kind and beautiful man you'll ever meet. Whatever he wants, whatever he needs, I'm there. No questions asked. And he knows that. He knows. He could have all my money. It's not about the money.

Trains, Telephones, and Job Applications

Dexter used to try being as supportive of his two closest cousins as he could be, but now he's actually avoiding them a bit. The last time he saw them, he almost "wrung their necks" after he helped get them jobs at a store where they allegedly stole something from the back office. Or at least that is what the white man who hired them claimed. And this very same person "had the nerve to act like he thought I was in on it, that I took some shit. So I just told him 'fuck you' and said I was never going to do some shit like that again for somebody." After that, one cousin went to jail (but is now out) and the other was wounded in a fight. "That's the kind of shit they like," Dexter offers in disgust, almost throwing his hands up in defeat over the entire thing.

The ability to be soiled and tainted by another person's misdeeds or underachievement is another vital factor affecting relationships across socioeconomic distances in black people's social networks. Stories like Dexter's, about extending a hand, getting burned, and then being unfairly implicated by that burning, offer important insights into how differently the calculus of black class stratification might work from class stratification within all-white social networks. In fact, some Harlemites speak very directly to that difference, arguing that a broad-bristled brush can unfairly paint over more successful blacks with its clumsily applied strokes:

DEXTER: The managers tried to help me, they said, and they got messed up. Look what they got in return and shit. And I was like, fuck them, but I was kind of feeling the same way about [his cousins]. That's if they did it. I know they could have, but they always said they didn't. But the thing is, they wouldn't have treated me the same way if I was a white man. I don't think so. If I had been a white man, and I brought some people in, it wouldn't have been the same thing. Because what they basically was saying was, you're black, they're black, they stole, you must be stealing, too.

Toney, 27, is an aspiring writer who lives in West Harlem. He has just landed an agent and may be close to a book deal for his first novel. He keeps his fingers crossed. Toney tries to stay in touch with his buddies, especially Lloyd, a chronically unemployed 26-year-old man who lives with his mother and younger sister in a two-bedroom East Harlem apartment. They were on

AFDC, but changes in the way the system is restructured under Temporary Assistance to Needy Families (TANF) have serious implications for what their household will look like in a few years – and for what they will need to do to keep themselves afloat. Toney tries to see Lloyd as often as he can. "I can't turn my back on him," he says. "Now he has to save his own self, you know, save himself, and get his life in order, but as rough as the brother is on the outside, he is all heart in here. He's just having a hard time." Toney doesn't go to Lloyd's house very much these days because he thinks it's "too depressing." He describes it as "dank" and "claustrophobic," and says he usually just tries to avoid all of that by calling Lloyd on the telephone instead of visiting.

Who speaks to whom on the phone (and about what) has important implications for how some individuals negotiate class differences in their social networks. Telephones may be a bit under-theorized in cultural anthropology as sites of moral suasion, value boosting and even class interaction.[10] Some of the people who don't like to visit use the telephone as a way to make contact without having to put tremendous amounts of time and energy into travel and face-to-face social niceties, especially when class differences also translate into a significant geographical distance:

ZELDA: I know this girl, Carmen, I haven't seen her in a while, like a year, but she is mad cool, and she's off in California and she calls like every couple of months. She's an actress. Not rich, but I seen her on commercials. Maybe she's rich. I don't know. Like a computer commercial or something she was on. She comes in New York and sometimes we hook up, but she's always busy doing her thing. So we don't see each other a lot.

As Zelda argues in the context of her relationship with this actress, sometimes the telephone can be an important conduit for keeping the lines of communication open between people who live very different lives and move in different socio-economic circles. Paul called his mom during his second birthday party just to thank her again for the earlier one and to tell her how much he loved her and enjoyed seeing her that evening. Cynthia makes sure to call around asking for Karen whenever she hasn't seen her in a while. And she sometimes has to call quite a few different people, because Karen's phone is almost as often disconnected as not. When it is out of service, Cynthia will try to call Liz's mother, provided *her* phone is on, and ask her to walk across the street and tell Karen to call Cynthia back on a pay phone or something. Or she'll just ask if anyone's seen Karen recently, and if so, she'll inquire about how she seems to be doing. If none of that phone-calling works, Cynthia will head out looking for Karen herself.

Janet remembers her first four months in Harlem as a kind of culture shock. It was a far cry from Ohio. During that time, when Janet seriously considered leaving the city for good, she would use the telephone to call her slightly younger cousin, Shelly, in Cleveland. Shelly's life has been very different from Janet's on various levels. Although Janet has advanced degrees from top-tier institutions, Shelly doesn't have her GED and still she lives with her mother, Janet's aunt, in a small one-bedroom apartment in one of the rougher parts of town. Janet believes that those long-distance phone calls to Shelly (all on Janet's dime) were extremely important factors in helping her adjust to Harlem when she first moved to New York:

JANET: We would spend hours on the phone. She kept me alive. And I never saw her that entire time. Not once. She always wanted to come, and hopefully, one day, I'll maybe send her a ticket or help her buy a ticket, or something. But she knows. I would call her, four nights a week.

JOHN: What would you talk about?

JANET: Everything. What's going on in Cleveland. She's never been to New York so I would tell her New Yorker stories and about Harlem. Literally anything. But it helped me talk my fear and the newness out of my system I think. And it worked, mostly.

These telephone calls to family and friends beyond the boundaries of Harlem are another explanation of ways in which Harlem becomes Harlemworld – as Harlemites describe their exploits in this famous neighborhood to other people all over the world.

Carl has his own story about when his brother Lee got his phone disconnected, and it was off for so long that Carl eventually decided to pay the bill himself. Lee says that his daughter had run up the phone bill on the Internet, and he wasn't able to find extra cash in his checks to get it turned back on, at least not quickly enough for Carl. "If I didn't pay it," Carl laughs, "I thought I would never hear from his ass again, so I just paid it."

Sometimes, the telecommunications revolution also provides ready strategies for not communicating, and class differences are often the excuse for such evasive telephone tactics. Paul, for one, has phone number juggling down to a science:

PAUL: Someone will have my pager number and not my home number. So they can't just reach me whenever they want and talk about bullshit, that's like for the people at work. My mom has everything, of course, but she knows not to give my cell and pager numbers out to Jimmy and them. That way I can make sure they don't page me whenever they want to.

Access to cellphones, answering machines, pagers, and inexpensive prepaid calling cards become ways to keep in touch along class-inflected routes. People can touch base with one another quickly and easily. However, it can also be the mechanism for stalling potential interactions indefinitely and segregating one's calling circles along various demographic lines, even and especially if the individuals involved don't live in the same community or hang out in the same daily haunts. Dexter still talks to some of his old school friends from the Brooklyn of his youth, but he can't always take the time to travel back and forth to do it:

DEXTER: I don't make it down there much, it's mad far on the train, but I speak to some heads. I'll give them a buzz or they give me a buzz and we catch up. You gotta keep in touch and get fueled.

Even leaving a short and sweet message on an answering machine is often the easiest and least time-consuming way to touch base across class lines without "drama," "bullshit," or any of the other potential problems that come along with social interactions of all sorts. People care for one another's babies, pay one another's phone bills, encourage or discourage one another's dreams, play some physically grueling games of basketball, and call one another on the phone daily, often using these as techniques for navigating the choppy waters of class difference. The jury is still out on whether these relationships across class lines and phone lines can translate into better jobs, schooling, housing and other opportunities for the lower-classed members of the relationship.

"I can't save him," Toney laments about his friend Lloyd in Spanish Harlem. "He has to save himself. The worst thing I could do is give him a push for something, a job or something.... And I don't want to be preaching to him all the time. That wouldn't be fair, either.... I'm not going to judge him. I just want him to know that I am here if he wants to talk or something like that. He should just know that." This is almost exactly what Paul says about assisting Tim, his basketball buddy. Instead of plying him with job announcements and the like, Paul just tries to beat him in a quick basketball game every once in a while, using that as an informal way to make sure that the two of them keep up with one another.

Zelda's present job came from a recommendation she got from "this woman with some clout who put a word in" at the drug counseling clinic. Zelda was riding on the subway with one of the administrators at her drug treatment program, and the two struck up a brief conversation. Zelda thinks the woman must have liked what she heard, because the next week they called her into the main office and offered her a job there. Another Harlemite, Vanessa, actually landed a job with the help of her anthropology friend, me. My landlord trusted me as a reference and hired her almost on the spot to work as an administrative assistant for his real estate business. It worked out for a bit, but she quit after schedule conflicts with school and other responsibilities made the job's hours infeasible. When Dexter was looking to change jobs, I tried to be at the front line of his search, also. He appreciated my help but claimed that potential occupational benefits are not the only things he can take away from our relationship. "Just seeing you," he maintains, "is like an inspiration. I feel like I can be where you are." Here, Dexter voices a kind of role-model notion of what is most important to him about class-stratified social relationships. It's not just that they can help one parlay an interest into an occupation, but also that they can let one know where else one could be located on the social ladder – and an example of just what that position might look and feel like. Most important, these differently negotiated relationships exemplify the continued meaningfulness that social stratification has for the everyday lives of black Americans after civil rights reforms.

Fleeting Moments in the Public Sphere

Many Harlemites recognize the significance of class-stratified interactions not only within familial and friendship-based networks but also in less substantial, more utilitarian interpersonal relationships in quickly passing social instants. For example, just going to the welfare office is a seriously class-stratified moment that people often think about and specifically theorize. Karen, for one, has many long stories about why she prefers interacting with white social workers in social service agencies than black ones:

KAREN: I hate, hate, hate them over there in social services. They are nasty and make you feel that way, like pieces of garbage. Black people keeping black people down. They the worst, much worse than the whites. Much worse. Trying to mess people up with that, their own kind, their own people. It's a shame.

Liz also singles out black social service providers to level a cross-class critique that is both strong and pointed, speaking to the power issues implicit in those specific moments of interaction:

LIZ: You know, sometimes that is the worst thing of all. That is really the worst thing. Because your own people are the problem. Not the white ones; they aren't the ones. It's the blacks.

Bernice, thinking back to her pre-college days when she was still struggling on public assistance, would concur with the point that Liz and Karen both raise:

BERNICE: These black house niggers, I tell you. I've gone over there to the Department of Welfare on 125th....I go in there and I deal with those people from one level to another and I hate to really say this, sometimes I get my needs handled by my own kind and they send me through the wringer. I deal with somebody that's Caucasian, that's part of the conspiracy, and I get what I need done....I think some of them [black social service providers] be taking out stuff that happened at home or in their personal life out on the job, on the clients.

Brian, another black male social worker, a member of Jordan's network, has many African American clients around the city, and he offers the flipside to these arguments:

BRIAN: They come at you as if to say, well, you are black, you can break the rules. Hook me up. We're like brothers. You can hook me up. And they are so disingenuous. They don't mean a word of that. They just think they can work on your sympathy strings. But I don't go for it. You build up a kind of immunity....These are people who have been making excuses and getting over all of their lives. And they are just trying it again. I don't fall for it.

Social service providers often invest in their occupation as a kind of calling. Jordan and Brian are no exceptions. But some of the luster of their professional mission has faded with time. Cross-class frustrations can make them question their job choice every now and then. Jordan and Brian feel that their work does a lot of good for a lot of people in the black community, and they offer that up as one of its benefits. However, they also feel that success sometimes occurs in spite of the attitudes of many of their black clients.

Shopping is another area where issues concerning class can swirl and simmer. Tim, Paul's basketball buddy, maintains that he hates it when "a man in a suit and tie can come into a store and they [the people behind the counter] try to act like my money ain't as good. He's black just like me, no? And his money got the same picture mine got." The local store is an oft-discussed locale for class-based intraracial conflicts. The black petite bourgeoisie are characterized as pushy elites whose merchandise is often considered overpriced. Some blacks also portray them as decidedly disrespectful to black customers:

ZELDA: Some of these black business people are nasty. Like they doing you a favor. Or like you got nigga money and that ain't real money. I'll take my stuff to the Chinese just as fast. Not that they any better. At least it ain't your own doing it to you. I know we're supposed to keep it in the community, but some of them make you want to go outside.

Zelda invokes the inner city's proverbial outsider entrepreneur ("the Chinese") to ground her response to black business owners' dismissal of her purchasing power.[11] Dexter, playing the role of devil's advocate, takes the opposite position, arguing that it is the black masses who abuse black-owned businesses and business owners:

DEXTER: Some black people want to think they can do what they want when they walk into a black store. "Everything should be free, we all from Africa." They want to take advantage, like being black means you want to be broke from not being a good businessman.

One black business owner in Harlem jokingly contends that she needs to hire a white person to stand in front of her store just so black people brainwashed from years and years of institutionalized racism will believe that it really is a legitimate place of business. Without that, she claims, black shoppers would just continue to take their money to more recognizably Jewish and Asian establishments nearby.

Another area where people interact across what they consider to be important class-inflected intraracial lines is on the street itself, on city sidewalks.[12] Tim sees black people "with suits on" in the street, and "some days I just feel like I want to drop [punch] them." At other times, he says, "it's like I feel a little proud." Paul talks about walking past homeless people and feeling like they expect more from him just because he's black and wears expensive-looking business attire. Sometimes it makes him feel bad; sometimes it just makes him angry and frustrated. David, who used to be homeless himself, thinks that homeless people deserve to expect more from blacks than they do from whites. After all, he argues, "we know what it's like to be without."

Class-stratified relationships and interactions aren't reducible to the presence or absence of role models – or to the mere possibility of utilizing others' social networks and financial resources. The class differences that people see in their friendship circles, their family relationships, and even more ephemeral social settings (during a trip to the store or to a social service provider) craft complicated topographies of self that help define one's relation to the rest of the world. The people in Harlem are living and negotiating complicated, stratified worlds, and the choices they make in such contexts are contingent on complex rationales for interacting with or avoiding certain individuals based on what that sociality tells them about themselves and their place in the world.

The New York City Police Department is often invoked as a tentacle of a racialized governmental bureaucracy pitted against the black community time and time again – through the confrontational handling of things like the Million Youth March, through the remorseless shooting of unarmed black males, through the Mollen commission scandal, which exposed corrupt Brooklyn cops, and through the highly publicized racial profiling cases that Harlem's community leaders and black law enforcement agents have marched to publicize. Black officers themselves become a particularly interesting point of discussion in the context of cross-class concerns within the black community:

DEXTER: I always stay away from any police shit, because the last time I tried to even just exercise my rights, they were like they were gonna lock me up and all of this kind of stuff.

JOHN: Black cops?

DEXTER: Both. The black cops will do things to you only because they know you can't really do nothing back. They wouldn't do it to white people. They wouldn't do it to blacks who have money to sue they asses. But they love to flex their muscles on us and try to get their rocks off by making us feel like shit because we struggling, and they know that nobody gives a damn about what happens anyway.

Dexter sees different classes of blacks (those "who have money to sue they asses" and those who don't) getting very different treatment from their race-mates in uniform. Bernice offers a strikingly similar class argument:

BERNICE: I've had interactions [with black police officers] because I have a son who got into a little incident with those police, and the guy that interviews me and my son at the same time, he has dreads in his head and he's full of locks and all that –

JOHN [interrupting]: The police officer?

BERNICE: Yeah. Yeah, the police officer. And I'm looking for some understanding. Some humility. You know, let's work on this incident. Oh no, he went there. He went to the other level "and this is the bottom line" and "this is what has to be done" and we ran back and forth for over a year. And I guess they gotta do what they gotta do because they have to eat too. But see, somewhere along the line what I see as the problem is that black folks forget where they came from. You know what I mean? They get these different positions, and then they run up against somebody that's under them in the lower class or the underclass and they step on that individual. You know? And it's sad because you gotta go home and sleep with yourself after doing this to folks.

Comparing Bernice and Dexter's position to Carl's, one finds a decided contrast:

CARL: I've never really had a bad run-in with a black police officer. I just speak to them, and they listen. They can see I'm not trying to get over. I am not just running around in the street. Most people aren't, but I can articulate that in a way that they understand. "Okay, leave this guy alone," you know.... Not that it couldn't happen tomorrow, but it hasn't yet.

Black police officers are sometimes considered the most pernicious class-based race traitors around. Like the elitist black business owner who is said to disrespect black customers, the black police officer is sometimes characterized as being extra willing to carry out the racist will of the state. The hip-hop artist KRS-One pleads with them to put down their guns and stop shooting other black folks in his underground hit "Black Cop." And the filmmaker John Singleton immortalized the trope of the self-hating black officer in *Boyz 'n the Hood*, which depicts a black policeman who has so internalized his denial of black humanity that he can't even understand why the lead character finds his indifference to black life so problematic. However, there is something about Carl's ability to talk his way out of confrontations with black officers that seems to hint at the relevance of class-inflected behavioral differences (in terms of speech patterns, mannerisms, and so on) to concerns about the interactions between black police officers and black civilians.[...]

Conclusion

Many of the Harlem residents I met argued that they didn't have serious social contacts across class lines. Even when people may initially say otherwise, they sometimes do have such interactions. Class differences within one's social circle can mean you celebrate with two separate parties for two "very, very different" and seemingly separable parts of your social network. Or it can mean that you designate your everyday interactions with poorer African Americans as other than clear friendships – even when they might seem to have all the trappings thereof.

Some Harlemites have people they work with, as in Zelda's case, whom they know pretty well – people they hang out with at nightclubs but who never, say, invite them over to their suburban home in New Jersey. Other Harlemites seem to know that they have friends who could use their help but approach that fact very carefully: either because they don't want to offend by appearing superior (not wanting to "preach") or because they can't justify risking such assistance when the person isn't ready to receive it. If friendships are difficult to hold onto amid class differences, familial ties can be just as hard. Some people live fairly close to relatives of different classes or status positions and purposefully avoid them. Maybe the person who has achieved a bit of socioeconomic success doesn't want to feel the guilt of that success juxtaposed against other people's failure. Or maybe they feel a potential danger in mingling too closely with the disillusionment and cynicism that sometimes burdens the lives of the poor. On the other hand, some people who have "made it" try to stay around specifically and self-consciously to model behaviors for the less successful.

Class-stratified interactions don't necessarily have to be substantive to be important and formative. Sometimes a fleeting moment or a brief encounter with a stranger or a series of short interactions with acquaintances can have tremendous significance in terms of how people think about class. Even small and seemingly minor contact across class lines can have benefits. Cynthia, for instance, traces some of her present successes back to her next-door neighbor's uncle, Montgomery, whom she knew when the girls were not even teenagers. He only came over a few times a year, as she remembers it, but he wore fancy suits, had lots of money for candy, and always told Cynthia and her friend Robin that they could do anything they put their minds to, anything in the world they wanted to do:

> CYNTHIA: He's still around, retired I think. But he really made an impression on me. He lived far away, but every time he came, it was cool. He loved Robin so much, and he was just a good role model. And he was just nice.

Role models may be important, but that is not the only way class differences affect people's lives. In Zelda's case, interactions up the class ladder landed her a job as a drug counselor. And people can sometimes take advantage of occupational opportunities that their networks provide – if, as Paul put it, they are ready to benefit from a friend's ability to help. Even when people see a dichotomously classed world, they are not necessarily invoking that dichotomy to talk about class homogeneity in their social networks as much as to think about the different types of people with whom they do have contact. As important as these interactions are, their mere existence is hardly the end of the story. I'm also interested in whether interactions across class lines have serious implications for how people behave, for their actions and activities, for how they perform belonging and social solidarity.

Many African Americans have family members, friends, former friends, acquaintances, colleagues, bosses, social workers, and case managers who occupy various class positions. Often, the significance of these interactions is downplayed (by both the people themselves and the social scientists who analyze them), but they exist nonetheless. Class isolation is not the only possible narrative model for discussing how blacks of various socioeconomic positions experience their social worlds. Surely, it is a convincing enough argument to make if one wants to offer that isolation as an explanation for transgenerational poverty and inequality. However, if you look at the relationships people actually have (social workers dealing with recipients on the dole, parents interacting with full-grown children, doctors treating patients, "friends" helping or not helping each other), these relationships often push and pull at the boundaries of belonging in several different directions at once. Class-stratified interactions don't always translate into occupational opportunities for the poorer partners (it might only mean a free meal on an occasional Sunday or a ride to church where class "ain't got nothing to do with it"), but these exchanges are important nonetheless – if for no other reason than the fact that they don't let social scientists off the hook with easy explanatory models for perpetual poverty.

Social scientists offer truncated social networks and inadequate social skills as an important part of the explanation for perpetual poverty. Surely, social networks can translate into gainful employment and other opportunities more easily for the rich than the poor.[13] And maybe some people who have interactions across class lines are unwilling (as Paul, Dexter, and Toney are) to extend an extra hand once they've been burned after offering such hospitality in the past. My argument is not that class-stratified interactions always or necessarily lead to socioeconomic advancement, but only that the lack of such advancement is not reducible to the idea that there are no such networks at all. People often do have relationships across class lines – even when they might hastily offer that they do not, or question the term used (friend, acquaintance, former friend) to define such persons. They often have relationships that reach up and down the class ladder. Sometimes such relationships land people jobs. Other times, as in Paul's case, they can mean little more than semiregular pick-up basketball games where the class-stratified social world is left out of bounds and out of play, if only for a few sweat-filled hours. Or, it might mean a free breakfast for one person and the sense, for the other, that one is "just doing the right thing" for someone who "used to be" a friend. Whatever the case, Harlemites are constantly dealing with the socioeconomic stratification inherent in their social networks – even if that just means attempting to impose class isolation and trying, with different degrees of success, to keep purportedly "very, very different worlds" apart.

NOTES

1 See Sarah Lawrence-Lightfoot, *I've Known Rivers: Lives of Loss and Liberation* (Reading, MA: Addison-Wesley, 1994); Lawrence Otis Graham, *Our Kind of People: Inside America's Black Upper Class* (New York: HarperCollins, 1999); Mary Pattillo-McCoy, *Black Picket Fences: Privilege and Peril among the Black Middle-Class* (Chicago: University of Chicago Press, 1999). See also Sam Fulwood, *Waking from the Dream: My Life in the Black Middle Class* (New York: Anchor, 1996).

2 See Bart Landry, *The New Black Middle Class* (Berkeley: University of California Press, 1987); Joe Feagin and Melvin Sikes, *Living with Racism: The Black Middle Class Experience* (Boston: Beacon, 1993); Ellis Cose, *The Rage of a Privileged Class* (New York: HarperCollins, 1993).

3 The notion of the "culture of poverty" was given one of its first comprehensive articulations in Oscar Lewis's 1959 work on poverty in Mexico. Lewis argued that behaviors associated with life in poverty-riddled areas (alcoholism, violence, crime, male desertion, hypermasculinity, female-headed households) could be explained by two very distinct kinds of causes. The initial or ultimate causes of these behaviors, he claimed, were "macrostructural" constraints on the poor, constraints linked to unemployment and underemployment. Lewis then added to this formulation by suggesting that these macrostructural conditions give rise to a poor people's "culture" that perpetuates and promotes the kinds of behaviors initially molded by structural constraints. This "culture," he concluded, is a more immediate cause of the deviant behaviors emerging from the depths of poverty, a kind of transgenerationally learned model for living with a stability, persistence, and agency independent of the ultimate source (those macrostructural conditions) that originally created it. This culture of poverty is thus considered to be a kind of ready-made "cultural repository" for a new generation's expedient learning of an older generation's deviant ways. See Oscar Lewis, *The Children of Sanchez: Autobiography of a Mexican Family* (New York: Vintage, 1961) and *The Culture of Poverty* (New York: Scientific America, 1966). Once created, this culture becomes a self-sustaining cause of persistent poverty across generations. Important to point out with respect to Oscar Lewis and his model of the culture of poverty is the fact that he did see macrostructural constraints as key ingredients in the formation of this so-called deviant ghetto culture. However, in recent discussions utilizing Lewis's notion, this macrostructural side of his equation disappears almost entirely. See Charles Murray, *Losing Ground: American Social Policy, 1950–1980* (New York: Basic, 1984); George Gilder, *Wealth and Poverty* (New York: Basic, 1981). In these versions of the culture of poverty, links between cultural patterns of behavior and macrostructural conditions are downplayed and even dismissed. Ghetto residents' moral shortcomings and deviant cultures alone are said to produce their social problems, and the only solutions offered in the wake of such perspectives seek to intervene with culturally and psychologically based remedies to save the poor from themselves and their self-destructive activities. Social analysts took the policy recommendations a step further by maintaining that welfare, one of the government's major attempts to assist the urban poor, merely fortifies and endorses their deviance and cultural depravity. They claim that the "liberal welfare state" adversely affected the incentives governing the behavior of poor people with its overly permissive welfare policies. These policies, they say, resulted in even greater degrees of poverty and cultural pathology because the regulations governing welfare made marriage and menial labor undesirable while promoting unwed childbearing and laziness. In one of the most popular and often-cited articulations of this perspective, Charles Murray argues that the welfare policies developed during the War on Poverty made it profitable for poor people to behave in the short term in ways that were detrimental and self-destructive in the long run.

A major problem some critics have had with the culture of poverty argument has to do with its rather uncritical pathologizing of a vast number of inner-city behaviors – some of which, detractors argue, may not be pathological at all. See Annette Weiner, "The False Assumptions of Traditional Values," in *The Family on the Threshold of the 21st Century: Trends and Implications*, ed. Solly Dreman (London: Lawrence Erlbaum & Associates, 1997). For instance, what is so "wrong" with the inner-city family structure (female-headed households, and so on)? Is the nuclear family (with father, mother, child, dog, and a white picket fence) any more valid than some of the family structures pathologized by culture of poverty proponents? Moreover, are these inner-city families in poverty simply because they haven't learned how to defer immediate gratification for more long-term goals? Carol Stack *All Our Kin: Strategies for Survival in a Black Community* (New York: Harper & Row, 1975), offers an oft-cited answer to these questions. She claims that the black family and its extended kinship organization are an extremely "rational" (not pathological) response to societal constraints. In the inner city, with its ever-present economic hardships, one could not survive, she argues, without the extended family kinship network, a network that not only requires frequent injections of one's own funds (for the benefit of others in the network) but in return provides social bonds that allow each and every participating member a social safety net during exceptionally rough economic times. It is this social group that does not allow for the growth of individual and personal wealth, but it is also these very individuals, she says, who provide much-needed financial support when one of their lot faces economic hardships. Furthermore, these networks conduct vital services that would be unaffordable otherwise – child care being a prime example. Stack even goes so far as to argue that the child-raising units in poorer black families are often not domestic but interdomestic, communal (or transgenerational), existing over many households and sharing parental rights, duties, and responsibilities for children among several members. But this, Stack maintains, is not necessarily deviant and pathological. Instead, she paints it as a vital strategy necessary for survival against the material constraints of an economically marginalized inner-city existence.

4 Ulf Hannerz did a good job trying to show this in his 1969 ethnography *Soulside: Inquiries into Ghetto Culture and Community* (New York: Columbia University Press, 1969). He makes it quite clear that not all people living in the ghetto are the same. Hannerz makes this case with respect to "lifestyles," arguing that some residents of the ghetto are "mainstreamers," others "swingers," others "street families," and still others "streetcorner men." Here, Hannerz's four social categories are based, fundamentally, on differences in behaviors – sharp distinctions in what people do and how they behave. The mainstreamers "conform most closely to mainstream American assumptions," "are homeowners," "are employed," "married and living in nuclear families with a quite stable composition" (pp. 38–39). The swingers "have not yet married" and "spend relatively little of their time just sitting around at home alone or with the family. Weekday nights and particularly weekends are often spent going visiting" (p.42). Streetcorner men are the ghetto dwellers who "return day after day to the same hangout. There they talk and drink, play cards, shoot crap, or just do nothing.... There is continuous drinking.... If they are not yet alcoholics, they are well on their way" (p. 54).

Hannerz unequivocally affirmed that ghetto neighborhoods were not just home to black poverty or deviance. He recognized a black middle class residing there, a fact other social analysts had a harder time seeing. There were "better-off" residents ("mainstreamers") around as well as those deviant, do-nothing, soon-to-be alcoholic streetcorner men. However, Hannerz's job as a researcher was to explain the causes of black poverty, and these mainstreamers were, therefore, not as relevant to his research as the streetcorner men, especially if the underlying question had to do with the extent to which black poverty was unlike white poverty. Hannerz was being a social problems researcher, and the black middle class simply wasn't a social problem that merited study. Still, Hannerz at least recognized class-based differences within black communities.

As the burgeoning body of literature on ghetto communities (so-called pockets of poverty) increased steadily, it decreased the value of social scientific discussions about black Americans whose actions were other than indicative of ghetto difference. For Hannerz, the point was not necessarily to look to black "mainstreamers" but to the blacks behaving in supposedly ghetto-specific ways associated with black poverty. "There are people in the ghetto who have good, stable jobs," he offers, "help their children with their homework. Eat dinner together at a fixed hour, make payments on the car, and spend their Saturday night watching Lawrence Welk on TV – to their largely mainstream way of life we will devote rather little attention" (p. 15). Hannerz notices class heterogeneity based on actions (everything from television watching to making payments on automobiles) but focuses our attention on what he offers up as ghetto-specific behaviors: "[A]ll ghetto dwellers will not get equal time here. There are many who are in the ghetto but not of the ghetto in the sense of exhibiting much of a life-style peculiar to the community" (p. 15). Hannerz delineates the behaviors setting black ghetto residents apart from other blacks not behaving that way (and ultimately separating them, as the other-older binary social model would have it, from white Americans as well). The mainstreamers behaved too much like middle-class Americans to be of interest to most poverty researchers, and it was through poverty studies that a substantial portion of the social science discourse on black America took root. These same emphases on what some black ghetto residents did (how they acted) justified the foregrounding of culture (shared actions and beliefs) and the mobilization of culture of poverty arguments as a means of solidifying assumptions about black racial difference in the growing social science discourse on America's race problem. Behavior was mistakenly reduced to a proxy for culture, and that conflation opened the floodgates for one of the most popular and destructive explanatory models of poverty ever argued.

5 *Peops* is a derivative of *peop(l)e*, meaning very close friends and relatives. It's a commonly used term among many of the folks I spoke with in Harlem.

6 It is also important to note that a binary model of class differences within black America [...] rears its dichotomous head here. [...] It is not an "etic" analytical category that social scientists impose on subjects from above. Instead, it is an "emic" articulation of the social world based on Paul's own subjective understandings of class differences within his social networks. One cannot simply rail against Paul's conception as wrongheaded and mistaken; one must understand why this binary folk-analysis exists as a categorization in the first place – and try to understand the cultural work it achieves.

7 Pattillo-McCoy, *Black Picket Fences*, and Douglas Massey and Nancy Denton, *American Apartheid: Segregation and the Making of the Underclass* (Cambridge, MA: Harvard University Press, 1993).

8 The anthropologist's relationship is often a precarious one in terms of class dynamics that serve to structure his or her interactions in the field, even if a "native." Some of my informants would categorize me as a friend, others as an acquaintance, and often class would rear its ugly head either way. The first time Dexter introduced me as his "ace" (at a house party another one of his friends threw on Long Island), I thought he was being funny or trying to exaggerate our relationship to make me seem like more a part of the in-crowd to his friends than I actually was. This was early in my fieldwork, and I had only known Dexter about a month. Eventually, I began to accept that Dexter was not as burdened by the need for objectivity and scientism as a pretext for our social interactions as I was, and genuinely found our conversations (with or without tape recorders) as wonderful opportunities to get to know one another as friends. And I only began to believe that I was really engaging in fieldwork and becoming an anthropologist when I was able to view our interactions in the exact same light. Furthermore, I have found that my socioeconomic position makes me useful on a great many levels to the people whose views are included in this book. For example, I've loaned money and resources to Zelda many times – always getting it back whenever a check comes in. I've tried to connect Dexter with a Columbia professor when he was expressing interest in medical anthropology. And I even helped a few people get jobs with verbal and written recommendations. Some of these exchanges between informant and ethnographer are class-marked sites of social interaction. Class is still important when dealing with more clearly middle-class, professional and upwardly mobile residents. My status as a doctoral student signified class similarity among many of them and helped me to enter certain spaces that might have been closed to me otherwise.

9 Katherine S. Newman, *Falling from Grace: The Experience of Downward Mobility in the American Middle Class* (New York: Vintage, 1988) looks at intergenerational downward mobility within the white middle class. For a quantitative look at class permeability, see Erik Olin Wright, *Class Counts: Comparative Studies in Class Analysis* (Cambridge: Cambridge University Press, 1997).

10 For a discussion of telephones as technologies of transnational conversation and community building, see Roger Rouse, "Mexican Migration and the Social Space of Postmodernism," *Diaspora* 1(1) (1991):13. For an analysis of how these cross-cultural conversations transform the relationships people have with their closest neighbors, see Deborah A. Thomas, "'Tradition's Not an Intelligence Thing': Jamaican Cultural Politics and the Ascendance of Modern Blackness" (Ph.D. diss., New York University, 2000).

11 See Kyeyoung Park, "Use and Abuse of Race and Culture: Black-Korean Tension in America," *American Anthropologist* 98(3) (September 1996): 492–499, for a discussion of these issues.

12 See Elijah Anderson, *Streetwise: Race, Class, and Change in an Urban Community* (Chicago: University of Chicago Press, 1990).

13 See Mark Granovetter, *Getting a Job* (Chicago: University of Chicago Press, 1995) for a discussion about the importance of "weak ties" in the transformation of social capital into more than just lateral occupational movement.

16

Nike's Reign

Mary Pattillo-McCoy

Groveland youth use their own bodies and the accessories that adorn them as status markers and symbols of identity. For the girls and young women, each long, acrylic press-on fingernail is accented with intricate colored brush strokes and sometimes even a hint of glitter. For young men, the placement, color, or brand of a baseball cap may pledge allegiance to a certain gang, or may clearly distinguish someone from that crowd. From the top of a girl's 12-inch-high french-twist hairstyle to the underside of a pair of Nike Air Jordan basketball shoes – which carry the infamous "Jump Man" trademark – and with all the personalized tattoos, Georgetown jogging suits, Girbaud jeans, 14-carat-gold necklaces, Karl Kani leather jackets, and Tommy Hilfiger boxer shorts in between, Groveland's young people are walking mega-malls, forever trying to stay in material dialogue with their friends, as well as with their enemies.

Groveland styles are proof that black youth are particularly vulnerable to the messages they view on television about what to buy, why they should buy, and who they could be (or, at the very least, be like) if they buy. Black youth are conspicuous consumers. They watch more television and view it more favorably and as more realistic, and they respond more positively to marketing stimuli, than their white peers.[1] Using the example of Nike sports apparel, this chapter illustrates the coincidence of the growth in mass marketing with the rising brand-consciousness of Groveland youth. Nikes are just one component of an elaborated discourse about clothes and other personal fashion items, their worth, and their meaning to young Groveland residents. The story of Nike in Groveland elaborates on the previous discussion of ghetto styles. By exploring the targeting of black youth by mass marketers, and the status-enhancing properties of consumer goods, the draw of the streets becomes more comprehensible.

The Black Market

In the 1960s, not only were African Americans slowly brought into the economic and political spheres of American life, but they were also incorporated into some social and cultural spheres as well. As television became more generally accessible, it was possible to visually reflect the diversity of Americans. Advertisers then recognized blacks as an important and sizable target market. Black newspapers had been trying to convince white businesses of the loyalty and eagerness of black consumers since the 1930s; they urged companies to spend advertising dollars in their publications. Yet it was not until the late 1960s, and especially the 1970s and 1980s, that white companies took heed (Nightingale 1993; Pitts et al. 1989). Since the 1960s, the use of African American actors in advertising has increased, and black celebrities have proved particularly successful for reaching black audiences (Lee and Browne 1995; Williams and Qualls 1989). The success of advertisers' increased use of black models, celebrities, and cultural themes has meant the inclusion of blacks, particularly black youth, within the reaches of marketing culture.

People use material goods to level the playing field, buying things they often cannot afford in order to give others the impression that they can. African Americans have done this for years, and with decidedly more vigor than whites. The real gap in economic status can be minimized at least symbolically by just looking good. Historian Carl Nightingale (1993:143) writes that for blacks, material items have always "been the stuff of intense emotional importance." African Americans use material goods as symbolic affronts to the power of whites. From the early 1950s through the 1960s, poor black men were more likely to buy expensive and prestigious cars (such as Cadillacs) and goods (like Scotch) than poor white men. A 1949 issue of *Ebony* magazine gave an answer to the query of "Why Negroes Buy Cadillacs." "Basically, a Cadillac is an instrument of aggression," argued the article's author, "a solid and substantial symbol for many a Negro that he is as good as any white man" (quoted in Nightingale 1993:144). In dress, too, blacks consume more and are more fashion-conscious than whites with comparable incomes (Alexis 1970; Stith and Goldsmith 1989; Nightingale 1993). A new car, good whiskey, and a designer suit are not simply to level the field with rich whites, but they make a statement to fellow blacks as well. A Cadillac serves to sort among the African American community. The driver buys it to signify first to him- or herself, then to friends, and finally to "the white man," that he or she has made it. This affront, however, is always at the symbolic level. It does nothing to alter the actual inequalities that consumers try to overcome. Because of its limited transformative utility, Cornel West (1994) blames consumer culture for the formation of decadent "market moralities."

Young people in Groveland are sometimes uncritical in their acceptance of fads and fashions, but they also use those fashions to resist and reinterpret their racially marginalized position, and they surely wield their clothes and accessories as weapons among each other. All the while they are enacting these seemingly contradictory behaviors, they are having fun. Nikes are an important component of the style of Groveland, and young people like those in Groveland are a big part of Nike's profits. The story of the two together illuminates the cultural milieu in which Groveland youth are embedded.

It's Gotta Be the Shoes

On a Wednesday evening in early February, I sat with Spider in the small office next to the gym in Groveland Park field house, where volleyball was supposed to begin at 7 o'clock. It was nearing 7:30, but I enjoyed the leeway to sit around and shoot the breeze. Spider always kept me entertained with his stories about the neighborhood, told with the detail of a painter. Spider and I were joined this night by Chris, a 19-year-old young man who carried the belly of a 40-year-old couch potato. Chris didn't seem to have any set schedule. He hung around the gym at all hours, making me pretty sure that he didn't have a regular job. That is, he didn't have a regular *legal* job. I had become convinced that Chris worked for Lance, the notorious South Side gang and drug kingpin who grew up six blocks away from Groveland Park. Lance would drop by Groveland Park quite often. It was a home base, and it was familiar. Lance would talk to Spider, use the phone, play dominoes, and get business reports from any number of young workers like Chris.

This evening, the television droned in the background. When there was a lull in the conversation, the TV guaranteed that we all had something to look at, instead of staring into the uncomfortably silent air between us. In one of the quiet moments, I noticed that Chris had on new gym shoes. These particular shoes were the newest of the new. Not only were they a new purchase for Chris, but they were the most recent addition to the line of Air

Jordan basketball shoes created by Nike. In the local sneaker shorthand, they were called the "North Carolinas." I inspected the impeccable white shoelaces, the soft white leather upper, and the gleaming light-blue patent-leather trim along the bottom (God's favorite color, according to Tar Heels). But before I could comment on how I liked them, Vince – the six-foot-three-inch, 275-pound park instructor – walked in and stepped on Chris's $150 toe, leaving a smudge that damned those shoes to the far reaches of the attic.

The dream had ended. The way I saw it, there were two lines of action that Chris could take. He could turn on his old friend Vince with a strong right to the nose, and demand retribution, not only for the monetary value of the shoes, but for the lost days when Chris could have used them to impress women, his neighborhood friends, and the admiring preteen boys who kept him feeling like he was Michael Jordan himself. Or he could run to the nearest water fountain, grab a clean towel, and engage in the usually private ritual of making once-worn gym shoes once again presentable.

Instead, no one saw it the way I saw it. It wasn't until a year later that I would see Chris whip out two $100 bills to make a whimsical bet. Another time, he pulled out a wad of $100 bills while he and Spider talked quietly among themselves about something I was clearly not meant to hear. I did not know at first that Chris had money like that. Once I did, I could interpret his unruffled composure when Vince stepped on his new shoes. While he paid big bucks for those shoes and for the awesome looks they could bring, it was well within his means to replace them with some other, even more spectacular, piece of status. Spider was the only one to comment on Vince's ruination of Chris's newest of the new North Carolinas. "He don't care," Spider said, directing his explanation to me. "Shiiit, he wear them outside."

At least Spider understood my astonishment. Some people don't wear their immaculate new gym shoes outside, unless God has painted the sky with Carolina blue, and the weatherman has forecast no rain, snow, or dog shit. Some people (like me and Spider, I guess) see those shoes as investments. And such a sudden depreciation in any sane person's investment would call for, at the very least, an irritated growl at the person who made the market crash. But for Chris, who could wear his gym shoes outside, these were the concerns of peons. Luckily, I figured all this out quickly enough not to give myself away as the ultimate peon, who would have cried had the same tragedy befallen her. When I had regained my composure, we picked up the conversation, reviewing the players in the NBA with whom Chris shared the distinction of sporting the "North Carolinas."

How had it come to be that what Chris wore on his feet could prompt a full conversation with impressive knowledge about which famous people wore the same thing on their feet? How could the most trampled piece of our wardrobe, taking from some wearers 300 pounds of abuse with every step, and subject to the violence of someone else's 300 pounds if we're not careful, inspire such high regard? What's more, gym shoes are charged with protecting the part of our body that, when we were children, we considered almost as gross as our private parts. Feet sweat, they breed fungi, they grow callouses, and with the new exercise craze, they are often pummeled into unsalvageable deformation and ugliness. And worst of all, feet stink. Still, we are willing to pamper them in $150 gym shoes, while we may spend only $1.49 on the soap to wash our faces with. Why? The reason is part of an intricate story of marketing decisions, local cultures, timing, and originality on the part of both producers and consumers.

In the late 1960s, before Chris was even born and in faraway Oregon, entrepreneur Phil Knight dreamed up what has become the Nike empire. According to an executive at a Portland investment firm who worked with Nike at its inception, "They managed to create a need where none had existed" (Labich and Carvell 1995).[2] Nike began with shoes for runners. Phil Knight had been a distance runner on the track team at the University of Oregon. After Stanford Business School, he thought that there might be a market for high-quality running shoes. He began by importing a Japanese brand and selling them out of the back of his car. Frustrated with the slow returns, Knight and his old track coach created their own brand. They paid a Portland State design student $35 to think up what is now worth over $6 billion – the

Nike "Swoosh" (Lane 1996). By the 1980s, Phil Knight's concerns were no longer the possibility that a heavy rain might wash out his car trunk and spoil the day's sales. Instead, his company had graduated to sponsoring athletes in the 1984 Los Angeles Olympic games, competing with the world's largest shoe companies.

While the Olympics were a far cry from hawking in Oregon, there was still more work to be done. Nike athletes took home only 63 gold medals, compared to the 259 gold medals that Adidas athletes won. Equally upsetting was the fact that an upstart shoe company had acquired the right to market the Reebok brand in the United States. They made rapid inroads in sports apparel through their domination of the women's aerobic market. In 1980, Reebok profits were a mere $300,000, but that figure jumped to $1.5 million by the next year. Despite the exposure of the Olympics, Nike now battled with Adidas and Reebok over the market of feet and bodies. Nike needed new ways to be number one, and stay number one.

Like most companies, Nike did not begin to recognize the black consumer market until the 1970s. Before that it was considered a substantial risk to use blacks as product endorsers, no matter how prominent they were. But after the turbulent 1960s, there wasn't much more that could ruffle America's feathers. So on the sidelines, Nike moved into basketball. To their number-one hoops consultant, Sonny Vaccaro, basketball meant moving into the black market. In his first meeting with Nike executives in 1977, Vaccaro told them, "Nobody's taking on these young kids in the colleges. *Black and East is basketball. It isn't pros. It isn't West Coast white kids.* You guys are missing the playgrounds and you're missing the colleges and that's what it's all about" (Strasser and Becklund 1991:286). Nike took Vaccaro's advice and gave him the authority to corral the East Coast playground scene and the college game.

One strategy Vaccaro used to get to the young kids on the playgrounds was the Dapper Dan basketball tournament – half All-Star game, half auctioning block. The top high-school players in the country received the honor of being invited to Pittsburgh to play against one another and show off their skills at the Dapper Dan. The top college recruiters were also invited to appraise the players and mutter among themselves about who might be bidding on whom. By 1978, 17,000 people attended the Dapper Dan tournament. Most important, it was officially sponsored by Nike. This meant that the most spectacular of players were outfitted in what would become the most spectacular of urban fashion symbols. After the weekend's festivities were over, the teenage participants were sent home as uniformed ambassadors of Nike.

Hooking the high-school players was relatively easy compared to making headway in the college game. College basketball was a bit more sticky because of the watchdog National Collegiate Athletic Association (NCAA). To infiltrate the colleges, Vaccaro had to use the connections he made from his Dapper Dan tournament to court college coaches. Backing Vaccaro's plan to woo college coaches, Nike gave him a hefty expense account to meet with coaches, wine and dine them, and make offers of free shoes for themselves and their teams, and yearly trips for the coaches and their wives to warm, relaxing, Nike-sponsored getaway destinations. This was not a new strategy. Converse had long since figured out that the way to the urban basketball market was through the college player, and the way to the college player was through the college coach. The major difference was that Vaccaro had a special knack for this business. By 1979, 50 college basketball coaches had signed on with Nike. At 12 players a team, that meant there was a new army of 600 college basketball players wearing Nikes. The players in those college programs later became the personnel of the pro league, so that by 1984, about half of the National Basketball Association's players wore Nike.

The NBA was just an idealistic dream for Tommy Smith, who was growing up in Groveland in the 1970s. He played basketball every day on the playground of Groveland Elementary School, a few blocks from his house. Shooting hoops into the late evenings, Tommy saw himself and the other kids who hung out there as rising athletes. But when he reached the tenth grade, Tommy was routinely buying jeans that were just 31 inches in length. This was his signal that he was not "rising" much above about five-nine, a little too short for the pros. His basketball career dreams faded, but he did not stop playing, because basketball was more than a dream. It was the divider between the in and the out crowds. "I was on the basketball team my senior year," Tommy remembered. "I've never been much of a student council person, or student government or anything like that in college or in high school. I was more of a cool type, and those things kept you away from that." Nike was just starting to work its way into the urban market when Tommy was in high school, looking to be cool.

How I came across Tommy's first Nike memory was quite serendipitous. It is amazing how the human brain works to recall information. Major events in our lives seem to act as anchors for a host of less significant activities that surrounded the event. Someone may remember the exact date he changed jobs because it was the same day that John F. Kennedy was killed. Someone else may remember taking an uneventful trip to the museum only because when she got home that evening her infant child took its first step. I thought that, perhaps, Tommy would remember his first talk with his mother or grandmother about sex or drugs; that it would have been such a monumental occasion (either for its gravity or for its awkward hilarity) that he would be able to tell me about it in detail. Instead, he came up relatively blank on the subject. His mother's friend Pam was the one who talked to Tommy about the birds and the bees, although the details he gave of that conversation were pretty vague. What he did remember was that Pam was the bearer of great gifts – his first pair of Nikes.

> [Me and my mother] never had any talks. She had a friend named Pam Rhodes, and that's where I think my girl talk and my, as I think about it, and my drug talk came from. From her friend Pam, who bought me my first pair of leather gym shoes, when Nikes first came out. I think I was in the seventh grade, seventh or sixth. I think it was seventh. She bought me my first pair of white Nikes with the black stripe and the suede around the toe.

At 29 years old, Tommy described the new Nikes of his childhood as if he had stored them in a glass case in a sacred room, peeking in on them periodically ever since. Remembering those shoes brought back his mother's old friend (her first and last name), chronologically situated the occasion in his seventh-grade year, and called up the less significant lessons he was taught about girls and drugs.

Tommy was in the seventh grade in the late 1970s, just around the time when Sonny Vaccaro convinced Nike of the gold mine in black neighborhoods. From the Dapper Dan tournament and the ranks of predominantly black and wildly popular college teams like the Georgetown Hoyas to little Groveland Elementary School playground, Nike made inroads into the black urban basketball market, just as Vaccaro had imagined it. And Tommy was probably one of the first of his friends to have a pair. Tommy was cool. Tommy was a trendsetter. Tommy had Nikes before anyone else in the neighborhood. Even as he got older, Tommy continued to see himself at the cutting edge of fashion. Reveling in the originality that he was proud of as a child, Tommy talked about his shopping routine.

> I just wouldn't go where everybody goes. I'm that individual that likes to be unique. And I like the compliments. I have a necklace, for instance, that's a gold beer or pop top. And everywhere I go, people, you know, wow! So, that's the kind of response I like to get. I don't want, "Oh, I got a pair of those." I don't really enjoy that. So, I try to go places that people usually wouldn't go or don't go.

As Tommy sat behind the desk in his home office sharing his strategies for being unique, he was dressed in an attractive but plain blue-and-gray striped shirt and green army pants. On his feet he wore a pair of blue Nikes that matched his shirt. It was true, I had not seen them on anyone before, and I had made it a practice in Groveland to greet people and then immediately size up their footwear. Maybe he really *did* know "unique" places to shop where other people did not go. Tommy was setting trends. And he had the admiration of those who were less innovative, those not patient enough to look for a gold pop-top charm (especially since cans no longer feature pop tops). Others settle for a gold cross, or the first letter of their name, or maybe even their whole name. (In an entirely different setting, an equally innovative fashion connoisseur had a gold charm of

Michael Jordan's "Jump Man" logo, where the ball at the end of Jordan's outstretched arm was a single diamond. He of course got lots of wows for that.) With every "wow" Tommy knew he was on the right track to being unique.

But Tommy found himself in a bit of a dilemma. His 11-year-old son, Corey, was also a part of that admiring crowd, not to mention the 20 boys that he counseled at the group home where he worked. The boys at the group home were not really Tommy's concern. Someone else would have to worry about where to get the $150 for their gym shoes. Most likely, Tommy's charges at work would just not get any new gym shoes. Instead they would be condemned to coveting Tommy's expensively covered feet every day that he arrived at work. Now his son was another matter altogether. "He wants Air Jordans this, he wants this and that," Tommy said, but he was not convinced that buying new Nikes was the best thing for Corey. "First I let him know exactly what those shoes really cost," he began.

> And they're exploiting the people who makin' 'em in the first place, and then overcharging me to get 'em for you. But then I'll let you know that you're gonna have to get these $100, these $150 shoes yourself. And you're not gonna wanna spend *your* $150. And then we go through that.

"But, Dad!" I can imagine Corey protesting to his father's reasonable explanation for why he should not expect an oblong box that smelled anything like leather and rubber under the Christmas tree that year. I can also imagine 11-year-old Corey accompanying his father on the shopping trip of the week, traveling far from the neighborhood and down confusing side streets to find the obscure store that sold Tommy the few-of-a-kind Nikes of which he was so proud. It is probably safe to assume that most fathers are not giving introductory lectures to their children on the political economy of gym shoes. Most kids just beg and they get. Corey could possibly get if he continued begging, but he had to first endure Tommy's internal conflicts over staying in style while supporting a system that, in his estimation, cheated both the makers and the buyers.

Tommy had some ammunition for his somewhat leftist convictions. When our conversation was winding down, Tommy got up from his chair, left the room for a moment, and returned with a book he had been reading entitled *Wealth and Poverty*. He sat back down and began answering a general question I had posed.

> Why do I think all this is happening, which is the people in our community striving to do what they wanna do and yet and still these things are happening? This answers your question exactly, key, important.

From there, Tommy began to read extensively (but not verbatim) from the book's text.

> Capitalism. Can a, can a man live in a free society if if if they feel no reason to believe that that society is just? Okay, um, a man cannot long tolerate the sense of spiritual meaninglessness in their individual lives, so they cannot long accept the society in which power, privilege, and property are not distributed according to some moral um meaningful criteria. Um, capitalist freedom leads to a vulgar and decadent civilization, afflicted by um libido for the ugly and trivial, the shallow and the ungodly and lacking in discipline and courage, or the values to be worth preserving. Capitalism is not only morally vacant, it also perpetuates gross immorality, racism, sexism, environmental abuse. It is a practical failure as well because it brings on inflation and unemployment. Above all, capitalism creates and perpetuates um the differences between the rich and the poor, rich countries and poor ones, men and women, and destroys the balance between men and women, I mean, between man and nature, consumption and individual appetites and social needs. Capitalism is an edifice without an inherent foundation in morality and religion, and that therefore it engenders a shallow and dubious order of human life. The system is immoral because it is based on greed.

I had not expected to stumble upon a Marxist in my ethnographic interviews. I was even less prepared for a Marxist in Nikes.[3] Nike's production practices made it difficult for Tommy to reconcile his politics with his participation in the dialogue of commodities. In the end, though, and however tortured he might have been, Tommy seemed to have found a way to wear his Nike gym shoes with confidence.

In the early years, Nike had small factories in Exeter, New Hampshire, and Saco, Maine. But even then, most of the manufacturing was done in

Korea and Taiwan. In 1985, the Maine factory closed because of the unremarkable fact that American workers just cost too much money. Korean and Taiwanese workers earned just over $1 an hour in the 1980s, while American workers were making between $8 and $11 for producing the same quality shoe (Strasser and Becklund 1991: 559). After 1985, only a small factory in Oregon remained open in the United States; the rest of production was overseas. By the 1990s, even Korea and Taiwan were becoming too expensive. Nike began expanding to Indonesia, Vietnam, and Thailand, where the labor was cheaper and the governments promised a cooperative and eager workforce. By 1996, an $80 pair of Nike shoes in the United States cost the company about $2.60 in labor costs (Gargan 1996). As a result, Nike came under fire for its labor practices (Jones 1996). But the berm around Nike's 74-acre corporate campus proved too tall and too thick for much of this criticism to get through. Moreover, Nike's popularity was too well fortified by the star personalities of its athletes for much of anything to get through.

The first solid brick in Nike's wall of athletic fame was basketball player Michael Jordan. In 1984, Michael Jordan decided to leave college to enter the NBA. Shoe companies lined up to dress his feet. Nike was trailing in the athletic shoe race with Adidas (worldwide, and in the heart of Michael Jordan), and saw Reebok picking up speed in the inside lane. Dapper Dan coordinator Sonny Vaccaro met with Nike executives to discuss what to do about Nike basketball. They had a lot of players on their team, but there was no go-to guy to get them closer to their ultimate desire: "To get Swooshes on everybody's feet.... To Swoosh the world" (Strasser and Becklund 1991). Nike was founded on risk, and it was once again time to gamble. It was all or nothing.

Nike offered Jordan "all" – a reported $2.5 million over five years, which included annuities, signing bonuses, and, most important, royalties from his own shoe, a first in the endorsement business. Adidas offered Michael Jordan close to nothing – $100,000, and no special shoe. In October of 1984, at the Palmer House Hotel in Chicago, just before he was to play his first regular-season home game with the Chicago Bulls, Michael Jordan signed with Nike, and history was made. The Michael Jordan/Nike marriage approximated the divine. Describing the scene at an Air Jordan photo shoot near a Chicago housing project, an ex–Nike executive (Strasser and Becklund 1991: 566) wrote:

> When Jordan left the playground, the kids mobbed him and begged for one of his Air Jordan T-shirts. A little girl standing in the middle was Jordan's favorite. He bent down, handed her the shirt, much to her delight, and walked away. The mini-mob followed him to the car, wanting to touch and be touched by him.

This larger-than-life portrayal is no exaggeration of Michael Jordan's stature among youth. B. J. Brown – a quiet Groveland 14-year-old who made the interview process feel more like a visit to the dentist's office than a friendly conversation – was finally able to muster up a few thoughts when I asked about his role models. He wanted to be like Michael Jordan, simply because "e'rybody like him. I wanna be like somebody, somebody bigger." There's no discerning whether Nike made Michael Jordan a superstar or vice versa. But there is no denying that the two together have become a part of many American dreams.

With the right publicist, the St. Mary's boys basketball team in Groveland could make a case for being showcased in one of Nike's and Michael Jordan's clever commercials. On the team of ten fourth-, fifth-, and sixth-grade boys, each player had star quality for a different reason. One of the boys was nearly five and a half feet tall, pretty impressive for a sixth-grader. "Girl, and you see how big his feet are," his mother pointed out to another mother in the bleachers during an evening game. "He gotta get men's clothes already. He gon' cost me a fortune." Another player stood out for his athletic skills. He was the shortest player on the team, nearly swallowed by his jersey and shorts. But he was also the most creative, handling the ball like a seasoned pro, and shooting with a confident touch. What nickname did the St. Mary's boys give to the best player on their team? Baby Jordan, of course.

Baby Jordan and seven of his teammates wore Nikes. (The two unfortunate misfits – or fashion rebels – had on Converse and Champion brands.)

Four of the pairs of Nikes were Air Jordans, and two of those were the most up-to-date edition. When Steven, one of the boys who had on the new Jordans, was fouled and went to the free-throw line, his mother commented about his gym shoes, "Girl, them the ugliest things I ever seen. His grandparents bought him those. He told them exactly what he wanted for Christmas and his grandparents bought him those. I think they the ugliest things. Butt-ugly!" Ugly or not, Air Jordans were a hot ticket. If Steven's mother refused to buy them for him, he had surely found some way to get them.

Elsewhere in Groveland, Ray Gibbs was growing up just when Sonny Vaccaro got really good at targeting black youth, and just around the time when Michael Jordan became Nike's ticket to success. But as a youngster, Ray Gibbs was not nearly as cool as the eight Nike-clad boys on St. Mary's basketball team. He wasn't as cool as Tommy Smith either, who got his first pair of Nikes five years before Michael Jordan made them popular. In 1984, when Ray was 9 years old, he was still subject to the unfashionable consumer decisions of his mother.

> You know when you a shorty everybody mother used to put 'em on some Pro-Wings. You used to think you had some name-brand shoes on. Come to find out it was a big disappointment when you got to school and the older kids start [asking], "What-chu got on there?" "Aw man leave me alone." In those days, I mean it was kinda funny. I mean, it didn't hurt you as much. But, you know, nowadays some of us wouldn't be caught dead going into Payless [shoe store].

On the sunny day nearing noon when I talked to the older and more fashion-conscious Ray Gibbs, he had long since said goodbye to Pro-Wings. Running late for our scheduled interview, Ray was just getting out of the shower, and spent much of the time we talked putting lotion on his basketball-calloused hands and dry knees. He had thrown on blue shorts and a T-shirt. His choice of footwear was a pair of Nike Air Max. Top of the line. In this particular shoe, he could go walking in the morning, maybe lift some weights in the afternoon, and play a leisurely pickup basketball game in the evening. Introducing the cross trainer.

Even though Michael Jordan jump-started Nike in 1984, bringing in over $100 million in new revenues, Reebok just would not go away. In the 1987 straightaway, Reebok overtook Nike with $1.4 billion in revenues. Again, Phil Knight and the other top managers needed something new. The answer, they decided, was in the "air." Nike designers wanted to capitalize on the "Air" moniker that had done so well selling Michael Jordan's shoe. The expanded Nike Air line, featuring this strange invention called the "cross trainer," fit the active lifestyle of people who were generally into fitness, but not avid athletes – like Ray Gibbs. Mixing this new idea with old marketing strategies, Nike got versatile football and baseball star Bo Jackson to be the poster child for this versatile shoe.

To regain the lead over Reebok, however, Nike needed a double whammy this time. So, along with the new ad campaign featuring Nike Air, cross trainers, and Bo Jackson, Nike also went back to Michael Jordan, who had been "the most successful athlete endorsement in history" (Strasser and Becklund 1991:574). This time, Nike (and its ad agency) brought in black film director Spike Lee to simultaneously market black culture and the shoe itself. Nike was no doubt aware of the studies showing that African Americans especially identified with brands that used themes from black culture in their advertisements.[4] Their marketing tactics were a success, and Nike regained supremacy in 1990, with revenues of $2.24 billion.

Over his 22 years, Tyson Reed's contribution to that mammoth sum has surely been no more than a tiny fraction of a percent, even though he has always been a Nike loyalist. He played football at Groveland Park and at his high school, and wore Nikes for all his games. The worn and grimy pair that he had on as he cleaned the oven during our conversation was probably left over from his old football days. During his high school years, Tyson was determined to stay in style. He remembered begging his mother for new shoes and clothes, with no success. So Tyson searched around for other ways to get what he wanted. [...] [I]t was Tyson who asserted: "Your parents give you what you need. And sometime they get you what you want. But when you sell drugs, *you* get you what you wanted." He went on to elaborate on this sentiment: "And then from there, you'on think about my mother. Man, I'on give a fuck if my mother don't never buy me nothin'. I'ma buy myself something."

When he was 16, Tyson felt he was a man because he could use his drug profits to buy whatever he wanted. And the first things he wanted were clothes and shoes.

> Man, no bullshit, every time I used to mess with [sell] drugs for like one day, I used to make like $1,800. And I'm sixteen making that kinda money. You know what I used to do? I used to go to the mall. I went to the mall one time, I ain't gon' never forget it. Tricked off! Just to talk to some broads. Just to let my homey [friend] talk to some broads. I went, I swear to God, I spent $1,200 on Guess? jeans. Not shorts. On Guess? jeans, that's it. Then I went to Foot Locker and brought [*sic*] like eight pair of gym shoes. And that ain't shit. I know people now who go in Foot Locker and spend $5,000.

Tyson punctuated his memories of teenage wealth with the intonation of an excited 12-year-old. He flashed back to the days when he was on top of the style world. He remembered how the drug money and the things he could buy with it were sexy enough not just to get a girlfriend for himself, but to make his friends attractive as well. That's a double-duty dollar.

Tyson eventually got out of the drug business. Since then, he believed, he had gained more respect for money. His impetuous spending sprees were things of the past, but his taste for Nikes was not. Nike need not worry about losing Tyson Reed to financial sobriety, for in him they still had a loyal follower. But with less disposable cash to work with, Tyson had to come up with a new solution to the problem of affording his favorite footwear. Tyson described his new shopping strategy.

> If I want some gym shoes, instead of going to Foot Locker and buying one pair of gym shoes, I'll go to one where I know somebody, and get me about four or five pair of gym shoes. So I'll get like a couple pairs free or something.

"Buy one, get three free" was Tyson's new motto. Buy one pair of shoes and get four pairs in the bag. In fact, Tyson's consumer fraud-inspired math was just about right. In 1992, the retail price for a pair of Nike shoes was just about four times what Nike paid for that pair from its Asian manufacturers (Clifford 1992).

Two blocks up on Groveland street, at Neisha Morris's house, a young Tyson was in the making. Neisha's son, Little Tim Ward, was not yet 1 year old. About the time when some children are repeating simple words like *cat* or *dog*, Tim will be jumping straight to two syllables – *Ni-ke*.

Neisha sat relaxed in her mother's living room, which was furnished with new off-white furniture, a plush brown rug, and a large painting of a quaint nature scene on the wall. Neisha had taken on the demeanor of a new mother, affectionately asking, "What's wrong, Boo?" when Little Tim made any gurgling noise. But she did not miss a beat as she told me about the neighborhood and her life. In the privacy of her home, and in the company of women, Neisha lounged around in just a long faded T-shirt and discolored slippers. This was a long way from the style she exhibited when she went to Groveland Park gym. In theory she went to the park to play volleyball, but really she went there to flirt with the young men who hung around the gym talking to Spider or Lance. Neisha, her cousin Kima, and their friends treated volleyball hour like a fashion show – Coach purses, primped hairstyles, leather coats, Timberland boots, and Nike gym shoes. They staged grand entrances, they smiled models' smiles, and they walked with their eyes to the lights.

But when Neisha had Little Tim and got more serious with Big Tim, her trips to the gym became less frequent. She began to move into life's next stage – motherhood and girlfriendhood. Neither role lessened her sense of style, but the energy that she had once put into keeping *herself* "clean" was now redirected to her son. Little Tim surely could not understand what he was worth when he was all suited up in his pricey clothes and gym shoes, but the fashion statements were worth much more to his mother than what they cost in dollars. Neisha was proud that the mothers of her generation made sure that their babies looked good.

> You know, I see older people that have kids. They just be lookin' nasty and dirty, you know. But like our age group, I guess 'cause maybe we are more materialistic and into things like that or something,

> but our age group keep our kids clean, you know. Everytime I go out the door, unless I'm just really runnin', Tim's always dressed. Dressed and I'm dressed. And my friends, they kids be dressed. Even though, like my friend Shauna, her boyfriend [is] not there for her. So she can't really, she buy her baby gym shoes like once a month. [Whereas] Tim been here for five months and got seven pair of gym shoes. That don't make no sense. Every Jordan that done came out from the white ones, to the black ones, to the black and white ones, the all-black. He got all four of them plus the Dennis Rodmans and two more pair of Nikes. And my friends, you know, they might buy they kids shoes once a month. I feel like, you know, some of 'em are under me, you know.

If babies are not even walking at 5 months, do they really need shoes? They do if shoes are not for walking. Shoes are to gauge who is "under" someone, or who doesn't have it as good. "It's a lotta people that's below average," Neisha judged. "You know, [people] that my mother give my old gym shoes to, or my old clothes to, or they just don't have it. They don't have Nike gym shoes. They don't have this, they don't have that."

The pecking order was clear to Neisha when she looked toward those less fortunate, but she was less able to focus on her own situation. Mrs. Morris had just recently kicked Mr. Morris out of the house. He no longer contributed much to the household bills, and there was Neisha's 9-year-old little brother to take care of (and to outfit in Nikes as well), house payments, car payments, and Little Tim. Mrs. Morris had a stable job, but Neisha was not working (although she received food stamps). And Big Tim's drug business was not something on which Neisha could fully depend. Her situation was not as privileged as she had projected, but she was nonetheless going to get full fashion mileage out of that collection of resources. Her pity for her less-well-off friends became her own words to live by. "It ain't always what you got," she counseled. "It's how you make with what you *do* have."

In using her son to pledge allegiance to the Nike Swoosh, Neisha was only following the lead of the "role models" created by the mass market. Nike is, after all, nearly as venerated as the red, white, and blue itself, and its citizens have proved to be loyal. At the top of the list are the professional athletes, who sometimes make more from their shoe contracts than they make playing their sport. These enormous endorsement contracts ensured that two Nike-ists on the 1992 gold-medal U.S. Olympic basketball team – Michael Jordan and Charles Barkley – would drape the American flag over their shoulders in order to conceal the blasphemous Reebok symbol on their warm-up suits, which they were compelled to wear, since Reebok paid the high price to sponsor the team. But it does not even take millions of dollars to elicit such fanaticism. Nike corporate salespeople – young, fresh, and moderately paid – make sure their clients understand the depths to which they believe in Nike and the eternality of their allegiance. Tattooed on some of their calves, ankles, shoulders, and inner thighs is the Nike Swoosh (Labich and Carvell 1995). It is indeed possible (and perhaps probable) that when Little Tim grows up, he may wear some brand of gym shoe that has not yet even been thought of. But for now, the zealous devotion to Nike exists from the top of its ranks to the very smallest of its disciples.

While Neisha was just following a fad by buying her son Nikes, and Baby Jordan's teammates were less than creative in deciding on a nickname for him, Groveland's Black Mobsters did occasionally push the fashion envelope in their use of brand names.[5] One afternoon, Kareem and Lucky, two Groveland Park regulars and members of the Black Mobsters, walked around the gym looking important in their jobs as Lance's bodyguards. Lucky's outfit was the most obviously coded. Lucky wore a blue Georgetown warm-up suit. When Georgetown basketball players wear their warm-up suits before a game, the message is benign: this is the uniform of Georgetown players, and as a team we all dress alike. At Groveland Park, however, the Georgetown uniform enjoyed added popularity because its colors were the same as the colors of the Black Mobsters. It is unlikely that Georgetown's African American basketball coach, John Thompson – respected for his "uplift the race" views in the area of college sports, but less known as a $200,000-a-year Nike "consultant" – intended for his team's predominantly blue uniforms to correspond to the color scheme of one of Chicago's most notorious gangs. But Thompson should take solace in the fact that Georgetown is not alone; a number of college and professional sports teams are unwitting accessories to the crime of gang-style posturing.[6]

Lucky's simple blue-is-the-color-of-the-Black-Mobsters outfit was a blatant use of popular fashion for locally significant ends. Kareem's fashion statement, on the other hand, took a bit more decoding. On the chest of Kareem's white T-shirt was a blurry picture of Michael Jordan encircled in a cartoonlike border. The caption read, "What's up, Folks?" Recall that the Black Mobsters are a part of the Folks gang nation. In effect, the decal portrayed Michael Jordan issuing the Black Mobster greeting, "what's up, Folks?" Despite this T-shirt's symbolic claim, Michael Jordan is, of course, not a member of the Black Mobsters or the Folks nation. The mere suggestion of gang affiliation is probably an affront to Michael Jordan's wholesome image. But as a popular-culture icon, Michael Jordan's image is prone to manipulation, just as in the more obvious (and less creative) practices of appropriating team colors, cocking a hat to the side, revering Italian gangster movies, or imitating the body language of big-time rappers.

The layers of signification in Kareem's T-shirt, while not immediately apparent, are noteworthy. In 1992, Nike and the National Basketball Association fought over the right to market Michael Jordan's likeness on sports apparel. Initially, Jordan gave sole rights to Nike, which meant that neither Jordan's face nor his likeness could appear on anything that Nike did not make, such as Bulls or Olympic jerseys with the team's picture. By the end of that year, however, Nike and the NBA had reached an agreement to allow the NBA to use Jordan's likeness after all (see Vecsey 1992). It was unlikely, however, that the makers of Kareem's T-shirt cleared their creation with Nike or the NBA. And they were probably not paying royalties to the superstar himself. They had, in essence, stolen Michael Jordan for their own purposes. It was also in 1992, during the Superbowl, that Nike premiered its "Hare Jordan" commercials. The "Hare Jordan" concept teamed Michael Jordan with popular Warner Brothers cartoon characters. There was Bugs Bunny – whose signature saying is, of course, "What's up, Doc?" And there was fellow animated animal Porky Pig, who ends all his shows with, "That's All, Folks." Michael Jordan plus Bugs Bunny plus Porky Pig equals "What's up, Folks?"

Kareem's T-shirt was not one-of-a-kind, but rather represented the Black Mobsters' small-business ventures. It played on the communal adoration of Michael Jordan (especially in Chicago) while simultaneously pledging allegiance to the Black Mobsters. The Black Mobsters' T-shirt business communicated a certain refusal to pay for the use of Jordan's face. Why should Folks pay for Michael Jordan's image when Nike and the NBA (among others) have made it abundantly available for the stealing? After contributing so much to the coffers of both the NBA and Nike, and since they admired him as much as most Americans, the Black Mobsters were determined to make a little money off Michael Jordan themselves. Folks appropriated, repackaged, and redefined all-American Michael Jordan to be an all-American Black Mobster.

Postscript

Nike's defeat seems assured by the cycles of capitalism; the only question is when. Revenues for 1994 neared $4 billion, and 1996 revenues surpassed $6 billion, with $550 million in profits. Phil Knight's challenge to his employees to make Nike a $12 billion company by the year 2000 shows that Nike is not going to fall without a fight (Lane 1996). And there will be quite a few challenges. In 1996, Nike lost one of its celebrity endorsers when basketball player Chris Webber decided that the $140 price tag on his signature Nike shoe was just too much to ask young people like the ones in Groveland to pay. Nike seems unaffected by his departure, however. In 1990, the civil rights organization Operation PUSH announced a boycott of Nike (Jackson and Schantz 1993). PUSH charged that Nike did not reciprocate the support that African Americans gave it through their purchases of Nike gear. PUSH claimed that blacks made up 30 percent of Nike's clientele. Nike put the figure somewhere between 10 and 15 percent, and boasted that three-fourths of its yearly $10 million in philanthropy goes to inner-city neighborhoods. The ever-increasing Nike revenue figures suggest that the PUSH boycott has also had little effect (Royko 1990).

In 1995, Reebok and Nike controlled over 40 percent of the global market in athletic footwear, and Phil Knight was the sixth richest person in America. In the year 2005, both giants could be cut down to the mere 10 percent global share (5 percent domestically) to which the once mammoth Adidas has been reduced. Someone will always be on top, and someone will be on the bottom. There will always be money to be made, because there will always be fashion battles to be won on the streets of Groveland. Tyson Reed explained it with profound simplicity.

> With kids, I would say, nowadays, regardless of if your parents own Sony, or regardless if your parents work for Sony, or regardless if your parents buy tapes from Sony, e'rybody and they mama gon' be listening to the same thing, wearing Jordans. If you po' you gon' have on Jordans. If you rich you gon' have on Jordans. If you middle class you gon' have on Jordans. Your parents buy 'em when you rich, you gon' have 'em. If you middle class, you work for 'em and you get 'em. If you po', you sell dope, you gon' have 'em.

The race to stay in style by whatever means continues. At present, those young Grovelandites with the Swoosh on their feet are in the lead.

It is not enough to investigate the economic and spatial contexts in which Groveland youth are embedded. The cultural context is crucial to fully understanding the crossroads that black middle-class youth face, the "street" and "decent" balancing act that they perform, and the diverse trajectories that their lives take. Nike is just one part of the popular-culture and mass-market context. There is nothing so peculiar about the company that it should warrant a full chapter of discussion, except for the fact that it reigned over other sneaker brands during the time of my research. Yet a similar point could be made about any number of fashion or consumer items: there is a local discourse that surrounds the act of purchasing and the act of showcasing the latest styles. Styles are generated by the strong messages delivered in advertising, and transformed through local processes of redefinition. It is clear that Nike has made a strategic pitch to the African American community, especially its youth, and that Nikes have in turn been incorporated into a dialogue of symbols that matter for courtship, for self-esteem, for aesthetic enjoyment, for gang affiliation, and for distinction-making in Groveland. Groveland youth grow up within a popular-culture milieu that targets them as consumers and inundates them with exciting images of the gangsta lifestyle. White youth receive the same messages, but the *interaction* of popular culture with the economic and spatial realities of the black middle class (and of course the black poor) imbues the gangsta image with more serious repercussions for black youth.

NOTES

1 George Moschis (1987:128) summarizes the literature on black youth consumer practices and the relationship between television advertising and consumption. He writes, "Nearly all studies examining the negative effects of advertising on children and adolescents have found correlations between the amount of television viewing and several 'undesirable' consumer orientations such as materialistic attitudes and social motivations for consumption." He also found that watching more television decreases consumer skills.

2 Marxist theorists of the Frankfurt School argue that mass marketing is an insidious capitalist tool to control the social and cultural aspects of people's lives, buttressing capitalist control in the economic sphere. The mass media are the vehicles through which capitalists market items that are invented purely to make a profit, not to satisfy the needs of the consuming public. In perfect correspondence with the assessment of the quoted Nike executive, Frankfurt School theorists argue that mass culture creates false needs. See Longhurst 1995.

3 While the excerpt that Tommy earnestly read aloud expressed clear anticapitalist sentiments, the book from which this passage comes is actually a neoconservative argument for the possibilities of entrepreneurial capitalism (see Gilder 1981:7). Tommy quoted a passage in which the author was laying out the radical critique of capitalism, not the author's own arguments. He was clearly selectively reading the book.

4 Pitts et al. (1989) investigate this culturally specific strategy and find that whites and blacks have very different readings of advertisements that contain

cultural messages. Black experimental subjects rated commercials that were produced by a black advertising agency with all-black casts and portraying various scenes of black life more positively than similar white subjects. The authors (Pitts et al. 1989:322–323) conclude: "We found that when marketing communication utilizes a strong cultural orientation…[they] elicit not only a stronger, more positive response to the brand and the commercial itself from the targeted audience (compared with the nontargeted white audience), but they generate a markedly different response in terms of perception of the value message."

5 Mass-produced styles and lifestyles can be transformed into vehicles for protest. The tattered clothes of 1960s hippies and the black leather jackets and berets of the Black Panthers were the uniforms of racial and class resistance. English scholars have most fully developed the idea of style as rebellion. Youthful rebellion, however, exists primarily at the "imaginary level"; it does not often alter the material relationship between classes (Hall and Jefferson 1976; Hebdige 1979; Brake 1985).

6 I say the "crime" of gang-style posturing because school districts across the country have instituted dress codes to ensure that gangs do not wear their colors or emblems in school (Gursky 1996; LaPoint, Holloman, and Alleyne 1993). From particular clothing items to shoelace colors, schools have restricted what students can wear. To add a twist to this fashion crackdown, shopping malls have also made rules against certain clothing, especially hats. Thus, the ironic reality is that even shopping malls – the ultimate sites and profiteers of consumerism and style – are actually stifling their patrons' ability to showcase their purchases.

REFERENCES

Alexis, Marcus. 1970. Patterns of Black Consumption, 1935–1960. *Journal of Black Studies* 1:55–74.

Brake, Michael. 1985. *Comparative Youth Culture: The Sociology of Youth Culture and Youth Subcultures in America, Britain and Canada*. London: Routledge & Kegan Paul.

Clifford, Mark. 1992. Spring in their Step: Nike is Making the Most of All That Cheap Labour. *Far Eastern Economic Review* 155:56–60.

Gargan, Edward A. 1996. An Indonesian Asset Is Also a Liability. *New York Times*. March 16, section A, 35–36.

Gilder, George. 1981. *Wealth and Poverty*. New York: Basic Books.

Gursky, Daniel. 1996. "Uniform" Improvement? *Education Digest* 61:46–48.

Hall, Stuart, and Tony Jefferson. 1976. *Resistance through Rituals: Youth Subcultures in Post-war Britain*. London: Routledge.

Hebdige, Dick. 1979. *Subculture: The Meaning of Style*. London: Routledge.

Jackson, Janice E., and William T. Schantz. 1993. Crisis Management: The Boycott of Nike by People United to Serve Humanity. *Business Horizons* 36(1):27.

Jones, Del. 1996. Critics Tie Sweatshop Sneakers to "Air" Jordan. *U.S.A. Today*, June 6, section B, 1.

Labich, Kenneth, and Tim Carvell. 1995. A Battle for Hearts, Minds and Feet: Nike vs. Reebok. *Fortune* 132:90–106.

Lane, Randall. 1996. You Are What You Wear. *Forbes* 158:42–46.

LaPoint, Velma, Lillian Holloman, and Sylvan Alleyne. 1993. Dress Codes and Uniforms in Urban Schools. *Education Digest* 58:32–34.

Lee, E. Bun, and Louis A. Browne. 1995. Effects of Television Advertising on African can American Teenagers. *Journal of Black Studies* 25:523–536.

Longhurst, Brian. 1995. *Popular Music and Society*. Cambridge, England: Polity Press.

Moschis, George. 1987. *Consumer Socialization: A Life-Cycle Perspective*. Lexington; MA: Lexington Books.

Nightingale, Carl Husemoller. 1993. *On the Edge: A History of Poor Black Children and their American Dream*. New York: Basic Books.

Pitts, Robert, E., D. Joel Whalen, Robert O'Keefe, and Vernon Murray. 1989. Black and White Response to Culturally Targeted Television Commercials: A Values-Based Approach. *Psychology and Marketing* 6:311–328.

Royko, Mike. 1990. No, Nike's Still Not Shaking in its Boots. *Chicago Tribune*, 2 October, section C, 3.

Stith, Melvin T., and Ronald E. Goldsmith. 1989. Race, Sex, and Fashion Innovativeness: A Replication. *Psychology and Marketing* 6:249–262.

Strasser, J. B., and Laurie Becklund. 1991. *Swoosh: The Unauthorized Story of Nike and the Men who Played There*. New York: Harcourt, Brace, Jovanovich.

Vecsey, Peter. 1992. Jordan, League Fashion a Compromise. *U.S.A. Today*, November 20, section C, 4.

West, Cornel. 1994. *Race Matters*. New York: Vintage Books.

Williams, Jerome D., and William J. Qualls. 1989. Middle-Class Black Consumers and Intensity of Ethnic Identification. *Psychology and Marketing* 6:263–286.

17

Black Like This: Race, Generation, and Rock in the Post-Civil Rights Era

Maureen Mahon

Rock 'n' roll, a great American innovation, is also a great American hybrid. Music critics and historians usually recognize rock "n" roll as a fundamentally black American music form developed through the creativity of young black and white working-class, southern musicians in the late 1940s and 1950s.[1] Their innovative blend of blues, rhythm and blues, and country music; lyrics about youthful subject matter; and outlandish performance practices created this post-World War II product that permanently changed popular music in the United States and, eventually, worldwide. As rock 'n' roll expanded beyond its core black constituency and began to appeal to white teenagers, the form itself became associated with whites in the American popular imagination. Indeed, by the mid-1980s, black Americans who engaged in rock as musicians or listeners stood out from the black mainstream for their allegiance to a music that no longer seemed to be "really black." The impulse to escape and contest this essentializing critique led guitarist Vernon Reid,[2] artist manager Konda Mason, and writer Greg Tate to found the Black Rock Coalition (B.R.C.) in New York City in 1985. They formed a chapter in Los Angeles, California, in 1989.[3] At the first B.R.C. meetings, members commiserated about the peculiar difficulties they faced as African American rock musicians: the idea that black people wanted to play rock 'n' roll was implausible to many record executives – and indeed many music consumers – who held rigid opinions as to what constituted authentic black music. Since its inception, the B.R.C. has welcomed Latino members and viewed Latino rockers as facing similar struggles; its membership, however, is almost entirely African American and its discourses emphasize black and white racial categories, effectively constructing non-African American members as "discursively black." The majority of men and women who became B.R.C. members were college-educated African Americans born between 1954 and 1964, a race-, class-, and generation-specific segment of artists and activists whose experiences, practices, and ideologies are inextricably connected to the social, political, and cultural shifts associated with the post-civil rights era, the period from the late 1960s to the present. In this article, I analyze the central roles generational position and the experience of school integration played in B.R.C. members' formation of identity and their involvement with an organization dedicated to the proposition that African Americans have a right to rock.

As predominantly middle-class African American veterans of public school integration efforts of the late 1960s and 1970s, B.R.C. members amassed mainstream skills and ideological perspectives, or "cultural capital" (Bourdieu 1984), in a charged context. Black nationalists identifying with Stokely Carmichael, and Huey P. Newton, and black integrationists identifying with Martin Luther King Jr. and the National Association for the Advancement of Colored People (N.A.A.C.P.) struggled to advance their competing visions of black identity and culture in the United States. According to the discourses of black nationalism ascendant as B.R.C. members came of age, engagement with and investment in the dominant Euro-American milieu implied a diminished commitment to the black community. From the integrationist perspective, forceful assertions of black pride and black difference indicated shortsighted resistance to mainstream inclusion (Harper 1995; Omi and Winant 1994:108–112; Van Deburg 1992). Thus, as B.R.C. members gained cultural competence in Euro-American contexts, friends and family worried that they were losing it in African American ones. Products of the competing ideologies and expections that permeated their era, B.R.C. members often occupied conceptual and aesthetic terrain "betwixt and between" (Turner 1974) both mainstream black and white worlds as well as between discourses of black nationalism and black integration.

My discussion of B.R.C. members' experiences takes their doubly liminal position as a point of departure for examining the significance of race, class, and generation differences among African Americans and for discussing the relationship between historically situated processes of identity construction and cultural production. To explore cultural politics, I follow recent work by anthropologists who examine the processes through which actors construct social identities and develop cultural practices in order to rearticulate dominant definitions and contest existing structures (Abu-Lughod 1986; 1993; Domínguez 1986; Fox and Starn 1997; Ginsburg 1991; Gregory 1992, 1998; Kondo 1990; Myers 1991; Turner 1990; Williams 1991). I argue that through their public performance of rock, B.R.C. members negotiate what might have been a debilitatingly paradoxical position by developing cultural practices that critique both the dominant discourses of black authenticity and the persistence of racism in the United States. These activist musicians have claimed their liminal position as a place from which to challenge what they see as the prevailing wisdom of the black and white mainstreams. Cognizant of the limitations racialization places on black American lives, B.R.C. members use their music as a performed analysis and critique that circumvents media and public conventions of race, inventing new (or at least infrequently recognized) forms of African American identity in the process.

Between 1993 and 1995, I conducted fieldwork in New York and Los Angeles with a cross-section of the B.R.C.'s 400 members, the majority of whom are men.[4] They worked for independent and major record labels, at advertising agencies, for periodicals, as freelance publicists and artist managers, and as studio musicians. In responding to my request to describe the path that led them to the B.R.C., many of the men and women I interviewed focused on their experiences with integration in public and private school contexts. In school, they encountered people from different racial, ethnic, and class backgrounds and began to incorporate ideas, music, and activities that reflected this experience. These forays into desegregated arenas were not entirely harmonious. Many members remarked on their battles with racism; some described the negative consequences of not following what their peers viewed as black norms. All were careful to include historical and social context in order to explain how they got to be who they are. Taken together, their stories provide grounded perspectives on the linked but often abstract issues of race, class, cultural capital, and generation.[5] Through my discussion of their life stories, I show how B.R.C. members framed their divergence from the expectations of black and white mainstreams in terms that gave new meanings to the black identities they constructed and enabled them to negotiate their apparently contradictory positions as black rockers (Ginsburg 1989:143).[6] B.R.C. members told these stories to me, and presumably to themselves, to assert the validity of their choices. Thus, I view these anecdotes as their own testimony to the long-standing myths of black authenticity and as responses to the challenge of double-consciousness.[7]

Black Authenticity and Double-Consciousness

Sociologist Pierre Bourdieu's detailed analysis of the relationship between aesthetic dispositions, cultural practice, and class in France during the 1960s is relevant to this discussion of racial authenticity and black rock (1984). His study underscores the fact that seemingly objective categories of taste and aesthetics depend on and constitute relations between different social classes. Further, he demonstrates the ways in which "taste classifies" objects and behaviors into categories like high culture and low culture. At the same time, it "classifies the classifier," marking people as cultured or uncultured and enabling them to "distinguish themselves by the distinctions they make" (1984:6). Applying this insight to my own evidence from the post-civil rights era United States, a taste for rock music classifies an African American as someone who has either misunderstood which music is appropriate for his or her consumption or has deliberately abandoned black culture by investing in what is perceived as a white music form. People who make this classification intend to attack the absence of authenticity in the individuals they classify, while demonstrating their own familiarity with contemporary black cultural norms.[8] They use music genre as both a sign of status and a tool for policing racial categories. Significantly, one does not have to be African American to classify the tastes of African Americans, and a number of B.R.C. members remarked on the bitter irony of having white music executives tell them that their music was "not black enough."

Concepts of black authenticity, a central component of these classifications, reinforce a limited vision of what black identity can be and suggest that behaviors and beliefs that fall outside certain parameters are not "really black."[9] An investment in black authenticity is buttressed by what anthropologist Renato Rosaldo characterizes as a tendency to "conflate the notion of culture with the idea of difference" (1993:201).[10] Blacks and nonblacks assume that sustaining authentic black culture and blackness, especially in an increasingly if imperfectly integrated United States, requires maintaining difference and separation from what they regard as contaminating cultures. In short, their view implies that "real" black culture and "real" black people must be "really" different, preferably elaborating and guarding practices they identify as authentic, a process of "cultural protectionism" (Gilroy 1993:96). Blacks and nonblacks alike may base their understandings of black authenticity on stereotypes that portray blacks as spiritual, sensual, and artistic, but also predisposed to criminality, poverty, and other pathologies. Assumptions about class status are embedded in these stereotypes, which make a poor or working-class position part of authentic blackness. In his study of African American popular culture, media scholar Todd Boyd critiques the belief "that there is a correct formula for Black identity that should in some way address working-class politics. Inherent in this notion is the assumption that Blackness is indelibly linked to a working-class ethic and singularly informed by the struggle of overcoming poverty" (1997:22). In such a context, asserting a black middle-class perspective is easily interpreted as diminishing the seriousness of the economic, educational, and social marginalization of poor and working-class African Americans. It is taken as evidence of a lack of concern about "the race." The roots of this tendency may be based in the late 1960s black political discourses and cultural productions that characterized middle-class African Americans as assimilated, self-hating "Negroes" and contrasted them to progressive, independent "Blacks" who had liberated themselves from the damaging effects of Euro-American middle-class culture by embracing a "pure and uncompromising" blackness and committing themselves to fight for "the people" (i.e., the black poor and working class) (Van Deburg 1992:54; see also Harper 1995; Kelley 1994). This critique of intraracial difference depended on a claim that "Blacks" were more authentically black than "Negroes." The habit of making this kind of claim – African Americans colloquially refer to it as acting "blacker than thou" – persevered into the 1990s and contributed, I suspect, to the B.R.C.'s decision to call its second CD compilation *Blacker Than That*, a title that underscores the organization's assertion of alternative images of black identity.

Although concepts of black authenticity have changed over time, they are embedded in an ahistorical vision of black identity as a static category that transcends time and space. As a consequence, it becomes necessary for black Americans and scholars who write about black Americans to reiterate what should be obvious: that there is no single black identity shared by all black Americans, that black Americans are not a monolithic group, and that multiple versions of blackness coexist.[11] For example, African American studies scholars have emphasized the significance of ethnic, class, gender, sexuality, and nationality distinctions among blacks as well as the social and historical processes that produce these differences (Carby 1998; Giddings 1984; Gilroy 1991, 1993; Hall 1992; Harper 1996; hooks 1990; Kelley 1994; Lorde 1984; Mullings 1997; Sutton and Chaney 1987; West 1990). The persistent debates about black identity in the United States and elsewhere indicate the extent to which it is a constructed and contested category, one that different groups – whether they be radicals or conservatives, academics or rockers – struggle to define and defend, often in terms that advance and legitimate their positions. In short, the construction and representation of identity are crucial components of cultural politics (Domínguez 1986; Ginsburg 1991; Gregory 1998; Kondo 1990).

The situation of black rock musicians whose musical tastes defy the rules of black authenticity is the condition African American scholar-activist W. E. B. DuBois called "double-consciousness." In his famous 1903 reflection on the question of African American identity, DuBois asks how blacks can, at once, be "American" and "Negro" (1989[1903]:3). Black Americans, DuBois argues, are historically and sociologically an inseparable part of U.S. society but are also marginalized from the American mainstream because of racism (1989 [1903]:187). According to DuBois, this material reality has a tangible impact on the psyche; black Americans, he asserts, are unable to achieve "true self-consciousness" and instead experience a "peculiar sensation" that he calls "double--consciousness" (1989[1903]:3). He describes this condition of double-consciousness as being:

> [a] sense of always looking at one's self through the eyes of others, of measuring one's soul by the tape of a world that looks on in amused contempt and pity. One ever feels his twoness, – an American, a Negro; two souls, two thoughts, two unreconciled strivings; two warring ideals in one dark body, whose dogged strength alone keeps it from being torn asunder. (1989[1903]:3)

DuBois saw that one challenge for African Americans would be to create a political and ideological climate in which it was possible to share in the opportunities the American dream promised without assimilation to the dominant Euro-American norms that disparaged blackness and black people. He recognized that black Americans have to fight part of this battle against racism and exclusion on the terrain of identity – at the level of consciousness – where so much damage had already been done. Throughout the history of the United States, DuBois argues, every black American has struggled to "merge [this] double self into a better truer self" and to draw on the resources of both Euro-American and African American cultures "without being cursed and spit upon by his fellows, without having the doors of Opportunity closed roughly in his face" (1989[1903]:3). In DuBois's time, efforts to achieve the "true self-consciousness" he idealized were thwarted by deeply entrenched *de facto* and *de jure* racism. When black rock musicians went knocking on opportunity's door in the mid-1980s, they discovered that a version of the situation DuBois described in 1903 continued to exist in the post-civil rights era. The tendency to rank black below white persisted, and efforts to address the relationships between black and white identities were still emotionally and politically charged.[12] Experiences with integration, black cultural nationalism, interracial conflict, and intraracial tension influenced the ways B.R.C. members approached the hostile environment they encountered in the music industry and among friends and family who questioned their taste in music. Rather than capitulating to one-sided and exclusionary constructions of an authentic black identity or an authentic rock musician, B.R.C. members responded to what I see as their contemporary condition of double-consciousness through their insistence on the legitimacy of black rock, a seemingly oxymoronic genre linking *black* and *white* categories. Identifying themselves as black rockers enables them to negotiate tensions between the expectations of both black and white communities, while creating music and articulating cultural critiques that reflect both their individual histories and their group concerns.

Since 1985, B.R.C. members have produced band performances, CD recordings, and educational panels that have introduced an alternative black sound and vision into the largely white rock context. As a fieldworker, I was particularly interested in the black rock scene that B.R.C. members constituted through their performances in the rock clubs of New York and Los Angeles. By 1993, when I began my research, these shows were a well-established part of life in the B.R.C. and much of the energy of the Coalition's most active members was devoted to conceptualizing, booking, and promoting them. As a result, one of the primary ways I learned about black rock, black rockers, and black rock scenes was by attending concerts at clubs like Wetlands, the Cooler, the Mercury Lounge, and the Knitting Factory. These lower Manhattan rock clubs in which B.R. C. members produced and displayed their music and sensibilities comprise what one member wryly referred to as "The Downtown Chitlin Circuit," the small clubs where dark, run-down interiors are understood as authentic rock 'n' roll atmosphere, as are the always evident aroma of beer and clouds of cigarette smoke. No one gets rich playing on this contemporary chitlin circuit, but these venues do allow bands to get some exposure, try out new material in front of an audience, and generate a fan base. On most weeks, I was able to see several B.R.C. band performances, usually in audiences that included other B.R.C. members. Nights in the clubs provided opportunities for members to catch up with old friends and to talk about things like the availability of cheap rehearsal space and the best way to promote a self-produced CD. Going to shows was also a way for them to find out what other musicians – friends and rivals – were doing musically; they could evaluate how audiences were responding and decide among themselves whether that last guitar solo was deliberately weird or brilliantly transcendent. By meeting together in the dim confines of these clubs – listening to a riff, cheering for a soloist, swaying with the music, joking, and talking – B.R.C. members (and, for a short time, I) participated in and perpetuated a black rock scene. The music, networks, sociability, and visibility that members developed through their performances and presence at rock clubs put black rock into local music scenes and also into the consciousness of local audiences, challenging existing assumptions about race and rock.

At a general member meeting, Geoff, a rock club manager and bass player born in 1954, explained in succinct terms the purpose of the B.R.C., the organization behind the black rock scene: "For me, it's an outlet for black musicians who had the same problem I did in high school: you couldn't play for black kids *or* for white kids." Geoff expanded on this theme in an interview that took place a few days after the meeting. He described the responses he and his black friends encountered when playing in a high school rock band:

> Now the problem [was]...that we were playing rock 'n' roll then....We listened to Motown and all the other quote unquote black music back then, but we were also listening to Led Zeppelin and Grand Funk Railroad...and I dug all that stuff so that's the type of thing we were playing....But the problem came in that we really couldn't play for any of the events in [our black] neighborhood because they didn't dig the rock music. I remember even playing on one event...and everybody in the audience is saying, "Yeah, these guys are going to be hip," and then we break out into this heavy metal kind of rock 'n' roll....These people were looking at us [like], "What are these Negroes about?" And when we would play with the white kids, they just didn't respect us. The only thing they wanted to hear us play was "I Wanna Take You Higher" [by Sly and the Family Stone]....So I was kind of caught in the middle between two worlds, so to speak.

Explicit in B.R.C. meeting conversations about the difficulties black rock musicians routinely encountered in a segregated rock community was a critique of racism and stereotypes that operated in both the music industry and in the common sense assumptions of black and white Americans. As an African American of a similar background and generation, I share B.R.C. members' interest in critiquing contemporary racial conventions.[13] As a social scientist, therefore, I have elected to study their work rather than that of black rappers whose music emerged at roughly the same time as the B.R.C. (In fact, B.R.C. member band Living Colour's first album features a guest appearance by members of the rap group Public Enemy.) During the 1980s and 1990s, however, rap achieved a level of public visibility and commercial success that black rock generally did not. This was because audiences, critics, and music executives found rap to be sonically fresh and appealing

(Rose 1994) and also, I suspect, because listeners could more easily match rap's lyrical content and public image to familiar understandings of black music and black identity. I say this neither to condemn rap nor to suggest that it is a monolithic form. It is undeniable, however, that rap conforms to many dominant stereotypes of black identity both negative (e.g., rappers represent the vulgar and violent tendencies of blacks) and positive (e.g., rappers draw on the colorful verbal style and rhythmic abilities blacks possess to tell the truth about the black experience in America). In contrast, black rock stands outside conventional conceptions of black authenticity, for although it is easy to accept blacks as musicians, the image of a *rock* musician is, for most Americans, a white man with a guitar.[14] Consequently, black rockers must explain themselves and their difference; they did so eloquently in the life stories they shared with me. Their interpretation of black identity is marked by a refusal to choose between the two poles that might be characterized as black nationalism and Americanist integration. For B.R.C. members, these are false choices. Instead, they approach the challenge of their liminal position and the condition of double-consciousness by constituting identities and cultural productions that draw on the range of resources and experiences to which they have had access. Through these processes, they celebrate and extend African American cultural contributions while attacking the institutionalized U.S. racism that continues to affect African Americans.

A "Postliberated" Generation

In the United States, the post-civil rights era marks a division between the generation of civil rights activists and supporters and the generation of their fortunate sons and daughters. B.R.C. members were not the architects of civil rights agitation, but its beneficiaries. They entered adolescence in the 10-year period after the movement's victories were concretized in the Civil Rights Act of 1964 and the Voting Rights Act of 1965. The material and ideological effects of this legislation intersected with other factors that B.R.C. members identified as influencing them as they embarked on their secondary education: Black Panthers advocating autonomy and armed self-defense within black communities, writers associated with the Black Arts Movement conceptualizing a black aesthetic, anti-war protesters challenging traditional notions of citizenship, and a counterculture celebrating experimentation with sex, drugs, and music – among other things. Together, these conditions informed B.R.C. members' political and cultural consciousness, contributing to their concerns as artists and activists.

Members explained their involvement with the B.R.C. by discussing adolescent experiences with music that occurred in the integrated contexts that were beginning to open up in the post-civil rights United States. In a typical example of the musical paths of B.R.C. members, Paul, an entertainment professional born in 1959, explained:

> I had a pretty wide range of influences in terms of music....Besides whatever my peers were listening to, I was listening to whatever [my older sister] was listening to....She was into the Beatles and the Rolling Stones and that kind of stuff. So even though we lived in a black neighborhood – and I think this is something that is pretty common in the background of B.R.C. people, most of whom lived in black neighborhoods –...[we] grew up listening to all kinds of stuff. I think sometimes people are amazed at these black people who were listening to all kinds of stuff. But...I remember [a B.R.C. member] pointing out...a picture of Huey Newton at his stereo in his house about to put on a Bob Dylan album which is a completely believable kind of scene because I remember those days. I was a kid at that time, but I was in that kind of a progressive, political, sort of countercultural, black kind of environment. Black hippies, if you will. [I was] also influenced by going to mostly white schools and also going to mostly white summer camps and youth groups and things like that, so I was exposed to a whole range of stuff and I think all the black stuff just came very naturally just by being black and living in that neighborhood.

Paul went on to describe his record collection that included white artists like Roxy Music, Emerson, Lake and Palmer, and Yes as well as black artists like James Brown and the Isley Brothers. These listening habits are evidence of the kind of crossing back and forth experienced by many, black and white, who came of age in the late 1960s and early

1970s. Paul points out that Huey P. Newton, the consummate black radical, crossed racial boundaries in his music listening in a way similar to B.R.C. members. This black rock nugget was presumably shared – in the original version and in Paul's retelling – to remind the listener that African Americans can and do go beyond black borders of music, culture, and politics.

The music that B.R.C. members perform and celebrate reflects these border crossings, but also excavates the history of black American popular music. Bands mix heavy metal, progressive rock, and punk with ska, reggae, jazz, fusion, and funk. A consequence of their love for sixties rock and, particularly, for sixties rocker Jimi Hendrix, the guitar is the focal instrument in most bands and guitarists with a facility for inventive soloing are highly regarded. Vocal styles vary from throaty screams to jazz improvisational scats to technically proficient rhythm-and-blues-style singing. Lyrics encompass both professions of love (or laments of love lost), ruminations about life's pleasures and its rough spots, and commentaries attacking the recording industry (a popular trope in "alternative" rock) as well as racism and other social ills. In spite of their shared identity as black rockers, no two bands approached these musical materials in exactly the same way. Indeed, reviews of B.R.C. band performances frequently commented on the "sprawling diversity" and "hyperkinetic, polyglot style" of member bands like Living Colour, Civil Rite, Michael Hill's Blues Mob, Me'Shell NdegéOcello, Faith, and Screaming Headless Torsos (Kot 1991:6; Sinclair 1991:18). This tendency to combine styles creatively was also evident in the distinctive look associated with the black rock scene at the time I started my research in New York. Some members wore their hair in braids or cropped close in short naturals, but dreadlocks were the dominant visual marker of B.R.C. membership. On-stage, members demonstrated the versatility of this New World hairstyle by allowing their locks to flow freely, occasionally swinging them with the sharp, rhythmic nod heavy metal fans call headbanging. People made sartorial statements in black leather ensembles, West African print fabrics, and brightly colored lycra; but jeans and sweaters were also prevalent. Both men and women had pierced ears (sometimes, multiply pierced), and rings, necklaces, and bangles made of silver, gold, leather, or shells were popular (in varying combinations) across the membership. Laden with references to musical precursors like Hendrix, Miles Davis, Sly Stone, Led Zeppelin, and Parliament-Funkadelic, and to the stylistic conventions of downtown New York art scenes, the African diaspora, and hard rock sensibilities, B.R.C. members fused disparate musical and visual elements into the somewhat genre-defying form they called "black rock."

Paul's catalog of bands and their influence on B.R.C. members underlines the specificity of the historical moment in which he and other B.R.C. members encountered the cultural and social trajectories that led them to develop certain interests, including an interest in rock. In an essay that explores the relationship between generation and social change, German sociologist Karl Mannheim emphasizes the importance of the coexistence and contemporaneity of people who are born in the same era and who are subject to the same combination of prevailing historical, social, intellectual, and political influences (1952:282). He stresses that these generations must be examined in conjunction with factors like ethnicity, social structure, nationality, and zeitgeist when attempting to analyze the consciousness and activities of a specific cohort (1952:313). According to Mannheim, the constant arrival of new generations results in "the continuous emergence of new human beings in our society" and "facilitates reevaluation of our inventory and teaches us both to forget that which is no longer useful and to covet that which has yet to be won" (1952:294). Central to this process is "fresh contact," in which individuals and generations come "into contact anew with the accumulated heritage" (1952:293). Typically, this encounter results in "a novel approach in assimilating, using, and developing the proffered material" (1952:293) as each new participant takes part in the culture while bringing novel, generation-specific attitudes "towards the heritage handed down by his predecessors" (1952:294). In the case of B.R.C. members, black identity and black culture are subject to these processes of historically situated redefinition of meanings (Ginsburg 1989:141). Informed by an appreciation of both integration and black pride, B.R.C. members produce what cultural critic and B.R.C. cofounder Greg Tate calls a "postliberated black aesthetic" (1992:200). Borrowing from Tate, I refer to B.R.C. members as part of the "postliberated generation" who, having grown up in the post-civil rights era of legislated racial equality, have access to institutions that previous generations of African Americans might not have dared to imagine.

Mannheim distinguishes between "generation" and "generation unit," explaining that "those groups within the same actual generation which work up the material of their common experiences in different specific ways, constitute separate generation units" (1952:304). Recognizing distinctions within generations helps account for why all African Americans of this generation do not share B.R.C. member concerns and situates B.R.C. members in a specific historical location that is influenced by a range of factors – from demographics to aesthetics – that constitutes them as a generation unit. Describing his cohort of artists and musicians, Tate wrote:

> The present generation of black artists is cross-breeding aesthetic references like nobody is even talking about yet. And while they may be marginal to the black experience as it's expressed in rap, *Jet*, and on *The Cosby Show*, they're not all mixed up over who they are and where they come from.
>
> These are artists for whom black consciousness and artistic freedom are not mutually exclusive but complementary, for whom "black culture" signifies a multicultural tradition of expressive practices; they feel secure enough about black culture to claim art produced by nonblacks as part of their inheritance. No anxiety of influence here – these folks believe the cultural gene pool is for skinny-dipping. (1992:207)

Here, Tate acknowledges the historical specificity of his generation and the particularity of its creative predilections. B.R.C. members came of age in a context shaped by the intersection of civil rights gains, black middle-class commitment to racial uplift, a thriving late-sixties counterculture ripe with the possibility of cultural transformation, and black nationalist ideology. A reluctance to accept the kinds of black diversity resulting from this layered experience is evident in the responses B.R.C. members encountered when publicly embracing and performing rock: they were told by friends and music industry representatives that they were not "acting black" (or, worse, that they were "acting white").[15] It is this persistence of essentialist concepts of authentic black identity that contributed to the formation of an organization intended to support the interests of these postliberated African Americans.

While broadly speaking African Americans share a political and cultural history, there are also differences related to region, gender, sexuality, color, class, education, and generation that shape the ways African Americans construct identities. As social scientists, we must take note of these diverse "positionings" in order to analyze the ways different blacks experience their social worlds and understand their relation to them (Hall 1992:225). An ethnographically grounded analysis of the ways specific social actors arrive at their positionings or identities lends texture to the discussion. In the remainder of this article, I draw on the commentaries of B.R.C. members to indicate the ways they understand their experiences of race and music. These reports underline the significance of the complicated play of interracial and intraracial distinctions. I turn first to the intersecting categories of race and class that, in combination with generation, have been central in shaping the identities B.R.C. members have formed for themselves as well as the cultural project in which they are engaged.

Race, Class, and Consciousness

When I told one long-time B.R.C. member that one of my research goals was to identify common features that brought the membership together, she immediately observed, "Well, just about everyone is middle class." Defining the middle class in the United States with any precision can be difficult, especially when attempting to pinpoint a "black middle class."[16] Because of the inescapable connection between class identification and perceptions of loyalty to the black community, marking African American class status is as much a political move as it is a demographic one. As I listened to B.R.C. members from fairly similar economic backgrounds use different terminology – working class or middle class – to define themselves, I was reminded that there was more at stake in these categories than simply describing how much money one's parents earned or which neighborhood one grew up in. Historians and social scientists have noted that in the eyes of many African Americans, black middle-class status depends on behavior and ideology as much as (if not more than) economics (Banner-Haley 1994; Drake and Cayton 1993[1945]; Gaines 1996; Higginbotham 1993; Kelley 1994). In this context, in which being working class is often interpreted as being "authentic" and being middle-class is sometimes read as trying to escape one's roots, claiming black middle-class status is a loaded act.

As Paul noted in his comments above, most B.R.C. members grew up in black neighborhoods. Additionally, their parents often aspired to middle-class status. Here, for example, is Geoff's description of his upbringing:

> I grew up pretty much in a black neighborhood of a larger suburban town.... It was like one of these all-American cities, blah blah blah...and it's very, very kind of middle class. It was one of the top ten school systems in the state and as such my parents moved there in a kind of postwar type of baby boom thing that they were about. Now, as I say, I grew up pretty much in a black neighborhood. So I'd say up until the fourth grade, I just knew black people, but still not stereotypical black people. Not that *I* think there's a stereotype, but a stereotype that some people think. [The black people I grew up with were] not urban, not inner city. [They were] very much middle-class where the fathers went out to work and the moms stayed home. Whereas my father – and maybe one other father – was in a white-collar job, pretty much it was a blue-collar type of a neighborhood, but we all kind of lived a white-collar life.

In his remarks, Geoff struggles to articulate what was distinctive about his community without falling into the trap of essentializing black identity. His neighborhood was indeed black, but it was not populated by the black underclass, the group that has come to dominate both social science and popular understandings of blackness. His comments also draw attention to a number of salient features of black middle-class life. For example, the economic equivalent of "moving up" – making more money – was not easily available to blacks operating in a segregated, discriminatory marketplace. Further, until recently, segregated housing made it impossible for middle-class blacks to physically separate themselves from working-class blacks by establishing middle-class neighborhoods.[17] Instead, the different classes lived side by side. Consequently, in African American communities, symbolic criteria like education and respectability have been more critical in determining middle-class status than more concrete measures like occupation and income (Gaines 1996:16–17).[18] Thus, Geoff could describe his neighborhood as middle-class even as he points out that the majority of families were blue-collar. The fact that these were stable, two-parent households with breadwinning fathers and work-at-home mothers was as valid a marker of "white-collar life" as a white-collar job or income.

Geoff's perspective is rooted in a long-standing African American tradition of assessing a person's class not according to profession or income, but "by a pattern of behavior expressed in stable family and associational relationships, in great concern with 'front' and 'respectability,' and in a drive for 'getting ahead' " (Drake and Cayton 1993 [1945]:661–662). In short, steady employment in a blue-collar job could lead to middle-class status and what Geoff calls a white-collar life. Galvanized by postwar efforts to desegregate the public sector, the majority of B.R.C. parents became civil servants with only a few working in the private sector that remained segregated, in the north and south, well after 1964.[19] While they were not necessarily middle-class professions, civil service jobs allowed families to achieve home ownership and financial stability.[20] In some cases, these jobs enabled families to live comfortably on a single income; indeed, a number of B.R.C. members' mothers were full-time homemakers for at least part of the time they were growing up. From the African American point of view, all of these conditions were clear markers of black middle-class status.

When practiced before Black Power activists emerged in the mid-1960s with demands for black self-determination and a sharp critique of integration (Van Deburg 1992), this focus on upward mobility may have been criticized, but was nonetheless understood. Indeed, the rhetoric of the civil rights movement highlighted the assimilability of African Americans to the white mainstream by understating the cultural differences between black and white Americans, and by asserting that all U.S. citizens could be united harmoniously once race prejudice had been overcome. By the late 1960s, in a period of increased black cultural and political nationalism, however, the influence of Black Power discourse led a new generation to interpret the principles of the civil rights movement as an effort to subordinate black culture to dominant white institutions and practices. They were, in short, exemplary of the problems inherent in integration. Geoff offers his own critique of his parents' assimilationist aspirations in his derisive "blah blah blah," implicitly distancing himself from the "postwar type of baby boom thing that *they* were about." In this rapidly changing context, middle-class striving often was associated with "selling out," and to identify as middle class took on a negative meaning; meanwhile, working-class status could confirm authentic black identity.

By the 1980s, it had become a sociological commonplace to talk about the critical mass of African Americans who shared many economic, education, and, increasingly, neighborhood features with white middle-class Americans as a "new black middle class" (Banner-Haley 1994; Cose 1993; Landry 1987; Tatum 1987; Wilson 1978). When acknowledging these important economic advances, it is also crucial to attend to what anthropologist Steven Gregory calls "the *changing* significance of race and class" in African American communities (1992, emphasis added). Gregory warns against treating the middle-class status of blacks as an unproblematic indication of freedom from the barriers of race. He argues that this view "not only minimizes the effects of contemporary racism on all classes within the African American population, but also fails to take account of the diverse ways in which race and class intersect in specific sociopolitical contexts" (1992:257). Even in the post-civil rights era, race *and* class influence political organizing and identity formation among African Americans. This occurs not in spite of civil rights legislation, integration, and affirmative action, but within the new social and economic conditions they have created. The identities B.R.C. members construct and the issues with which they contend reflect this intersection.

Nearly all B.R.C. members described their upbringing as "comfortable," and regardless of economic circumstances, parents' occupations, and home ownership, they were raised with a similar set of values. So, while some define their upbringing as "very middle-class" and others identify as working-class, all members consistently noted the efforts their parents made to create stable home environments and to instill in their children a sense that they were capable of achievement. This was true in single-parent and two-parent households, in urban and suburban contexts, and whether parents were blue-collar or white-collar workers. Consistent in the life stories were recollections of being taught that with a good education and persistence, they could be successful. This perspective echoes traditional black middle-class uplift ideology. Significantly, the legal victories of the civil rights movement cleared the way for these achievements as, for the first time in U.S. history, a critical mass of African Americans began to gain access to integrated education and, ideally, desegregated opportunities.

Integrated Education and Cultural Capital

Bourdieu's observation that art and cultural consumption both mark and legitimate social differences illuminates the situation of B.R.C. members (Bourdieu 1984:7). As individuals whose tastes and practices cross usually rigid race and class boundaries, they are particularly aware of the extent to which their musical preference, especially in light of their race, constructs them socially. The life stories of B.R.C. members indicate the ways the combination of their race, class, generation, and education disposed them toward certain practices and aesthetics. Their desegregated education afforded them mainstream cultural competence – the knowledge of what to say and do in a given situation – and cultural capital – influence and power based on cultural rather than economic resources (Bourdieu 1984). In spite of the benefits that accrue to those conversant with mainstream practices, many B.R.C. members were critical of the processes through which they achieved this knowledge. They deconstructed an education that emphasized assimilation to middle-class (Euro-American) norms while marginalizing African American culture and history. Further, they noted the ways the capital and competence they acquired through their education constituted them – both in their own minds and in the minds of their peers – as "different," leading to the position Geoff described as being "caught in the middle between two worlds" and their eventual involvement in the B.R.C. For many, the recognition of intraracial difference was more significant than questions of interracial relations.

In Bourdieu's formulation, schools, with their "value-inculcating and value-imposing operations," train citizens not only in academics, but in the cultural preferences and practices associated with the dominant group; as a result, they are essential to the accumulation of cultural competence and cultural capital (1984:23). African Americans have long been cognizant of this relationship and, consequently, have viewed education as central to upward mobility, social equality, and inclusion in the United States.[21] The Supreme Court's 1954 decision to strike down legal segregation of public schools was a first critical step in ensuring equal educational opportunities for African Americans and, more broadly, in making all racial segregation illegal. It was followed, ten years later, by the Civil Rights Act of 1964 which included in the provisions of Title IV the desegregation of public education. Northerners seized on these rulings as opportunities to attack the *de facto* segregation of schools that resulted from segregated neighborhoods, exemplifying the "subtle" ways racism operated in the North (Ravitch 1974:245).

By providing B.R.C. members and other African Americans access to the information, skills, and dispositions associated with mainstream success, an integrated education had the potential to increase their cultural as well as economic capital. This opportunity was primarily available to African Americans with parents who had the economic means or the ideological disposition to move into jobs, schools, and housing that were slowly being desegregated. Indeed, for most B.R.C. members, the encounter with integrated education was not simply a matter of being in the right place at the right time, but a result of their parents' concerted efforts to secure for them the best education possible.[22] Some parents took their children out of inadequate local public schools and placed them either in private schools or superior public schools located in distant neighborhoods. Such individually focused efforts were complemented by more collective initiatives. For example, Geoff, who grew up in the Northeast, described how his parents were part of a group of African Americans who brought a suit against the local school district in order to desegregate the schools. As a result, Geoff became one of a handful of black students in a white school and began living what he called "a two-level life." He recalled:

> I didn't want to be left out, so I made myself deal with these people [at school]. But I also understood that because I was the only "spot" in the class, as it were, I wasn't really – you know what I mean. I wasn't really taken in and made to feel as comfortable as I would, say, back in the neighborhood. You know, with the fellas and stuff.

Geoff attempted to forge the interracial alliances that were touted to be one of the positive results of desegregation, but as his recollections reveal, these connections did not always come easily. Mandated school desegregation did not eradicate racism.

Integrated education was widely viewed as a first important step in more fully including blacks in the U.S. mainstream.[23] In the following remarks, Michelle, an artist manager born in 1964, drew on personal experience to critique the procedures taken to integrate schools in Queens, NY, and the assumptions underpinning them:

> MICHELLE: I went to…kindergarten through fourth grade…in my neighborhood.…Then the city got this bright idea that they needed little smart black children over in Forest Hills and they put us in this program at [another public school].… So they took me [and my three friends] …and they bussed us too far away for a ten-year-old to travel to go to elementary school to Forest Hills where we were able to mix and mingle with the natives [laughs].
>
> MAUREEN: [laughs] With the natives of Forest Hills, Queens.

MICHELLE: With the natives of Forest Hills. But I enjoyed it, I had a good time, I don't regret it, I had a good time. I just did not like that it wasn't a share-and-share-alike program....[They sent us] over into this other neighborhood and they didn't send anybody back. So there was no cultural sharing. And so I had to go to their ghetto, but they couldn't come to mine. That's the only thing that I really dread about that whole bussing thing. I don't mind bussing...but if it's not a two-way street, it's not necessary. I can learn right where I am.

At the time of the interview, I appreciated Michelle's wisecrack about mixing and mingling with the natives and took it as her playful nod to me, the anthropologist. Considering her comment in relation to other B.R.C. member narratives about integration, however, I realize it was not simply a joke for my benefit, but a pointed analysis of the experience of being bussed. Some of the ideals informing integration do have an anthropological tinge: that by communing with whites, blacks would be able to understand "their culture" and would be better equipped to succeed in it. (Perhaps this is a post-civil rights era twist on the traditional anthropological mission to study Others for scientific purposes.) What is significant about Michelle's critique of her forced fieldwork is the observation that it was "not a two-way street." The project of integration was not meant formally to train nonblack students in the ways of African Americans (although this occurred informally). Rather, in the integrationist project, unlike anthropology, preserving or validating the culture and practices of the nondominant group was not the focus. This oversight, underlined by calls for multicultural education in the 1990s, revealed the primary agenda of integration to be assimilation of African Americans into the white mainstream. As people influenced by black pride sentiment and identity politics of the late 1960s, Michelle and other B.R.C. members viewed this marginalization of black culture as an especially egregious error. Their own cultural productions are far less one-sided, drawing on multiple influences and revealing the "cross-breeding of aesthetic references" that Greg Tate celebrated in his characterization of the postliberated generation (1992:207).

These forays into the mainstream resulted in cross-fertilization that the architects of integration might not have anticipated. David, a guitarist born in 1954, explained how his parents insisted that he stay on a rigorous academic track throughout elementary school and junior high. This led to his acceptance to Stuyvesant, one of New York City's specialized public high schools, and his introduction to social movements that challenged the mainstream he was being prepared to enter.[24] He recalled:

> Stuyvesant High School was on the Lower East Side...and this is 1967, '68, '69 when the Fillmore East and the Lower East Side and the Love Generation and the Black Panthers, *all* that stuff, was happening and I was right down there. Student rebellion and stuff. It was near [New York University] and the Village. So I got involved in all of that. And I had a friend named Andy who went to Stuyvesant who lived [on the Lower East Side]. So after school we used to hang out at his crib on Fridays and we'd walk down to the Fillmore East....We all were into trying to learn guitar.

At Stuyvesant, an integrated school environment put David in contact with other students who were fascinated by the burgeoning counterculture of the late 1960s and drawn to the Fillmore East where musical acts, including black rocker Jimi Hendrix, performed. David and his friends formed connections across racial lines and based on shared cultural interests. Ironically, David's arrival at Stuyvesant, an educational institution intended to launch students into mainstream success, occurred at a historical moment when young white Americans were questioning mainstream values. Even as David and other future B.R.C. members were acquiring cultural capital through their education, the dominant cultural milieu encouraged them to challenge the assumptions underpinning the beliefs and practices they learned in school. In David's case, this accidental intersection confounded his parents' efforts to inculcate him with mainstream values; ultimately, he followed a bohemian path, formed a band, and became a professional musician.

Although the majority of B.R.C. members grew up in black or predominantly black urban neighborhoods and experienced integration at school, a few lived in predominantly white suburban neighborhoods, another post-civil rights era phenomenon (Cose 1993; Landry 1987; Tatum 1987; Wilson 1978). Patricia, a music industry professional born in the mid-1950s, described her family's move "up" from a black urban neighborhood to a white suburban one:

> Now mind you, we were in the suburbs, but on the outskirts of the suburbs; we were just barely in there. Like right on the other side of the street was [the city], but we were in. And there was a huge gap culturally. All of a sudden I was "a nigger." I had never heard that....Even though we were in [the suburbs] with all these people who were wealthy, we were not. We were still struggling and on the fringe....I had new friends who were white and Jewish. [Before], I didn't even know what that was. Had to. There was no black people in town.

The clarification that her family was in the suburbs, but "just barely in there" and that her family was "struggling" is another example of African Americans attaining aspects of middle-class status without being fully middle-class according to mainstream definitions.[25] Moving from the city to the suburbs was a step up from the perspective of blacks in the city, perhaps; but for white suburbanites, Patricia's family was still on the outside. Possibly more significant to Patricia than her family's financial position was the social status she was ascribed as an African American in a white community. Integration, she explained, was extremely difficult:

> I always did well in school. I was this, that, and the other in the school when I left [the city] in the fifth grade. So when I moved to [the suburbs] in the sixth grade, they immediately put me in the dumb reading class and in the slowest this and that class, math, everything. I was just appalled. I couldn't believe it. I was with these people who were just so, I thought, inferior to me. [laughs] Who were these white children who were calling me nigger? So it was an interesting time....There were like two black kids in the whole school. It was a trip. Anyway, I learned how to do the white people's game and how this thing worked and learned how to deal with them, because I didn't have a clue when I started. You know, I was a kid then, too, I just wanted to play and I wanted to be accepted.

Patricia's time in the trenches of predominantly white schools left her with an unforgiving take on what she was taught: "I learned how to do the white people's game," a statement that unromantically articulates one of the goals underpinning the integrationist project. Patricia's comments, like those of other members, acknowledge the extraordinary burden that was placed on African American students who were suddenly ambassadors to uncharted and not entirely welcoming territory. Although black students had been brought into predominantly white schools to achieve greater equality of access and opportunity, they were still racially marked. For example, Patricia, along with some other members, recalled being tracked into remedial classes. The gap between attending integrated schools and feeling fully accepted at the schools is a recurring theme both in the narratives of B.R.C. members and in those of other members of the postliberated generation.[26] Still, the existence of these often stressful conditions did not deter black parents from seeking integrated education for their children, and their expectations, along with those of educators and legislators, were great. But young African Americans who attended integrated schools were, as Patricia reminded me, just kids who wanted to play and be accepted.

Of course, school desegregation took place in a context where race and class continued to operate. Anna, a writer who was born in the early 1960s, compared her elite, white college to her white, working-class high school:

> Even though I was always in...advanced classes [in high school], I realized how deeply inferior my education was when I got to college. [This also happened in] high school because, I went to an integrated high school, which was very racially charged, in a white neighborhood. So I started to get an indication [then], because I saw a lot of stupid white children who knew more than me and it would really frustrate me because...I knew they weren't smarter than me, they just had access to better education. That used to really upset me because...in certain ways I couldn't compete with them even though I knew I was as qualified, if not more so....College just concretized those misgivings I had....I just realized how poor the education was....I would go into these literature classes – I was always a big reader – and [the white students] would just say stuff, just mention things that I had never even heard of. Just mention. And I was always in the *top* class [of my high school].

In distinguishing her high school and college experiences, Anna analyzes race, class, and cultural capital. She observes that even though she was a top student at her predominantly white, working-class high school, the quality of the education there was far below that of her peers at college. She poignantly describes her frustration at the realization that she had not been exposed to the books, authors, and ideas that her classmates would "just mention." Although Anna and other African Americans attended "white" schools that their parents presumed to be superior to black ones, schools in white, working-class neighborhoods were subject to inequities related to class difference. In the United States, where class is rarely acknowledged directly and whiteness is associated with higher status, it is understandable that African American parents would assume that predominantly white schools would provide a good education. They overlooked the fact that the working-class whites served by the schools were, like working- and middle-class African Americans, marginalized from the mainstream.

Race, class, and cultural capital intersected in different ways for different B.R.C. members. Paul, who attended one of New York's specialized high schools and an Ivy League university, pointed out that his middle-class background and the fact that his parents and siblings had attended college gave him an advantage in the college search process that many of his African American peers did not have:

> I was really up on the whole college thing which was good because I did not get very good advice in high school and this is a common problem, I think, for black students. Either [teachers and guidance counselors] aim you low or they just don't know themselves.... I think it's of some relevance here because I think a lot of people that were maybe the oldest people in their families or whose parents didn't come from a college background did not get good advice...and were not directed to the right places.

Paul's analysis of the role class and cultural capital play in shaping individual experience and, in his case, undercutting the effects of institutional racism, supports Bourdieu's contention that in cases where educational capital is the same, "the amount of cultural capital directly inherited from the family" influences the success with which schools transmit cultural capital to students (Bourdieu 1984:23). Paul pointed out that few parents of his black peers attended college; this, coupled with the racialized expectations of what black students should or could do in terms of higher education, influenced the assistance parents were able to offer and the advice school officials gave. Paul recalled being discouraged from applying to Ivy League colleges because his teachers believed he would not be accepted, but he applied to the "difficult" schools, supported by his parents who insisted that he "aim high." In underlining the limits often placed on academically gifted African American students, Paul's comments highlight the extent to which racialized thinking can impede the acquisition of cultural capital and, by extension, class mobility – even in situations ostensibly geared to countering the effects of racism.

Like Paul, many B.R.C. members drew attention to differences between themselves and their black peers and described the ways in which intraracial relations were inflected with class dynamics. As indicated by the persistent concern over black authenticity, there is more than one cultural system to which African Americans are accountable. Contact with white communities was a highly charged symbol of difference within black communities and B.R.C. members were marked because they attended recently desegregated schools through bussing and other programs. As a result, they confronted contradictory standards for success; frequently, the markers of mainstream cultural competence they were attaining at school were understood by black peers as signs of abandoning African American identity – in other words, as indications of "cultural *in*competence." Some members commented on how their anticipation of racial differences between themselves and whites coincided with jarring and less expected differences between themselves and other blacks. Yvonne, a vocalist born in 1964, explained that having piano lessons from the time she was 6 years old and attending an elite private high school in Manhattan distinguished her from other children in her black working-class neighborhood in the Bronx. Reflecting on her mother's opinion of the high school, Yvonne observed:

> I think she was into the fact that I was getting a private school education and she thought that...I was more like [the private school students] than I was like the kids that were in my neighborhood and in that regard she was absolutely right. Because I had always had problems in my neighborhood with kids who were neighborhood kids. You know, every year my mom used to take me to Rockefeller Center to go ice skating and then we'd go and see that corny-ass Christmas show, every year. And the other thing we used to do on Sundays after church: we would ride the number two bus down Fifth Avenue and we would go to *every* museum, *every* museum....And after we left the museum we would walk down to Lincoln Center and see some kiddie puppet show there. But that's stuff that my mom did with me all the time and those were things that other kids in my neighborhood did not do. So when I would get home and say, "I'm learning Mozart and Beethoven and my mom took me to see *Swan Lake*," they would be like, "What are you, you freak?" [laughs] "You're not black." All of that bullshit. So it was a safer environment for me to be in [laughs] I think than to go to public school.

In giving her piano lessons, sending her to a private high school, and taking her to museums and theaters, Yvonne's mother, a single parent who held a blue-collar job for much of Yvonne's life, was attempting to provide her daughter with cultural capital. Even the "corny-ass Christmas show" at Radio City Music Hall, hardly high art by the standards of most theater aficionados or Yvonne herself, is still the kind of live theatrical entertainment that could lay the groundwork for an appreciation of the arts associated with a high degree of mainstream cultural competence. These forays into Manhattan's visual and performing arts arenas created and highlighted differences between Yvonne and her neighbors, the kinds of intraracial variations that are not always acknowledged in discussions of "the Black Community."

The act of learning behaviors that were marked as racially different was a source of conflict for many B.R.C. members and their black peers. Angela, a bass player who was born in the early 1960s and who grew up in a midwestern town during the 1970s, described how the intersection of her race and her music taste separated her from the town's growing black community and caused alarm among family members:

ANGELA: I really got into rock just probably – honestly – by the old association breeds assimilation....I was surrounded by Caucasian teenagers who were listening to that and I dug it....I had grown up on that kind of music....I was not into soul music or funk. The only time I really heard funk and soul was when I [visited] my father's side of the family, his brothers and sisters....The few black kids that were going to [my] junior high, they didn't think rock was weird because they were listening to it, too. It wasn't until I got into high school...[that] I started meeting up with a lot of black kids who were into funk. That's when they thought I was a total alien. I mean seriously. I caught hell.

MAUREEN: What did they do?

ANGELA: First of all, they called me all kind of names: "White Girl," or [they would say] "You like that whiteboy music." They put me down because they thought I couldn't dance....That's a funny story in itself.... Like I said, I would go to my aunts' houses and they would be listening to funk and they used to watch *Soul Train* – I used to watch *American Bandstand*....One day I was just dancing – probably a-rhythmically – and my aunt looked at me and she went to my mother. She said, "You know, we got to get some rhythm into Angela. She dances like a little white girl." [laughs]...She was that concerned that I had no rhythm. So she taught me how to dance to funk. Yeah, she did.

An integrated context expanded African Americans' repertoire and interests, frequently augmenting their distinctiveness from other African Americans. Even the decision to watch Dick Clark's *American Bandstand*, the music show targeted to white teenagers, instead of *Soul Train*, Don Cornelius's black response to Clark's predominantly white program, is significant. The fear that "association breeding assimilation" would have damaging, long-term effects was real enough for her aunt to make a special effort to "get some rhythm into Angela," and by so doing, reconnect her to appropriately black culture and practices. Presumably, this was a valiant effort on the part of an aunt to prevent a niece from being permanently scarred by integration.

Angela's story underlines the fact that authentic blackness, a state of mind often perceived to be the natural birthright of all African Americans, is in fact a set of behaviors that social actors construct, reproduce, and change over time. If Angela's affinity for white cultural productions demonstrated that she had not properly learned blackness, her aunt's response indicates that it is possible and preferable to correct the problem – no matter how belatedly – in order to guard against being left out of the African American mainstream.

Linking B.R.C. member narratives of school integration to their eventual participation in the Coalition underscores the interplay of race, class, and generation, drawing attention to the competing demands faced by African Americans in the post-civil rights era. On the one hand, their blackness often limited full acceptance by whites in situations where integration did not eliminate racialization. On the other hand, their association with what were perceived to be white institutions and practices compromised their blackness. Specifically, their participation in rock, a form originated by blacks but by the late 1960s categorized as white, marked them as outsiders. Among the things the post-civil rights era is noted for is a persistent if subdued racial tension, but one point on which mainstream blacks and mainstream whites seemed to agree was that black rockers were playing the "wrong" music. It was the coexistence of this prevailing view and the maverick tastes of young African Americans who embraced rock that led to the formation of the Black Rock Coalition.

Enacting Identity

The B.R.C. provided a network of African Americans who shared rather than questioned a black interest in rock. The lively meetings were opportunities to let off steam, exchange information, and develop projects with people who shared common goals. Paul, who attended the B.R.C.'s first meeting in Manhattan in the fall of 1985, explained how the passion for rock combined with similar class identification and education experience to bring together what he and other members referred to as "like-minded people." He observed:

> It's a really interesting phenomenon because...there was a real feeling of almost like an Alcoholics Anonymous kind of a vibe where you're in a room with all these people who had the same interests, but they had no way of meeting each other....All these closet rock 'n' rollers come crawling out of the woodwork, out of bizarre towns in Jersey, Queens, the Bronx...into a meeting somewhere [laughs]....Some of the people [recognized each other] because they'd go to the big rock clubs and they'd see this one other black person. Maybe there's 20 people going to rock clubs on a regular basis, but maybe on a given night, there's only one or two.... But here is someone with a whole roomful, so it's a really interesting thing. There's this...feeling of "Wow, all these people are people who I don't have to explain shit to. People who have a haircut just as bizarre as mine."...So you have all these people that are maybe the hippie in their neighborhood or the rocker in their neighborhood; now everybody from all the neighborhoods...[is] in the room. You've got 30 people with common interests and it's very interesting to see how that developed... in terms of connecting with each other musically, connecting with each other with friendship, connecting with each other romantically. *That's* a deep concept.

According to Paul, the B.R.C. brought together "black bohemian, black intellectual types," people who had always been outsiders – "the hippie in their neighborhood" – and who shared demographic, musical, and political similarities. These like-minded people organized themselves around *black rock*, a term linking two categories that, for the most part, have been conceptually separate since the early 1960s. The seeming incompatibility of *black* and *rock* echoes the seeming incompatibility of *Negro* and *American* that is articulated in the concept of double-consciousness. Here, it is worth mentioning that in both cases, the categories marked as white – rock and American – have embedded in them a great deal of blackness.[27] B.R.C. members set out to draw attention to these forgotten black roots by developing practices intended to upset prevailing racialized conditions. Members articulated their position and explained their music in the "B.R.C. Manifesto." Written in 1985, this one-page document lays claim to the black legacy of rock music in order to counter dehistoricized assumptions about contemporary black rockers who frequently suffered the accusation that they were playing "whiteboy music." Part of the "Manifesto" reads:

> The B.R.C. also opposes those racist and reactionary forces within the American music industry which deny Black artists the expressive freedom and economic rewards that our caucasian [*sic*] counterparts enjoy as a matter of course.
>
> For white artists, working under the rubric *rock* has long meant the freedom to expropriate any style of Black music – funk, reggae, blues, soul, jazz, gospel, salsa, *ad infinitum* – then sell it to the widest possible audience.
>
> We too claim the right of creative freedom and total access to American and International airwaves, audiences and markets.
>
> Rock and roll is Black music and we are its heirs. (B.R.C. 1985)

B.R.C. members circulated this document to prospective members and to journalists, who quoted it in their coverage of the new organization. Guided by the analysis and critique set forth in the "Manifesto," members worked to put themselves and their interests into the public eye in ways that negotiated their black difference and their American belonging. Addressing what DuBois described as the struggle to be both a Negro and an American, B.R.C. members played rock while insisting that doing so did not compromise their blackness. Indeed, they viewed their embrace of rock as a process of reclaiming an African American contribution to American music and of continuing to create in the genre. Invoking the names of black rock forebears like Chuck Berry, Jimi Hendrix, Sly Stone, Funkadelic, and Labelle, all of whom are recognized as significant figures in the development of American popular music, the "B.R.C. Manifesto" rejected "the demand that Black musicians tailor their music to fit into the creative straitjackets the industry has designed" and asserted, "We are individuals and will accept no less than full respect for our right to be conceptually independent" (B.R.C. 1985).

The identities and interests that they had developed as they came of age led to artistic and ideological allegiances that ultimately had a concrete impact on the New York and Los Angeles music scenes as B.R.C. members brought their music and politics into local music communities. Starting in New York with the irreverently named "Drop the Bomb Party" on December 7, 1985, black rock bands, under the auspices of the B.R.C., produced concerts that displayed the musical breadth of the organization.[28] Performing at local rock clubs like New York's CBGB and Club Lingerie in Los Angeles, members proudly displayed all of the facets of their musical heritage. As performers and as panelists, B.R.C. members have participated in alternative music industry conferences like the New Music Seminar and the College Music Journal Music Marathon in New York and the South By Southwest Music and Media Conference in Austin, Texas.[29] The B.R.C. has also created a forum for exploring music industry issues by sponsoring panel discussions on topics of interest to musicians and music industry professionals. Responding to debates in the media about the vulgarity of rap and heavy metal lyrics, Los Angeles members held a panel in 1991 called "Messages in the Music: Sexism, Lyrical Content, and Censorship." In New York in 1993, "The Incredible Shrinking Black Music Executive" panel provided an opportunity for panelists and audience members to discuss the decreasing number of and limited power held by African American decision-makers in the music industry. B.R.C. members have hosted a radio show on public station WBAI-FM in New York, and in Los Angeles they produced a cable TV program on United Artists TV, a community access station. Members have produced two compilations of music by member bands, *The History of Our Future* on Rykodisc in 1991 and *Blacker Than That* in 1993 on its own B.R.C. Records label. Members also have developed a web page that offers general information about the B.R.C., sells B.R.C. CDs and T-shirts, features interviews with black rock musicians, and provides links to web pages of member bands and other alternative black musicians.[30] In addition to these B.R.C.-sponsored projects, individual members work together to produce and promote band performances and independently record and distribute CDs. Together, these productions entertain while countering dominant representations of black music and black identity.

As they came of age, B.R.C. members confronted questions of class and race, of education and taste, of sociological conditions and historical trajectories, and of personal choices and collective concerns. B.R.C. members could not take who they were for granted because they were so often challenged – by black friends, white classmates, family members, and music industry executives – about their apparently contradictory identities. Their decision to confront these questions directly through the formation of an organization enabled them to express publicly identities that incorporated issues, aesthetics, and politics absent from static notions of authentic black identity. For academics in the post-civil rights era, the concept of identity as a fluid production that is always in process, multilayered, and contingent has become a commonplace. Social science and humanities scholars emphasize the relationship between identity construction, difference, social change, power, and resistance in their research. A leader in this effort, black British cultural studies scholar Stuart Hall, argues that this more nuanced treatment of black identity is necessary in the late 20th century:

> It is to the diversity, not the homogeneity, of black experience that we must now give our undivided creative attention. This is not simply to appreciate the historical and experiential differences within and between communities, regions, country and city, across national cultures, between diasporas, but also to recognize the other kinds of difference that place, position, and locate black people. (1992:30)

My purpose has been to locate B.R.C. members through an ethnographically grounded discussion of the relationship between the construction of their identities and the social contexts in which these constructions have occurred. B.R.C. members act according to the terms in which they have understood themselves, but they must also contend with the ways other social actors and social institutions construct them. Influenced by black nationalist and black integrationist discourses, they formed the Black Rock Coalition as a response to the contemporary racial conditions they encountered. As they negotiate the conditions of double-consciousness and liminality, B.R.C. members produce music and identities that synthesize black and white, recognizing the complex and necessary connections between these usually opposed categories while also proudly affirming blackness and black culture. As black rockers, B.R.C. members created pluralist artistic productions, but did not lose sight of the continuing significance of race and class. Indeed, they formed an organization in order to address the racialization they encountered as *black* rock musicians, represent their concerns to a wider public, and reinforce among themselves the validity of their project to reclaim the right to rock.

NOTES

1 Several studies of popular and rock music draw attention to these racial dynamics and describe the sociological shifts – especially increased urbanization during and after World War II – that contributed to the emergence of rock 'n' roll (Bane 1982; Chapple and Garofalo 1977; Gillett 1983; Guralnick 1971, 1979; Jones [Baraka] 1963; Lipsitz 1990; Small 1987).

2 In accordance with the agreements I made with the B.R.C. members I interviewed and worked with while conducting fieldwork, I have changed identifying details and used pseudonymous first names to protect their anonymity. I use real first and last names of B.R.C. members and real band names in instances where their names and identities are part of the public record. In naming other groups referred to in this article, I use the terms *black*, *black American*, and *African American* interchangeably, and the terms *white* and *Euro-American* interchangeably. In quoted material, I preserve the author's capitalization and hyphenation of these terms.

3 The B.R.C. is a 501(c) 3 nonprofit educational organization. It has operated since 1985 with volunteer staff.

4 During the time I conducted my fieldwork, B.R.C. leaders estimated the combined membership of New York and Los Angeles B.R.C. chapters to be 400. The majority of members lived in the New York and Los Angeles metropolitan areas, although the Coalition claims members in Atlanta, Philadelphia, Chicago, and San Francisco.

5 While the B.R.C. includes men and women, neither men nor women emphasized the gender dimension of their integration experiences. In discussions of social relations within the B.R.C., however, women

and some men commented on the intersection of gender and race, echoing black feminist critiques of the tendency of black organizations to marginalize the specific concerns of black women and to emphasize the race and gender concerns of black men (Giddings 1984; hooks 1990).

6 In her study of abortion rights activists, anthropologist Faye Ginsburg argues that life-story narratives connect individual life cycles to historical circumstances, situating the speaker and demonstrating the logic behind his or her choices (1989:134). She treats the activists' life stories as "counter-discourses" in order to determine the extent to which "activists reframe experiences they originally felt were dissonant with social expectations by constituting them as new cultural possibilities" (1989:143).

7 This practice is connected to the kind of intellectual process that anthropologist John Gwaltney asserts is critical to the survival of African Americans (1980). In *Drylongso*, an eloquent compilation of life stories collected from urban blacks, Gwaltney observes that African Americans must depend on their ability to produce "indigenous analysis" in order to make sense of their lives in the United States, an experience dominated by the central paradox "of being separate yet inseparable from the fabric of American life" (1980:xxviii). These life stories are also related to the tradition of African American autobiography in which self-naming and self-fashioning are central features. Michael M. J. Fischer suggests that, ideally, an anthropological analysis of this type of "ethnic autobiography" reveals the "reinvention of ethnicity" that occurs in each generation and that demonstrates the fluidity of ethnic identities in contrast to the static or authentic versions that are often presumed (1986:195).

8 Black Arts Movement poetry of writers like Amiri Baraka and Sonia Sanchez provides literary evidence of this tactic. Literary critic Phillip Brian Harper has observed that in spite of its discourse of solidarity based on common race and common condition, black nationalism in the 1960s depended on a rhetoric that underlined the social divisions within the black community (1995). In short, the articulation of an authentic black consciousness required a black Other; indeed, whites were only marginally important to the project.

9 Interrogative book titles like *Am I Black Enough for You?* (1997) by Todd Boyd and *Are We Not Men?* (1996) by Phillip Brian Harper indicate the defensiveness that accompanies the expression of diverse black identities.

10 Rosaldo is critiquing what he calls a classic norm of anthropology which holds that "to pursue a culture is to seek out its difference, and then show how it makes sense...on its own terms" (1993:201) This investment in difference as the mark of culture is also found within communities with histories of being marked as different or Other by dominant groups. An embrace of black difference from the Anglo-American mainstream as an organizing principle of cultural identity was articulated by DuBois and other black intellectuals at the beginning of the 20th century and continues in the post-civil rights era (DuBois 1989[1903]; Omi and Winant 1994).

11 Addressing such myths has been a part of the anthropological project and anthropologists have struggled, with varying degrees of success, to explain the distinctiveness of African American cultures and communities while also relating them to the U.S. mainstream (Aschenbrenner 1975; Hannerz 1969; Herskovits 1990[1941]; Liebow 1967; Powdermaker 1939; Stack 1974, 1996; Whitten and Szwed 1970). Ironically, anthropological and other social science representations of African Americans have in some cases inadvertently contributed to the stereotyping and mythologizing of blackness (Szwed 1972). Throughout the 20th century, African American anthropologists have used their research to attack these simplistic images (Harrison 1988; Harrison and Harrison 1998; see also Davis et al. 1941; Drake and Cayton 1993[1945]; DuBois 1996[1899]; Gregory 1998; Gwaltney 1980; Hurston 1978[1935]; Mullings 1997; Valentine 1978). These studies deconstruct distorted conceptions of African Americans and African American culture, and almost without exception critique institutionalized practices of racism and economic injustice.

12 A classic anthropological example of the problem is Herskovits's *The Myth of the Negro Past* (1941), in which he identifies links between West and Central African culture and Negro culture in the United States (1990[1941]). His work was controversial precisely because its search for African retentions seemed to underscore the differences between black and white Americans at a moment when stressing commonalities between the two seemed more politically expedient (Jackson 1986; Szwed 1972). This was the case in spite of Herskovits's belief that his research would lessen interracial tension by demonstrating that, contrary to the dominant myth, Negroes, like all other Americans, were a people with a history. Notably, DuBois wrote one of the only positive contemporary

reviews of the book (Jackson 1986). Tracing African retentions or Africanisms in the New World continues to be a productive and occasionally provocative undertaking (Holloway 1990; Mintz and Price 1992; Sudarkasa 1982; Thompson 1983).

13 In 1986 (a year after the B.R.C. was founded), George Marcus and Michael M. J. Fischer advanced the concept of "anthropology as cultural critique" and suggested to anthropologists that "the challenge of serious cultural criticism is to bring the insights gained on the periphery back to the center to raise havoc with our settled ways of thinking and conceptualization" (1986:138).

14 Black guitarist Jimi Hendrix is, as they say, the exception that proves the rule.

15 Marlon Rigg's documentary *Black Is...Black Ain't* (1995, distributed by California Newsreel) offers a cinematic exploration of the difficulties associated with defining what blackness "truly" is.

16. Although the black middle class has grown to its largest size in the history of the United States, its existence is barely reflected in contemporary anthropological literature. This absence is in keeping with the discipline's focus on the "authentic" black working class (Szwed 1972) and the field's general lack of attention to U.S.-born middle-class groups (Nader 1972; Ortner 1991). As a result, "underclass" communities of African Americans have received most of the attention in social science literature and represent authentic black identity in most mainstream imaginings. Increasingly, however, anthropologists are countering this tendency to conflate race and class by analyzing the social processes through which African Americans formulate race and class identities and negotiate race and class difference (Bell 1983; Gregory 1992, 1998; Mullings 1997).

17 It is important to keep in mind that there are class variations within extended black families and that even the most solidly middle-class blacks may be quite close to the working class through connections to extended family. For example, a B.R.C. member whose father was an upper-level federal government employee recalled the uneasiness he felt when he and his siblings passed down their old clothes to less well-off cousins; he also commented on the heated discussions his parents had over how much financial support to contribute to relatives going through hard times.

18 Scholars of African American studies have detailed the ways pre-World War II black middle-class political ideology deployed a concept of uplift under which elite African Americans strived "for bourgeois respectability in the absence of rights or freedom. Their hope was that rights and freedom would accrue to those who had achieved the status of respectability" (Gaines 1996:16–17; see also Giddings 1984; Higginbotham 1993). This approach underscored differences within black communities, for even though "the material condition of many blacks with these aspirations was often indistinguishable from that of impoverished people of any color," striving blacks invoked what historian Kevin Gaines calls "a *moral economy* of class privilege, distinction, and even domination *within the race*, often drawing on patriarchal gender conventions as a sign of elite status and 'race progress' " (1996:16–17, emphasis in original). In short, separating oneself from the cultural practices of the masses and adopting the ways of the Euro-American mainstream were, for many, key steps in black American efforts to achieve higher status.

19 In 1941, Roosevelt issued Executive Order 8802, creating the first Committee on Fair Employment Practice and calling for the desegregation of employment under federal contracts. Still, a federal law desegregating all places of employment was not enacted until the passage of Title VII of the Civil Rights Act of 1964, after most B.R.C. members' parents had established themselves professionally and started families. It is important to note that these pre-1960s efforts to end segregation were executive orders; Congress was unable to pass a comparable law. Further, these efforts were undercut by the lack of jurisdiction given the committees; they could not sanction employers for discriminating against blacks. Indeed, even government jobs were still largely segregated, limiting blacks to lower-level positions within offices (Newman et al. 1978:106).

20 For example, parents of some B.R.C. members held blue- and pink-collar civil service jobs, working as subway motormen or as secretaries in city agencies.

21 Ultimately, the battle for school desegregation, intended to improve the quality of education, was driven by larger issues of race, power, and access. One commentator observes: "The black struggle for desegregation did not arise because anyone believed that there was something magical about sitting next to whites in a classroom. It was, however, based on a belief that the dominant group would keep control of the most successful schools and that the only way to get a full range of opportunities for a minority child was to get access to these schools" (Orfield 1993:242).

22 Possibly as a result of parental insistence, over three-quarters of the members with whom I had contact attended college. Of this group, approximately two-thirds graduated.

23 If upward mobility for blacks included attending an integrated school, upward mobility for whites meant leaving neighborhoods and schools that were becoming "too colored" (i.e., African American and Latino) for the greener (or whiter) pastures of the suburbs. In the 1950s, for example, New York City's white population had already begun to decline, dropping by 800,000; at the same time, the black and Puerto Rican population increased by 700,000 (Ravitch 1974:261). By the late 1960s, African American and Puerto Rican students had become the majority in the public school system, complicating efforts to integrate schools (Ravitch 1974:246, 331). Still, enclaves of predominantly white schools continued to exist as New York City's population became less white.

24 These magnet schools were part of an effort to encourage voluntary desegregation while also enhancing public school education (Orfield 1993:247). Specialized or magnet schools were widely viewed as a stepping stone to admission to a prestigious college. New York's specialized schools, like others in U.S. urban centers, offered courses of study that were unavailable elsewhere in the district; ideally, these new curriculum options would encourage black, white, and Latino parents to transfer their children to desegregated schools (Orfield 1993:247).

25 Gaines notes that "occupations within the black community widely perceived by historians as middle-class, including that of teacher, minister, federal officeholder, businessman, and professional, cannot be regarded as equivalent with the business, managerial, and craft labor occupations among whites from which blacks were largely excluded" (1996:14). Further, he observes that we must avoid using "a false universal standard for class formation that ignores the extent to which the very notion of the black middle class – indeed, of class itself – is built on shifting ideological sands" (1996:14).

26 Post-civil rights coming-of-age novels (Beatty 1996; Ellis 1988) and memoirs (Carter 1991; Cary 1992; Lamar 1991; Tarpley 1995) detail the complexities related to being one of a handful of blacks in predominantly white contexts. In these fictional and autobiographical texts, narrators struggle to maintain a balance between the middle-class ideals of upward mobility and loyalty to black identity.

27 Black intellectuals have written on this theme in order to "set the record straight" and to acknowledge the black contributions to American culture. LeRoi Jones's [Amiri Baraka] *Blues People* (1963), for example, is an elegant polemic that historicizes and problematizes the white American appropriation of black American music. His description of the "hopelessly interwoven fabric of American life where blacks and whites pass so quickly as to become only grays!" (1963:111) provides a provocative answer to the question that closes DuBois's *Soul of Black Folk*: "Would America have been America without her Negro people?" (1989[1903]:187).

28 B.R.C. shows at rock clubs and other music venues include the following: In 1986, "Rock against Apartheid" took place at the now defunct New York club The World and presented Bad Brains, Living Colour, and Sirius featuring Ronnie Drayton; a portion of the proceeds from this event went to benefit the African Arts Fund Inc. Scholarship Program for Black South African Artists. On the 10-year anniversary of Elvis Presley's death, the B.R.C. celebrated the music of Otis Blackwell and featured a performance by Blackwell, the African American who wrote Presley's hits "All Shook Up" and "Don't Be Cruel" (as well as "Great Balls of Fire" and "Breathless" made famous by Jerry Lee Lewis); this performance, "Otis Blackwell Meets the Black Rock Coalition Orchestra," took place in August 1987 at the Prospect Park Bandshell in Brooklyn. The Los Angeles chapter was inaugurated with an event called "All is Not Quiet on the Western Front/Black Rock Coalition Invasion Part II" at Music Machine, Los Angeles, in July 1989; performers included Los Angeles bands Civil Rite and Hello Children and New York band Eye and I. The show was hosted by B.R.C. cofounder Vernon Reid and black rock diva Nona Hendryx. Los Angeles hosts an annual Malcolm X Birthday Tribute and each year both chapters produce Jimi Hendrix birthday celebrations.

29 These music conferences feature performances by well-known and up-and-coming rock and rap artists. In addition to promoting the music, the conferences use panel discussions to educate musicians and managers about the labyrinthine music industry and to discuss industry controversies and concerns. The New Music Seminar folded after its 1994 conference due to financial trouble, but the other two seminars continue to operate.

30 The address for the B.R.C. homepage is http://users.aol.com/brcny/home.html.

REFERENCES

Abu-Lughod, Lila. 1986. *Veiled Sentiments: Honor and Poetry in a Bedouin Society*. Berkeley: University of California Press.

Abu-Lughod, Lila. 1993. Finding a Place for Islam: Egyptian Television Serials and the National Interest. *Public Culture* 5(3):493–513.

Aschenbrenner, Joyce. 1975. *Lifelines: Black Families in Chicago*. New York: Holt, Rinehart, & Winston.

Bane, Michael. 1982. *White Boy Singin' the Blues: The Black Roots of White Rock*. New York: DaCapo Press.

Banner-Haley, Charles T. 1994. *The Fruits of Integration: Black Middle-Class Ideology and Culture, 1960–1990*. Jackson: University Press of Mississippi.

Beatty, Paul. 1996. *The White Boy Shuffle*. New York: Houghton Mifflin.

Bell, Michael J. 1983. *The World from Brown's Lounge: An Ethnography of Black Middle-Class Play*. Urbana: University of Illinois Press.

B.R.C. (Black Rock Coalition). 1985. The Black Rock Coalition Manifesto, flier.

B.R.C. 1991. *The History of Our Future*. Various artists, Rykodisc, compact disc, RCD 10200.

B.R.C. 1993. *Blacker Than That*. Various artists, Black Rock Coalition Records, compact disc, BRC–000.

Bourdieu, Pierre. 1984. *Distinction: A Social Critique of the Judgement of Taste*. Richard Nice, trans. Cambridge, MA: Harvard University Press.

Boyd, Todd. 1997. *Am I Black Enough for You? Popular Culture from the 'Hood and Beyond*. Bloomington: Indiana University Press.

Carby, Hazel. 1998. *Race Men*. Cambridge, MA: Harvard University Press.

Carter, Stephen L. 1991. *Reflections of an Affirmative Action Baby*. New York: Basic Books.

Cary, Lorene. 1992. *Black Ice*. New York: Knopf.

Chapple, Steve, and Reebee Garofalo. 1977. *Rock 'n' Roll is Here to Pay: The History and Politics of the Music Industry*. Chicago: Nelson-Hall.

Cose, Ellis. 1993. *The Rage of a Privileged Class*. New York: HarperCollins.

Davis, Allison, Burleigh G. Gardner, and Mary R. Gardner. 1941. *Deep South: A Social Anthropological Study of Caste and Class*. Chicago: University of Chicago Press.

Domínguez, Virginia R. 1986. *White By Definition: Social Classification in Creole Louisiana*. New Brunswick, NJ: Rutgers University Press.

Drake, St. Clair, and Horace R. Cayton. 1993[1945]. *Black Metropolis: A Study of Negro Life in a Northern City*. Chicago: University of Chicago Press.

DuBois, W. E. B. 1989[1903]. *The Souls of Black Folk*. New York: Bantam.

DuBois, W. E. B. 1996[1899]. *The Philadelphia Negro: A Social Study*. Philadelphia: University of Pennsylvania Press.

Ellis, Trey. 1988. *Platitudes*. New York: Vintage Books.

Fischer, Michael M. J. 1986. Ethnicity and the Post-Modern Arts of Memory. In *Writing Culture: The Poetics and Politics of Ethnography*. James Clifford and George E. Marcus, eds. Pp. 194–233. Berkeley: University of California Press.

Fox, Richard G., and Orin Starn, eds. 1997. *Between Resistance and Revolution: Cultural Politics and Social Protest*. New Brunswick, NJ: Rutgers University Press.

Gaines, Kevin. 1996. *Uplifting the Race: Black Leadership, Politics, and Culture in the Twentieth Century*. Chapel Hill: University of North Carolina Press.

Giddings, Paula. 1984. *When and Where I Enter: The Impact of Black Women on Race and Sex in America*. New York: Morrow.

Gillett, Charlie. 1983. *The Sound of the City: The Rise of Rock and Roll*. New York: Pantheon Books.

Gilroy, Paul. 1991. Sounds Authentic: Black Music, Ethnicity and the Challenge of a *Changing* Same. *Black Music Research Journal* 11(2):111–136.

Gilroy, Paul. 1993. *The Black Atlantic: Modernity and Double Consciousness*. Cambridge, MA: Harvard University Press.

Ginsburg, Faye. 1989. *Contested Lives: The Abortion Debate in an American Community*. Berkeley: University of California Press.

Ginsburg, Faye. 1991. Indigenous Media: Faustian Contract or Global Village? *Cultural Anthropology* 6(1):92–112.

Gregory, Steven. 1992. The Changing Significance of Race and Class in an African American Community. *American Ethnologist* 19(2):255–274.

Gregory, Steven. 1998. *Black Corona: Race and the Politics of Place in an Urban Community*. Princeton, NJ: Princeton University Press.

Guralnick, Peter. 1971. *Feel Like Going Home: Portraits in Blues and Rock 'n' Roll*. New York: HarperPerennial.

Guralnick, Peter. 1979. *Lost Highway: Journeys and Arrivals of American Musicians*. New York: HarperPerennial.

Gwaltney, John L. 1980. *Drylongso: A Self-Portrait of Black America*. New York: Vintage Books.

Hall, Stuart. 1992. What Is This "Black" in Black Popular Culture? In *Black Popular Culture*. Gina Dent, ed. Pp. 21–33. Seattle, WA: Bay Press.

Hannerz, Ulf. 1969. *Soulside: Inquiries into Ghetto Culture and Community*. New York: Columbia University Press.

Harper, Phillip Brian. 1995. Nationalism and Social Division in Black Arts Poetry of the 1960s. In *Identities*. Kwame A. Appiah and Henry L. Gates Jr., eds. Pp. 220–241. Chicago: University of Chicago Press.

Harper, Phillip Brian. 1996. *Are We Not Men? Masculine Anxiety and the Problem of African-American Identity*. New York: Oxford University Press.

Harrison, Faye, V. 1988. Introduction: An African Diaspora Perspective on Urban Anthropology. *Urban Anthropology* 17(2–3):111–142.

Harrison, Ira E., and Faye V. Harrison, eds. 1998. *African-American Pioneers in Anthropology*. Urbana: University of Illinois Press.

Herskovits, Melville J. 1990[1941]. *The Myth of the Negro Past*. Boston: Beacon Press.

Higginbotham, Evelyn Brooks. 1993. *Righteous Discontent: The Women's Movement in the Black Baptist Church, 1880–1920*. Cambridge, MA: Harvard University Press.

Holloway, Joseph E., ed. 1990. *Africanisms in American Culture*. Bloomington: Indiana University Press.

hooks, bell. 1990. *Yearning: Race, Gender, and Cultural Politics*. Boston: South End Press.

Hurston, Zora Neale. 1978[1935]. *Mules and Men*. New York: Perennial Library.

Jackson, Walter. 1986. Melville Herskovits and the Search for Afro-American Culture. In *Malinowski, Rivers, Benedict and Others: Essays on Culture and Personality*. George W. Stocking Jr., ed. Pp. 95–126. Madison: University of Wisconsin Press.

Jones, LeRoi [Amiri Baraka]. 1963. *Blues People: Negro Music in White America*. New York: Morrow Quill.

Kelley, Robin D. G. 1994. *Race Rebels: Culture, Politics and the Black Working Class*. New York: The Free Press.

Kondo, Dorinne. 1990. *Crafting Selves: Power, Gender, and Discourses of Identity in a Japanese Workplace*. Chicago: University of Chicago Press.

Kot, Greg. 1991. *Musical Apartheid: Black Rockers Trying to Break Down Stereotypes*. Chicago Tribune, October 27:6.

Lamar, Jake. 1991. *Bourgeois Blues: An American Memoir*. New York: Plume.

Landry, Bart. 1987. *The New Black Middle Class*. Berkeley: University of California Press.

Liebow, Elliot. 1967. *Tally's Corner: A Study of Negro Streetcorner Men*. Boston: Little, Brown.

Lipsitz, George. 1990. Against the Wind: Dialogic Aspects of Rock and Roll. In *Time Passages: Collective Memory and American Popular Culture*. Pp. 99–132. Minneapolis: University of Minnesota Press.

Lorde, Audre. 1984. *Sister Outsider: Essays and Speeches*. Trumansburg, NY: Crossing Press.

Mannheim, Karl. 1952. The Problem of Generations. In *Essays on the Sociology of Knowledge*. P. Kecskemeti, ed. Pp. 276–320. London: Routledge & Kegan Paul.

Marcus, George E., and Michael M. J. Fischer. 1986. *Anthropology as Cultural Critique: An Experimental Moment in the Human Sciences*. Chicago: University of Chicago Press.

Mintz, Sidney W., and Richard Price. 1992. *The Birth of African American Culture: An Anthropological Perspective*. Boston: Beacon Press.

Mullings, Leith. 1997. *On Our Own Terms: Race, Class, and Gender in the Lives of African American Women*. New York: Routledge.

Myers, Fred R. 1991. Representing Culture: The Production of Discourse(s) for Aboriginal Acrylic Painting. *Cultural Anthropology* 6(1): 26–62.

Nader, Laura. 1972. Up the Anthropologist: Perspectives Gained from Studying Up. In *Reinventing Anthropology*. Dell Hymes, ed. Pp. 284–311. New York: Pantheon.

Newman, Dorothy K., Nancy J. Amidei, Barbara L. Carter, Dawn Day, William J. Kruvant, and Jack S. Russell. 1978. *Protest, Politics, and Prosperity: Black Americans and White Institutions, 1940–1975*. New York: Pantheon Books.

Omi, Michael, and Howard Winant. 1994. *Racial Formation in the United States: From the 1960s to the 1990s*. 2nd edn. New York: Routledge.

Orfield, Gary. 1993. School Desegregation after Two Generations: Race, Schools, and Opportunity in Urban Society. In *Race in America: The Struggle for Equality*. H. Hill and J. E. Jones Jr., eds. Pp. 234–262. Madison: University of Wisconsin Press.

Ortner, Sherry B. 1991. Reading America: Preliminary Notes on Class and Culture. In *Recapturing Anthropology: Working in the Present*. Richard G. Fox, ed. Pp. 163–189. Santa Fe, NM: School of American Research Press.

Powdermaker, Hortense. 1939. *After Freedom: A Cultural Study of the Deep South*. New York: Viking Press.

Ravitch, Diane. 1974. *The Great School Wars: New York City, 1805–1973: A History of the Public Schools as Battlefields of Social Change*. New York: Basic Books.

Rosaldo, Renato. 1993. *Culture and Truth: The Remaking of Social Analysis*. Boston: Beacon Press.

Rose, Tricia. 1994. *Black Noise: Rap Music and Black Culture in Contemporary America*. Hanover, NJ: Wesleyan University Press.

Sinclair, Tom. 1991. No Rap. No Jazz. They Want to Rock. *New York Times*, September 1:18–19.

Small, Christopher. 1987. *Music of the Common Tongue: Survival and Celebration in Afro-American Music*. London: Calder Publications.

Stack, Carol B. 1974. *All Our Kin: Strategies for Survival in a Black Community*. New York: Harper & Row.

Stack, Carol B. 1996. *Call to Home: African Americans Reclaim the Rural South*. New York: Basic Books.

Sudarkasa, Niara. 1982. African and Afro-American Family Structure. In *Anthropology for the Eighties: Introductory Readings*. Johnnetta B. Cole, ed. Pp. 132–160. New York: Free Press.

Sutton, Constance R., and Elsa M. Chaney, eds. 1987. *Caribbean Life in New York City: Sociocultural Dimensions*. New York: Center for Migration Studies of New York, Inc.

Szwed, John F. 1972. An American Anthropological Dilemma: The Politics of Afro-American Culture. In *Reinventing Anthropology*. Dell Hymes, ed. Pp. 153–181. New York: Pantheon.

Tarpley, Natasha. 1995. *Testimony: Young African-Americans on Self-Discovery and Black Identity*. Boston: Beacon Press.

Tate, Greg. 1992. Cult-Nat Meets Freaky Deke. In *Flyboy in the Buttermilk: Essays on Contemporary America*. Pp. 198–210. New York: Fireside.

Tatum, Beverly Daniel. 1987. *Assimilation Blues: Black Families in a White Community*. Northhampton, MA: Greenwood Press.

Thompson, Robert Farris. 1983. *Flash of the Spirit: African and Afro-American Art and Philosophy*. New York: Random House.

Turner, Terence. 1990. Visual Media, Cultural Politics, and Anthropological Practice: Some Implications of Recent Uses of Film and Video among the Kayapo of Brazil. *Commission on Visual Anthropology Review* (Spring):8–13.

Turner, Victor. 1974. *Dramas, Fields, and Metaphors: Symbolic Action in Human Society*. Ithaca, NY: Cornell University Press.

Valentine, Bettylou. 1978. *Hustling and Other Hard Work: Lifestyles in the Ghetto*. New York: Free Press.

West, Cornel. 1990. The New Cultural Politics of Difference. In *Out There: Marginalization and Contemporary Cultures*. R. Ferguson et al., eds. Pp. 19–36. Cambridge, MA: New Museum/MIT.

Whitten, Norman E., and John F. Szwed, eds. 1970. *Afro-American Anthropology*. New York: Free Press.

Williams, Brackette F. 1991. *Stains on My Name, War in My Veins: Guyana and the Politics of Cultural Struggle*. Durham, NC: Duke University Press.

Wilson, William J. 1978. *The Declining Significance of Race*. Chicago: University of Chicago Press.

Van Deburg, William L. 1992. *New Day in Babylon: The Black Power Movement and American Culture, 1965–1975*. Chicago: University of Chicago Press.

PART VII

Privilege, Power, and Anxiety of the Norm

18

It Hurts To Be a Girl: Growing Up Poor, White, and Female

Julia Hall

In this investigation, I contend that a group of poor, white, middle-school young women in the postindustrial urban Northeast are living among high concentrations of domestic violence. I refer to this group as "Canal Town" girls.[1] These young women are envisioning lives in which, by charting a course of secondary education, they hope to procure jobs and self-sufficiency. As their narrations indicate, such plans are fueled by the hope that they will live independent lives as single career women and, therefore, will bypass the domestic violence that currently rips through their own and their mothers' lives. This research is one piece of a large-scale ethnographic study on the production of identities among poor white urban girls and boys. For more than a year, I observed and interviewed a group of 18 middle-school youth in neighborhood streets, the bilingual school, and the local community center (Hall 2001).

While there are many analyses that focus on the ways in which institutions and the formation of female youth cultures contribute to inequitable futures (Finders 1996; Holland and Eisenhart 1990; McRobbie 1991; Raissiguier 1994; Smith 1988; Valli 1988; Weis 1990), none of this work picks up on the issue of violence. Fine and Weis (1998) examine this theme as it boldly emerges in data on the lives of poor and working-class adult white women and the production of identity. They found that white working-class women experience more abuse, as compared with working-class women from other cultural backgrounds, and are more apt to treat their abuse as a carefully guarded secret (Weis et al. 1997; Weis, Marusza-Hall, and Fine 1998).[2]

Informed by such work, I turn this critical lens on middle-school girls. What I found is that their lives are also saturated with domestic abuse. They are not talking about it, not reporting it, and covering their bruises with clothes. They are also hiding it from others and themselves to such an extent that it is not openly dealt with at a critical level at all. Nowhere in their narrations is there any sense that males are accountable for their violent behavior.

This research is contextualized in a postindustrial economy characterized by the systematic dismantling of the basic productive capacity of a nation, a trend sharply experienced in the United States during the 1970s and 1980s. During these decades, the U.S. steel industry had already begun a process of shifting to foreign, less expensive, less regulated markets, as did other areas of manufacturing and production. As a result, smaller businesses that were dependent on industry also closed (Bluestone and Harrison 1982). No longer able economically to support its own populace, the city in this analysis currently relies on shrinking state resources. Left in the wake of global restructuring are empty factories, gutted warehouses, and people who can no longer make a decent living. Canal Town is an urban neighborhood reflecting these changes.

No longer able to find the wage-earning jobs they once enjoyed, today residents are often unemployed (Perry 1996). Many rely on food stamps and Aid to Families with Dependent Children (AFDC). The demography of Canal Town has also shifted from white to racially diverse. This change is reflected in the neighborhood school, which was transformed into a Spanish-English bilingual magnet in the late 1970s. The community center, which has traditionally been staffed by white adults, however, is almost exclusively visited by local white youth. The extent to which racism emerges in this neighborhood and the middle school, encouraged by white adults in the community center, is explored in other work (Hall 2001).

Although still socially and economically privileged by their whiteness, among most white former workers a family wage has disappeared. The cushion of wealth that white laborers were often able to amass for their families across generations is quickly eroding. Still, there may be pockets of accumulated resources that are shared among white families in Canal Town, for example, in the form of home ownership or a pension (Fine and Weis 1998; Oliver and Shapiro 1995).

To take part in the shaping of responsive public policy, it is increasingly important for educators to understand how *poor* youth from *all* cultural backgrounds make sense of their world. Up until now, the voices of many poor adolescents have not been given room in the literature. Research that does focus on poor youth looks at rural culture (Borman, Mueninghoff, and Piazza 1988; DeYoung 1995). Yet, as economic retrenchment becomes even more invasive in the lives of urban residents who struggle to earn a living, more and more people are being forced into lives of poverty. With contemporary welfare cutbacks, the nature of life in poor families across race is arguably beginning to change. White middle-school youth are at an ideal age for exploring many of these issues as they are just beginning to think seriously about the future (Everhart 1983; Finders 1996; Hall 2001).

The Canal Town girls' families have historically been working-class, most having fathers and grandfathers who worked in industry while their mothers and grandmothers stayed home. The subordination of women to men within white working-class families has been heavily investigated (Smith 1987). Others explore this subordination through the notion of the *family wage*. The family wage appeared advantageous to all family members, but in reality it supported the notion that women should receive lower wages than men or stay home (May 1987; Woodcock Tentler 1979). Although the young women in this investigation contend that the adult men around them are no longer employed in full-time labor jobs, present-day gender arrangements in the Canal Town community are linked to the ideology prevalent during the days of heavy industry.

While the Canal Town girls share their stories of abuse, I am ultimately responsible for the shape their words take in this text. As a white, female, relatively young critical ethnographer, I was born south of the city in which this research takes place. My family, however, traces its roots to environs outside of Canal Town. As a graduate student, I volunteered as a tutor at the community center in Canal Town, where I became interested in the role the organization played in the lives of area children. The white youth who attended the center appeared to be extremely committed to the staff and activities. After tutoring for more than one year, my curiosity evolved into questions that would eventually comprise this research. Having been a presence in the neighborhood, I easily gained access to the community center and the bilingual school as sites for investigation. The question that interested me most, and which became the overall objective of the project, was to understand what poor youth living in a post-industrial economy might expect from the future.

I began formal interviews with the youth after one year of observations. Interview protocols were constructed to capture thoughts on neighborhood, friends, future jobs, and relationships. I feel the girls were forthright in their responses since I was someone they had come to know. I did not intend to ask the girls about violence. After initial interviewing, however, many of the young women began to talk about abuse. Upon this realization, I began to explore this issue. Questions included probes on domestic violence in their community and in their own lives, what neighborhood women were doing about abuse, and the school's response to violence. The particular young women were selected for this research as they were members of a tight peer group.

Canal Town Girls

To obtain some sense of the nine poor white sixth-, seventh-, and eighth-grade girls who participated in this research, I share information from the individual interviews pertaining to their home life. Out of the nine girls – Anne, 11; Rosie, 11; Sally, 11; Jamie, 12; Elizabeth, 12; Lisa, 12; Katie, 13; Christina, 13; and Lisette, 13 – only Jamie says she lives with both parents. Elizabeth, Anne, and Katie maintain they live with their mothers, siblings, and their mothers' steady boyfriends. The rest of the girls – Christina, Lisette, Lisa, Rosie, and Sally – report they live with their mothers, siblings, and on occasion, their mothers' different boyfriends. Only Jamie and Christina said they were in contact with their biological fathers, while the remaining girls contend they have no knowledge of their fathers' whereabouts. In terms of employment, seven of the girls state their mothers are not presently working, nor have they been in the past. Only Elizabeth says that her mother used to work as a secretary before she was born. Of the adult men who contribute to household expenses, Jamie's father holds a part-time job in the trucking industry, while Katie is the only girl to claim her mother's boyfriend earns money for their family. As Katie explains, he collects items on trash day that he sells to pawn shops. Jamie says her family receives food stamps, while all of the other girls say their families rely on food stamps and AFDC. Jamie lives in a house that her parents inherited from her grandparents, while the rest of the girls say they live in apartments.

Dream Jobs

As the Canal Town girls begin to talk about what they want their lives to look like after high school, they stress going to college and/or obtaining a good job, and only mention marriage or family after being asked. Since the girls are only in middle school, their plans for the future may not yet be specific or thought out, but the positioning of a job or career as central to the production of identity is worth noting.

CHRISTINA: I want to be a doctor...I'll have to go to college for a long time...I don't know where I'll go [to college], hopefully around here...I'm not sure what type of doctor, but I'm thinking of the kind that delivers babies.

LISETTE: I want to be a leader and not a follower...I want to be a teacher in [the neighborhood] because I never want to leave here...I want to go to [the local] community college, like my sister, learn about teaching little kids...I definitely want to be a teacher.

KATIE: I want to be a scientist; I just love math...I want to stay [in the neighborhood]. If I live someplace else I won't be comfortable...I'm shy...I want to work with, like, chemicals, test tubes.

LISA: I probably see myself as an educated person with a good job. The one thing I hate to see myself as is to grow up being a drunk person or a homeless person on the streets...I would like most of all to be an artist, you know, with my own studio... I'm going to start with cosmetology when I go to [the local high school] and then take it from there.

JAMIE: I'd like to go into carpentry. I already help my dad fix stuff, like the table...I just want to be a carpenter. I want to go to college and also be a carpenter, which is something you don't got to go to school for; you just become one....It's just what I want to be.

All of these young girls envision further education in their future, but most do not yet have a clear sense of what school they hope to attend or how long they plan to go. Christina is the only one who talks about a career that absolutely requires a four-year degree and beyond, while it is uncertain whether Lisette, Katie, Lisa, or Jamie might pursue their goals by obtaining a two- or four-year degree. Christina, Katie, and Jamie intend "nontraditional" careers in male-dominant fields, while Lisa and Katie choose those that are typically female. Lisa seems the least committed to any career and tells me she is encouraged by her guidance counselor to sign up for the female-dominated occupation, cosmetology, in high school. Any of these girls may switch ideas about careers a number of times, yet when asked about the future, all of them focus their energies on the single pursuit of furthering their schooling and landing a job. Christina says she worries about being homeless, which is likely a chronic fear among poor youth.

These white young adolescents are the daughters of presently poor adults. None of their parents continued their education beyond high school and a few did not graduate from grade 12. College, they say, is not an option that is really discussed much at home. Perhaps Lisette has the clearest idea of where she would like to go to school because she is the only white girl who I worked with who has an older sibling enrolled in an institution of higher education. Lisette's sister attends a nearby community college and studies early childhood education, a circumstance that likely influenced her little sister's plans. Interestingly, three of these white girls indicate that although they want to break out of cycles of dependence and have careers, they do not want to leave their neighborhood – whether for school or work.

The importance of a job or career is emerging within the identities of these girls, but it is too soon to say whether they will follow through on their plans for further education or training. The outlook is not promising, as all but a few of their older siblings are negotiating lives riddled with substance abuse and early pregnancies. My conversations with the principal of the area high school reveal that very few local teenagers are enrolling in any form of advanced studies.

Even though the Canal Town girls view education as important in obtaining their goals, they both accept and reject academic culture and knowledge. I observed that on a daily basis while in class, these girls copy homework, pass notes, read magazines and/or books, or, in other words, participate in the form rather than the content of schooling. Time spent in school involves passively skipping across the surface of learning.

In only a few instances did the girls actually narrate resentment toward school authority. As part of a tradition of working-class women whose personal choices have been mediated by structural constraints, the Canal Town girls, by virtue of gender, are not part of this legacy of expressed resentment. Animosity toward institutional authority is typically male and is linked to the historical contestation between capital and workers (Everhart 1983; Weis 1990). Since white women generally labored in the private sphere or as marginalized wage workers, they did not directly engage in such struggles.

Family Planning

The Canal Town girls, like the older white working-class girls of Freeway (Weis 1990), view jobs and careers as a central part of their futures, which is in vivid contrast to working-class girls in previous studies (McRobbie 1991; Raissiguier 1994; Valli, 1988). While the Freeway girls mention the desire for marriage and family only after they are financially secure, most of the Canal Town girls, with the exception of Lisa, contend they do not wish to have husbands, homes, and families at all. Rather, the Canal Town girls claim they are looking to the life of a single career woman as a way to circumvent the abuse that they see inscribed in future families or relationships with men. It quickly becomes clear that seeking refuge from domestic violence plays a big role in constructing identities. For many of these girls, the future includes avoiding marriage and family altogether and getting a job so they can rely on themselves.

CHRISTINA: I don't want to be married because if I was married, my husband would want a kid. I don't want to have a kid because its father may not treat us right...hitting and stuff. ...There's not enough for everybody and the kid shouldn't have to suffer...I want to always stay in [this neighborhood]... live alone....At least I know trouble here when I see it.

LISETTE: I don't want to get married and be told to stay at home...and be someone's punching bag...I'll get a one-bedroom apartment and live alone and just try to be the best teacher I can be.

KATIE: I can't see myself being with a guy because they don't know how to not hit... that's, like, why I don't want to be married or have, like, a kid...I'm going to go to school and be something really good.

LISA: I guess I sort of want to be married, but I want to be free at the same time, and that's not going to happen. I won't be able to do what I want if I'm married....

He's got to treat me good and respect me for who I am and not for what he wants me to be, and not for what I did in the past...not a lot of hitting...I just don't know if that exists...I'd rather live by myself, focus on a career.

ELIZABETH: I don't know yet [if I want to marry]. With the problems that happen, you never know. A person can act nice before you marry them and then after they can be mean to you. They have all the power. They can make us do everything. My uncle is as lazy as hell. He makes my mom go to the store all the time. He makes us walk. My mom likes it, but I hate it....We don't have a car, but he gets cable and my mom pays for it. He makes my mom pay for all the bills. We get our clothes from other people, but he buys his new....I don't know if it's fair to have kids. If you don't put your kids first, you shouldn't bring them into the world....If I get married, it will be to someone who's intelligent, willing to help, someone who doesn't drink, and someone who isn't violent...I don't think it exists, so I want to just get a good job and live alone.

The girls are not devising career-oriented plans simply to escape a patriarchal-dominant home. Rather, they specifically say they view a job as the ticket to a life free of abuse. By concentrating energies on the world of work instead of family, some of the Canal Town girls feel they can spare bringing children into the world, whom they feel often bear the brunt of adult problems. As Elizabeth resolves, "If I get married, it will be to someone...who doesn't drink, and [to] someone who isn't violent...I don't think it exists, so I want to just get a good job and live alone."

While the girls say they want to live as independent women in the public sphere, they are developing such identities in response to violent men. Nowhere, in more than one year of observations and interviews, did I hear these girls hold men and boys accountable for their abusive behavior. While it may be the case that they hold such a critique, the absence of any such discourse in the data is glaring, especially given the frequency and detail in which abuse was mentioned in the private space of an interview or in hushed conversations with friends.

It Hurts to be a Girl

When these young girls are asked to describe their neighborhood, they soon begin to tell stories of women being abused at the hands of men. The women in their narrations seemingly work to conceal their abuse from authorities and ultimately end up "going back."

JAMIE: It's a pretty good place to live....There's lots of auto crashes, drunk people. Lots of people go to the bars on Friday and Saturday and get blasted. They're always messing with people. Some guy is always getting kicked out of the bar for fighting. Guys are mostly fighting with their girlfriends and are getting kicked out for punching so they continue to fight in the street; I see it from my bedroom window; only the girl mostly gets beat up really bad...but later she was saying it was her fault.

CHRISTINA: There's lots of violence in this neighborhood. Like there's this couple that's always fighting. When the guy gets mad, he hits her. It happens upstairs in their house. She's thrown the coffee pot at him and the toaster, they [the coffeepot and toaster] landed in the street...I saw it while walking by....The guy would show off all the time in front of his friends. One day when he was hitting her, she just punched him back and told him she wasn't going to live with him anymore. He used to hit her hard. She used to cry but she would still go out with him. She said she loved him too much to dump him. A lot of people go back.

LISETTE: It's overall a nice neighborhood.... There's like a lot of physical and mental abuse that goes on. Just lots of yelling. I know one mother that calls her daughter a slut. She tells her, "You're not worth anything; you're a slut"...There's one family where the mother's boyfriend sexually abused her little girl, and stuff like that. The girl was like seven, and like he's still with them. The mother didn't care....It's like fathers and boyfriends beat on the kids. They [the mothers] don't take a stand. They don't say, "Well you know that's my daughter" or "that's my son." It's like they don't care. They think that they're just to sit down and be home...they just sleep all day or watch TV. Some of them drink all day and are high and spend a lot of time sleeping it off.

ROSIE: My neighborhood's quiet sometimes. It's a nice neighborhood, I guess. Sometimes it could be violent....Like there was my mom's friend who came over once with bruises all over. Her boyfriend beat her up because she had a guy from downstairs come up to her house. The boyfriend got real mad and he was going to kill her because he was jealous. I didn't see the fight but I saw her. She looked like a purple people eater....There's this one girl who got beat by her boyfriend. She did drugs and had another boyfriend, and the first boyfriend found out and got jealous....She went back with him though.... Violence is pretty much common in people's lives. About 95 percent of the world is angry. They attack things or litter, abuse people, and do other bad things like rape or kill. It's just the way it is.

Even though the community is seen as "a pretty good place to live" and "overall a nice neighborhood," the girls' descriptions of residency quickly devolve into stories of violence – mostly violence directed toward women by the hands of men in both public and private spaces. As Jamie – who lives across the street from a tavern – watches out the window from her second-storey flat, it is a normal occurrence for men to hit women in public sites, such as in a bar or on the street. As Christina walks through her neighborhood, she observes that violence also exists between men and women behind the closed doors of homes. Christina also notes that women often return to their abusive partners. Lisette distinguishes between different types of abuse – physical and mental – and gives examples of abuse between mothers and boyfriends, daughters and sons.[3] Rosie, it can be argued, is so desensitized to abuse that she humorously recalls how a badly beaten friend of her mother resembled a "purple people eater." In Rosie's view, "About 95 percent of the world is angry...it's just the way it is."

Although these girls may look at abuse differently, they all are quick to recognize violence as a defining feature of their community. Many mention that women "go back" to their abuser as if it were acceptable or normal for men to abuse women, and that it is the women's duty to negotiate their way around this violence. Again, missing in these arguments is the recognition that men are responsible for their abusive behavior. The only critique articulated is raised by Lisette, but it is directed toward neighborhood mothers whom she feels are not adequately putting their children's needs first.

Despite their young ages, the Canal Town girls have heard of abuse in a variety of different contexts and forms and, according to their narrations, women in this neighborhood do not always endure their violence in isolation. Rosie, for example, reveals that a neighbor sought refuge with her mother after a severe beating. Abuse, however, is seemingly concealed within the community – that is, complaints rarely reach a more public forum.

For girls, abuse does not just exist in public places and in the private dwellings of others. Violence also occurs in their own homes. In talking about personal experiences with abuse, they typically contextualize violence as part of the past, as "things are better now." The younger girls, though, are not consistent in packaging such events in history. For instance, Elizabeth and Sally shift from present to past in describing the abuse in their homes. Many women recall chilling vignettes of unbridled rage that pattern their upbringing.

ELIZABETH: I want my mother's boyfriend to stop drinking so much. He drinks a lot. Like a sink full of beer cans because his friends come over a lot too. They bring over cases and he usually gets drunk off a 12 pack....Like every other day he will start screaming and blaming things on my sister me and my mom. My mom tells him, "No, it's not our fault." He forgets a lot too, like what he did with his money, or where he puts his pens and pencils. He starts screaming at us because he thinks we take them. The house has to be a certain way. If one thing is out of place, he'll hit us or lock us in the closet for awhile until my mom screams so much he lets us out...but things are better now.

SALLY: I used to think of myself as a zero, like I was nothing. I was stupid; I couldn't do anything...I don't anymore because we're all done with the violence in my house...I've tried to keep it out since I was a kid....My mom and John [her mother's boyfriend] will argue over the littlest things. My mom is someone who is a violent person too. Sometimes she hits us, or he does. Then she would take a shower and we would get all dressed up, and we would all go out somewhere. After something bad would happen, she would try to make it better. She's a real fun person....We're really close. We make cookies together and breakfast together.

ANNE: My mom and her boyfriend constantly fight because they drink. When I was little, I remember being in my bed. I was sleeping, only my other sisters came and woke me up because my mom and her boyfriend were fighting. We [Anne and her sisters] started crying. I was screaming. My sisters were trying to calm me down. Our door was above the staircase and you could see the front door. I just had visions of me running out the door to get help because I was so scared. My oldest sister was like nine or ten and I had to go the bathroom and we only have one and it was downstairs. She sneaked me downstairs and into the kitchen and there was glasses smashed all over, there were plants underwater, the phone cord was underwater in the kitchen sink. It was just a wreck everywhere. But most of all, there were streams of blood mixing in with the water, on the floor, on the walls.

ROSIE: I remember one Christmas my mom and my uncle were fighting. I escaped out the window to get help for my mom. We were living on the bottom floor at the time. I didn't have time to take a coat or mittens, I just grabbed my goldfish bowl...I think it was because I didn't want to ever go back there. I immediately ran to the [community] center but it was closed, being like three in the morning or something. So I just ran around the neighborhood and water was splashing out of my goldfish bowl, and the fish were dying, and I was freezing, and I couldn't even scream anymore.

As these narrations indicate, domestic violence patterns the lives of these girls. In a moment of desperation, Rosie seeks refuge at the community center, but it has long closed for the night. Mom can offer little salvation as she is often drunk, violent herself, or powerless as the man in her life is on an abusive rampage. As they escape into the icy night or are locked in closets, these females have little recourse from the extreme and terrifying conditions that govern their lives. In Sally's case, her mother is also violent yet is thought of as making up for that abuse by involving her daughter in family-style activities. Sally learns, therefore, not to see or feel pain. Given these accounts, it is easy for me to conclude that the effects of domestic violence are not something that can be contained at home, and the Canal Town girls indicate that exposure to abuse profoundly shapes their behavior in other places, such as school.

ELIZABETH: About twice a month they [her mother and mother's boyfriend] fight. But not that far apart. Last time he [the boyfriend] smacked me, I had a red hand on my face. I walked around with a red hand on my face, only I wouldn't let anybody see it...I skipped school and the [community] center for, like, three days so no one would ask me about it...I hid in my closet until you could barely see it. Then when I went back to school, I stayed real quiet because I didn't want people to look at me, notice the hand on my face.

CHRISTINA: When I had a boyfriend, he [her father] got so mad at me. He told me I wasn't allowed to have a boyfriend. I didn't know that because he never told me. He said that if he ever saw him again, I would get my ass kicked. So one day he heard that Robbie [her boyfriend] walked me to school. Well, he [her father] came over that night and pulled down my pants and whipped me with his belt. I was bloody and the next day full of bruises. But I hurt more from being embarrassed to have my pants pulled down at my age. It hurt to sit all day long at school; that's all I could concentrate on. I couldn't go to the nurse because then she would find out. Nobody knew how I hurt under my clothes. I couldn't go to gym because people would find out, so I skipped. I hid in the bathroom but got picked up by the hall monitor who accused me of skipping gym to smoke. I just got so mad when I heard this, I pushed her [the hall monitor] away from me and yelled. I was out of control with anger when they were dragging me down to the principal's. I got suspended for a week and had to talk to a school psychologist for two weeks about how bad smoking is for your health.

ROSIE: My mom got money from her boyfriend for my school pictures, and when they came back, he saw them as I was getting ready for school...he threw them and said that I messed up my hair. But I got up an hour early that day to fix it, I remember, only my hair just flattened, not on purpose. He got real mad and picked up a lamp and threw it at her and it hit her but I tried to block it and got hit too. It fell on the floor all in pieces. She was crying because she was hurt and because he left and I was crying because I knew she would let him come back. So we were both crying picking up the glass. Then I walked to school and I didn't open up my mouth once all day because I thought I would cry if I did.

ANNE: Sometimes at school I just avoid teachers because they might feel sorry for me because they might see like bruises or something....Sometimes I act bad so they won't feel sorry for me, then if they see a bruise or something they would think I deserved it. I would rather have them think that than getting the principal or nurse.

The glimpses into these lives suggest children from violent homes are learning at very young ages how to negotiate lives that are enmeshed inside a web of overwhelming circumstances. Elizabeth talks about how her mother's boyfriend blames her and her mother and sister for all that is wrong, while Rosie gets hit with a lamp while trying to protect her mom. As they devise ways to conceal their bruises, they each face their pain alone. Elizabeth skips school and seeks shelter from the world in the same closet in which she is punished by her mother's boyfriend. Christina is choked on her anger and pain and separates herself from school activity only to become embroiled in another set of problems. As Rosie quietly sits through class, her physical and mental pain renders her completely disengaged from academic and social life at school. Anne deliberately acts bad to distract teachers from focusing on her scars of abuse.

The narrations of the poor white girls in this study reflect findings in much of the existing research (Weis, Marusza-Hall, and Fine 1998). As these girls indicate, abuse at home makes it difficult to concentrate in school, and the hurt, anger, and fear that they harbor inside often render them silent, which also corroborates these studies (Elkind 1984; Jaffe, Wolfe, and Wilson 1990). According to Afulayan (1993), some children blame themselves for the abuse and skip school to protect a parent from the abuser, while other children become ill from worry. Depression, sleep disturbances, suicidal tendencies, and low self-esteem are other symptoms exhibited among children living in violent homes (Hughes 1988; Reid, Kavanaugh, and Baldwin 1987).

All of these girls reveal they spend incredible energy on keeping their abuse a secret while in school. This is likely in response to a number of fears, including fear of public embarrassment, fear of further angering an abuser, or fear that families will be torn apart by authorities. While observing the girls at school, I noticed that some of them sustained bruises that could not be so easily hidden under long sleeves or turtlenecks. One day, for example, Christina came to school wearing an excessive amount of eye makeup, which was noticeable, considering she usually did not wear any. While talking to her outside after school, I realized this was probably an attempt to conceal a black eye, which could clearly be seen in the harsh light of day.

Interestingly, I did not hear any talk of domestic violence at school – critical or otherwise. This finding parallels the poor and working-class white women in the study of Weis et al. (1997) who also were silent about the abuse in their lives, which was similarly not interrupted by schools, the legal system, and so forth. It did not seem to me that any of the girls sought help at school from their white female peers, teachers, or anyone else in coping with abuse. Instead, in the space of the school, a code of silence surrounding domestic violence prevailed, even though the girls articulate an awareness of others' abuse throughout the community. Not once did I hear students or teachers query others about violence, nor was abuse even mentioned as a social problem in classes in which human behavior was discussed. Even on the day that Christina came to school attempting to camouflage a bruised eye, I did not observe a teacher pull her aside to talk, nor did I hear her friends ask her if she was all right. Dragged by their families from one violent situation to the next, it is remarkable that these girls are, for the most part, able to get through the school day, go home, and come back again tomorrow.

Conclusion

The Canal Town girls are from families that had been working-class for generations. Born into the snares of a postindustrial economy, today these girls are growing up in poverty. As their narrations on work and family indicate, gender arrangements in their lives echo those of the working class in which women are subordinate to men. Embedded in this subordination is a silencing of domestic violence.

Domestic violence runs painfully deep in the lives of the Canal Town girls. These girls are socialized at an early age to conceal abuse from those outside the community who might take action. As a method of coping, they have learned to work around abuse to such an extent that by envisioning their future lives as financially independent, they hope to sidestep violence. The sting of abuse provides much of the scaffolding for how these girls wish to construct their lives, and men are seemingly not taken to task. In this tight-knit community, it often hurts to be a girl.

During an entire year of field work, I never saw or heard a teacher approach a student concerning domestic violence. I also never witnessed a teacher initiate a discussion on the topic of abuse in class. Throughout the year, I had the opportunity to ask all of the teachers if they had knowledge of the extent of violence in the Canal Town community or the possibility of abuse in the lives of their students. The teachers had little to say on this topic, many indicating they had not thought much about domestic violence, although they "wouldn't be surprised."

By not responding to violence in the home, institutions that structure the lives of these girls, such as schools, arguably contribute to its concealment. The guidelines already in place in some schools, the counselors, and child abuse training for teachers do not typically address the needs of battered youth. Due to shame or punishment that awaits at home, youth do not always visit a counselor. It is often the case that teachers also are afraid to report abuse – afraid of upsetting the students, parents, and school administrators. Perhaps educators feel "unsure" about their suspicions and "wait" to see more evidence. Indeed, alerting Child Protective Services many times leads to further abuse by an angered parent. Likewise, police investigations and court appearances often prove unproductive and humiliating for women and children (Weis, Marusza-Hall, and Fine 1998).

Educators must come to the conclusion that at least some students in their classes go home to abusive situations. Teachers and policy-makers, therefore, are confronted with the task of formulating more tangible responses. In English and history classes, boys and girls can often be led in critical discussions about domestic violence – as it relates to classroom material and to daily life. Through these lessons, abuse must be positioned as abnormal behavior, with social and historical roots that can be unraveled. Older kids can also be encouraged to enter internships at domestic violence shelters and hotlines, so youth can learn that abuse is wrong, it is not a personal problem, and there is some recourse (Weis, Marusza-Hall, and Fine 1998).

Educators and social scientists must additionally seek out other safe spaces in students' lives where critical conversations can take place (Fine and Weis 1998; Weis, Marusza-Hall, and Fine 1998). The Canal Town girls, for example, are regular visitors to a neighborhood community center. Places such as community centers, arts programs, and youth groups offer a location that is unbounded by state guidelines where such talk can happen. By conducting workshops in these sites by those who run domestic violence shelters, youth can be led to think critically about abuse and can come realize they are not alone and that there is a possibility for a different way of life.

NOTES

1 This name is based on the fact that during the early 1800s, this area of the city was selected as the last stop on a major canal that was constructed across the state. This opened up the city, transforming it into a formidable site for the production and transport of steel. During the past few decades, however, most of this industry has left the area.

2 Boys living in violent homes may experience more abuse than girls. This has been found to be the case because, when angry, boys typically act out more than girls. Because this acting out is more apt to enrage a violent adult, boys often end up as a more primary target (Jouriles and Norwood 1995).

3 This sophisticated way of looking at abuse is likely attributed to the extremely close relationship Lisette has with Ruby, the white middle-aged activities director at the local community center, who also serves as an informal counselor to white neighborhood youth.

REFERENCES

Afulayan, J. 1993. Consequences of domestic violence on elementary school education. *Child and Family Therapy* 15:55–58.

Bluestone, B., and B. Harrison. 1982. *The Deindustrialization of America: Plant Closings, Community Abandonment, and the Dismantling of Basic Industry*. New York: Basic Books.

Borman, K., E. Mueninghoff, and S. Piazza. 1988. Urban Appalachian girls and young women: Bowing to no one. In *Class, Race, and Gender in American Education*, ed. L. Weis. Albany: State University of New York.

DeYoung, A. 1995. *The Life and Death of a Rural American High School: Farewell Little Kanawha*. New York: Garland.

Elkind, P. 1984. *All Grown Up and No Place To Go*. Reading, MA: Addison-Wesley.

Everhart, R. 1983. *Reading, Writing and Resistance: Adolescence and Labor in a Junior High School*. Boston: Routledge & Kegan Paul.

Finders, M. 1996. *Just Girls: Hidden Literacies and Life in Junior High*. New York: Teachers College Press.

Fine, M, and L. Weis. 1998. *The Unknown City: The Lives of Poor and Working-Class Young Adults*. New York: Beacon.

Hall, J. 2001. *Canal Town Youth: Community Organization and the Development of Adolescent Identity*. New York: State University of New York Press.

Holland, D., and M. Eisenhart. 1990. *Educated in Romance: Women, Achievement, and College Culture*. Chicago: University of Chicago Press.

Hughes, H. 1988. Psychological and behavioral correlates of family violence in child witnesses and victims. *American Journal of Orthopsychiatry* 58:77–90.

Jaffe, P., S. Wolfe, and S. Wilson. 1990. *Children of Battered Women*. Newbury Park, CA: Sage.

Jouriles, E., and W. Norwood. 1995. Physical aggression toward boys and girls in families characterized by the battering of women. *Journal of Family Psychology* 9:69–78.

May, M. 1987. The historical problem of the family wage: The Ford Motor Company and the five dollar day. In *Families and Work*, ed. N. Gerstel and H. E. Gross. Philadelphia, PA: Temple University Press.

McRobbie, A. 1991. *Feminism and Youth Culture: From Jackie to Just Seventeen*. Boston: Unwin Hyman.

Oliver, M., and T. Shapiro. 1995. *Black Wealth, White Wealth: A New Perspective on Racial Inequality*. New York: Routledge.

Perry, D. 1996. *Governance in Erie County: A Foundation for Understanding and Action*. Buffalo: State University of New York Press.

Raissiguier, C. 1994. *Becoming Women, Becoming Workers: Identity Formation in a French Vocational School*. Albany: State University of New York Press.

Reid, J., T. Kavanaugh, and J. Baldwin. 1987. Abusive parents' perception of child problem behavior: An example of paternal violence. *Journal of Abnormal Child Psychology* 15:451–466.

Smith, D. 1987. *The Everyday World as Problematic: A Feminist Sociology*. Boston: Northeastern University Press.

Smith, D. 1988. Femininity as discourse. In *Becoming Feminine: The Politics of Popular Culture*, ed. L. Roman, L. Christian-Smith, and E. Ellsworth. London: Falmer.

Valli, L. 1988. Gender identity and the technology of office education. In *Class, Race, and Gender in American Education*, ed. L. Weis. Albany: State University of New York Press.

Weis, L. 1990. *Working Class without Work*. New York: Routledge.

Weis, L., M. Fine, A. Proweller, C. Bertram, and J. Marusza-Hall. 1997. I've slept in clothes long enough: Excavating the sounds of domestic violence among women in the white working class. *Urban Review* 30:43–62.

Weis, L., J. Marusza-Hall, and M. Fine. 1998. Out of the cupboard: Kids, domestic violence, and schools. *British Journal of Sociology of Education* 19:53–73.

Woodcock Tentler, L. W. 1979. *Wage Earning Women: Industrial Work and Family Life in the US 1900–1930*. New York: Oxford University Press.

19

White Means Never Having To Say You're Ethnic: White Youth and the Construction of "Cultureless" Identities

Pamela Perry

Culturelessness can serve, even if unintentionally, as a measure of white racial superiority.

"How would you describe white American culture?" I ask Laurie, a white, middle-class senior at Valley Groves High,[1] a predominantly white, suburban public school near the Pacific Coast of northern California. She pauses, her face looking visibly perplexed as if she did not understand the question or her mind was drawing a blank. Wondering if she heard me over the roar of the cappuccino machine in the background, I awkwardly reiterate, "Like, you know, what would you say white American culture is like?"

"I wouldn't be able to tell you. I don't know." She pauses again and laughs nervously. "When you think about it, it's like – [a longer pause] – *I don't know!*"

About 20 miles away from Valley Groves is the postindustrial city of Clavey. Clavey High School is composed of a brilliant mosaic of students from different ethnic and racial groups, about 12 percent of whom are white. In an interview with Murray, a white, Jewish, middle-class senior, he and I talked a great deal about the consequences of race in the United States and what privileges come with being a white person here. When I probed into his identification with being white or Jewish, he said,

> [Cultural pride] doesn't make sense to me. To me it doesn't. I mean, what difference does it make what my great-great-grandfather was or his whole generation. That's not affecting my life....I'm still here now. I've got to make what's best for me in the future. I can't harp on what the past has brought.

Laurie and Murray express what the racial category "white" means to each of them. Although their responses differ markedly, they share something fundamental; they perceive white raciality as cultureless. For Laurie, whiteness is not culturally defined. She lives within it but cannot name it. It is taken for granted. For Murray, to be cultural means having emotional attachment to tradition and history. He eschews culture, in this regard, and lives in the present, looking forward.

I chose these two excerpts from qualitative research I carried out in 1994–97 at Valley Groves, a predominantly white, suburban high school, and Clavey, a multiracial, urban high school. The focus of this research was on what differences, if any, the two demographically distinct contexts made on the ways white youth reflected on and constructed white identities. I found that it made a large difference: white students at Valley Groves did not reflect on or define white identity as a culture and social location to the extent that the white youth at Clavey did. Moreover, white identities at Clavey tended to be altogether more variable and contradictory than at Valley Groves. Elsewhere, I argue that these differences in white identities were conditioned by different experiences and structures of interracial association (Perry 1998).

I make a similar argument in this article but with a focus on the only similarity between the ways whites at both schools defined white identity. They defined white as cultureless. By that, I mean that white identity was understood to have no ties or allegiances to European ancestry and culture, no "traditions." To the white youth, only "ethnic" people had such ties to the past. The students would agree with George De Vos (1975) that a "feeling of continuity with the past" distinguishes an "ethnic" group from peoples with more "present-oriented" or "future-oriented" identities (p. 17) – such as whites.

However, although white students at Valley Groves and Clavey shared this perception of white identity, they did not arrive at it by the same processes. In what follows, I present and interpret ethnographic and interview data to argue that at Valley Groves, the tendency for youth to explicitly define themselves and other whites as people without culture came about through processes of *naturalization* – the embedding of historically constituted cultural practices in that which is taken for granted and seems "normal" and natural. At Clavey, culturelessness was achieved through processes of *rationalization* – the embedding of whiteness within a Western rational epistemology and value paradigm that marginalizes or subordinates all things "cultural."

Although there is some scholarly debate over whether there is such a thing as "white culture" (Ignatiev and Garvey 1996; Roediger 1994), my argument here is not so much about whether there is or is not a white culture but about the power whites exercise when *claiming* they have no culture. Culturelessness can serve, even if unintentionally, as a measure of white racial superiority. It suggests that one is either "normal" and "simply human" (therefore, the standard to which others should strive) or beyond culture or "postcultural" (therefore, developmentally advanced).

This work seeks to advance on theories and research in critical white studies, the sociology of education, and racial-ethnic identity formation by vividly illustrating the social construction of white identities and culture in schooling and the ways that different social-structural contexts differently influence constructions of whiteness, including the construction of white as cultureless or the norm.

Previous Scholarship on White Culture

While I was conducting my research, the field of "critical white studies" was birthing with a dizzying amount of literature on whiteness. Widely interdisciplinary, whiteness scholarship cannot be reduced to any small set of theoretical currents, but it may be safe to say that it has been preeminently concerned with exposing the ways white domination is sustained and reproduced in invisible ways. Scholars within critical white studies have revealed the perniciousness of whiteness as it hides in literature, art, and popular culture (Dyer 1997; Giroux 1997; Hill 1997; hooks 1992; Morrison 1993; Pfeil 1995); work and educational institutional structures (Essed 1996; Fine et al. 1997); pedagogy (Giroux 1997; McCarthy and Crichlow 1993); the law and property rights

(Haney Lopez 1996; Harris 1993; Lipsitz 1995); the values and identities of whites in the historical past (Allen 1994; Almaguer 1994; Goldberg 1993; Ignatiev 1995; Jacobson 1998; Lott 1993; Roediger 1991, 1994; Saxton 1990; Ware 1992); and the historical present (Frankenberg 1993, 1997; Gallagher 1995, 1997; Hartigan 1997, 1999; Kenny 2000b; Segrest 1994; Wellman 1977; Wray and Newitz 1997).

Among whiteness scholars, *whiteness* and *white culture* are frequently conflated, especially when whiteness is understood as a whole symbolic system and way of life through which whites make sense of themselves and their social relations. Possibly because of this, few have directly addressed the invisibility of white culture as a set of "bounded" – that is, clearly named and defined – practices and values with historical antecedents. Among those who have, Ruth Frankenberg (1993) has best articulated a widespread understanding that white culture is "invisible" because it is constructed as "normal." The white women she interviewed felt that they were culturally empty. Frankenberg argues that the women's discourses suggest that their felt sense of cultural emptiness stems from a dualistic sense of unbounded white versus bounded (nonwhite) others. As the norm and standard, white culture has no definition, only those who *deviate* from the norm have "culture." And therein lies the toxicity of the construction of white as the (cultureless) norm: it serves as a basis on which to measure the humanity and social standing of others.

Historian David Roediger (1994) has a slightly different critique of white culture. Like Frankenberg (1993), he observes that white culture is devoid of a kind of bounded quality. He asserts that whites lack any community or direct continuity with some past, unlike African Americans or even white ethnics like Italian Americans. However, Roediger does not believe that culturelessness is merely a false consciousness but the truth about whiteness. For Roediger, there is no white culture, and white domination is exercised not from a racial norm–other dualism but through "an identity based on what one isn't and on whom one can hold back" (p. 13). I understand Roediger to be arguing that white culture is not merely absent, it is, in a sense, anticulture – predicated on subjugating those "with" culture.

I do not agree with Roediger (1994) that white culture is altogether nonexistent. It may be invisible and taken for granted for many whites, but it is "real," often oppressively so.[2] One objective of this and my wider work is precisely to make white culture visible and thus disarm its cloaked perniciousness. However, Roediger's implication that white culture is by definition anticulture is more descriptive of the power of whiteness than, merely, white as "norm," which can imply that it is "neutral" or passive in its effects. Two other scholars, anthropologist Renato Rosaldo (1989) and philosopher David Theo Goldberg (1993), have produced elaborated arguments on the theme of white anticulture. Rosaldo points out that everyone has culture; it fundamentally shapes all people's understanding of themselves and the world. But the *visibility* of one's culture differs according to social status. Drawing on observations in the Philippines, Mexico, and the United States, Rosaldo argues that cultural invisibility is a characteristic of all those who hold full citizenship and institutional power in the nation state. Cultural invisibility is a privileged status marking the most "rational" (and, hence, deserving of power and privilege) peoples against those who are not rational, those who are "cultural" (pp. 198–199). He introduces the concept "postcultural" to define cultural invisibility and to codify how the *denial* of culture marks one's place on the high end of the social hierarchy. Rosaldo's argument suggests that, if at one time Western Europeans had to define themselves as cultural to set themselves apart from and superior to "savages," today, with much of the world "civilized" under Western domination, whites must claim a new and higher rung – the postcultural – to maintain their privileged status.

Evident in the above arguments is the understanding that white culture has historically been molded by the values and sociodiscursive constructs of the European Enlightenment and, specifically, the rule of reason. Goldberg (1993) lays this out thoroughly in his book *Racist Culture*. He asserts that racial exclusions and inclusions have historically been made and authorized by Western rational authority. The grounds for exclusion of non-Westerners have been reason or, rather, the claimed absence of reason. However, the standards of "Reason in modernity arose against the backdrop of European domination and subjugation of nature, especially human nature" (p. 119). Hence, Goldberg argues, irrationality does not refer to the inability to meet expectations of "logical noncontradiction or consistency" but rather the inability to "exhibit the values, metaphysical attitudes, epistemological principles, or cognitive styles of 'whitemales'" (ibid.). Those values, attitudes, principles, and styles include individual responsibility and self-determination, a self-concept that is wedded to freedom from the past, and the primacies of the mind over the body, the intellect over emotion, and order over chaos.[3]

These scholars, to varying degrees and in divergent ways, point out that white culture *is* Western European rational culture and that whites (white propertied males especially) are the unconditional beneficiaries of rationalism in that they are constructed as the most rational and, therefore, the most superior of all peoples.[4] Being rational, whiteness must deny culture to the extent that culture is understood as sets of practices that carry affective and valued continuities with the past. Rational whiteness is postcultural. It is anticulture.

This explains, in my view, the persistence of cultureless whiteness in the two different schools in this study; cultureless whiteness is a form of hegemonic power and, therefore, widespread. However, my work suggests that different contexts may require different strategies to maintain the illusion of cultureless whiteness. I propose that the naturalization of whiteness most easily occurs where white cultural practices are ubiquitous and self-confirming, such as at Valley Groves High. In contexts in which naturalization processes are weak, such as Clavey High, where whites are a numerical and cultural minority, then rationalization processes come into the foreground.

Method and Reflections

The vast wealth of excellent scholarship on the social construction of identities in schooling fundamentally shaped my research focus and methodology (Bourdieu and Passeron 1977; Davidson 1996; Eckert 1989; Fordham 1996; Fordham and Ogbu 1986; Kinney 1993; MacLeod 1987; Thorne 1993; Valenzuela 1999). The main focus of my work was what role, if any, close interracial association in school had on the racial consciousness and identities of white youth. Therefore, in choosing my research sites, I looked for two schools: one predominantly white and located in a predominantly white town or city; the other multiracial, minority white and located in a minority white town or city. It also concerned me that the schools be in the same geographical region, of similar size and academic standing, and with student bodies of similar socioeconomic backgrounds to keep those factors as "constant" as possible. I studied census data and school statistics for different towns and cities across the United States before I decided on Valley Groves, which was 83 percent white, and Clavey, which was 12 percent white. Although Clavey was located in a city and Valley Groves a suburb, Clavey was very similar to Valley Groves in all respects besides racial composition, largely due to the fact that Clavey's catchment area encircled a largely middle- to upper-middle-class population. Particularly important for my research was that white students at Clavey were primarily middle-class, which allowed me to focus on middle-class whites in both schools.

I spent two and a half years in the schools doing participant observation and in-depth interviewing. Daily practices included sitting in on classrooms with students, hanging out with them during breaks and lunch, attending school club meetings, and participating in student-administrator advisory committees, especially those concerned with race and cultural awareness on campus. I also observed or helped out with after-school programs and events, such as school plays, major rallies, games, and the junior and senior balls of each school. To familiarize myself with the music and leisure activities the students were involved in, after hours I listened to the local rap, R & B, punk, alternative, and classic rock radio stations; bought CDs of the most popular musical artists; went to live underground punk and alternative concerts; read fanzines and other youth magazines; watched MTV; studied music that students dubbed for me; and attended a large rave produced by some Clavey students.

Although I looked somewhat younger than my age (38 when the research began), I made concerted efforts to minimize the effects of age difference on how students related to me. I did not associate with other adults on campus. I dressed casually in attire that I was comfortable in, which happened to be similar to the attire students were comfortable in: blue jeans, sandals or athletic shoes, T-shirt or sweat-shirt, no jewelry except four tiny hoop earrings – one in one ear, three in the other. I had students call me by my first name, and I did not talk down to them, judge them, or otherwise present myself as an authority figure. To the contrary, I saw the students as the authorities, and they seemed to appreciate that regard. Those efforts, on top of having developed some popular-cultural frames of reference with the students, contributed to my developing some very close relationships with several of the students and fairly wide access to different peer groups and cliques on campus. Having stood in the middle of secret hideouts, food fights, fist fights, tongue lashings, and over-the-top fits of goofiness, I can say that in most cases, I seemed to have little impact on students' behaviors.

My other most apparent traits – race, gender, and middle-class/intellectual appearance – had both positive and negative effects. I connected most readily and easily with girls. The results were that I have more narrative data and in-depth material from girls than boys. At Clavey, however, I did make a few close relationships with boys that I believe helped balance my findings at that school. Similarly, my class background made crossing class differences awkward at times for me and for some participants, particularly working-class males. However, since I was focusing on middle-class white students, my own middle-class whiteness seemed to work mostly on my behalf. With respect to students of color, of which I interviewed quite a few, my race limited my ability to hang out with them in groups at school. Because my focus was on white students, I do not feel this limitation seriously compromises my argument, but deeper perspectives from students of color would certainly have improved it.

I formally interviewed more than 60 students at Valley Groves and Clavey. They included, at Valley Groves, 14 white youth, one Filipino female, and a group of 10 African American students. At Clavey, I interviewed 22 white youth, 10 African American youth, two Chinese American, one Filipino, and two Latino youth. A little more than half of my interviewees were female and the rest male. Most were middle-class, but six were working-class.[5]

I did not randomly sample interview participants because I had very specific desires regarding to whom I wanted to speak: liberals and conservatives; whites, blacks, Asians, and Latinos; punks, hippies, homies, alternatives, rappers, and such; high achievers and low achievers; girls and boys; middle-class and working-class. So I sought out interviewees through multiple methods. Mostly, I directly approached students I observed in classrooms or in their cliques, but I also went to club meetings and asked for volunteers and, for the hard-to-find students, sought recommendations or introductions from youth.

Interviews took place on campus, in coffee shops, and in students' homes and generally lasted two hours. Students and their parents signed consent forms that explained that I was examining racial identities and race relations in the two demographically distinct contexts. In the interviews, I explored youth's experiences at school, their experiences of racial difference, how they thought of themselves racially, how they thought of racial-ethnic others, their cultural interests and other significant identities, and what types of meanings they gave to their interests and identities. Interviews and informal discussions were also a time for me to discuss with youth my interpretations of school practices, youth cultures, and other events around campus. Students spoke candidly and openly; they seemed eager to talk to an adult who would listen to and treat them respectfully.

The interviews were tape-recorded and transcribed. They and my field notes were manually coded and analyzed along the way to illuminate processes, practices, terms, and conceptions calling for deeper investigation or changes in focus. Along the way, also, I read widely, looking for existing studies and theories that might shed analytical light on my observations. My final coding and analysis were carried out without the aid of software – only colored markers, a Xerox machine, and lots of post-its.

Identity Naturalization at Valley Groves High: Passive Construction of White as Cultureless

Valley Groves is a suburban city of roughly 115,000 people. Its residents are solidly white and middle- to upper-middle class. In 1990, 83 percent of the population of Valley Groves was white, and the median household income was $42,095. Inside Valley Groves High School's catchment area is Mapleton, a small suburb of about 7,500 people. Ninety percent of Mapleton residents are white, and their median household income in 1989 was $70,000.

The racial and class demographics of Valley Groves and Mapleton cities were reflected in the composition of the Valley Groves High student body and staff. In the 1995–96 school year, white youth made up 83 percent of the school population, followed by Hispanics (7 percent), Asians (5 percent), Filipinos (2 percent), and African Americans (2 percent). The 53 teachers, five administrators, three campus supervisors, and 50-odd service and administrative staff were 85 percent non-Hispanic white. There was only one African American among them.

Raymond Williams (1976) wrote,

> Hegemony supposes the existence of something that is truly total...which is lived at such a depth, which saturates the society to such an extent, and which, as Gramsci put it, even constitutes the limit of commonsense for most people under its sway. (pp. 204–205)

At Valley Groves, whiteness "saturated" youth's lived experience. White youth and adults overwhelmed the demographic landscape. When I asked white students at Valley Groves how they would rate their experiences of people of color, most said "very little" or "none at all." In the school yard during lunch or break, students sauntered into the "quad," a large patio area in the center of the campus, to meet with friends and grab a bite to eat. At these times, the most open and public spaces were a sea of blonde-and brown-haired white girls and boys in blue jeans and T-shirts sporting logos of their favorite rock band or skateboard company. The popular and nondescript kids (usually called "normal") occupied the main quad, and the counterculture white students – druggies, skaters, hicks – claimed territory in outside areas adjoining the quad.

Some African American, Asian, or Latino students joined with white friends, and, when they did, they assumed the styles and demeanors of the crowd they were in, be it "popular," "skater," or merely "normal." Then, there were the students of color who clustered in groups of like-kind, racial ethnically. They wore their own styles; spoke in Tagalog, Spanish, or black English; and usually hung out in the cafeteria, classrooms, or distant corners of the campus, locations that kept them virtually invisible to the majority of students in and around the quad.

Similar spatial demographics, in which racial-ethnic difference was placed where it did not challenge the white norm, existed in the classroom structure (Fine 1989). The mainstream students – the popular kids, athletes, and college-bound youth – were in the honors and other high-tracked classes. The "regular" classes were made up of a hodge-podge of different types of youth – middle-class mainstream, working-class, countercultural. With the exception of some of the high-tracked math classes, in which Asian American students were overrepresented, high and regular-tracked courses were disproportionately white, with small numbers of minority youth distributed equally among them. Just where the students of color were I am sorry to say I never learned the answer to, except that one day I saw a large (disproportionate) number of them in a remedial class.

Whiteness saturated Valley Groves school life not only demographically but culturally as well. The dominant culture at Valley Groves – that which oriented the social organization of students, common styles and practices, and expected behaviors – was homologous with the dominant culture outside of the campus, namely, a white European American culture. By "white European American culture," I refer to two features of American culture, broadly. First, although the dominant culture in the United States is syncretic, that is, composed of the different cultures of the peoples that populate the United States, several of its core characteristics are of European origin. These include, as I have already suggested, the values and practices derived from the European Enlightenment, Anglican Protestantism, and Western colonialism, such as rationalism, individualism, personal responsibility, a strong work ethnic, self-effacement, and mastery over nature. I include, also, carryover or "melted" material cultures of Western, Eastern, and Southern European peoples, such as hamburgers, spaghetti, cupcakes, parades, and line dancing. Second, by virtue of being numerically and politically dominant, whites tend to share certain dispositions, worldviews, and identities constituted by that, especially in predominantly white communities. Currently, a race-neutral or "color-blind" worldview and sense of oneself as normal are examples of that.

At Valley Groves, student cliques and social categories revolved around a norm–other dichotomy in which normal meant that one conformed to the dominant culture and expectations placed on them, and other meant one did not. For example, when I asked Billy how he would describe his group of friends he said,

> "Normal. We don't smoke or drink or anything and [we] wear clothes we would call normal."
> "And what is that?" I asked.
> "Not oversized, baggy clothes like the skaters wear, or, obviously, we don't wear cowboy hats or boots."

The normal clothes Billy referred to were the styles one might find at mainstream department stores like The Gap: loose, not overly baggy blue jeans; cotton T-shirts and blouses; sundresses; khaki shorts. The kids who did not dress or act normal served to define the boundaries of what was and was not normal. For instance, skaters wore excessively baggy pants and overall filthy clothes; "hicks" wore ten-gallon cowboy hats, tooled-leather boots, and tight jeans with big brassy pants buckles; and druggies flagrantly carried and consumed illicit drugs. (*Flagrant* is the key word here since, as a popular girl told me, "Popular kids do drugs. They just don't want anyone to know it.") Carli, a white girl who considered herself "hippie," referred to the non-mainstream kids as "rebels." She said, "I call them rebels 'cause they know the system sucks."

This norm–other dichotomy was race-neutral. Maria, a popular senior of Mexican American descent on her mother's side, told me that the "first cut of students starts with who is popular" and who fits in with the other cliques on campus. Anyone, regardless of racial-ethnic ascription, could be popular, a skater, a druggie – even a "homie," which, as groups went at Valley Groves, was the most nonwhite. Price of admission was conformity to the styles and demeanor of the group. Hence, black kids who were skaters were not "black skaters," nor were white kids who were homies "white homies"; they were simply "skaters" and "homies," respectively. A white skater I spoke to pointed to an African American boy in his crowd and said. "That doesn't matter. We all love to skate together, hang out together." And when I asked black students if the white kids who were homies were considered "wanna-be black," they looked flatly at me and said, "No." Ron, who was a homie himself, said, "One of the guys who hangs out with us is white. He's not a racist and we've known each other for years."

Students' measuring sticks for gauging normal styles, behaviors, and expectations were the common, everyday practices and the system of rewards at school. On any given day at Valley Groves High, students attended classes and romped into the quad at break and lunch to purchase anything from fresh cinnamon rolls, cupcakes, rice crispy bars, and fudge for snacks to pizza, hamburgers, meat loaf, and spaghetti for something more substantial. On occasion, leadership students played rock music over the loudspeakers while students talked among themselves in their friendship groups. Circulating through the youth were members of the administrative staff, who would greet students by their first names and engage them in casual conversation, and the team of grounds supervisors, all of whom were greying, middle-aged women. One was affectionately referred to as "Grandma."

"These are all good kids," is what administrators, teachers, and ground supervisors would say to me nearly every time I spoke with them. As Bourdieu (1977) argues, the embodiment of practices and ideas into that which feels normal, natural, and "common sense" requires collective reinforcement and approval. Adult approval rating of the students was high, and they let students know that with their smiles and friendly banter. It was demonstrated also, I believe, through the grounds supervisors, who, by virtue of their title (as opposed to "security") and appearance, demonstrated an implicit trust the adults had that students would, for the most part, comply with expected behaviors. (At least, adults trusted that the white students would comply. Students of color, especially black boys who wore hip-hop styles, told me that they experienced considerable racial profiling by school administrators and the grounds supervisors. This explicitly racial treatment of students of color was either not witnessed by whites or rubbed out of their minds, which I believe played a role in maintaining the pretense of race neutrality on campus.)

At schoolwide rallies and events, collective consensus, reinforcement, and approval of white American norms came from an even wider span of individuals: school adults, other students, and the outside community. Such events seemed to secure a broad consensus of what is true, right, and white but always through nondiscursive practice, never by saying and, thus, never sayable. For example, homecoming – a high-school tradition that celebrates the school football team – was a time to raise school spirit and, thus, excite the interest and imagination of the most students possible. It was, for me, an excellent time to observe shared assumptions and normative expectations of students and observe the rewards and sanctions applied to different types of behaviors.

One day during homecoming week, students held rallies in the gym for the entire student body. To the thunder of heavy-metal music, rivers of white students flowed into the gym and took seats in different quadrants of the auditorium reserved for different grade levels. Just before the official ceremony began, two big, husky white males (appearing to be seniors) dragged into the center of the auditorium a small boy (appearing to be a freshman) whose feet and legs were bound with silver duct tape. The crowd laughed and applauded. The two husky guys pumped their fists in the air to encourage the crowd then dragged the boy off center stage. After a brief greeting, members of the student leadership committee introduced the junior varsity and varsity football players. The players came out in succession and formed a line across the middle of the gym floor. The boys were all white except for three black players on the junior varsity team and, on the varsity team, two boys with Hispanic surnames. As his name was called, each player stepped forward to acknowledge the applause. Most did so with an air of shyness or humility, their heads bowed, cheeks blushing, shoulders pulled up to their ears. Two boldly strutted out, trying to play up the roar of the crowd, but their efforts fell flat.

Then, the varsity cheerleaders bolted to center stage, leaping energetically before getting into formation for their choreographed performance. The girls were all thin, some overly so, and wore uniforms with close-fitted bodices that made them look all the smaller. But their body size betrayed their strength. Their routine, driven by the firm beat of a heavy-metal tune, was rigorously gymnastic, with lots of cartwheels, flips, and pyramid constructions that were punctuated by the top girls falling trustingly into the arms of their comrades. Long, silky blonde hair parachuted out with each acrobatic stunt. Through the performance, the audience remained silent and attentive, with an occasional collective gasp at the girls' athleticism, until the show was over. At that time, the cheerleaders received roaring, vocal applause.

On the day after the rally was the homecoming parade. The parade took off from the basketball courts and wound its way onto a residential side street. Four adult males, two of whom appeared to be Mexican American, led the parade mounted on prancing horses and wearing Mexican serapes and sombreros. The front two carried large replicas of the California and American flags. Following the horsemen were two convertibles, one of which was a white Corvette carrying the (white) city mayor, who waved ceremoniously to the onlookers on the sidewalks.

The music of the marching band, which followed closely behind the mayor, announced the arrival of the parade along its path. A group of eight white and one African American female dancers led the band, tossing and spinning colored flags in sync with the beat of the band's percussion section. The 50 musicians in the band, most of whom appeared white with five or six exceptions, marched militarily in tight formation and played their instruments with competence and finesse. Following the band was a procession of American-built pickup trucks carrying, first, the varsity and junior varsity football players, then the "royalty" – the senior "king" and "queen" and underclass "princes" and "princesses" – and finally, an open-bed truck loaded with seniors, hooting and cheering as if their graduation day had already arrived.

The parade made its way through several blocks of residences before returning to the main street and slowly making its way back to the school. Proud parents were perched on the sidewalks with their 35-millimeter and video cameras in hand. Community residents stepped onto their front landings to wave and cheer as the parade passed their homes. Others peered out through large pane windows with cats in arms and dogs at heel.

The homecoming rally and parade were, in my view,[6] packed with assumptions, values, behaviors, and origin stories that privileged white European American perspectives as well as gender, sexuality, and class-based norms (all of which tend to coproduce one another). At the rally, for example, the display of the hog-tied freshman reinforced that white (male) dominance is sustained not only through the subordination of nonwhite others but of "other" whites as well (Hartigan 1997, 1999; Thandeka 1999; Wray and Newitz 1997). Second, the virtues of personal mastery and self-effacement were exemplified by the humble postures of the football players and reinforced by the slights the audience gave to those who presented themselves with more bravado. And, finally, the cheerleaders' thin, bounded physiques and gravity-defying athletic feats demonstrated that the girls had successfully learned to subjugate their bodies and overcome nature.

The homecoming parade, with its display of the national and state flags, American cars, marching band, and school royalty, was a stunning way to observe the coproduction of whiteness, Americanness, citizenship, and gendered codes of conduct. Included was even an origin story of white American colonial victory over Mexico. And, by virtue of who was there and who was not, the knitting together of the themes of mastery, domination, nationhood, and industry with whiteness was seamless. Other cultures in the school and community were not represented in the parade. There were no Filipino dancers, Asian martial artists, or African American rappers. The event was performed by whites and for whites and, thus, little contradicted the cultural and political assumptions at play.

In sum, at Valley Groves High, white people and white European American culture saturated school life. White youth had little to no association with people or cultures that would place whiteness in relief in such a way that students might reflect on it and consciously define it.

No Ties

Given this sociocultural milieu, white youth could say nothing when I asked them to describe white culture; they had no words to describe that which comes naturally. Laurie, whom I quoted at the beginning of this article, struggled to describe white culture and finally succumbed to "I don't know!" Billy, a popular white senior, had a similar response. I asked him what he thought was culturally specific about white American culture. After a long pause in which he said only, "hmmm," he asked, "Like, what's American culture?"

> "Uh-huh," I replied.
>
> "Hmmm. [Another long pause] – I don't really know, 'cause it's like [pause] – just [pause] – I'm not sure! I don't know!"

However, Valley Groves' white students were not always speechless about white identity. When my questions probed into the youth's social experiences and identities as whites and not their cultures, they could find something to say. Not too surprisingly, most told me that being white meant you had no cultural ties. Students I spoke to would explain that they had mixed European roots that held no significance for them; therefore they were "just white." For example, I asked Mara, a Valley Groves senior, what she would say if a census taker asked her, straight out without any prompting, "What are you?"

MARA: Like a race?

PGP: Could be a racial category.

MARA: I'd have to answer "Very white." I am, yeah. I am 100 percent white.

PGP: I noticed on your [consent form] you said you had a mix of European backgrounds, and you wrote, "Pretty much WHITE." Is that what "white" means to you, a European mix?

MARA: I just think that there's not much – I don't really think of myself as European. I think of myself as a white American girl. . . . I don't really go back to my roots, though I know I have family and where they come from but they're all white races.

PGP: You don't have any heartfelt devotion to your European past?

MARA: Not really. My family has lived here for generations, so I don't really draw on that.

Laurie had a similar response:

> We're a bunch of everything. My great-great-grandmother is Cherokee. Whenever I fill out [questionnaires] about what's my ethnic background I write "white" because everything is so random. We have German, some family from Wales – but that means nothing to me. . . . I don't have ties to anything. I haven't heard about anything my parents have been through except for my grandparents in wars. It's all been about people, not culture.

Answers like Mara's and Laurie's, of which there were many, reflect that, although white youth at Valley Groves may not have thought about whiteness as a culture, they did think about it as a social category (Phoenix 1997), as a "group position" (Blumer 1958) with respect to other racial-ethnic groups. To Valley Groves students, whites were a group because they did not have culture, and "minorities" did. Through mixed-European and other cultural amalgamation, whites were a new breed, a hybrid, removed from a past that was meaningless to them and for the loss of which they held no remorse.

Valley Groves whites were speaking from the "postcultural" perspective that Rosaldo (1989) asserts is the perspective of all who are members of the dominant group of Western-style nation-states. Naturalized whiteness complements and helps constitute this kind of postcultural identity because of the stability garnered from the fit between societal norms and the constructed identity of whites (powell 1997). The us–them construction revolves around "majority" (those who all look and act normal to one another) and the "minority" (those who do not look or act like the majority). Naturalized whiteness is securely grounded in and validated by the normal way of things in the present and therefore does not seek meaning in a cultural or past orientation.

Clavey High School: When White is Not the Norm

Once a port of entry for African American, Mexican, and Asian immigration into northern California, Clavey City today has one of the most racially/ethnically diverse populations for its size in the United States. Of its 372,000 residents, 33 percent are white, 44 percent are black, 19 percent are of Hispanic origin, and 15 percent are of Asian origin. Median household income in 1989 was $27,095. More than 16 percent of families in Clavey City live below poverty.

Clavey High School stands like a fortress overlooking a dense urban landscape. The school's magnet academies draw in youth from all over the city, bringing in a mosaic of students from different racial and ethnic groups. At the time of my research, whites comprised 12 percent of the 2,000 students at Clavey. African Americans were the majority, making up 54 percent of the school. They were followed in numbers by Asian Americans (23 percent), then Hispanics (8 percent), Filipinos (2 percent), and a few Pacific Islanders and Native Americans. At any given moment during lunch break, one could tour the campus and hear students speaking in standard English, black English ("ebonics"), Eritrean, Cantonese, Mandarin, Korean, Spanish, Spanglish, Tagalog, Samoan, Russian, and Vietnamese, among others.

The racial composition of the administrative and teaching staff at Clavey was also quite diverse. The principal of Clavey was a white male, but the other top administrators, two assistant principals and the dean, were African American. Of all the administrators and their staff, 50 percent were African American, 25 percent were Asian, and 25 percent were white. Clavey teachers were 53 percent white, 30 percent African American, 8 percent Asian American, 6 percent Hispanic, and 3 percent Pacific Islander.

Life at Clavey High was very different from that at Valley Groves. White youth at Clavey were in daily, up-close association with marked racial and cultural difference to whiteness, and race was the primary means of sorting out who was who and where one belonged in the social organization of the school. Clavey's tracking structure, which I say more about later, was racially segregated, with whites and Asians disproportionally represented in the high-tracked classes and African Americans and Latinos overrepresented in the low-tracked classes. As well, certain areas on the campus were "where the white kids hang out"; others were "where the black (or Asian American or Latino) kids hang out." And student cliques and subcultures were racially marked such that "straights" (who were like "normal" kids at Valley Groves), alternatives, hippies, and punks were all "white people's groups"; rappers, athletes, gangsters, and "fashion hounds" were "black people's groups"; housers, natives, newly arrived, and martial artists were "Asian people's groups"; and so forth. This meant that the styles, slangs, vernaculars, and demeanors that marked identification with a certain clique or subculture simultaneously implied racial identification. In a word, peer group activities *racialized* youth.

Speaking to this fact and the sanctions that came with crossing racialized boundaries in styles or leisure activities, Gloria, an immigrant from El Salvador, said to me,

> For my race, if you start wearing a lot of gold, you're trying to be black. If you're trying to braid your hair, you'll be accused of trying to be black. I'm scared to do things 'cause they might say, "that's black!" Or if you're Latino and you listen to that, you know, Green Day – that [alternative rock] kinda thing. If you listen to that, then you wanna be white...."Oh my god, why you listening to that music?" they'd say...Aren't you proud of who you are?

Also different from Valley Groves was the dominant school culture. Overall at Clavey, African American youth claimed the majority of open, public spaces, and black popular cultural forms and practices shaped the normative culture of the school. By "black popular culture," I refer to the music, styles, and other meaningful practices that have risen out of black communities; are linked, if remotely, to diasporic traditions; and, most significantly, mark black identity and peoplehood (Gilroy 1991, 1993; Rose 1994; Wallace 1992). Hall (1992) defines three things that are distinctive of black diasporic culture: (1) *style* as the "subject of what is going on," (2) *music* as the "deep structure of [black] cultural life," and (3) the *body* as "canvases of representation" (p. 27). Gilroy (1991) adds that the body in black culture carries "potent meanings" (p. 226) because it rests at the core of historical efforts of blacks to assert their humanity.

Unlike at Valley Groves, where the dress code did not diverge much from white adult mainstream style, at Clavey, basic elements of black hip-hop style were generalized into the normative styles for all youth. One informant called it the "leveler" style because it made all who wore it "the same." This basic style included clean, oversized, and sagging denim pants or sweatpants; large and long untucked T-shirts or hooded sweatshirts; large, bulky parkas; and sparkling-clean athletic shoes. The look was particularly common for boys, but girls' styles were also influenced by it. Only if and when students wanted to mark a distinctive style and/or racial identification did they embellish on this basic, baggy theme. Duncan, a middle-class, white male skater and "raver" (someone who frequents rave parties) told me,

> We all wear baggy pants, right? So parents think! But you find that ravers have cut-off bottoms to their [sagging] jeans, they wear bigger t-shirts they have hanging out of their pants, they carry packs that's full of crap that they take everywhere.

What Duncan specified as "raver" style, other students specified as "white," particularly the cut-off bottoms to large pants. Other markers of white kids' styles were Van shoes, instead of Nike or Fila brands (which marked black style), and macramé or silver-chain neck chokers.

Informal and formal activities on campus were also shaped by black popular culture. During breaks or at lunchtime, the ambient din of casual conversation was composed of the sounds, words, and inflections of black English and the most recent innovation in "street" slang. Lunchtime events, school rallies, and dances were enlivened with rap and R & B music, predominantly, with an occasional reggae tune or specially requested techno or alternative song. Often, students performed raps on the steps in front of the cafeteria or graced an audience with a spontaneous hip-hop dance performance.

Homecoming week at Clavey, like at Valley Groves, was a time to unite the school and raise the collective spirit. So, leadership students made attempts to appeal to the breadth of diverse interests and cultures of the school with "fashion shows" of traditional or native garments and a variety of games designed to mix students up. At lunch, they played a range of music, from R & B to techno and alternative rock, but songs by African American and Afro-Caribbean artists were predominant. The main events – the rally and game – were attended by and played predominantly to a majority black audience.

The rally took place during lunch on the day of the "big game." Students, of whom all but a few were black, crammed into the auditorium to the heartbeat pulse of a rap song. The rally opened with a greeting from the student body president and a soulful a cappella song performed by three African American students. Then the cheerleaders, composed of one white and 10 black girls, sprung out onto the gym floor. Their choreographed routine was fluid, rhythmic, and dance-like, with movements drawn from traditional and contemporary African and African American dance forms. To the infectious beat of an upbeat R & B song, the girls playfully flirted with their appreciative audience with beckoning hand and eye gestures. Several boys succumbed to the urge to dance in dialogue with the girls and leapt down to the floor to join them, but they were met by the arresting hands of campus security. Others, boys and girls alike, stood up and swayed or danced in place until the performance was over. Then, the varsity football players were called to line up in the center of the auditorium. The players were African American with the exception of two white boys and one Latino. When each name was announced, the football player leapt forward a few steps and embraced the cheers from the crowd. Each took his moment in the limelight proudly, with his fist in the air or maybe a little dance to augment the roar of his audience.

At Clavey, there was no homecoming parade that extended into the community, like at Valley Groves. At the game, a small procession of vehicles featuring the elected school "emperor" and "empress" circled the football field during half-time. There was no marching band, either, but the award-winning school gospel choir sang several lively songs at halftime.

In short, school life at Clavey was heavily infused with styles, music, and activities that marked the identities and cultures of the majority black students. This had a few important implications for the experiences and identities of the white students. First, white was not the norm, either numerically or culturally. Barry, a middle-class, "straight" white male, told me, "School is like a foreign country to me. I come here to this foreign place, then go home where things are normal again." When I asked white students why they did not attend the rallies and dances, they said things like, "I don't enjoy the people," "They don't play my kind of music," and "I can't dance to that music." All in all, the message was that they could not relate to the dominant school culture.

Furthermore, whiteness was not entirely taken for granted. The racial organization of Clavey's social life, curricular structure, and schoolwide activities meant that white students were forced to grapple with their identities as whites and participate in active contestation over the meanings of white identity and culture. No white student I spoke to at Clavey was completely unable to describe something about white culture. All had reflected on it to some extent, even if only to ruminate on how difficult it was to define. And some youth could say a lot about white culture. One white, middle-class senior girl, Jessie, elaborated extensively on differences in attitudes toward food consumption that she noticed between her white, Filipino, and Chinese American friends, and she commented on how much more visible white culture is to her in places outside of California. She said, "Minnesota, Denver and...places like that. It seems like...you know, you've got the whole thing going on – beer bread, polka, parades, apple pie and things like that."

Most stunning to me about the white students at Clavey was not what they said explicitly about white culture but what they said implicitly. In our discussions about the types of music they liked and why, white students would tell me that they liked rock or punk or alternative music and not rap or R & B because "their" music spoke more to their "interests" or experiences as whites. For example, Kirsten and Cindi were good friends. They both were from middle-class homes, were juniors at the time, and liked alternative rock. Kirsten was white, European American, and Cindi was part white and part Chinese, although she admittedly "looked white" and hung out solely with other white youth. I asked them why they thought students tended to self-segregate on campus:

CINDI: I think there is...the factor that some people feel like they may not have very much in common with someone from a different race, which in some ways is true. Because you have, like, different music tastes, different styles of clothes. Also, like what your friends think.

KIRSTEN: Or like different things you do on weekends.

CINDI: Yeah, so I think that's something that separates the races.

KIRSTEN: It's kind of interesting because my musical interests have changed....It seems like [in junior high school] everyone, regardless of if they were black or white or Asian... listened to the [local rap and R & B station.] But then I think when you are little you don't really...have too much of an identity of yourself. As you get older and mature more you, like, discover what your "true being" is. So then people's musical tastes change. [Later in the conversation.] I think punk is more of a "I don't get along with my parents" kind of music and rap is more of "let's go kill someone" music.

CINDI: Punk...expresses a simpler anger. It's just kind of like "Oh, I broke up with my girlfriend"...something like that. Usually rap has more to do with killing and gangs – stuff that doesn't really relate to me.

In this discussion, Kirsten and Cindi defined white identity and culture in terms of interests and tastes in leisure culture. This "discourse of taste" (Dolby 2000) was the language of choice among all groups of students for articulating racial-ethnic differences. Behind it was the belief that different life experiences accounted for different tastes. Sometimes, white youth named fairly explicit experiences they believed were most common to or defining of whites. Class experience, expressed by Kirsten and Cindi in terms of the type of neighborhood one lived in, was often evoked by youth. Other times, white youth spoke in terms of intangible but presumably race-based, emotional, aesthetic, and ethical sensibilities they felt when they listened to, say, punk or alternative music but not when they listened to rap.

Active Construction of White as Postcultural

Ironically, even as Clavey whites demarcated white culture and identity boundaries through their popular cultural tastes and leisure activities, they also imagined whiteness as cultureless, as postcultural. This was not as explicit as it was at Valley Groves. It would show its face when white students referred to people of color as people with "race" or "ethnicity," as though whites had neither. Tina, a working-class junior who had always been a racial minority in school and had many close black and Latino friends, told me that she "had a lot of ethnicity in [her] family...Hispanic, Korean. We all get along." By this she meant that white relatives had married "out" of whiteness and into culture, ethnicity.

Common also was the explicit and implicit definition of white as empty, meaningless, bland, and without tradition. This comment by Eric touches on all of those:

> I think it's more difficult [to define white culture] for Americans because the culture of America is more just consumption. In America, we buy stuff, and that's the basis of our culture. If you talk to people who want to come to America? – They want things. TV is a very American thing. We don't have lengthy traditions....A lot has been lost because of the good ol' melting pot. I heard a cool one about a salad bowl – that's what America is, and along comes the dressing and turns everything into dressing flavor. Vegetables all got that white American spin on it.

Note, too, that Eric equates "white" with "American" until his last line, when he specifies "white American." That is a faux pas that whites often fall into because of the dominant construction of white as the "unhyphenated" American standard.

Finally, several Clavey white students told me that they did not like to think about themselves as "white" but as "human." These students also expressed a more explicitly rationalist construction of whiteness that denied the significance of a past orientation and exalted a more individualistic and present- or future-oriented construction of the self. White, middle-class boys expressed this most boldly, which might be expected given that they are triply constructed as the most rational by race, class, and gender.

Murray, whom I quoted at the beginning of this article, best exemplifies this latter perspective. In Murray's comments, we can read several tenets of Western rational thought and a postcultural identity: the irrationality of past-oriented values, the future orientation of the self, and individual responsibility. Daniel was a white, middle-class, "straight" male with some Portuguese ancestry. He made comments similar to Murray's:

> People have suggested I am a person of color or mixed. Then I decided, no, I'm European American. Ancestry doesn't matter.... People look back in the past and judge you for it, and I don't think that's right. Sure, people enslaved people. At one time every race had slaves. I think you need to move on and see what's going on now. History is important but you have to work on getting together now and don't use that as a divide.

A few scholars have observed a propensity among whites to deny the significance of the past, slavery particularly, in affecting the life chances of African Americans today. Some argue that this denial is a kind of defensive mechanism whites adopt to exonerate themselves from taking responsibility for the legacies of slavery and past discrimination against African Americans and other minorities (Gallagher 1995). I take a slightly different position and suggest that white identity and culture is constructed in such a way that the values of individuality, personal responsibility, and a future-oriented self create a cognitive inability to see things any other way (see also Alba 1990; Blauner 1989). A past orientation simply does not make sense to many whites from their cultural perspective.

In sum, at Clavey, white culture was not entirely naturalized and taken for granted; it was reflected on and even defined somewhat, particularly through the language of tastes and popular culture. To an extent, however, white students also considered themselves unmarked American, nonethnic, unmarked human, and/or present-oriented. In a word, they saw themselves as cultureless. I might add that several students of color I spoke to also were quick to define white culture in terms of styles and tastes but not in terms of tradition. Johnetta, an African American senior, said, "It's hard to generalize [about white culture] because there's no ready answer to what is white culture."

Whereas I have proposed that the naturalization of whiteness greatly facilitated the passive construction of postcultural whiteness at Valley Groves, I suggest that at Clavey, different and more active social processes were in play. Namely, Western rational ways of knowing and making sense of social relations permeated Clavey school and social practices. As I have argued, Western rationalism exiles tradition and culture from the realms of truth and relevance and replaces them with reason. That which is reasonable or rational is separated from and raised above that which is not, like the elevation of mind over body, intellectual over emotional, and order above chaos. Whiteness benefits from those hierarchical dualities by being linked with the higher value of each – with orderliness, self-control, individualism, and rationality, which, not coincidentally, are recognized as standard or normal behaviors. Otherness is defined in terms of that which is passionate, chaotic, violent, lazy, irrational, and – since marginal to the norm – cultural.

Two school practices in particular stood out for me in terms of the ways they seemed to structure the meanings all youth gave to their experience through a Western rational value paradigm. The first and most obvious of those was the tracking structure. Scholars have long argued that racial segregation in tracking reproduces racial inequalities in the wider society, largely by preparing high-tracked students, who tend to be middle-class white and Asian, better than low-tracked students, who tend to be black, Latino, and poor white and Asian (Gamoran et al. 1995; Oakes 1985, 1994; Oakes and Guiton 1995). Tracking also reproduces racial inequalities by reinforcing, if not constituting, racial stereotypes. Jeannie Oakes (1994) has argued that "all but the most extraordinary schools have their stereotypes and prejudices reinforced by racially-identifiable high- and low-tracked classes" (pp. 86–87). She asserts that tracking "institutionalizes racist conceptions of intellectual capacity" (ibid.). I would add to her argument that tracking also institutionalizes the values of mind over body and self-control over lack of restraint and racializes those who are superior and inferior in those respects.

At Clavey, the high-tracked classes, those designed to prepare students for high-ranking colleges and universities, were 80 percent white and Asian, according to a school survey. Conversely, "preparatory" classes, which filled graduation requirements, were overwhelmingly black and Latino. Remedial classes were 100 percent black and Latino. Although, officially, youth were tracked according to their intellectual or achievement levels, the discourses that surrounded tracking at Clavey suggested that *behavior* (including expected behavior) was just as relevant.

Students in the high-tracked classes were generally understood to be "well-behaved," "good" students. In those classrooms, students acted in the utmost orderly fashion: always listening attentively and taking notes, speaking only when called on. They considered themselves hard-working and sophisticated in their ability to defer gratification, such as to study during lunch instead of hang out and have fun with their friends. They justified their privilege to be in the accelerated classes on these grounds and blamed underachievement on the behaviors of the underachieved. Linda, a white Jewish girl in accelerated classes, represented this viewpoint in the following comment:

> It's so sad because these kids could be pushed so far beyond what they are [doing]. Like, it's unbelievable. When I see a twelfth grader holding a geometry book, I cringe inside me. Because, *you can learn*, you can do it! People are so lazy, they don't care. They have no goals, no ambitions. It's frustrating! I don't get it!

The "lazy" and unambitious kids Linda referred to were black and Latino students in the preparatory classes. Other commonly used terms to describe those classes and the students in them were "bonehead," "rowdy," and "out of control." And, indeed, some of those classes had students who were inattentive or disruptive and who could, on occasion, set the whole class off into a blaze of rowdiness. But those students were aware that they had been assigned to the least valued and negatively stereotyped classes in the school. If they did not hear it through common discourse, they deduced it from the classes themselves. They were overcrowded and short of chairs, books, and other course materials. Sometimes, they did not even have full-time teachers. It is not a stretch to suggest that preparatory students behaved in "bonehead" ways that they thought were expected of them (Baron, Tom, and Cooper 1985; Eder 1981; Ferguson 1998; Lightfoot 1978; Steele and Aronson 1998).

In sum, tracking at Clavey asserted more than, simply, intellectual superiority but also the values of mind over body and self-control over lack of restraint. Furthermore, it marked standard, acceptable forms of behavior – standards within which middle-class whites and Asians were squarely located practically and symbolically.

"Multicultural" programs and discourses were other school practices that positioned whites as the school's most rational and postcultural. At Clavey, there were two main, formal multicultural events: the "cultural assemblies" and "multicultural week." Once every other month or so, an ethnic club – the African American Student Union, the Asian Student Union, Latino Student Union, or the Inter-Tribal Student Union – would put on a schoolwide assembly. A common assembly featured traditional ceremonial dances and rituals, music and song, poetry readings, historically informative slide shows, and clothing displays, all arranged and performed by the students.

Lunchtime activities during multicultural week were another opportunity for students to publicly display elements of their cultural heritage. Each day of the week was designed to feature a particular aspect of a culture – the music, dance, clothing, written texts, or narratives. For example, on a day featuring traditional or national clothing styles, youth held a fashion show in which African American youth in dashikis, Chinese American girls in brocade gowns, and Mexican American youth in ceremonial dance costumes paraded before youth gathered outside the cafeteria.

These events had their merits. They gave voice and visibility to the cultures and perspectives of people historically silenced by white colonialism. African American and Asian youth told me that they enjoyed having the opportunity to present their culture as well as learn about others. I propose, however, that multicultural events at Clavey coterminously reproduced white supremacist, rationalist tenets of white colonialism by making whiteness culturally invisible.

Rosaldo (1989) argues that, "as the Other becomes more culturally visible, the self becomes correspondingly less so" (p. 202). I believe this was true for many Clavey whites. When white students spoke about the assemblies, they usually expressed enthusiastic appreciation for "the chance to learn about so many cultures." But learning about other cultures merely gave them more references by which to define what they were not. As well, when they spoke in this way, it was as if "cultures" were like books – objective things that existed outside of the self but could be consumed to pleasure the self (Farley 1997). In a conversation with four middle-class white girls at Clavey, I asked them how they thought their experience at Clavey would influence their adulthood.

ANN: I think it's going to be a very positive thing. [Melissa interjects: Yeah.] Because it teaches us how to deal with different kinds of people.

SERA: Yeah, you learn more about others....It's a positive experience.

MELISSA: Yeah, you gain street smarts. You gain stuff.

Greater knowledge of other cultures was something Ann, Sera, and Melissa appreciated because it gave them tools to enhance their sociability, but it did not make them reflect on their sociocultural location as whites. When other white students at Clavey spoke to me about the value of the multicultural events, they made very similar kinds of statements and inferences. Overall, multicultural events, as "add-on" school practices in which white students could pleasurably gaze on racial-ethnic others without putting themselves on the line, reinforced a sense of whiteness as center and standard (cultureless) and racial-ethnic others (by virtue of having culture to display) as different and marginal to that.

Furthermore, no white students I spoke to questioned why there was not a white-American cultural assembly. Granted, to most this was untenable, largely because it might be taken as a white supremacist act. I talked to students about school clubs for whites only, and they categorically dismissed the idea. One said, "There'd be a riot!" Another said, "It wouldn't be right. It would be taken all wrong." But it was also untenable because, as another student put it, "White is all around. It doesn't need special attention." The idea that white culture does not need special attention (read: white is the norm and standard) seemed to be another message multicultural events gave to white students. As if for the eyes of whites only, multiculturalism at Clavey gave white students new references to add to their mental cache of exotic others while further obscuring the invisible power of white culture.

Conclusion

For a while now, scholars of race and whiteness have understood that the construction of white culture as the invisible norm is one of the most, if not *the* most, pernicious constructions of whiteness in the post-civil rights era. However, very few have examined the everyday social processes by which white people come to think of themselves as normal and culturally empty (Frankenberg 1993; Kenny 2000a, 2000b; Twine 1997), and among those, no one has done a comparative study illuminating the ways that different social-structural institutional contexts influence different constructions of white identity as cultureless. My research suggests that, at Valley Groves, a predominantly white high school, white identity seemed cultureless because white cultural practices were taken for granted, naturalized, and, thus, not reflected on and defined. At Clavey, a multiracial school, white culture was not taken for granted – white youth thought about and defined it to an extent, particularly through their interests and tastes in popular culture. However, in part, whites also reflected on their sociocultural location through the lens of European American rational authority, which school structures and practices helped construct and reinforce. That lens refracted whiteness into all that was good, controlled, rational, and cultureless and otherness into all that was bad, out of control, irrational, and cultural. It may be that when naturalization processes are not possible because of close interracial association, then rationalization processes must come into play to preserve white hegemony.

This argument has theoretical and practical implications for critical white studies, the sociology of education, and general theories and research in racial-ethnic identity formation. Within critical white studies, there are two prevalent sets of assumptions about white culture that this research advances. The first is that white people experience themselves as culturally empty because whiteness is hegemonic and, therefore, undefined. To disrupt the insidious power of white culture, then, we must expose and define it. My study suggests that this is true but not everywhere the truth. The multiracial experiences of white youth at Clavey suggest that making white culture visible is not sufficient for challenging the construction of white as norm. What is also necessary are efforts to expose, challenge, and transform the rule of reason that frames white culture as rational and, therefore, *beyond* culture, postcultural or even anticultural.

Another assumption among some scholars of critical white studies, particularly "New Abolitionists," is that white culture is experienced as empty because, simply, there is not white culture. I am less concerned with the question of whether there really is a white culture than with what is reproduced through *denying* there is a white culture. The argument I have presented here proposes that the concept of culture denotes more than, simply, a way of life organized around sets of symbolic practices. It connotes a relationship of power between those who "have" culture (and are, thus, irrational and inferior) and those who claim not to (and are, thus, rational and superior). More research and thought needs to go into examining the ways postcultural whiteness is inculcated in daily practice and into the profits whites gain by denying that they have a culture.

This research also contributes to the growing scholarship on social and cultural reproduction in education. Although considerable research has examined the reproduction and subversion of societal norms in schools, including racial norms (for example, Carter 1999; Conchas 2000; Davidson 1996; Fine et al. 1997; Fordham 1996; Kenny 2000a; McCarthy and Crichlow 1993; Valenzuela 1999), more is still needed that closely examines the symbolic impact of certain school practices on how white students make sense of their own identities and the identities of people of color. This research only touched the surface of that and came on some disturbing and unexpected findings, namely, the active construction of postcultural whiteness. Research and evaluations of multicultural and other programs designed to redress racial inequalities have focused primarily on students of color. Important insights might be gained from more attention to white students and the meanings they assign to their experiences of those same programs.

Finally, this research embellishes on theories of racial-ethnic identity formation by vividly illuminating the socially constructed and contingent nature of race. Racial identities are made, not born, and they are made through the interaction of the specific social, structural, political, and cultural composition of a given context (Blumer 1958; Pinderhughes 1997). This means that racial identities are not fixed or uniform but variable and multiple. They may even be contradictory. These observations are often lost among scholars of whiteness and white racism who tend to represent whites and white identities as everywhere and always the same and contradictions as a form of "contemporary race prejudice" (Williams et al. 1999). My research affirms that the hegemonic construction of white as cultureless is stubbornly persistent but that even *it* is not the same across all contexts. To more effectively dismantle white domination, we need to be aware of and ready to work with its different manifestations and internal contradictions. Future research and anti-racist scholarship may benefit from deeper exploration of the variability of white racial identities and the processes by which white racial domination is reproduced and subverted in distinct contexts.

NOTES

1 All names of cities, schools, and individuals in this article are pseudonyms.

2 Please do not interpret my assertion that culture is "real" to mean that I see it as a fixed and immutable "thing" that is consistent with all members of a culturally defined group. Cultures are constituted by social, geographical, historical, and political processes, which make them variable and always changing (see Rosaldo 1989). However, in a given time and place, a culture may appear fixed and stable, especially in conditions of domination and oppression (Hall 1996). The same argument applies to my use of the concept "race." However, I have yet to find a way to satisfactorily resolve the tension between, on one hand, analyzing and deconstructing racial categories and stereotypes to dismantle them and, on the other, reifying and reproducing those same categories and stereotypes in the process. I acknowledge that my assertions in this piece about white and black culture uncomfortably balance on that tension.

3 See also Ferguson (1997).

4 Ferguson (1997) argues that the property qualification in the U.S. Constitution for the right to American citizenry was used to justify the exclusion of nonwhites, women, and unpropertied men on the grounds that land ownership "epitomizes a *rational*, virtuous, masculine, and politically necessary control of the world" (my emphasis, p. 157). Only the most rational had the right to be citizens.

5 I judged socioeconomic class by considering both parent occupation and quality-of-life issues.

6 Although I tried throughout this research to reflect on and take into consideration the race, class, gender, and other biases I bring to my representations and interpretations of the students' practices and assumptions at both Valley Groves and Clavey, I cannot claim to have succeeded in that 100 percent.

REFERENCES

Alba, Richard. 1990. *Ethnic Identity: The Transformation of White America*. New Haven, CT: Yale University Press.

Allen, Theodore. 1994. *The Invention of the White Race*, vol. 1: *Racial Oppression and Social Control*. London: Verso.

Almaguer, Tomas. 1994. *Racial Fault Lines: The Historical Origins of White Supremacy in California*. Berkeley: University of California Press.

Apple, Michael W. 1995. *Education and Power*. New York: Routledge.

Baron, Reuben, David Y. H. Tom, and Harris M. Cooper. 1985. Social class, race and teacher expectations. In *Teacher Expectancies*, ed. Jerome B. Dusek. Hillsdale, NJ: Lawrence Erlbaum.

Blauner, Bob. 1989. *Black Lives, White Lives: Three Decades of Race Relations in America*. Berkeley: University of California Press.

Blumer, Herbert. 1958. Race prejudice as a sense of group position. *Pacific Sociological Review* 1(1):3–7.

Bourdieu, Pierre. 1977. *Outline of a Theory of Practice*. Cambridge, UK: Cambridge University Press.

Bourdieu, Pierre, and J. C. Passeron. 1977. *Reproduction in Education, Society and Culture*. Beverly Hills, CA: Sage.

Carter, Prudence L. 1999. Balancing acts: Issues of identity and cultural resistance in the social and educational behaviors of minority youth. Ph.D. diss., Columbia University, New York.

Conchas, Gilberto Q. 2000. Structuring failure and success: Understanding the variability in Latino school engagement. Working paper, Harvard Graduate School of Education.

Davidson, Ann Locke. 1996. *Making and Molding Identity in Schools: Student Narratives on Race, Gender, and Academic Engagement*. Albany: State University of New York Press.

De Vos, George, 1975. Ethnic pluralism: Conflict and accommodation. In *Ethnic Identity: Cultural Continuities and Change*, ed. George De Vos and Lola Romanucci-Ross. Chicago: University of Chicago Press.

Dolby, Nadine. 2000. The shifting ground of race: The role of taste in youth's production of identities. *Race, Ethnicity, and Education* 3(1):7–23.

Dyer, Richard, 1997. *White*. New York: Routledge.

Eckert, Penelope. 1989. *Jocks and Burnouts: Social Categories and Identity in High School*. New York: Teachers College Press.

Eder, Donna. 1981. Ability grouping as a self-fulfilling prophecy: A micro-analysis of teacher–student interaction. *Sociology of Education* 54(3):151–162.

Essed, Philomena. 1996. *Diversity: Gender, Color and Culture*. Amherst: University of Massachusetts Press.

Farley, Anthony Paul. 1997. The black body as fetish object. *Oregon Law Review* 76(3):457–535.

Ferguson, Robert A. 1997. *The American Enlightenment, 1750–1820*. Cambridge, MA: Harvard University Press.

Ferguson, Ronald F. 1998. Teachers' perceptions and expectations and the black–white test score gap. In *The Black–White Test Score Gap*, ed. Christopher Jencks and Meredith Phillips, 318–374. Washington, DC: Brookings Institution.

Fine, Michelle. 1989. Silencing and nurturing voice in an improbable context: Urban adolescents in public school. In *Critical Pedagogy, the State, and Cultural Struggle*, ed. Henry Giroux and Peter McLaren, 152–173. Albany: State University of New York Press.

Fine, Michelle, Lois Weis, Linda C. Powell, and L. Mun Wong, eds. 1997. *Off White: Readings on Race, Power and Society*. New York: Routledge.

Fordham, Signithia. 1996. *Blacked Out: Dilemmas of Race, Identity, and Success at Capital High*. Chicago: University of Chicago Press.

Fordham, Signithia, and John Ogbu. 1986. Black students' school success: Coping with the "burden of 'acting white.'" *Urban Review* 18(3):176–206.

Frankenberg, Ruth. 1993. *White Women, Race Matters: The Social Construction of Whiteness*. Minneapolis: University of Minnesota Press.

Frankenberg, Ruth. 1997. *Displacing Whiteness: Essays in Social and Cultural Criticism*. Durham, NC: Duke University Press.

Gallagher, Charles A. 1995. White reconstruction in the university. *Socialist Review* 24(1&2):165–187.

Gallagher, Charles A. 1997. White racial formation: Into the twenty-first century. In *Critical White Studies: Looking Behind the Mirror*, ed. Richard Delgado and Jean Stefancic, 6–11. Philadelphia: Temple University Press.

Gamoran, Adam, Martin Nystrand, Mark Berends, and Paul C. LePore. 1995. An organizational analysis of the effects of ability grouping. *American Educational Research Journal* 32(4):687–715.

Gilroy, Paul, 1991. *"There ain't no black in the Union Jack": The Cultural Politics of Race and Nation*. Chicago: University of Chicago Press.

Gilroy, Paul. 1993. *The Black Atlantic: Modernity and Double Consciousness*. Cambridge, MA: Harvard University Press.

Giroux, Henry. 1996. *Fugitive Cultures: Race, Violence, and Youth*. New York: Routledge.

Giroux, Henry. 1997. Rewriting the discourse of racial identity: Towards a pedagogy and politics of whiteness. *Harvard Educational Review* 67(2):285–320.

Goldberg, David Theo. 1993. *Racist Culture: Philosophy and the Politics of Meaning*. Cambridge, UK: Blackwell.

Hall, Stuart. 1992. What is the "black" in black popular culture? In *Black Popular Culture*, ed. Gina Dent, 21–33. Seattle, WA: Bay.

Hall, Stuart. 1996. Introduction: Who needs identity? In *Questions of Cultural Identity*, ed. Stuart Hall and Paul du Gay, 1–17. London: Sage.

Haney Lopez, Ian F. 1996. *White by Law: The Legal Construction of Race*. New York: New York University Press.

Harris, Cheryl. 1993. Whiteness as property. *Harvard Law Review* 106:1707–1791.

Hartigan, John, Jr. 1997. Locating white Detroit. In *Displacing Whiteness: Essays in Social and Cultural Criticism*, ed. Ruth Frankenberg, 180–213. Durham, NC: Duke University Press.

Hartigan, John, Jr. 1999. *Racial Situations: Class Predicaments of Whiteness in Detroit*. Princeton, NJ: Princeton University Press.

Hill, Mike, ed. 1997. *Whiteness: A Critical Reader*. New York: New York University Press.

hooks, bell. 1992. *Black Looks: Race and Representation*. Boston: South End.

Ignatiev, Noel, 1995. *How the Irish became White*. New York: Routledge.

Ignatiev, Noel, and John Garvey, eds. 1996. *Race Traitor*. New York: Routledge.

Jacobson, Matthew Frye. 1998. *Whiteness of a Different Color: European Immigrants and the Alchemy of Race*. Cambridge, MA: Harvard University Press.

Kenny, Lorraine Delia. 2000a. Doing my homework: The autoethnography of a white teenage girl. In *Racing Research, Researching Race: Methodological Dilemmas in Critical Race Studies*, ed. France Winddance Twine and Jonathan Warren. New York: New York University Press.

Kenny, Lorraine Delia. 2000b. *Daughters of Suburbia: Growing up White, Middle Class, and female*. New Brunswick, NJ: Rutgers University Press.

Kinney, David A. 1993. From nerds to normals: The recovery of identity among adolescents from middle school to high school. *Sociology of Education* 66 (1):21–40.

Lightfoot, Sara Lawrence. 1978. *Worlds Apart: Relationships between Families and Schools*. New York: Basic Books.

Lipsitz, George. 1995. The possessive investment in whiteness: Racialized social democracy and the "white" problem in American studies. *American Quarterly* 47(3):369–387.

Lott, Eric. 1993. *Love and Theft: Blackface Minstrelsy and the American Working Class*. New York: Oxford University Press.

MacLeod, Jay. 1987. *Ain't No Makin' It*. Boulder, CO: Westview.

McCarthy, Cameron, and Warren Crichlow, eds. 1993. *Race, Identity and Representation in Education*. New York: Routledge.

Morrison, Toni. 1993. *Playing in the Dark: Whiteness in the Literary Imagination*. New York: Random House.

Oakes, Jeannie. 1985. *Keeping Track: How Schools Structure Inequality*. New Haven, CT: Yale University Press.

Oakes, Jeannie. 1994. More than a misapplied technology: A normative and political response to Hallinan on tracking. *Sociology of Education* 76(2):84–89.

Oakes, Jeannie, and Gretchen Guiton. 1995. Matchmaking: The dynamics of high school tracking decisions. *American Educational Research Journal* 32:3–33.

Perry, Pamela. 1998. Beginning to see the white: A comparative ethnography in two high schools of the racial consciousness and identities of white youth. Ph.D. diss., University of California, Berkeley.

Pfeil, Fred. 1995. *White Guys: Studies in Postmodern Domination and Difference*. New York: Verso.

Phoenix, Ann. 1997. "I'm white! So what?" The construction of whiteness for young Londoners. In *Off White: Readings on Race and Power in Society*, ed. Michelle Fine, Linda C. Powell, Lois Weis, and L. Mun Wong, 187–197. New York: Routledge.

Pinderhughes, Howard. 1997. *Race in the Hood: Conflict and Violence among Urban Youth*. Minneapolis: Minnesota University Press.

powell, john a. 1997. Reflections on the self: Exploring between and beyond modernity and postmodernity, *Minnesota Law Review* 81(6):1481–1520.

Roediger, David. 1991. *The Wages of Whiteness: Race and the Making of the American Working Class*. New York: Verso.

Roediger, David. 1994. *Towards the Abolition of Whiteness*. New York: Verso.

Rosaldo, Renato. 1989. *Culture and Truth: The Remaking of Social Analysis*. Boston: Beacon.

Rose, Tricia. 1994. *Black Noise: Rap Music and Black Culture in Contemporary America*. Hanover, NH: Wesleyan University Press.

Saxton, Alexander. 1990. *The Rise and Fall of the White Republic*. New York: Verso.

Segrest, Mab. 1994. *Memoirs of a Race Traitor*. Boston: South End.

Steele, Claude M., and Joshua Aronson. 1998. Stereotype threat and the test performance of academically successful African Americans. In *The Black–White test Score Gap*, ed. Christopher Jencks and Meredith Phillips, 401–427. Washington, DC: Brookings Institution.

Thandeka. 1999. The cost of whiteness. *Tikkun* 14 (3):33–38.

Thorne, Barrie. 1993. *Gender Play: Girls and Boys in School*. New Brunswick, NJ: Rutgers University Press.

Twine, France Winddance. 1997. Brown-skinned white girls: Class, culture, and the construction of white identity in suburban communities. In *Displacing Whiteness: Essays in Social and Cultural Criticism*, ed. Ruth Frankenberg, 214–43. Durham, NC: Duke University Press.

Valenzuela, Angela. 1999. *Subtractive Schooling: U.S.-Mexican Youth and the Politics of Caring*. Albany: State University of New York Press.

Wallace, Michelle (a project of). 1992. *Black Popular Culture*, Ed. Gina Dent. Seattle, WA: Bay.

Ware, Vron. 1992. *Beyond the Pale: White Women, Racism and History*. New York: Verso.

Wellman, David. 1977. *Portraits of White Racism*. Cambridge, UK: Cambridge University Press.

Williams, David R., James S. Jackson, Tony N. Brown, Myriam Torres, Tyrone A. Forman, and Kendrick Brown. 1999. Traditional and contemporary prejudice and urban whites' support for affirmative action and government help. *Social Problems* 46 (4):503–527.

Williams, Raymond. 1976. Base and superstructure in Marxist cultural theory. In *Schooling and Capitalism: A Sociological Reader*, ed. R. Dale, 202–210. London: Routledge & Kegan Paul.

Wray, Matt, and Annalee Newitz, eds. 1997. *White Trash: Race and Class in America*. New York: Routledge.

20

"I Want To Be the Minority": The Politics of Youthful White Masculinities in Sport and Popular Culture in 1990s America

Kyle W. Kusz

> *I'm talking about the disadvantages of being a white guy in America.* I'm sick of minorities hogging the good complaints. Whitey's been silent for too long...whitey's been getting a constant pounding. I've been taking so many lefts I'm begging for rights.
>
> Spade 1998:52 (emphasis added)

> It is also the era of the multicultural. And the challenge of this multicultural era is the challenge of living in a world of difference. It requires generating a mythology of social interaction that goes beyond the model of resentment that seems so securely in place at these times....*Indeed, as the purveyors of "white reign" assert themselves, they simply underscore their own vulnerabilities and fragilities.*
>
> McCarthy 1998a:339 (emphasis added)

As I search the radio for background music to facilitate my writing process, I tune into Green Day's latest release, "Minority."[1] For the uninitiated, Green Day is a West Coast punk band whose music was surprisingly embraced by the pop music mainstream in 1995. Characteristic of punk music, Green Day's music is fast, hard, and defiant. Yet, many of its songs, particularly those that have received airplay on mainstream radio stations and MTV, are also distinguished by great melodies and infectious choruses. "Minority," Green Day's first song off their new CD, features a catchy tune that invites listeners to bob their heads and sing along with the chorus ("I want to be the minority"). Since its release, the song has regularly appeared on MTV's show, *Total Request Live*,[2] an unofficial measuring stick of what's popular with America's teens.

As I listen to Green Day's song, I contemplate the seemingly peculiar popularity of a punk song performed by three young White guys proudly proclaiming a desire to be "the minority."[3] In all honesty, I am not surprised that such a song would find its way into mainstream pop music radio stations and MTV in 2000. "Minority" was preceded in the 1990s by the popularization of "alternative" music, a malleable label used to describe a variety of music (grunge rock, indie rock, and 1990s punk, to name a few). Perhaps the most notable and unifying elements of alternative music are its performance and consumption by Whites, particularly White males, and its appropriation of language and imagery associated with "working class and underclass white cultures" (Newitz 1997:146).[4] Green Day's anthem can be located within this 1990s popular music context in which we hear a number of songs by White male artists who express a desire for alterity and make claims of being disadvantaged and victimized. But as the alternative music trend lost some of its momentum in the late 1990s, the popularity of Green Day's "Minority" demonstrates that, in the new millennium, there is still a market and demand for songs by White male bands expressing sentiments of being victimized and ill treated.

Alternative music represents just one of several sites of contemporary American popular culture in which one encounters images and narratives of victimized young White males. In this article, I examine such images and narratives of disadvantaged young White males as they are produced in a number of best-selling books that address the social-psychological development of adolescent boys, written in the wake of the rash of school shootings perpetrated by young White boys in 1997–1998 (Garbarino 1999; Gurian 1997, 1998; Pollack 1998) and a 1997 *Sports Illustrated* cover story titled, "Whatever Happened to the White Athlete?" which forwards a panic-driven tale about the declining position of White male athletes in American professional and high-school sports (Price 1997). My aim is to offer a contextualized cultural analysis of these discourses that explains how their representations of "youthful" victimized White males are not only constituted by, and constitutive of, the representational strategies of 1990s White male backlash politics, but signal a new inflection of these representational strategies.

My project draws on David Savran's (1998) observation that the 1990s marked "the ascendancy of a new and powerful figure in U.S. culture: the white male as victim" (p. 4). But unlike Savran's work, which ignored the context of American sports and focused on older White masculinities that largely conform to the biographical dimensions of the baby boom generation, my study examines more youthful White masculinities produced both within and outside of the context of American sports. Building on Savran's work, I contend that these representations of disadvantaged and victimized youthful White masculinities signify a new representational strategy of White male backlash politics – the youthification of the "White male as victim" trope. I highlight the youthful character of these White masculinities for a couple of reasons. First, I use the term *youthful* because the ages of the representations of White masculinities that orient this study range from adolescent boys to 20-something professional athletes. Second, within the discourses I examine, there is a frequent slippage back and forth between the use of terms like *boys* and *young males* and *males* or *White males*, suggesting that these images and narratives about young White boys/males signify something more than just innocent stories about disadvantaged (White) boys (namely, they serve to deny and disavow the privileges of being White and male not only in fin-de-siècle America but also in the future as we move into the new millennium). Finally, I use the term *youthful* to signify how these texts use the terms *boys* and *youth* in ways that are meant to invoke connotations of innocence, lack of constraints, and hope for the future. Such innocent images of young White boys become political when they are produced within a post-Columbine context in which the violent practices of at least a few young White boys complicate such an articulation between innocence and youthful White masculinity.[5]

At first glance, these seemingly unrelated sites of American popular culture – the discourse on the development of adolescent boys and a *Sports Illustrated* report about the disappearance of a White majority within American professional sports – would not seem to share very much in common. But, through my analysis, I articulate these sites together as localities of the national popular involved in the production of images and narratives of victimized and disadvantaged young White males that both reflect, and reproduce, the discursive logics of the contemporary White male backlash. By making connections between these popular sites – one that exists outside of sport and the other within sport – I highlight the pervasiveness of this strategy of representing young White males as vulnerable, victimized, or otherwise disadvantaged subjects. I am interested in these seemingly banal sites of popular culture (what Berlant [1997] called the "waste material of everyday communication," p. 12) because they are the places where conservative backlash ideologies that seek to reconceal, protect, and resecure the representational and material privileges of White masculinity are being translated into a "non-ideological" and "common sense" viewpoint and where they are learned and mobilized by real social actors to make sense of their everyday lives (Kellner 1995).

On Whiteness

whiteness is...intimately involved with issues of power...[and] profoundly influenced by demographic changes, political realignments, and eco-

> nomic cycles. Situationally specific whiteness is always shifting, always reinscribing itself around changing meanings of race in the larger society. (Kincheloe and Steinberg 1998:4)

To illuminate the politics of these "victimized" youthful White masculinities, my analysis is theoretically informed by the recent critical scholarship on Whiteness that has been produced across a wide range of disciplines – including literary studies, sociology, history, speech communication, and cultural studies (Frankenburg 1997). This contemporary interest in examining Whiteness is, following Dyer (1988), a response to the fact that critical studies of race have tended to focus on historically marginalized racial and ethnic groups, thereby overlooking Whiteness "as if it is the natural, inevitable, ordinary way of being human" (p. 6). In an effort to denaturalize the idea of Whiteness as the "privileged place of racial normativity," these critical studies of Whiteness have viewed it as a social construction rather than as a "natural" biological category (Wray and Newitz 1997:3). Such a social constructionist view of Whiteness emphasizes that its meanings are produced by "socially and historically contingent processes of racialization, constituted through and embodied in a wide variety of discourses and practices" (Wray and Newitz 1997:3). In addition, the meanings of Whiteness are understood as always being intimately constituted by and constitutive of relations of power (Kincheloe and Steinberg 1998).

Critical readers of Whiteness also have pointed out that the discursive and social power of Whiteness resides, at least partially, in its ability to be both everything and nothing (Dyer 1988; Nakayama and Krizek 1995). Nakayama and Krizek (1995) suggested that "whiteness makes itself visible and invisible, eluding analysis yet exerting influence over everyday life" (p. 293). Keeping with the tendency of Whiteness to be invisible, Aanerud (1997) argued that it is important to read Whiteness into texts that are not explicitly about race if one is to disrupt Whiteness as the unchallenged racial norm. Shome (1996) reinforced this point by arguing that the goal of critical Whiteness research is to expose and illuminate "the everyday, invisible, subtle, cultural and social practices, ideas, and codes that discursively secure the power and privilege of white people, but that strategically remains unmarked, unnamed, and unmapped in contemporary society" (p. 503).

This recent research on Whiteness also illuminates that Whiteness is not a monolithic, unchanging, and fixed category that always already embodies a certain set of meanings within any and all cultural spaces (Kincheloe and Steinberg 1998). The exemplary historical studies on Whiteness done by Roediger (1994, 1999), Allen (1990), Nelson (1998), and others have illuminated the historical contingency of the meanings of Whiteness. Also, Hartigan's (1997a) ethnographic work on the meaning of Whiteness for poor Whites in Detroit in the 1990s – a space where Whiteness is not equated with economic or social privilege – called attention to the fact that within a specific historical moment in the United States, multiple forms of Whiteness always exist. Thus, Whiteness cannot be understood in an essentialist or overly reductive manner that obfuscates the polysemic, contingent, and dynamic characteristics of Whiteness – how Whiteness is inscribed with different meanings within various cultural spaces and historical moments. Critics of Whiteness must be aware of how Whiteness always already interacts with such things as gender, class, nation, generation, age, and sexuality, thereby inflecting the meaning of Whiteness in subtle ways (Kincheloe and Steinberg 1998).

Given its multiplicity, the meanings of Whiteness within a specific historical era can even be conflicting and contradictory. Critics of Whiteness have keenly pointed out that these conflicting and contradictory meanings of Whiteness facilitate the hegemonic force of Whiteness. As Davy (1997) argued, Whiteness has the capacity for "a number of sometimes conflicting ideologies used differently and differentially depending upon the historical needs of White control. Whiteness is not a totalizing force, but one which changes and shifts in response to historical conditions" (p. 213). Davy's point here highlighted the need to recognize that the internal contradictions and conflicts of representations of Whiteness often mask the insidious and not so obvious ways in which the normative position of Whiteness in American culture is reproduced. Thus, one must be particularly attentive to the ways in which constructions of Whiteness as unprivileged, victimized, or otherwise disadvantaged – images that seem to contradict the ideology of Whiteness as privileged – can work in particular contexts as a mechanism to resecure the privileged normativity of Whiteness in American culture.

Taken together, this recent research on Whiteness highlights the need for critical studies of Whiteness that are conjuncturalist in their approach and that seek to make visible the discourses, practices, and material conditions that produce discourses of Whiteness (and that very often render it invisible and hide its dominating effects). With these points in mind, I turn my attention toward outlining the specific historical and cultural conditions of post-1960s America that implicitly figured the victimized youthful White masculinities that were constructed in a number of books about the development of boys and *Sports Illustrated*'s "crisis" narrative about the position of the White athlete in American professional sports.

Representational Politics of White Masculinity in 1990s America

> You cannot understand an intellectual or artistic project without also understanding its formation: that the relation between a project and a formation is always decisive; and that the emphasis of Cultural Studies is precisely that it engages with both, rather than specializing itself to one or the other. (Williams 1997:168)

Post-1960s America has been marked by a conservative backlash politics that, on one front, sought to arrest the scant gains that historically marginalized groups (women, people of color, gays, and lesbians) have made since the 1960s (Giroux 1997a; Savran 1998). Savran (1998) identified a number of forces of this time period that have produced this conservative backlash:

> the reemergence of the feminist movement; the limited success of the civil rights movement in redressing gross historical inequities through affirmative action legislation; the rise of the lesbian and gay rights movements; the failure of America's most disastrous imperialistic adventure, the Vietnam War; and, perhaps most important, the end of the post-World War II economic boom and the resultant and steady decline in the income of white working- and lower-middle-class men. (p. 5)

As these changing historical conditions made visible the structural privileges of White masculinity in the United States, they simultaneously engendered a crisis of identity for a number of American White males (Weis, Proweller, and Centrie 1997; Wellman 1997). Popular symptoms of this crisis are the appearance of television shows like *Men Behaving Badly* and *Becker*,[6] the popularity of Robert Bly's "Iron John" stories and the Promise Keepers, the rise of White militias epitomized by Timothy McVeigh's bombing of the Oklahoma City federal building, and the resurgence of White supremacist groups like the Ku Klux Klan (Faludi 1999; Kimmel 1996; Savran 1998). Amidst this growing anxiety among a number of White men, a conservative backlash politics developed that used a number of strategies to resecure the structural privileges of White masculinity just as it simultaneously disavowed the existence of these privileges.

This conservative backlash politics was underpinned and motivated by specific race- and gender-based interests. For example, the main mouthpieces and figureheads of backlash discourses are White men like radio personalities Rush Limbaugh and Bob Grant, or columnist Mickey Kaus (Giroux 1997a), or even fictional figures like D-Fens, from the immensely popular early 1990s film, *Falling Down* (1993). Consequently, I rename conservative backlash politics as "White male backlash politics." By White male backlash politics, I mean those images, representations, and discourses that are currently being deployed in American culture in a symbolic (and material) struggle over the meanings articulated with White masculinity in the United States (McCarthy 1998b).

Backlash politics particularly intensified during the 1980s with mean-spirited discourses about welfare, drugs, and crime, which demonized African Americans (particularly young males, single moms, and welfare recipients) and represented their social problems as individual shortcomings and deficiencies. Such discourses blamed already vulnerable minority populations for their economic and social difficulties and disadvantages while obscuring the devastating effects of the economic policies of Reaganism and deindustrialization on these groups (Cole 1996; McCarthy 1998b; Reeves and Campbell 1994). In the early 1990s, widely reported struggles over the academic canon, affirmative action, multiculturalism, illegal immigration, and English-language-only legislation became key sites of this White male backlash (Kincheloe and Steinberg 1998:11).[7] Within each of these struggles, the combatants were largely divided along racial lines between Whites and people of color. At stake in these debates was whether to extend or contain the rights given to these marginalized social groups (Giroux 1994:29–30) and whether Whites and males would bear witness to (and rectify) the racial and gender-based injustices that occurred in the United States in the past and those that persist in the present. Historically marginalized groups – namely, people of color – used a strategy of identity politics[8] in an effort to demand their inclusion as full American citizens (economically, culturally, and politically). Within the logic of identity politics, minority subjects (women, people of color, and gays and lesbians) took the offensive by arguing that their oppressed and marginalized positions were a direct result of the privileged positions of the dominant groups of the United States (Whites, males, heterosexuals).

One notable change within these backlash offensives of the 1990s was that Whiteness – or more often, White masculinity – was increasingly marked publicly as the "oppressive, invisible center" of the American social formation (Giroux 1997a:286). This public scrutiny of White masculinity as always already dominating, oppressive, insensitive, and uncaring is exemplified in a 1993 *Newsweek* cover story titled, "White Male Paranoia," which announced that "feminists, multiculturalists, P.C. policepersons, affirmative action employers, rap artists, Native Americans, Japanese tycoons, Islamic fundamentalists, and Third World dictators, [are] all...saying the same thing [about White males]: *You've been a bad boy*" (Gates 1993:48).

In response to these critiques of White masculinity, a conservative backlash formed that took issue with this construction of White masculinity as oppressive, dominant and dominating, uncaring, and socially and economically privileged. American media culture (television shows, mainstream Hollywood films,[9] popular music, talk radio[10]) became an important terrain that never simply reflected such backlash narratives but was instrumental in producing and disseminating the logics and the key figures constitutive of White male backlash discourses. Figures like Rush Limbaugh and D-Fens became frequently cited popular embodiments of a new simulated figure – the "angry White male" (Gates 1993). The cultural function of the simulated angry White male figure was that it enabled the rage and resentment of White males embittered by the public criticisms of White masculinity to be conveyed publicly. Yet, this repressed rage and resentment, expressed in simulated angry White males[11] like D-Fens, simultaneously allowed such derogatory sentiments to be disavowed by "real" White males as an exaggerated representation of their feelings.[12]

But the angry White male was not the only representational strategy employed by the White male backlash. In fact, this conservative backlash reconfigured White masculinity in a number of ways to contest the emergent view of White masculinity in the 1990s as always already dominant, privileged, and oppressive. One very prominent strategy constituted White men as the besieged victims of the 1990s American social formation. This strategy of constructing White men as victims exemplified how Whites could also engage in identity politics (McCarthy 1998b). This strategy also involved a measure of fantasy. For example, affirmative action programs were imagined as having unfairly slanted the economic playing field against White males despite plenty of sound information that clearly proved the economic advantages that White men still enjoyed in the 1990s (better pay, more opportunities, lower rates of unemployment) (Wellman 1997). This strategy of constructing White males as victims is deeply problematic because it requires a "sociohistorical amnesia" that refuses to bear witness to the histories of racial and gender inequalities in the United States, as well as the cultural, economic, and political privileges that White men still enjoy in the present (Kincheloe and Steinberg 1998:13).

Another representational strategy used by White male backlash politics of the 1990s is the use of a populist rhetoric that, without explicitly mentioning race or gender or class, implicitly reproduces and protects the practices, institutional arrangements, and social relations that enable the central and normative position of White masculinity to be produced. The racial and gender politics of this project are very often expressed through rhetoric about protecting American families, the nation, "traditional" American values, and individualism (Giroux 1997c). This populist rhetoric is often employed to portray multiculturalist and feminist forces and discourses as threats to the values, practices, and social relations on which American families, traditional values, and the nation are said to have been founded.

It should also be noted that the White male backlash was particularly effective in interpellating many White men to its ideologies because of the economic anxieties that many middle- and working-class White men were experiencing in the 1980s and into the early 1990s (Fine and Weis 1998). These anxieties were produced by the globalization of many American corporations; the flight of high-pay manufacturing jobs with good benefits overseas, replaced by low-pay service industry work with few or no benefits; as well as the development of new computer technologies that eliminated (or threatened to eliminate) many white-collar, middle-management positions. From 1973 to 1992, the median income of White males decreased steadily (from $34,231 to $31,012) (Wellman 1997:315). Unable to make sense of their loss of work or their declining or stagnating wages, the rhetoric of the White male backlash offered a variety of narratives that blamed the economic woes of "hard-working Americans" (read: White males) on a host of racially and gender-coded scapegoats. Again, affirmative action programs were offered as a scapegoat. These programs, created to remedy the long histories of structural inequalities and institutionalized discriminatory practices against women and people of color, were strategically (mis-)represented as the sources of White men's declining or stagnating economic circumstances. Such (mis-)representations also masked how post-Fordist processes of deindustrialization or the laissez-faire U.S. economic policies of the 1980s had significantly contributed to the declining (or stagnating) economic fortunes of American White men. Even further, these conservative backlash narratives concealed how the decline in White men's median incomes did not mean any deterioration (by any measure) of their economic advantage over non-Whites and women (Wellman 1997). In fact, Wellman (1997:315) provided evidence that, since 1973, women and non-Whites have experienced relatively similar declines to White men in their median incomes. Consequently, the main effect of these strategic (mis-) representations offered by the White male backlash is that they turned White men's economic fears and anxieties (whether real or perceived) into a rage directed at women and people of color. In this case, racism and sexism became the conduits through which many middle- and working-class White men's feelings of rage and resentment were (re-)directed away from perhaps a more appropriate source for their anxieties – corporate America and their global, late capitalist policies (McCarthy 1998a). Xenophobic desires were produced and legitimated to stave off any White-on-White, class-based conflict between White "haves" and "have-nots."

The creation and repetitive presence of these backlash representational strategies are part of a broader trend in which mainstream American popular culture developed a seemingly insatiable appetite for representations of nonnormative, deprivileged Whites (whether in racial or economic terms) and even "trashy" White figures (many of whom are male) (Hartigan 1997b; Newitz 1997; Newitz and Wray 1997). Hartigan (1997b) argued that the generation of these "bad images of Whiteness" is a symptom of the way in which the meanings ascribed to racial categories have changed due, at least in part, to the criticisms of Whiteness ushered in by the identity movements of the late 1960s (p. 325). Meanwhile, Newitz and Wray (1997) offered two primary reasons for the appearance of stories about White trash in American popular culture during this time period. On one hand, they contend that White trash can function as a "politically conservative protest against so-called multiculturalist agendas such as affirmative action, revisionist education, and social welfare programs" (p. 173). Alternatively, the proliferation of representations of White trash might signify "the first wave of white assimilation to multiculturalist identity...[by] articulating racial dis-empowerment and whiteness together" (p. 173). Although I would optimistically like to believe the latter view, I think Newitz and Wray's former point more accurately captures the political/cultural function of these images of White trash – or, more generally, of Whites who are coded as unprivileged, disadvantaged, victimized, or somehow "trashed" victims – they serve as a means of denying and disavowing the structural privileges of Whiteness that have come under attack in the past decade.

Building on Hartigan's (1997b) and Newitz and Wray's (1997) findings about 1990s American culture, I have observed a number of popular films of the mid- to late-1990s that feature disadvantaged or otherwise unprivileged youthful White male figures that have been constituted by, and are constitutive of, the discursive logics of the White male backlash politics. Mid- to late 1990s Hollywood films like *Good Will Hunting*, *Gattaca*, *Great Expectations*, and even *Titanic* offered narratives that featured young White males whose lack of social, cultural, economic, or genetic privilege (in the case of the futuristic film *Gattaca*, in which genetics determined the class structure of that society) is a central and featured aspect of their identity. Unlike an angry White male figure like D-Fens, American film audiences were asked to like and identify with these youthful, and seemingly unprivileged, White male protagonists. The narratives of these films could be aptly described as contemporary versions of a Horatio Alger-like upward mobility tale. In each of these films, the White male protagonist is represented as coming from unprivileged origins but is able to transcend these origins because of his superior innate capabilities and extraordinary will. Another key aspect of these films is that they highlight class (or genetic) differences within Whiteness in ways that allow the protagonist's social advantages of being White and male to be effectively overlooked by many viewers of the film. By focusing on class differences, and by offering representations of likeable, lower-class (and otherwise unprivileged), young White male protagonists, these films signal a trend in which White viewers are interpellated to identify with unprivileged youthful White male subjects. At the same time, the protagonist's explicit lack of social and economic privilege opens a space where White viewers could use the film as evidence to disavow the social and economic privileges of Whiteness and masculinity.

I take time to briefly discuss these films because their representations of disadvantaged young White masculinities are resoundingly similar to the constructions of young White masculinities in the discourse about the development of adolescent boys and *Sports Illustrated*'s special report on the contemporary plight of the White (male) athlete. Again, I identify these representations of disadvantaged, "victimized," or otherwise unprivileged youthful, White masculinities across the landscape of late 1990s American popular culture to further demonstrate how they represent a reconfiguration of White male backlash politics – the youthfication of the White male as victim figure. Now, I turn my attention to the late 1990s popular discourse of boys' development.

"Lost Boys": Young White Males as Social Victims

> [There's] something very wrong with the adolescence our boys live today...adolescent boys are now, arguably, our most undernurtured population...social structures that over the ages have honored boys are getting dismantled, and there is no increase in the number of equally strong structural elements for teaching duty, meaning, and purpose. (Gurian 1998:3)

In the late 1990s, a popular discourse about a youthful White masculinity was constituted through a number of books explicitly concerned with the development of adolescent boys into "exceptional men" (Gurian 1998: cover). Some of these books, like Michael Gurian's *The Wonder of Boys* (1997), *A Fine Young Man* (1998), and *The Good Son* (1999) and William Pollack's *Real Boys* (1998), garnered national acclaim and national best-seller status. The appearance of others, like Eli Newberger's *The Men They Will Become: The Nature and Nurture of Male Character* (1999), Daniel Kindlon's (with Teresa Barker and Michael Thompson) *Raising Cain: Protecting the*

Emotional Life of Boys (1999), and James Garbarino's *Lost Boys: Why Our Sons Turn Violent and How We Can Save Them* (1999), speaks to the proliferation of interest and concern with the development of "our nation's boys." This widespread cultural concern with the development of adolescent boys intensified after the highly publicized school shootings committed by (White) suburban adolescent boys during 1997–1998 in Paducah, Kentucky; Pearl, Mississippi; Jonesboro, Arkansas; Springfield, Oregon; and Littleton, Colorado. What I find most interesting about this discourse about boys is its construction of young (White) boys as victimized and disadvantaged subjects. It is this repetitive construction of young boys as disadvantaged subjects that implicates these books as a site involved in the reconfiguration of White male backlash politics.

Rather than examining these books individually (noting their points of convergence and divergence), I will limit my discussion to the remarkable similarity of how the category of boys is constructed throughout these books. In each book, boys are rendered visible as suffering, confused, afraid, and vulnerable subjects who, beneath their hard exterior, have an innocent and good essence. Yet, the Whiteness of these boys is not explicitly mentioned in most of the books. In Gurian's (1998) best-selling book, *A Fine Young Man*, boys are represented in essentialist terms, as fragile and emotionally disadvantaged subjects. Throughout much of this book, Gurian describes boys through a rhetoric of suffering, victimization, and disadvantage. In various chapters, he writes, "our adolescent males are suffering privation we have not fully understood" (p. 11); they are the "primary victims of school violence," as well as victims of girls' emotional manipulation (p. 41). According to Gurian, the fragility and emotional disadvantage of boys are biologically determined by such things as the "inherent intellectual fragility in the male brain system" (p. 17), or their "biological hardwiring" (p. 30). Through this biological determinist argument, young adolescent males are figured as disadvantaged victims of their own biology. In contradiction to this biological determinist argument, he also contends that boys are additionally disadvantaged by the development of an allegedly "female culture" that has "collapsed" the social structures set in place to "honor" males and nurture them into their proper roles as men (Gurian 1998). So, not only does Gurian find it important to note how boys are figured as innocent victims of biological processes beyond their control, but his victimized representation of these White-unmarked boys is coupled with the strategy of shifting the blame for boys' abuses to an allegedly feminized American culture that has failed to properly nurture them. These representational strategies set the stage for Gurian to offer his solution to the boys' improper behaviors – our society needs to re-erect those structures that will honor and return them to their proper roles of society's leaders.

Although it does not subscribe to Gurian's (1998) biological determinist view of the behaviors of boys, in *Real Boys*, William Pollack (1998) similarly discusses boys as being "in serious trouble" (p. xxvi). For him, boys' trouble (their confusion and alienation) is the result of conflicting messages about masculinity in post-1960s America that require boys to be both "New Age men" (sensitive, unselfish, and caring) and "cool dudes" (strong, stoic, nonemotive, and in control). Meanwhile, Garbarino (1999) notes in his discussion of lost boys that boys might exhibit hard exteriors, but these displays are merely superficial façades that mask a "vulnerable inner self" (p. 22) and a "wounded soul" (p. 35). These authors even instruct the reader that although the vulnerability, disadvantage, woundedness, or innocence of these boys may not be easily seen because of the hard, cool, and confident masks that boys often present to the world, we should learn to read such masks as further symptoms of the silent suffering and vulnerability of these boys, harboring no doubts about the essential innocence and goodness of boys. Masterfully, the discourse on boys produced in these books is able to rearticulate the dominating and prohibitive behaviors that boys/men often enact on others as further proof of their own vulnerability, suffering, and need for compassion from our culture. In a language of compassion and care for our nation's sons, these books offer a solution to the contemporary problems of boys that, when examined critically, must be read as endorsing a project of remasculinizing men.

Within these books, readers are urged to discard gender stereotypes of males that do not allow them to see boys as they "truly" are – innocent, fragile, vulnerable, scared, and essentially good. They contend that these gender stereotypes of men as uncaring, selfish, nonemotive, and insensitive not only act as a "gender straitjacket" for boys (Pollack 1998:xxiv) but also unfairly constrain the actions of boys and lead our culture to neglect the alleged "real" needs of boys, which are defined as being the center of attention, living without constraints on one's actions, and being placed into positions of control. In this case, where the normative and invisible character of masculinity has been exposed by feminist critiques and led others to categorize men in stereotypical ways, this discourse on boys, through its calls to stop using "unfair" gender stereotypes of men, seeks to resecure the invisibility of masculinity. It also calls for the shoring up of social structures for the purpose of developing young boys into "fine young men" (to paraphrase Gurian). At the same time, the discourse on boys has the effect of working to resecure masculine norms and values and institutional supports that men, within the logic of the backlash imaginary, fear have been unfairly eroded.

Although gender is the social force most explicit within this discourse about boys, race also plays a constitutive role in it. It is significant that this concerned discourse about our nation's boys is produced, not following stories of violence in urban schools in the 1990s (which are racially coded as Black or non-White in the popular imagination) or following the alarming tales of everyday violence in Black, urban communities showcased in early 1990s films like *Boyz in the Hood*, *Juice*, or *Menace II Society*.[13] Instead, this discourse about boys is produced only in the midst of the multiple school shootings involving White suburban boys. Only in Garbarino's (1999) book is the racial dimension of this discourse on boys openly acknowledged. Taken as a whole, Whiteness is largely represented as normal or neutral within this discourse on the development of boys (Aanerud 1997). Although Whiteness is largely rendered invisible through this "normal" and "neutral" discourse about boys, its presence can also be viewed in small traces, usually through imagery. For example, most of the book covers display images of frail-looking, innocent, blond- and brown-haired, White-skinned boys. Or, the Whiteness of this discourse is revealed by making explicit how the discourse uses coded language to evoke race in the reader's mind without having to discuss it explicitly. The use of racial codes within this discourse on boys is evident in Gurian's (1998) book, in which he begins the first chapter with this description of the type of troubled boy his book seeks to help:

> He was a hard shell of a boy already at twelve. Though he and I lived in a middle-sized American city in the Pacific Northwest, he reminded me of urban youth who feel they have nothing going for them at all, trapped in inner cities, dangerous schools, and more dangerous streets. Jason dressed in the hip-hop style, and he had a buzz cut, his baseball cap on backwards, baggy jeans, and a flapping belt. He liked to talk about music, rap music, of course. He liked to show off. (p. 9)

Here, the comparison of Jason, a boy from a middle-sized American city in the Pacific Northwest who has an affinity for rap music, to an urban youth dressed in the hip-hop style invokes a series of racial signifiers (both White and Black) that implicitly connotes his White identity and implies that part of his trouble is his "inappropriate" identifications with styles and music popularly imagined as authentically belonging to African Americans.

The power of Whiteness within this discourse about boys is also evident in its marked difference from the highly racialized contemporary discourses of urban crime and punishment of the 1980s and 1990s in which young Black males are demonized as "menaces to society" who are prone to violence, unsuitable for rehabilitation, and must be incarcerated. Instead, in this discourse about boys, which is implicitly centered on White boys, these boys are constituted as our nation's sons and are not demonized. In fact, they are instead rendered visible as innocent, suffering, and unfairly disadvantaged subjects in need of our nation's compassion and support. Furthermore, rather than blaming (White) boys for their poor behaviors and expressions of rage, blame is shifted onto American culture. The usual suspects repeatedly held responsible for the waywardness of youth are identified – breakdown of the family or absent parents, violence in the media and video games, and "that crazy rock music that kids listen to today." In this case, American culture writ large is also indicted for becoming a feminized culture that has allowed the collapse of "traditional" social structures that once nurtured boys into proper men. Here, the power of Whiteness (and masculinity acting together) resides in the production of a discourse about White boys that does not blame them for their transgressions but instead blames American culture for failing boys while calling for reforms of American society and culture that serve to protect and resecure the hegemonic position (socially and culturally) of White masculinity.

Through its representations of victimized and disadvantaged White boys, this discourse about the proper development of boys can be read as being produced by, and productive of, the representational strategies and discursive logics of the White male backlash. In fact, the discourse's images of victimized and disadvantaged White boys are remarkably similar to the images of victimized and disadvantaged adult White males in other backlash texts like Robert Bly's *Iron John* books; films like *Falling Down*, *Forrest Gump*, and *The Fan*; or Rush Limbaugh's conservative rhetoric about the embattled White guy (see Gates 1993; Giroux 1997a; Savran 1998; or Spade 1998). Like these other backlash texts, this discourse on boys offers interventions that have the effect of attempting to resecure the patriarchal institutional structures and masculine cultural norms and values in the name of facilitating the proper development of adolescent boys who are represented as being naturally (biologically) and culturally victimized and disadvantaged.

When subjected to close analysis, what also becomes notably apparent within this discourse about boys and what further signals its link to the conservative backlash is how the terms *boy*, *young male*, and *male* are often used interchangeably. At times, the books' discussions of the forces that negatively affect the development of boys or young males become discussions of the forces affecting adult males or males without any mention of age. This slippage is readily apparent in Gurian's (1998) text through his frequent use of his own and other middle-aged men's recollections of their adolescent years as his empirical "data," or through statements like, "Testosterone, then, is a major factor in naturally cutting *males* [rather than *boys* or *adolescent males*] off from emotional development" (p. 36). In this rather easy substitution of males and adult males for boys and adolescent males, one begins to see how the alleged "truths" about the needs of boys produce a series of effects that, whether intended or not, effectively seek to reconstruct a social formation (values, norms, and institutional structures) that recenters White masculinity within American social, cultural, and familial life. Even further, the link between this discourse on boys and the discursive logic of backlash politics is revealed through Gurian's (1998) identification of notorious male backlash proponent Warren Farrell's book, *The Myth of Male Power* (1994), as a "must-read" for anyone who wants to understand what "men and boys" (notice the slippage) suffer in all human health indicators (p. 280).

Finally, this innocent, vulnerable, and victimized depiction of the racially unmarked category of boys serves as a brilliantly effective means of promoting (whether intended or not) the interests of the White male backlash. When the goal of the politics of the White male backlash is to, in Savran's (1998) words, "recoup the losses they [White males] have allegedly suffered at the hands of women and people of color" (p. 4), such things as bolstering social structures that honor males and promoting social practices that avoid putting constraints on boys (because constraints of any kind are represented as being unhealthy to boys' proper development) implicate the discourse on boys' development as an armature of the conservative backlash politics. The category of boys is, perhaps, even more effective in generating support for the ideas of backlash politics because the connotation of the term boys with "innocence" and with "the future" helps to allow the discourse to appear to be nonideological – just an innocent, nonpoliticized discourse interested in promoting the health and well-being of boys who represent our nation's future. But it is also because of the supposed innocence and good intentions of this discourse about boys that the backlash politics constitutive of it largely go unnoticed. That is, because the discourse is presented through noble rhetoric about making "adolescent boys into exceptional men" (Gurian 1998: front cover), one might miss how it inconspicuously promotes a set of values and social arrangements that seeks to ensure the reproduction of the hegemonic social and cultural position of White masculinity. Not only does the use of the term boys, where race is erased and "boy" stands as a sign of a youthful White masculinity, allow the racial and gender politics of the discourse to be masked (or easily denied even if they are made visible), but the youthfulness of "boys" urges the reinvestment in social structures that honor (White) males not just in the present but, perhaps even more important, promotes the reproduction of these structures (and masculinist norms and values) in the future.

Sports Illustrated's Crisis of the Young White (Male) Athlete: American Sports as a Site of the White Male Backlash

> The white athlete – and here we speak of the young men in team sports who ruled the American athletic scene for much of the century – doesn't want to play anymore...the playing field [American professional sports arena] had become the nation's common ground, the one highly visible stage on which blacks and whites acted out the process of learning to live, play and fight together as peers. Today fewer whites stand on that common ground. (Price 1997:32–33)

Sports Illustrated's December 6, 1997, issue offered readers a special report titled, "What Ever Happened to the White Athlete?" (Price 1997). The article is represented as a six-month-long inquiry into the subject of race and sports that included "dozens of interviews with coaches, athletes, executives and academics and a nationwide poll of 1,835 middle school and high school kids" (p. 33). Despite its best efforts to give this article the gloss of an objective and soundly researched scientific report, the end product of *Sports Illustrated*'s work is a panic-driven news story focused on the increasing absence of the White athlete in contemporary American professional sports. In my analysis, I implicate this article about the declining position of White (males) in sport as another site of 1990s America in which the representational strategies and discursive logics of the White male backlash politics are deployed and disseminated for public consumption. Then, I make visible how *Sports Illustrated*'s report uses representations of youthful White males, configured by the logics and strategies of the White male backlash, as opposed to adult White males. These young White masculinit(-ies) first get figured as suffering and victimized minority subjects and then get contradictorily refigured, by the article's end, as having an extraordinary will and self-determining agency as well as a restored confidence. In addition, through critically interrogating the functions and contradictions of the article's depictions of youthful White masculinities, we gain insight into how the article's conflicting and seemingly incongruous representations of White masculinity work to reproduce the hegemonic power of Whiteness.

The first evidence of how *Sports Illustrated*'s special report on race and sports is produced by, and reproduces, the White male backlash ideologies is the magazine's conspicuous choice for the cover photo that accompanied the report. The cover displayed a nostalgia-laden, black-and-white image of four high-school-aged, clean-cut, affable White male basketball players whose uniforms and hairstyles unmistakably code them as pre-1960s figures. Each player has a conservative, closely cropped haircut; big ears; and inviting boy-next-door smile. Each dons Chuck Taylor sneakers and playing uniforms that are notably white. The players could easily be mistaken for the all-White high-school basketball team featured in the 1986 blockbuster film *Hoosiers*. Each player is shown kneeling with one hand extended forward touching a single basketball resting in the center between them. This positioning of the athletes, each with a hand on the basketball, signifies them as a team that presumably works together toward a shared goal rather than as a group of individuals. Their smiling faces, oozing with optimism and innocence, and their unifying pose invite (White male) readers to nostalgically identify with them and a set of traditional values that they project – teamwork, competition, camaraderie, winning, hard work, and playing for the love of the game. Of course, these are the values that many sports pundits and fans resentfully decry as having been lost in today's professional athletes and sports. So, then, this 1950s team-oriented, sacrificial White male athlete constructed in *Sports Illustrated*'s article is implicitly defined over and against the African American NBA or NFL player who is said to be more concerned with making money and achieving celebrity status than with winning championships and being a solid role model.

Sports Illustrated's decision to use a picture of pre-1960s White male youths rather than an image of contemporary youths is quite noteworthy for a number of reasons. Like other texts framed by the White male backlash ideologies, *Sports Illustrated*'s decision to use this image evokes a pervasive nostalgia (invested in by many adult White males) for a historical moment imagined as a less complicated and innocent time, particularly for White males. A moment absent from such things as the "annoying" sensitivities of political correctness and affirmative action, the increased public marking of Whiteness, and directives to emphasize and celebrate multiculturalism and cultural diversity. This recollection of 1950s America, embodied in these smiling and wholesome young White males, invokes a longing for imagined good old days – prior to the "disrupting" events of the 1960s – when the centrality and pre-eminence of the White male was taken for granted, when the position of White males was rarely publicly challenged.

This nostalgic longing for a pre-1960s America expressed in this *Sports Illustrated* cover photo is a variation of the backlash strategy discussed earlier in which populist rhetoric that does not explicitly mention race, gender, or class is deployed to reproduce social practices, institutional arrangements, and ideologies that center and normalize the position of White masculinity. In this case, by invoking these backlash ideologies through the photo without actually expressing them, this nostalgia (with its racial and gender implications) can be conveyed in a seemingly innocent and inconspicuous manner.

Sports Illustrated's cover image also begs the question: What audience would be interpellated by this image and special report on the plight of the professional White (male) athlete? *Sports Illustrated*'s nostalgic black-and-white choice rather than a contemporary color photo of White youth may signal an effort to appeal to middle-aged White men who recognize themselves in the image. But *Sports Illustrated*'s repeated framing of the crisis of the White athlete as a contemporary crisis of *young* White male athletes suggests that the intended audience is a young White male who is allegedly turning away from sport. Rather than arguing that the article is intended to appeal to either older White males or younger White males, I contend that the article's framing – its choice for the cover image, use of statistics collected from a national survey of current high-school athletes, and stories of contemporary young White male professional athletes – invites the interpellation of White males across different generations. On one level, the article's focus on young White (male) athletes signals how representations of unfairly disadvantaged youthful White masculinities, in this case within sport, are increasingly being employed as symbols to serve the ideological ends of White male backlash politics – generating anxiety, resentment, and a sense of crisis about the supposed declining position of White males within American society and culture. On another level, the interweaving of these images and stories about both former young White (male) athletes and current White (male) athletes suggests an effort to construct a narrative that interpellates younger White males to invest in the White male backlash imaginary.

Henry Giroux (1997a) has noted that during the 1990s, "whiteness" was increasingly made visible at times when Whites were constituted as victims. *Sports Illustrated*'s special report exemplifies Giroux's observation. In bold white letters that stand out in relation to the black-and-white photo, the question, "What Ever Happened to the White Athlete?" is posed. The word *White* appears in a much larger font; its prominence demonstrates how, in the late 1990s, Whiteness is often made visible and marked in popular culture at those times when the practices of a white-skinned person or group do not conform to, or fit within, the dominant meanings associated with Whiteness. Stated a bit differently, Whiteness is often made visible in the national popular when particular performances of White-skinned subjects or historical events (such as the changing racial configuration of athletes within certain professional sports in the United States) potentially challenge, and threaten to disrupt, our "naturalized" ideas about the cultural meanings of Whiteness (its invisibility and/or normativity) or its centered social positioning. Even further, Whiteness is not only made visible in the article to signify the disruption of its naturalized meanings or the social position of Whites in society, but it is paradoxically made visible to restore the invisibility of Whiteness and, thus, to resecure its normative and central sociocultural position.

Moving to the text of *Sports Illustrated*'s special report, the article begins and ends with a story about a 29-year-old White male American sprinter named Kevin Little. We are first introduced to Little recalling a recurring incident in his life in which, to his dismay, he has to explain to disbelieving others (Whites and Blacks) that he is a professional sprinter. Little laments about how he commonly receives a look of surprise, a slight chuckle, and the words, "But you're white?" when he identifies himself as a sprinter (Price 1997:32). We are told that Little is tired of the disbelief and skepticism he encounters when he tells others that he is a sprinter. Next, we learn that in March of 1997, Little not only tied the American indoor record in the 200 meters at the world championships in Paris, but he was the first White American since 1956 to win a major international sprint title (Price 1997).

This story about Little is not mobilized simply to highlight his remarkable on-track performances (although his athletic success is an important facet to his story). Rather, Little's story gains its currency because it figures him as a young White male athlete who is "suffering" from self-doubts brought about by fans, friends, and (Black) competitors stereotyping him as an inferior athlete because he is White. In the typical manner of a backlash text, Little is initially rendered visible to the reader as a victim. In this case, Little is constituted as a victim of the negative stereotypes about White athleticism. Here, the increased public marking of Whiteness by others is represented as having unfairly caused Little much suffering and unfairly constrained him by erecting social and psychic forces (people's unsupportive comments and his own self-doubts) that constrain his efforts to fulfill his aspiration of being the best sprinter he can be. In contradistinction to the arguments White conservatives often proffer that race does not affect a person's life outcomes (usually applied in cases in which people of color speak of disadvantages that are the result of their racial identity), Little's story asserts that the recent public marking of Whiteness – particularly, the limiting stereotypes of White athleticism – produces significant debilitating effects that unfairly restrict his actions and aspirations. Thus, within *Sports Illustrated*'s report, race is deemed important in those moments when the public marking of Whiteness negatively affects the life possibilities of White males. Furthermore, through its exposition of the way in which making Whiteness visible has had derogatory effects on Kevin Little, *Sports Illustrated*'s story implicitly endorses a desire to make Whiteness once again invisible.

It should be no surprise that *Sports Illustrated* begins its report by featuring an athlete like Kevin Little. As a White person participating in a sport commonly understood as being dominated by Black athletes (200-meter run), he is the perfect figure to play the role of the unprivileged, minority White male subject within contemporary American sports. By making Little's story the lead, *Sports Illustrated* presents him as "Exhibit A" in its crisis narrative about the ground that the White (male) athlete has unfairly lost. Through its survey of middle-school and high-school youth's attitudes about sport participation, *Sports Illustrated* attempts to show that Little is not alone; that he is just one of many young White (male) athletes who have either turned away from sports or whose confidence in their athletic abilities has waned due to the disappearance of White (male) athletes on the national athletic stage. Young White males are represented as dropping out of the "big three" American sports (football, baseball, and basketball) at a rapid rate or as being unfairly deterred from participating in these sports by parents, coaches, and the media, all of whom see African American males as a dominating athletic presence that impedes White male athletes' chances to compete at either the youth or professional levels. These young, White male athletes are figured as being unfairly subjugated (having their agency constrained), not only because of the debilitating effects of negative stereotypes about White athleticism but because of the overwhelming success of Black males in American professional sport. Within this story line, Black male athletes are depicted as a dominant, discriminating, and exclusionary force whose success unfairly constrains the life possibilities of White male youths by forcing them to abandon their dreams of being a professional athlete. This narrative of Black dominance and White male disadvantage in sport enables the U.S. racial hierarchy to be turned on its head so that White males can be positioned as a seemingly legitimate unprivileged subject. But by inverting the social order, this story of White male disadvantage represents an attempt to forget or render inconsequential the long histories of racial inequalities, institutional racism, and White privilege that have existed in the past and that still persist in the present, both within and without sport (Rodriguez 1998).

Sports Illustrated's special report, then, alleges that perhaps the most alarming effect of the disappearance of the White male professional athlete is that it has caused "a spreading White inferiority complex" for young White males (Hoberman, cited in Price 1997:44). Although *Sports Illustrated* makes this claim, it does not support this allegation with evidence. In fact, it actually provides evidence that contradicts such a claim. The article provides pie charts with shocking titles like "White Flight" and "Feeling Inferior" that catch readers' eyes and reinforce its thesis of White (male) athletes being in crisis. But closer inspection of these graphs and charts reveals that only 34 percent of the White male youths surveyed agreed with the statement, "African-American players have become so dominant in sports such as football and basketball that many Whites feel they can't compete at the same level as blacks," whereas 45 percent of the White male youths surveyed disagreed with the statement (Price 1997:34). Although short on evidence, these graphs and statistics, with their veneer of scientific objectivity and their prominent titles, create the impression that *Sports Illustrated* has sufficiently supported its hyperbolic claims of White male victimization within sport.

The articulation of this White inferiority complex is also important because it shows how youthful White males, as opposed to middle-aged White men like a Promise Keeper, or Rush Limbaugh listener, or the celluloid figure D-Fens, are being mobilized within this backlash politics. The relative youthification of the White male backlash figure within this narrative about sport is significant because it is his youth – a traditionally subordinate subject position – that, in part, facilitates the production of his victimized identity. In *Sports Illustrated*'s narrative, constructing American professional sport as a site of African American dominance and White inferiority requires that one selectively forget two things. First, that the commercialized and mediated American sports formation also includes sports like tennis, golf, extreme sports, professional wrestling, and soccer, which are (numerically) dominated by Whites. Second, professional sports are almost exclusively administered (coached, owned, and operated) by White males. But, by focusing on relatively young White athletes (whether at the professional or youth levels of sport) within its narrative of White athletic crisis, such irrefutable evidence can be conveniently forgotten or overlooked.

In addition, as in the discourse of boys development, the connotation of "the future," which is often articulated with the category of youth, implies that the "spreading inferiority complex" being felt by these White males is not merely a problem of today but could escalate into a potential problem of the future. The unspoken anxiety that underwrites this claim of a spreading White inferiority complex among young White male athletes is, "If young White males feel inferior to African American men in sport will this sports-specific inferiority complex translate into feelings of inferiority in other spaces and practices unrelated to sport?" Suddenly, what is at stake is not simply the cultural position of White males in sport but the cultural and social position of White masculinity in American culture as a whole.

Similarly, the category of youth is also frequently articulated with notions of "hope" and "limitless opportunities." Consequently, the alleged African American dominance in sport becomes a force that unfairly limits the life possibilities of White male youths afflicted by this supposed inferiority complex. It supposedly does so by influencing young White male athletes to give up their optimistic dreams of athletic stardom and effectively arrest their athletic development. The notion that taking away a young person's dreams is equivalent to arresting their development is subtly at play within this articulation of this White male crisis to youthful White males, especially as sport is understood as providing youths with valuable lessons about the merits of hard work, perseverance, meritocracy, and optimism that transcend their sporting experiences. Thus, the youthfulness of the victimized White male athlete intensifies what is at stake in the African American dominance of American professional sport. Not only is the alleged growing White inferiority complex with young White males implicitly cast as a symptom of the eroding position of White masculinity within American culture in the present, but its articulation with youthful White males further suggests that it may have deleterious effects on them in the future.

Meanwhile, the article also produces another important image of White masculinity through a story about the athletic success of White NBA player, Brent Barry. Although Barry garners much attention as the son of NBA legend, Rick Barry, his story is important for *Sports Illustrated*'s narrative because he defied conventional racial logic when he won the 1996 NBA Slam Dunk Championship. Thus, Barry is introduced into the article's narrative because he represents a young White male who has achieved a relatively high level of athletic success in a sport dominated by Black athletes in the 1990s (basketball). He is valorized for his strong will to succeed and his ability to be a self-determining agent who is not constrained by forces outside of himself (i.e., Black dominance in basketball, derogatory stereotypes of White athleticism). This representation of a youthful White masculinity as an unconstrained, self-determining agent is needed within *Sports Illustrated*'s special report to counter its initial image of White masculinity as a suffering, disadvantaged, minority subject within American sports. In addition, this counterimage of White masculinity functions to resecure the normative way in which White masculinity is imagined within American culture (as sovereign, individualistic, self-determining agents), thus providing an imaginary solution to any possible anxieties created (in White male readers) by its initial construction of White masculinity as a suffering, constrained victim within contemporary American sports.

The construction of Barry as possessing an extraordinary will relies on the stereotype of Whites' athletic inferiority to Blacks and is enabled by the depiction of suburban culture (implicitly coded as White) as a social barrier for White (male) athletic success because it is overwrought with comforts and distractions like video games and abundant opportunities outside of sport. In addition, the supposed lack of community-wide support of White athletes is used to constitute suburban culture as a social constraint on White (male) athletes. Quite ironically, suburban comfort is cast in *Sports Illustrated*'s narrative as a gigantic social barrier that young White male athletes have to overcome to become professional athletes. This peculiar representation of "suburban comfort as constraint" is necessary to constitute youthful White male athletes, like Barry, as possessing an extraordinary will. Coupled with its reliance on the stereotypical notion of White athletic inferiority, this depiction of suburbia allows young, White male athletes to be represented as having to work harder than the inner-city Black athlete. A testimonial from Barry is used within the article to legitimate this representation of suburban culture:

> "It almost takes more effort to get out of a situation where you could sit back and be comfortable" he says. "If you're struggling you could say, 'I don't need to do this anymore. My parents have great jobs, I could go to any college I want.' It's a much different set of social barriers; the pressure on you to perform isn't so great. If you're the white kid and you've got glee club after school, the ski trip on the holidays and Stratomatic baseball in the spring, well, that's what you're going to do. I pride myself on the fact that I had to have a lot of desire and will and competitiveness to get out of white suburban America and make it in a game dominated by great black athletes." (quoted in Price 1997:50)

Through his comment, Barry offers an amazing inversion of the customary sporting upward-mobility tale usually associated with basketball and African American, inner-city males in the

1990s. Within Barry's statement, the dire economic and social conditions (deindustrialization, drugs, rampant crime, institutionalized racism) that often leave economically disadvantaged, inner-city Black males few viable avenues for success other than sport are trivialized and rendered incomparable to the alleged social barriers facing the suburban White male athlete. In fact, these bleak social and economic conditions are constituted as advantages for the Black athlete because they produce pressure to succeed in athletics and community-wide support for athletics in the Black community. Incredibly, *Sports Illustrated* does not merely equate the social conditions of the suburban White male athlete and the inner-city Black male athlete; rather, it constitutes the plight of the White male suburban subject who has to overcome the "distractions" of suburban comfort and a White community that does not fully support his athletic investments as being more difficult than the condition of his Black male counterpart. The economic and social privileges of being White, male, and from the suburbs are reconstituted to become social barriers hampering White males' athletic success. *Sports Illustrated*'s contradictory narrative of White male athletic disadvantage (a variation of the construction of the "White male as victim" trope) represents a unique and troubling attempt to disavow White male privilege. Yet, its framing of Barry's story also enables White masculinity within the *Sports Illustrated* article to be rendered visible not just as a social victim but also to be figured as a self-determining agent whose strong will and determination propelled him to overcome the social and psychological barriers necessary to achieve athletic success.

The configuration of Barry as a White male with an extraordinary will is reinforced by a final story about the lone White sprinter, Kevin Little. In the closing two paragraphs, Little re-enters the narrative and is much different than the Kevin Little the reader met at the opening of the article. He is constituted as no longer being afflicted by feelings of self-doubt and defensiveness brought about by the negative stereotypes of White athleticism. Instead, Little is represented as using his newly visible Whiteness to gain an advantage on his Black competitors:

> No one [African American] wants to lose to him. "Then the edge goes to me," he says. "I can look into their eyes and their faces, and if they have a little fear of losing to a white sprinter, I've won right there. *I'm holding the cards*. (Little, quoted in Price 1997:51, emphasis added)

Little's quote is employed to both reaffirm the need to make Whiteness once again invisible while also serving to reassure the (White male) reader through this fabrication of White men as self-determining subjects who are not and will not be constrained by social conditions (like stereotypes, Black dominance, and lack of social support for their athletic endeavors). Little re-emerges at the end of the article as a pedagogical figure for White males – an example of an unfairly disadvantaged White male who not only proves the superior will of White males but has even learned to use "black dominance as his weapon" (Price 1997:51). Thus, by the article's end, White masculinity is reconfigured not as a suffering and constrained social victim but as many White American men would like to imagine themselves – as self-determining subjects of history (rather than its objects) who author their own life outcomes and who are not constrained by social forces beyond their control.

Conclusion

> Forms of media culture induce individuals to identify with dominant social and political ideologies, positions, and representations. In general, it is not a system of rigid ideological indoctrination that induces consent to existing capitalist societies, but the pleasures of the media and consumer culture...[that] seduce[s] audiences into identifying with certain views, attitudes, feelings, and positions. (Kellner 1995:3)

Several other cultural critics, influenced by the critical work being done on Whiteness, have illuminated how a number of popular culture sites – like Hollywood films (Clover 1993; Giroux 1997b; Kennedy 1996; McCarthy 1998a; Savran 1998); AM radio (Giroux 1997a), television (Newitz and Wray 1997), and grunge music (Newitz 1997) – have been instrumental in not only disseminating but also generating the representational strategies and logics of this White male backlash politics. Surprisingly, little work has examined how contemporary discourses involving sport, as a site of popular culture, have been influential in the production and dispersal of the logics of this White male backlash politics, whose implicit goal is to resecure the central and dominant cultural position of White masculinity in the late 1990s. My interrogation of *Sports Illustrated*'s special report is an initial effort in this direction. Such critical attention of contemporary discourses and developments in sport can illuminate how sport has become an important site of the White male backlash because the overrepresentation of African American males in these sports enables the fabrication of a crisis narrative about the precarious and vulnerable cultural position of White males that can be seemingly defended through a quick glance at the "empirical" evidence of the contemporary racial makeup of American professional athletes.

Furthermore, my analysis provides evidence of how images of more youthful White masculinities are increasingly being employed within White male backlash texts. The youthification of the White male backlash figure suggests that an effort is being made to interpellate younger White males into the White male backlash ideologies. Such an effort might produce a cross-generational investment by White men of various ages in these ideologies that would facilitate the continuation of the White male backlash's political goals in the future. Or, the youthification of the White male backlash figure might also be symbolically useful as it enables the popular acceptance of backlash ideologies that seek to resecure the hegemonic position of White masculinity within American culture in the name of such things as improving the lives of boys or in the name of enabling young White males an opportunity to pursue their interests in traditional sports, like basketball or football or track. Nonetheless, what can be said with some reasonable certainty is that the production of these representations of disadvantaged and victimized young White males within popular music, popular literature, and popular sport operates, as Kellner (1995) stated, as sources of cultural pedagogy that attempt to seduce (White male) audiences to "deny what is most obvious: the privileged position of whiteness" (Kincheloe and Steinberg 1998:15).

NOTES

1 The title of this article is taken from Green Day's song, "Minority."

2 *Total Request Live* is a show in which mainly teen viewers can call and e-mail to vote for their favorite songs and videos.

3 Of course, it should be noted that Green Day's "Minority" chorus also contains the line, "Down with the Moral Majority," which could suggest that the song is meant to resist the contemporary conservative backlash politics. Nonetheless, rather than trying to pin down the song's meaning, I want to emphasize that it is the precisely polysemic character of the song – allowing many meanings both reactionary and resistive to be articulated to it – that allows it to be embraced unproblematically by mainstream radio and MTV as simply a recurrent expression of teen rebellion against adult authority. Perhaps more germane to my present discussion, the desire to be a minority expressed in the song allows it to fit nicely within the discursive boundaries of the White male backlash by reproducing images and narratives of White males as minorities, as disadvantaged, and as victims.

4 White male artists and bands like Beck (with his song "Loser" and its popular chorus, "I'm a loser baby, so why don't you kill me"), Pearl Jam (with their lamentful ballad, "Nothing Man"), the Offspring (with their Top 40 hit, "Self-Esteem" and its signature line, "I'm just a sucker with no self-esteem"), and Nirvana (with their infamous tune, "Smells Like Teen Spirit") make up the key contributors to this alternative musical trend.

5 I thank Dr. Cheryl Cole on this point. Our discussion helped me to see how the events of Columbine make the articulation of White boys with "innocence" and "hope for the future" a more fervently politicized representation.

6 *Men Behaving Badly* was an NBC sitcom that aired in the mid- to late 1990s and whose humor was predicated on watching two White, male 20-somethings attempt to reclaim their masculine privileges. C.B.S.' show *Becker* (1998) was one of the first to bring the "angry White male" (who, in 1998, can be constructed to elicit laughter and identification in its audience rather than discomfort and abjection) into American living rooms.

7 The White male backlash of the 1990s was also precipitated by the severe recessions of the late 1980s and early 1990s that even affected the middle classes (if not materially at least psychologically). White working- and middle-class men's fears

about downward economic mobility due to these recessions and the increasingly globalized, post-Fordist American economy led to an intensification of racism for White men as they tried to draw distinctions between themselves and Black men, imagined as an inferior other (Weis, Proweller, and Centrie 1997:217).

8 By identity politics, I mean the political practices and mobilizations based on cultural and social identities that involve marking one's group as a victim of discriminatory practices in the past or present (Clarke 1991).

9 See Berlant (1997), McCarthy (1998b), and Savran (1998), for analyses of how contemporary films like *Forrest Gump*, *Disclosure*, *Falling Down*, and so forth can be read as crucial cultural, pedagogical sites in producing, authorizing, and gaining momentum for this conservative White male backlash politics.

10 Giroux (1997a, 1997b) argued that talk radio, specifically Rush Limbaugh, is an important site through which this White backlash politics is constructed, popularized, and made desirable to the (White middle-class) public.

11 I use "simulated" in the Baudrillardian (1983) sense to mean a copy for which there is no original. Thus, I am not trying to argue that there is sufficient empirical proof to say that "real" American White men espoused the views attributed to the angry White male. In fact, I think such evidence is inconsequential. What I argue is that the very ambiguity of the actual existence of the angry White male (his simulated quality) enabled the complaints of real American White men to be publicly expressed, yet simultaneously denied, because real White American men did not exactly fit the extreme, paranoic profile of a D-Fens or the angry White male figure constructed in the *Newsweek* cover story.

12 The simulated character of the angry White male even allowed "real" White men like Rush Limbaugh to express such "angry" racist or sexist or homophobic sentiments and later disavow them by claiming that he was just performing this alleged angry White male to the delight of his audience.

13 By citing these films, I do not claim that they reflect a pre-given reality or provide a window on contemporary Black, urban life. Instead, as these films were very often interpreted as mirror images of the lives of young Black male youths in the early 1990s, such interpretations did not produce a mainstream discourse that called for compassion and understanding of the lives of urban Black male youths. In addition, within mainstream discourse, the films did not call for changes in the culture that produced such violence in urban America like this "discourse about boys" (which focused on White boys) did.

REFERENCES

Aanerud, R. 1997. Fictions of Whiteness: Speaking the names of Whiteness in U.S. literature. In R. Frankenburg, ed., *Displacing Whiteness: Essays in Social and Cultural Criticism*. Durham, NC: Duke University Press.

Allen, T. 1990. *The Rise and Fall of the White Republic*. London: Verso.

Baudrillard, J. 1983. *Simulations*. Semiotext(e). New York: Columbia University Press.

Berlant, L. 1997. Introduction: The intimate public sphere. In *The Queen of America goes to Washington City: Essays on sex and citizenship* (pp. 1–24). Durham, NC: Duke University Press.

Clarke, S. A. 1991. Fear of a Black planet. *Socialist Review*, 21(3/4):37–59.

Clover, C. 1993. "Falling Down" and the rise of the average White male. In P. Cook and P. Dodd, eds., *Women and Film: A Sight and Sound Reader* (pp. 138–147). Philadelphia: Temple University Press.

Cole, C. 1996. American Jordan: P.L.A.Y., consensus, and punishment. *Sociology of Sport Journal* 13:366–397.

Davy, K. 1997. Outing Whiteness: A feminist/lesbian project. In M. Hill, ed., *Whiteness: A Critical Reader* (pp. 204–225). New York: New York University Press.

Dyer, R. 1988. White. *Screen* 29(4):44–65.

Faludi, S. 1999. *Stiffed: The Betrayal of the American Man*. New York: William Morrow.

Farrell, W. 1994. *The Myth of Male Power: Why Men are the Disposable Sex*. New York: Simon & Schuster.

Fine, M., and Weis, L. 1998. *The Unknown City: The Lives of Poor and Working Class Adults*. Boston: Beacon.

Frankenburg, R. 1997. Introduction: Local Whitenesses, localizing Whiteness. In R. Frankenburg, ed., *Displacing Whiteness: Essays in Social and Cultural Criticism* (pp. 1–34). Durham, NC: Duke University Press.

Garbarino, J. 1999. *Lost Boys: Why our Sons Turn Violent and How We Can Save Them*. New York: Free Press.

Gates, D. 1993. White male paranoia. *Newsweek* 121 (13),48–53.

Giroux, H. 1994. Living dangerously: Identity politics and the new cultural racism. In H. Giroux and

P. McLaren, eds., *Between Borders: Pedagogy and the Politics of Cultural Studies*. New York: Routledge.

Giroux, H. 1997a. Rewriting the discourse of racial identity: Towards a pedagogy and politics of Whiteness. *Harvard Educational Review* 67(2):285–320.

Giroux, H. 1997b. White noise: Racial politics and the pedagogy of Whiteness. In *Channel Surfing: Race Talk and the Destruction of Today's Youth* (pp. 89–136). New York: St. Martin's.

Giroux, H. 1997c. White squall: Resistance and the pedagogy of Whiteness. *Cultural Studies* 11 (2):276–289.

Gurian, M. 1997. *The Wonder of Boys*. New York: Jeremy T. Parcher/Putnam.

Gurian, M. 1998. *A Fine Young Man*. New York: Jeremy T. Parcher/Putnam.

Gurian, M. 1999. *The Good Son*. New York: Jeremy T. Parcher/Putnam.

Hartigan, J. 1997a. Establishing the fact of Whiteness. *American Anthropologist* 99(3):495–506.

Hartigan, J. 1997b. Unpopular culture: The case of "White trash." *Cultural Studies* 11(2):316–343.

Kellner, D. 1995. *Media Culture*. New York: Routledge.

Kennedy, L. 1996. Alien nation: White male paranoia and imperial culture in the United States. *Journal of American Studies* 30(1):87–100.

Kimmel, M. 1996. *Manhood: A Cultural History*. New York: Free Press.

Kincheloe, J., and Steinberg, S. (1998). Addressing the crisis of Whiteness: Reconfiguring White identity in a pedagogy of Whiteness. In J. L. Kincheloe, S. R. Steinberg, N. M. Rodriguez, and R. E. Chennault, eds., *White Reign: Deploying Whiteness in America* (pp. 3–30). New York: St. Martin's.

Kindlon, D., Barker, T., and Thompson, M. 1999. *Raising Cain: Protecting the Emotional Life of Boys*. New York: Ballantine.

McCarthy, C. 1998a. Living with anxiety: Race and the renarration of public life. In J. L. Kincheloe, S. R. Steinberg, N. M. Rodriguez, and R. E. Chennault, eds., *White Reign: Deploying Whiteness in America* (pp. 329–341). New York: St. Martin's

McCarthy, C. 1998b. The devil finds work: Re-reading race and identity in contemporary life. In C. McCarthy, ed., *The Uses of Culture* (pp. 135–146). New York: Routledge.

Nakayama, T., and Krizek, R. 1995. Whiteness: A strategic rhetoric. *Quarterly Journal of Speech* 81:291–309.

Nelson, D. 1998. *National Manhood: Capitalist Citizenship and the Imagined Fraternity of White Men*. Durham, NC: Duke University Press.

Newberger, E. 1999. *The Men They Will Become: The Nature and Nurture of Male Character*. Cambridge, MA: Perseus.

Newitz, A. 1997. White savagery and humiliation, or a new racial consciousness in the media. In M. Wray and A. Newitz, eds., *White Trash: Race and Class in America* (pp. 131–154). New York: Routledge.

Newitz, A., and Wray, M. 1997. What is "White trash"? Stereotypes and economic conditions of poor Whites in the United States. *The Minnesota Review* 47:61–77.

Pollack, W. 1998. *Real Boys*. New York: Owl.

Price, S. L. 1997 (December 6). Whatever happened to the White athlete? *Sports Illustrated* 87(23):32–51.

Reeves, J. L. and Campbell, R. 1994. *Cracked Coverage: Television News, The Anti-Cocaine Crusade, and the Reagan Legacy* Durham, NC: Duke University Press.

Rodriguez, N. 1998. Emptying the content of Whiteness: Toward an understanding of the relation between Whiteness and pedagogy. In J. L. Kincheloe, S. R. Steinberg, N. M. Rodriguez, and R. E. Chennault eds., *White Reign: Deploying Whiteness in America* (pp. 31–62). New York: St. Martin's.

Roediger, D. 1994. *Towards the Abolition of Whiteness: Essays on Race, Politics, and Working Class History*. London: Verso.

Roediger, D. 1999. *The Wages of Whiteness: Race and the Making of the American Working Class* (2nd edn). London: Verso.

Savran, D. 1998. *Taking it Like a Man: White Masculinity, Masochism, and Contemporary American Culture*. Princeton, NJ: Princeton University Press.

Shome, R. 1996. Race and popular cinema: The rhetorical strategies of Whiteness in city of joy. *Communication Quarterly* 44(4):502–518.

Spade, D. 1998 (April). White man blues. *George*, 52.

Weis, L., Proweller, A., and Centrie, C. 1997. Re-examining "A moment in history": Loss of privilege inside White working-class masculinity in the 1990s. In M. Fine, L. Weis, L. Powell, and L. M. Wong, eds., *Whiteness: A Critical Reader* (pp. 209–226). New York: New York University Press.

Wellman, D. 1997. Minstrel shows, affirmative action talk, and angry White men: Marking racial otherness in the 1990s. In R. Frankenburg, ed., *Displacing Whiteness: Essays in Social and Cultural Criticism* (pp. 311–331). Durham, NC: Duke University Press.

Williams, R. 1997. The future of cultural studies. In J. Storey, ed., *What is Cultural Studies? A Reader* (pp. 168–177). London: Arnold.

Wray, M., and Newitz, A. 1997. *White Trash: Race and Class in America*. New York: Routledge.

Part VIII

Language, History, and Specificity

21

The Politics of Labeling: Latino/a Cultural Identities of Self and Others[1]

Suzanne Oboler

"I am what I am." Thus begins "Ending Poem," by Aurora Levins-Morales and Rosario Morales (1986:212–213), a mother-and-daughter statement that reaffirms the existence of the self and is almost a challenge to those who question the existence in the United States of a Latina identity and culture. It supports the critique by Eliana Ortega and Nancy Saporta-Sternbach (1989:3) of the claim that minority literatures express a search for identity rather than a "paradigm of self-affirmation in the Latina writer, a self-perception and self-definition." Certainly the Morales' "Ending Poem" would support Ortega and Saporta-Sternbach's (1989:3) view that among U.S. Latina writers, the issue is more a question of searching for "the expression or articulation of that identity, but not for...identity itself." Throughout the poem, mother and daughter alternate in their affirmation of their respective identities and use historical, geographical, ancestral, culinary, and other cultural aspects to characterize their (Latina) selves.

Still, reading the Morales' poem, one is struck by the ways in which *both* self (I am what I am) and other (I am not what I am not) are fundamental to the construction of the identities of these individual Latinas – and, one might say, to the ethos of the (Latino) group:

> I am not African.
> *Africa waters the roots of my tree, but I cannot return.*
>
> I am not Taína.
> *I am a late leaf of that ancient tree*
> and my roots reach into the soil of two Americas.
> *Taíno is in me, but there is no way back.*
>
> I am not European, though I have dreamt of those cities.
> *Europe lives in me but I have no home there.*[2]

Characterizations of the self necessarily evoke those of the other, and there are many "others" to be portrayed, recreated, and redefined in the process of constructing and affirming the Latina self. As Ortega and Saporta-Sternbach have argued (1989:14), "In constructing herself as a subject, a Latina must dismantle the representation of stereotypes of her self, constructed, framed, and projected by the dominant ideology." The need to dismantle stereotypes is well known and can be traced to the dichotomizing of self and other apparent, for example, in the essentializing practices of classical anthropology. Recent critiques of traditional anthropology suggest that the study of the other has been as much about the affirmation of the anthropologist's self as about the construction of the native's otherness.[3] If this is true, then one might ask, how are the dichotomies of self versus other problematized when dealing with bicultural or multicultural peoples? Is not the affirmation of the self, and the examination of stereotypes of it, also the affirmation of the internalized (stereotyped) others within it (Lorde 1990; Fanon 1967; Anzaldúa 1990)?[4]

One could argue, for example, that these various "others" are also (although certainly not only) aspects of the ethos of the Latino/a[5] ethnic group. Let me enumerate some of them: (1) There is the Latino as gendered other, (2) there is the Latino self as a Hispanic other, (3) then there is the notion of Latino as a class-specific other. (4) There is the

Latino self as a racial other – whether that racial other is called *Mestizo/a*, the nonwhite, the white-Hispanic, the person of color, *la raza*, etc. (5) There is the Latino self as an American other – and, within that otherness, one must distinguish whether one is referring to the self as U.S. citizen or as a member of the population of the Americas as a whole. (6) There is the Latino self as a Latin American national other: the Puerto Rican self, the Mexican self, the Chicano/a, Colombian, Peruvian, Dominican, etc.[6] The question is how, if at all, is this internalized identity-tension between self and other(s) articulated and dealt with by those who identify themselves or are designated as Latinos in the United States? Are they indeed affirming the self, even as they redefine the other(s)? And if so, how?

These questions are important if we are to better understand the notion of Latinos as constituting a "social movement" (Flores and Yudice 1990). Given the varying meanings in daily life in U.S. society of ethnic/racial identities – whether self-defined or imposed – there is a need to further explore the construction of Latino identity and "ethnic consciousness" both within and beyond the context of the "situational ethnicity" that Félix Padilla (1985) has described in his important study on "Latinismo" among Mexican Americans and Puerto Ricans in Chicago.[7] Indeed, the fact that with the gradual dissemination of the term Hispanic since the 1970s a significant number of second- and later-generation Latinos have grown up identified and self-identifying as Latinos or Hispanics raises the question whether Latinismo can be viewed, in certain regions around the country, solely as a "situational" identity, particularly in urban areas like New York City.[8] Preliminary observations among second and later generations of Chicanos, Puerto Ricans, Cubans, Dominicans, and Central and South Americans raised in the United States appear to suggest that for some, Latinismo is not only or necessarily "situational." Latino-Americans are growing up in the borderlands of at least two cultures and are affected by and aware of the discrimination and prejudice against them *as Latinos*. It is therefore not surprising that some might want to take the term farther by constructing their identities as a group in the U.S.A.[9] The result seems to be the creation of new Latino histories and traditions that may in effect be eroding these later generations' consciousness of the historical discrimination against Mexican-Americans and Puerto Ricans since 1848 and 1898, respectively, and of the differences in modes of incorporation into the U.S. economy between these groups and the Latin American and Caribbean immigrants arriving in the past two decades.

I will therefore focus on some of the internalized others within and against which the Latino/a self is asserted in the United States to suggest (1) that class and race background and values shape the meaning and social value individuals attribute to the terms they adopt to define both self and other and (2) that, at least in the present conjuncture, both self and other are fundamental to the formation of the ethos of the Latino/a ethnic group in the United States. I will explore the self/other dichotomy through an analysis of interviews with middle- and working-class Latinos currently living and working in New York City.[10]

The Latino/a as Other

The gendered other

Gender ideologies throughout the world have traditionally privileged men with better employment possibilities (Leacock and Safa 1986). Latin American societies have been no exception to this rule. Indeed, in spite of the economic realities on the continent, Latin American societies continue to hold that a respectable woman's place is in the home (Brown 1975; Rubbo 1975).[11] Discussing women and work in the United States, Rubin (1976:171) has pointed out that "historically, it has been a source of status in working-class communities for a woman to be able to say 'I don't *have* to work.'" This observation is applicable to Latin America, although status considerations there are not limited to working-class communities. As one male informant whose social status was middle-class in his home country explained:

> I had to work for so many people in the family that it got very difficult for me because in Colombia, the wife doesn't work. When one reaches a certain pos-

ition, the wife becomes the gracious hostess. She's the one who takes care of the children, she's the person who collaborates, but she doesn't really produce any money through work...the social side has to be kept up. There are those who say, "How can so-and-so's wife go to work! It's impossible!" (Francisco, Colombia)

While immigration had directly affected men's perceptions of women's traditional roles, it was the women I interviewed who provided the best interpretations of the types of cultural adjustments men have to make when women enter the workforce in the United States: "It's harder for men because they have to forget their *machismo* and depend on themselves here" (Soledad, Colombia). The women reported that many men begin to help with the household chores, which may lead some to feel that their masculinity and pride is undermined in the immigration process – a finding confirmed in Pessar's (1987) study of Dominican households in the United States. Both the men and the women I interviewed agreed that men had better job opportunities in the United States, but only the women expressed negative feelings about men's working lives: "He's got to pay the rent, the big bills. They have to have two jobs here. It's easier to buy a house there than it is here. Come to think of it, he hasn't gone up in life as I have" (Milagros, Peru).

Coming from a male-privileged employment context, the women incorporate these changes into their own sense of self, challenging the stereotyped gendered other within. As a result of immigration, a woman's sense of self begins to shift back and forth between her previous "othered" socialization and values and the "new self" constructed in a daily life of active participation in the workforce, which often (as noted by Pessar and Grasmuck 1991) results in her becoming the primary or at least an equal contributing member of her household.

Comparing their juggling of work and household chores in the United States and in their own countries, some women explained why life for them was easier in the U.S. "It's better because you don't have to wash all day long, and you can get clothes that don't have to be ironed. You can study. Back home, I wouldn't be able to do what I do here" (Milagros, Peru). This woman added that the ability to pay some of the bills gave her a new sense of freedom and of self. It also made her feel that she had bettered herself. But for some of the women life in the U.S.A. raised other issues: "It's not better here, because here mothers have to leave their children with someone outside of their circle of family and friends to go to work" (María, Dominican Republic). The need to rely on people other than family and friends is a forced departure from the traditional cultural patterns of the Latin American extended family. Dealing with this break – and with the struggle not only for daily survival but also to recognize oneself and adapt to changes in gender roles, values, and expectations – is at the heart of both immigrant men's and women's lives in the United States.

Still, people in the United States with ties to Latin America and the Caribbean are not seen merely as men and women struggling with the changes in their gender values brought on by immigration. Rather, regardless of the way or time of their arrival in U.S. society, they are identified as Hispanic men and women, and this identity interacts with their experiences in the United States and hence also challenges their already shifting sense of self.

The Hispanic other

Over the past two decades, the term Hispanic has come into general use in the United States to refer to all people living there whose ancestry is predominantly from one or more Spanish-speaking countries. The term therefore assigns people of a variety of national backgrounds to a single "ethnic" category. It encompasses great racial and class diversity, obscures gender differences, and even includes people whose primary language is not Spanish (Flores 1985; Hayes-Bautista and Chapa 1987; Giménez 1989). The Hispanic othered-self is, through its implicit homogenization, a denial of the diversity of national, linguistic, social, historical, cultural, gendered, racial, political, and religious experiences of at least 25 million people. Despite this, the term Hispanic is increasingly used, as Treviño (1987) notes, by Hispanics and non-Hispanics alike to establish the idea of a homogeneous Hispanic ethnic group.

Not surprisingly, the term has caused much confusion among government agencies, scholars, the media, and the public at large. It directly affects both policy decisions and the individual selves of many immigrants, residents, and citizens with ties to Latin America and the Caribbean. In failing to do justice to the variety of backgrounds and conditions of the individuals to whom it has been applied, the term Hispanic can have the effect of denying their sense of self. This became clear in my interviews with Latinos as they sought to define themselves in relation to the Hispanic other attributed to them. Informants rejected the term Hispanic as a self-identifier, but this rejection took many forms and was particularly differentiated in terms of social class.

The class-specific other

One of the revealing points that emerged again and again in the interviews was the extent to which people's sense of self contrasted, sometimes dramatically, with the connotations they attributed to the label Hispanic. While many informants had been forced by immigration to re-examine their gender roles and values, they did so through the prism of the values shaped in their own countries. And, although all of the informants were working in the garment industry in New York City and so had what are there considered traditional working-class occupations, not all of them had had working-class occupations or status in their own countries. Social class values were clearly a determinant of both their sense of self and the ways in which they positioned themselves in a society that applied to them a label with negative connotations.

People with a middle-class background immediately pointed out that the term was derogatory, but they recognized that, derogatory or not, that is what they were called. One informant, for example, explained the term this way: "They invented the word Hispanic to discriminate against us. We are at the bottom of the pile here" (Francisco, Colombia). Another middle-class person said, "I'm Colombian, but in the census I wrote Hispanic. That's what they call us here."

In contrast, working-class informants appeared reluctant to call themselves Hispanic or even to discuss the term in relation to themselves. They clearly saw it as identifying a group of people with negative attributes, and they implied that these people had absolutely nothing to do with them. Not surprisingly, many informants simply distanced themselves from the term and asserted their sense of self in terms of their continental and national origins: "It's wrong to call us Hispanic, because that word applies to the Spaniards. We're not Spaniards. We're from Latin America" (Alicia, Colombia). Others explicitly recognized the existence of the Hispanic as other by expressing deep disapproval of those they identified as Hispanics in this society. Thus, one person began by denying any knowledge of the meaning of the term and ended up by specifying its negative connotations. In her interpretation, Hispanic was a term that "they" (i.e., mainstream U.S. society) used as a synonym for "pigs," people who were "dirty," had "bad habits," lacked morals, and were "noisy." She concluded, "So because of those two or three families, they call us all Hispanics" (Rosa, El Salvador).

Hence this informant expressed her fear of being labeled Hispanic and openly distanced herself from the term. That is very different from the middle-class perception that "Hispanics are at the bottom of the pile here." This suggests that while middle-class informants may recognize themselves as Hispanic and simultaneously distance themselves from the label by *sociological* interpretation, working-class people interpret the implications of the label for their sense of self in strictly *personal* terms.[12]

The racial other

One key aspect of the effects of the imposition of a homogenizing label that classifies people with ties to Latin America and the Caribbean in ethnic terms is the ways in which the informants adopted U.S. racial/ethnic classifications to articulate their sense of self. Again, the informants' responses corresponded to the values stemming from their social class positions in their own countries, including not only class-based values but also the *culturally specific* racial prejudices that accompanied them in Latin America. Thus, for example, when asked to comment on whether his life had changed in the United States, one worker who had middle-class status in his native country first established his class background, pointing out that there was considerable social distance between him and the other Latin Americans with whom he worked in the factory:

> They [i.e., "Americans"] exploit us with very low salaries, and they delude us into thinking that life is owning a car. Here it's common for people to have a car – you can get one dirt-cheap; there's no status in it. You see, having an acceptable car, a good house does bring you status in any South American country. They delude people who could never have had a car in their own country. But the comforts of a good kitchen, of being able to wash your plates, of having a dishwasher, a refrigerator, a good sound system, a television – none of that is really life. There is no pride in acquiring any of it for anyone who comes here with an education. (Francisco, Colombia)

This informant proceeded to speak of the shift in his social status using the U.S. racial/ethnic hierarchy:

> The fact is that they've got us [Latin Americans] poorer here.... The problem is that we Latin Americans are considered the lowest race here. We are only here to work at the bottom. Because there's a bad policy here in the U.S. There are around 32 or 33 million of us, and yet we are considered a minority. The percentage of Greeks, Germans, Poles, is very low, yet they have special privileges that we don't have.

In comparing his position and aspirations with those of the Latin American working-class immigrants with whom he worked and not with those of other middle-class immigrants like himself, the informant was adopting the U.S. ethnic/racial system of classification. On the one hand, he was distancing himself from the other workers as a middle-class person "with an education." On the other hand, as a middle-class person himself, he was claiming the same rights accorded to what he perceived as the white middle class ("Greeks, Germans, Poles") and, in the process, excluding African-Americans and other minorities from the "special privileges" accorded to the (white) middle class. Moreover, his discourse seems to suggest a desire for incorporation into U.S. society – an incorporation that he defined in terms of access to the rights and privileges of the (white) middle class.

While the middle-class informants tended to measure themselves in terms of social status – comparing themselves to people whom they considered their equals in the U.S. – working-class people seemed to assess themselves in material terms, that is, by comparing what they had achieved in the U.S. with what they had had back home: "I'm much better off here than there. After paying all the bills, it's almost the same here [as in the Dominican Republic], but you are more comfortable here."

Still, like the middle-class informants, these working-class people also knew that they were identified as Hispanic and were aware of the prejudice against them. Not surprisingly, their sense of self as members of U.S. society was shaped by their awareness of the barriers to their incorporation; which dictated the ways they positioned themselves in the United States:

> I would like my children to go into the U.S. army. You know why? Because what I've achieved here I've gotten thanks in part to this country. I did it with my efforts, but they gave me the opportunity to come, to survive. So to show my gratitude I would like that.... The problem is that in the army, or in the navy, Hispanics are always given the worst jobs. If my daughter is educated and qualified, why should the Americans give her the worst positions just because she's Hispanic? (María, Dominican Republic)

In this statement, María expresses not only her ability to integrate into U.S. society, but also the limits to her doing so, as defined by the label Hispanic and its connotations. Although she recognizes that her daughter is qualified, she fears the latter will never be considered to be American because she will always be treated as a Hispanic.

The American other

Although second- and later-generation Latin Americans may never be considered "American," it is important to keep in mind that the identity of Latin America as a unified continent has itself long been debated and is yet to be fully forged (Oddone 1987; Giordano and Torres 1986). Thus, it is perhaps not surprising that the notion of exploring the existence of an identity shared by Latin American people (and the meaning of that identity) was new to some informants, regardless of their time of arrival in the United States.

> I went to the factory the very next day after our last conversation and asked my colleagues at work what they understood by Hispanic. I asked an Ecuadorian, a Dominican, and a Puerto Rican. They all gave the same answer. They said it was because we all speak Spanish.... They didn't seem to care what the Americans call us. But I think it's interesting. I think we should know why they call us Hispanic. So I began to think about it. (Rosa, El Salvador)

Asked whether she thought of herself as Hispanic, Rosa answered:

> No, I don't. I'm Central American. Because you know there's the North Americans and the Central Americans and the South Americans. We're all Americans, right? But then we have to differentiate ourselves. Some are in the North, some in the Center, and others in the South, right? So when someone asks me what I am, I say, "I'm Salvadoran. I'm Central American from El Salvador," and that's it. A Colombian can say "I'm South American, from Colombia."

As did most informants, Rosa defined herself in terms of her nationality. Her reluctance to use the term Hispanic was at least partly due to her negative perception of the term. At the same time, contextualizing her national identity in terms of the continent's geography, narrowing the latter down to particular nationalities, was an approach echoed by most other informants as they sought to assert their identities in the U.S. context.

The Latin American national other

For most informants, the Hispanic was in many ways the external other. At the same time, through its negation, the label Hispanic became the basis on which the self was being constructed. Thus, several informants rejected the application of Hispanic to themselves and others from the Latin American and Caribbean region: "I will call myself by my nationality, no matter where I live" (Irene, Ecuador); "We should be called South Americans, or Central Americans. It depends on where you're from" (Julián, Peru). Indeed, for many of the informants, the root of the problem with the term Hispanic was the discrimination attached to the grouping of all Spanish-speaking people and their awareness that labels such as this one efface what are for them obvious national, ethnic, and social distinctions.[13] Thus, for example, for the most part, the informants perceived the erasure of their national differences as being caused by the ignorance of non-Hispanic Americans about Latin America and the Caribbean: "Neither Americans or Europeans know much about geography. In this respect they are very ignorant. That's why they group us all together. They don't know the difference, because they don't know their geography" (Soledad, Colombia). The extent to which the informants resented what they perceived as Americans' lack of knowledge about their culture can be seen in the relationship they established between the ways they defined their identity in the U.S. context and their attempts to be specific about the continent's geography:

> We are all of us Americans. (Julián, Peru)

> I never call people from this country "Americans." I use that word for everyone from Alaska to Patagonia. In my city – I can only speak of my city, because, you know, each one has its own customs – we call them *yanquis* or *gringas*, but not Americans.
>
> I only know one America. Its geographical position may be North America, Central America, or South America. But we're all American. Colombia isn't located in Europe, it isn't located in Asia, and it isn't in Africa, either. So if they take the name of the entire continent for their country, what is left for ours? What is the name of the continent that Colombia is on? (Alicia, Colombia)

Comments such as this point to the tension that has historically existed between the populations of the Latin American and Caribbean nations, on the one hand, and the United States on the other. For some informants, the tension is overtly political: "I'm American only by accident, because Puerto Rico is a territory of the United States. I don't think that's by choice, because they've got American bases there" (Juan, New York-born Puerto Rican). Asked about his American citizenship and passport, Juan continued to deny that he was American, explaining, "I'm Americanized, but I'm not American" – by which he means "I believe like they say, work hard, you get ahead, you get whatever you want, you get your house, your cars, your mortgages." Thus he refuses the identity of American, recognizing that it has been imposed in much the same way as the identity of Hispanic: "From whites you came up with the word Hispanic.... Puerto Ricans never call each other Hispanic." Not surprisingly, then, Juan defined his identity in (Puerto Rican) national rather than ethnic (Hispanic or Latino) terms: "First I'd say I'm Puerto Rican. I would consider myself that because that's what I was taught to believe in... you know, to be proud of your nationality. You're proud of what you are and what the people in your country fought for."

For the most part, among the non-Puerto Rican informants, the tension between the "two Americas" is further manifested in the need to recognize the boundaries of the identity of the other – whether that other be a Latin American national or a U.S. citizen – in the process of shaping one's own identity in the U.S. context: "I once had a discussion with a Puerto Rican who said to me, 'I'm American,' and I answered, 'I'm as American as you are, because there is only one America'" (María, Dominican Republic). Thus Latinos specify their national origins especially among themselves: "If I introduce you to someone I would say, 'This is my friend, she's from Peru.' Or else I'd say, 'She's South American, or Peruvian'" (Verónica, Dominican Republic).

Indeed, regardless of their social class, informants did not necessarily understand the purpose of grouping everyone collectively as Hispanics:

> It just doesn't sound right to me. For example, if I'm with my people, I might say "South Americans," as others would say "Central Americans" or "Caribbeans."...we're not just a lump, we know who everyone is – because even though we may use the same language, our cultures are different, and we have to think about what we're going to say to different people and how we're going to say it. (Soledad, Colombia)

Thus, while mainstream U.S. society tends to erase the differences among populations with ties to Latin America and the Caribbean through a label such as Hispanic, my informants are more concerned with focusing their assertion of self in relation to other Latin American nationalities in the United States. Although they are fully aware of their commonalities (e.g., language use, geographical origins), they also affirm their respective selves through pointing to, and emphasizing, the distinctions – both subtle and otherwise – among themselves.

Defining the Self: Race, Class, National Origin, and Language

In defining the meaning of the term Hispanic for themselves, most informants showed themselves to be conscious of the differences among the various Latin American and Caribbean nationalities yet aware of the prejudices that indiscriminately group Hispanics in the United States. It is not surprising, then, that they speculated about the weight of the various aspects of the definition that they identified, ranging from the geographical to the linguistic, national, and racial. Inevitably, they included their life experiences as immigrants as they tried to make sense of these various aspects in defining their selves vis-à-vis the value of the term Hispanic in their lives.

Some made specific reference to the term's linguistic element: "They call us Hispanics because we speak Spanish" (Julián, Peru). Others related the term specifically to nationality:

> I don't really know what Hispanic means: I think it's all the people who come from Latin America, but I'm not sure. I know that people who are born here in the United States aren't Hispanic. So, for example, one of my children, the one born in Peru, is Hispanic; the other isn't because she was born in this country. (Milagros, Peru)

Asked how she would categorize the child born in the United States, Milagros didn't hesitate to answer: "Well, if she was born here, of course she's an American." Thus she views the term Hispanic as having a precise regional connotation, although she perceives its meaning to be strictly tied to people's birthplaces rather than to their ethnicity. Another version of this approach combined the regional and the linguistic elements of the term: "It's an undefined group name given to all the countries where Spanish is spoken" (Mónica, Dominican Republic).

Cynicism was also not absent from some of the informants' explanations of the origins and meaning of the term:

> White people have a name for everybody else. From whites you came up with the word Hispanics, and spic. I mean, Puerto Ricans never call each other Hispanic. They never called each other spics. They never did. When they said Hispanics, that's just a group of people that they've put together that speaks Spanish....
>
> They just count all Latin people in one bunch. They do it to the blacks, too. I mean, come on, there're more than just blacks. You got your American blacks, you got your African, your Jamaican; then you got your Puerto Rican blacks; some guys are darker than me. Then you got your Dominican blacks, you got white people that are dark-skinned...
>
> So you got your Hispanics over here, which includes whatever race you want to put in it south of the border. Then you got your blacks, anything from the Congo down. Then you got your whites, which is Americans...(Juan, New York-born Puerto Rican)

In view of the prevalence of race-related representations in New York City, it is perhaps not surprising that a New York-born Puerto Rican discussed the meaning of Hispanic in strictly racial/ethnic terms. Although Juan recognized the diversity within the various groups, he also had a firm perception of a two-tiered racial hierarchy made up of whites and everybody else in the United States. He defined Hispanic as including "whatever race you want to put in it south of the border," while singling out whites as Americans. Indeed, although he clearly rejected Hispanic as a term of self-identification and focused instead on his nationality rather than race, Juan nevertheless implicitly recognized that in this society his nationality and his race were conflated. Hence, as a Puerto Rican, his identity in this society was not white.

Interpreting the weight of the various components of the term Hispanic – race, class, national origins and language – becomes an essential part of informants' self-definitions and strategies of survival. Perhaps the clearest example of the extent to which this is true can be seen in one informant's description of the problems raised for Hispanics by the 1990 census questionnaire:

> If I were black and I spoke Spanish, I don't know how I would have answered that census questionnaire. They put black down as a race and separated it from people who speak Spanish, and they didn't have anything down for mestizos or for white Latin Americans. So when I was answering the census I said to myself, "Whoever did this made a lot of mistakes. Whoever did the census form wasn't educated enough about race." Because how could someone who is really black but speaks Spanish write down that he's black? I kept wondering about that. (Soledad, Colombia)

This criticism of the separation of race and language points to the prejudices Latin Americans confront in themselves as they come to terms with the prevalence of racial over national classifications in the United States. In fact, it illustrates Latin Americans' *public* assignment of greater social value to cultural/linguistic attributes (speaking Spanish) than to skin color.

What emerges from this study is the extent to which informants drew on their social and cultural backgrounds and their life experiences as they tried to come to terms with the label Hispanic. Juan's cynicism about the classification of Hispanics was the result of his lived experience as a Puerto Rican in the racially charged environment of New York City, where he grew up. Soledad's questions stemmed from her own socially and culturally shaped Latin American perception that "whoever did the census form wasn't educated enough about race." Where she comes from, Colombia, as in all other Latin American countries, the discourse on race distinctions has more gradations, and each gradation is strictly related to the individual's social class position (Wade 1985).

U.S. Latinos: Being and Becoming

The interviews in this study show that the way in which people with ties to Latin America and the Caribbean choose to identify themselves in the United States is less a cultural imperative than a reflection of their direct experiences and their needs at a given conjuncture in their lives. It also expresses their expectations of and strategies for incorporation into the U.S. social structure. While as Latin Americans they may insist that they are as American as the *gringos*, their confrontation with race and class representations in U.S. society forces them to incorporate both these dimensions into their imagining of the "American community" (Anderson 1983) and their construction of a sense of self in relation to the label Hispanic and the racial, class, national, and linguistic others attributed to them.

Whereas the middle-class informants tended to project their integration into North American society and immediately adopt U.S. categories to measure their progress, the working-class informants appeared more divided and ambivalent. They tended to continue to assess their sense of self in relation to their progress in terms of the standards of their old society – how much better off they were in the U.S.

Both groups knew that they were classified as Hispanic, but the way in which they positioned themselves in relation to this classification differed. Working-class informants positively evaluated their lives in the United States relative to what they perceived to be their life chances in their home countries, but they were not naive about the extent to which they could advance in economic terms in U.S. society. The ambivalence they expressed toward the United States reflects an awareness of the limits imposed on their upward mobility by what they perceived as the prejudice and discrimination against Hispanics. The prejudiced, "low-class," and negative connotations of the term Hispanic seemed to place a ceiling on how far they could rise. For them, ambivalence had become a way of positioning themselves in relation to both the old and the new society. In contrast to the working-class informants, the middle-class Lations I interviewed appeared to expect immediate incorporation into U.S. society on the grounds of their class, their education, and their social status in their own countries. Their sense of self and positioning vis-à-vis their new society did not *necessarily* correspond to that of the working-class informants.

Thus, in constructing the Latino self and a Latino social movement in the struggle for social justice in the United States, it is important to acknowledge the many "others" within – and against – which Latinos' identities and sense of self are being forgotten. "I am what I am" *is* a dare, a challenge to all those who would question the existence of a Latino/a self in the United States. But it is also a reminder that identity is, as Stuart Hall (1990:222) has argued, "a 'production,' which is never complete, always in process." The homogenizing quality of the label Hispanic is the result of mainstream U.S. society's indifference to the distinctions within the Latino/a population – whether the indifference refers to the diverse races, classes, languages, nationalities, linguistic or gendered experiences of the more than 25 million people identified as Hispanics or Latinos/as currently living in the United States. Yet the richness of the Latino ethos lies precisely in incorporating the individual life histories and experiences as processes of being and becoming – in recognizing and acknowledging the internalized others in the process of defining the self.

Padilla (1985:167) points to the need for research focusing on "the collective and emergent character" of Latino/a ethnic behavior. Although that behavior clearly depends on the extent to which Latino/a interests can be politically articulated, aspects of personal identity may promote and/or hinder it. Given the diversity of national, racial, and class-based histories and experiences within the populations with ties to Latin American and the Caribbean, to identify oneself as a Latino/a is a conscious choice not only acknowledging one's history and sociocultural background but also recognizing the need to struggle for social justice. In this sense, more than solely a culturally dictated fact of life, identifying oneself as Latino/a and participating in a Latino social movement is a *political* decision. By making that decision in these terms, those who recognize one another as Latinos through their ideological advocacy of social justice will be able to express the strength of *la comunidad* with greater force. They will also be more likely to assert, as do the Morales in their poem, that "We are whole."

NOTES

1 I use the word "politics" in the sense of a "political ethos" or "political culture," following the definition of the Chilean political scientist Norberto Lechner (1987, my translation): "The set of shared beliefs and values which, in influencing the practice of strategic actors (reinforcing and reproducing it in daily life), constitutes the common ground – the political culture – upon which proposals to conserve or transform reality are presented."

2 "Ending Poem," in *Getting Home Alive* by Aurora Levins-Morales and Rosario Morales, copyright© 1986 by Firebrand Books, Ithaca, New York. Used by permission.

3 The question of the other has been central to the debates on what West (1990) has called "the new cultural politics of difference." For varying perspectives and approaches to theorizing "the other" in anthropology and literary and cultural studies, see Clifford (1988), Clifford and Marcus (1986), Spivak (1987), Said (1983), Bhabha (1989; 1990), and Hall (1990). For a useful overview and critique of the recent debates on these various approaches to multiculturalism and cultural studies in the United States, see Chicago Cultural Studies Group (1992).

4 West (1990) has noted the need to explore "blackness-whiteness" in order "to conceive of the profoundly hybrid character of what we mean by 'race,' 'ethnicity,' and 'nationality'" (see also Morrison 1992; Bhabha 1989).

5 Latino/a was coined as an alternative to the term Hispanic imposed by government agencies and the society at large in the 1970s and 1980s. Like Hispanic, ethnic, minority, marginal, alternative, and Third World, it is "inaccurate and loaded with ideological implications" (Gómez-Peña 1989). Hayes-Bautista and Chapa (1987). Treviño (1987), and Giménez (1989) have discussed the implications of a standardized terminology for people with ties to Latin America and the Caribbean.

6 Language, generation, religion, and sexual preference are additional ways of understanding Latino/a "othering."

7 According to Padilla (1985:163), "Latinismo is *political ethnicity*, a manipulative device for the pursuit of collective political, economic, and social interests in society."

8 Padilla's analysis of the emergence of Latinismo among Puerto Ricans and Mexican-Americans focuses on "situations involving inequality experienced in common by Puerto Rican and Mexican American groups" in Chicago (1985:68). His pioneering study focuses on Latino ethnic consciousness resulting from interest-group articulation. Of particular relevance here is his discussion of the implications of regional differences in the United States. His point that Latino interests may sometimes conflict with the interests of national groups is also well taken. As he notes, the fact that different national-origin groups are settling in different areas of the United States and have diverse needs and historically rooted reasons for being in this country requires more localized research into the different possibilities for and meanings of Latino identity as well as of Latinismo as situational ethnicity.

9 For some, the term "Latino" is taking on a clearly nationalist connotation. As one second-generation Colombian youth recently told me, "I'm not American; but I'm not Colombian either. My nationality is Latino."

10 In-depth interviews were conducted over a two-year period with 22 immigrants from nine countries – men and women, old and young, of different genders, races, classes, and generations – who were garment workers in New York City (Oboler 1995).

11 Latin American gender ideologies notwithstanding, only one of the informants had never worked outside the home in her country of origin – attesting both to the difficult economic conditions in the Latin American countries (MacEwan 1985) and the increasing integration of Third World women into the development process as a result of change in the world economic order (Leacock and Safa 1986; Fuentes and Ehrenreich 1983; Portocarrero 1990).

12 The complexity of self-identifying through an imposed ethnic label can be seen in this and other informants' responses. The distance they place between themselves and the term "Hispanic" should not, however, be mistaken for a rejection of themselves (or others) as Latin American and Caribbean people or a lack of pride in or awareness of their cultures and language. As workers in ethnically diverse factories and members of an ethnically conscious society, they were fully conscious of their geographical, cultural, and linguistic commonalities. Moreover, in the workplace, for example, these commonalities would of course differentiate them as a group from their non-Latino co-workers.

13 The extent to which differences are erased by the other depends on how socially and culturally "distant" the other is from the self. For many people with ties to Latin America and the Caribbean, "the American" (the external referential other) may be perceived as much more distant from the cultural experience of a Latino/a self than another Latin American national. Closer distinctions (the internal boundary), however, are essential for constituting the cultural horizon of the Latino/a self, and in specifying this strategic internal boundary class, gender, and race biases are easily identifiable. Hence, many informants were prone to erase the differences among those they designated as "Americans" while stressing the subtle distinctions between self and other within the Latino population. I thank Teresa Caldeira for discussion and clarification of this idea.

REFERENCES

Anderson, B. 1983. *Imagined Communities: Reflections on the Origin and Spread of Nationalism.* New York: Verso.

Anzaldúa, G. 1990. How to tame a wild tongue. Pp. 203–212 in R. Ferguson et al., eds., *Out There: Marginalization and Contemporary Cultures.* New York and Cambridge: New Museum of Contemporary Art/M.I.T. Press.

Bhabha, H. K. 1989. Remembering Fanon: Self, psyche, and the colonial condition. Pp. 131–150 in B. Kruger and P. Mariani, eds., *Remaking History.* Seattle: Bay Press.

Bhabha, H. K. 1990. The other question: difference, discrimination, and the discourse of colonialism. Pp. 71–89 in R. Ferguson et al., eds., *Out There: Marginalization and Contemporary Cultures.* New York and Cambridge: New Museum of Contemporary Art/ M.I.T. Press.

Brown, S. E. 1975. Love unites them and hunger separates them: poor women in the Dominican Republic. Pp. 322–332 in R. Rapp, ed., *Toward an Anthropology of Women.* New York: Monthly Review Press.

Chicago Cultural Studies Group. 1992. Critical multiculturalism. *Critical Inquiry* 18:530–555.

Clifford, J. 1988. *The Predicament of Culture: Twentieth-Century Ethnography, Literature, and Art.* Cambridge, MA: Harvard University Press.

Clifford, J. and G. Marcus, eds. 1986. *Writing Culture: The Poetics and Politics of Ethnography.* Berkeley and Los Angeles: University of California Press.

Fanon, F. 1967. *Black Skin, White Masks.* New York: Grove Press.

Flores, J. 1985. "Qué assimilated, brother, yo soy Assimilao": the structuring of Puerto Rican identity in the U.S. *Journal of Ethnic Studies* 13(3):1–16.

Flores, J. and G. Yudice. 1990. Living borders/*buscando América*: languages of Latino self-formation. *Social Text* 8(2):57–84.

Fuentes, A. and B. Ehrenreich. 1983. *Women in the Global Factory.* Boston: Institute for New Communications/South End Press.

Giménez, M. E. 1989. "Latino/Hispanic" – who needs a name? The case against a standardized terminology. *International Journal of Health Services* 19:557–571.

Giordano, J. and D. Torres, eds. 1986. *La identidad cultural de Hispanoamérica: Discusión actual.* Santiago de Chile: Monografias del Maitén.

Gómez-Peña, G. 1989. The multicultural paradigm: an open letter to the national arts community. *High Performance* (Fall 1989):20.

Hall, S. 1990. Cultural identity and diaspora. Pp. 222–237 in J. Rutherford, ed., *Identity, Community, Culture, Difference.* London: Lawrence & Wishart.

Hayes-Bautista, D. E. and J. Chapa. 1987. Latino terminology: conceptual bases for standardized terminology. *American Journal of Public Health* 77:61–68.

Leacock, E. and H. L. Safa. eds. 1986. *Women's Work.* South Hadley: Bergin & Garvey.

Lechner, N. 1987. *Cultura política.* Santiago: CLACSO/FLACSO.

Levins-Morales, A. and R. Morales. 1986. *Getting Home Alive.* Ithaca, NY: Firebrand Books.

Lorde, A. 1988. Age, race, class, and sex: women redefining difference. In R. Ferguson et al., eds., *Out There: Marginalization and Contemporary Cultures.* New York and Cambridge: New Museum of Contemporary Art/M.I.T. Press.

MacEwen, A. 1985. The current crisis in Latin America and the international economy. *Monthly Review* 36:1–17.

Morrison, T. 1992. *Playing in the Dark: Whiteness and the Literary Imagination.* Cambridge, MA: Harvard University Press.

Oboler, S. 1995. *Ethnic Labels, Latino Lives: Identity and the Politics of (Re)presentation in the United States.*

Oddone, J. M. 1987. Regionalismo y nacionalismo, Pp. 201–238 in L. Zea, ed., *América Latina en sus ideas.* Mexico: Siglo XXI/UNESCO.

Ortega, E. and N. Saporta-Sternbach. 1989. At the threshold of the unnamed: literary discourse in the eighties. Pp. 2–26 in A. Horno-Delgado et al., eds., *Breaking Boundaries: Latina Writings and Critical*

Readings. Amherst: University of Massachusetts Press.

Padilla, F. 1985. *Latino Ethnic Consciousness: The Case of Mexican Americans and Puerto Ricans in Chicago*. Notre Dame: University of Notre Dame Press.

Pessar, P. 1987. The Dominicans: women in the household and the garment industry. Pp. 103–130 in N. Foner, ed., *New Immigrants in New York*. New York: Columbia University Press.

Pessar, P. and S. Grasmuck. 1991. *Between Two Islands*. Berkeley: University of California Press.

Portocarrero, P., ed. 1990. *Mujer en desarrollo: Balance y propuestas*. Lima: Flora Tristán.

Rubbo, A. 1975. The spread of capitalism in rural Colombia: effects on poor women. Pp. 333–357 in R. Rapp, ed., *Toward an Anthropology of Women*. New York: Monthly Review Press.

Rubin, L. B. 1976. *Worlds of Pain*. New York: Basic Books.

Said, E. 1983. *The World, the Text, and the Critic*. Cambridge, MA: Harvard University Press.

Spivak, G. C. 1987. *In Other Worlds: Essays in Cultural Politics*. New York: Routledge.

Treviño, F. M. 1987. Standardized terminology for standardized populations. *American Journal of Public Health* 77:69–72.

Wade, P. 1985. Race and class: the case of South American blacks. *Ethnic and Racial Studies* 8:233–249.

West, C. 1990. The new cultural politics of difference. In R. Ferguson et al., eds., *Out There: Marginalization and Contemporary Cultures*. New York and Cambridge: New Museum of Contemporary Art/M.I.T. Press.

22

"Heart Like a Car": Hispano/Chicano Culture in Northern New Mexico

Brenda Bright

In its idiomatic usage in the United States, *bad* means *good*, not as in *nice*, but as in *well-executed*. *Bad* connotes the paradoxical dangerousness and respectability of minority social actors and oppositional cultural forms. *Badness*, as both desirable and pleasurable, is the product of social tensions. Chicano car customizers highlight these meanings in their creations, their cars, known as "lowriders." Lowriders are beautiful *bad* cars of every make and model, designed to ride "low and slow" and to appear "mean and clean."[1] Throughout the Chicano southwest United States, and increasingly beyond, they sport spectacular paint jobs in pinks, greens, oranges, deep purples, and reds that are highlighted with coatings of metal flake and as many as 18 layers of lacquer. The interiors are elegantly upholstered and detailed. Many are lowered and have hydraulic pumps installed at the wheels to make the cars lift up and down, bounce, and even dance on demand. Small, wide wheels accentuate the low, lean look. As the pictured New Mexico license plate commandingly reads, the cars are "4U2SEE" (see figure 22.1). Their owners, also referred to as lowriders, drive these beautiful, luxurious roadway spectacles very slowly, literally taking over the road and forcing other drivers to "deal with" their slow, deliberate driving style.

When interviewed at a car show in Española, New Mexico in the summer of 1990 for a national television special on America's car mania, Dennis Martinez, a Hispano lowrider from nearby

Figure 22.1 "4U2SEE" (For you to see) vanity plate, Santa Fe. Photograph by author

Chimayó, explained lowriding in terms of its cultural features: "It's my culture, man. It's like my inheritance. My family all lowride, so I just keep lowriding myself. It's something that's *traditional*. I have a heart that's like a car, you know. My heart is in my wheels" (Lynch-Frost Productions 1990). At the same show, Vicky Gutierrez said, "Here in Española we love our cars!" Martinez describes the love of lowriding as *traditional* and Gutierrez the love of cars as *local* – particular to Española (see figure 22.2).[2] These assertions of local specificity contain the kernels of other significant connections being made by Hispano lowriders through the cars, namely to commodities and to ethnopolitical culture. Northern New Mexico Hispanos take the car, a general feature of American culture, and customize it into a lowrider, one of several politicized Chicano cultural forms adapted in the area in the wake of the Chicano Movement. In light of widespread incorporation of cars in the cultures of the United States, the statements of Martinez and Gutierrez indicate a seemingly contradictory aspect of consumer culture that is only beginning to be addressed within anthropology – how people experience and create mass-produced culture as a form of local culture.[3] Here, Hispanos customize a mass-produced commodity into an ethnic cultural form and subsequently create the car as a form of local culture. Lowriders are evidence of the creation of a simultaneously local and extralocal ethnopolitical identity.

Figure 22.2 Map of the Española area

The presence of these elaborately "bad" cars and their linkage to local culture and tradition raise questions about culture, commodities, tradition, and locality important to anthropology. How is local culture constructed in the presence of mass-produced and mass-circulated commodities (Miller 1994)? How "local" is local culture (Appadurai 1995; Bright 1995)? The statements by Martinez and Gutierrez suggest an intermingling of local popular traditions with the collective imaginary in which mass culture is not something external invading the popular from outside but instead develops out of certain potentialities already within the popular itself – noted here as "traditional" or "local" propensities (Rowe and Schelling 1991:8). Given the intermingling of the local with the mass, the potentialities are twofold, those developing from within local culture and those developing from within mass and mediated culture. An analysis of such cultural productions requires careful attention to both dimensions. Their intermingling in the Española area of northern New Mexico is the subject of this essay.

A growing body of work within anthropology and cultural studies details how the products, practices, and politics of modernity are radically changing the relationships between the imagination and social life (Abu-Lughod 1990; Appadurai 1990, 1991; Ferguson and Gupta 1992; Fischer 1986; Foster 1991; García-Canclini 1992; Marcus 1995; Shank 1994; Thornton 1988; Urla 1996). Because of translocal and transnational flows in capital, people, ideas, technology, and media, the realms of social life are increasingly disjunctive. In many ways, they have become deterritorialized, or perhaps reterritorialized.[4] At the very least, they are not so resolutely local as anthropologists have historically assumed. Increasingly, media and commodities provide important materials for the creation of social relationships and social identities. Accordingly, Appadurai (1991) identifies the contemporary need within anthropology to interpret how local historical trajectories flow into complicated transnational and translocal structures. The ethnographic study of commodity forms that circulate widely, yet are ultimately localized in some sense, enables us to attend to socially generated cultural meanings. Such a project requires a threefold approach. First, genealogical research on relevant objects, media, and social movements is necessary to articulate the conditions of generation, adaptation, and circulation within broader meanings. Second, historicized social research on a particular locale details the contexts under which objects and media become part of social life. Third, ethnographic research delineates the work of making mass media and commodities suitable to creating social relationships and social identities (Carrier 1991).

Given the changing relationships between the imagination and social life, it is increasingly important to consider how locality influences cultural production and ethnographic accounts of that production. The ubiquitous presence of mass-produced commodities and localized versions of mass culture challenges single-site ethnography. To ask how local is local culture, paying careful attention to translocal dynamics in their local inflections, is to ask what sorts of ethnographic approaches are appropriate to the conditions of contemporary culture (Ferguson and Gupta 1992; Marcus 1990; Thornton 1988). Marcus (1995) argues that the world-system context has radically changed the grounds of contemporary social life, and with it, the grounds for anthropological accounts. In response to these shifts, he suggests, two key approaches have emerged. While the single-site approach is maintained by many, providing full attention to the local conditions and responses of groups to macroprocesses, a second multisite mode of ethnographic research is emerging. Multisite ethnographies address the disjunctive contexts in which subjects act and are acted upon. As Marcus details, multisite ethnographies develop strategies to follow a set of connections particular to the research topic at hand, and in so doing, they reveal both a particular cultural formation and aspects of the system itself.

Theorizations of social life in the world-system context indicate that locality is never simply a constraint. It is produced through material means, social relationships, and ethnographic accounts.[5] Locality as a staple of social life – as well as the grounding of ethnographic research and writing – is a problematic arena only recently examined by anthropologists. Is it the case that access to mediated images frees people from the constraints of their more circumscribed local lives? If so, then how? With careful attention to locality as a form of cultural production, anthropological approaches can ascertain under what conditions, and how, mediated cultural forms are incorporated into local cultural landscapes. Methods for studying local culture, however, must be crafted carefully and supplemented with complementary translocal approaches to account for the specificities of contemporary cultural formation.

The questions I explore in this essay are the products of a multisite ethnography of a translocal phenomenon, lowriding in the U.S. Southwest. In the broader project, I trace the meanings of lowriding, a form of car customizing associated with Chicanos. I study lowriding in three distinct sites, asking how locality affects the meanings of a mass yet customized cultural form.[6] The sites are Los Angeles, California; Houston, Texas; and Española, New Mexico. In all three sites, there is a significant discourse of local culture: how Houston lowriders differ from Los Angeles lowriders, how Los Angeles lowriders consider themselves years ahead of all other lowriders, and how to tell Chimayosos – New Mexicans of Hispano descent from the village of Chimayó – from other New Mexican lowriders.

Each locality has dimensions that exceed such comparative glosses. In metropolitan areas, forms of lowriding work according to the logics most often ascribed to mass-produced popular culture – they provide alternative communities and potential identities. They also communicate experiences and desires (Lipsitz 1995). In Los Angeles, lowriding activities provide alternatives to strictly local and often limiting forms of identity, such as gang participation. At the same time, lowriding aesthetics construct a style considered unique to Chicano experiences of social relationships and structured marginality (Bright 1995, in press).[7] In its early period in Houston (1977–84), lowriding provided a form of community that integrated newly arrived Chicano migrants with Chicano locals in the context of an expanding economy. In most metropolitan settings, lowriding provides a means of self-identification as well as opportunities for unique community construction. In such settings, lowriders participate in the pleasures of consumer culture through the aesthetics and performances of the cars. They also use their cars and the images on them to challenge and mediate the boundaries of marginality particular to minorities in metropolitan areas of the United States. These boundaries are marked in part by police surveillance, racism, and spatial segregation.

In metropolitan settings, lowriding is primarily associated with the broader concerns and practices of working-class Chicano culture, albeit with local influences and ramifications. In contrast, lowriding in the rural yet semiurban Española area links local Hispano culture and tradition with the ethnopolitical concerns of the Chicano movement. In northern New Mexico, tourism and craft commodification have fostered an intercultural economy that traffics in the cultures of native inhabitants – Hispano and Native American – and in the unique New Mexican landscape (Babcock 1990a, 1990b; Rodríguez 1987). Area Hispanos provide much of the working-class labor force for the area, especially for the state government in Santa Fe, the area tourist industry, and nearby Los Alamos Laboratories. Given these factors, it is not surprising that lowrider aesthetics in northern New Mexico exhibit a concern with boundaries, emphasizing autonomy and locality as the significant factors of identity. I argue that in northern New Mexico, lowriders merge regional ethnicity, working-class ideologies, and Chicano nationalism in a discourse of tradition in order to claim a "place" and a unique identity for themselves. This article explores the interaction between traditional and mass forms in the development of culture, identity, and locality in northern New Mexico. More broadly, it analyzes how commodities are re-created, or customized, in local relationships and webs of significance.

The term *lowrider* was coined in California in the 1960s and lowriding has subsequently become an important part of Chicano popular culture throughout the Southwest.[8] Lowriding's popularity is fueled in part by the publication of *Lowrider Magazine*, based in California. *Lowrider* began regional distribution in the late 1970s, prompting increased lowrider and lowrider car club participation throughout the Southwest, including the Española area.[9] Española is an important regional town and local trading market in northern New Mexico with a population of more than 8,000 that is 84 percent Hispanic. It is located along the Rio Grande River between the tourist towns of Santa Fe and Taos. Seven miles east of Española is Chimayó, with a population of 2,789 (93 percent Hispanic). The Española and Chimayó area is a well-known lowriding haven, often referred to as "the lowriding capital of New Mexico" (see figures 22.2 and 22.3). In Española, the favorite cruising strip is Riverside Drive, also known as Highway 68, the road that links Santa Fe to Taos. It is a major commercial strip, with hotels at either end of town. The town's main strip malls front Riverside Drive as do the major grocery stores, auto parts stores, service stations, and hamburger stands. Most area residents come to Española for shopping, making Riverside Drive the central place in a town that has no real center. Highway 68 is also the road traveled by tourists as they pass through Española on their travels between Santa Fe and Taos. Lowriders are a familiar sight on this road, elaborately decorated automobiles slowly making their way down Riverside with barely visible drivers. This is especially true on Saturday nights, when they cruise a loop from one end of town to the other, sometimes stopping in a frontage parking lot to meet with friends and enjoy the view. Lowriders are one of the few local "sights" that tourists stop to view as they make their way between Santa Fe and Taos.

Less visible than cruising are the ways cars, like other commodities in this area, are constantly repaired and remodeled as they circulate in familial, gifting, and trade networks. Lowriding takes place within these networks, within and across familial and cohort group ties. Cars and trucks have long lives and are often passed from parents to children. Twenty-three auto-body shops in Chimayó alone attest to the amount of repair and customizing work done in the area. Local lowriders constitute roughly 10 percent of the area population, although they are an ever-shifting group as people move in and out of interest in lowriding practice.

Locale

The northern New Mexico region is best known to outsiders as the cultural and geographical center of the "land of enchantment." Its unique landscapes of semiarid mountains, wind-carved sand outcroppings, beautiful forests, and verdant agricultural river valleys are home to long established Native American Pueblos and Hispano villages. Each year thousands of tourists are attracted to the area stretching from Albuquerque north to the Colorado border. This region, originally settled by Pueblo Indians, was a northern province of New Spain, then Mexico, and later a southwestern territory of the United States. Under Spain and then Mexico (1540–1846), New Mexico's political economy was subject to the frontier

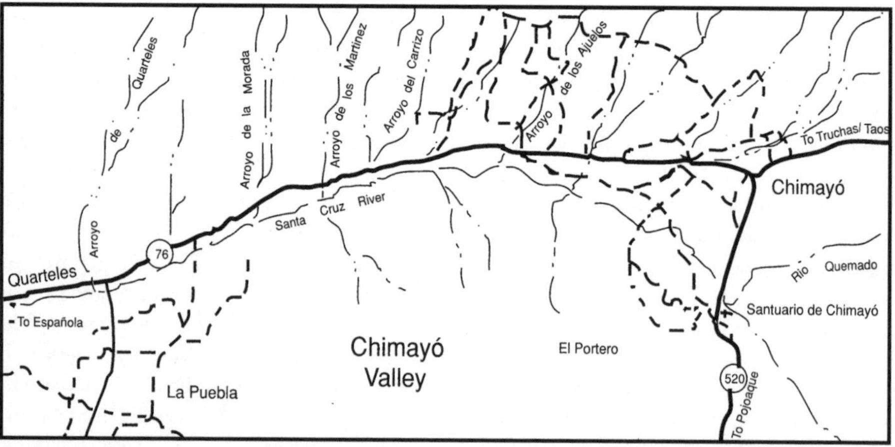

Figure 22.3 Map of the Chimayó valley

modes of governmental and ecclesiastical management that operated at a far distance from Mexico City. As a U.S. territory (1846–1912), it was subject to colonial modes of management that fostered increased social and economic marginality among the area's native residents. New Mexico was late in receiving statehood in 1912.

Throughout the Spanish, Mexican, and U.S. periods, Santa Fe has been an important governing, trading, and ecclesiastical center. Taos is significant for its location at the northern end of the Santa Fe trail. By contrast, the importance of Española is strictly regional, and its ethnic and class composition is in stark contrast with that of Santa Fe and nearby Los Alamos.[10] As mentioned earlier, Española's population of 8,389 is predominantly of Hispanic origin (84 percent), as is Chimayó's population of 2,789 (93 percent). Most of Española's non-Hispanic population is Native American, with the Santa Clara Pueblo just to the south and the San Juan Pueblo just to the north. Los Alamos's population of 11,455 is predominantly white (83 percent white non-Hispanic origin) with 12 percent of Hispanic origin while Santa Fe's population of 55,859 is more mixed, with 47 percent of Hispanic origin. The median income in Española is $19,785 per household, and in Chimayó it is $19,858. In contrast, Santa Fe's median income is $30,023, while the Los Alamos median income is the largest in the state at $48,330 (Bureau of the Census 1990).

As the home of the majority of area lowriders, Chimayó is of particular importance to this article.[11] It is located seven miles east of Española. Route 76, which connects them, runs along the Santa Cruz River. The river valley is bounded to the north by a sawtooth line of sand cliffs. People live on either side of Route 76, predominantly along arroyos, or dry creek beds, that drain from the sand cliffs into the river. Over the past 15 years, a series of earthern dams have been built to the north and parallel to the river, between the sand cliffs, to control flooding. Arroyos are the major residential roads and landmarks of the area.

For many, Chimayó is best known as the home of one of northern New Mexico's most famous Hispano landmarks, the Santuario de Chimayó (see figure 22.4). The Santuario functions as a spiritual center for many religious and cultural activities (Borhegyi 1956). The chapel is used by both locals and tourists, and the Santuario is the site of a variety of pilgrimages. Perhaps the best known of these is the Easter procession during which pilgrims walk the road from Santa Fe to the Santuario. In the summer, Española's Fiesta de Oñate begins at the Santuario with a convocational Mass and blessing of the Fiesta's King, Queen, and their court. After the blessing, Fiesta runners carry the torch the seven miles from the Santuario to the fiesta grounds in Española. The village fiesta in July honoring patron saint Santiago, or St. James, begins with a procession of church auxiliary groups, locals, ex-residents, and a handful of tourists who carry a small glass case with the *bulto* (statue) of Santiago from the Santuario to the more recently built and much larger Sagra Familia church a few miles away on Route 76. Tourist buses run regularly from Santa Fe to Taos, stopping in Chimayó at the Santuario, at Ortega's Weaving and Gallery, and at the Rancho de Chimayó restaurant. Tourism has spawned a supplemental economy for this area.

Local residents often identify the land with one family group or another, as family plots along particular arroyos are often subdivided generation after generation (Crawford 1989; Rodríguez 1987, 1992). When Victor Martinez named the owners of body shops for me, he was unsure of the last name of one owner whose shop was near Ortega's Weavers and Gallery. He identified the owner in terms of location: "I think he's Trujillo because the Trujillos live more over there." In the summer of 1990, I lived with my family in the Arroyo de los Martinez, also known as Daniel's Arroyo after the trailer park at its entrance off Route 76. Named for the deceased son of the trailer park's owners, the site testifies to the importance and presence of family groups in the area.

Historically Catholic, Chimayó's population is now Catholic and Evangelical Protestant. Most lowriders are Catholic and use the symbols of Mexican American Catholicism on their cars. Area Protestants are often critical of these practices as inappropriate, interpreting this usage of religious images as an expression of culture rather than faith. While locally contested, such

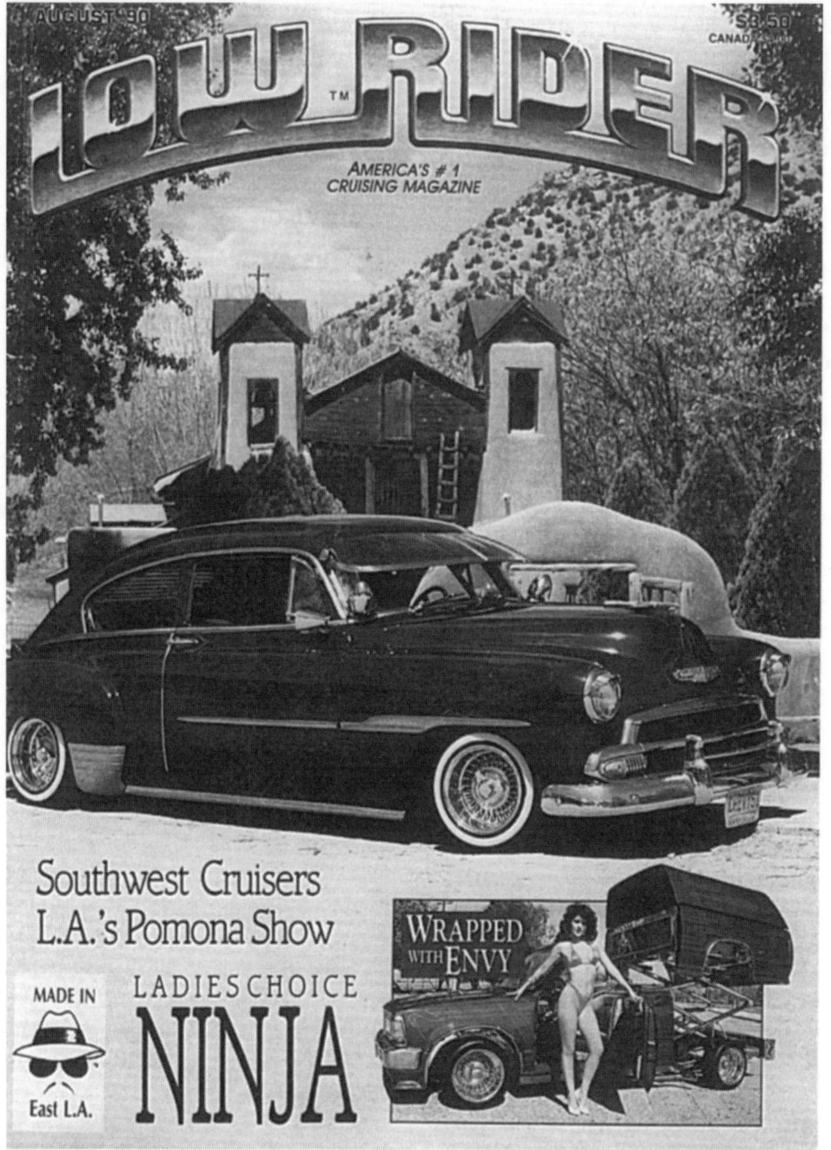

Figure 22.4 *Lowrider Magazine* cover featuring the Santuario de Chimayó. © 1990 Lowrider Publishing Group. Used by permission

practices participate in the broader dynamics of representation and cultural objectification of the region.

Over the course of the 20th century, the northern region of New Mexico has developed a tourist and commodity economy that objectifies local landscapes and culture, and in the process produces locality as a form of identity. Changing modes of government and persistently distant relations to the cultural centers of the ruling nation-states have generated long struggles over tradition in this area (Briggs 1980; Briggs and Van Ness 1987; Deutsch 1987; Forrest 1989; Grimes 1976; Rodríguez 1987, 1992; Weigle 1976).

One example of this struggle can be seen in the history of image carving. In this area, wood carvers have long made religious figures for worship. In his study of New Mexican wood carvers, Briggs argues that the history of image carving in New Mexico reveals a process of localization during the Spanish, Mexican, and early U.S. periods (1980). The area was regularly without clergy, due to the remoteness of the region and its small population. In the absence of clergy, area residents adapted their religious practices. Early attempts to imitate the religious iconography of metropolitan artists were transformed over time to an internal adherence to local tradition. This period also saw the transformation of various patron saints according to local cultural patterns. The function of such saints and images in Hispano life has been one of mediation, enabling the symbolic connection of individuals, groups, and social movements.

Processes of localization and mediation continue into the present. The 20th century has featured the large-scale commodification of the cultural goods of Hispano and Native American groups. The area has received large numbers of mass-produced commodities from outside the state. This circulation of goods has contributed to local discourse about culture and the boundaries of goods and practices. For example, New Mexican carved images have increasingly become cultural commodities produced for purchase by outsiders attracted to their imagery and craft, but who rarely use them in spiritual practices.[12] Artists who produce religious objects such as saints and biblical scenes for sale to outsiders or nonpractitioners are faced with the dilemma of how to justify their work. According to carver George Lopez, objects sold to outsiders were not yet blessed and hence did not have the status of full cultural objects (Briggs 1980). Other carvers refuse to sell religious images to nonbelievers. Contemporary carvers combine traditional materials and aesthetics with modern techniques and prototypes while consciously seeking to evade the control that Anglo elites exercise over the form and content of carvings as well as the context for their exhibition and marketing. Such dilemmas are particular to members of a group whose material culture is valued by nonmembers.

Two processes influencing localization in wood carving are particularly noteworthy. In contrast with other historical periods, the contemporary period features the use of writings about the works of local carvers and the local industry, a new kind of prototype used as a resource by a number of carvers (Briggs 1980:187). The second process is the increasing economic integration of local Hispanos since the 1960s, influential for cultural production generally as well as for wood carvers and lowriders. Significantly this change occurred in the context of continued political and economic marginalization along with the heightened risk of loss of language, culture, and history. It is in concert with these developments that New Mexicans draw on symbols of locality – land, water, and New Mexican religion – in order to articulate their existence and their grievances (Briggs 1980:210).

That such cultural and economic trends give rise to an intensified symbolic representation of the area creates important effects and challenges for local residents. Many local residents are involved in producing traditional Spanish colonial arts or tourist crafts for sale, often subsidizing incomes from working-class jobs. They are employed to construct images of their land and cultures in styles that foster tourist consumption, perhaps best exemplified in "Santa Fe style" (Babcock 1990b).[13] For example, several Chimayosos were employed to paint, but not design, a mural for the interior of the La Fonda Hotel on the plaza in Santa Fe. While they are called upon to re-create their culture for others, they also create their own art works and use them to represent themselves – for example, these same people make representations of their culture on their lowriders. For many, religious images are not only mediators, but also icons of identity and resistance.

As in earlier centuries, Hispano lowriders engage in a process of localization, adapting commodities to an internal orientation; however, the isolation of earlier centuries is no longer the dominant constraint on local practices and forms. Lowriders are faced with the dilemma of making extrinsic objects, such as cars, cultural while living in a milieu that features labor outmigration as well as tourist commodification and class difference. Most of the original lowriders in the area spent some of their early work lives in Californian industries or in regional mines, later returning to set up households near their families. At home, lowriders experience Hispano culture both as their native culture and as it is commodified for non-Hispano tourists while facing the pressures of a growing market for their familial land among outsiders. Under these circumstances, lowrider adaptation strategies are highly inflected by concerns with place, social relationships, and identity.

The Chicano Movement and Mass Communication

In New Mexico, the traffic in culture – and the culture of traffic – between the Chicano Movement and local cultures is multifaceted and linked to mass communication. The popularity of lowriding expanded broadly in the late 1970s with the publication of *Lowrider Magazine*, then produced and distributed in San Jose, California. The magazine itself was greatly influenced by the rhetorics of the Chicano Movement, an important premise of which was to incorporate traditional Mexican American crafts and aesthetics into modern Chicano life (Lujan 1970; Ybarra-Frausto 1991). The movement mobilized people to appreciate Chicano cultural productions, in part through its use of popular symbols. As New Mexico wood carving and lowriding demonstrate, the symbols and forms forged within the movement became important forms for adaptation. Cultural, political, and institutional networks promoted this traffic in culture, linking the imagination, culture, and social life of people of Mexican descent across the United States.

Area ethnopolitical movements responded directly to historical experiences of political, economic, and cultural alienation. Reies Tijerina's La Alianza Federal de Mercedes (Federal Alliance of Land Grants) was organized in Rio Arriba Country in 1963 to reclaim lands from the Spanish land grants that Hispano residents lost to the U.S. government (Acuña 1981; Nabokov 1969; Rodriguez 1987). Simultaneously, these experiences were accompanied by the development and mass distribution of Chicano culture in the form of music such as War's song "Low Rider," Cheech and Chong movies, Hollywood gang films, and magazines such as *Q-Vo* and *Lowrider*. In New Mexico, the appreciation of these newly politicized traditional Chicano art forms complemented the production of tourist and ethnic arts – both Hispano and Native – in the Rio Grande valley. Hence the loss of land and increased tourism – the very things that threatened to erode Hispano culture – instead created the conditions under which the Chicano Movement strengthened local conceptions of culture.

Cars and Social Life

Lowrider cars belong to a social life based in large part on gifting, tinkering, and bartering within kinship and friendship networks. Family incomes mostly derive from working-class jobs, craft production, and the waning practice of agriculture. Area households also rely on resources gained from gardening, trading labor, and sharing efforts as in acequia management and wood collecting. Agriculture, especially the growing of chiles, is practiced mainly by older men. Many local women work for the government, either in maintenance or administration for Los Alamos Laboratories or for the state government in Santa Fe. Some run fast-food restaurants in Española. Others take in children, enabling them to stay home with their own. Many men work at construction in Santa Fe, as machinists or contractors for Los Alamos, or in businesses in Española. Prior to the 1970s many young men and their wives left the area to work in industries in California, in mines in Grants and Colorado, or to find work in Utah. Often they returned within 10 years with savings to set up their own households. Because of the dangerous nature of their work, many of the area residents have been disabled temporarily or permanently. The plethora of body shops mentioned earlier indicates how cars are part of a large secondhand economy. Cars are used and reused. Dents are repaired. Rust is removed and metal replaced. If a car is beyond use, then it is used for parts. Sometimes the car bodies are used as barriers for flood control in the sandy arroyos (see figure 22.5). Parts of old cars are often sold at swap meets.

Figure 22.5 Car bodies used as drainage control. Photograph by author

Many people are involved in the transformation of a car to a lowrider. A car can be handed down or bought from a family member, bought new, bought used, or salvaged. Junior Trujillo bought his father's Impala and fixed it up. Ana Flores inherited her family's Monte Carlo, and with a little help from her father and her boyfriend, renovated and customized it. Herman Herrera salvaged his parents' '37 Chevy from under a collapsed shed and restored it with the help of Eliseo and Melecio Martinez. Often, some portion of the work is done professionally. Julian Quintana has an upholstery business and reupholsters many of the local cars; hence, his car is known as "Stitches." Vicky Gutierrez had her '77 Mustang's "girlish look" painted by Marshall Martinez and the upholstery done at Floyd's Upholstery (see figure 22.6). Dennis Chavez bought his '73 Ford Ranger used and started customizing it in 1979. Now it belongs to his son, who shows it. Victor Martinez's grandfather used to drive Victor's uncle's lowrider and his family called him the "oldest lowrider around."

Customizing transforms a used car, which is often inherited or bought from a family member, into a beautiful "bomb," as cars from the forties and fifties are known. Many local lowriders, like Dennis Martinez, trace the customizing practices back to their fathers and uncles. Martinez's father had a '50 Mercury with spinners, white walls, and spinner skirts. His uncle had a '52 white Chevy, "down on the ground." Ana Flores's uncle was one of the first lowriders in Española. In this area, family members of both sexes are often involved in customizing. These intergenerational links also become a link to family tradition that provides evidence of the pervasiveness of area lowriding through time.

Even though the Española area is predominantly rural, it is subject to the influences of urbanization and industrialization. As mentioned earlier, many of Chimayó's older generation of lowriders, born in the 1940s, moved to California cities for industrial jobs in the sixties and often brought cars back with them when they returned to set up their households. These experiences have influenced their working-class sensibilities and heightened their value of local connections. Eliseo and Melecio Martinez, who live near the western boundary of Chimayó, are brothers who married in the early 1960s and moved with their wives to

Figure 22.6 Vicky Gutierrez and family. Photograph by author

California to work. Both men were early members of "Los Paisanos," a car club that began around 1976 and became more official in 1981 when Herman Herrera joined. Eliseo and his wife lived in Compton (in the Los Angeles area) for two years. While there, he worked in an airplane factory and his wife worked assembly for *TV Guide*. In 1967 they returned to Chimayó, and in 1970 Eliseo began work on the truck he currently drives, a modified '38 Ford. The truck rests on a shortened '76 Grand Prix frame. The truck bed is from a '50/'51 and has been shortened and made thinner. The truck has been several colors in its long life but is currently painted orange with red flames. Inside it has black upholstery and an orange ceiling. Melecio has constructed several cars, among them a customized '55 Hillman van that he brought back from California in 1965. The Hillman lasted about ten years; then, he installed a new engine and began customizing it anew. The two brothers have been instrumental in helping others make their cars, especially their nieces Liz and Rene and their friend Herman Herrera.

Dennis Chavez lives near the Santuario on the eastern side of Chimayó. Once owned by his family, the Santuario was sold by Chavez's great-great-grandfather to the Archdiocese of Santa Fe in 1926, through the intervention of Mary Austin and others (Kay 1987). Chavez and his wife lived in Los Angeles from 1965 to 1966, in Germany from 1966 to 1968, and back in Los Angeles and Oakland from 1968 to 1971. During this time, Dennis had several customized automobiles, including a '47 Studebaker with suicide doors (doors that are hinged at the rear rather than the front) and baby moon rims, a '59 Ford and a '56 Mercury with tuck and roll upholstery. From 1971 to 1979, he was informally involved with friends and family members who also had customized cars. They in turn "hung around" with guys from nearby Nambe who formed one of the valley's first car clubs, the Rod Angels, in 1978. Many of Chavez's group formed the Chimayó Valley Cruisers in 1979.

Dave Jaramillo, owner of "Dave's Dream," conceived of his car as an object that would bring his family closer together. (He worked for several years in the mines of Grants, New Mexico, returning on weekends to work with his cousin Dennis Martinez on the car, a 1969 Ford LTD. Their work on the car began in 1976 and lasted until 1978 when Dave died in a car accident. At the time of his death, the car was unfinished, but since then it has fulfilled his expectations in several ways. Martinez's wife, Irene, and his cousin, Dennis Martinez, have completed it. Dave and Dennis were close friends and members of the same car club. Dennis and Irene commissioned a Santa Fe artist to paint a family portrait, featuring Dave, Irene, and Dave Jr. on each side of the car. Irene showed the finished car at car shows where it was known as "El Gran Chimayoso." The car was purchased in 1990 by the Smithsonian Institution for their transportation collection and for exhibition with "American Encounters." Its purchase was facilitated by Dennis and Irene, who were again active in conceiving and facilitating the car's restoration, including the restoration of the family mural. The car, commonly known as "Dave's Dream," could also be known as "Dennis's Dream" or "Dennis, Irene, and Dave Jr.'s Dream." Such family relations are the foundation for the production of lowriders in this area (Brewer 1990).

Cars are most often communal or familial projects, but the motivations for modifying the cars are often related to local trends in popular culture.[14] For example, while Ana Flores had always loved her family's 1972 Monte Carlo, her interest in lowriders was sparked in high school when she and a girlfriend, Yvonne, began reading *Lowrider Magazine*. Noting how the magazine's emphasis on east L.A. style and lowriders excited them, Ana remarked, "We were east L.A. this and lowrider that!" After she was 18 and began working at Los Alamos, Ana started customizing the Monte Carlo Super Sport given to her by her mother. Ana learned about cars, including engines, from her father. At the time of my research, her boyfriend was helping her customize her car.[15] In the summer of 1990, Ana was a member of La Reina's court for the Fiesta de Oñate. Her high-school friend, Yvonne, is now married to Chris Sanchez. *Lowrider Magazine* featured the couple's car on the cover of the August 1990 issue (see figure 22.4).

To be sure, participation in lowriding has gendered dimensions. Lowriders are important carriers of customary practices *and* expressive vehicles for identity in the Española area. Men's interest in cars often begins as a predominantly – but not exclusively – male adolescent concern with style, personal identity, and mechanical skills. After high school, increased independence in work and familial relations frequently paves the way for men's cohort relationships to develop into car clubs. Women's interests, as such, are similarly constituted, but tend to be initiated later and made manifest during their years of employment prior to marriage. After marriage, women's direct participation wanes dramatically as their activities and priorities shift to their own families. In addition, it is very difficult to open the trunk of a car with "shaved" door handles while trying to juggle children and groceries. While there are women who drive lowriders, men predominate and usually participate in some kind of organized lowrider group. In a few clubs, wives of members are allowed voting status, but for the most part, women do not form or join clubs. When they do join clubs, they tend to be active for a shorter period of time than men do. Women like Ana Flores, who learned to work on cars, meet with some local resistance.

When lowriding is a family activity, it is organized around men's interests and family participation. Moreover, men are more likely than women to claim that their car is a "family" project or that their car connects them to their family. In one case, an Española man claimed that his car was his family – he was divorced from his wife and no longer lived with her or their children. Instead, he "took care" of the car which features a mural of a beautiful blonde on the trunk (see figure 22.7). Men's cars function as representations of masculinity and male relationships. In addition, cars are sites of mechanical and aesthetic proficiency. They are material sites for the imagining and construction of men's relationships and responsibilities, and they occupy a central location in the lives of many men. Not surprisingly, they can become the subject of domestic tension. The time, effort, money, and care they require is seen by some wives as in direct conflict with familial responsibilities and relationships. In this rural area, families can feel quite fragmented because members must work away from home in Los Alamos or in Santa Fe. As a result, the meanings of family and of gendered identity become heightened in a culture that values family relationships. When Dennis Martinez says, "My heart is in my wheels," and adds "I have a heart like a car," he alerts his audiences to the multiple meanings that cars have. Cars carry people and feelings, and car customizing allows a man to express his

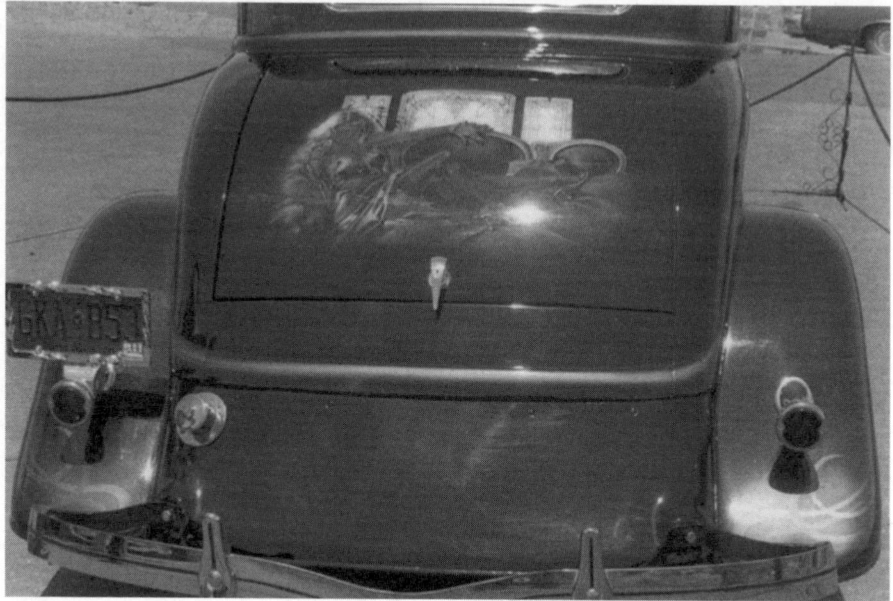

Figure 22.7 Car as family. Photograph by author

feelings. Men care for their cars, they care for their families, and having a nice car is one way of being a man. For some, it is a way of being a man who cares for his family. The socioeconomic context of these car-related practices – rural area, working-class jobs, employment outmigration, heavy tourism, and cultural appropriations – coupled with a history of marginalization from the land, make the cars themselves an important surface for assertions of personal and cultural identity.

I suggest that we think of tradition as invoked by lowriders as a process of improvisation, a process that reconverts cultural practices for current conditions. García-Canclini defines reconversion as follows: "to reconvert cultural capital means to transfer symbolic patrimony from one site to another in order to conserve it, increase its yield, and better the position of those who practice it" (1992:32).[16] A symbolic process akin to what García-Canclini describes can be seen at work in lowrider aesthetics. In northern New Mexico, where representation is a key economic and cultural practice, lowriders incorporate the emblematic images of their culture – their families, their land, their religion, their struggle – onto the many surfaces of their cars.

Local/Translocal Inscriptions

In the aesthetic of Española area lowriders there is one particularly striking indication of the simultaneous localization and translocalization of culture: the pairing of an image with personal meaning, often drawn from local culture, with an image or reference to extralocal identities and processes. Dennis Martinez's statement, "It's something that's *traditional*. I have a heart that's like a car, you know. My heart is in my wheels," links the historical importance of lowriding practice to its affectivity. His statement situates the car within a particular narrative construction that suggests how the car, a mass-produced object, becomes embedded within a cultural context through relationships, material practices, and textualizations.

A "heart that's like a car" suggests the ways in which the car is an embodiment, enhancing both bodily mobility and affectivity. In this vein, the car is similar to the human body, a site of cultural inscription. In contemporary contexts where most aspects of our lives are disjointed, cars simultaneously isolate us and provide continuity between people and places. Customizing a car enlarges the possibilities of bodily inscription, exhibition, and, for many lowriders, social relations. These activities take place on cars that are in reality mobile canvases. Given the broad range of aesthetic practices and representational forms in this heavily touristed area, cars provide a site relatively free from the potential commodification to which many other forms are subject.

The simultaneous presence of local and translocal symbols is seen in Dennis Martinez's salmon pink 1970 Monte Carlo (see figure 22.8). The ghostly painted images on the car ally him with two traditions – one local Hispano and the other Chicano. The mountainous landscapes on the rear panels of the car are reference to the local mountains (see figure 22.9). The depiction of the land in this area signifies culture, family, community, continuity, and, importantly, conflict (Rodríguez 1992). The roses between the rear and side windows are a metonymic symbol invoking the owner's Hispano culture as well as his deceased mother and her garden (see figure 22.10). The rose also represents la Virgen de Guadalupe, who provides her believers with a means to know God's love and acts as a sign of God's acknowledgment of the Hispanic New World. In both cases, the rose symbolizes empowerment and tribute, just as Martinez – as a descendant of Mexicans and his mother's son – has been empowered by the love of these two women.

In the foreground of the mountainous landscape stands a third ghostly image – the pachuco. An invocation of Chicano consciousness signifying cultural awareness, integrity and self-determination (see figure 22.9), pachucos were Mexican American male youths in the 1940s, members of the early generation of U.S.-born Mexicans. They too had a style to "deal with" – zoot suits with fingertip-length sleeves, broad shoulders, baggy pants pegged at the ankles, and ankle-length watch chains. During World War II Mexican American zoot suiters in Los Angeles were hunted down and beaten by American soldiers stationed there.[17] For the servicemen, zoot suits symbolized excess – their styling required additional fabric during a time of limited resources when such constructions were outlawed – and lack of proper patriotic feelings (Mazón 1984). In the historical reconstructions of the Chicano Movement, the pachuco represents the first Mexican American to embody Chicano consciousness. Through style, pachucos defiantly express the contradictions of being Mexican American (of being neither Mexican nor American) yet suffering violence and discrimination because of cultural difference.

For lowriders, the pachuco serves as a powerful symbol for claims to difference made through style. It became one of the symbols adapted and promoted by *Lowrider Magazine* in the late 1970s as lowriding's popularity grew throughout the Southwest (Plascensia 1983). Martinez uses it here as an emblem of empowerment. Concerned with working-class empowerment (in part as a result of an accident he suffered while employed at Los Alamos Laboratories – he lost an eye), and with cultural empowerment for area Hispanos, Martinez sees his car as an opportunity to express his skills and culture (see figure 22.11). For him, these two arenas are linked and simultaneously represented in the images on his car. The challenge to viewers is how to contextualize and understand these acts of representation.

Arthur Medina's white '75 Cadillac is called "Lowrider Heaven." The front license plate says "little LA," a nickname of Española, tying local experiences to extralocal processes and larger identities (see figure 22.12).[18] Medina, who aspires to be known for his art work, has painted the head of Jesus on the trunk. He also has painted Jesus on the exterior of his house (see figure 22.13). When I asked him if he was a religious man, he replied, "I believe in God a lot." When I pressed him to tell me why it was important to him to have Jesus on his car, he said, "Well, like, he did a lot for us! Like, I could be putting knights or something on my car, but I feel better if I put him on it. I just feel better. It's like he's guiding me." His explanation, while seeming to posit a choice between popular culture and religious culture, actually unites them within a single repertoire, indicating the extent to which religious iconography is a local form of popular culture. As both cases show, traditional forms become the popular culture of the area. The car for Arthur Medina is a place where he expresses his feelings. He says, "I put on it what I feel." Since he thinks of his work as art, he prefers that his car be hand painted, a

Figure 22.8 Dennis Martinez and his 1970 Monte Carlo. Photograph by author

technique that he considers more conducive to expressing feeling. Thus, these lowriders indicate two symbolic trends among lowriders from the Española area. One is the use of tradition as central to the popular culture of the area. The second is the connection of local culture to extralocal processes and identities.

Given the wide range of images that lowriders use on their cars, cars from the Española area are distinguished to the extent that religious images

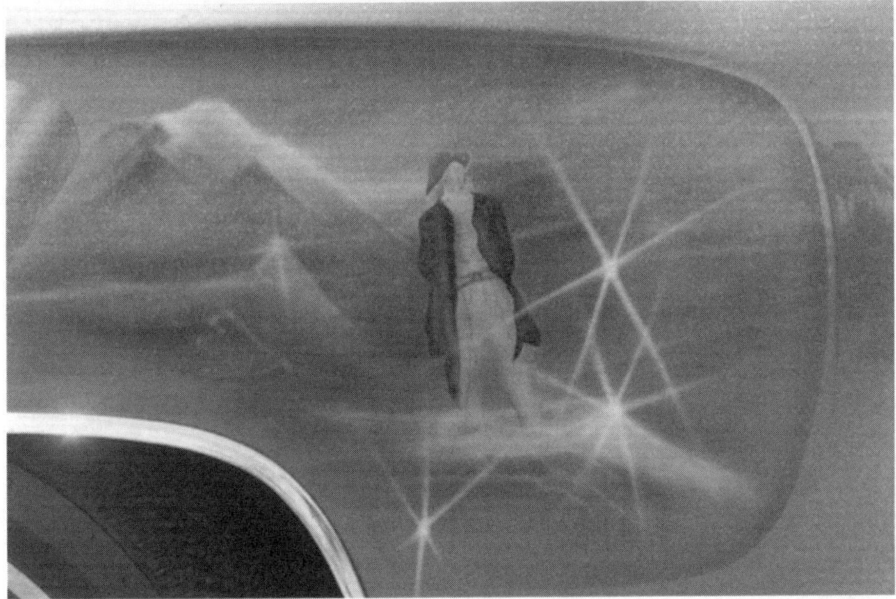

Figure 22.9 Sangre de Cristo mountains and pachuco. Photograph by author

Figure 22.10 Rose mural. Photograph by author

Figure 22.11 1970 Monte Carlo. Photograph by author

Figure 22.12 Arthur Medina's 1975 Cadillac. Photograph by author

are prevalent. For Chimayó lowriders, the Santuario de Chimayó plays a consolidating role influencing which symbolic forms they choose and circulate (see figure 22.4). An important regional landmark and spiritual center, the Santuario symbolizes Chimayó and is the backdrop for many photographs. In addition to those seeking its spiritual powers, people interested in folk art

Figure 22.13 Cadillac in front of Arthur Medina's home. Photograph by author

and Hispano folklore are drawn to the Santuario. The carving of Jesus over the altar in the Santuario is well known. The west wing of the Santuario contains the healing dirt, many images of Jesus, la Virgen and saints as well as appeals, *testimonios* (testimonials), and thanks for help received.

Victor Martinez's '50 Ford is customized in the style of a '50s customized car – complete with continental kit extending the support of the rear bumper, flame paint job, and original option rims (see figures 22.14 and 22.15). But just above the continental kit is a mural depicting the sacred heart of Jesus, an invocation of cultural authority and a symbol of suffering, sacrifice, and love (see figure 22.16). With these two aesthetic devices – the replication of an "American" cultural style through the '50s motif and the image of Jesus – the owner ties himself to an "American moment" while also invoking local and extralocal cultural authority. The skill with which he makes his vehicle is his particular and very personal claim to self-respect.

Place provides an important context for the display of cars in addition to being a meaningful reference for images on cars. Victor Martinez and his family attend the Catholic church in nearby Santa Cruz, but his wife's family owns a hamburger stand directly across from the Santuario. Both Victor and his wife Barbara work there on the weekends. He often parks his car outside the stand in full view of the Santuario and its visitors. Hence, Victor is aware of the symbolic significance of whatever image he puts on his car, and this awareness has influenced his choice to exhibit a religious image instead of another form. Arthur Medina's family also owns a food, folk art, and souvenir stand across from the Santuario. Arthur is an artist in that he not only made his car, the Cadillac described above, but in 1991 was in the process of teaching himself wood carving and trying to define his own craftwork, much of which also carried religious themes. This work was made for sale to tourists visiting Santuario.

These examples provide a sense of the narrative constructions and connections made possible through customizing activities. Each car is an individual project, a family project, and a local reference. Each requires structuring a "vehicle" for family togetherness as well as for personal and group narratives. It is a "vehicle" for claiming

Figure 22.14 Victor Martinez's 1950 Ford. Photograph by author

Figure 22.15 Victor Martinez's 1950 Ford, rear view. Photograph by author

local and extralocal identity. In this sense, the car is a "cultural vehicle" enabling the reinvention of culture. It is in this creative sense that the low-rider says, "It's my culture, man" while explaining that the best metaphor for the building of a low-rider is "giving new life to an old soul."[19] In New Mexico, customizing aesthetics are influenced by a sense of cultural difference that is rooted in highly localized identities – related to family, land, and local cohorts – but inflected by responses to

Figure 22.16 Sacred heart of Jesus mural. Photograph by author

economic and cultural appropriations in the area that necessitates appeals to a larger-scale, extra-local identity.

The Smithsonian

For the 1992 quincentennial, the Smithsonian produced an exhibition entitled "American Encounters" to be on display for roughly 10 years (Morrison 1992). They wanted to use the cultures of the Rio Grande valley area of New Mexico to demonstrate a long history of multiculturalism in the United States. In the process of preparing the project, the Smithsonian purchased the previously mentioned lowrider car, "Dave's Dream," from Irene Jamarillo in Española (Brewer 1990). During the course of the Smithsonian's research, lowriders, more than any other group researched, emerged as controversial in New Mexico culture.

In 1990, the Smithsonian lobbied the New Mexico state government to contribute $1,000,000 to the "American Encounters" exhibition. New Mexico residents expressed concern that they were going to be "represented" by the lowly and exotic lowrider car. Given local concerns with autonomy and self-representation, many New Mexican residents saw this as an opportunity to express their views and represent themselves broadly as they found themselves being incorporated into the Smithsonian's imagining of the nation. The Smithsonian responded to editorials in the local papers with assurances that the exhibition was not focusing on lowriders per se, but on the complexities of New Mexican cultures and intercultural relations (Kennedy 1991; Miller 1991).

The message of this discussion was that lowriders play an important symbolic role in the larger discussion of New Mexican "culture," a message not lost on Española lowriders or their audiences. This discussion of cultural representation indicates one of the important controversial features of popular culture: that the objectification of culture disrupts established class and cultural hierarchies. While lowriders see themselves and their cars as positively engaged in representing their culture, this vision is not always shared by others. Some Anglos see them as bothersome troublemakers and are often afraid of them.

Some Hispanos likewise think of them as troublemakers and worry that they give all Hispanos a bad name. Others deride them for their attachment to religious symbols in the name of having a good time. The cars are thought by some to be excessively adorned and in bad taste. Tomás Ybarra-Frausto cites lowriders as a key example of *rasquachismo*, a Chicano aesthetic sensibility that turns ruling paradigms upside down and produces "a sort of good taste of bad taste" (1991:155). It is in the context of conflicts over culture and representation that lowriding has the important effect of carving out a niche of pleasure, autonomy, and self-authored and authorizing representation for working-class Chicanos throughout the Southwest.

Reconversions

Lowriding in New Mexico is at once a historically situated series of social practices and a form of local "Chicanoized" Hispano culture. The customizing techniques that characterize lowriding in the upper Rio Grande valley have been employed since the 1940s among Mexican Americans and Hispanos throughout most of the Southwest. But lowriding as a popular social practice and the clubs and competitions associated with it date from the 1970s. New Mexico adaptations of lowriding are based in part on the development of the form in California, knowledge gained by outmigrating and returning New Mexican workers, and the ideology of ethnic empowerment – communicated through the regionally distributed *Lowrider Magazine* that stresses lowriding as a uniquely "Chicano" form of customizing. Potentialities already within the form made it suitable for translocal adoption. Potentialities at the local level included local conditions (tourist commodification, land appropriation, and work conflicts), local social practices (such as kin-based trading and gifting), as well as local popular cultures (religious images as icons of identity and resistance).

Understanding lowriding as a form of Chicano culture practiced by northern New Mexican Hispanos requires a frame of elaboration for analyzing ethnic identity processes in northern New Mexico. Issues of Hispano identity are most cogently addressed in Sylvia Rodríguez's work on Taos Hispanos and the dynamics of identity processes in northern New Mexico. Rodríguez examines "Hispano ethnicity and its relation to contemporary Mexicano-Chicano ethnopolitical identity and mobilization" (1992:96). She notes that constituencies for Chicano (national-political) and local Hispano forms of ethnopolitical and ethnocultural expression tend to overlap, especially in ritual revivals, Danza Azteca, lowriders, and Cinco de Mayo celebrations. In "The Hispano Homeland Debate Revisited" (1992), she elaborates the contours of the recent debate about Hispano distinctiveness. Certain academics, key among them geographer Richard Nostrand (1984), claim that a significant portion of Hispanos of all classes in northern New Mexico see themselves as related to but distinct from other Mexicanos and Spanish-speaking people. The problem that concerns Rodríguez is that Norstrand and his supporters assume "that any sense of Hispano distinctiveness, whether true or false, will impede the development of a broader, more progressive Chicano (or American or working-class) political consciousness and therefore is undesirable or retrograde" (1984:104). But Rodríguez's work suggests that the two forms of identity are in fact not incompatible. The process, as argued by Michael Hannan, proceeds as follows:

> When modern centers penetrate the local community, they undermine the salience of small-scale identities....Sustained mobilization in opposition to further penetration by the center must be on a scale commensurate with that of the center. Therefore, successful penetration by the center alters the condition of competition among the various bases of collective action in a direction that favors large-scale identities. (Hannan 1979:255–256, quoted in Rodríguez 1992:105)

Extrapolating the significance of this argument for northern New Mexico, Rodríguez proposes the following:

> Rather than being an impediment to the emergence of a broad-based, extralocal Chicano identity, the traditional, small-scale organization has become the medium through which a larger identity is realized. Rooted in the village community, Hispano identity has become "Chicanoized" through modernization, outmigration and resistance. (1992:105)

Rodríguez asserts that lowriders are among the forms of ethnic cultural resurgence that indicate the "Chicanoizing" of Hispano identity.

The broader question here is the part cars play in modernization, outmigration, and resistance. A further answer to how lowrider cars can be both traditional and a response to processes of development and modernization is found in Donna Haraway's meditation on the relations of bodies and machines in the late 20th century, what she calls the potential politics and myths of cyborgs. The idea of cyborgs – hybrids of machines and organisms – as contemporary reconversions transcends the dualisms that posit what seem to be more clearly bounded, somewhat autonomous relations between people and machines, and people and commodities. These dualisms wrongly promise some ideal state of humans apart from machines. "Cyborg imagery can suggest a way out of the maze of dualisms in which we have explained our bodies and tools to ourselves" (1991:181). Cyborg imagery posits a way of thinking about people and machines in which "intense pleasure in skill, machine skill, ceases to be a sin, but an aspect of embodiment. The machine is not an *it* to be animated, worshipped, and dominated. The machine is us, our processes, an aspect of our embodiment" (1991:180). For Haraway, this meditation is necessary in order to adequately understand, envision, and participate in the ontology of the late 20th century. She defines a cyborg as a creature of social reality, lived social relations, and fiction.

"I have a heart like a car" and "my heart is in my wheels" imply just such a dialectic between body and machine and between person and commodity, as the unique features of the car are being called into the service of local personal and cultural concerns. Machinelike qualities (emulating transportation) are extended to the body as the heart becomes a vehicle of transport for loved ones. This is coupled with the extension of affectivity to the purpose of the machine itself. Haraway's person–machine hybrid is Briggs's mediator, a vehicle for social relations that enables pleasurable textualizing of social reality in a way that allows mobility, social location, and a mobile canvas. Lowriders collapse the seeming dualities between persons and machines and persons and commodities as they engage in reconverting tradition and customizing modernity. If modernity promised products and techniques to free us from the constraints of locally based culture, it did so with the threat of uprooting us from social relationships. In response, lowriders engage in traditionalizing commodities by customizing them with meanings that enable a continuity of relationships. As reconversions, lowriding practices reinterpret and reinscribe local meanings into the surfaces and materials of modern life.

Given this context, Dennis Martinez makes perfect sense when he says, "My heart is in my wheels." His statement stresses the personal dedication expected from any car customizer. It is similar to saying "I love my car" or "Here in Española we love our cars." But indeed it is a more interesting assertion than that. "My heart is in my wheels" claims the car as a lowrider's purpose, empowerment, sacrifice, and joy. It is the expression of aspirations and affections, the execution of vision and skill. To make a lowrider, Chicano customizers must draw upon and simultaneously create culture. These cars are pleasure, the sort that comes through the responsible mastery of circumstance through skills that are both cultural and technological. These cars bring pleasure from performing "culture," disrupting boundaries and derailing expectations.

When Dennis Martinez says, "I have a heart like a car," he implicitly identifies the most dramatic aspects of these cars. Namely, the car is a repository and a carrier – for the owner's "work," his family, and his tradition. Each car is the product of a baroque sensibility. This is demonstrated in the process. The making of a car requires a vision of aesthetics and meaning. Said another way, it requires customizers to link narratives of commodities to cultural and personal histories, thereby implicating themselves in the design of the car. The making of a customized car requires the recreation of tradition from the intermingling of popular traditions and mass culture. Such practices are highly inflected by the horizontal coexistence of a number of symbolic systems that are the products of modernization processes. Traditions are not simply practices passed on from one generation to the next; they are practices that enable cultural continuity and require maintenance.

Lowriders intertwine tradition and history with personal vision, deploying cultural and personal symbols to localize commodities. The aesthetic details reveal a dialectical appeal to self-respect and cultural authority (Ross 1989). This appeal plays out in specific ways in New Mexico, where tradition becomes a form of improvisation and an important resource for popular culture productions. As Néstor García-Canclini suggests, the separation of tradition from modernity no longer works:

> The traditional and the modern are mixed together all the time....Modernization is not a matter of replacing traditional high and popular forms but of reformulating their function and meaning....Instead of the death of traditional cultural forms, we now discover that tradition is in transition, and articulated to modern processes. Reconversion prolongs their existence. (1992:30–31)

As lowriders indicate, local culture is creative, appropriating symbols of modernity to assert autonomy and difference. Commodities are localized in social networks, material practices, and textualizations. Simultaneously, local practices and social relationships are nested within broader translocal processes. Lowriders exemplify contemporary modes for the translocal production of locality, demonstrating how local culture is produced in a globalizing world.

NOTES

1 *Hispano* refers to the people of Spanish and Mexican descent in New Mexico. *Chicano* is an ethnopolitical term that refers to Mexican Americans and all people of Mexican descent living in the United States. *Chicano* is used primarily by those who have incorporated an explicitly political component in their group identity. This component stresses culture (heritage, practices, and creations) and the conditions of its production within the United States. While *Chicano* designates an ethnopolitical identity for many, it has been used historically as both a nickname and as a slur. Its politicized usage was adopted in the Chicano Movement of the 1960s. This movement developed among Mexican American activists and students as part of the civil rights struggles in the United States. Important locations of radical political activity were the University of California; Denver, Colorado; Crystal City, Texas; and Tierra Amarilla in Rio Arriba County, New Mexico. See José Limón 1981. See also Anaya and Lomelí 1991; Muñoz 1989; Rodriguez 1992; Saldívar 1990; Ybarra-Frausto 1977.

2 Española is located on the highway between Santa Fe and Taos. Primarily a Hispano town with a population of 8,389 according to the 1990 census, it is the regional trading town and destination for people migrating from the area villages of northern New Mexico in order to participate in the cash economy. Significantly, it is also a town that many tourists pass through on their way to and from the more popular tourist destinations of northern New Mexico.

3 By and large, studies of car culture focus on manufacturing, aesthetics, and subcultures. The greatest shortcoming of automotive and subcultural studies is that they do not adequately investigate the relationships between local cultures, work cultures, and networks of mass production and mass culture. See Gradante 1982, 1985; Moorhouse 1991; Plascensia 1983; Plath 1990; Stone 1990; Watkins 1991; Wolfe 1965.

4 These are Appadurai's finanscapes (money), ethnoscapes (people), ideoscapes (ideas), technoscapes (technology), and mediascapes (media). His argument is for conceptualizing these particularities as part of larger formations with their own particularities and sets of perspectives (1990:6).

5 As Appadurai argues (1995), the ethnographic record can be read as presenting the technologies and teleologies of localization. In short, a rereading of the ethnographic record foregrounding the idea of locality itself can be informative and provide new avenues for ethnographic conceptualization and representation. Other writers on the conditions of modernity and postmodernity call for a rethinking of the intersections of locality and the material and cultural conditions of social life (Battaglia 1995; Ferguson and Gupta 1992; Marcus 1995; Miller 1994) as well as locality and ethnographic accounts (Fischer and Abedi 1990; Marcus and Fischer 1986).

6 The central questions of my project, *Lowrider: Chicano Culture in the Time of the Automobile*, are fourfold (Bright in press). First, how is popular culture utilized in the creation of contemporary communities? Second, how do local cultures and political economies influence the process by which Mexican Americans create and adapt an extralocal ethnopolitical identity in the process of creating and

adapting lowrider styles? Third, how is gender constructed in local and extralocal versions of popular culture, sexuality, and ethnicity? Fourth, how do so-called minorities address the challenges of structured inequality, mass media, and commodity culture through their participation in popular culture?

7 While it is true that gangs as corporate entities are not strictly local, gangs are typically comprised of sets that come from a shared geographical area, and for whom a territory-based identity is foundational. In Los Angeles, many lowriders narrate their participation as having been decided in a choice between gang membership or car customizing (see Bright 1995). Los Angeles lowriding most nearly resembles Appadurai's suggestion that the presence of multiple mediated forms provides alternatives in culture and identity that are not so resolutely local (1991). The Houston example suggests that migrants also use popular forms to create communities for themselves.

8 The widespread use of the label *Chicano* dates from the 1960s as does the term *lowrider*, although for reasons that are both different and related. Lowriders share customizing techniques with other customizing enthusiasts – especially chopping and channeling. While cars customized by Mexican Americans have primarily emphasized appearance over performance and speed, many Mexican Americans have also wanted fast cars. Before the 1960s, the differences between Mexican American and Anglo cars were subtle and not so clearly identified with any one style of customizing. In fact, early hot rods looked much like today's lowriders, with bodies close to the ground. Three developments during the 1960s distinguished lowriders from hot rods. First was the production of muscle cars (often with "raked" front ends and raised rear ends) and with them the solidifying of Anglo aesthetics emphasizing speed and high performance. Second was the adaptation of hydraulic lifts so that Mexican American cars could be lowered, allowing the owner to have a "low" car with the ability to raise it up to legal associated limits as necessary. Third was the identification of this style with a Mexican American experience and identity, and competitive cruising scenes developed. The most notable was Whittier Boulevard in East Los Angeles. See Bright 1995. See also Rodriguez 1984, Stone 1990, and Wolfe 1965.

9 *Lowrider Magazine* was published from 1977 until 1984 when it went bankrupt. Alberto Lopez bought *Lowrider* and renewed its publication in 1988. Since then, lowriding has increasingly migrated across ethnic and racial lines. Los Angeles has a long history of African American car customizers and lowriders. With the advent of gangster rap out of Los Angeles in the late 1980s and MTV air time for hip hop videos, lowriders have been increasingly known as part of hip hop, with origins in African American and Afro-Caribbean youth culture (Rose 1994). See Bright 1997.

10 The class antagonisms between Española and its wealthy neighbors of Los Alamos and Santa Fe can be seen in a series of jokes known as "Española jokes," similar to Texas Aggie jokes and Pollack jokes. These jokes make fun of Española for its residents' backwardness and lack of intelligence. They ridicule Española as a poor, rural, underdeveloped area populated by social undesirables. Española area residents typically do not tell these jokes (Cordova 1990; Sagel 1993). See Battaglia 1992 for an insightful reading of the ways jokes are located within power relations and serve to displace culture.

11 Around the state, Chimayosos are known as tough, proud, and somewhat countryish in their ways, a characterization many of them accept. I argue that their self-image has developed in part because of their experiences with cultural appropriation and subordination.

12 In New Mexico, the partial transformation from spiritual object to cultural commodity has been influenced by Anglos involved in the study and "preservation" of "native" art and architecture and through their fascination with exotic practices such as interest in *penitente* practices, which were stimulated in part by Anglo encroachment (Briggs 1980:44; Weigle 1976:75, 90–91). See Sylvia Rodríguez's writings on the cultural politics of the Taos area for a full historical examination of these processes (1987, 1992).

13 In a related example, the city of Española, which lies in between the tourist centers of Santa Fe and Taos, is badly in need of more revenue dollars and has instituted an urban development program aimed at attracting what appears to be the area's last untapped resource, the tourist business. The residents are constructing a new town plaza and church. They are simultaneously enacting legislation creating an "Old Town" zone with building code restrictions similar to those in place in Santa Fe. This will create an identifiable, albeit romanticized, dehistoricized, and rehistoricized image of the town as a picturesque "Spanish" town and the home of Spanish conqueror and colonizer, Don

Juan de Oñate. This in a town that, unlike Santa Fe, never had a central plaza.

14 The cars are detailed to be unique. For example, special taillights from a 1959 Cadillac are added to a 1964 Chevrolet Impala. Other special touches include undersized steering wheels, dice knobs on the gearshift, and double "frenched in" antennae. One addition cinches the lowrider's uniqueness among customized cars – hydraulic lifts that allow the car to "hop" front, back, and side to side. This kind of work is done on almost any vehicle, for example, a 1938 Ford truck with a 1950 truck bed placed on a modified 1976 Grand Prix frame and given a flame paint job and double antennas.

15 An early boyfriend insisted that she could not have a nicer car than his.

16 See also Stonequist (1937). He discusses "reviving" and "modernizing" local culture as a way to keep old issues alive and point out new ones. This prevents "accommodation on any particular level from becoming too fixed and crystallized, thereby helping to raise the ultimate status of...[the] group" (1937:174).

17 For a historical analysis of the zoot suit riots, see Mauricio Mazón 1984. The Chicano interpretation of the pachucos as the first Mexican Americans has been promoted in the works of Luis Valdez. His play *Zoot Suit*, produced as a movie in 1978, depicts the racism and persecution that pachucos experienced and links their distinctive style of dress with their experiences as the first Mexican and American generation that was neither Mexican nor American (Sanchez-Tranquilino 1987; Valdez 1978a and 1978b).

18 Just as Los Angeles is the largest settlement of Mexican migrants outside Mexico city, Española is the regional destination for people migrating from the area villages of northern New Mexico in order to participate in the cash economy.

19 Making a car can be productively compared with making family photo albums. The difference is that cars are quintessentially paternal vehicles when compared to photo albums, which are predominantly maternal projects.

REFERENCES

Abu-Lughod, Lila. 1990. The Romance of Resistance: Tracing Transformations of Power through Bedouin Women. *American Ethnologist* 17:41–55.

Acuña, Rodolfo. 1981. *Occupied America: A History of Chicanos*. 2nd edn. New York: Harper & Row.

Anaya, Rudolfo, and Francisco Lomelí, eds. 1991. *Aztlán: Essays on the Chicano Homeland*. Albuquerque: University of New Mexico Press.

Appadurai, Arjun. 1990. Disjuncture and Difference in the Global Cultural Economy. *Public Culture* 2 (2):1–23.

Appadurai, Arjun. 1991. Global Ethnoscapes: Notes and Queries for a Transnational Anthropology. In *Recapturing Anthropology: Working in the Present*. Richard G. Fox, ed. Pp. 191–210. Santa Fe, NM: School of American Research Press.

Appadurai, Arjun. 1995. The Production of Locality. In *Counterworks: Managing the Diversity of Knowledge*. Richard Fardon, ed. Pp. 204–225. New York: Routledge.

Babcock, Barbara. 1990a. A New Mexican Rebecca: Imaging Pueblo Women. *Journal of the Southwest* 32 (Winter):400–437.

Babcock, Barbara. 1990b. By Way of Introduction. *Journal of the Southwest* 32(Winter):383–399.

Battaglia, Debbora. 1992. Displacing Culture: A Joke of Significance in Urban Papua New Guinea. *New Literary History* 23(4):1003–1017.

Battaglia, Debbora. 1995. On Practical Nostalgia: Self-Prospecting among Urban Trobrianders. In *Rhetorics of Self-Making*. D. Battaglia, ed. Pp. 77–96. Berkeley: University of California Press.

Borhegyi, Stephen F. de. 1956. *El Santuario De Chimayo*. Santa Fe, NM: Ancient City Press.

Brewer, Steve. 1990. Stereotypes Disintegrate in Lowriders. *Albuquerque Journal* September 20:C-1.

Briggs, Charles. 1980. *The Wood Carvers of Córdova, New Mexico*. Albuquerque: University of New Mexico Press.

Briggs, Charles L., and J. R. Van Ness, eds. 1987. *Land, Water, and Culture: New Perspectives on Hispanic Land Grants*. Albuquerque: University of New Mexico Press.

Bright, Brenda Jo. 1995. Remappings: Los Angeles Low Riders. In *Looking High and Low: Art and Cultural Identity*. Brenda Jo Bright and Liza Bakewell, eds. Pp. 89–123. Tucson: University of Arizona Press.

Bright, Brenda Jo. 1997. Nightmares in the New Metropolis: The Cinematic Poetics of Lowriders. *Journal of Latin American Popular Culture* 16:13–29.

Bright, Brenda Jo. In press. *Lowrider: Chicano Culture in the Time of the Automobile*. University of California Press.

Bureau of the Census. 1990. *Census of Population and Housing*. Washington, DC: U.S. Government Printing Office.

Carrier, James. 1991. Gifts, Commodities, and Social Relations: A Maussian View of Exchange. *Sociological Forum* 6(1):119–136.

Cordova, Gilberto Benito. 1990. *The 3 ½* Cultures of Española. Albuquerque, NM: El Norte Publications/Academia.

Crawford, Stanley. 1989. *Mayordomo: Chronicle of an Acequia in Northern New Mexico*. New York: Anchor Books, Doubleday.

Deutsch, Sarah. 1987. *No Separate Refuge: Culture, Class and Gender on an Anglo-Hispanic Frontier in the American Southwest, 1880–1940*. New York: Oxford University Press.

Ferguson, James, and Akhil Gupta. 1992. Beyond "Culture": Space, Identity, and the Politics of Difference. *Cultural Anthropology* 7(1):6–23.

Fischer, Michael, M. J. 1986. Ethnicity and the Post-modern Arts of Memory. In *Writing Culture: The Poetics and Politics of Ethnography*. J. Clifford and G. Marcus, eds. Pp. 194–233. Berkeley: University of California Press.

Fischer, Michael M. J., and Medhi Abedi. 1990. *Debating Muslims: Cultural Dialogues in Postmodernity and Tradition*. Madison: University of Wisconsin Press.

Forrest, Suzanner. 1989. *The Preservation of the Village: New Mexico's Hispanics and the New Deal*. Albuquerque: University of New Mexico Press.

Foster, Robert J. 1991. Making National Cultures in the Global Ecumene. *Annual Reviews in Anthropology* 20:235–260.

García-Canclini, Néstor. 1992. Cultural Reconversion. In *On Edge: The Crisis of Contemporary Latin American Culture*. G. Yúdice, J. Franco, and Juan Flores, eds. Pp. 29–43. Minneapolis: University of Minnesota Press.

Gradante, William. 1982. Low and Slow, Mean and Clean. *Natural History* 91(4):28–39.

Gradante, William. 1985. Art among the Lowriders. In *Folk Art in Texas*. F. E Abernethy, ed. Pp. 70–77. Dallas, TX: Southern Methodist University Press.

Grimes, Ronald. 1976. *Symbol and Conquest: Public Ritual and Drama in Santa Fe, New Mexico*. Ithaca, NY: Cornell University Press.

Hannan, Michael. 1979. The Dynamics of Ethnic Boundaries in Modern States. In *National Development and the World System: Educational, Economic and Political Change, 1950–1970*. John Meyer and Michael Hannan, eds. Pp. 253–275. Chicago: University of Chicago Press.

Haraway, Donna J. 1991. A Cyborg Manifesto: Science, Technology and Socialist-Feminism in the Late Twentieth Century. In *Simians, Cyborgs, and Women: The Reinvention of Nature*. Pp. 149–182. New York: Routledge.

Kay, Elizabeth. 1987. *Chimayó Valley Traditions*. Santa Fe, NM: Ancient City Press.

Kennedy, Roger. 1991. Museum Director Promises State Quality Exhibition at Smithsonian. *Rio Grande Sun*, July 25: A4.

Limón, José. 1981. The Folk Performance of "Chicano" and the Cultural Limits of Political Ideology. In *Other Neighborly Names: Social Processes and Cultural Image in Texas Folklore*. R. Bauman and R. D. Abrahams, eds. Pp. 197–225. Austin: University of Texas Press.

Lipsitz, George. 1995. Their America, and Ours: Intercultural Communication in the Context of "Our America." Ethnic Studies Department, University of California, San Diego. Unpublished Manuscript.

Lujan, Gilberto Sánchez. 1970. El Arte del Chicano. *Con Safos* Winter:11.

Lynch-Frost Productions. 1990. Auto Obsession. *American Chronicles*. Fox Network. October 4.

Marcus, George E. 1990. Imagining the Whole: Ethnography's Contemporary Efforts to Situate Itself. *Critique of Anthropology* 9(3):7–30.

Marcus, George E. 1995 Ethnography in/of the World System: The Emergence of Multi-Sited Ethnography. *Annual Review of Anthropology* 24:95–117.

Marcus, George E., and Michael M. J. Fischer. 1986. *Anthropology as Cultural Critique: An Experimental Moment in the Human Sciences*. Chicago: University of Chicago Press.

Mazón, Mauricio. 1984. *The Zoot Suit Riots: The Psychology of Symbolic Annihilation*. Austin: University of Texas Press.

Miller, Daniel. 1994. *Modernity: An Ethnographic Approach*. Oxford: Berg.

Miller, Jay. 1991. Inside the Capitol. *Rio Grande Sun*, July 11: A5.

Moorhouse, H. F. 1991. *Driving Ambitions: An Analysis of the American Hot Enthusiasm*. Manchester: Manchester University Press.

Morrison, Howard. 1992. *American Encounters: A Companion to the Exhibition at the National Museum of American History, Smithsonian Insitution*. Washington, DC: Smithsonian Institution.

Muñoz, Carlos. 1989. *Youth, Identity, Power: The Chicano Movement*. London: Verso.

Nabokov, Peter. 1969. *Tijerina and the Courthouse Raid*. Albuquerque: University of New Mexico Press.

Nostrand, Richard. 1984. Hispano Cultural Distinctiveness: A Reply. *Annals of the Association of American Geographers* 74(1):164–169.

Plascensia, Luis F. B. 1983. Low Riding in the Southwest: Cultural Symbols in the Mexican Community. In *History, Culture and Society: Chicano Studies in the 1980s*. Mario T. Garcia et al., eds. Pp. 141–175. Ypsilanti, MI: Bilingual Press.

Plath, David W. 1990. My-Car-isma: Motorizing the Showa Self. *Daedalus* 119(3):229–244.

Rodriguez, Roberto. 1984. *Assault with a Deadly Weapon: About an Incident in E.L.A. and the Closing of Whittier Boulevard*. Los Angeles: Rainbow Press.

Rodríguez, Sylvia. 1987. Land, Water, and Ethnic Identity in Taos. In *Land, Water, and Culture: New Perspectives on Hispanic Land Grants*. C. L. Briggs and J. R. Van Ness, eds. Pp. 313–403. Albuquerque: University of New Mexico Press.

Rodríguez, Sylvia. 1992. The Hispano Homeland Debate Revisited. In *Perspectives in Mexican American Studies* 3(1992):95–116.

Rose, Tricia. 1994. *Black Noise: Rap Music and Black Culture in Contemporary America*. Hanover, NH: Wesleyan University Press.

Ross, Andrew. 1989. *No Respect: Intellectuals and Popular Culture*. New York: Routledge.

Rowe, William, and Vivian Schelling. 1991. *Memory and Modernity: Popular Culture in Latin America*. London: Verso.

Sagel, Jim. 1993. Lowdown Laughs: The Española Joke. In *Dancing to Pay the Light Bill*. Pp. 55–58. Santa Fe: Red Crane Books.

Saldívar, Ramón. 1990. *Chicano Narrative: The Dialectics of Difference*. Madison: University of Wisconsin Press.

Sanchez-Tranquilino, Marcos. 1987. Mano a Mano: An Essay on the Representation of the Zoot Suit and Its Misrepresentation by Octavio Paz. *Journal: A Contemporary Art Magazine* Winter:34–42.

Shank, Barry. 1994. *Dissonant Identitites: The Rock'n'roll Scene in Austin, Texas*. Hanover, NH: Weslayan University Press.

Stone, Michael C. 1990. "Bajito y Suavecito": Low Riding and the "Class" of Class. *Journal of Latin American Popular Culture* 9:85–126.

Stonequist, Edmond. 1937. *The Marginal Man: A Study in Personality and Culture Conflict*. New York: Scribner's Sons.

Thornton, Robert. 1988. The Rhetoric of Ethnographic Holism. *Cultural Anthropology* 3:285–303.

Urla, Jacqueline. 1996. Outlaw Language: Creating Aternative Public Spheres in Basque Free Radio. In *The Politics of Culture in the Shadow of Capital*. Lisa Lowe and David Lloyd, eds. Pp. 280–300. Durham, NC: Duke University Press.

Valdez, Luis. 1978a. *Zoot Suit*. Los Angeles, CA: Center for Theatre Groups, Mark Taper Forum.

Valdez, Luis. 1978b. *Once Again, Meet the Zoot Suiters*. Los Angeles Times, August 27: V:54.

Watkins, Evan. 1991. "For the Time Being, Forever": Social Position and the Art of Automobile Maintenance. *Boundary* 2 18(2):150–165.

Weigle, Marta. 1976. *Brothers of Light, Brothers of Blood: The Penitentes of the Southwest*. Albuquerque: University of New Mexico Press.

Wolfe, Tom. 1965. The Kandy-Kolored Tangerine-Flake Streamline Baby. In *The Kandy-Kolored Flake Streamline Baby*. Pp. 62–89. New York: Pocket Books.

Ybarra-Frausto, Tomás. 1977. The Chicano Movement and the Emergence of a Chicano Poetic Consciousness. *New Scholar* 6:81–109.

Ybarra-Frausto, Tomás. 1991. Rasquachismo: A Chicano Sensibility. In *Chicano Art: Resistance and Affirmation*. Richard Griswald del Castillo et al., eds. Pp. 155–162. Exhibition Catalog, Wight Art Gallery, UCLA, Los Angeles. Tucson: University of Arizona Press.

23

"Checkin' Up on My Guy": Chicanas, Social Capital, and the Culture of Romance

Angela Valenzuela

The purpose of this paper is to examine the culture of romance among regular track Chicanas in a large, inner-city, virtually all-Mexican high school in Houston, Texas, fictitiously known as Juan Seguín High.[1] By culture of romance, I refer to a romanticized view of heterosexual relations where love, warmth, and intimacy are dominant emotions. In their classic study of romance among college-going women, Dorothy C. Holland and Margaret A. Eisenhart refer to the culture of romance as one of the main factors explaining why women scale back their own aspirations. That is, to achieve love and attention from males, women often make compromises to the detriment of their careers. An irony of romantic love for these college-going women is that as they become more deeply involved in their relationships and as they envision more traditional roles for themselves as future spouses, women minimize their investment in academics and their pursuit of careers becomes less important.[2]

Romantic relationships at Seguín clearly involve similar kinds of compromises. However, qualitative evidence gathered from fieldwork lends support to a complementary hypothesis: At least for the more seriously involved, when young women provide support to their male friends, however excessive, they enact or perform a version of femininity that promotes school as a goal. For reasons that are largely related to context, the evidence suggests that a cultural meaning system can develop that runs in the opposite direction of what Holland and Eisenhart would predict. That is, romantic love can evolve into a pro-school ethos. Whether this ethos translates into higher academic achievement, however, depends on the levels of social capital that students possess.

By social capital, I mean the social ties that connect students to each other, as well as the levels of resources (like academic skills and knowledge) that characterize their friendship groups.[3] In contrast to other better-known forms of capital, like human and cultural capital,[4] social capital is known by its function. That is, through the interactive web of social relationships, social capital enables the attainment of goals that cannot be accomplished solely by the individual. This collectivist ethos is evident among youth at Seguín when, in the context of their peer group and even their romantic relationships, exchanges involve a marshaling of academically productive social capital.[5]

Holland and Eisenhart maintain that the shape that the culture of romance takes will vary depending on social context. For this reason, I do not see my findings as seriously challenging theirs. The present discussion instead highlights the capacity of social context to engender a pro-school ethos within the boundaries of romance. After describing the larger study and addressing some of its key findings, I turn to the primary sources of data, participant observation and group interviews, that permit me to explore my hypothesis.[6]

The Seguín High School Study

This research is part of a larger study that investigates generational differences in achievement and schooling orientations between immigrant and U.S.-born Mexican youth.[7] Data were collected through a survey, participant observation, and open-ended interviews with individuals and groups of students between 1992 and 1995.[8] My study helps explain a widely observed empirical pattern of higher immigrant achievement vis-à-vis their acculturated, U.S.-born counterparts found in both small-scale ethnographies and national-level data.[9] Rather than revealing the upward mobility pattern historically evident among European-origin groups, research on generational attainments points to an "invisible ceiling" of blocked opportunity for Mexican American people.[10]

Although these widely observed differences between early- and later-generation youth are regarded by scholars as reflecting a "decline in achievement,"[11] the framework I elaborate recasts the evidence as reflecting how schooling subtracts resources from youth. Borrowing from Robert D. Putnam, I argue that Mexican immigrant and U.S.-born Mexican youth alike are subjected to forces of "social decapitalization" (or loss of social capital in students' networks) through a process I term "subtractive schooling."[12] This means that the ways that youth are schooled or assimilated translates into the following interrelated outcomes: students' cultural and linguistic divestment, including their de-identification from Mexican culture and the Spanish language; psychic, social, emotional, and cultural distance between immigrant youth and their more culturally assimilated U.S.-born peers; and finally, a limited presence of academically productive social capital in the peer group networks of U.S.-born youth.[13]

As I argue in *Subtractive Schooling*, institutionally mediated social decapitalization is the antithesis of social capital. It not only fails to build on the cultural value that Chicanas and Chicanos attach to the sharing of norms, values, and resources, but also obstructs the transference of human and cultural capital. James C. Coleman forcefully argues that without social capital, human capital, embodied in individuals' levels of training and educational attainment, is negligible for the goal of academic success.[14] In Coleman's view, it is therefore not enough to possess human capital. One must also be enmeshed in exchange networks characterized by bonds of trust that permit an easy flow of resources and support that benefit both the individual and the collective.[15]

I describe the divisions I observed between youth and the paucity of social capital among U.S.-born youth, in particular, as two sides to the same coin. If one assumes as I did that achievement is a social process whereby orientations toward schooling are nurtured in familiar contexts among those with similar dispositions, then divisions between those with more and those with less social capital will be especially consequential to the latter.[16] More directly, the broader Mexican community's collective interest to achieve academically gets compromised by a schooling process that exacerbates differences among youth and makes them inaccessible to each other.

Analyses of gender within peer groups reveal that, were it not for the females in these groups, U.S.-born youth would be virtually devoid of social capital. Both quantitative and qualitative sources of evidence illuminate this finding: Regular-track females in every generational group tend to outperform their male counterparts.[17] However, placement in the honors track appears to erase the differences of both gender and generational status. Taken together, these findings suggest that regular-track placement cannot be overemphasized as an organizational feature of schooling that exacerbates differences between males and females, as well as between immigrant and U.S.-born youth.

Moreover, since never more than 10 percent to 15 percent of Seguín's entire student population is ever located in the honors college-bound track, the academic trajectories of the vast majority are circumscribed by regular-track placement. The salience of tracking is also underscored by Laurie Olsen, who similarly observes how immigrants' placement in the ESL track and U.S.-born youths' placement in the regular track compromises the achievement possibilities of the group as a whole.[18]

The first-hand accounts provided below show that romantic involvement for the females translates into helping boyfriends with their school work, even at their own expense. Females' support ranges from giving advice on courses, translating assignments, offering encouragement to stay in school, and acting as sounding-boards for problems, to providing assistance on written assignments and exams. While the discussion that follows suggests that social capital can flow through romantic relationships, a countervailing force that mutes its impact is an uneven system of exchange occurring at young women's expense.

The data further suggest that Chicanas are cognizant of gender inequality in their relations with the young men in their lives. They nevertheless seem willing to persist in such relationships. Irene I. Blea sheds light on this tendency with her suggestion that, in contrast to white women, Chicanas prefer unity with over distance from Chicano males.[19] This sense of unity, she argues, is born out of a shared experience of racial subordination that they must collectively confront. Another complicating factor Blea mentions is that Chicanas are socialized to believe that marriage, children, and family are to constitute their highest aspirations. When such cultural issues intersect with institutional barriers like tracking and low expectations, Chicanas might very well be more tolerant of uneven exchange relationships than their more socioeconomically privileged counterparts.

My exploration into youths' culture of romance below begins with a finding from participant observation that simultaneously allows me to address further the conditions of schooling at Seguín that influence the likelihood of a pro-school, romantically involved peer group culture. I then follow with detailed accounts of three couples who belonged to three different groups of students that I interviewed. Though the females in these groups accorded varying degrees of emphasis to family, peers, and school as rationales for both their romantic involvement and personal investments, their references to their social context help explain how their culture of romance translates into its unique, pro-school form.

The Culture of Romance and the Conditions of Schooling

Several weeks into the fall 1992 semester, while observing scores of students on the school's front steps as they make their way to their third-period class, I spy a nervous-looking young female who seems to be desperately trying to find someone. Though only a few feet away, she seems not to notice me and continues glancing furtively into the building, across the school lawn, and across the street. With a preoccupied look on her face, she pauses momentarily to smile widely and yell to a group of three young males, presumably friends, cruising by in a white, small-wheeled truck listening to Tex-Mex music blaring through large speakers spread across the truck's bed. "Go to class!" she screams as the driver waves to her. "Ah, they can't hear me," she mumbles to a female friend who chances upon her at that very moment. "They're crazy," she continues. "Those guys are skipping class already and school's barely started!"

"What's happenin'?" her friend asks.

"Checkin' up on my guy," the first girl replies in an anxious tone.

At first, I think she is referring to one of the young men in the truck. I soon realize, however, that she is talking about another male who is her boyfriend. The two friends exchange several concerns they have about their schedules. I overhear them grumbling about courses to which they have been assigned that they already do not like and changes in their lunch schedules that mean that they will not be able to eat lunch together.

"At least I'm still with Andy [for lunch]," the first girl says. "He needs me."

Though I have trouble hearing how her friend is responding, I can tell that she is mainly in a listening mode because the other is dominating the conversation.

I overhear Andy's girlfriend say with concern in her voice, "He's not such a great student, but I promised myself that I would help him out in any way I could this year."

She informs her friend that Andy has gotten off to a bad start. Andy has apparently been moved to several different classes in the past couple of weeks because the counselors keep confusing him with another student with the same name. Though a freshman, Andy keeps getting assigned to junior-level courses. "He still has to go to class, even if it's not the right class!" exclaims his girlfriend excitedly as she begins again to glance nervously about the school's front lawn.

Since the bell is about to ring, only a few remaining students are within sight. As her friend gets drawn into the action, her words become audible: "I can help you find Andy. Maybe he's hiding behind the T-[temporary] buildings. But we have to hurry!"

Showing embarrassment, Andy's girlfriend backtracks and confesses, "Naw, it's a waste of time. He's not the skipping type."

Her friend then waves her arms, palms up, in disbelief. After exhaling loudly, she shouts, "Girl, what are you putting me through? Did you even try to check in his room to see if he was there?"

As Andy's girlfriend doubles over, bursting with laughter, I can only hear her friend's voice, which gets louder with each passing word: "Oh man, I know what this is about. It's like you gonna tell Andy how much you love him, how much you care for him today. It's like you gonna tell him what you did for him today, all lovey-dovey!"

Andy's girlfriend's face turns bright red as tears of laughter stream down her face.

In sheer delight, her friend snaps, "Busted! I got your number, girl!"

The bell rings, and they dart into the building and disappear. As I assemble my thoughts about the significance of this emotional display, the males in the white truck drive by again.

Before addressing my interpretation of this exchange, it is worth elaborating further on the schooling context wherein youths' capacity to prevail is severely put to the test. Since the first few weeks of school in any semester at Seguín are always chaotic, the kind of scenario presented by the students above is hardly unusual. According to school officials, the school was built to hold only 2,600 students. However, the school is typically responsible for enrolling several hundred more beyond that limit. With no obvious plans for any new construction, classrooms in "temporary buildings" provided by the district have proliferated annually to accommodate the demand for space. Too few counselors to process too many students results in a scheduling nightmare with frequent placement errors. In a "good" year, by the third week of school most students' schedules are "fixed," meaning that students are assigned to the classes they should have been enrolled in from the first day of school.[20]

In the first few weeks, teachers typically face huge classes composed of a random mix of students, only some of whom belong where they are. Even larger than the actual classes are the rosters of students who are supposedly present in their classrooms. Students' displeasure over schooling combines with massively long class rosters, teachers' and students' conflictual relations with counselors, extraordinarily large class sizes, insufficient numbers of desks, books, and teaching materials, and inadequate space to make for a state of high tension and normlessness. Under such circumstances, the administration's attempts to both keep students in class and minimize disorderly conduct are often futile – hence the three males in the white truck.

With soaring dropout rates, freshmen invariably make up more than half of the school's student population of 3,000. Academic failure is so common that a full quarter of the students have to repeat the ninth grade for at least a second time. In this kind of environment, students tend to gather fairly quickly that they need to look out for themselves and for each other lest they "fall through the cracks." By assuming a special responsibility for her boyfriend, Andy's girlfriend cogently illustrates how caring for one another can become an institutionally driven imperative. That females tend to take care of males also suggests that the ancient, one-way, woman-as-helpmate-to-man role persists.

What remains unanswered in the preceding account, however, is why Andy's girlfriend acted like she was desperately trying to find Andy if she knew all along that he was most likely in his classroom. Either skipping class was within the realm of possibility or something else was operating. While, at face value, little more than childish play could have been at hand, the girlfriend's intense embarrassment after having been "busted" by her friend lays bare her hidden desire:

to act in a caring way toward her boyfriend so that she could later tell him just how much she cared for him. Though away from him during the day, she nevertheless attended to him in a "caring" way, even if this involved momentarily convincing herself about his chances of skipping class. In a state of romantic love, Andy's girlfriend thus performed a version of femininity that combines several important elements that also appear in the group interviews that follow. That is, romantically involved females not only express their caring by promoting school as a goal, but this caring also gives them a sense of self-worth, connectedness, and status. Such benefits appear to accrue in schooling contexts that are especially difficult, challenging, or alienating.

Group Interviews

Close to half of the 25 groups I interviewed contained both females and males, the majority of whom were "just friends," or not romantically involved. I also interviewed gender-mixed groups in each generation (four groups are first-generation, one is mixed-generation, and six are U.S.-born). Across my sample of 11 gender-mixed groups, females exhibit a clear pattern of being the providers of academic-related support.[21]

Although there were numerous instances I came across of females helping out males who were friends, I focus on romantically involved couples because they allow me to address my concern with how the culture of romance translates into the everyday lives of young women and men whose groups are differentially endowed with social capital. These issues are examined through the experiences of three couples presented below in order from lowest to highest level of social capital.

The "Achievement Gang"

These students jokingly refer to themselves as the "Achievement Gang." The females play the role of encouraging and overseeing their male friends in the group. None of these students actually does very well in school, and, as a group, they have only a low level of social capital. They nevertheless see themselves as an "achievement gang" because they combine the elements of a pro-school ethos with gangster-like attire.

Betty, a sophomore, regularly checks up on her friends Jerry, a sophomore, and Benny, a freshman, throughout the day. She monitors whether they come to school, show up at their classes, and turn in their assignments on time. I ask Betty whether she provides other kinds of assistance, like helping her friends with their homework. In a bantering tone, with Jerry and Benny listening and laughing, Betty responds, "Man, I'm the one who needs help! And do I get it? No! From these guys? You know we're in bad shape if I am helping them." She throws some hard punches, but the young men are unfazed.

In a matter-of-fact tone, Jerry states that Betty helps him not to "mess up." This is important because he says he's "very weak" and easily tempted when someone asks him to "skip and go get high." Benny contends that his only weakness is his best friend, Jerry. He appreciates Betty's riding hard on Jerry because he knows that "if Jerry's in line, I won't skip." Jerry and Benny argue over which of them is the worst influence, but they both agree that Betty is a great influence. Jerry mentions that his mother encourages him to hang around with Betty because, in the past, whenever he's gotten into a group with "all guys," he inevitably "take[s] a wrong turn": "She knows I'm in good hands with Betty," he says, confidently. ("From one woman's arms to another," I mutter to myself.)

Jerry's comment about his mother reminds me of a conversation I had with a parent whose son, David, had run into serious trouble with some boys at school who threatened his life. Throughout middle school, this parent had cautioned her son to avoid other children, telling him, "At school, you are to have no friends! After school, you are to come straight home!" In practice, this directive led David to hang out exclusively with girls. This made his mother feel more comfortable, but David told me that having female friends was a mixed blessing, for it made other males extremely jealous. These jealousies followed him into high school and led to death threats. David's reaction was to transfer to another school before the end of his first six weeks.

Jerry's and David's mothers apparently believe that their sons' interests are best served by females who nurture and watch over them. For their part, the young women in the gender-mixed groups seem very comfortable with and uncritical of this role. The only resistance to gender-role expectations that I heard young women at Seguín express was directed at their parents' expectations.

Several weeks after the interview, I see Betty and Jerry holding hands as they walk slowly to class together. Out of curiosity, I ask them if they were already going steady at the time that I had interviewed their group. They reply that they had been going steady but were on shaky ground at that point.

In response to my question about what made the difference, Betty explains that she threatened to leave the group if Jerry and Benny skipped to get high one more time. After a big fight about this, Jerry and Betty again realized just how much they cared for each other. Jerry grits his teeth and admits that Betty has her "act together." Filling me in quickly on a great trip that he took with her family to Mexico one weekend, he also indicates that he likes and admires her family. A pensive Betty suggests that she's really not as together as she appears. "Next time, it's going to be me [messing up] and you'll do the same for me," she says.

Had I not spoken to Betty and Jerry this second time, I would have remained concerned about her relationship to these young men. As a friend, she helped Jerry to assess his academic trajectory and his goals. This process encouraged them to explore their relationship further. They both shared with me that they really want to graduate from high school and go farther than their parents had. It was Jerry who best expressed the relation between romance and achievement: "When you're steady, guys and girls leave you alone. I've seen enough of the 'punk scene.' Now it's time to focus on getting out of here." Hence, Betty and Jerry's relationship enabled them to articulate and act on instrumental goals at the same time that it foreshadowed their impending status as responsible future adults. While the support in this relationship was definitely tilted in Jerry's direction, the growth that he had undergone led Betty to expect that it would eventually tilt in her direction as well.

The rappers

This group is comprised of two females and three males. All three males in the group share an interest in rap music. I meet them during the lunch hour in fall 1992 as they are huddled around a TV monitor that has somehow found its way into the school cafeteria. Unabashedly, the three males in the group dance to the beat of the rap tunes being sung by the rap artists on the music video that is being broadcast at the moment. With their baggy Girbaud jeans folded at the cuff, their gold necklaces, and a couple with baseball caps turned sideways, the three dancers come across as rather stylish in their appearance.

As students make their way into the cafeteria, the audience around them grows. After the rap tune ends, their dancing stops, and everyone observing them, including myself, applauds loudly. After their performance, they playfully bow, taking their caps off. With the crowd dispersing, their girlfriends laugh as the two males with the baseball caps fall backward into their arms. In the interview that I conduct with this group, I learn most about Norma and her relationship to her boyfriend, Chach. Norma and I hold the group's place at a nearby table as the rest enter the cafeteria lines to get food. During this several-minute interval, we warm up quickly to each other. After telling her that I'm writing a book and would like to see if she and her friends would like to be in it, Norma expresses immediate interest, "Sure, that sounds great!" Asking her to tell me about the guy who fell into her arms seems a logical place to start.

"So, who is that guy?" I ask.

"Oh, that's Chach!" she says. "He's a nut!"

After telling me that he dances really well, Norma shakes me head in disapproval. I ask her what is wrong. She then explains that, while she likes rap, she doesn't like it "if it gives you an attitude." I quickly confirm that he is her boyfriend and that she is very concerned about his cultural identity and commitment to school. She seems to think he needs her help in all kinds of ways.

Knowing that her group will be joining us shortly, she crams a lot of explanation into a few minutes. She divulges how her relationship to

Chach has led her to spend more time on his homework than on her own. Admitting that her school work has begun to suffer, Norma justifies her investment in her boyfriend's school work by saying that if she does not help him, "Chach will definitely drop out of school." She confesses that she is working on both her boyfriend's attitude toward school "and his taste in music." Norma explains that none of Chach's teachers like him. He got in trouble with the law just once, and it was all downhill after that. "Don't take much to get a bad rep, you know." She claims that "helping Chach helps him to feel good about himself – you know, getting a good grade now and then." After every good grade, Chach takes Norma for a "really nice evening out on the town." She adds that doing Chach's homework teaches her "a lot." "It just doesn't show in my grades," she remarks, smiling.

Since both Norma and Chach are freshmen, I take the liberty of mentioning that they seem rather young to be dating. Norma replies that now that she's had her *quinceañera*, or her sweet 15 ceremony, her parents feel that she is old enough to date. I ask her if her parents know how much she helps Chach. She says that she would never tell them, partly because they are not "too excited" about him.

"They think he's *agringado* (too white)," she explains.

"What about the time it takes away from your own work?" I probe.

"I make Bs and some Cs. Not bad if you ask me. As long as I'm not failing, they don't notice anything."

With respect to his taste in music, Norma is critical of Chach's interest in gangsta rap, which she believes is too violent and "talks too much about 'bitches and hos.'" She says that he needs to listen to more Mexican and Tejano (Texas Mexican) music.

"It's like he doesn't know who he is, like he wants to be black. So I always tell him to take me to Tejano clubs when we go out. He's starting to get into Selena, La Mafia, and Emilio Navaira. I feel kinda sorry for him."

Out of curiosity, I ask her if her boyfriend's attitude toward school and his taste in music have anything to do with one another.

"I think so. It's like he's angry and the music's angry. He can't understand why I'm not angry."

"Like with what?" I press her.

"You know, with whites and the system gettin' you down. It's a black thing. What I think is if he's more Mexican or Tejano, there's more to live for."

"What do you mean?" I query.

Norma either would not or could not explain.

"I don't know...but he's Mexican and I'm helping him to know it and feel good about it."

I am glad to have had these few minutes with Norma because she probably could not have made any of these statements before any of the members of her group. The group interview reveals the students to be friends from both the same neighborhood and the middle school that feeds into Seguín. Despite these similarities, the differences at least between Chach and Norma seem great enough to make me wonder how long they will remain together.

Fortunately, I run into Norma the following semester. Without my even asking, Norma volunteers, in halting speech, that she and Chach are no longer together. Since I can tell that she is hurting, I hug her and tell her that I am sorry.

"So you're no longer with your group either, huh?" I ask.

"No, how could I be? This is all so upsetting to me."

I ask Norma what happened. She replies that "the beginning of the end" happened one night toward the end of the fall semester when she was helping Chach study for an exam. In the middle of their session, he expressed his dismay with the whole "setup." He said that he was tired of school and that all of his teachers were against him. Norma responded by telling him that he was exaggerating. But then when he said that none were "for him," she couldn't disagree. "So I told him, 'I'm for you, Chach.'" "But this didn't work either," Norma continues. "He then got an attitude toward me and told me that he didn't need me either." At this point, Norma stops talking, attempting to remain in control of her emotions.

After a long pause, I tell her I am sorry. I then suggest to her that maybe with more time on her hands, she can dedicate herself more to her own studies.

"It's his self-esteem," she explains. "You can't love anyone if you can't love yourself." "You know," she continues, "I don't want to do this school thing alone. I know I can, but I don't want to," she responds, quietly. She tells me how now that Chach is not part of her life, school is less interesting. Somehow, Chach made her feel like everything was "in its place."

"It's like it made me feel important," she says.

"What did?" I ask.

"To know that I was helping him out," Norma reminisces.

"Even if it meant that your grades went down?" I suggest.

She defends Chach, saying that it wasn't his fault. She then rationalizes that her grades are not any better this semester anyway. With anxiousness in her voice, she says, "I just can't get into school right now. I'm not going to fail, but I'm not going to do too well this year. Maybe next."

This young woman is clearly in need of as much help and support as Chach ever was. Unfortunately, the only sense of direction that she conveys is that provided by her relationship with Chach. We spend a long time talking through her difficulties. Fortunately, as she has many other friends and is not one to withdraw into herself, her school work seems more at issue for me at the moment. She responds well to my suggestion that she try to organize a study group for her more difficult courses. I also suggest that it is not too early for her to be planning for college. She says that no one has ever talked to her about college but that she will definitely consider it.

While I at first thought that her breakup would get her out of an exploitative situation, I realized that matters were not so simple. Except for her grades, most things actually did seem to fall into place while she was with Chach. She went out on dates, was part of an interesting group of friends, and she was also more interested in school. She further derived a strong sense of stability and self-worth from having someone like Chach whom she felt needed her. I was able to glean from this and other discussions I had with students that in a fairly capricious environment, where students drop out in great numbers and where youth have few attachments to adults at school, they place a premium on the stability and continuity that relationships provide.

A number of unique conditions thus combine to form this kind of meaning system that equates romantic love with a pro-school orientation. I am not suggesting that Norma's orientation toward schooling was ever sufficient for her to reap unequivocal success. I merely suggest that within the confines of her social world, where few peer models of achievement exist for reasons that are largely attributable to subtractive schooling, Norma's interest in school – both for herself and her boyfriend – may be appropriately characterized as a pro-school orientation. While Norma understood her disaffection from schooling as related to her loss of connection to Chach, I doubt whether such a responsible and intelligent young woman would have arrived at such a conclusion in an academically rich environment comprised of adults interested in her well-being and where numerous peer models for achievement existed.

Current events/ESL students

I labeled this group this way because they most enjoy reading Spanish-language newspapers and watching Spanish-language television news. Graciela, a sophomore immigrant in the group, regularly completes her boyfriend Armando's homework assignments, forging his handwriting. She explains that she does his homework because the long hours he works at a local meat market leave him little time for school work. "Lo hago porque él trabaja mucho [después de la escuela] y no tiene suficiente tiempo" ("I do it because he works a lot [after school] and he doesn't have the time"). Graciela does not have a salaried after-school job, but her daily responsibilities at home include housework and taking care of three younger siblings for several hours until her parents return home from work. Given her own time constraints, I cannot help wondering whether what Graciela really means is that Armando's time is more valuable than hers.

I suggest to them that their actions will minimize Armando's learning if he doesn't do the work himself. "Como quiera aprendo" ("I learn no matter what") he counters. They maintain that he simply skips a step by reading over the work

Graciela has already done. This arrangement, which evolved over time, began with Graciela translating the homework assignments Armando received in his regular (non-ESL classes) such as math and social studies, which are taught in English. Graciela fears that without her help, her boyfriend might fail.

"But what good is passing if you don't know the material?" I object.

With no apparent misgivings, both assure me that Armando is indeed learning. What strikes me as I talk with them is how perfectly able Armando appears. When I first joined the group for lunch that day, I interrupted a discussion they were having about the aftermath of the L.A. riots. Mentioning ex-Police Chief Darryl Gates, Peter Ueberroth – the political leader in charge of rebuilding South Central Los Angeles – and the impending trial of the three African American men accused of beating white trucker Reginald Denny during the riot, Armando demonstrated a thorough and up-to-date understanding of the intricacies of L.A. politics. Despite the many hours he may work at his after-school job, he clearly has time and energy available for watching and listening to news media.

The conversation then turns to a discussion about Graciela's parents, who are really strict and do not yet know about their romantic involvement. Since their relationship has gotten pretty serious, Graciela eventually plans to tell them. One of their friends, Jesús, asserts jokingly, "¡Se quieren casar!" ("They want to get married!") Perhaps out of nervousness with the subject of marriage, this comment makes us all laugh. Graciela nevertheless holds firm, saying in Spanish that she wouldn't be doing all that she is doing for Armando if they didn't have big plans.

"¿Cuáles son sus planes?" ("What are your plans?") I ask. Armando then explains that they would like to get married, go to college, and have children…"algún día" ("someday").

"Qué jóvenes están ustedes" ("How young you two are") I note. Graciela responds by saying that her parents were young, too, when they got married, and everything turned out fine. She feels confident that after her parents meet Armando that they, too, will understand why she's in love with him. Armando then interjects that Graciela tells him that he's exactly like her father's side of the family and that he'll fit in perfectly. Graciela then elaborates that her father is a musician who plays many instruments and that Armando plays guitar and sings. Like her father, Armando also loves going to the *pulga* (flea market) on Saturdays "y tantas otras cosas" ("and many other things") Graciela says, beaming.

"Tú quieres mucho a tu papá" ("You love your father a lot") I note.

With affection, she responds, "Ay, sí" ("Oh, yes").

In Spanish, I ask her how she thinks she'll break the news about their dreams to her parents. Graciela says that she plans to emphasize her college-going plans. When I ask them when they think they might go to college and when they think they'll get married, they are unclear how it will all work out for them. Graciela is especially unclear whether "manteniendo a una familia" ("maintaining a family") should occur before or after she goes to college. She phrases this concern in a way that suggests an inevitable sacrifice to her career rather than to Armando's. What is clear, however, is that what would most legitimate their relationship in Graciela's parents' eyes is her continued interest in education.

These rationalizations do not erase the fact that Armando is taking advantage of Graciela's generosity, especially in light of her many household responsibilities. As Graciela is a very bright and articulate student, I question whether she cannot or will not grasp the unfairness of this arrangement. Since her strategy is so deliberate, I am inclined to believe the latter. That Graciela herself dreams of someday "maintaining" her own family suggests how a mix of traditional and liberal gender role expectations form her own personal ideology.

Olsen's ethnography of immigrant high-school youth has direct bearing on Graciela's situation.[22] Olsen finds that when females' behavior is subject to strict parental monitoring, schools – and the relationships that naturally develop within them – become liberating places. At school, immigrant girls can exercise more fully their quest for individuality and independence. However, when this quest lands them into demanding and exploitative relationships, the sense of independent thought and action in a system of patriarchy is mere illusion. Ironically, it may be the girls' lifelong experience with stronger social control mechanisms that results in their ability to provide "safe spaces" for potentially wayward males. Thus, while the culture of romance that Graciela and Armando enact relies on the quest for education as its key source of legitimation, their system of exchange occurs at Graciela's expense – and ultimately at Armando's own, as well.

Conclusion

What I identify as problematic in *Subtractive Schooling* is the lopsidedness of the support system, with males not adequately reciprocating females' support. I interpret this uneven pattern of support as a reflection of females' nurturing role extending into the life of the peer group. While the data continue to suggest this imbalance, a more focused analysis of intimate relationships among youth reveals how the young women in these relationships have practical concerns, either about school or their futures. That is, rather than simply finding ways to express heterosexual love and attention, they also express a level of pragmatism that is more often characteristic of adult relationships. Building social captial and romantic relationships thus work in tandem to help these young women imagine and prepare for their future adult roles in society.

These young women's failure to see their inordinate contributions to their male friends' well-being as exploitative is attributable to a number of factors. While love is blinding, traditional gender role expectations are, too. Indeed, the power of convention helps explain why I never came across a situation in which a male assumed full responsibility for a female's school work. Another blinding factor is their enhanced sense of self-worth that derives from their enactment of stabilizing, adult-like roles. As a result, they neither see their support as a chore nor as the fulfillment of sexist expectations.

Instead, the girls appear to be involved in exchange relationships akin to the culture of romance that Holland and Eisenhart observed in their study of college-going white women. That is, the construction of a female identity in traditional terms invariably translates into compromises women – and, in this case, girls – make to secure the love and affection of a male. As Holland and Eisenhart suggest, young women derive pleasure from the thought that their interventions are crucial to their boyfriends' academic success and/or to their psychological well-being.[23] In contrast to the college-going women in their study, however, a pro-school ethos among the seriously romantic at Seguín is an entirely compatible proposition. Jerry may capture best an internal dynamic that may be operating for many couples: "When you're steady, guys and girls leave you alone." As the words of the young females also tend to convey, romantic relationships provide a secure, loving space that provides some measure of stability and protection in a difficult and capricious environment.

Unfortunately, the school unwittingly promotes a "survivalist" rather than an achievement-oriented mentality. When the hallways themselves are jam-packed with anxious students attempting to maneuver their way to the next class within a brief, five-minute time span, it's not hard to feel objectified and preoccupied with one's own survival in this overcrowded, heavily bureaucratized environment. Since so much effort is dedicated to either avoiding or rectifying the kind of bureaucratic harm that often accompanies the processing of huge masses of students, one's placement within the academic hierarchy is scarcely an afterthought for most students within the regular track. Against this backdrop, it comes as no surprise to find a cultural meaning system that equates romance with a pro-school ethos.

The quality of school-related support that females are able to provide, as Betty explicitly notes, is contingent on their own abilities and prior academic training. The more academically adept, like Norma and Graciela, have much more to provide their boyfriends than the more academically challenged Betty. All three nevertheless purvey whatever measure they seem to possess. Since the provision of support appears to be a given, these young women would do well to assess how they provide the support they do provide. This concern especially emerges in the case of

Norma and Chach, with Norma perhaps investing too much in Chach and, in so doing, repelling him. In the other cases, imbalances in the provision of support remain a central concern.

As social capital theory predicts, the potential of those enmeshed in exchange relations to achieve success increases, especially if a give-and-take process, like the one Betty expresses, develops. Indeed, within Betty's own group, Benny, her boyfriend's friend, benefits from Betty's concern for both. Taken together, the findings at once reveal how social capital and a culture of romance can work hand in hand. Although more research is needed on the subject, the evidence suggests that, for these young women, a culture of romance can provide both the connective interpersonal tissue that cements students to one another and the justification for social capital investments.

Although young females seem to indeed find academics more meaningful in and through these relationships, the precariousness of their schooling environment also seems to enhance the salience and hence the probability of close-knit relationships of various kinds, including heterosexual unions. It is unfortunate that regular-track females' capacity to give is oftentimes blunted by their weak academic skills even if their average grades are higher than those of their male peers. It is also unfortunate that gender inequality minimizes what would otherwise be a stronger collective impact of social capital. Institutional policies and practices like tracking that subtract resources from youth thus persist as a concern. They neutralize students' social capital and compromise the educational mobility of even the most talented. If Latinas are to emerge as leaders in the coming century, institutional constraints and traditional gender role expectations must be equally challenged.

NOTES

1 All names herein are pseudonyms.

2 Dorothy C. Holland and Margaret A. Eisenhart, *Educated in Romance: Women, Achievement, and College Culture* (Chicago: University of Chicago Press, 1990).

3 For more on social capital, see James S. Coleman, "Social Capital in the Creation of Human Capital," *American Journal of Sociology* 94 (1988):95–120, and *Foundations of Social Theory* (Cambridge, MA: Belknap Press, 1990); and Angela Valenzuela and Sanford M. Dornbusch, "Familism and Social Capital in the Academic Achievement of Mexican Origin and Anglo Adolescents," *Social Science Quarterly* 75:1 (1994):18–36.

4 For more on these forms of capital, see Pierre Bourdieu and Jean-Claude Passeron, *Reproduction in Education, Society, and Culture*, trans. Richard Nice (Beverly Hills, CA: Sage, 1977).

5 Ricardo Stanton-Salazar, "A Social Capital Framework for Understanding the Socialization of Racial Minority Children and Youth," *Harvard Educational Review* 67:1 (1997):1–40.

6 I attended, either as an observer or as a participant, numerous school and community functions. School activities included pep rallies, orientation and registration activities, football games, speaker presentations, and parent and faculty meetings. I deliberately sought out students at times and in places when/where they were likely to congregate. These included the cafeteria area during the lunch hour, the hallways between class sessions, the girls' restrooms during some physical education classes, in front of school buildings before or after school, and under the stairwells and in other out-of-the-way places students favored throughout the day, especially when they were skipping classes.

I also conducted open-ended interviews with 25 groups of students from fall 1992 through the spring 1993 semester. I spoke with student groups of between two and eight members during their lunch hour. To qualify, group members had to be either ninth- or tenth-graders and to describe themselves as "close." My questions about their shared interests and factors that made them "close" resulted in the information for the present analysis.

Groups corresponded to the following major categories: immigrant, U.S.-born, and generationally mixed friendship groups comprised of both immigrant and nonimmigrant youth. First-generation students were, along with their parents, born in Mexico. Second-generation students were born in the United States but have parents born in Mexico. Students were classified as third-generation if they and their parents were born in the United States. I use the self-referents "Mexican American" and "Chicana/o" and the term "U.S.-born" to refer to nonimmigrant, later-generation youth. Most of the interviews with immigrants were conducted in

Spanish, while most of the interviews with U.S.-born and mixed-generation groups were conducted in English or "Spanglish," a combination of English and Spanish.

In addition to differences in generational status, the groups I interviewed also varied in their gender composition, some being mixed and some being single-sex. The romantic couples investigated herein belong (or belonged) to gender-mixed friendship groups.

7 Angela Valenzuela, *Subtractive Schooling: U.S. Mexican Youth and the Politics of Caring* (Albany: State University of New York Press, 1999, forthcoming), and "Subtractive Schooling: U.S.-Mexican Youth and the Politics of Caring," in *Reflexiones 1998: New Directions in Mexican American Studies* (Austin: University of Texas Center for Mexican American Studies, forthcoming).

8 In November 1992, I administered a questionnaire to all 3,000 students at Seguín. It included questions about students' family backgrounds, English and Spanish language abilities, generational status, school climate, teacher caring, and academic achievement. With a 75 percent response rate, a sample of 2,281 students for analysis resulted.

9 For an example of a small-scale ethnography, see Mara Eugenia Matute-Bianchi, "Situational Ethnicity and Patterns of School Performance among Immigrant and Nonimmigrant Mexican-descent Students," in *Minority Status and Schooling: A Comparative Study of Immigrant and Involuntary Minorities*, ed. Margaret A. Gibson and John U. Ogbu (New York: Garland Publishing, 1991), 205–247. For examples of national-level data, see Alejandro Portes and Rubén G. Rumbaut, *Immigrant America: A Portrait* (Berkeley: University of California Press, 1990); Alejandro Portes and Min Zhou, "The New Second Generation: Segmented Assimilation and its Variants," *Annals of the American Academy of Political and Social Sciences* 530 (1993):74–96; Grace Kao and Marta Tienda, "Optimism and Achievement: The Educational Performance of Immigrant Youth," *Social Science Quarterly* 76:1 (1995):1–19; and Barbara A. Zsembik and David Llanes, "Generational Differences in Educational Attainment Among Mexican Americans," *Social Science Quarterly* 77:2 (1996):363–374.

10 Jorge Chapa, "The Question of Mexican American Assimilation: Socioeconomic Parity or Underclass Formation?" *Public Affairs Comment* 35:1 (1988):1–14, "The Myth of Hispanic Progress," *Harvard Journal of Hispanic Policy Issues* 4 (1990):3–17, and "Special Focus: Hispanic Demographic and Educational Trends," in *Ninth Annual Status Report: Minorities in Higher Education* (Washington, DC: American Council on Education, Office of Minority Concerns, 1991); Herbert J. Gans, "Second-Generation Decline: Scenarios for the Economic and Ethnic Futures of Post-1965 Immigrants," *Ethnic and Racial Studies* 15:2 (1992):173–192; Frank D. Bean et al., "Educational and Sociodemographic Incorporation among Hispanic Immigrants to the United States," in *Immigration and Ethnicity: The Integration of America's Newest Arrivals*, ed. Barry Edmonston and Jeffrey S. Passel (Washington, DC: Urban Institute Press, 1994), 73–100; and Valenzuela, *Subtractive Schooling*.

11 Alejandro Portes and Min Zhou, "Should Immigrants Assimilate?" *The Public Interest* 116 (1994):18–33, and "The New Second Generation."

12 Robert D. Putnam, "The Prosperous Community: Social Capital and Public Life," *The American Prospect* 13 (Spring 1993):35–42, and "Bowling Alone: America's Declining Social Capital," *Journal of Democracy* 6:1 (1995):65–78.

13 A number of assimilationist policies and practices are implicated in the process of subtractive schooling, including the consequences of "cultural tracking" (see Valenzuela, *Subtractive Schooling*). Cultural (nonacademic) tracking refers to the practice of separating Spanish- from English-speaking students through the English as a Second Language (ESL) program. ESL is a stigmatized track within the regular track. Inasmuch as there is any mobility out of the ESL track, it occurs horizontally, with students moving into the English-only, regular-track curriculum. Never mind that many immigrant youth I came across entered U.S. schools with well-developed cognitive skills about which their ESL teachers frequently boasted. Indeed, many had attended *secundaria* (known more formally as *educación media*) in Mexico.

Since only 16.9 percent of the total middle-school-age population in Mexico attends *secundaria*, any *secundaria* experience is exceptional (see Gerald L. Gutek, *American Education in a Global Society: Internationalizing Teacher Education* [White Plains, NY: Longman, 1992]). Though members of an elite group, they are seldom recognized or treated as such by school officials, including counselors, who either do not know how to interpret a transcript from Mexico or who are ignorant about the significance of a postprimary educational experience. At least for youth emanating from the urban centers, anecdotal evidence suggests that *secundaria* is more rigorous than post-primary education in the United States. Comparisons are difficult to make, however, since the two systems are quite distinct. In Mexico, occupational and academic tracking occur immediately after *primaria*, depending on whether students are anticipating entering the labor market or university-level schooling, respectively.

14 Coleman, "Social Capital in the Creation of Human Capital," and *Foundations of Social Theory*. See also, Valenzuela, *Subtractive Schooling*; Annette Lareau, *Home Advantage: Social Class and Parental Intervention in Elementary Education* (New York: Falmer Press, 1989); and Stanton-Salazar, "A Social Capital Framework."

15 Although Coleman fails to extend this reasoning in his writings to the concept of cultural capital, a parallel logic can be inferred. See also Lareau, *Home Advantage*.

16 In contrast to U.S.-born youth, immigrants were typically found marshaling their resources to promote the academic well-being of their entire group. In accordance with their esprit de corps, pro-schooling ethos, their teachers often affectionately referred to them as "organized cheaters."

17 Although she did not control for track placement, Matute-Bianchi similarly observed this pattern in her study of generational differences in achievement at Field High, a school located in a central coast California agricultural community ("Situational Ethnicity").

18 Lauric Olsen, *Made in America: Immigrant Students in Our Public Schools* (New York: The New Press, 1997). Neither Olsen nor I should be interpreted as suggesting that immigrants should not be accorded their much-needed, and oftentimes deficient, language support systems. Instead, we both take issue with how schooling fosters and legitimates divisions among youth, most notably through the stigmatizing ESL curriculum. While youth do enter schools with certain prejudices and attitudes, schooling is shown in both of our works to exacerbate these differences. In *Subtractive Schooling*, I suggest that a more inclusive, culture-affirming pedagogy would help reverse the effects of subtractive schooling, particularly the "loss" of students' language and culture.

19 Irene I. Blea, *La Chicana and the Intersection of Race, Class, and Gender* (New York: Praeger, 1992).

20 With counselors carrying caseloads of over 300 students each, expediency rules in placement decisions. Because of their status, seniors are always attended to first and are therefore always among those whose schedules are "fixed" first.

21 Valenzuela, *Subtractive Schooling*.

22 Olsen, *Made in America*.

23 Holland and Eisenhart, *Educated in Romance*.

Index

Index compiled by Meg Davies (Registered Indexer, Society of Indexers)